BCL –
3rd ed

ASIA

ASIA

A Regional and
Economic Geography

by

SIR DUDLEY STAMP

C.B.E., D.SC. (Lond. and Exeter), D.LIT.(Lond.), LL.D.(Clark and Edinburgh)
EKON.D. (Stockholm), D.SC.NAT. (Warsaw)

Professor Emeritus of Social Geography in the University of London
Formerly Professor of Geography and Geology in the University of Rangoon
Gold Medallist of the Mining and Geological Institute of India, 1922
Medallist of the Tokyo Geographical Society, 1957
Honorary Member of the Geographical Societies of Madras and Calcutta
Special Lecturer, Universities of Bombay and Calcutta, 1938
University of Hong Kong, 1955, 1961
University of Malaya, 1960

LONDON: METHUEN & CO LTD
11 New Fetter Lane, E.C.4

First published October 31st, 1929
Second Edition, revised, July 1931
Third Edition, enlarged and partly rewritten, March 1936
Fourth Edition, revised, July 1939
Reprinted 1944 and 1946
Seventh Edition, revised, June 1948
Eighth Edition, revised throughout, February 1950
Reprinted with minor corrections 1952
Ninth Edition, revised and reset, 1957
Tenth Edition, 1959
Eleventh Edition, 1962
Twelfth Edition, 1967
Reprinted 1969

12.2

SBN 416 30400 1

PRINTED AND BOUND IN GREAT BRITAIN BY
BUTLER AND TANNER LTD, FROME AND LONDON

Distributed in the U.S.A.
by Barnes & Noble Inc

To

MY WIFE

In memory of
Bullock-cart days
and Irrawaddy nights

PREFACE TO THE NINTH EDITION

IT is now more than a quarter of a century since the publication of the first edition of this book in 1929. In the intervening years it is probably true to say that in no other continent has the world picture changed so fundamentally as in Asia. Those European powers which in 1929 controlled a quarter of Asia's area and a third of Asia's people have handed over the mantle of government to Asia's own leaders. The mandated areas of Syria and Palestine have become the Republics of Syria, Lebanon and Israel and the Hashemite Kingdom of the Jordan; the erstwhile Indian Empire is now the Republic of India and the Islamic Republic of Pakistan; the former province of Burma is now an independent republic; the Dutch East Indies have been succeeded over most of the territory by the Indonesian Republic. The United States' possession of the Philippines, taken over from Spain after the war of 1898, is now the independent Commonwealth of the Philippines, and French Indo-China has given place to a welter of states. In the years since 1929 the Japanese Empire had a brief period of expansion to become a Greater East Asian Empire, only to be reduced to a core corresponding to Japan proper of old. China, but newly a republic, has passed through the phase of Japanese dominance, and the terror of civil war, to become a communist state and ally of Soviet Russia. Korea, from Japanese dominance, became the first battle-ground of United Nations' forces, only to be divided by a troubled peace. Last, but not least, is the upsurge of national consciousness throughout all the countries of the continent.

It is scarcely surprising that the first edition of this book reads rather as an historic document. The basic facts of physical geography—of structure, relief, climate, soils and vegetation—remain unchanged but vastly more fully studied and better understood than in the past. Where no literature formerly existed much research, albeit of varying quality, has now been published and authoritative regional studies have been made.

When first I went to Burma in 1921 it was to explore for oil and other minerals. I travelled there leisurely by sea; I took my portable gramophone to districts where European music never before had been heard. When I revisited my old haunts seventeen years later, radio had brought the whole world into instantaneous contact. When again I went to India on the eve of independence I stepped out of the plane on Indian soil within thirty-six hours

vi

of leaving my London flat. When, in the course of revisiting old
scenes during the re-writing of this book in 1955, I found myself
in Hong Kong I was within a couple of days of London either
way around the world.

It is little wonder that this book has had to be completely
recast, the greater part rewritten. Recent personal visits to Turkey,
Cyprus, Lebanon, Syria, Iraq, India, Pakistan, Ceylon, Burma,
Malaya and the Far East have enabled me to readjust my viewpoint and I trust that in the pages which follow I have presented
a picture of Asia today as well as its evolution over the past
twenty-five years.

L. D. S.

June, 1956

NOTE TO THE TENTH EDITION

THE past two years have continued the story of rapid change
in Asia. The reorganization of Indian States which came into
force on November 1, 1956, took place too late to be noted in the
last edition except for a map slipped into the final page proofs. In
this edition maps have been redrawn to show the new state
boundaries.

In August and September 1957 Japanese geographers organized a Regional Conference in Japan under the auspices of the
International Geographical Union. The Conference afforded me
a delightful opportunity of travelling widely in Japan under expert
and very efficient leadership and of seeing the work of many Asian
geographers at first hand. I was able to make study visits to Hong
Kong and the Philippines and later in the year enjoyed the hospitality of Thailand at the Pacific Science Congress in Bangkok. I am
also much indebted to Professor S. P. Chatterjee for showing me
the remarkable work of his National Atlas Organization in
Calcutta, to many Iranian friends who entertained me in Tehran
and to Professor D. K. Amiran of the Hebrew University of Jerusalem for invaluable guidance and hospitality in Israel.

L. D. S.

August, 1958

NOTE TO THE ELEVENTH EDITION

THE pace of change continues and again it has been my good fortune to revisit many old haunts and to gather new material to incorporate into appropriate sections. In particular I would record my intense pleasure in being invited as a guest in December 1959–January 1960 to my old university, Rangoon, to help in the celebrations of the 50th anniversary of the founding of the Burma Research Society. To Professor R. Wikkramatileke and Professor Robert Ho and their colleagues in the University of Malaya at Singapore and Kuala Lumpa I am greatly indebted for hospitality during my visit early in 1960. As United Kingdom delegate to the Sub-Commission on Land and Water Use of F.A.O. at Conferences in Turkey (1959) and in Israel (1961) I was able to travel extensively in those countries and to note in particular many developments, some of which are recorded in the pages which follow. Only minor alterations have been made in other parts of the book.

L. D. S.

July, 1961

NOTE TO THE TWELFTH EDITION

THE main changes in this edition result from the incorporation of recent statistics especially of population and trade. Note has been taken of political and economic changes notably in south-east Asia. I am greatly indebted to Professor R. Ishida of Tokyo who has very carefully revised the sections on Japan.

L. D. S.

April, 1966

CONTENTS

PART I—THE CONTINENT OF ASIA

PART II—THE COUNTRIES AND REGIONS OF ASIA

MAPS AND DIAGRAMS

xi

PART I
THE CONTINENT OF ASIA

A CONTINENT OF CONTRASTS

EACH of the great continental land masses has features distinctively its own and each in a sense may be described as unique. But Asia has very many features which entitle it to that description. There is first its vast size—of the order of 17,256,000 square miles and embracing between a quarter and a third of the land surface of the globe, estimated at 57,168,000 square miles. In consequence there are parts of the heart of the continent over 1,500 miles from the nearest point on tidewater. The huge complex of mountain chains with intervening plateaus and basins occupying the whole core of the continent and sending out offshoots or spurs towards the periphery is certainly unique and has had an overriding effect on the whole life of the continent. Politically and historically the concept of the continent of Asia is little more than an academic abstraction so separated are its constituent peripheral parts from one another. At the present day the U.S.S.R. stretches from eastern Europe across Siberia to the far north-east of Asia and the boundary between 'Europe' and 'Asia' finds no place on the political map. It is commonly accepted as following the crest of the Urals, themselves but a low divide, and then the Ural River to the Caspian, finally along a line from the Caspian to the Black Sea which some would identify with the crest of the Caucasus, others would place farther south. For this reason the area of Asia cannot be precisely measured: it depends what one accepts for the boundary between Asia and its peninsular extension of Europe.

In its different parts Asia is essentially a continent of contrasts. It includes the highest spot on the earth's surface—the peak of Everest—as well as the lowest in the Dead Sea rift. It has the lowest recorded temperature on the earth's surface outside Antarctica and may at least lay claim to the highest. It has the rainiest known spot in the world as well as localities with reasonable claim to be the driest. Its total population is of the order of 1,933,000,000—more than half the world's people—yet the areas with by far the highest known densities can be matched by vast uninhabited deserts.

To some extent the continent falls into a number of areas large enough to be called sub-continents. Some are well defined and it has long been usual to talk of the Indian sub-continent—now the Indo-Pakistan sub-continent. But other parts are less well defined. Cressey talks of a division into five 'realms' (which he divides into 22 provinces and 93 geographic regions) which he names the Soviet Union, China-Japan, South-east Asia, India and South-west Asia. East and Spate also divide Asia into realms but find six—South-west Asia, India and

Pakistan, South-east Asia, The Far East, Soviet Asia and High Asia. The last named is carved out of Cressey's China-Japan, otherwise the boundaries are identical except that Cressey includes Afghanistan with South-west Asia, East and Spate with India-Pakistan.

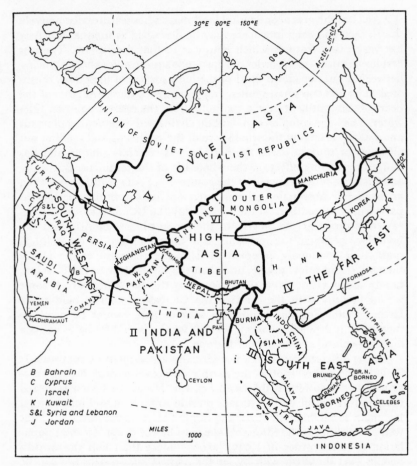

Fig. 1.—The Asian realms, *after* East and Spate

The islands of the Indonesian archipelago, part of the South-east Realm, straddle the Equator but the mainland of the continent lies entirely in the Northern Hemisphere and also entirely in the Eastern Hemisphere.

THE OROGRAPHY OF ASIA

THE continent of Europe is frequently referred to as a peninsula of the larger land mass of Asia, a description which is readily confirmed by a glance at a map. So it happens that geographers and geologists who have studied a mere appendage have attempted, in the past, to apply the lessons learnt to the interpretation of the structure of the main body. It is to such explorers and geographers as Prince Kropotkin that we are indebted for pushing to the fore a somewhat different outlook. The basal structure of Asia is different from that of the remaining continents: moreover, as the principal land mass of the globe, Asia deserves to be studied *de novo*. The heart of Asia consists of a great series of lofty plateaus, buttressed by mountains and flanked on north and south by extensive plains; a statement which cannot be made of any other continent. Unlike the great mountain chains of Europe and the Americas, those of Asia do not act as the main water partings of the continent, and the supposition that a water parting must be formed by a mountain chain was responsible for the insertion on maps of Asia of numerous mountain chains which have no existence in fact.

The inaccessibility and the comparative uselessness of the dry heart of Asia long hindered its exploration—with two results. In the first place, the detailed structure of the interior is still imperfectly known, there are large blanks still on the geological maps and it is impossible definitely to confirm or to refute theoretical reconstructions of the build of the continent. In the second place, the wide unknown spaces in the heart of Asia have been a convenient hiding-place for many of the mysteries which still puzzle scientists. Stages in the evolution of mammalian groups which have been difficult to understand have been inferred to have taken place in central Asia: the evolution of Man himself has been, with good reasons it is true, relegated to the mountain-girt fastnesses of the interior of the great continent.

Modern scientific exploration is slowly but surely clearing away the mists: long continued work such as that of Sven Hedin both as an individual and team leader is still needed, whilst great expeditions like that of the American Museum of Natural History show how much remains to be done. Latterly the results of scientific exploration in the U.S.S.R. and Communist China are being made available to western scholars.

This survey of the geography of Asia may be begun by attempting to summarize very briefly what is known of the orography of the continent, leaving considerations of underlying geological structure to a later stage.

5

In broad outline Asia consists of a number of great physical units.

(1) There is a great central triangle of plateaus of varying elevation, buttressed by huge mountain chains, which occupies the heart of the continent. The Pamir Knot to the north-west of India forms the western apex of the triangle: the northern apex lies in the north-east of the continent: the south-eastern apex in the interior of China.

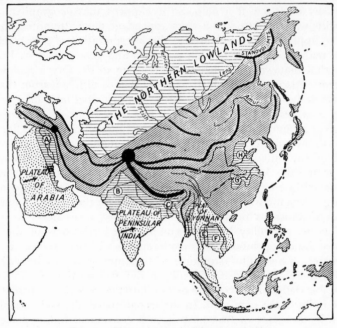

FIG. 2.—The main physical features of Asia

The great alluvial river-plains are lettered: **A.** Tigris-Euphrates; **B.** Indus; **C.** Ganges-Brahmaputra; **D.** Irrawaddy; **E.** Menam Chao Phaya; **F.** Mekong; **G.** Yangtse Kiang; **H.** Hwang Ho.

(2) A second series of plateaus stretches from the Pamir Knot, through Afghanistan, Persia and Anatolia. These two series of plateaus entirely separate the north-west of Asia from the south and east.

(3) A great lowland triangle occupies the whole of Asia to the north of the central mountainous triangle and forms the greater part of Soviet Asia.

(4) The east of Asia is occupied by a series of lowlands, separated by mountain spurs and flanked on the outside by a long and complicated succession of fold mountains, arranged as festoons.

(5) In the south of Asia are three large plateaus—those of Arabia, Peninsular India and Indo-China—separated from the main central triangle by a series of river-plains—the plains of the Tigris-Euphrates, Indus-Ganges-Brahmaputra and Irrawaddy.

These five units may now be considered separately. Many years ago an excellent summary—which has since become a classic—of the orography of Asia was given by Prince Kropotkin [1] and his broad generalizations are still applicable.

The Plateaus of Central Asia. The high plateaus of central Asia occupy more than a fifth of the whole surface of the continent. It is scarcely correct to refer to the interior of Asia as a 'plateau', since it consists of a series of plateaus of unequal altitude. The plateaus have their mountain ridges rising above the general level, and also have their high, in places gigantic, border ranges. But the depressions on the plateau surfaces rarely sink to the level of the lowlands; generally their lowest parts are still 2,000 or 3,000 feet above sea-level; whilst the chains of mountains, although rising to high absolute altitudes, are still relatively low, as one foot is upon the level of the plateau. On the north-western borders several broad trenches are cut into the plateau-mass 'like gigantic railway cuttings, leading with an imperceptible gradient from the lowlands to the plateaus'. The plateau regions of central Asia do not offer such variety of scenery as do fold ranges. 'Unvaried monotony—monotony of orographical features, climate, flora and fauna—remains the distinctive feature of the plateaus over immense distances. Over thousands of miles the traveller finds the same broad and open valleys, the same harsh climate, the same species of plants and animals, the same unfitness for agriculture.'

Taking the plateau triangle as a whole, it is fringed or bounded by a succession of mountain ranges. On the south is the Himalayan Chain; forming the south-west corner is the Pamir Knot or the Pamir Plateau. Along the north-west border aligned obliquely to the general edge of the plateau are the Tien Shan, the Altai, Sayan, Barguzin, North Muya and the Konam Mountains. Along the eastern and south-eastern borders are the Great Khingan 'Mountains' which pass northwards into the Stanovoi 'Mountains'. In the south-east the structure is complex and obscure. [2]

The plateaus of central Asia do not fade into one another, but are usually separated by well-marked ranges. They form a series of level basins, often quite cut off from one another. It is therefore simplest to consider the separate plateaus by studying in the first place the arrangement of the ranges. The Asiatic mountain system may be considered as grouped around the Pamir Plateau, 'the roof of the world'. From this great Knot huge chains are given off in four main directions:

(a) To the south-east is the Himalayan Chain, reinforced on the north by the Karakoram.

---

[1] 'The Orography of Asia', *Geog. Jour.*, **23**, 1904.

[2] On this vexed question see F. Kingdon Ward, 'The Mekong-Salween Divide as a Geographical Barrier', *Geog. Jour.*, **58**, 1921, 49–56; also the work of the Gregorys (see p. 411).

(*b*) To the east is the Kunlun.

(*c*) To the north-east is the Tien Shan.

(*d*) To the north-west are the Trans-Alai, Alai and Hissar Mountains.

(*e*) To the south-west is the Hindu Kush.

(*f*) To the south-south-west lie the mountains of Gilgit and the Sulaiman Mountains.

Each of these great chains may be followed further.

(*a*) The Himalayan Chain sweeps in a great curve along the north of India and into China. What happens structurally to the folds is one of the chief problems of Asian geography. Perhaps the folds continue across the high plateau of western China into one of the great chains of China; possibly the folds are, as it were, redoubled on themselves

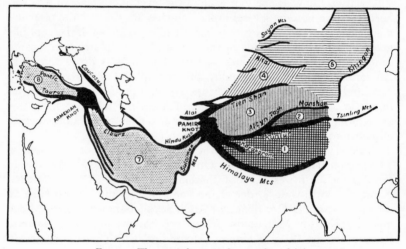

Fig. 3.—The central mountain complex of Asia

Plateaus: **1.** Tibet; **2.** Tsaidam Basin; **3.** Tarim Basin; **4.** Dzungarian Basin; **5.** Gobi Plateaus; **7.** Iranian Plateau; **8.** Anatolian Plateau. The Vitim and Aldan Plateaus (6 of the text) lie to the north-east of the map.

and form the great chain between India and Burma. The latter line is continued through the Andaman and Nicobar Islands, Sumatra and Java into the festoons of mountains of the East Indies generally.

(*b*) The Kunlun itself passes south of the Tsaidam Swamp and eventually into the Tsinling Mountains of China, but the Astin Tagh (formerly called the Altyn Tagh), which really forms its northernmost range, passes eastwards into the Nanshan or Southern Mountains of China.

(*c*) The Tien Shan pass eastwards into the Pei Shan or Northern Mountains of the Chinese; mention must also be made of their western extensions into Russian Turkistan.

(*d*) The Trans-Alai, Alai and Hissar Group fade into the plains of Russian Turkistan.

(*e*) The Hindu Kush continues westwards along the north of Persia, passing into the Elburz Mountains after having given off a great branch which becomes the Caucasus. The Elburz pass into the Armenian Knot and are then continued along the north of Asia Minor as the Pontic Ranges.

(*f*) The Sulaiman Mountains are continued to form the Kirthar Hills and the bounding ridges of the Seistan-Iran Plateaus on the south, then as the Zagros system to the Armenian Knot, passing then as the Taurus Chain along the south of Asia Minor.

These chains are followed much more easily in Fig. 3.

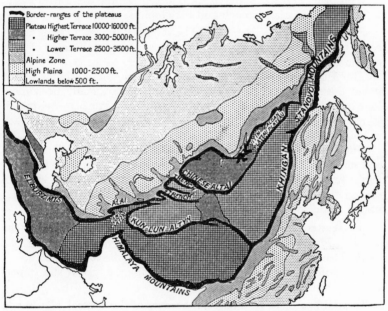

FIG. 4.—Kropotkin's conception of the structure of Asia

The plateaus may be regarded as basins lying between these ranges.

(1) The Plateau of Tibet is the loftiest of them all, and lies between the Himalayas or Karakoram on the south and the Kunlun on the north.

(2) The Tsaidam Basin lies between the main branch of the Kunlun on the south and the Astin Tagh on the north.

(3) The Tarim Basin is an extremely well-defined one, lying between the Kunlun and Astin Tagh on the south and the Tien Shan on the north.

(4) The Dzungarian Basin lies between the Tien Shan on the south and the Altai on the north.

(5) The Gobi Plateaus and the Ordos Basin lie to the north-east of the three last mentioned.

(6) The Vitim and Aldan Plateaus lie farther north-east.

It should be noted that these plateaus occur at very varying elevations, hence Kropotkin divides the whole great plateau region of central Asia into three 'terraces':

(a) Highest Terrace: 10,000 to 16,000 feet, including the Pamir Plateau and Tibet.

(b) Higher Terrace: 3,000 to 5,000 feet, including the north-eastern plateaus, Vitim and Aldan Plateaus.

(c) Lower Terrace: 2,500 to 3,500 feet, including the Tarim Basin, Dzungarian Trench and the Gobi.

Prince Kropotkin's scheme must be modified in view of later knowledge, but the main features are reproduced as Fig. 4, because of their historic value.

The Plateaus of Western Asia. The mountain chains which bound these tracts on the north and south have already been mentioned, and it remains to note the basins or plateaus—Seistan in Afghanistan and Baluchistan; Iran in Persia; and Anatolia in Turkey or Asia Minor.

The Great Lowland Triangle of the North-west. When examined more carefully, it is very evident that the whole of this area must not be regarded as a great plain. In the section on Siberia we shall analyse its component parts with some care, but we may note here that Siberia alone consists of at least three main parts:

(a) Western Siberia is a true lowland, bounded on the west by the low range of the Urals.

(b) Central Siberia is of the nature of a low dissected plateau.

(c) Eastern Siberia is a complex of hills and plains still imperfectly known.

In addition there is, along the borders of the central plateaus, a belt of what Kropotkin called high plains edged by an alpine zone. South-west of the lowland triangle, in Russian Turkistan, distinct hill ridges separate a number of basins bordering the main Aralo-Caspian depression.

The Lowlands and Mountain Festoons of Eastern Asia. The great lowlands of eastern Asia are the river plains of the Amur, of central Manchuria, of the rivers of north China; of the Yangtze Kiang in central China, of the Si Kiang in south China, of the Mekong in Indo-China and of the Menam in Siam. Of the spurs of ancient mountains which separate these basins and the curves of more recent mountains which guard them on the Pacific side, we will speak later.

The Plateaus of Southern Asia. These plateaus include two which are particularly well defined—those of Arabia and Peninsular India. Each has a general slope from south-west to north-east and merges gradually into great plains—the plains of the Tigris and Euphrates in the one case and of the Indus and Ganges in the other. The third plateau, that of Yunnan and the Shan States of Burma and China, is less well defined.

Before leaving the orography of Asia we must refer to the drainage. Asia falls into four main drainage areas—the Arctic, Pacific and Indian Ocean drainages and the areas of inland drainage. The consistent way

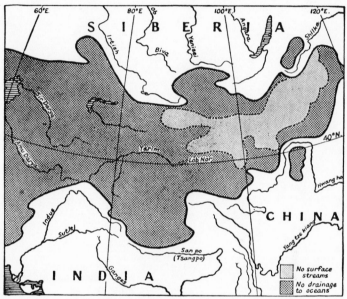

FIG. 5.—The rivers and drainage basins of Asia

This diagrammatic map shows that the heart of Asia is a great area of inland drainage, and that there is no main 'continental divide' as understood in other continents.

in which nearly all the rivers ignore the great chains and rise on the surface of the central plateaus, where their sources are separated from one another by very insignificant barriers, is worthy of special note.

The rivers flowing to the Arctic Ocean—Ob, Yenisei and Lena—have but short upper courses amongst the mountains of the central complex and very long courses across the plains. Their mouths and lower courses are frozen over in the winter months; the middle courses thaw before the mouths are free from ice, with the result that in the spring the rivers flood enormous areas of their broad open valleys. The rivers flowing to the Pacific Ocean have much longer courses on the plateau and frequently pass down through a series of basins—as does the Yangtze—before reaching the ocean. The chief are the Amur, Hwang Ho, Yangtze, Si Kiang and Mekong. Several of them afford valuable highways, but all have rapids.

The great rivers flowing into the Indian Ocean rise beyond the first rampart of mountains; they are all of them snow-fed and come down in flood in summer. In all the drier regions they provide important sources of water for irrigation. These rivers include the Salween, Irrawaddy, Brahmaputra, Ganges, Indus, Tigris and Euphrates.

THE STRUCTURE OF ASIA

THE orography of Asia is naturally determined by the underlying structure, and one should, theoretically, consider the two together. But orography is a matter of surface surveying; the determination of structure demands a more intimate examination, one which probes beneath the surface. Whilst, therefore, the general character of the surface of Asia is comparatively well known, authorities differ widely in their conception of its structure. The two have therefore been divorced; the foregoing chapter dealt in the main with ascertained facts, the present chapter enters, quite frankly, the realm of theory.

General Facts. In the first place there are certain features in the broad structure of Asia upon which there is general agreement. We may divide the structural units into four groups:

(*a*) The ancient blocks of the south, believed to have formed part of the old continent of Gondwanaland. They consist of a great complex series of pre-Cambrian rocks, highly folded and metamorphosed in the pre-Cambrian period and which have formed 'stable blocks'. Later sediments lie spread on their surface and occupy hollows, showing that the blocks have undergone changes of elevation, but they have been resistant to folding, and the sediments, where present overlying the ancient foundation, are but slightly disturbed. There are now two of these stable blocks, Arab-Asia and Peninsular India. Both blocks now slope towards the north or north-east and are there covered by alluvium of the Tigris-Euphrates in the one case and the Indus-Ganges-Brahmaputra in the other.

(*b*) The ancient blocks of the north, generally similar in character to those of the south. One of these blocks, though it does not lie in Asia, is profoundly important in a consideration of the structure of Asia, and that block is the Russian Platform, underlying practically the whole of European Russia. A similar block, the existence of which seems to be generally agreed, and to which the name Angaraland has been given, occupies practically the whole of the plateau of central Siberia. Argand, as will be noted later, believes that two other ancient massifs exist, one underlying the Tarim Basin (Serindian massif) and one underlying the plains of northern China and Manchuria (Chinese massif).

(*c*) A conspicuous series of fold ranges—including the greatest ranges of Asia—which were formed at a comparatively recent date in the earth's history, during the period of the great Tertiary or Alpine earth-movements. The Tertiary Fold Ranges of Asia include the mountains of Asia Minor, Armenia, Persia, Baluchistan and Afghanistan, the great ranges of western Burma and all the great festoons of mountains of eastern Asia.

(d) The fourth division comprises all that is left—consisting mainly of sedimentary rocks of Palaeozoic and Mesozoic ages; folded by pre-Tertiary and especially by the Caledonian movements, which took place at the close of the Silurian and in the Devonian periods, and the Armorican or Hercynian movements of late Carboniferous and Permian times,[1] as well as by movements in the Mesozoic period, more characteristic of Asia than of Europe. These older fold ranges have often cores of old rocks; they are often separated by minor stable blocks of varying character. Some of the latter are of great size—notably that of southern China.

Argand's Conception of the Structure of Asia. The veteran Swiss geologist Emile Argand read a paper before the International Geological Congress at Brussels in 1922 entitled 'La Tectonique de l'Asie'.[2] The paper created a great deal of interest, not only because of the author's interpretation of the structure of Asia, but also because of his novel ideas on tectonics in general. It is impossible here to enter into the latter and in the summary which follows certain considerations outside M. Argand's thesis have been introduced to make clear the general position.

Fig. 6 has been simplified from Argand's diagrammatic tectonic map of Asia. It will be seen that he distinguishes—

(a) Two old platforms, of pre-Cambrian rocks, in the south (Arabia and India).

(b) Four old platforms, of pre-Cambrian rocks, in the north (the Russian Platform, Angaraland, the Serindian and Chinese massifs).

(c) A broad belt, shown in black, of Alpine or Tertiary folds (chaînes géosynclinales et chaînes liminaires du cycle alpin).

(d) Large areas consisting mainly of palaeozoic sediments and folded before the Alpine movements took place.

Here we must diverge for a few moments into certain matters affecting the earth's structure as a whole. It is probable that the original crust of the earth consisted of two concentric shells: an outer

---

[1] Perhaps it is unwise to refer to 'Armorican' or 'Hercynian' movements in Asia since their importance is doubtful. But these movements are so significant in Europe, that it seems probable they had a counterpart in Asia.

[2] *Comptes rendus de la XIII Session, Congrès géol. intern.*, **I**, 171–372.

lighter shell with roughly the composition and character of granite, and an inner heavier shell with roughly the composition and character of the well-known volcanic rock basalt. Or the outer shell may have

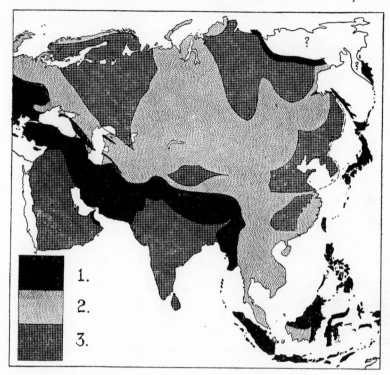

FIG. 6.—The structure of Asia, *simplified from* Argand

1. Tertiary folded belts; **2.** Regions of post pre-Cambrian and pre-Tertiary folding; **3.** Ancient blocks.

been discontinuous and the original continental masses like gigantic icebergs of granite floating in a sea of basalt. The processes of denudation and sedimentation, which we are ordinarily able to study, take

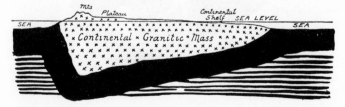

FIG. 7.—Diagram of a continental granitic mass floating on a substratum of basaltic material (in black). Below the latter there may be another layer—the peridotic

(*After* Holmes and others)

A.—2

place on the continental masses and in the epicontinental seas, so that although the continental masses of today show little, if any, traces of the original crust of the earth, they can still be regarded as masses of

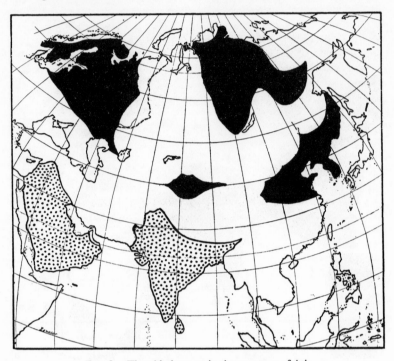

FIG. 8.—The old elements in the structure of Asia

(*After* Argand) In black, the old massifs of the north; dotted, the remnants of Gondwanaland.

FIG. 9.—The old massifs of the north of Asia before disruption and dispersal according to the theory of continental drift. The present position of these blocks is shown in Fig. 8

(*After* Argand)

comparatively light rock buoyed up on the heavier basaltic layer, as shown in Fig. 7. Given this fundamental conception of the continents, there is nothing inherently impossible in the idea that the continental masses can split and the fragments drift apart. This is, broadly, Wegener's famous theory of Continental Drift. Applying these theories to Asia, the old stable blocks of the south, Arabia and India, were originally part of one great continental block (Gondwanaland), which included also the western half of Australia, nearly the whole of Africa and the eastern half of South America. Gondwanaland split up and the fragments drifted apart. Similarly, if one accepts Argand's interpretation of the northern parts of Asia, one can imagine the four old platforms there (Fig. 8) originally part of one mass. Fig. 9 shows them reunited as they may have been. They drifted apart gradually: the intervening areas became seas in which huge quantities of sediment were deposited and then rucked up into folds by successive earth-movements, finally forming a solid mass.

Actually, it may be noticed, Wegener's theory of Continental Drift is unnecessary to explain the structure of northern Asia: the four ancient platforms may still represent portions of an ancient North Asian continent, the areas between them having been worn away by the ordinary processes of denudation and filled with masses of sediment.

An Orthodox Conception of the Structure of Asia. In attempting to outline a rather different conception of the structure of the continent it has been labelled 'orthodox' for want of a better title, since the hypotheses of Wegener (despite recent work on paleomagnetism) and Argand may still be regarded, perhaps, as 'unorthodox'.

In any case we have the fundamental threefold division of the continent into central and northern Asia, the Alpine fold belt, and the old blocks of the south. Northern Asia includes at least two main units:

(a) Angaraland or the plateau of central Siberia.
(b) The west Siberian lowland.

To the south of these lies a great series of basins, of varying elevation, separated by mountain ranges of varied origin. It is of course well known that there are certain parts of the earth's crust which are relatively stable—the stable blocks or ancient massifs to which we have already referred; other parts where strain is relieved by fracture or 'faulting'; other parts where strain is relieved by crumbling or folding. In northern and central Asia Angaraland is an ancient stable block; west Siberia is probably a sunken stable block, that is, one whose surface is relatively low; most of the basins of central Asia consist of slightly sunken blocks which have not been subjected to folding since early Mesozoic times, and which are separated by mountain ranges of two types. The mountains are either folded belts or are block mountains left as ridges because of the downfaulting around them. It will be necessary to refer again to this question in the section on Mongolia. Of one thing there is little doubt: central Asia has been a continent since Mesozoic times.

Coming now to the question of the Alpine fold belts, towards the close of the Mesozoic one can picture a long narrow sea or ocean separating the continent of central Asia from the continental masses of Gondwanaland—a long narrow sea of the type of the Mediterranean but much larger and known in geological literature as a geosynclinal

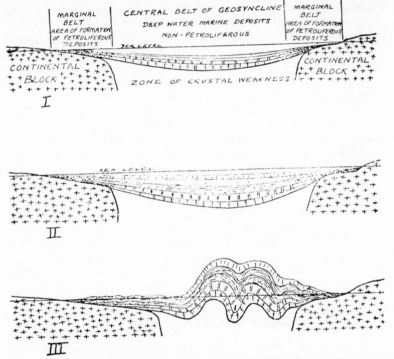

FIG. 10.—Diagrams showing the gradual infilling (**I** and **II**) of a geosynclinal trough and its deformation (**III**) into an anticlinorial mountain chain

basin. To this particular basin the name Tethys has been given. In this sea were deposited great thicknesses of sediment. At the same time epicontinental seas and great gulfs fringed the south and east of Asia. Then, intermittently during the Tertiary period, came a great series of earth-movements. The seas lying between or on the flanks of the continental masses formed the lines of weakness; their sediments were folded and overfolded into the greatest chains of the Asiatic continent. Fig. 10 is an attempt to illustrate the process of deformation of the great geosyncline. Fig. 11 illustrates the rock structures actually found in the Himalayan Chain and shows the overfolding of the rocks. Fig. 13 shows the disposition of the Alpine folded belts in Asia.[1] It will be shown later that the individual ranges are not necessarily parallel to

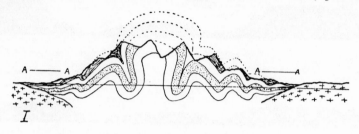

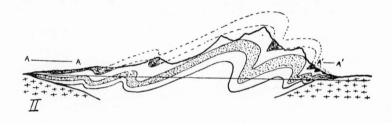

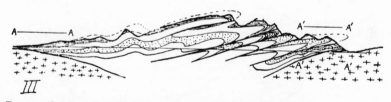

FIG. 11.—Sections through fold mountain chains, showing three types of structure to be studied in the fold mountains of Asia

I. Symmetrical anticlinorium, probably rare; II. Asymmetrical anticlinorium; III. Overthrust anticlinorium of the type exemplified in the Himalayas.

the edge of the folded belts, but tend to be arranged *en echelon* within those belts.

That there is much still to be learnt before the structure of Asia is fully understood will be apparent from the broad survey given by

[1] The writer has attempted to show elsewhere (*Jour. Inst. Petr. Techn.*, **14**, 1928, 28–53) that the oilfields of Asia are associated with the margins of these Alpine fold belts, hence their indication on Figs. 10 and 13.

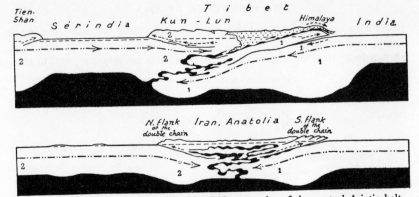

FIG. 12.—The structure of the Tertiary fold mountains of the central Asiatic belt, *according to* Argand

It will be noted that the overthrusts seen in the Himalayas are attributed to 'under-riding' by the great stable blocks and that complementary to the southern flank of each chain (overthrust southwards) there is a northern flank overthrust northwards. **1** = The Gondwanaland continental mass; **2** = The Serindian-Russian mass.

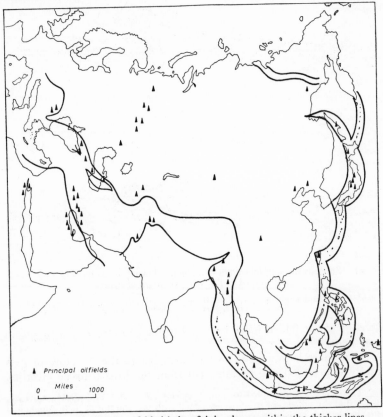

FIG. 13.—The Tertiary folded belts of Asia, shown within the thicker lines

The small symbols are oilfields.

the veteran Chinese geologist J. S. Lee in a paper written in 1950 and published later.[1] In addition to the well-known series of arcs bordering the Pacific, he finds running right across the continent from east to west series of ε type of arcs with their main convex front facing south. These are regarded as consistent with the southward movement of northern blocks towards Gondwanaland.

[1] 'Distortion of Continental Asia', *The Palaeobotanist*, **1**, 1954, 298–315.

REFERENCES

In addition to the works quoted above, the mine of information is Suess' great work, *Das Antlitz der Erde*. The French edition of this work is the best, because of the full documentation. See also Hobbs, *Earth Features and their Meaning* (New York: Macmillan, 1920); L. de Launay, *La Géologie et les Richesses minérales de l'Asie* (with structural maps of Asia) (Paris: Béranger, 1911); W. A. Obrutschew, *Geologie von Sibirien* (Berlin: Borntraeger, 1926); Grabau, *Stratigraphy of China* (Peking: 1925–6); C. P. Berkey and F. K. Morris, Publications of the Asiatic Expeditions of the American Museum of Natural History, Nos. 29, 30 and 31. An important work is *The Structure of Asia*, edited by J. W. Gregory (London: Methuen, 1929). In particular, the introductory chapter of this work should be consulted. An important summary of the structure of the Himalayas is given by D. N. Wadia—Presidential Address, the Section of Geology, Indian Science Congress, Calcutta, 1938. A similar service for China has been rendered by J. S. Lee—*Geology of China* (London: Murby, 1939). An important summary of the whole is given in K. Leuchs, *Geologie von Asien*, Berlin, 1937. See also W. E. Pratt and D. Good, *World Geography of Petroleum* (Amer. Geog. Soc., 1950), D. N. Wadia, *Geology of India* (Second Edition, 1949) and J. S. Lee. *op. cit. sup.*

All these earlier ideas will be found summarized and brought up to date in Lester C. King, *The Morphology of the Earth* (Edinburgh and London: Oliver & Boyd, 1962).

THE CLIMATES OF ASIA

THERE are two features of Asia which exercise a controlling influence in determining the climates: the one is its size; the other is the great central core of lofty plateaus and its buttresses of great mountain ranges.

From a meteorological point of view Eurasia—and indeed the north of Africa as well—must be considered as a single land mass, a land mass having a total area which approaches 25,000,000 square miles. The heart of Asia is more than 1,500 miles from the nearest seaboard,[1] a circumstance which is alone sufficient to ensure conditions of extreme continentality, and might, in any case, be expected to result in a great difference between summer and winter conditions.

The orographical structure of Asia is such as to accentuate the climatic features due to the vast size of the land mass. The central plateaus are flanked by ranges which effectively prevent the penetration of oceanic influences to the interior; further the succession of plateaus and ranges stretching without a break from Asia Minor to the extreme north-east of the continent forms a practically impassable wall in the lower strata of the atmosphere. As a result the winters are exceedingly cold in the plains lying to the north of this central barrier, the 'cold pole' of the earth being situated, as shown in Fig. 14, in the north-east of Siberia on the Arctic Circle. Conversely, the plains of India are completely shut off from Arctic influences, and in summer some of the highest recorded temperatures on the surface of the earth are found in northern India.

It is impossible, therefore, to divorce the meteorology of Asia from its structural features. Sea-level isotherm maps and isobar maps, in particular for the summer months, are apt to convey very erroneous impressions, and special attention should be given to temperatures and pressures not reduced to sea-level.

Conditions in Winter. In the winter months of the Northern Hemisphere, when the earth's thermal equator shifts to the south of the Equator, the centre and north of Asia become extremely cold. The northern plains are far removed from the oceanic influences—notably the influence of the warm North Atlantic Drift—which modify so profoundly the winter rigours of western Europe and at the same time are completely cut off by mountain barriers from any warming influence of the Indian or Pacific Oceans, yet open to cold influences from the frozen Arctic. The higher layers of the atmosphere, over the great ranges of mountains and tremendous lofty plateaus of central

[1] Contrast North America, just over 1,000 miles.

Asia, are naturally cold. Hence in winter the whole of central and northern Asia is occupied by a great cushion of cold, heavy air forming naturally a region of high pressure. In terms of modern airmass meteorology this forms a great continental polar (cP) mass.

We may express the matter in another way by saying that the winter cold intensifies the sub-tropical high pressure in south Asia, but the prominent feature is the 'cold' anticyclone, a cushion of very cold, dry, dense air centred over the Gobi, which is an extension and an intensification of the Arctic high pressure.[1] The Arctic low-pressure belt,

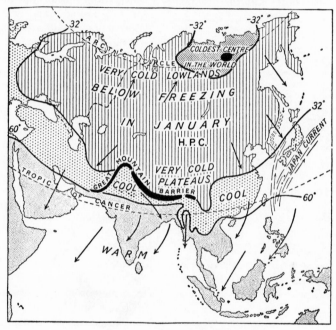

FIG. 14.—Winter climatic conditions in Asia

The temperatures shown are the approximate average temperatures in January (not reduced to sea-level) and stress the cold heart of the continent more than do sea-level isotherms. **H.P.C.** = the high-pressure centre (very approximate). 'Coldest centre' excludes Antarctica.

which exists over the North Atlantic (as the semi-permanent depression off Iceland) and over the North Pacific, is completely obliterated over the Asiatic continent.

Obviously the heavy air over the heart of Asia in winter will flow out in all directions, giving rise to cold, dry winds blowing outwards from central Asia. Where the barometric gradient is steep and the progress of the winds comparatively unimpeded by mountain ranges, the winter winds are not only bitterly cold but strong and continuous.

[1] W. G. Kendrew, *The Climates of the Continents*, Oxford, 4th edition, 1953, 147.

Such is the case over northern China. On the south, however, the mountain barrier afforded by the Himalayas is sufficiently high to stop their progress entirely. They fail completely to reach India. The last sentence might well have been put in italics, for the central Asian high pressures are frequently credited with being the cause of India's north-east monsoon. Actually the comparatively feeble northerly winds experienced in India in winter, as will be described later, originate from subsidiary high-pressure centres over the northern plains of India itself.

In the winter months practically the whole of Europe lies in the

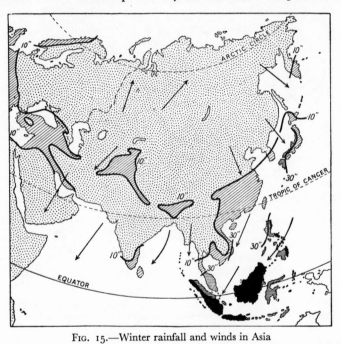

FIG. 15.—Winter rainfall and winds in Asia

The isohyets shown are 10, 30 and 60 inches for the half-year November 1 to April 30.

westerly wind belt and is under the influence of the succession of cyclones which roll eastwards across the Atlantic. The further passage of these cyclones is effectively prevented by the high-pressure centre of Asia: one current of the westerlies is deflected to the north and results in a winter snowfall in north-western Siberia; a second current is deflected to the south and penetrates as far eastward as Baluchistan and the Punjab.

The outward blowing winds of winter will obviously be dry winds: it is only after they have crossed some stretch of water that they are able to pick up moisture and become rain-bearing. As will be noticed in the sequel, they bring snow or rain to Japan, central and south China, the coast of Indo-China, the Philippines and Ceylon. Elsewhere, as shown in Fig. 15, Asia is practically rainless in the winter half of the year, except for the East Indies which lie in the Equatorial belt. It may indeed be said that to the general rainlessness of Asia in winter there are five exceptions:

(a) The snowfall of north-western Siberia (not sufficiently heavy to be shown on Fig. 15) brought by cyclones of the westerly wind belt.

(b) The rainfall of Asia Minor, south-western Asia, Persia, Baluchistan, Afghanistan and north-western India brought by the southern stream of depressions of the westerly wind belt.

(c) The rainfall of Ceylon and the Madras Coast brought by disturbances in October to December which have picked up moisture from the Bay of Bengal.

(d) The rainfall of the East Indies, lying in the Equatorial belt.

(e) The rainfall of certain east-coast tracts due to oceanic influences affecting the normal character of the winter winds.

Conditions in Summer. As the summer months approach, the land heats rapidly, and not only is the great high-pressure system of winter completely dissipated, but it is actually replaced by a succession of low-pressure areas. Again, the influence of the mountain barriers is paramount. A sea-level isobar map shows a low-pressure area stretching from Arabia over Baluchistan, north-western India and Tibet. Actually there is no connection between the intense low-pressure centre which develops over the plains of north-western India and those which develop over the plateaus of the continental interior. The heating of the land and the change from high pressures to low take place slowly and progressively. The outblowing winds become feebler and feebler; April and May are months marked in many areas by light irregular breezes. It might be expected that these feeble breezes would gradually strengthen into the summer monsoon. Such, however, is not the case. The equilibrium is upset suddenly, and the monsoon 'bursts', blowing suddenly with its full violence. This is particularly the case in India, and an attempt at explanation will be offered later. The winds which flow in towards the low-pressure centres vary greatly in strength and regularity. They are strong and constant in India, where the low-pressure centre over the north-western plains is well marked. They are much feebler over China and Japan, where the low-pressure centres of the interior lie over the central plateaus and are less insistent in their attraction for the inflowing air. Thus in India it is the winter monsoon which is light, the summer monsoon strong; in China the winter monsoon is strong and the summer monsoon comparatively feeble.

But in all cases the inflowing winds are from the ocean; they are moisture-laden, and the summer months are the rainy months over practically the whole of Asia. The amount of rainfall is determined by orography: the mountain ramparts of the central plateaus effectively prevent a heavy fall anywhere in the heart of Asia. Only in one part of Asia is the summer normally rainless: south-western Asia (excluding southern Arabia) as far east as Baluchistan and Afghanistan forms a continuation of the Mediterranean region of Europe and North Africa just as it does in winter.

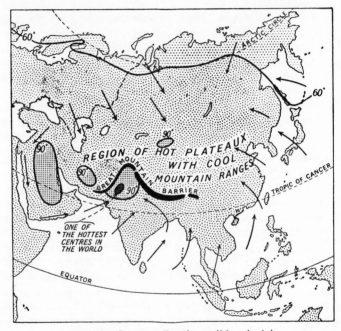

FIG. 16.—Summer climatic conditions in Asia

The temperatures shown are the approximate average temperatures in July (not reduced to sea-level) and stress the generally high temperature of the whole continent, despite the elevation of the interior. This map also emphasizes the independence of the Indian monsoon.

In the above remarks we have used the word 'monsoon' in the way in which it is usually used amongst climatologists as meaning the periodic *winds* of Asia. Actually the word should mean *season* and is often used, especially by residents in India, as equivalent to the rains or the rainy season.

The Climates of Asia. The three essential elements in the climates of Asia are the dry outblowing winds of winter, the wet inblowing winds of summer and the controlling influence of the relief. Owing to the vast extent of the continent, a number of climatic types may be distinguished.

(1) *The Equatorial Climate*, as its name implies, occurs as a belt on either side of the Equator, normally extending roughly between 5° North and 5° South. It therefore occurs almost throughout the East Indies, in Malaya and, in a modified degree, in Ceylon.

The temperature is high all the year round, and is characterized by its very small variation. In typical localities the average for the year is between 78° and 80° F.; the range between the hottest and coldest months is normally less than 5°. Similarly, the differences between day

FIG. 17.—Summer rainfall and winds in Asia

The isohyets shown are 10, 30 and 60 inches for the half-year May 1 to October 31. All parts shown in black have more than 60 inches in this period.

and night temperatures are small, and may be taken as usually less than 20°. The Equatorial regions are popularly, but erroneously, regarded as the hottest in the world. The average temperature, it is true, is uniformly high, and the constantly damp, steamy atmosphere may be enervating, but the Equatorial climate is far from being the most trying in the world. The absence of really high temperatures—the thermometer rarely rises above 100° F.—and the pleasantly cool rains which accompany the afternoon thunderstorms make the climate quite pleasant. This is particularly the case in maritime situations such as the island of Singapore, where land and sea breezes impart a welcome movement to the air. The climate is found at its worst in the interior of the great Equatorial forests where the air is absolutely still. The effect of elevation is to lower the average temperature and, sometimes, to result in a slightly greater range.

In Equatorial regions the rain falls at all seasons of the year and there is, typically, no 'dry season', except in a relative sense. The

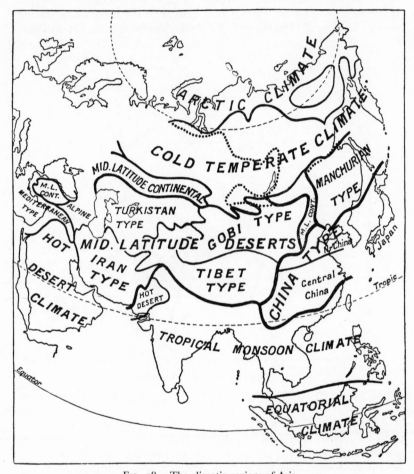

Fig. 18.—The climatic regions of Asia

The dotted line shows the limit of permanently frozen ground or permafrost.

Equatorial lands may be considered as lying in the Belt of Calms or Doldrums, and the rains are mainly, sometimes entirely, convectional rains. During the early part of the day bright sunshine induces rapid evaporation and an upward current in the atmosphere. The ascending moisture-laden air becomes cooled and clouds form. The formation of clouds in the afternoon and the subsequent precipitation is frequently accompanied by thunder. The rain falls in torrential downpours, usually of short duration. This daily programme is not evident from the statistics, which show an 'average' of cloud of between 3 and 7 throughout the year. The relative humidity in regions of Equatorial climate is uniformly high, being on an average over 80 per cent. the year through.

Although rain falls throughout the year, stations near the Equator usually have two periods of maximum rainfall; stations towards the northern or southern fringes of the belt usually one. In most cases the rainfall maximum or maxima occur shortly after the period when the sun is vertical. The farther one goes away from the Equator the longer will be the duration of the dry or relatively dry period; hence the gradual passage into the Tropical Monsoon climate.

EQUATORIAL CLIMATE—TEMPERATURES IN ° F.[1]

Station	Latitude	Height above sea, ft.	Jan.	Feb.	Mar.	April	May	June	July	Aug.	Sept.	Oct.	Nov.	Dec.	Average	Range
Singapore	1° N.	10	78	79	80	81	81·5	81	81	81	80	80	79	79	80	3·2
Amboina (Moluccas)	4° S.	40	81	81	81	79	79	78	77	78	78	79	80	81	79	3·6
Jakarta	6° S.	23	78	78	79	79	80	79	78	79	79	80	79	78	79	2·0
Penang	5° N.	23	80	80	81	82	81	81	80	80	80	80	79	79	80	2·9
Sandakan (Borneo)	5° N.	98	79	79	81	82	82	81	81	81	81	81	80	79	80	2·9

EQUATORIAL CLIMATE—RAINFALL IN INCHES

Station	Jan.	Feb.	Mar.	April	May	June	July	Aug.	Sept.	Oct.	Nov.	Dec.	Total
Singapore	8·5	6·1	6·5	6·9	7·2	6·7	6·8	8·5	7·1	8·2	10·0	10·4	92·9
Amboina	5·6	4·5	5·4	10·9	20·5	23·9	23·2	16·0	9·1	6·9	4·1	5·7	135·8
Jakarta	13·0	13·6	7·8	4·8	3·7	3·6	2·6	1·3	2·6	4·1	5·0	8·7	70·8
Penang	3·9	3·0	4·7	7·0	11·0	7·2	8·9	12·8	19·0	16·1	10·9	4·8	109·3
Sandakan	19·4	9·9	7·8	4·1	5·1	8·6	10·0	6·9	9·5	10·2	16·4	19·3	127·2

(2) *The Tropical Monsoon Climate* occurs mainly within the Tropics.[2] The typical monsoon lands are India, Indo-China and southern China. Central and northern China and Japan are often called 'monsoon lands'; their rainfall is due to similar causes, but they lie outside the Tropics, and have distinctly cold winters, thus necessitating their

[1] Figures quoted from Kendrew, *Climates of the Continents*. The figures given for the range of temperature are calculated from more accurate data than are given in the monthly columns. In the latest edition Kendrew has given some more recent figures.

[2] For a modern view of the origin of the monsoons see under Indo-Pakistan.

separation from the tropical monsoon lands. In winter the monsoon lands are under the influence of the normal Trade winds—the 'winter monsoon'; in summer these winds, as we have already seen, are completely reversed. It is customary to distinguish three seasons in tropical monsoon lands, though details will be found later under India of a more scientific division into four seasons. The three seasons are:

(a) The cool season, with little rain, from November to about the end of February.
(b) The hot season, also rainless, from February to the middle of June.
(c) The rainy season, when the rain cools the atmosphere and temperature is generally lower, from the middle of June to about the end of October.

Generally speaking, the drier the place the less the cooling influence of the rain is felt and the greater the range of temperature. There is thus a very large range in the Punjab (plains of North-west India). The wetter places, on the other hand, and those under the influence of the sea, have a much smaller range of temperature. Bombay is a good example. It should be noted that in October, when the rains are drying up, there is a slight rise in temperature.

The rainfall in monsoon lands depends largely on relief. Where the monsoon comes in contact with high mountains near the coast, and is forced to rise, the resulting rainfall is very great. Average annual falls of over 500 inches are known, and such exposed situations may be classed as the rainiest in the world. On the other hand, near the low-pressure centre in India, towards which the winds blow for great distances overland, they arrive practically dry, and certain stations have less than 5 inches of rain per year. Other details of the monsoon climate will be found later under India. In studying the following figures, notice the special position of Hué, facing north-east and receiving but little of its rain in the period of the south-west monsoon.

TROPICAL MONSOON CLIMATE—TEMPERATURES IN ° F.

Station	Latitude	Height above sea, ft.	Jan.	Feb.	Mar.	April	May	June	July	Aug.	Sept.	Oct.	Nov.	Dec.	Year	Range
Bombay	18° 54'	37	74	75	78	82	**85**	82	79	79	79	**81**	79	76	79	10·1
Rangoon	16° 46'	18	75	77	81	**85**	82	80	79	79	79	**80**	78	76	79	10·3
Mandalay	21° 59'	250	69	74	82	**89**	88	85	85	85	83	82	76	69	81	20·4
Delhi	28° 39'	718	58	62	74	86	92	**92**	86	85	84	78	68	60	77	34·3
Karachi	24° 51'	13	65	68	75	81	85	**87**	84	82	82	80	74	67	78	21·5
Hong Kong	22° 16'	108	60	58	63	70	77	81	**82**	81	80	76	69	63	72	24·0
Hué	16° 26'	23	69	67	74	80	83	**85**	84	85	81	78	73	70	78	17·6

TROPICAL MONSOON CLIMATE—RAINFALL IN INCHES

Station	Jan.	Feb.	Mar.	April	May	June	July	Aug.	Sept.	Oct.	Nov.	Dec.	Total
Bombay	0·1	0	0	0·1	0·5	20·6	24·6	14·9	10·9	1·8	0·5	0·1	74·1
Rangoon	0·1	0·2	0·2	1·7	11·7	18·3	21·4	19·6	15·9	7·1	2·5	0·1	98·8
Mandalay	0·1	0·1	0·2	1·2	5·2	5·7	3·3	4·1	6·2	4·5	1·7	0·3	32·6
Delhi	1·0	0·6	0·7	0·3	0·7	3·2	8·4	7·4	4·4	0·4	0·1	0·4	27·6
Karachi	0·6	0·3	0·1	0·1	0	0·4	3·2	1·8	0·7	0	0·2	0·2	7·6
Hong Kong	1·0	1·3	3·3	5·4	12·4	16·3	15·9	14·8	12·5	5·2	1·1	1·0	90·2
Hué	4·0	4·8	1·8	2·4	3·6	2·8	3·4	4·0	16·2	26·3	22·4	10·2	101·9

(3) *The China Type of Climate*,[1] or the Warm Temperate East Coast Climate, is found in central and northern China. Central and northern China form part of the great monsoon region of Asia, but the climate differs from the Tropical Monsoon climate of India and southern China in the coldness of the winters. The rainfall, like that of India, is due to the development of low-pressure centres in the interior of Asia in summer, towards which rain-bearing winds from the ocean blow. Whilst India is protected in winter from the cold outblowing winds from the heart of Asia by the mountain barrier of the Himalayas, China is not so fortunate. The January isotherm of 32° almost reaches the Tropic of Cancer; snow is common in winter, even on the plains. The essentially summer rainfall is greatest near the coast, but as will

THE CHINA TYPE OF CLIMATE—TEMPERATURES IN ° F.

Station	Latitude	Height above sea, ft.	Jan.	Feb.	Mar.	April	May	June	July	Aug.	Sept.	Oct.	Nov.	Dec.	Year	Range
Shanghai	31° 13′	33	38	39	46	56	65	73	80	80	73	63	52	42	59	42·8
Hankow	30° 35′	118	39	40	49	61	71	78	83·5	83	76	65	54	43	62	44·7
Peking	39° 55′	131	23	29	41	57	68	76	79	76	68	55	38	27	53	55·3
Tokyo	35° 40′	69	37	38	44	54	61	69	75	78	72	61	50	41	57	40·5

THE CHINA TYPE OF CLIMATE—RAINFALL IN INCHES

Station	Jan.	Feb.	Mar.	April	May	June	July	Aug.	Sept.	Oct.	Nov.	Dec.	Total
Shanghai	2·2	2·3	3·4	3·8	3·7	6·5	5·5	5·9	4·7	3·2	1·7	1·2	44·1
Hankow	2·1	1·1	2·8	4·8	5·0	7·0	8·6	4·6	2·2	3·9	1·1	0·6	43·8
Peking	0·1	0·2	0·2	0·6	1·4	3·0	9·4	6·3	2·6	0·6	0·3	0·1	24·8
Tokyo	2·0	2·6	4·3	5·3	5·9	6·3	5·6	4·6	7·5	7·2	4·3	2·3	57·9

[1] The types of climate here called 'China Type' and 'Manchurian Type' may, perhaps, be better considered together as the 'East Asian' or 'Temperate Monsoon' climate. The rainfall is monsoonal and hence different from that on the east coast of North America; its seasonal distribution in Manchuria is very different from what it is in the St. Lawrence area.

be explained later under 'China' winter rainfall is not completely absent. Three sub-types may be distinguished:

(a) Central China (examples Shanghai and Hankow).
(b) Northern China (example Peking).
(c) Japan type, modified by Japan's insular position. The varied climates of Japan will be considered later.

(4) *The Manchurian Type of Climate*, or Cold Temperate East Coast Climate, may be assimilated with the climate which is found around the mouth of the St. Lawrence in North America in the large temperature range but not in the rainfall régime. The climate is found in Manchuria and Amuria, and one might, indeed, include the north China region mentioned above. The range of temperature is very large, the winters are long and severe. The monsoonal influence is still seen in the rainfall régime.

THE MANCHURIAN TYPE OF CLIMATE—TEMPERATURES IN ° F.

Station	Latitude	Height above sea, ft.	Jan.	Feb.	Mar.	April	May	June	July	Aug.	Sept.	Oct.	Nov.	Dec.	Year	Range
Harbin	45° 45′	325	−2	5	24	42	56	66	**72**	69	58	40	21	3	38	73·8
Vladivostok	43° 10′	50	5	12	26	39	49	57	66	**69**	61	49	30	14	40	64·6

THE MANCHURIAN TYPE OF CLIMATE—RAINFALL IN INCHES

Station	Jan.	Feb.	Mar.	April	May	June	July	Aug.	Sept.	Oct.	Nov.	Dec.	Tota
Moukden	0·2	0·2	0·6	1·0	2·4	3·2	**6·7**	4·3	2·6	1·7	0·5	0·2	23·6
Vladivostok	0·1	0·2	0·3	1·2	1·3	1·5	2·2	**3·5**	2·4	1·6	0·5	0·2	15·0

(5) *The Hot Desert Climate* is found over wide areas in south-western Asia about the latitude of the Tropic of Cancer. These regions lie along the sub-tropical high-pressure belts, and are so situated that they are practically outside the influence of either the monsoon or the Mediterranean belts. We say 'practically' because actually it is possible to resolve the hot deserts of south-western Asia into two types —those which have a very dry type of monsoon climate (Lower Indus Valley and the Thar Desert of India) and those which have a very dry type of Mediterranean climate (Syria, Iraq and part of Iran).

The absence of clouds allows the sun's rays to shine down with un-mitigated force on the unprotected soil during the day, whilst the absence of cloud at night permits rapid radiation of heat, so that the nights are often very cold. Similarly there is a big contrast between the hot season, when the sun is almost vertically overhead, and the cold

THE HOT DESERT TYPE OF CLIMATE—TEMPERATURES IN ° F.

Station	Latitude	Height above sea, ft.	Jan.	Feb.	Mar.	April	May	June	July	Aug.	Sept.	Oct.	Nov.	Dec.	Year	Range
Jacobabad	28° 17′	186	57	62	74	85	94	**98**	95	92	89	79	67	59	79	40·4
Aden	12° 46′	94	76	77	78	81	86	**89**	88	86	87	82	79	77	82	12·9
Baghdad	33° 21′	220	49	53	59	68	79	87	92	**92·5**	86	76	61	52	71	43·7

THE HOT DESERT TYPE OF CLIMATE—RAINFALL IN INCHES

Station	Jan.	Feb.	Mar	April	May	June	July	Aug.	Sept.	Oct.	Nov.	Dec.	Total
Jacobabad	0·3	0·3	0·2	0·2	0·2	0·1	**1·2**	**1·2**	0·2	0	0·1	0·2	4·2
Aden	0·3	0·2	**0·7**	0·3	0·2	0	0	0·1	0·2	0	0·1	0·1	2·2
Baghdad	1·3	**2·1**	1·6	0·9	0·2	0	0	0·1	0	0	1·0	1·8	9·0

season. There is little or no rain to exercise a cooling influence on the summer temperatures; most of the hot deserts are low lying, so that there is not even altitude to temper the heat. As a result some of the highest temperatures of the world are recorded in these regions. Jacobabad, in the driest part of the Indus Valley of India (a very dry monsoon type), has an *average* temperature of nearly 98° in June.

(6) *The Mid-Latitude Desert Climate* is the climate of the high plateaus of Asia. These formerly misnamed 'Temperate' Deserts are cut off from the oceans by distance and mountain barriers. They agree in having wide ranges of temperature and a very low rainfall. Generally they are huge areas of high pressure—great masses of cold air—in winter, and areas of low pressure with inblowing winds in summer. The scanty rainfall is therefore mainly in summer, except in those regions which border the Mediterranean countries. Indeed, it must be observed that the climate of the mid-latitude deserts is obviously related to the climates of the surrounding regions. The deserts of the heart of Asia are bordered on the south-west by Mediterranean lands, on the south and south-east by monsoon lands, on the east by regions with the China and Manchurian types of climate, on the north by the cold forest lands, on the west by the mid-latitude grasslands. The desert may thus be a very dry grassland region, a very dry Mediterranean region, and so on.

At least four sub-types may be distinguished:

(*a*) The Tibet type—found on the highest plateaus (Leh in Kashmir is the nearest record available).

(*b*) The Iran type—found on the enclosed plateaus of Iran and Afghanistan, with a winter rainfall régime (example, Tehran in Iran).

(c) The Gobi type, found on the plateaus of lower elevation and in the basins north of Tibet (examples, Kamgar, Urga in the Gobi Desert, Lukchun in the Tarim Basin).

(d) The Turkistan or Turan type, found on the lowlands to the south-west of Siberia, the Turanian Basin—a very dry type of steppe (example, Tashkent).

The rarity of the atmosphere may result in some extraordinary freak phenomena of temperature. In Tibet the ground temperature in the sun may be over 130° whilst it is still freezing in the shade. There are similarly enormous differences between day and night temperatures. Some of the greatest known annual ranges are in the climates of the mid-latitude deserts. The rainfall varies from 15 inches downwards. Semi-desert conditions may even prevail where the rainfall is rather more. In the higher regions some of the precipitation is in the form of snow.

THE MID-LATITUDE DESERT TYPE OF CLIMATE—TEMPERATURES IN °F.

Station	Latitude	Altitude, ft.	Jan.	Feb.	Mar.	April	May	June	July	Aug.	Sept.	Oct.	Nov.	Dec.	Year	Range
Leh	34° 10'	11,503	17	19	31	43	50	58	**63**	61	54	43	32	22	41	45·3
Tehran	35° 42'	4,002	34	42	48	61	71	80	**85**	83	77	66	51	42	62	51·3
Kashgar	39° 30'	4,255	22	34	46	61	70	77	**80**	76	69	55	40	26	55	57·9
Lukchun	42° 40'	− 50	13	27	45	66	75	85	**90·5**	85	74	55	33	21	56	77·3
Urga	47° 58'	3,800	−15	−4	13	34	47	59	**63·5**	59	47	29	8	−7	28	78·7
Turt-Kul	41° 20'	295	23	29	43	58	72	80	**83**	79	67	52	38	30	54	60·5

THE MID-LATITUDE DESERT TYPE OF CLIMATE—RAINFALL IN INCHES

Station	Jan.	Feb.	Mar.	April	May	June	July	Aug.	Sept.	Oct.	Nov.	Dec.	Total
Leh	0·3	0·4	0·2	0·2	0·3	0·2	0·5	0·5	0·2	0·2	0	0·2	3·2
Tehran	1·2	0·9	2·4	0·9	0·4	0	0·4	0	0·1	0·1	1·2	1·3	8·9
Kashgar	0·3	0	0·2	0·2	0·8	0·4	0·3	0·7	0·3	0	0	0·2	3·4
Turt-Kul	0·2	0·4	0·5	0·6	0·2	0	0	0·1	0	0·1	0·1	0·1	2·1

(7) *The Mediterranean Climate* is, like the monsoon climate, a very distinctive type. It is found in Asia round the coasts of Asia Minor and Syria and in a modified form along the Kurdistan Mountains. The Mediterranean climate is a 'west coast' climate, occurring on the western sides of the land masses in roughly the same latitudes as the China type on the east. On the west the great land masses roughly between latitudes 30° and 45° are under the influence of the sub-

tropical high-pressure belt in summer when the regions are hot and dry, with outblowing winds. In winter, however, the regions come under the influence of the Westerly wind belt and so enjoy moist, mild winters. In other words this is, *par excellence*, the 'Winter Rain Climate'. Another characteristic of the Mediterranean climate is the large amount of sunshine. Almost cloudless skies are the rule in summer, and even in winter clouds are less numerous than would be expected.

The Mediterranean lands of south-western Asia belong to what is called the 'Eastern Mediterranean type', and suffer from colder winters than are usual farther west.

THE MEDITERRANEAN CLIMATE—TEMPERATURES IN ° F.

Station	Latitude	Altitude, ft.	Jan.	Feb.	Mar.	April	May	June	July	Aug.	Sept.	Oct.	Nov.	Dec.	Year	Range
Izmir	38° 25′	33	46	48	51	59	69	76	81	**82**	75	66	58	52	63·7	36
Haifa	33° 54′	115	54	57	60	66	70	76	80	**82**	80	75	64	58	68·5	28

THE MEDITERRANEAN CLIMATE—RAINFALL IN INCHES

Station	Jan.	Feb.	Mar.	April	May	June	July	Aug.	Sept.	Oct.	Nov.	Dec.	Total
Izmir	4·2	3·6	3·0	1·6	1·4	0·4	0·2	0·1	0·8	1·7	3·1	**4·9**	25·0
Haifa	**7·1**	5·7	0·9	0·7	0·1	0	0	0	0	0·5	2·7	6·7	24·4

(Figures from *The Climate of the Eastern Mediterranean*, H.M.S.O.)

(8) *The Mid-Latitude Continental*, or mid-latitude grassland climate, is found in the wide open grasslands or steppelands of western Siberia

MID-LATITUDE CONTINENTAL CLIMATE—TEMPERATURES IN ° F.

Station	Latitude	Altitude, ft.	Jan.	Feb.	Mar.	April	May	June	July	Aug.	Sept.	Oct.	Nov.	Dec.	Year	Range
Barnaul	53° 20′	480	− 2	1	13	33	51	62	**67**	62	50	35	16	4	33	69·3

MID-LATITUDE CONTINENTAL CLIMATE—RAINFALL IN INCHES

Station	Jan.	Feb.	Mar.	April	May	June	July	Aug.	Sept.	Oct.	Nov.	Dec.	Total
Barnaul	0·3	0·2	0·3	0·4	1·0	1·4	**1·8**	1·6	0·9	0·9	0·7	0·6	10·1

and, in a rather modified form, in such areas as the grasslands of Mongolia. This type of climate is characteristic of the interiors of the great land masses, removed from the influence of the sea and hence suffering considerable extremes of temperature. The light spring and summer rains encourage the growth of grass, but are insufficient for trees. The winters are long and severe; the summers short but warm. The rainfall in typical regions ranges between 10 and 30 inches, coming almost entirely in spring and summer. The great heat of late summer and the intense cold of winter are alike immaterial to the growth of grass: it seeds and withers. The winter precipitation where present is in the form of snow, and it should be noted that the snow covering keeps the ground warm in winter, whilst the melting of the winter snows in spring enhances the supply of moisture for the germinating grass.

(9) *The Cold Temperate Climate*, or climate of the northern coniferous forests, is found over a broad belt across the northern lowlands of Asia. The average temperature is low, and the greater part of the somewhat scanty precipitation is in the form of snow. The natural vegetation is everywhere of the evergreen coniferous forest type; the warmth of the summer sun is normally insufficient for the ripening of cereals. A feature of very great significance is the difference between the length of the very short winter days and the very long summer days. In the heart of northern Asia there are tracts with a temperature range of over 100° in the year—the greatest in the world. Nearly all stations have an average temperature for the year below 40° and over very large areas the average is below freezing. There is usually a short but surprisingly warm summer, with the average for the hottest month sometimes approaching 70°. Three months with a temperature of over 60° are needed for the ripening of wheat; in this climatic belt only the extreme southern margins are sufficiently warm, though the long summer days permit the hardier grains to ripen with great rapidity rather farther north. Owing to the small evaporation and the fact that much of the precipitation is in the form of snow, which lies on the ground in winter so that when the warmth of spring comes it melts and soaks gently into the ground and little is lost, a rainfall as low as 10 inches is adequate

COLD TEMPERATE CLIMATE—TEMPERATURES IN ° F.

Station	Latitude	Altitude	Jan.	Feb.	Mar.	April	May	June	July	Aug.	Sept.	Oct.	Nov.	Dec.	Year	Range
Berezov	63° 50′	100	−11	−2	11	21	35	51	**61**	56	42	25	4	−7	24	72·0
Verkhoy-ansk	67° 50′	330	−59	−47	−24	7	35	55	**60**	50	36	5	−34	−53	3	118·6

for tree growth. Most areas show a marked summer maximum in precipitation.

COLD TEMPERATE CLIMATE—RAINFALL IN INCHES

Station	Jan.	Feb.	Mar.	April	May	June	July	Aug.	Sept.	Oct.	Nov.	Dec.	Total
Berezov	1·0	0·6	0·8	1·3	1·6	2·2	3·4	2·3	2·3	1·1	1·3	0·5	18·4
Verkhoyansk	0·2	0·1	0	0·1	0·2	0·5	1·2	0·9	0·2	0·2	0·2	0·2	4·0

(10) *The Arctic Desert*, or tundra climate, is found along the northern shores of Asia. Within the Arctic Circle the winters are very long and very cold—there are at least some days on which the sun never appears—and the summers are very short but hot. Though for certain periods the sun never sets, it never rises far above the horizon. Temperature and rainfall are comparable with those in the northern parts of the coniferous forests, but summer temperatures are lower. Agriculture is impossible, for the ground is frozen for three-quarters of the year. In recent years much attention has been given to the regions of permafrost—where the soil remains permanently frozen at depth. A map of the Asiatic areas affected will be found in my *Our Developing World* (London: Faber & Faber, 1960, 41).

Before terminating this section it must be noted that no specific reference has been made to 'Alpine' climates. In a very broad way the altitudinal climatic zones resemble latitudinal climatic zones. Reference will be made in the regional sections to important local variations consequent upon elevation.

Köppen's Classification of the Climates of Asia. The scheme of classification which has been used for the climates of Asia in this book is a scheme based primarily on characteristic 'types', the types showing a close correlation with natural vegetation and with agricultural regions. It follows in general the scheme drawn up by A. J. Herbertson in his classic paper to the Royal Geographical Society.[1] It may be objected that these climatic types are not capable of exact mathematical definition and that in a scientifically exact and logical classification such a definition should be possible. Such a logical scheme has been drawn up by W. Köppen,[2] who distinguishes amongst the climates of the world six main zones, each of which is divided and subdivided into a number of climatic provinces and smaller areas. Each of the main zones is designated by an initial letter (A, B, C, D, E and F); the province by a descriptive letter (W = Wüste or desert—rainfall under 25 cm.; S = Steppe—rainfall 25 to 50 cm., i.e. 10 to 20 inches); special features of the area by small letters.

[1] A. J. Herbertson, 'The Major Natural Regions', *Geog. Jour.*, **25**, 1905, 300–12.
[2] *Die Klimat der Erde*, Berlin, 1923; also Petermann's *Mitteilungen*, **44**, 1918. See also *Geog. Rev.*, **8**, 1919, 188–91, and the *Köppen-Geiger Handbuch der Klimatologie*, Berlin, 1931.

The six main zones and the eleven climates are as follows:

A. Tropical Rainy Climates.
    1. Hot damp primeval forest climate.
    2. Periodically dry savanna climate.
B. Dry Climates.
    3. Steppe climate (S).
    4. Desert climate (W).
C. Warm Temperate Rainy Climates.
    5. Warm climate with dry winters.
    6. Warm climate with dry summers.
    7. Damp temperate climate.
D. Sub-Arctic Climates.
    8. Cold climate with wet winters.
    9. Cold climate with dry winters.
E and F. Snow Climates.
    10. Tundra climate.
    11. Perpetual frost climate.

The special features indicated by small letters are:
a = temperature of warmest month more than 22° C. (72° F.). b = warmest month less than 22° C. but more than four months above 10° C. c = one to four months more than 10° C. (50° F.); coldest above − 3·6° C. (26° F.). d = as c, but coldest month below − 3·6° C. f = constantly moist. g = Ganges type with maximum temperature before summer rains. h = hot, with mean annual temperature above 18° C. (64° F.). i = isothermal, difference between extreme months less than 5° C. k = winter cold, mean annual less than 18° C., warmest month above 18° C.; k′ as k, but warmest month less than 18° C. m = monsoon rains, heavy, giving evergreen forest. n = fog; n′ = high humidity. p = fog infrequent but high humidity and high temperature. s = dry in summer. w = dry in winter; s′ = rainy season in autumn; s″ and w″ = rainy season in two parts with short dry season intervening.

Köppen's scheme has been detailed here and a map of Asia given because of the extensive use of his classification. But in my own opinion the results in Asia are far from satisfactory and the arbitrary lines separating even the major zones have little meaning. Thus cutting India in half is the line separating 'A' and 'C' climates. Yet this line does not correspond to any which can be distinguished on the grounds of vegetation, agriculture or any phenomena of human occupancy. Actually it cuts right across a well-marked minor as well as a major natural region of the country. Similarly, Cressey concludes that this classification 'is not particularly suitable for the climates of China and Köppen's map needs considerable revision'.[1]

[1] *China's Geographic Foundations* (1934), 69.

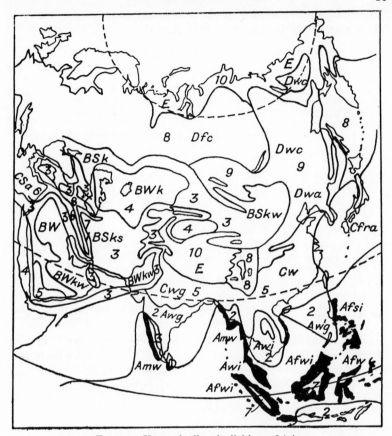

FIG. 19.—Köppen's climatic divisions of Asia

Thornthwaite's Classification of the Climates of Asia. The classification introduced by C. Warren Thornthwaite [1] is 'like Köppen's in that it is quantitative and attempts to determine the critical limits significant to the distribution of vegetation and also in that it employs a symbolic nomenclature in designating the climatic types. It differs in that it makes use of two new climatic concepts, precipitation effectiveness and temperature efficiency. It is inferred that in the tropical rain forest, the most rapidly growing and the densest vegetation type on the earth, the climate must be the most favourable of all for plant growth . . . precipitation effectiveness and temperature efficiency must be at a maximum.'

Five types based on humidity have been recognized and the

[1] 'The Climates of the Earth', *Geog. Rev.*, **33**, 1933, 433–40; see also *ibid.*, **21**, 1931, 633–55, and **23**, 1933, 433.

'precipitation effectiveness' (P–E Index) calculated according to a formula explained in the 1931 paper quoted on p. 39. These are:

Humidity type	Vegetation	P–E Index
A (wet) . . .	Rain forest	128 and above
B (humid) . .	Forest	64 to 127
C (sub-humid) .	Grassland	32 to 63
D (semi-arid) .	Steppe	16 to 31
E (arid) . . .	Desert	0 to 15

Six 'temperature efficiency types' are distinguished as follows:

		T–E Index
A′	Tropical	128 and above
B′	Mesothermal	64 to 127
C′	Microthermal	32 to 63
D′	Taïga	16 to 31
E′	Tundra	1 to 15
F′	Perpetual Frost	0

In addition four types of seasonal distribution of effective precipitation are distinguished:

r   rainfall abundant at all seasons
s   rainfall scanty in summer
w   rainfall scanty in winter (w′ = rainfall scanty in spring)
d   rainfall scanty at all seasons

Thus theoretically $5 \times 6 \times 4$ or 120 possible climates exist. Certain combinations are eliminated by definition and Thornthwaite finds there are 32 actual climatic types in the world. His scheme for Asia is shown approximately in Fig. 20, and the climates present are as follows:

1. AA′r   Equatorial forest belts
2. AB′r   Part of Kyushu (Japan)
3. AC′r   Eastern mainland of Japan, coast north of Vladivostok
4. BA′r   Absent in Asia
5. BA′w   Monsoon (deciduous) forest belt of south-eastern Asia and Burma, Ceylon, Java
6. BB′r   Interiors of large islands of East Indies, Korea, Japan, Caucasus
7. BB′w   Southern China, Assam, Formosa
8. BB′s   Absent in Asia
9. BC′r   Hokkaido, Sakhalin
10. BC′s   Absent in Asia
11. CA′r   Absent in Asia
12. CA′w   Most of Peninsular India, interior of Indo-China
13. CA′d   Absent in Asia
14. CB′r   Absent in Asia
15. CB′w   Dry belt of Burma, slopes of Himalayas
16. CB′s   Absent in Asia
17. CB′d   Coastal strips of Asia Minor, south-western Arabia
18. CC′r   Absent in Asia
19. CC′s   Absent in Asia
20. CC′d   Russian grassland belt, Manchuria

21. DA'w   Thar Desert (part)
22. DA'd   Western margin of Arabia
23. DB'w   Punjab (part)
24. DB's   Absent in Asia
25. DB'd   Plateaus of Anatolia and Iran, Syria and parts of Palestine
26. DC'd   Central Manchuria, much of heart of Asia
27. EA'd   Hot deserts of Arabia and Thar (part)
28. EB'd   Turanian and Tarim Basins, Iranian Desert, Indus Valley (part)
29. EC'd   Gobi Desert, northern Turanian Basin
30. D'   The Coniferous Forest of Taïga Belt
31. E'   The Arctic Tundra Belt, Tibet
32. F'   Absent in Asia

Clearly this carefully considered scheme needs prolonged study, but it is by no means certain that it will be acceptable to the student of the geography of Asia. As it stands it produces too many strange bed-fellows and there are too many anomalies. There are vast differences

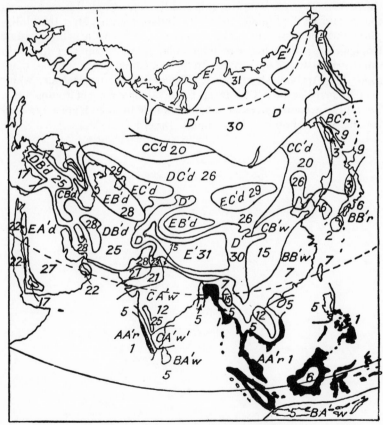

FIG. 20.—Thornthwaite's climatic divisions of Asia

between the climate of the Ganges Delta and Singapore (if vegetation is the criterion the rubber tree proves this), but why should Ceylon be relegated to an entirely different group with which neither its climate nor vegetation agrees (note the distribution of the teak tree, for example)? Is the wind-swept plateau of Anatolia rightly grouped with the orange-grove country of Palestine? Is the climate of Korea and the slopes of the Caucasus really comparable with the interior of Borneo? Perhaps a more fundamental objection to the classification is the implication that forest passes to grassland with decreasing precipitation efficiency. Actually trees demand a deep-seated water supply; grass a superficial supply in the growing season.

Asiatic Airmasses. In modern meteorological terms it is possible to restate the general Asiatic position by saying that in winter the whole continent is dominated by a mass of continental polar (cP) air. Over northern India and off the China coasts are areas of subsidence (where the movement of air is downwards and the inter-tropical front lies well to the south of the Equator across the Indian Ocean). Over the Philippines and Indonesia the cP air comes in contact with mT (maritime tropical) air along what is really a Polar front. In summer the main movement is of mT air towards India and China as the summer monsoon. The Arabian air stream is cT (continental tropical air) whilst over Manchuria the mT air meets the cP along a zone of frontogenesis. For a brief account reference should be made to F. K. Hare's *The Restless Atmosphere* (London: Hutchinson, 1953).

THE VEGETATION OF ASIA

IT will be necessary to deal in some detail with the natural vegetation of the countries of Asia in the sequel, and it is only possible here to give the very broadest outline. Even minor variations in rainfall are reflected so intimately in the vegetation that generalized descriptions are apt to convey entirely false impressions. For example, almost untouched evergreen rain forests, actively exploited timber forests, dry scrublands and thorn-bush deserts are all equally characteristic of India alone.

Broadly speaking, the major climatic divisions have each their dominant type of vegetation. Within those divisions rainfall or more correctly available moisture is the first factor in the determination of major variations in the lowland vegetation; soil, which is itself largely a product of climatic conditions, determines local variations.

It will be convenient, therefore, to review briefly the natural vegetation of Asia by taking each of the major climatic regions considered in the last chapter.

The Equatorial Regions. The natural vegetation of the Equatorial belt of Asia is lofty, evergreen forest mainly of hardwood species. The forest occurs in huge sweeps from the seashores to the hill-tops, interrupted only occasionally by areas, such as hill ranges, where the soil is insufficient to support forest growth, or by tracts where bamboos, grasses or other herbaceous vegetation have waged a successful war against the forest—usually as a result of man's intervention. The decrease of temperature, due to elevation, rarely affects vegetation in Equatorial regions below 5,000 feet; its influence is mainly due to the occasional frosts above that level. The Equatorial forests which have seized upon the popular imagination are the gloomy, vault-like forests of the Amazon, where the canopy is so dense that no sunlight, and indeed very little light at all, penetrates to the forest floor—an almost lifeless waste of decaying vegetable matter. Forests of this type rarely, if ever, occur in Asia. The canopy is dense, but sufficient light penetrates to the floor of the forest to permit the growth of a lower storey of trees, bamboos and canes, and often of a luxuriant ground vegetation. The larger trees are nearly all of hardwood species, tall and unbranched, tapering but very gradually and frequently exceeding 200 or 250 feet in height. Many of the trees are furnished with 'plank-buttresses', important supports for their great height. The trees are rarely gregarious; an acre of forest commonly contains but one or two specimens of a single species. This creates a fundamental difficulty in the commercial exploitation of the forests; the extraction of a single species, however valuable, may be wellnigh impossible; on the other hand, clear felling produces an immense variety of timbers of which the quantities of any one are but limited. A feature of the forests of south-eastern Asia is

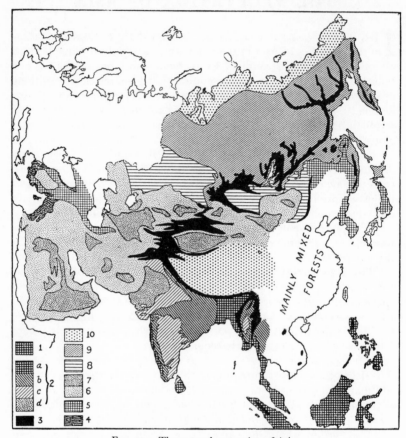

Fig. 21.—The natural vegetation of Asia

1. Equatorial vegetation—wet evergreen forests
2. Monsoon vegetation a—wet evergreen forests
                      b—deciduous monsoon forests
                      c—thorn woodland and scrub
                      d—desert
3. Mountain vegetation
4. Mediterranean vegetation—evergreen woodland
5. Mixed coniferous and hardwood deciduous forests
6. Dry steppes and steppe-deserts
7. True desert
8. Temperate grassland (steppe) and parkland
9. Taïga or coniferous forest
10. Tundra and Tibetan alpine vegetation

the large proportion of the trees which belong to the natural order *Dipterocarpaceae*, nearly all of which have winged seeds.[1] The numerous

[1] See P. W. Richards, *The Tropical Rain Forest*, Cambridge University Press, 1952.

epiphytes, especially ferns and orchids, which grow high up on the trees, are characteristic, as are the innumerable lianes or woody climbers. Often the trees by which the latter reached the canopy of the forests have died and decayed, leaving the lianes hanging from the heights, with snake-like coils trailing over the ground. The animal life of the forests is often concentrated in the tree-tops; one hears the groups of chattering monkeys rather than sees them. The interior of the Asiatic forests, however, is far from lifeless, and among the denizens is the Indian elephant. Like the Equatorial forests of the Congo and Amazon, those of Asia have formed the last refuge for primitive man—kind—the Veddas of Ceylon, the Semang of Malaya and the numerous tribes of Borneo. A. R. Wallace's famous classic, *Island Life*, gives an excellent account of the Equatorial regions of Asia.

The grassy stretches of the upland areas have already been mentioned; there remain two characteristic types of vegetation to be noted. The mangrove swamps of muddy coasts and deltas occur between tidal limits, and include an important variety of trees—some reaching heights of 200 feet (as do the Kanazo forests of Burma), although the true mangrove swamps consist of trees of only about 15 to 30 feet in height. They are provided with aerophores which project through the muddy soil and permit air to reach the roots during the period of low tide.[1] Then there is the vegetation of sandy coasts, where a narrow strip of the graceful Casuarina trees is very common, though the coconut has become so firmly established as to be regarded as 'natural' vegetation.

The Monsoon Regions. The natural vegetation of monsoon regions is forest, but it should be noted that the rainfall, coming as it does in the hot season, provides a climate which is not wholly inimical to grass. The frost-line is lower than in the Equatorial belt; it averages 3,000 feet above sea-level in Burma and is rather lower in northern India. Below the frost-line the vegetation is tropical; its actual character depends upon the amount of the rainfall. Where the rainfall is more than 80 inches per annum, evergreen, broad-leaved rain forest, so closely comparable with that occurring in Equatorial regions as to be identical, occurs. Where the dry season is a long one, certain species may not thrive—for example, the imported rubber, *Hevea brasiliensis*, will not flourish in Bengal, though the rainfall is in many parts over 80 inches and evergreen forest is the natural vegetation.

Where the rainfall is between about 40 and 80 inches—in localities favoured as regards soil and underground water supply even where it is as low as 30 inches per year—the typical 'monsoon forests' are found. They are broad-leaved forests which become leafless in the hot season, bursting into flower and then into leaf just before the rains break in

---

[1] A description of different types of mangrove forest, applicable to wide areas in Asia, will be found in L. D. Stamp, 'The Aerial Survey of the Irrawaddy Delta Forests', *Journal of Ecology*, **13**, 1925, 262–76.

earnest. Some of the trees, such as the sal of India (*Shorea*), are gregarious; in other cases two or three species form co-dominants (as in the 'indaing' forests of Burma, where *Dipterocarpus tuberculatus* and *Pentacme suavis* are the two dominant trees), but in most monsoon forests there are numerous species and pure stands of any one species are rare. This is the case with the 'teak forests', where teak (*Tectona grandis*) forms

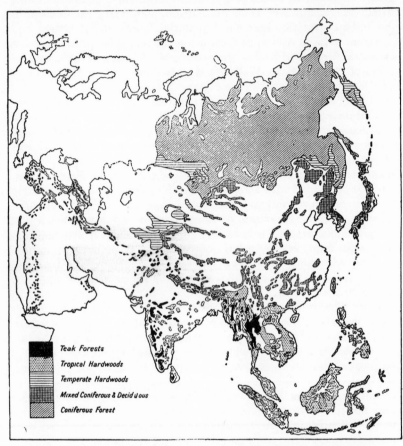

FIG. 22.—The forests of Asia (based on maps published by Zon and Sparhawk)

but a small percentage of the total number of trees. The number of species is not as large, however, as in the Equatorial forests. The monsoon forests, being the home of the teak and sal, as well as other important timbers, such as the Burma ironwood (*Xylia dolabriformis*), are economically far more important than the Equatorial forests. The timbers are nearly all hardwoods, but more tractable, generally speaking, than those of the latter forests. The monsoon forests are more open; there is often a dense undergrowth, especially of bamboos, and in the drier types of grass. It is a common practice, in reserved or scientifically managed forests, to burn off the undergrowth in the dry season by simply setting fire to it—it is rarely that the fire becomes sufficiently intense to damage the larger trees. The loss of leaves, it should be noticed, takes place in the dry, hot season, and not in the cold season as in temperate forests. Just when man and beast most desire shelter the forest gives none: anyone who has trekked through the drier type of monsoon forest in March or April will never forget the still, lifeless air, the motionless, deathly still trees and the shimmering heat which rises from the brown baked ground, blackened by recent fires suggesting in earnest the appellation 'stinking hot'.

Where the rainfall drops below 40 or 30 inches, it is, in general, too dry for the adequate growth of forests. Their place is taken at first by a woodland of thorny trees—amongst which *Acacia* is usually conspicuous—the trees decreasing in size as the dryness increases, till one has a scrubland of scattered thorny bushes 3 or 4 to a dozen feet high, separated by wide areas of ground—bare and brown for half the year, covered with green grass and herbs for the few months of the rainy season. This type of vegetation is, it should be noted, an impoverished woodland, but bears very close resemblance to the African savanna or tropical grassland with scattered trees. It is noteworthy that many of the species found as low bushes—such as *Acacia catechu* and *Acacia luecophloea*—occur under more favoured conditions as forest trees.

Where the rainfall drops below 20 inches the conditions may be said to approach those of semi-desert, succulent plants such as *Euphorbia* becoming important.

In monsoon lands one finds tidal or mangrove forests as in the Equatorial regions and fringing forests of Casuarina on sandy shores. Riparian forests are characteristic of the larger rivers in several parts of monsoon lands.

Hill forests of monsoon countries fall broadly into two classes—the evergreen, broad-leaved forests in which various species of oak (*Quercus*) are usually important and coniferous forests with such species as *Pinus longifolia*, *Pinus excelsa*, *Cedrus deodara*, *Picea* and *Abies*.

The Temperate Monsoon Regions of China and Japan (East Asian climate). It is more than a little difficult to say what is the natural vegetation of China. Broadly it may be described as temperate forest, but deforestation has been carried on to such an extent that forests are now found only in three main regions—the Nan Shan or Nanling Range; the Tsinling Range; and the Western Highland region. The general character of the forest is that of broad-leaved, frequently evergreen, trees mixed with conifers, especially in the higher parts. There are large areas of bamboo, whilst the widely distributed national tree of China is the T'ung or wood-oil tree (*Aleurites cordata*). The oil is obtained from the nuts, and is poisonous when fresh. Another characteristic tree is the Varnish tree (*Rhus vernicifera*), the tree which yields the lacquers of the Far East, the varnish being obtained by tapping.

In Japan, as detailed in the section on Japan, the south of the country is occupied by warm temperate forests with evergreen and deciduous broad-leaved hardwoods mixed with coniferous; farther north conifers and deciduous hardwoods predominate.

The Manchurian Region. Ecologically this region embraces most of the hilly parts of Manchuria and stretches into the adjoining parts of Russia. Grassland covers the lowlands, but forest covers all hilly tracts. Like the forests of the corresponding climatic region in North America, conifers and hardwoods are mixed. Conifers include spruce, silver fir, red pine, and larch, but the most valuable economically is the Manchurian pine (*Pinus mandshurica*). Hardwoods include oaks, ash, alder, beech and others.

The Desert Regions. It is impossible to attempt a description of the varied types of vegetation which occur in the tropical and mid-latitude deserts of Asia. Broadly it may be said that the vegetation in any given region is an impoverished representative of that found in neighbouring regions more favoured by Nature in water supply. A distinction may be made between true deserts, such as the heart of the Tarim Basin or the Ruba' el Khali in southern Arabia, which are virtually lifeless, and the tame deserts which support a measure of both animal and vegetable life, especially in good rainfall years.

The Mediterranean Regions. The xerophytic evergreen Mediterranean woodland of small trees with their numerous devices protective against excessive transpiration in the hot dry summer is well developed in south-western Asia. The small leaves of the olive, grey-green, with their protective covering of silky hairs, the leathery leaves of the myrtle or laurel, the bright green, waxy leaves of the orange, the excessively long roots of the vine suggest the types of modification found in the Mediterranean woodland. The ground vegetation is often reminiscent of English heathland or moorland, with its low shrubs, wealth of herbaceous plants in spring, but comparative absence of grass. One associates the reduction of leaf surface found in conifers with protection against cold, but it serves equally well as a protection against excessive loss of moisture in hot regions, and hence coniferous woodland, especially of rather small species, is also seen in Mediterranean regions.

The Grassland Regions. Grassland is typically developed in Asia in the south-west of Siberia and again as a fringe to the deserts and semi-deserts of the Mongolian plateau as well as in the lowlands of central Manchuria. The Mongolian steppes may be described as some of the least developed areas of mid-latitude grasslands still remaining in the world, and as such they have or have had a special interest to the neighbouring nations of Japan, China and Russia. The typical vegetation is a low growth of grass; the grassy sward is often interrupted by bare spaces, the grasses usually grow in tufts, and the tufts become farther apart in drier regions. Where creeping species are present they produce a more evenly covered surface. Steppe grasses have narrower leaves than those of damp meadowlands, and many species have leaves which roll up in dry weather. Small woody plants with small leaves, herbaceous, tuberous and bulbous plants are common.

Southwards the steppes of south-western Siberia grade gradually into steppe-desert; northwards they pass into a very fertile stretch of parkland which affords a gradual passage to coniferous forests. Steppe-land of a kind rather different from the typical area reappears in such areas as the Anatolian Plateau.

The Cold Temperate Regions. The cold temperate regions of Siberia are clothed with coniferous forest, of which a description is given later under Siberia. From the main belt of forest, tongues penetrate southwards along the mountains of central Asia. The extreme climate does not encourage rapid growth; the trees are smaller and poorer than in corresponding regions of North America. Moreover, because the rivers flow northwards their upper courses thaw out whilst their lower courses and estuaries are still blocked with ice, with the result that flooding melt-waters inundate vast areas of forest to the detriment of the quality of the timber.

The Arctic Regions. Beyond the last stunted trees, the cold desert or the tundra dominates the northern fringe of Asia. Only in a few more favoured localities do willows and dwarf shrubs exist; elsewhere the predominance of mosses and lichens and of dwarf xerophilous plants is the characteristic feature. In some places mosses, especially *Polytrichum*, are dominant, in drier places lichens, giving either a moss-tundra or a lichen-tundra. Swampy depressions are numerous, and a scanty peat may carry a layer of sphagnum; sheltered spots exposed to the sun's rays may be rich in flowers. But the summer is short and sharp; for the greater part of the year the ground is completely frozen.

The Agricultural Regions of Asia. A survey of the agricultural regions of Asia has been published by Dr. S. van Valkenburg in *Economic Geography*, beginning in the issue for July 1931. He adopts the scheme of climatic regions given in this book and finds the major land-use regions closely coincide. His coloured map presents the following major divisions:

1. Tundra and Alpine.
2. Desert.
3. Forest.
4. Grazing.

   5. Crop land, with four divisions: wheat, rice, millet-sorghum and oats.

   6. Plantations.

   7. Oases.

REFERENCES

General works giving references to literature include De Martonne, *Traité de Géographie physique*, successive editions, Vol. III (Paris: Colin); Schimper, *Plant Geography* (Oxford, 1903); *A World Geography of Forest Resources* (New York: American Geographical Society, 1956). Detailed references will be found under countries. See also S. R. Eyre, *Vegetation and Soils: A World Picture* (London: Arnold, 1963).

THE POPULATION OF ASIA

ASIA, in addition to being the largest continent, has also a larger population than any other. Yet the distribution of the people is curiously irregular. The majority of the people of Asia are found in two areas—India-Pakistan, with an average density of about 300 per square mile and a population in 1966 of about 600,000,000; and China, with a total population of probably 800,000,000 (density in China proper over 450). Three other areas, and three only, may be described as densely populated—Japan, with a population in 1966 estimated at 98,000,000 (density 666); Java, with probably over 65,000,000 (density 1,270); and Ceylon, with 11,500,000 (density 450).

On the other hand, vast stretches of Asia have a population meagre in the extreme. The million square miles which make up the peninsula of Arabia have probably only about 13,000,000 people; the vast stretches of Siberia have a population density of under 5; much of central Asia under 1. Even the East Indies, excluding Java, can only boast of a population density of a little over 50.

There is no doubt that climate is the primary determining factor in the present distribution of population.

The Tropical Monsoon, the China type and the China type as modified in Japan, are the climates which, by affording an abundance of food with a relatively small expenditure of labour, are those favouring a dense population. Within these climatic regions the relief of the land—and soil fertility so closely bound up with it—plays a leading part in the actual distribution; the crowded plains and the empty hills of China exemplify this to the full. It is scarcely too much to say that the great majority of the most densely peopled tracts of southern and eastern Asia are alluvial plains.

Within the monsoon tract of Asia there are anomalies which deserve attention. Even a very simple map like Fig. 23 brings out the relative emptiness of Burma, Siam and Indo-China, which climatically are just as favoured as their densely populated neighbours India and China. Inaccessibility, illustrated by the Arakan Yoma cutting off the fertile Irrawaddy Plains from India and by the mountains of Annam cutting off the fertile plains of Cambodia and Siam from China, is in the main responsible, but there are social and economic factors, outside the realm of geography, also at work. In a later section we shall examine the social and religious systems which till recently have bound the Chinese to his native soil and prevented emigration.

In the East Indies, with their Equatorial climate, one is struck at once by the contrast between Java on the one hand and the remainder of the archipelago on the other. The circumstances which have led to the present density of population in Java will be examined later, but the extraordinary fertility of the volcanic soils is one important factor.

Nearly all Asiatic countries remain predominantly agricultural and high densities are usually high rural densities. Urbanization and industrialization came late to Asiatic countries, but is now proceeding at a rapid pace. As late as 1941 India had only two 'million cities'; by 1951 this had increased to six. In south-east Asia five cities reached a million after 1945—Jakarta, Manila, Saigon, Bangkok and Singapore.[1]

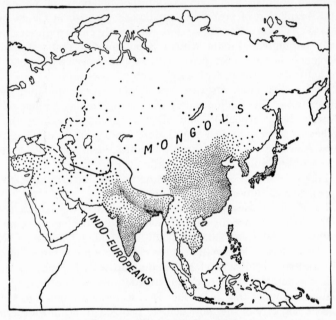

FIG. 23.—The population of Asia

Map showing the concentration of people in the monsoon lands excepting Indo-China. Each dot represents approximately 500,000 people. There has recently been a great increase in Soviet Asia not shown in this map.

Turning now to the races of Asia, the first outstanding feature is the function of the great mountain barrier, already emphasized in connection with climate, which clearly separates the two great divisions of mankind represented in the continent.

The plateaus of central Asia have probably formed a continental mass at least since the Mesozoic period; they were land before the Himalayas had even begun to appear. One is justified in assuming—and indeed recent discoveries lend much support to the assumption—that central Asia formed one of the great world centres of evolution and

[1] D. W. Fryer, 'The "Million City" in Southeast Asia', *Geog. Rev.*, **43**, 1953, 474–94.

dispersal of the mammals.[1] In this category comes man, and it is not improbable that man evolved from simian stock somewhere in central Asia during the Tertiary period. The on-coming of the Glacial period, which must have greatly affected the climates of central Asia, probably acted as a spur to human migrations; the close of the Glacial period saw

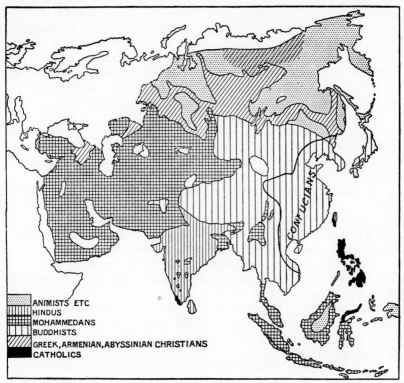

ANIMISTS ETC
HINDUS
MOHAMMEDANS
BUDDHISTS
GREEK, ARMENIAN, ABYSSINIAN CHRISTIANS
CATHOLICS

CONFUCIANS

FIG. 24.—The religions of Asia

Shintoism also is important in Japan, Taoism in China.

in central Asia much moister conditions than exist at present; [2] the shrinking of ice-caps, the retreat of mountain glaciers gradually resulted in a diminution of water supplies; glacial lakes became marshes

[1] Though Carl Sauer (*Agricultural Origins and Dispersals*, Amer. Geog. Soc., New York, 1952) favours south-east Asia.

[2] These statements are made on general grounds; they do not affect the much-debated question as to whether central Asia is still becoming drier or has done so in historic times. Kropotkin long ago recognized the gradual desiccation of most of Asia since glacial times (*Geog. Jour.*, **23**, 1904, 176, 331, 722). Ellsworth Huntington, in his famous book, *The Pulse of Asia* (1907), developed the thesis that the secular desiccation had been varied by cyclic fluctuations; in later works he has traced the influence of minor climatic pulsations and rainfall cycles in the history of certain peoples.

and then prairies and finally even arid deserts, and so the inhabitants were driven to seek fresh lands. Of these early movements of people there are but the slightest traces. In an instructive little book, Dr. A. C. Haddon has dealt with the fascinating subject of the wanderings of peoples in Asia.[1] Amongst the prehistoric migrations Haddon shows the Nordics (the peoples of northern Europe) moving westwards from central Asia; the Mongols south-eastwards to China; and the Alpine race from Turkistan through Asia Minor to south-central Europe.

It is impossible in the space available here even to summarize the present distribution of races in Asia. A brief but clear account will be found in Haddon's *Races of Man and their Distribution*.[2] A more recent and elaborate account, somewhat abstruse to the non-anthropological reader, has been given by L. H. Dudley Buxton.[3] Haddon distinguishes three main divisions of mankind:

Ulotrichi (woolly-haired: corresponding roughly to the black or negro race);

Cymotrichi (wavy-haired: corresponding roughly to the brown and white races);

Leiotrichi (straight-haired: corresponding roughly to the yellow races).

The Ulotrichi in Asia include certain very primitive pygmy races—the Andamanese, the Semang of Malaya and Sumatra, and the Aetas of the Philippines—as well as the larger Papuans of New Guinea.

The Cymotrichi include long-headed (dolichocephalic), medium-headed (mesaticephalic), and broad-headed (brachycephalic) groups, further subdivided by skin colour:

Dolichocephalic Cymotrichi, with dark brown to nearly black skins, include the Veddas of Ceylon, the jungle tribes (Pre-Dravidian) of Peninsular India, Malaya, Sumatra and Celebes, and also the Dravidians of India.

Dolichocephalic Cymotrichi, of intermediate shades, include the Indo-Afghans, who populate most of south-western Asia and northern India, the Indonesians of the East Indies; the Arabs and Jews.

Mesaticephalic Cymotrichi include the indigenous Ainu of Japan.

Brachycephalic Cymotrichi include the Armenians.

The Leiotrichi include practically all the inhabitants of northern and eastern Asia—the straight-haired, yellowish- or yellowish-brown-skinned races in certain cases only with eyes set obliquely, popularly and loosely called Mongols. The peoples of northern Siberia form one group, the Tungus and Manchus another, the Chinese proper a third, the Turki peoples a fourth, the Ugrians of western Siberia a fifth, the Tibeto-Chinese (including Malays) a sixth.

[1] *The Wanderings of Peoples* (Cambridge University Press, 1911).
[2] Milner, n.d. (*c.* 1911), rewritten and published by the Cambridge Press, 1924,
[3] *The Peoples of Asia* (Kegan Paul, 1925).

This is but a bald statement of one classification of the peoples of Asia. For other and diverse views reference may be made to the stimulating writings of Professor Griffith Taylor—conveniently summarized in his chapter on Racial Geography in *Geography in the Twentieth Century* (London: Methuen, 1951). The geographical interest lies in tracing the factors which have played a part in the differentiation of these races, the factors which have induced racial movements and the factors which have determined the direction of those movements and the preservation of remnants of early primitive tribes. We shall have occasion, in the latter part of this book, to deal with the peoples of certain areas, but it is only by attempting to trace human migrations on a good physical map of Asia and by plotting the location of the primitive tribes and the great civilizations that one comes to appreciate the great part which the orography and the climatology of Asia have played.

THE EUROPEAN EXPLORATION OF ASIA [1]

LONG before Europe had discovered Asia, Asia had discovered Europe. In the dawn of history the merchants of Phoenicia (the coastlands of what are now Syria and Lebanon) had pushed westwards through the Mediterranean for trade and even beyond the Pillars of Hercules (Straits of Gibraltar) to Britain. There is no doubt that there was regular intercourse between the Minoan civilization of Crete and the Levant (a name long used for the Mediterranean coastlands of Asia Minor and Syria), while in the seventh and sixth centuries B.C. the Greeks had established colonies along the shores of Asia Minor. The Greeks, by their close proximity to Asia and the high standard of civilization they had attained, were the natural pioneers in the discovery of Asia. The Persian menace served to unite the various independent cities of Greece under the single leadership of the Macedonian, Alexander, who was destined to carry out the conquest of the Persian Empire, already planned by his father, Philip of Macedon.

The first historic expedition by a European into Asia was made by Alexander the Great, who, in one of the greatest of military undertakings, marched through Asia Minor, defeating the armies of Darius at Issus and so gaining access to Syria and the Phoenician coast, later across the Tigris to the decisive victory of Arbela and on through Ecbatana, Susa and Persepolis to the valley of the Oxus (the modern Amu-Darya). Not content with the conquest of the Persian Empire, Alexander by way of Kabul crossed the Hindu Kush in 327 B.C. and advanced to the Indus Valley. Having penetrated as far as the Bias River at its junction with the Sutlej, he returned through the deserts of Babylonia which he had left seven years previously. Alexander was no mere world conqueror whose conquests had no ulterior motive. He appears to have aimed at merging Asia with Europe, and with that end in view planted colonies and military settlements and encouraged his soldiers to intermarry with the conquered. Evidence of Alexander's invasion can be seen in place-names, notably in Samarqand, originally Samarkander, a corruption of Alexander. With the establishment of the Graeco-Bactrian [2] Kingdom by Alexander and his successors the lands beyond the Euphrates came to bear the ineffaceable marks of Hellenistic culture, seen specially in architecture and sculpture.

As Greek dominance of the Western world gave place to Roman,

[1] The original draft of this chapter was by Miss D. M. Fisher, B.A. (Mrs. Andrew), and we were much indebted to the late Professor Eileen Power, D.Litt., for notes on the subject-matter.

[2] Bactria was the name applied to the country between the Hindu Kush and the Oxus.

gradually Europe became better acquainted with the East, though not for centuries did Europeans learn of the land that gave them their much-prized silk. Silk was probably the earliest cause of commercial intercourse between Europe and China. Virgil, Horace and others speak of the Seres, and the 'Land of the Seres' was one of the earliest names for China used by Western nations. The long-continued Parthian Wars had the effect of jeopardizing Rome's supply of silk, since the Parthians inhabited lands through which the early trade in this commodity was carried on—the modern Khurasan of north-eastern Iran.

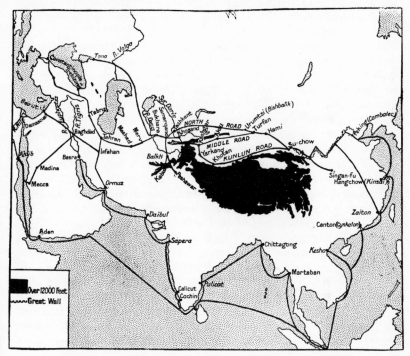

FIG. 25.—Medieval trade routes between Europe and the Far East

(Medieval names where differing from modern names are in italics)

The main routes by which the peoples of Europe and Asia gradually came to know one another have remained substantially the same throughout historic time. Routes to the East were either by sea or land. There were two main sea routes:

(1) From the central highway of trade, the Mediterranean, and the Black Sea, by way of the 'fertile crescent' to the Euphrates and the Persian Gulf, along the Malabar Coast to Ceylon, across to the East Indies and so to the south of China.

(2) The Mediterranean to Egypt, up the Nile, across to the shores

of the Red Sea and via the Red Sea to Ceylon, where the other route was joined. This sea route received great impetus about A.D. 50, when a Roman sea captain is said to have discovered the periodicity and hence the importance to sailing vessels of the south-west monsoon. Throughout ancient and medieval times the sea routes continued to be important trade channels, especially for the spices of the East, while the silk was carried by land caravan. The sea routes were considered safer, chiefly owing to the depredations across central Asia of successive barbarian hordes. Certain articles, notably Chinese porcelain, could withstand sea-travel better than the jolting inseparable from a land caravan.

The great land routes are more easily traced from east to west than from west to east.[1]

(1) The South or Kunlun Road. Starting from Singan-fu, the old capital, and in later times from Peking, this road followed the Great Wall to the modern Suchow, then across the dreary desert of the Lop Nor district and along the foot of the Kunlun Mountains to Khotan, Yarkand and Kashgar, an important junction of several roads. From Kashgar the road ran north-west to Khoqand, thence to Samarqand and Bukhara, the meeting-place of all the transasiatic routes. From Bukhara the approach to Europe was either south of the Caspian by way of Tabriz through Asia Minor to the Black Sea and Constantinople, or across Persia and the Tigris and Euphrates to the Mediterranean. A third route, during the thirteenth and fourteenth centuries, was from Bukhara across the Oxus and north of the Caspian to the Volga and northern shores of the Black Sea.

(2) The Middle or South Tien Shan Road. This road diverged from the first at the modern Suchow and went north to Hami and Turfan; thence to Aqsu and south-west to Kashgar, joining the first road.

(3) The North or North Tien Shan Road. This branched off from the Middle Road at Hami or Turfan, running on to Urumisi, north again to the Issyq Kol, on to Tashkent, across the Sir Darya (Jaxartes) to Samarqand, where it joined the other roads. In addition to these routes there were and still are the Mongolian routes and Dzungarian routes of which an account is given below, p. 595.

That these roads were of extreme importance from very early times is certain. Along them travelled people, religions and, above all, trade. The direction of earliest trade tended chiefly to be from east to west, partly because Chinese and Indian merchants were the pioneers of trade with the West and also because of the tremendous influence of the westward trend of nomadic hordes: Huns, Seljuks, Tartars and Ottoman Turks all threatened the peace of Europe at different times. By the dawn of the Christian era, however, Europe had become inspired with the desire to know more of the Land of the Seres, which came to be

---

[1] See also the section on central Asia, below. Reference may also be made to *Travel and Travellers of the Middle Ages* (London: Kegan Paul, 1926).

known as China from the feudal State of Ts'in. In A.D. 196 there is record of an envoy of the Emperor Marcus Aurelius in China. Christianity spread into Asia early in the fourth century, when there was an episcopal see in Merv (Russian Turkistan). The spread of Christianity during the fifth and sixth centuries was Nestorian in form. Nestorianism, in fact, soon became the only form of Christianity found in India and China. Meanwhile trade between east and west was increasing under the dominance of the Eastern Roman or Byzantine Empire with its capital at Byzantium (Constantinople or Istanbul) and which lasted till the fifteenth century. The Western world had long coveted the secret of the Chinese silk manufacture; at last it was known through the medium of monks who smuggled in silkworm eggs.

The earlier Byzantine emperors spent a good deal of their time trying to check the inroads of the Persians on their eastern frontier; but a more serious foe was yet to come in the forces pledged to extend the Moslem religion by the sword. The successors of Mahomet in the seventh and eighth centuries established an empire stretching from Samarqand to Spain, and made their capital, Baghdad, the richest emporium of its day, commanding routes by sea and land. The power of the Mahommedan Arabs in time gave place to that of the Seljuk Turks, who appeared near the river Oxus at the end of the tenth century, and with the collapse of the Mahommedan Empire took the opportunity to push westwards. By 1071 the Seljuks had captured Jerusalem and were persecuting pilgrims, who by this time journeyed from all parts of Europe to the sacred spots of the Holy Land. Thus was precipitated the great crusading movement as an offensive of the West against the East. Among the many important results of the Crusades may be mentioned the immense impetus that was given to missionary and trading enterprise in the Far East. Missionary expeditions beginning with St. Francis in the thirteenth century and travels of merchants and others throughout the Middle Ages gradually brought the great unknown continent of Asia into closer touch with the nations of Europe. Incidentally, the Crusades had the effect of re-opening up the sea route to the East by the Mediterranean and Red Sea and also the Persian Gulf, routes which had for long been in the hands of the Moslems, controlling as they did the western outlet at Gibraltar and the eastern at the Nile delta and Persian Gulf. Of the revived maritime trade Venice received the lion's share, closely rivalled, it is true, by Genoa.

Meanwhile contact between Europeans and the peoples of India and China was furthered on land by the widespread conquests of the Mongols, who were united at the beginning of the thirteenth century under the greatest of barbarian leaders, Ghengiz Khan. First eastern and then western Asia succumbed to the Mongol advance, until by 1259 lands from the banks of the Yellow River to the Danube and from the

Persian Gulf to Siberia owned allegiance to the Mongols. European travellers who were acceptable to the Mongols were secure from the Moslem danger.

The first traveller was a Franciscan monk, John of Plano Carpini, who was sent by Pope Innocent IV with a letter to the Grand Khan. He reached the Karakoram, but returned after two years with a haughty answer to the Pope's message. In 1254 another Franciscan, William of Rubruck, was sent to the court of Kublai Khan. The next travellers were of more importance. Two brothers, Nicolo and Maffeo Polo, Venetian merchants, left Constantinople in about 1251 and reached the court of Kublai Khan in Cathay (China). They were well received and asked by the Grand Khan to deliver a message to the Pope with the intent that numbers of missionaries might be sent to his people. They returned to Acre in 1269 to find the Pope had died. In 1271 the brothers set out again, taking with them Marco, Maffeo's son. They followed the sea route to Acre, then went via Baghdad to Ormuz, north through the Kerman desert and over the Pamirs to Kashgar, following the South Road to Peking, which was reached in May 1275. Marco was taken into the Khan's service and sent on his behalf to Shansi, Shensi, Szechwan and Yunnan. He was even made ruler over Yangchow, 'the only case recorded in history of a European being made a "mandarin" over Chinese territory'. The Polos contrived at last in 1292 to return. They followed the sea route to the Persian Gulf, being delayed in Sumatra, and arrived in Venice in 1295. Masefield says of Marco Polo—'that he created Asia for the European mind'.

In response to the request for missionaries, John of Monte Corvino was sent in 1289 with messages to all the Khans of Asia. He went by way of the Persian Gulf to the Malabar Coast and the Malay Peninsula, and finally reached Peking in 1292 or 1293. John's mission met with considerable success. In 1307 he was joined by colleagues designated 'bishops' by the Pope with authority to consecrate John Archbishop of Cambaluc (Peking). The letters of John of Monte Corvino bear witness to the progress of Christianity in China, and show that there were 6,000 or more converts in Peking, while missions also existed at Zaitun (modern Ch'ungchow) in the south-east in Fukien, as well as at many places along the caravan route into Europe. In 1318 Odoric of Pordenone, a friar from Padua, went by sea from Constantinople to Trebizon (Trabzon), thence through Persia to Ormuz, a route which at this time was favoured because the Mameluke Sultan of Egypt made the journey via Suez a dangerous one. Odoric visited Tane near Bombay, sailed along the west coast of India to Ceylon, across to Sumatra, Java, Cambodia, and so to Canton; after visiting the Chinese ports he spent three years with John of Monte Corvino in Peking. The return journey was by land through Shansi, Shensi, Szechwan and

Tibet. He is said to have been the first European to visit Lhasa. Others, missionaries and merchants, followed in the footsteps of the Polos to India and China until 1368, when Christian missionaries disappeared with the sudden overthrow of the Mongols. The accession of the Mings in China meant that the great land route was closed for approximately two centuries. At the end of the fourteenth century Tamerlane of Samarqand, a descendant of Ghengiz Khan, threatened to win the continent once more for the Mongols. He was prevented by death in 1405 from securing China.

The westward flow of yet another wave of barbarian Turks, the Ottomans, further restricted travel between Europe and Asia, and it remained for the sixteenth and seventeenth centuries to reopen the sea route to India and Cathay (China). The Crusades had done so only temporarily. Could not the infidel obstacle be circumvented by another route? The question was answered by nothing less than the discovery of America and the Cape route to India. The 'quest of the Indies' occupied the minds of navigators for hundreds of years, years which witnessed a decline in the importance of the Mediterranean as a commercial highway, together with the loss by Italy of supremacy as a trading nation. While Italy's maritime power declined, that of Western nations not limited to the Mediterranean 'backwater' developed; and so we find Spain, Portugal, Holland, England and France vying with one another for the wealth and trade of the East.

The last decade of the fifteenth century was a period of outstanding importance in maritime history. In 1486 Bartolomeu Diaz, a Spaniard, had sailed along the west coast of Africa and sighted the Cape of Good Hope. In 1492 Christopher Columbus, a native of Genoa, first sailed the Atlantic and discovered the West Indies for Spain. It may be, or it may not, that he believed he was on a new route to China, but one thing is certain. For the next fifty years the Spaniards were so busy conquering the New World that they left the rich prizes of the East to the Portuguese.

In 1498 the Portuguese Vasco da Gama rounded the Cape of Good Hope, sailed some distance north along the east coast of Africa, crossed the Indian Ocean and reached Calicut six months after leaving Lisbon. This voyage definitely opened up a new seaway to India. Within the next fifty years the Portuguese had established trading posts on the coasts of the Persian Gulf at Ormuz, the coasts of India at Calicut and Goa, Ceylon at Galle, Malaya at Malacca and, in 1557, as far afield as Macao off the south of China. At a time when refrigeration was unknown and meat was poor the great prize was the spices of the East with which stale, poor meat could be disguised. The Dutch followed on the heels of the Portuguese, sometimes (as in Ceylon) displacing them, but their influence was destined to be greatest in the East Indies. There they started active trading about 1595, established Batavia (now Jakarta) in

1619 and laid the foundation of the Netherlands East Indies. Also on the heels of the Portuguese and the Dutch were the English.

In the early sixteenth century the Spaniard, Magellan, had circumnavigated the globe in an endeavour to find a way to the Orient round the extreme south of South America. The same incentive led Willoughby and Chancellor, Englishmen, in 1554 round the north coast of Europe to the White Sea. In 1557 Jenkinson, likewise aiming at Cathay, penetrated inland through Russia from the north and on to Bukhara.

In 1577–80 Francis Drake made his famous voyage round the world, following Magellan's route. In 1592, Sir John Burrough captured a Spanish vessel, the *Madre de Dios*, which revealed much in relation to commerce with the Far East. Soon after, Benjamin Wood was sent with a letter from Queen Elizabeth to the Chinese Emperor asking for his protection of English traders. The expedition however failed to reach its destination.

Meanwhile English trade with the nearer East had increased so much that Elizabeth had granted a charter to the Levant or Turkey Company, which had its headquarters at Aleppo.

In the famous Elizabethan age (1558–1603) Sir Humphrey Gilbert and Martin Frobisher made efforts to find a North-West passage by way of North America to the East. This route was perhaps the one most eagerly sought at this period in history. Among many English explorers, Henry Hudson and William Baffin sailed in the same direction during the early seventeenth century. A publication by William Bourne in 1573 is of interest as indicating five possible sea routes to China:

(1) The Portuguese route, via the Cape of Good Hope.
(2) The Magellan Straits route.
(3) The North-west route—north of North America.
(4) The North-east and north of Russia route.
(5) The Northern route (presumably via the North Pole).

The history of Eastern commerce during the seventeenth century is a record of great trade rivalry between English, Portuguese, French and Dutch, who all began to form trading companies with trading stations round the coasts of India and China. The English, in particular, equipped numerous trading and diplomatic expeditions. In 1600 the East India Company was established with its headquarters in London in order to encourage trade with India and the Far East. It was followed a few years later by a similar French Company. In 1604 the East India Company, known as the Old Company, sent four ships to the Moluccas, where valuable cargoes of spices, pepper, ebony and sandal-wood could be obtained. The Keeling expedition in a voyage from 1606 to 1609 reached Java, where a factory or trading station was established. Japan was visited by an ambassador of James I of England, and tentative efforts were made to open Japanese ports to English ships. Though factories were set up, rivalry between English and Dutch brought about the expulsion of all foreigners from Japan in 1624. Possibly from these early connections with Japan, tea was first heard of in England. The first European known to have mentioned tea is the traveller Pinto, who visited the Far East in the middle of the sixteenth century; but not until the time that Samuel Pepys kept his diary (1660–9) was it called by the name of 'tay' or tea.

In 1636 the first Englishman to trade with China, Henry Bornford, opened up trading relations at Macao, where there was by that time an important Portuguese settlement. This trade, however, was not carried on directly with the Chinese; it was as much in the interests of the Portuguese as of the English. An attempt, though unsuccessful, was made to establish direct Chinese trade by John Weddell. Further attempts were made in 1643, 1658 and 1664. At last in 1671 an English factory was established at Amoy. The English had been more successful in India, where a factory at Masulipatam had been opened in 1611 and at Surat in 1612—the nucleus of the great hold of the British in India. In 1654 Fort St. George was built near the site of the present city of Madras; while in 1661 the island of great strategic importance, Bombay, was acquired as the marriage dowry of Catherine of Braganza. In 1684 the Company set up a temporary factory in Canton, and subsequently British trade began. Throughout the first half of the eighteenth century British ships sailed to Chinese ports, but only under sufferance. Despite vigorous efforts to obtain better trade conditions, the English, along with other Europeans, were confined to Canton by an imperial edict of 1757. It was the beginning of a long struggle due very largely to the aloofness of attitude pertaining to the imperial throne of China. In 1792 Lord Macartney was appointed British ambassador to Peking, with the aim of securing the opening to the British of Ningpo, Chusan Islands, Tientsin and a depot at Peking. The failure of the costly embassy is well known; it met with nothing but rebuff. In India, meanwhile, difficulties had arisen not from the people of India but from rival French traders. The English factories were soon opposed by French: on the west was Tellicherry with Mahé and on the east Pondicherry with Fort St. David, while the Portuguese were firmly settled in Goa. The opposition of the French was overcome after the Seven Years' War, and under the guidance of pioneers such as Clive and Warren Hastings permanent trading relations were established. The story of the British in India is one of slow but steady expansion.

The Spaniards despite their preoccupation with the Americas did not entirely neglect the East. In 1564 Miguel Lopez de Legazpi set out on a voyage of discovery, secured the Luzon Islands, which he renamed the Philippines after his sovereign, and founded Manila. The Spaniards held this strong position until 1898, when the islands were lost to the United States. In the early seventeenth century Spain, having been admitted to Formosa, began to trade with Japan, until the opposition of Holland proved too strong. Nevertheless, successful trade was maintained along the coast of China.

The rise of the Dutch as a maritime people came with the religious wars and persecutions of the Protestants at the hands of the Catholics at the end of the sixteenth century. When the Protestant cause had been championed by the House of Orange, the sea power of the Netherlands made rapid strides. Incurring fierce opposition from Portuguese and Spaniards over questions of trade, the Dutch began to look for markets

FIG. 26.—The political divisions of Asia

Showing the countries relative to the position of the Tropic and the major lines of latitude and longitude.

of their own. Between 1595 and 1597 they reached the Moluccas and Java. Trade was also carried on with China and Japan at the expense of the Spaniards, who were driven out of Formosa by the Dutch in 1642.

As to the French, their chief commercial interest was in India: in China their interest was rather in missions than in commerce. As early as 1604 a chartered company was formed for purposes of Oriental trade. Other companies were formed in 1611, 1642 and 1644, at the instigation of the able Colbert. Stations or factories were set up on the Indian coasts in opposition to those of the British East India Company. French influence in these regions was threatening to override the English, when

Clive's timely victories secured the supremacy of the English. For French trade with China the Compagnie de Chine was formed in 1698. Much credit is due to the French Roman Catholic missions—Dominican, Franciscan and Jesuit. In 1542 St. Francis Xavier, a Jesuit, reached Goa and began with considerable success to preach the Gospel in southern India, Ceylon and Malaya. Many others followed. Matteo Ricci, another Jesuit, is worthy of note. He spent many years in Nanking, Nanchang, Peking and Tientsin, leaving behind on his death in 1610 a noble tradition of learning. Friction between the different missionary bodies was inevitable and led to the expulsion from China of Christian priests during the eighteenth century.

The relations of the Russians with the East began with the downfall of the Mongols in China. Attempts at diplomatic relations were made many times during the Ming and Manchu dynasties. Ultimately by the Treaty of Nerchinsk (1689) trade, subject to strict regulations, was permitted. In 1727, 200 Russian merchants were to be allowed to visit Peking every two years. Eventually the trade connection which had found its beginnings in the Middle Ages when southern Russia was an important gateway into Asia, led to the acquisition by Russia of nearly half Asia, and the opening of the Trans-Siberian Railway with its terminus at Vladivostok.

The history of later intercourse between Europe and Asia is too long and complicated a narrative for this volume. The chief stages in the building up of the Indian Empire are well known to all readers of history; in China it was a story of advance in the face of many obstacles. Europeans slowly forced an entry into all Chinese ports. To do so the English fought the Opium and 'Arrow' Wars and endured the Taiping Rebellion in addition to becoming involved in China's wars with France and Japan.

The importance of the explorations and discoveries of individual travellers must not be overlooked—the journeys of Ralph Fitch, Thomas Roe, of Laval and Tavernier in the sixteenth and seventeenth centuries, to mention only a few of the earlier travellers; and the valuable geographical explorations of men like the Swede Nordenskiöld, who between 1878 and 1880 in his famous ship the *Vega* sailed round the northern shores of Europe and Asia to the Bering Straits, thus finding the north-east passage. Recent travels by land in Asia are far too numerous even to mention. Especially in the thirty years before the First World War men like Sven Hedin, Francis Younghusband, Aurel Stein, Prince Kropotkin, and Ellsworth Huntington achieved some of the most extensive investigations on record throughout central Asia, so that the Pamirs, Tien Shan, Tibet, Chinese Turkistan and the Gobi Desert were no longer unknown regions to the Western world. Yet that these vast tracts still have secrets to be revealed was shown from such later discoveries as those of Roy Chapman Andrews, whose expeditions were arranged under the auspices of the American Museum of Natural History in the nineteen-twenties.

Modern routes linking Europe and Asia tend to follow those of medieval times. The opening of the Suez Canal in 1869 brought back some of the importance of the Mediterranean and led to the abandonment, to a great extent, of Vasco da Gama's Cape route. On land the Trans-Siberian Railway, built from 1891 to 1905, though a long way farther north, emphasized the old transasiatic routes. Later aerial communication was opened up largely by land through the pioneer flights to India of Sir Alan Cobham and Sir Samuel Hoare. Airplanes are thus following the old caravan routes in going via Baghdad and Karachi.

Regular air services are now operated by British lines from London to India, Malaya, Hong Kong and Australia; by Dutch lines to the Far East; by French lines to Indo-China; by Russian lines across Siberia. American lines serve especially east Asia. A new contact between Europe and Asia was initiated when SAS (Scandinavian Air Services) began using the direct route from Copenhagen to Tokyo across the North Pole. Both India and Pakistan have international lines and practically all Asian countries have their own air lines. In particular vast countries such as China, India and Persia not well supplied with railways and roads have become very 'air-minded' and have numerous internal services.

ASIA'S POSITION IN THE WORLD

THE diversity of character presented by different parts of the Asiatic continent is such as to prevent the whole being considered to any extent as a unit. One might attempt to give an account of the

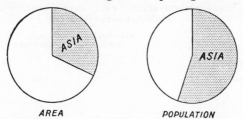

FIG. 27.—The area and population of Asia compared with those of the world as a whole

Out of a total land surface, including Antarctica, calculated at 57,168,000 square miles, Asia occupies 17,256,000 square miles. If the 4,410,000 square miles credited to Antarctica is excluded, Asia occupies approximately a third of the land surface. If the world population at 1966 be taken as 3,400,000,000 the total for Asia of approximately 1,933,000,000 is rather more than half.

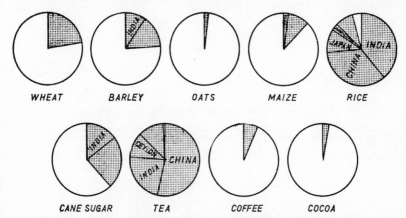

FIG. 28.—The position occupied by Asia in the production of certain staple foodstuffs

The total world production for the principal foodstuffs is not known accurately because of the uncertain figures, little more than guesswork, for China, and estimates only for some other countries. Approximate figures from United Nations (FAO) sources for 1960–62 including U.S.S.R. are as follows:

	World acreage, million acres	World production, million metric tons	Asia production, per cent.
Wheat	495	244	35
Barley	155	93	36
Oats	108	60	3
Maize	269	224	12
Rice	296	240	93
Cane sugar	—	31	30
Tea	—	1·02	97
Coffee	—	3·86	4
Cocoa	—	1·16	0·5

Comparing this with the earlier periods shown in previous editions of this book, Asia now grows a larger proportion of the world's wheat and barley. The once huge sugar production of Java has largely disappeared. Other proportions are little changed.

67

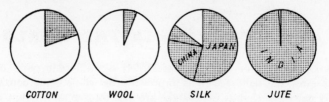

FIG. 29.—The position occupied by Asia in the production of four staple textile materials, 1962

					World production, metric tons	Asian percentage
Cotton	.	.	.	.	11,700,000	20
Wool .	.	.	.	.	2,579,000	8
Silk .	.	.	.	.	310,000	90
Jute .	.	.	.	.	2,500,000	98

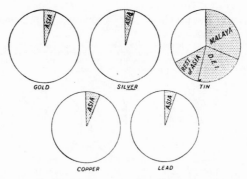

FIG. 30.—The place occupied by Asia in the production of five leading metals

This diagram was drawn for 1962, but it is difficult to state the present position fairly or accurately. The mineral production of the Asian parts of the U.S.S.R. is not published and figures are not available for China.

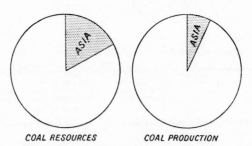

FIG. 31.—The position occupied by Asia in connection with coal

Coal reserves of Asia are estimated with difficulty because of the widely fluctuating totals given for China and Asiatic Russia. Out of an estimated world total of 7,397,553 million tons of anthracite, bituminous coals and brown coals Asia is believed to have 1,281,038 million or about 17 per cent. Out of a world production of about 2,210 million tons (excluding lignites) about 20 per cent. is from Asia including Asiatic Russia.

forests of Asia, but little of what one might say about the forests of Siberia would apply to India; one might discuss the wheatlands of Asia, but the description of conditions in south-western Siberia would be inapplicable to India; what may be true for China is far from being correct for India; even what is true in Turkey may not apply to Syria. The greater part of this volume is therefore devoted to a regional account of the countries of Asia, and this introductory section dealing with the continent as a whole has been made correspondingly brief.

For certain purposes, however, it may be useful to realize the position which Asia, as a whole, occupies in the world today. Unfortunately complete figures are very rarely available for all Asiatic countries; those for China are largely guesswork, whilst it is usually impossible to separate Asiatic Russia from European Russia even when figures for the Soviet Union are available.

Very roughly, as Fig. 27 shows, Asia covers a third of the land surface of the globe and has more than half the world's people. As the diagrams which follow—Figs. 28–31—demonstrate, it is rarely that Asia's production of leading commodities reaches a like proportion.

PART II

THE COUNTRIES AND REGIONS OF ASIA

TURKEY—THE THRESHOLD OF ASIA [1]

IT is perhaps appropriate that we should begin the study of the countries and regions of Asia with modern Turkey. The Turks, it is true, are an Asiatic race; the oriental character of Turkey was long recognized by its inclusion as one of the countries of the 'Near East', though the connotation of the terms 'Near East' and 'Middle East' has undergone marked changes in recent years. Yet Turkey has been modernized and Europeanized under the policies initiated by the late Mustapha Kemal Pasha (Kemal Ataturk) at a rate almost without parallel in the annals of history. Miss Grace Ellison, in a book published shortly after his rise to power,[2] summarized the creed of Kemal Pasha, not inaptly, as 'we will be modern *and* Turkish'.

So important is the new outlook in its influence on the development

FIG. 32.—The extent of Turkey as determined in 1922–3 [3]

of Turkey since the First World War that we will follow the course of briefly recapitulating the main points of Turkish history before proceeding to an account of the geography of the country. In this historical introduction the old conventional names for towns and regions are used; modern names are used in later sections.

In the latter part of the thirteenth century, the former Seljukian dominions in Asia Minor were already broken up into a number of petty kingdoms and were hard pressed by invading Mongols. The Ottoman Turks at this time were but bands of nomadic horsemen haunting the Anatolian highlands. One day, when riding within sight of Angora, a band of four hundred Oghuz Turks saw on the plain

[1] I am greatly indebted to my good friend Professor Cemal A. Alagöz for comments on this section.
[2] *Turkey Today*, London, 1928. See also H. Luke, *The Old Turkey and the New*, London, 1955.
[3] A small area around Alexandretta (now Iskenderun) was ceded by France in 1939.

below them a fierce battle in progress and, through their love of a conflict, bore down to assist the losing side—not knowing until afterwards
that they had won the day for the Seljuk Sultan of Rûm against the
Mongols. The grateful Sultan allowed the Turks, who were led by
Ertoghrul, to settle in his dominion. Othman, the son of Ertoghrul, has
for long been regarded as the founder of the Turkish Empire, and for
more than 600 years his house provided an unbroken succession of
sultans. It was from so curious and humble a beginning that the Turkish
Empire grew. The Turks were victorious against all comers until pitted
against the Mongolian hordes under the great Tamerlane at Angora at
the beginning of the fifteenth century. But Turkish history throughout
emphasizes one thing—the Turk's peculiar genius for reinvigoration.
So it was not until after the disastrous meeting with Tamerlane that the
Empire reached the height of its power. This was during the reign of

Fig. 33.—The Ottoman Empire, 1566, at the period of its greatest extent

Suleiman the Magnificent (1520–66), when the Turks ruled in undisputed sway from Budapest to Mecca and from Upper Egypt to the
Black Sea.

Then followed three hundred years of decline, till the 'Sick Man of
Europe' became a byword. Towards the end of last century there arose
the 'Young Turk Party', and in 1908 the Young Turks compelled the
Sultan to elect a chamber of deputies. Western Europe began to feel
that the fortunes of Turkey had at last changed for the better, but in
1912 came the Balkan War and the further humiliation of Turkey. In
1914, full of hope that at last her opportunity had come, Turkey entered
the War as an ally of the Central Powers. But the result was disastrous.
The Treaty of Sèvres wrested from her all her Asiatic dominions except
Asia Minor. Even there the independent state of Armenia claimed a
large share of mountainous country in the east; Greece was allotted an
important zone round Smyrna, whilst a neutral zone was determined on

either side of the Dardanelles and Bosporus. In Europe the boundary of Turkey was fixed within a few miles of the walls of Stamboul.

Then came the Turkish revolution—a nationalist movement headed by Mustapha Kemal Pasha. Acting in complete defiance of the provisions of the Treaty of Sèvres and of the Sublime Porte Government in Constantinople, this 'Napoleon of Modern Turkey' raised an Anatolian army with the avowed object of regaining Smyrna from the Greeks. The Kemalists, as they were called, adopted Angora as their headquarters and set up there a provisional government. On September 17, 1922, the Kemalists entered Smyrna—only four days later a disastrous fire commenced which destroyed all the foreign quarters of

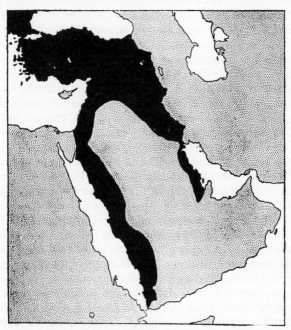

Fig. 34.—The extent of the Ottoman Empire in 1910 prior to the Balkan Wars and the Great War

the town and left only the old Turkish section. It was apparent that the real power in Turkey was the Angora Government and not the fragment of the old administration remaining in Constantinople. At Mudania, on the shores of the Sea of Marmara, representatives of Angora met the Allied generals under the chairmanship of General Sir Charles Harrington and drew up the famous Mudania Convention (October 11, 1922). The Turkish right to Smyrna and the whole of Asia Minor (excepting the neutral zones along the Dardanelles and Bosporus) was confirmed, and the immediate evacuation of Eastern

Thrace (the portion of Europe between the Maritsa River and Constantinople, including Adrianople) by the Greeks was provided for—thus defining, roughly, the present limits of Turkey.

From then, till his death in 1938, Kemal Pasha was engaged in consolidating and building up the new State. The *de facto* Government at Angora assumed the title of the Turkish Grand National Assembly in 1920; on November 1, 1922, it voted a resolution declaring that the office of Sultan had ceased to exist. At the same time the office of Caliph, or head of the Mahommedan religion, which had always been held by the Sultan, was divested of all temporal power, and it was provided that it should be filled by election from among the princes of the House of Osman. The administration of Constantinople was quietly taken over on November 4, 1922, and the Sultan himself left the city on November 17. On October 13, 1923, Angora was declared to be the capital of Turkey—despite certain difficulties of access which will be noted later, the associations of Angora as the birthplace of the old Empire and the ancestral home of the Turks fit it to be the capital of the new Turkey far more than cosmopolitan Constantinople or mercantile Smyrna. On October 29, 1923, the Grand National Assembly proclaimed that Turkey (the new official name in place of the Ottoman Empire) was a republic and elected Mustapha Kemal Pasha first President. Although Islam was declared the State religion, the Assembly decided on March 2, 1924, to abolish the office of Caliph and the princes of the House of Osman were expelled from Turkey. In April of the same year the religious courts were abolished. In the days of the Ottoman Empire enormous power was exercised by the various religious Orders of Dervishes—whose position may be compared with that of the Monastic Orders in England at the time of their conflict with Henry VIII. It is not surprising, therefore, that the Orders were abolished in September 1925, the Dervishes driven out of the country and their 'tekkes', or monasteries, closed. The Ulema, or official priesthood, was suppressed in 1926, and the care of the mosques and the ministrations of Islam passed into the hands of a single Imam for each mosque. The final stage in the State's anti-religious campaign came during my first visit to Turkey in the spring of 1928 with the order disestablishing Islam as the State religion. To one who has lived in the East it is indeed strange to go through a country full of mosques, yet not to hear the muezzin's call to prayer; not to see the befezzed pious bowing down towards Mecca at the hour of sunset. Nevertheless the majority of the people remain Moslems.

The orders abolishing the fez and directing the unveiling of women were, in many ways, strokes of administrative genius. There is no doubt that the age-old antagonism between Moslem, Christian and Jew was responsible for the numerous disturbances which made civil administration so difficult. The fez was almost a Mahommedan or a Turk uniform, and made it easy to distinguish the hated Christian or Jew. Hence petty personal quarrels often developed into civil brawls. The abolition of the fez and the insistence upon Turkish as the only language has rendered much more difficult the development of religious quarrels. One does not now see a single fez; but the unveiling of the women has been more difficult to enforce. To the Western woman who is accustomed to think of her sex fighting for liberty and equal rights and to compare with some pride the state of affairs today with the Victorian era, it is curious to observe the effect in a nation whose women have had liberty thrust upon them. In Constantinople and Angora it soon became rare to see a fully veiled woman, and the younger generation took readily enough to the silk stockings and the bright-coloured frocks of the West—but not to the hat, the place of which is taken by a scarf. In the smaller towns and villages the tendency to escape from the sombre black of the old costume was much slower. This consisted of a black skirt, a black cape and a black draped head-dress, the whole not unlike the outdoor dress of an English nurse. From the head-dress a thick black net veil hangs over the face, but can be lifted at will. Though the veil is now often worn thrown back over the head, it is usually lowered by the older folk as a stranger passes.

Turkish has been adopted as the one and only language. All signs of Greek and Roman lettering were obliterated, and even the names of stations were written only in the difficult Arabic script. That this was a mistake and militated against the Westernization of Turkey soon became apparent. In 1928 came the resolution to use the Roman alphabet in all official documents. This resulted in the adoption of official spellings of all place names, often quite different from previous transliterations from the Arabic. Angora became Ankara, Adalia became Antalya, and so on. This is quite apart from actual changes, such as Izmir for Smyrna and Istanbul for Constantinople. The European system of first name and surname was also adopted, and so Mustapha Kemal Pasha became Kemal Ataturk or, more correctly, Atatürk since a system of diacritical signs is retained.

Such radical changes in the life of a nation have not been made and cannot be maintained without recourse to forceful persuasion. The power behind Kemal Pasha's government was apparent to the public eye in the Army (which was larger than the army of any European power if we exclude the U.S.S.R.) and the Police Force. The latter, with smart dark grey uniforms with red facings, became one of the most efficient in the world and for some years kept an exact record of the movements of everyone in Turkey, Turk and stranger alike—a permit being necessary for all journeys.

We have entered somewhat fully into the development of modern Turkey for two reasons. It will be apparent at once that all older descriptions of the country are now absolutely and entirely false. In the second place it is essential to realize that the Turkish Republic under a President is fundamentally different from the Ottoman Empire which it replaced. The Sultan was not only head of the Empire, but, in his capacity as Caliph, was the leader of Moslems the world over. In other words, he was intimately concerned, not only with the wide Turkish dominions, but with such predominantly Mahommedan countries as Egypt, Persia, Afghanistan and large parts of the Indian sub-continent. The force which might have built up a nation was dissipated by the very breadth of its international interests. The President of the Turkish Republic, on the other hand, is devoted to the task of consolidating a nation, one in race and language, and of administering a single country. The change is symbolized by the change of capital from the cosmopolitan port of the erstwhile Constantinople to Ankara, the natural, geographical centre of the present Turkish domains and the ancestral home, not of the Moslem religion, but of the Turkish people.

We turn now to consider the geography of the country which Kemal Ataturk—like Alexander the Great, a Macedonian—set himself to modernize.

The modern Republic of Turkey has an area of 294,500 square miles with a population, according to the Census of October 23, 1960, of 27,754,820, which is a huge increase on the 20,934,638 of 1960. The Republic includes a small tract of European territory, only 9,256 square miles but embracing Istanbul (Constantinople) and extending as far west as Edirne (Adrianople) and the Meriç (Maritsa) River. The population of the European portion was 2,284,625 in 1960; leaving 25,754,820 in Asiatic Turkey. Asiatic Turkey embraces the whole of Asia Minor, including most of the great mountainous mass of Eastern Anatolia (the old Armenia) but excludes the islands in the Aegean except Imroz (Imbros), Bozcada (Tenedos) and Rabbit Islands, which remain Turkish. The following account deals with the Asiatic portion of Turkey—now the bulk of the republic—almost entirely.

Physical Features. Asia Minor has been likened to a hollow-crowned, narrow-brimmed hat with very ragged edges. The analogy is not a good one, but it serves to emphasize one main point. Asia Minor is essentially a plateau with a slight tendency to slope towards a hollow in the centre wherein lies the great but shallow salt lake of Tüz Göl. The surface of the plateau has an average elevation of about 2,500 feet; apart from the dip in the centre there is a general tendency to rise eastwards towards the Armenian massif.

The plateau is not bounded by a simple rim. On the north the Pontic Mountains consist of a succession of ranges placed *en echelon*, with a general east-west trend, separated by deep valleys. Thus from the plateau one climbs the innermost rim and then descends to the coast by a succession of deeply hollowed steps. The discontinuity of the individual ranges is a feature which must be insisted upon. Most of the

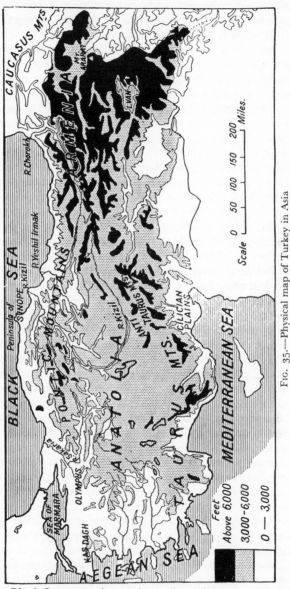

FIG. 35.—Physical map of Turkey in Asia

rivers of the Black Sea coast rise on the surface of the plateau and break through the confining mountains at intervals, having long intermediate courses, parallel to the coast, in the inter-range valleys. Along the greater part of the Black Sea coast the mountains descend right to the shore. The ranges are parallel to the coast, and there are few harbours.

A.—4

The few tracts of cultivable flat land which do exist are the gifts of the larger streams—the Bafra Plains of the Kizil River and the Charshembé Plains of the Kalkid River. Here, where ports are still more needed, the sediment brought down by the rivers results in the general shallowing of the sea near the coast. The mountains of the northern rim rise in places to 8,000 and even 9,000 feet, but the terraced drop to the sea robs them of any marked grandeur of scenery.

The southern rim of the plateau is formed by the Taurus—narrower and less complex than the northern rim, but grander and more imposing. Again it is built up of short echeloned ranges which in the west reach heights of 10,000 and even 11,000 feet and drop almost sheer to the Mediterranean. Cruising along the coast, the snow-capped heights of the Taurus present a picture not easily forgotten, with the wonderful blue of the Mediterranean in the foreground, an occasional dot which denotes a village near the shore and the darkly forested slopes beyond. There is not the same series of parallel valleys as along the Black Sea coast, and the streams find their way more directly to the sea. Again a coastal plain is absent, the only considerable plains are between Antalya and Alaiye and the very important Cilician Plains bordering the north-east corner of the Mediterranean. Leading from the Cilician Plains to the surface of the plateau is the famous pass known as the Cilician Gates, now followed by a motor road. Near by the 'Baghdad Railway' cuts through the chain.

Towards the east the Taurus takes on a general north-easterly trend, and becomes reinforced on the north by the parallel chain of the Anti-Taurus. This trend brings it gradually towards the Pontic Mountains, and the fusion of the two results in the great complex of mountains which occupies the east of Turkey. This complex is conveniently termed the Armenian Knot, and culminates in the lofty peak of Ararat. Many other peaks of the massif are volcanic, and activity in the not very distant past is indicated by the presence of hot springs, geysers and frequent earthquakes. Few parts of the Armenian crown drop below 5,000 feet. The level of the great lake of Van is 5,300 feet; the surface of the Erzurum Plain is about the same. The deep lake of Van owes its origin to a lava stream blocking a valley, and for many years it was increasing in depth and area, overwhelming rich fertile land to the north-east. It is among the high Alpine valleys that the headwaters of the great Mesopotamian rivers take their rise.

Returning now to the western end of Asia Minor, the mountain ranges do not there fuse as they do towards the east, but run out into the Aegean Sea as bold fingers of land separating deep inlets. Between the ranges the rivers descending from the plateau have built up broad deltaic plains, and much of the richest and most fertile land of Turkey lies in these valleys. The numerous hill-screened inlets afford excellent harbours; the river valleys themselves ready (though not exactly easy) routes to the plateau. The discontinuous nature of the ranges which make up both the Pontic and Taurus Mountains is well shown by their westward prolongations. In addition to the main spurs there are numer-

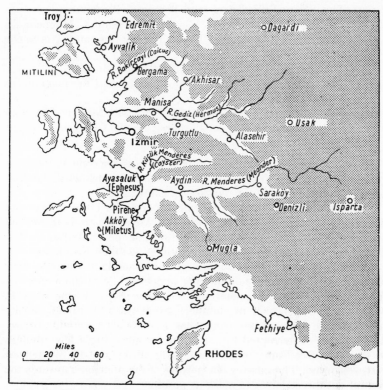

FIG. 36.—The west coast valleys of Turkey and the Izmir (Smyrna) hinterland.

Important hydro-electric plants are now developed on the Gediz above Manisa (Demirköpru Dam) and on the tributary of the Menderes east-south-east of Aydin (Kemer Dam).

Land over 1,000 feet stippled.

ous subsidiary ranges, but all have a general east to west alignment. There are four main spurs from the Pontic Mountains.

(a) One extends to Scutari opposite Istanbul.

(b) A second extends to the promontory in the Sea of Marmara south of Istanbul and is continued in the peninsula of Cyzicus.

(c) A minor one extends along the southern shore of the Sea of Marmara.

(d) A fourth gives rise to the glorious height of Olympus, overlooking the fertile plain of Bursa, and is continued much farther west as Mount Ida (Kas Dagh) overlooking the plains of Troy.

Southwards other spurs from the plateau separate the great valleys of the west coast—valleys all familiar from their associations in Greek history. From north to south the important valleys are:

(1) The valley of the Caicus with Bergama (Pergamus).
(2) The valley of the Hermus (Gadiz) with Manisa (Magnesia ad Sepylum), Ak-hissar (Thyateira), Sardis and Ala-Shehr (Philadelphia).
(3) The riverless valley which contains Izmir (Smyrna).
(4) The valley of the Cayster with Ayasuluk and the magnificent ruins of Ephesus.
(5) The valley of the Meander (Menderes) with Miletus, Magnesia ad Maeandrum, Aydin (Tralles), Priene, Colossae, Laodicea and Hierapolis.

South of the Meander and the site of Miletus, we come to the great spurs of the Taurus Mountains. Here is included much fertile land, at present undeveloped, in the old land of Caria.

Most of the river valleys already mentioned afford route-ways on to the plateau. The valleys of the Gadiz and Menderes are both utilized by railways, but for long only that up the Gadiz penetrated to the surface of the plateau, joining the plateau lines at Afyon Karahisar.

Returning now to the surface of the Anatolian Plateau, large stretches are flat or gently undulating steppeland, over much of which the scenery is dreary in the extreme. Snow-covered and wind-swept in winter, dry and brown in summer, interrupted by broad marshy stretches and salt-pans, the region has a character essentially Asiatic. The surface is interrupted by numerous ranges rising a few hundred or thousand feet from the surface, nearly all again with the general east-west trend. The main water parting of the plateau is towards the centre, but there is little to mark its position.

Geology.[1] It is impossible here even to summarize the geology of the Anatolian Plateau except to remark that the whole of Asia Minor lies in the main geosynclinal area of Alpine folding. Much of the heart of the plateau is covered with late Tertiary and recent rocks; the hills which appear from beneath this cover are built up of folded Palaeozoic and Mesozoic rocks; there are large stretches of volcanic rock—as around Kayseri and at, and north of, Ankara—as well as extensive masses of granite. In the folded belts which flank Asia Minor to north and to south Mesozoic and Tertiary rocks are mainly involved, but there are extensive cores of metamorphic and older sedimentary rocks. In the north-east of Asia Minor younger volcanic rocks cover large areas. The important valleys of the west of the peninsula, Philippson interprets as 'senken'—valleys let down between parallel faults.

[1] See A. Philippson, 'Klein Asien', *Handbuch der reg. Geologie*, Vol. V, Part 2, n.d. *c.* 1919.

The connection between the intervening horsts and the mountainous islands of the adjacent archipelago should be noted.

Climate.[1] Climatically Asia Minor comprises two belts—the coastal tracts and the plateau.

The *coastal tracts* have essentially a Mediterranean climate. The Mediterranean coastal strip is the warmest—the annual isotherm of 15° C. (59° F.) runs east and west roughly along the coast—most of it, except the Cilician Plains, is above 50° F. on the average in January and between 75° and 84° in July. The valleys of the Aegean coast have slightly cooler summers (July average generally below 75°) and colder winters (January average between 40° F. and 50° F.). By this big variation it will be seen that the Aegean shores have a climate of the Eastern Mediterranean type. Sometimes the winds which sweep down

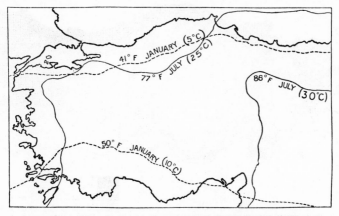

Fig. 37.—The climate of Turkey—January and July isotherms

from the plateau are bitterly cold (compare the Mistral from the Alps). The rainfall of the south and west coasts is almost entirely in winter and is moderate in amount—not exceeding 30 inches.

Along the southern shores of the Sea of Marmara the winters are distinctly colder—about 40° in January.

The Black Sea coast of Asia Minor is in several respects remarkable. It is remarkable, in the first place, for its heavy rainfall, the average exceeding 100 inches per annum in the mountainous east. Autumn and winter are the rainiest seasons, spring the driest. The rainfall decreases towards the west. The climate may be classed as Mediterranean, and Mediterranean vegetation flourishes (including the typical olive), but only as far west as the peninsula of Sinop. Between Sinop and the Bosphorus the vegetation is poorer and the olive is absent. It has been

[1] For a modern analysis see Sirri Erinç, 'Climatic Types and the Variation of Moisture Regions in Turkey', *Geog. Rev.*, **40**, April 1950 .224–35.

suggested that the Caucasus Mountains, distant as they are, protect the coast east of Sinop from the bitter north-east winds which have their origin in the great high-pressure system of central Asia. It is possible that these winds, warmed by the descent after crossing the Caucasus, are enabled to pick up much moisture from the Black Sea, hence the heavy autumn and winter rainfall.

On the *plateau* the climate is akin to that of the steppelands of Russia, with which the flora and fauna, as well as the human geography, are closely allied. The surface is little protected by the low rim of mountains and is swept by bitter north-east winds in winter and often late into the spring. The mean winter temperature is not much above freezing-point. Snow lies in the valleys continuously for two to four

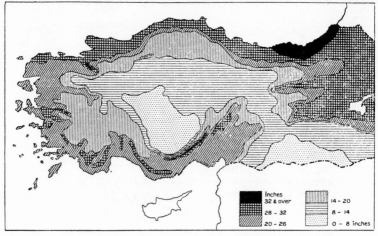

FIG. 38.—The rainfall of Asiatic Turkey
(*After* R. Fitzner)

months. When I have crossed the Anatolian Plateau in early April I have seen the snow still lying in patches and felt the winter winds still blowing with an icy tang. The summers, on the other hand, are very hot and dry. Even the spring has its unpleasant features, including violent dust storms which drive impalpable dust into everything and obscure the sun for hours like a thick fog. The rainfall régime on the plateau is of the Mediterranean type, but otherwise the climate is that of an arid steppeland. The total precipitation over considerable areas does not exceed 10 inches and in addition varies greatly from year to year.

In the mountains of Armenia in the east of the plateau the conditions are still more continental. Erzurum—infamously known as the 'Siberia of Turkey'—has a six months' winter with a temperature below 15° F., and the temperature has been known to fall below − 17° F.

every night for three weeks. Nearly all the valleys and plains in the mountain mass of Armenia are blocked with snow for four or five months.

Vegetation. From what has been said it will be gathered that there are at least two main vegetation regions:

(a) The Mediterranean tracts of the coastlands.
(b) The steppelands of the plateau.

This simple arrangement is profoundly modified by elevation. We may note the vegetation zones distinguished on a valuable and in-structive map—old but packed with information remaining true at the present day.[1]

In the *Mediterranean zone* may be distinguished on the slopes of the Taurus (reading downwards)—

Dwarf willow belt, up to 2,800 m. (8,500 feet).
Coniferous Forest (to the tree limit), up to 2,000 m. (6,000 feet).
Deciduous (summer green) Forest, up to 1,700 m. (5,000 feet).
Evergreen Mediterranean Woodland, up to 600 m. (1,800 feet).

It is further noted that in the Taurus region myrtles, oleanders and the typical thorny Mediterranean bushes occur up to 1,800 or 2,000 feet; Mediterranean pines up to 3,000 feet; the vine and valonia oaks to 4,000 feet; other oaks to 5,000 feet and cedars to 6,000 feet.

In the *Pontian zone* may be distinguished—

High pastures.
Deciduous Forest.
Evergreen (Mediterranean) Woodland.

On these slopes the box ascends to 1,000 feet; the walnut to 3,000 feet; the rhododendron and azalea to 6,000 feet.

The *Anatolian zone* is essentially a steppeland. Over vast areas it is treeless except for lines of stunted willows along the watercourses. The herbage is often scanty, of grass and small shrubs. In spring millions of tiny yellow and purple crocuses do their best to make splashes of colour amongst the limestone-strewn slopes.

Production and Industry. Despite the great developments of recent years which are changing Turkey from an agricultural to an agricultural-industrial state, the mainstay of the country is still in the land. Two-thirds of the people (against four-fifths in 1935) derive their livelihood directly from the cultivation of the land and the tending of flocks and herds. Grain and livestock are the dominant interests of the plateau, the vine and fruits of the seaboard.

Taking the country as a whole, rather less than a third (32 per cent.) of the surface is described as cultivated, rather more than a third

---

[1] 'Kulturkarte von Kleinasien, nach den authentischsten Quellen entworfen von Ammand v. Schweiger-Lerchenfeld', *Mitt. d. K.K. geogr. Gesellschaft*, 1878, Tafel IV.

of the surface (38 per cent.) is officially 'pasture'—most of it rough grazing with scanty herbage. In the drier parts of the plateau stock-raising is almost limited to goats, of which there were, in 1960, over 25,000,000. About a quarter of the goats are those which yield mohair, of which Turkey is the world's leading producer and exporter. Most of the 34,000,000 sheep are also found in the *plateau* and on the hill slopes of the eastern mountains the numerous shepherds still use some form of transhumance. Of necessity about a third of the land classed as cultivated lies fallow for periods of two to four years. Wheat and barley occupy up to 95 per cent. of the land actually sown in the drier parts of the plateau. In many areas tools and methods have changed little since Hittite days and ploughing consists of scratching the surface with an ox-drawn wooden plough tipped with iron. But, where isolation has been broken down by improved communications, there have been some phenomenal changes. Under Ataturk the state set up model farms demonstrating modern machinery and providing good quality seed as well as producing much of the wheat entering commercial channels. There are also village agricultural institutes where selected pupils become practical teachers of the peasants. Especially since 1950 many thousands of tractors and much other equipment have been brought to the country, mainly through the American aid-programme. Aridity places a severe limit on agricultural expansion on the plateau and irrigation is the obvious answer wherever water is available. There are some 200 projects of varying size: some of the larger are providing also hydroelectric power. Of these the Sariyar Dam (north-east of Eskisehir) and the Hirfanli Dam (south-east of Ankara) are the most important. The great Seyhan Dam (completed 1956–7) is north of Adana. The Almus Dam near Tokat is a multi-purpose project.

An old-established specialized crop of the plateau, grown especially near Konya and Afyon Karahisar, is opium.

The agriculture of the *coastal tracts* is much more diversified but many of the crops are curiously localized. The well-known Turkish tobaccos are grown on the alluvial tracts of the north coast around Samsun, Bafra, Çarsamba, Sinop, Inebolu and Zonguldak and in the valleys of the west around Izmit and Izmir. In the rainy north-east tea has been introduced and citrus fruits are grown, and here are the groves that make Turkey the world's largest exporter of hazel nuts. In the Bursa Plains, long famed for silk, vegetables are grown for the Istanbul market. The economic hinterland of Izmir is famed for figs, raisins and other dried fruits and almonds; olives and olive oil are produced specially around Aydin in the Menderes Valley and in the Bursa Plains. The cotton of the Adana or Cilician Plains has become the country's largest industrial crop with a value exceeding that of tobacco. The introduction of rice of Italian types has made Turkey self-sufficient in this grain.

Although the rolling plains of eastern Thrace between Istanbul and Edirne (European Turkey) resemble somewhat the Anatolian Plateau the population is denser and industrial crops include sugar beet and sunflower.

Again taking Turkey as a whole, there were in 1963 over twelve million cattle, over a million horses and 2·1 million donkeys and mules. Turkey does not escape the age-old struggle between nomad pastoralist and settled farmer and both with the forester. If the population goes on increasing at the present rate it has been estimated that the remaining forests (covering 13·5 per cent. of the surface) will be destroyed within twenty-five years by the peasant and his goat. As a result forest conservation has been undertaken by the State, which owns most of the forests.

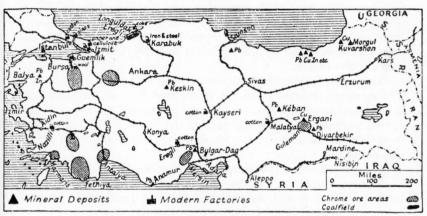

FIG. 39.—Railways and industries in Turkey
See also G. M. Wrigley, 'Turkey', *Focus Amer. Geog. Soc.*, Jan. 1953.

Turkey is richly endowed with *mineral wealth*, but the minerals are only now being developed, largely as a result of lack of communications. A rapid increase in mineral production may be expected in the near future. Coal is found especially among the mountains of the northern rim of the plateau, and a railway has been built to tap the coalfield of the Zonguldak Basin between Ankara and the coast. Most of this coal goes to the great government iron and steel works at Karabuk, erected on a site chosen for strategic reasons some 45 miles from the coal, and using iron ore from central Anatolia (Divrik or Divrigi near Sivas) up to 600 miles away. Iron ores are also known in the Adapazar region (lower Sakarya Valley) and near Ayvalik (Kazdag).

Turkey has numerous and large deposits of lignite, many now used locally and for the railways.

At Arghana Maden (Ergani) to the south-east of the plateau the copper mines are said to be potentially amongst the largest and richest in the world; copper is also known in eastern Trabzon. Chrome ore is found especially in the west coast tracts—near Bursa, Kütahya (mines on the slopes of Olympus between Bursa and Kütahya are especially famous) and Izmir as well as near Mersin. But the most important chrome ores are in Hatay, near Iskenderun; the Guleman mines near Diyarbakir are also important. Chromite forms Turkey's most interesting mineral contribution to international trade. Over two-thirds of that mined in 1950–60 went to the United States, which is deficient in this strategic mineral. There are Government silver mines at Bulgar Maden (near Konya), where gold is also found; silver, lead and zinc occur at Balikesir. Zinc, manganese, antimony and mercury are among the other metallic minerals. Amongst non-metallic minerals borax is exported from the Marmara (pandermite or boracite being found 30 miles south of Panderma); emery is obtained in the vilayet of Aydin; meerschaum at Eskisehir; arsenic in Aydin and Sivas; whilst there are salt works near Izmir, Erzurum and elsewhere. Salt is increasingly demanded by the chemical industry and so is sulphur, which is also mined.

There were good geological grounds for believing that south-eastern Turkey might embrace extensions of the Iraq-Iran oil belt. Contrary to the previous policy of nationalization of mineral resources, foreign capital was encouraged to take part in the search for oil. An output from fields in the Taurus near Mersin of 375,000 metric tons in 1960 had doubled to 745,000 in 1963.

Fisheries are also of considerable importance.

In 1934 a five-year industrial development plan was inaugurated by Kemal Ataturk, with the object of changing Turkey from an agricultural to an agricultural-industrial state. During that year were begun large state cotton mills at Kayseri and Eregli, a paper mill at Izmit, a glass factory at Istanbul, a coke and coal product factory at Zonguldak, as well as modern installations to deal with sulphur, milk products and otto of roses. There are now over 30,000 factories employing over 2,500,000 in Turkey—the majority established since 1923. The chief industrial towns are Istanbul and Izmir. There is an important sugar factory at Alpullu in European Turkey, another at Usak near Izmir, and a third at Eskisehir. With the completion of six later ones at Turhal (near Tokat), Erzurum, Konya, Kayseri, Ámasya, and Kütahya, Turkey became self-supporting in sugar. There are many woollen factories, but carpets are less important than formerly. A modern cotton-ginning, spinning and cotton oil-cake factory exists at Adana.

The textile factory at Kayseri claims to be the largest in south-west Asia and altogether Turkey is producing at home two-thirds of her requirements in cotton goods and 80 per cent. in woollen goods.

The greatest enterprise of the State however was the iron and steel mill at Karabuk. Its operation proved uneconomic and the recent tendency in industry has been to encourage private enterprise. From 1949 to 1951, for example, the output of cement was doubled—mainly from new privately owned works. Great development in hydro-electricity is now taking place. Early in 1961 14 major projects were either completed or nearing completion.

Population. For the first time in the history of Turkey a general census was taken in 1927. This has been followed by regular censuses in 1935, 1940, 1945, 1950, 1955 and 1960 with the following results:

Date	Total	Urban, per cent.	Density per sq. km.	Density per sq. mile
1927	13,648,270	24·2	18	47
1940	17,820,950	24·4	23	60
1945	18,790,174	24·9	24	62
1950	20,934,670	25·2	27	70
1960	27,754,820	—	36	92

The 1950 results were analysed by W. C. Brice[1] who pointed out that an increase of 50 per cent. in under twenty-five years has been achieved with very little movement by migration either inwards or outwards. Despite the great growth of Instanbul (1,466,500 in 1960), the capital Ankara (287,000 in 1950 but 650,000 in 1960) and Izmir there has been little increase relatively in the urban population. The net growth of population is of the order of 3 per cent. per annum—approaching double the world average.[2] Nevertheless density is still low. Turkey's new prosperity is associated with the development of the remoter country districts and the villages. The area referred to in the above table is the same throughout except that four remote eastern districts were not included in the enumeration of 1927 and Hatay was added to Turkey in 1939 and is included first in the 1945 census.

Population distribution is closely related to physical conditions, notably of relief, soil and adequacy of rainfall. It is concentrated in the fertile valleys of the west coast, the cultivable plains of the north and south coasts and the damper parts of the plateau. The valleys bordering the Aegean were already well peopled in 1927 and apart from the over-spill of Istanbul and the growth of the Ankara region and industrial Zonguldak greatest increases have been in the eastern parts of the plateau, north-east coast and extreme eastern borders. The vigorous expansion of the railways has greatly helped the development of the eastern plateau—as evidenced by such towns as Sivas and Kayseri—whilst the growth of Trabzon indicates its function as the outlet for the Gümüshane mines and the north-eastern areas generally.

[1] 'The Population of Turkey in 1950', *Geog. Jour.*, **120**, 1954, 347–52.
[2] Estimated in 1965 to be 3·0 per cent. per annum—amongst the highest in the world. Total exceeded 32,500,000 in mid-1965.

Before the First World War there was a very large alien population
in Asia Minor. There were very large numbers of Greeks especially in
Smyrna (Izmir) and western towns. There were also large numbers of
Armenian Christians and numerous Jews and Italians.

After 1919 a large proportion of the Armenian population emigrated
to the Republic of Erivan and the Jewish element in the towns decreased. But far more remarkable was the disappearance of the Greeks.
An agreement between Turkey and Greece, signed at Lausanne, provided for the compulsory exchange of the Greeks of Turkey, not including Constantinople, against the Turks of Greece, not including western
Thrace, as from May 1923. From the point of view of numbers there is
no doubt Turkey was the loser. The hellenization of Asia Minor dates
back to the days of classical Greece, and many of the towns, especially

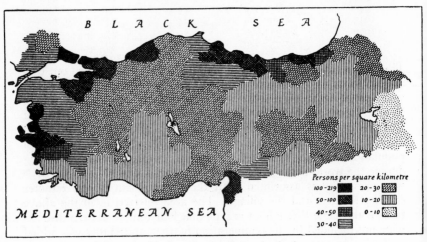

FIG. 40.—Turkey: the population density in 1950
(*After* W. C. Brice)

in the south-west of Asia Minor, were Greek rather than Turkish in
that the wealthy influential merchant and manufacturing classes were
Greek. In purging their country of this foreign element the Turks were
thorough. All the rayahs (Greek Christian peasants of Turkish nation-
ality) were included in the banished. It is difficult to estimate the
numerical loss to Turkey; the effects were more apparent in the growth
of many Greek towns. Although Constantinople (Istanbul) was excluded from the exchange, many of the Greeks left the city. The Greek
Government estimated the number of Greek refugees from Asia Minor,
Constantinople and Thrace between August 1922 and January 1925
at 1,400,000—10 per cent. of the 1927 total population of the whole
great Republic of Turkey. Athens alone increased in population from
300,000 in 1921 to over 600,000 in 1928. The Greeks took with them

their trades. The Turkey carpets which they formerly manufactured in Smyrna they now manufacture in Greece. Their departure disorganized the whole economic fabric of such Turkish towns as Izmir and Aydin, and flourishing industries were entirely destroyed. At the time it looked like economic suicide but time has shown how Turkey could rebuild a Turkey of and for the Turks. The country has continued to lose her foreign population. Greeks, Circassians, Armenians, Jews and Bulgars have continued to drift back to their own countries, Turkish-speaking peasants from the Balkans have drifted in. Only o·2 per cent. of the present Turkish population are considered as foreigners: many of these are in cosmopolitan Istanbul. This must not be allowed to obscure the existence of the two large minority groups—a million and a half

Fig. 41.—Turkey: changes in population density, 1927–50
(*After* W. C. Brice)

Kurds, closely allied to the Turks, in the south-east and scattered else-where, and the quarter million Arabs, also in the south-east.

Despite the development of industry and commerce, Turkey is still predominantly agricultural. Agriculture is the occupation of more than two-thirds of the employed population—75 per cent. in 1945. Consequently most of the population is found in some 40,000 village units; in 1950 only the five towns of Istanbul, Izmir, Ankara, Adana and Bursa had more than 100,000 people, but this had increased to nine in 1960 by the addition of Eskisehir, Gaziantep, Konya and Kayseri. By 1960 eighteen other towns had over 50,000 including Erzurum, Sivas, Malatya, Diyarbakir, Samsun, Urfa, Maras, Mersin, Balikesir, Zonguldak and Izmit.

The great cosmopolitan city of Istanbul which entered into the 'millionaire' class in 1950 is in striking contrast to the rest of the country. Contrary to some prophecies, its growth has not been adversely affected by the transfer of the capital to Ankara. Uniquely sited on crossroads of exceptional international importance—the Bosporus, sole entrance to the Black Sea, is only from 800 yards to $2\frac{1}{2}$ miles wide—it has a superb natural harbour in the Golden Horn. Cut off from the plains of Thrace by magnificent walls which still survive, Istanbul has many relics from the past side by side with varied industries such as shipbuilding, munitions and fishing. Its incomparable mosques now jostle with luxury hotels, its bazaars with modern stores.

Izmir is Turkey's third city in population and its first export port, serving especially the productive valleys of the west coast.

Ankara, capital of Turkey and the largest inland city, is in the main a modern creation which spreads out on to the plain at the foot of the ancient Hittite citadel and now to the surrounding hills from one of which the great monument to Kemal Atatürk looks down on the metropolis so largely his creation. It had 650,000 people in 1960.

Despite, therefore, the gloomy prognostications of the time, in the twenty-five years which followed the expulsion of the Greeks, the Turks succeeded in rebuilding completely their economy. Agriculture has been vastly improved not only in the old semi-luxury export items formerly handled by the Greeks such as tobacco, dried fruits and nuts but also, and especially, in the staple crops such as cereals and cotton which have come to lead among exports.

As the years have passed Turkey has come more fully into the European orbit. An important bulwark against Communism, the country is a full member of NATO (North Atlantic Treaty Organization). In 1954 old quarrels with Greece were so far forgotten that Turkey, Greece and Yugoslavia formed a defensive alliance. Many recent developments have been aided by American funds and technical assistance.

Communications. Foremost amongst the needs of the new Turkey were improved communications. Enormous areas were formerly accessible only by pack animal and that only in certain seasons. The need is still there but great strides have been made.

At first the emphasis was on building up an open network of main railways. From a route mileage of 2,173 at the end of 1925, the total had increased to 4,755 by 1947. A fifteen-year plan was produced in that year for the construction of a further 1,500 miles but was later shelved in part in favour of the prior claim of a nine-year road programme. Mileage was still under 5,000 in 1964. This reflects a change of emphasis to all-weather highways. In 1926 there were only 8,500 miles of national roads and a 1927 map published in earlier editions of this book showed that existing roads were mainly feeders to the railways. The 1948 programme envisaged the construction or reconstruction and maintenance of about 15,000 miles of all-weather standard roads. The work has been greatly facilitated by the mechanized road-building equipment supplied by the American Mission for Aid to Turkey. By

1951 nearly 10,000 miles of road were being maintained; by 1962 there were 16,000 miles of national highways and 20,000 of provincial. Motor transport both short and long distance is extensively used and broadly speaking where there is a road (sometimes where there is not) there is certain to be a bus service.

Extensive use is now made of air travel. Internal lines are operated by Turkish Airlines, formerly state-owned but now a mixed company with B.O.A.C. a partner since 1957. Officials and business men normally make the journey between Istanbul and Ankara in two hours by air; external services are operated from Istanbul by B.E.A. and other international lines.

The early railways of Turkey were largely British or French constructed and owned. The old Anatolian Railway ran from Haydar Pasa (opposite Istanbul) to Ankara and Konya. Its extension beyond Konya

FIG. 42.—The railways of Turkey, showing those in existence before 1914
The Turkish and Iran railways were linked directly in 1964.

as the 'Baghdad Railway' was the German bid to secure a land route to the Indian Ocean in rivalry of British-French control of the Suez Canal sea route. It was completed by the Germans during the First World War through Aleppo to Nisibin but for many years—indeed until 1940—the Turkish and Iraqi railways remained without a link. The famous Orient Express via Vienna and the Simplon Orient Express from Paris to Istanbul via the Simplon have, with certain changes in route and fortune, long figured amongst the world's famous trains. The Express is nominally continued on the far side of the Bosporus to Ankara. Turkish lines are all on, or being converted to, the standard gauge of 4 feet 8½ inches. For a time there was an all-rail route on this gauge along the Syrian-Palestine coastal plain to Egypt.

In January 1929 rather more than half the Turkish railways were Government owned. The Government completed their policy of buying up foreign-owned lines in 1936 and by 1948 the whole network became State property. The growth of the network can be seen from Fig. 42.

Apart from Istanbul, Izmir remains the chief port of Turkey but the development of communications has brought into prominence the several ports of both the Black Sea and Mediterranean coasts.

FIG. 43.—The countries and railways of western Asia

Foreign Trade. It is extremely difficult to generalize concerning the foreign trade since the leading exports are agricultural products depending largely on harvests which fluctuate widely according to season. Cotton, tobacco, fruits and nuts and cereals (wheat) may each at times lead. Other items include live animals, hides and skins, eggs, olive oil, opium, tanning extracts, etc. The bulk of the imports are manufactured goods but include such foodstuffs as tea, coffee and sugar. In years of bad harvest there is even an import of wheat. The industrial countries of Europe—Britain, France, Italy, Germany—are normally the chief customers for Turkey's exports and suppliers of her needs.

THE NATURAL REGIONS OF TURKEY

When the first edition of this book was being written in 1928 little had been published on the regional geography of Turkey. By far the most thorough study was that made by Ewald Banse, which covered also the lands of the old Turkish Empire (*Die Türkei: eine moderne Geographie*, 3rd Edition, Brunswick; Westermann, 1919). It had been briefly summarized in English (with a map) by E. C. Semple (*Geographical Review*, **11**, 1921, 338–50). In a brief paper on the 'Regional Geography of Anatolia' (*Economic Geography*, **2**, 1926, 86–107) G. P. Merriam had dealt with the western half of the country. Using these accounts and a large amount of unpublished material collected during my travels in Turkey in 1928 I attempted a general regional division and description. In recent years geography has come to occupy an important place in the universities of Turkey and the division of the country into natural regions received the attention of the first Turkish National Geographical Congress in 1941. Later a careful study of 'The Agricultural Regions of Turkey' was published by Sirri Erinç and Necdet Tunçdilek (*Geographical Review*, **42**, 1952, 179–203). Their map is shown in Fig. 45 and bears close comparison with my earlier map. In the account which follows, this later work has been used to modify my previous descriptions.

The Pontic-Aegean-Mediterranean Coastal Region

The North-eastern Region. As already noted, the coastal strip from Sinop to the eastern border has a climate which is a much modified Mediterranean. The rainfall is heavy and there is no month wholly without rain. As a result such a typical Mediterranean tree as the olive will grow but the yield of oil is slight and olive cultivation is negligible. The most important parts of the coast are the alluvial plains of the Halys around Bafra, and of the Yeşil and Kelkit around Carsamba, together with cultivable stretches around Sinop, Samsun, and along the coast at intervals to Trabzon. A crop of special importance is tobacco. Samsun is the most important centre of Asia Minor and the quality of the leaf is excellent. Bafra leaf is famous for its exquisite taste and aromatic quality. The tobacco of Sinop is reported as inferior in quality. Maize is one of the chief grain crops of this region; various Mediterranean crops include, in particular, nuts and myrtles. The Region comprises sub-regions C1, C2 and C3 of Fig. 45. The Rize sub-region has a rainfall of over 80 inches with maize as the chief cereal, tea (a recent development) and tangerines as special crops. The Central sub-region (C2) is an important tobacco area with maize and beans as subsistence crops, hazel nuts as a cash crop on the lower ground. On higher ground maize gives place partly to barley and rye and butter is produced. Farther west (C3—the Samsun area) is drier and the agriculture more mixed.

The Marmara Region. The western prolongations of the Pontic ranges abut on to the charming Sea of Marmara in a series of hilly or mountainous promontories. Between them are broad cultivated valleys. Of the valleys the most important are the Izmit Valley, the Bursa

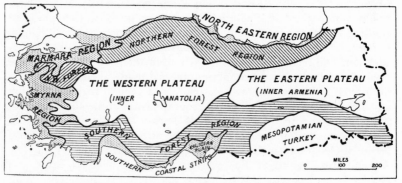

FIG. 44.—The natural regions of Turkey as delineated for the first edition of this book

Plains, and the Plains of Troy. The Izmit Valley is another important tobacco region—it is one of the largest producers in Asia Minor, though the quality is not good. The region under consideration is part of the warm, dry, porous soils of the lower hill slopes and shelter from cold northern winds is important. Between Gemlik and Banderma there is a low hill range along the shores of the Sea of Marmara, very largely covered with olive groves—400,000 trees are said to be in full bearing. In the Plain of Bursa, the olive is a very important crop; in the Plain of Troy and about Edremit it is the chief crop. Although the olive does not enter to any extent in foreign commerce, it plays a very important part in the domestic economy of the Turks, just as it does in nearly all Mediterranean lands, as a substitute for the butter and animal fats of other lands. Olives from the Marmara Region which is moister than areas farther south are, however, eaten as such rather than used for oil.

Of the towns in this region special mention must be made of the delightful old Turkish town of Bursa on the slopes of snowy Olympus.

Bursa is only 20 minutes from Istanbul by air, with half a dozen services a day. A good motor road across the fertile plain connects Bursa with its port Mudania, four or five hours by steamer from Istanbul. Banderma is the port and railhead farther west; Çanakkale on the Dardanelles is the chief town of the Plains of Troy. Izmit, the tobacco centre, at the head of the Gulf of Izmit, should be noted. The little islands in the Gulf are summer resorts for the inhabitants of Istanbul.

The West Pontic sub-region (C4 of Fig. 45) is transitional between the Black Sea and Mediterranean regions. Large areas are covered with low woodland or bush with small basins and plains in some of which cultivation has been stimulated by the nearness of the market of Istanbul—which is true also of the Marmara Region.

The Aegean Region or Izmir Economic Zone. The hinterland of the port of Izmir may be regarded as extending roughly from the

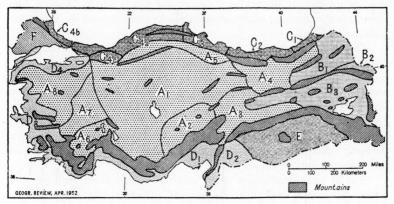

FIG. 45.—Agricultural regions of Turkey

(*After* Erinç and Tunçdilek)

A. Interior Anatolia: **1.** Central; **2.** Kayseri-Niğde sub-region; **3.** Malatya-Elaziz sub-region; **4.** Erzincan sub-region; **5.** Northern transitional belt; **6.** Lakes Region; **7.** Afyonkarahisar sub-region; **8.** North-western transitional belt.
B. Eastern Anatolia: **1.** Kars-Erzurum sub-region; **2.** Aras Valley sub-region; **3.** Van-Tunceli sub-region.
C. Black Sea Coasts: **1.** Rize sub-region; **2.** Giresun-Ordu sub-region; **3.** Samsun sub-region; **4.** West Pontic sub-region.
D. The Mediterranean Region: **1.** Sub-region of Mediterranean agriculture; **2.** Gaziantep sub-region; **3.** Aegean sub-region; **4.** Marmara sub-region.
E. South-eastern Anatolia.
F. Interior Thrace.

edge of the plateau—actually including certain border tracts on the plateau—to the Aegean and from latitude 39° 40′ north to the shores of the Mediterranean. It thus comprises the rich valleys of the rivers known in classical literature as Caicus, Hermus, Cayster, Meander and Indos. This may be described as the richest and therefore the most important region of Turkey; it was the old hellenized region of Asia Minor, but the inhabitants are now almost exclusively Turks. Apart from the settled Turks of the towns, special interest attaches to the 'yuruks' who shift their quarters according to season and are agro-pastoralists also occupied in gathering wood, making charcoal and collecting honey.

Agriculture is the chief occupation of the region. Taking first the field crops, cereals occupy the leading position. The largest crop is wheat, followed by barley. Tobacco is grown especially between Izmir and the Meander, hemp in the Meander Plain. Olive groves are every-where but especially on sheltered slopes in the north. Vineyards are widespread.

As in all parts of Turkey, agriculture is still carried on in a very primitive way. The cattle-drawn wooden plough is gradually being replaced by the iron ploughshare. Threshing is still done extensively on paved threshing floors by horses and cattle treading out the grain, but the demand for threshing machinery is increasing. The seed is sown on the low ground in November or later, the harvest is in May or June (compare the plateau, where sowing is in September and the harvest in July and August).

The wheat grown on the lowlands is a soft wheat (compare the hard wheat of the plateau) and the yields vary from 15-fold to 30- or 60-fold in the richest coastal districts. Thirty to forty per cent. of the crop is retained where grown for seed and for local milling, but the Izmir Region as a whole is roughly self-supporting in the matter of grain. Rice is grown, and the former large imports of this popular food grain have almost ceased.[1] Irrigation has been extended and im-proved; hundreds of motor pumps are used to raise and distribute the water of the Menderes River.

Special interest attaches to the cultivation of opium. Half the area under opium is in the Izmir vilayet itself, the remainder in the vilayets of Mughla and Denizli. Before the devastation of the Afyon Karahisar and Izmir districts during the Turko-Greek War of 1919–22 over a quarter of a million acres were sown with poppy, yielding on an average 5,000 to 6,000 cases of opium—in one year production reached 10,000 cases. In the twenties the average crop was estimated at 3,500 cases,[2] valued at £T6,000,000 or £640,000. Smyrna opium was in great demand because of its high content of morphine. Turkish opium con-tains between 11 and 14 per cent. against Persian (8–10), Egyptian (6–8·5), Indian (6–7), Chinese (3–6). The cultivation is mainly in the hands of peasant proprietors, who thoroughly pulverize the soil by double ploughing and sow thrice at intervals to ensure against failure and to afford a succession of plants. Light, rich soil is desirable. The plants flower from the end of April (lowlands) to June (uplands) and at this time gentle showers are beneficial. The juice is collected by making

---

[1] A typical national dish is 'pillaf', consisting of rice cooked (as in India) with each grain separate, and garnished with sultanas, chopped-up meat and vegetables (cf. Indian pillau).

[2] A case is of 50 okes, or 50 × 1·282 kg. or about 141 lb.

an incision in the capsule by drawing a knife two-thirds of the way round it, care being taken not to penetrate the interior lest the juice should flow inside and be lost. The operation is usually carried out after the heat of the day and the exuded juice is later scraped off. The average yield is 7 lb. of opium and 600 lb. of seeds per acre. The seeds yield about 40 per cent. of oil, which is used for food. It is as sweet as olive oil and cheaper. The value of the oil produced is about two-thirds that of the opium. The oilcake is used for cattle food and manure. Although the old demand for opium for smoking is being eliminated

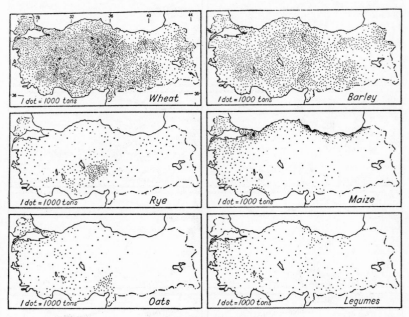

FIG. 46.—Cereals in Turkey

Turkey is essentially a grain-growing country and cereals occupy 88 per cent. of the cultivated area —wheat alone 52 per cent. and barley 26. The interior has a surplus which feeds the Turkish people but except for animal products the interior contributes little to foreign trade. (*From* Erinç and Tunçdilek.)

throughout the world, there is a continuing demand for medicinal purposes especially from European countries.

Tobacco is an important crop in the neighbourhood of Izmir and Manisa. The Izmir tobacco has a particularly fine taste and is in good demand for blending. The area produces half of Turkey's tobacco.

Cotton is not such an important crop as in the great cotton belt of the Cilician Plains, but is extensively grown in the plains of the Hermus and Meander (Menderes) Rivers, the finest being from around Aydin. Most of the cotton is of the short stapled 'Jerly', probably a native of Syria, but about 10 per cent. of the crop is of American cotton. The sowing is in March or April, the picking towards the end of September or in early October.

Grapes and Sultanas. Of all types of dried grapes perhaps the sultanas of Turkey are best known. They are produced from a small variety of yellow grape, which for long was cultivated exclusively in the Izmir Region, though in recent times it has been introduced into Greece, Crete, California, Australia and South Africa. These sultanas are produced now mainly in the lower Gediz plain near Manisa. The sultana

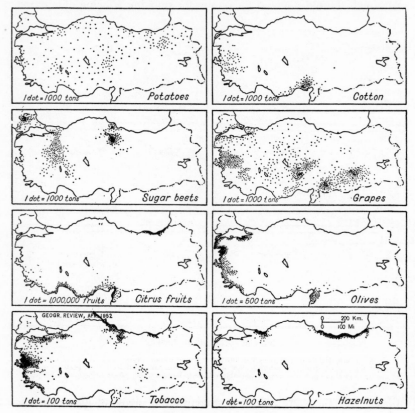

FIG. 47.—The specialist crops of Turkey

The marked localization in regions should be noted. (*From* Erinç and Tunçdilek.)

vines are grown from cuttings imported from America—which are disease resisting—or from native cuttings. The vines begin to yield in the fifth year, reach full yield after seven years and go on with full yield for thirty or forty years. A vine may yield as much as 450 lb. of grapes. In November and December the vines are trimmed by removal of weak branches, and in February and March are pruned again and the vineyards ploughed and kept clear of weeds. As the leaves develop, the vines are sprinkled with sulphur or, if the weather is wet, sprayed with a solution of copper sulphate. The grapes are harvested in the middle of August. The clusters are cut off and dipped into a strong lye of boiling water, potash and olive oil, spread on sheets of cardboard and left exposed to the sun for five or six days until dry. The fruit is then collected into small heaps and the stalks winnowed away. The bulk is now machine packed without hand or foot pressing—it was not so in the past.

Considerable quantities of ordinary grapes are consumed locally or made into pekinez. Mahommedanism forbids the use of wine, hence the manufacture of pekinez by boiling the grape juice, which is then prepared by beating with the open hand into a thick dark liquid like clouded honey.

Figs are indigenous to Asia Minor, and the region under consideration is one of the great areas of supply. Of all dried varieties those grown in the Menderes Valley are unrivalled. The orchards stretch from the river banks to the hill-slopes, the finest being on the hillsides. The figs of the Menderes Valley are thin-skinned, full of honeyed substance and aromatic in flavour. Figs are grown also very extensively along the banks of the Cayster, but the fruit is inferior to that of the Menderes Valley.

The fig trees are grown from cuttings, and begin to yield in the third or fifth year according to method of planting, but the full crop is only yielded from the tenth year. The most productive age of the trees is from twenty to thirty years: the yield definitely declines when the tree reaches fifty. The average yield of a fig tree in full bearing is about 70 lb.; there are 60 to 100 trees per acre giving a yield of $1\frac{1}{2}$ to 3 tons per acre. The fruit ripens in August and is allowed to dry on the branches. It is carefully collected, left to dry on strips of canvas, packed into horsehair sacks of about 250 lb. and sent to the packing houses. The packing houses are carefully controlled by the Municipality and the Health Department. The fruit is thrown into heaps on the floor, picked over and graded by women, then packed into the trays by men and boys who constantly dip their hands into salt water. Practically the whole is exported, especially to the United Kingdom and the United States.

Olives. The plains round Edremit and Ayvalik provide half the olive oil of Turkey and there are many olive groves round Izmir. Except in the Aydin district the groves are seldom more than 15 or 20 miles inland. An olive tree in full bearing yields 28 to 35 lb. of olives, equivalent to $5\frac{1}{2}$ to 7 lb. of oil. It is curious that the crop alternates, good and bad years succeeding one another. The olives vary in quality, but are mixed for extraction of oil. The trees are beaten to cause the olives to fall and there is no attempt at careful handling. Green and dry olives are used for food, but up to 95 per cent. of the crop is used for the extraction of oil. There is little or no surplus available for export.

Rose Industry. The Bourdon and Isparta districts have always been famous for attar or otto of roses, but many of the former growers went to Greece and the industry declined.

Leaving the purely agricultural products of the Izmir Region, there is an interesting product of commercial importance which comes from the Mediterranean woodlands of the hills or the edge of the plateau. This is *valonia*, a name applied to the cup of the acorn of the Valonia oak (*Quercus aegilops*). The oaks grow wild in thick woods at Usak, sparsely in other districts. The yield of valonia at low altitudes (75 kg. or 165 lb. per tree) is less than that at high altitudes (200 kg. or 440 lb. per tree). The trees are beaten with sticks between August and October and the valonia spread out in the sun to dry. The acorns, earth, etc., are then eliminated and the valonia sent to Izmir by rail. Only a little is used locally or in Istanbul; the bulk of the crop is exported from Izmir. The use of valonia is in tanning; the valonia extract, drummed into hides at the end of the tanning process, is particularly valuable in the preparation of sole leather, for it deposits 'bloom' (ellafic acid) and makes the leather solid and compact. An extract, 'valex', is also produced.

Regarding the mining industries of the Izmir Region, it may be said, as of Asia Minor as a whole, that the region is rich in minerals which are only now being exploited as communications improve. Chrome is mined at Dagardi and Fetige, also emery, antimony and boracite. Others which are or have been worked in the Region include emery, antimony, chrome, silver-lead, cinnabar (for mercury), manganese, lignite, sulphur, alum, arsenic and gold.

Turkey and Greece (the latter from the island of Naxos) have almost a monopoly of the world's emery, and the Turkish mines are most productive. The production of salt, from the northern shores of the Gulf of Izmir, is a Government monopoly.

The Izmir Region is also a manufacturing region. Carpet-making and tanning claim most employees; other industries include flour-milling, oil-pressing from olives and sesamum, soap-making, textile manufacturing (cotton and wool), and industries connected with the packing of fruit, including the manufacture of boxes. Special interest attaches to the manufacture of Turkey carpets, an industry which employs over 10,000 in the Izmir area alone. The wool used is all local native, mainly from the plateau. The carpet industry remains a cottage industry, and is centred in Isparta (highest grades) and neighbouring towns, Onshak, Ghiordes (poorer qualities), Konla (rugs) and Dernidgi (large carpets). The industry recovered from the exodus of the Greek and Armenian population but has suffered various fluctuations.

It will be noted that in the preceding pages the stress has been on the Izmir Region as an economic one, apart from its unity as one of Mediterranean agriculture. This is justified because it has long been concerned with foreign trade—passing through Izmir—far more so than any other part of Turkey.

The Cilician Plain and the southern coastal strip. The temperature conditions of the Cilician Plain have been likened to those of the Lower Nile Valley. The summer is excessively hot, shade temperatures of over 110° are frequent, and there is comparatively little cooling at night. The summer drought is intense; moisture-laden winds from the sea and coastal swamps make the air humid and extremely oppressive, but do not bring rain. The conditions are eminently suitable for cotton, which is grown mainly without irrigation. The soils include black humic soils, grey limy soils, and reddish soils. The bulk of the cotton grown is the short staple variety known as 'Jerly' (yerli), though American and Egpytian cottons are likely to increase in importance. The crop is grown on a three-year rotation, grain the first year, cotton or cotton and sesamum the second, fallow the third. The cotton is sown in March or April and harvested in October. Shortness of staple is the chief drawback of the Jerly cotton. In 1926 a very up-to-date cotton mill was erected at Adana and marked the beginning of a flourishing industry. With recent development of irrigation, use of machinery and fertilizers and large-scale holdings, the Cilician or Çukurova Plain is the best developed agricultural area of Turkey.

The influence of the higher summer temperatures of the south coast is seen in several ways. The olive is found mainly on the slopes of the hills, up to 2,000 feet; bananas, lemons and oranges are more characteristic than figs, with 80 per cent. of Turkey's citrus production.

The important town of Adana is the centre of the Cilician Plains; it is in road communication with the plateau through the Cilician Gates and the railway which follows almost the same route. New railways place it in direct touch with the south-east of the plateau and the mining region of Arghana. Mersin is the port of Adana, the railway between Adana and Mersin passing through the historic city of Tarsus, celebrated as the birthplace of St. Paul. Mersin has been selected for major developments. An oil refinery completed in 1962 can handle 10,000 tons a day of imported crude, as well as Turkey's own small production. The port has direct motor roads to Erzurum and is supplanting Izmir as Turkey's second port.

The fertile stretch of coastland around the towns and ports of Antalya and Alaya is quite separated from the Cilician Plains. Antalya has a modern flour mill as well as its macaroni, canning and spirit factories. It is linked with Mersin by an excellent road, as well as with the plateau, and this sheltered sunny coast is becoming the 'Riviera' of Turkey.

The Gaziantep sub-region (D2 of Fig. 45) is a small but important area of fruit and grain famed for its pistachio nuts. It lies to the east of the Amanus range which cuts it off from the Cilician Plains and has a natural outlet to the Mediterranean in the so-called Northern

Gateway shown on Fig. 45. Here lies the district of Hatay with the famous old port of Alexandretta (now Iskenderun) and the town long known as Antioch (now Antakya) ceded to Turkey in 1939.

The Regions of the Anatolian Plateau

The Western Plateau or Interior Anatolia. From the point of view of climate and vegetation it has been pointed out that the steppe-lands of the Anatolian Plateau are akin to the Russian steppes. So, too, is the human geography. Economically the Anatolian steppe has less importance than the coastal regions just considered, but it is the home of the Turkish race and 'dominates the life of all Asia Minor by the quality of the men it produces'. The rigorous climate has produced men of physique, self-reliance and at the same time with a likeable openness of character—the 'best individual soldier in the world'. The whole region is one of low rainfall, generally less than 14 inches a year, falling mainly in winter. In summer the winds blow inwards to the centre of low pressure, but the land surface is so hot as to increase their moisture-holding capacity. The soils over most of the plateau are poor—shallow, highly alkaline or stony. As is usually the case, rock-weathering proceeds slowly in a country where the rainy season and hot season do not coincide (contrast the thick lateritic soils of monsoon lands), and the little soil which is formed is carried off by sudden, short torrential downpours. Such water as penetrates dissolves some of the mineral matter, is drawn to the surface by capillary action and on evaporation deposits a crust of alkaline salts. Where the underlying rocks are impervious there are broad, unhealthy salt marshes, despite the low rainfall. The plateau is an area of extensive grain cultivation (wheat is the staple) over the favoured oases, pastoral nomadism over the less favoured steppelands.

Cattle are reared where the richer pastures beside a stream or a lake provide fodder, and oxen are the principal animals used for ploughing in those regions where agriculture is possible. In the marshy regions, the water buffalo is to be seen; on the drier parts of the plateau where the Ford and the railway have not yet penetrated, the camel is the principal beast of burden. But the chief wealth of the region lies in sheep and goats. The sheep yield wool, mutton and milk, and form the chief source of meat for the whole country. Large numbers are annually driven westwards to provide for the needs of Istanbul and Izmir. The wool is used for clothing for local use and provides the raw material for the rug and carpet industries to which reference has already been made. Reference has been made to that delightful national dish 'pillaf'; it is the milk of the Anatolian ewes—less frequently goats, cows and buffaloes—which provides the second great national dish. That is ya-ourt (or yoghourt) and nearly all the milk is consumed in that form. The milk is heated and poured into small bowls and, as it cools, a spoonful of old ya-ourt is introduced, causing the milk to set when cold like a blancmange—provided the few black seeds in the middle as a charm against the Evil Eye have not been forgotten. Ya-ourt is like a solid, sour junket—to the European a sprinkling of sugar and some stewed fruit renders it more palatable—and forms the unvarying food of the Anatolian peasant twice a day.

The goats of Anatolia are the long-haired Angora goats, famous for their long silky mohair. Turkey formerly had a monopoly of mohair, but for several decades now the production from the karoos and veld of South Africa has exceeded that of Asia Minor. Mohair is valuable in making hard-wearing plushes. The mohair is clipped off annually and baled before being sent to Istanbul for sale and export. The finest comes from the north-west of Ankara. Goats and sheep are often kept —one might say usually—in mixed herds and roam over wide expanses of country. The herd often moves with the wind, showing an almost uncanny knowledge of where the sheltered dips and valleys are to be found. The picturesquely garbed shepherd is the servant of his flock, following them in their wanderings. One windy spring afternoon I wandered with an Anatolian shepherd and his flock which moved on its own about two miles in three hours. Advantage is taken of the mountain pastures in summer; in winter the flocks are herded in rough mud compounds, the hollow walls of which provide the shepherds' quarters, and are allowed out when the covering of snow permits some pasturing.

Amongst the products of the plateau may be mentioned gum tragacanth, an exudation from a small spiny bush, *Astragalia*, common west of Konya and in the Ankara, Kayseri and Yoxgat districts. Gum mastic is similar, obtained from the mastic tree.

Agriculture in the steppelands is restricted to certain 'rainfall islands' such as the Kayseri district or where the streams can be used for irrigation. The greatest possibilities for development are offered by the south-west of the plateau, around Konya and Karaman. In a normal year Konya railway station alone handles 15,000 tons of wheat and supplies a considerable proportion of the needs of Istanbul. At Karaman, to the south of Konya, water is brought in a canal from the hills and a big scheme plans to use the waters of the Beyshehr Lake in the Taurus. Although the region as a whole produces up to 40 per cent. of Turkey's wheat, yields are irregular and crops may fail entirely in years of drought or after exceptionally severe winters. In bad years severe toll is also taken of stock.

Of the sub-regions shown on Fig. 45 A2 (Kayseri) has some better volcanic soils and is famed for rye and fruits (apples, pears, apricots and grapes). Increasing climatic severity marks A4 (Erzincan). Although opium has been discussed under Izmir, it is the Afyon Karahisar sub-region (A7) which produces half Turkey's total—indeed the word Afyon means opium.

The towns of the plateau are of great interest. Apart from the semi-permanent mud villages, the older and larger towns have nearly all taken advantage of positions of strategic importance. The old town of Ankara (Ancyra) occupies an impregnable position on top of a volcanic plug; so also Afyon Karahisar and Amasya, which are situated in gorges. Those on the plains, such as Karaman, were surrounded by a strong wall. The towns of the plateau worthy of note are Eskisehir and Afyon Karahisar, controlling respectively the railways to Istanbul and Izmir; Konya, the centre of the south-western plains, with Karaman and Eregli; Kayseri and Sivas, the centres of the south-east; Amasya and Tokat of the north-east; Ankara, the capital, in the heart of the whole.

The Eastern Plateau.[1] Whilst the surface of the western part of the plateau is by no means free from ranges of hills and mountains, these become the dominant feature of the east as one approaches the Armenian Knot. The climate, as already noted, is one of great severity. The human geography, as far as physical controls will allow, is similar to that farther west. Erzurum is a centre to be noted; Van lies to the south-east.

As a comparison of Figs. 40 and 44 suggests, the forested ranges of north and south are by no means devoid of valley settlements with cultivation where relief and soils allow.

The Forest Regions

The Northern Region. The forests which clothe most of the Pontic Ranges are particularly rich and dense towards the east, where the rainfall is greatest. Oak trees are particularly numerous, together with chestnut, beech, fir, elms, lime and pine. Wood is extracted for construction, shipbuilding and firewood, but vast stretches are untouched owing to communication difficulties. Stretches suitable for agriculture are few; the unhealthy town of Kastamonu lies in one of the east and west valleys, and is so far cut off from the rain-bearing winds that irrigation is necessary and the heat of summer is almost unbearable. It is in this region that the important coalfields are situated on which the iron and steel industry of Zongulduk-Karabuk has been based.

The North-western Region. The position of this small tract surrounded by agricultural lands is curious and is due to the rugged nature of the country. Only a small part of the region is exploited—pine wood is cut on the lower slopes in the west, valonia is gathered for export.

The Southern Region. This region is economically the most important of the three, largely because of the accessibility of parts and

[1] The 'Armenia' major region of Banse, including also part of his northern Mesopotamia.

the needs of near-by markets. For convenience in description we may include the whole of south-eastern Turkey in this region—including the rich mining districts of Arghana and the important town of Diyarbakir. The south-eastern boundary of Turkey—with Syria—lies along the plains below the forested mountains, and Turkey thus includes a strip of country similar to the north of Syria.

The need of the Cilician Plains for wood has resulted in extensive exploitation in the centre of the range, where the working both of hardwood and softwood species has been actively carried on. Here, as elsewhere, the cover of the lower slopes is sparse and cattle are numerous.

In the extreme west the timber has been extracted for shipbuilding for centuries, and forest products are exported both from Antalya and Izmir. Some further details of the forest exploitation of south-western Turkey may be useful. We include not only the main forested ranges of the Western Taurus, but the spurs between the great valleys of the south-west and west—in the hinterland of Izmir. Throughout most of the region the peasants, as usual, are apathetic to forest wealth; they use timber indiscriminately for firewood; the shepherd burns down tracts of valonia woodland to increase the pastoral area. The principal trees of commercial importance are:

Pines, yielding timber for export to Egypt and Syria, turpentine and colophon, pitch and tar resin, bark for tanning, and pine kernels. Pine and fir trees constitute 70 per cent. of the wealth of most of the south-western forests.

Oak, yielding timber, charcoal, bark for tanning and gall-nuts.

Plane and *elm* yield timber, used locally; *cedars* grow out on the mountains near the south coast, and the timber for building and cabinet-making is shipped from Antalya.

Walnut and *chestnut* are Mediterranean woods, used, amongst other purposes, for cabinet woods.

A little timber is brought by rail to Izmir, but the bulk of Izmir's requirements for building and for packing-cases is imported. There is no doubt that Turkish forests are capable of great development.

Amongst the miscellaneous forest products, the crop of gall-nuts (used in the manufacture of ink and dyes) was formerly considerable. Incense is obtained in large quantities from the forests of Kenidjegiz, which produce 100 tons a year—exported from Antalya to Egypt and Italy.

Mesopotamian Turkey (South-eastern Anatolia)

In this arid region suffering from climatic extremes and an inadequate and irregular spring rainfall, the bulk of the population is nomadic or semi-nomadic. Agriculture—a few crops in summer or winter stations—is subordinate to stock-raising. The extension of the Iraq oil belt into this region may prove important. Oil is produced at Bulgurdag in the Taurus near Mersin.

CYPRUS[1]

THE Republic of Cyprus, the third largest island in the Mediterranean, lying in the angle between Syria (60 miles to the east) and Turkey (40 miles to the north), has an area of 3,572 square miles (nearly half the size of Wales) and a civilian population of half a million. Formerly a Turkish possession, it passed by agreement under British control in 1878, the Sultan retaining nominal sovereignty. The island was formally annexed by Great Britain in 1914 on the outbreak of war with Turkey and was declared a Crown Colony in 1925. Rather less than one-fifth of the population are Turkish-speaking Moslems; four-fifths are Greek-speaking Orthodox Christians. Some of the latter desired union with Greece (*Enosis*) though there is little to connect the island with Greece except language and religion, and, after a period of

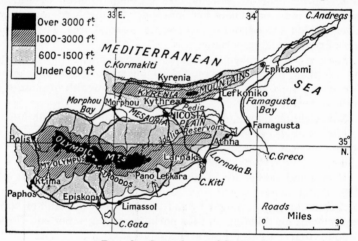

FIG. 48.—General map of Cyprus

unrest, the island became a Republic with a Greek-speaking President and a Turkish-speaking Vice-President in 1960. It remains a member of the Commonwealth.

Shaped like a bill-hook, with the handle extending to the north-east, the island has along the whole of the northern coast—a distance of 100 miles—the Kyrenia mountain range with peaks rising to 3,300 feet and consisting mainly of limestones highly folded in Alpine times. In the south-west is an old igneous mass, the Troödos massif, culminating in Mount Troödos (Olympus) with a height of 6,406 feet—

[1] I am much indebted to Dr. D. Christodoulou for his help in the revision of this section and for preparing the maps.

high enough to be snow-covered every winter and to permit of winter sports. Between the two ranges stretches a plain, the Mesaoria, 55 miles long and 20 to 35 wide. It is given over to farming but has near the centre the old walled capital, Nicosia, now rapidly expanding outside its walls.

Cyprus enjoys mild winters (coldest month: Nicosia 55° F.) with abundance of sunshine (the cloudiest month averaging 5 hours of sunshine a day or more than half the possible). Very cold winds may occur in February and March; summers are very hot but dry and relieved by sea breezes which blow regularly. Day temperatures are high and insolation intense. Nights may be cool, especially in the

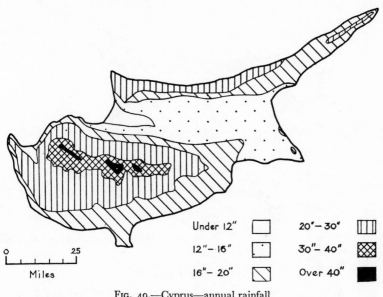

Under 12″ ☐   20″–30″ ▥

12″–16″ ⦂   30″–40″ ▨

16″–20″ ◩   Over 40″ ■

0 ———— 25
Miles

FIG. 49.—Cyprus—annual rainfall

interior. The hottest month in Nicosia is 84° F. but on Troödos only 69° F. Troödos during the summer carries the seat of government and has many summer resorts.

The rainfall map shows the amount and distribution of rainfall. Precipitation is concentrated in the months of October–March, but rain-days rarely exceed 50 or 60. In the central lowlands for nearly ten months of the year evaporation exceeds precipitation. Linked with the fact that rainfall is very variable and droughts all too common, water is a scarce and valuable asset. For four months, from July to October, the central plain is arid and sun-scorched, save where irrigation keeps alive the verdure, with little shelter from the pitiless rays of the sun save an occasional carob tree. 'The first rains fall in October or November, and a week after their arrival the country is covered with tiny green blades of grass. From November the dull green of the orange groves is relieved by the golden gleam of the ripening fruit. By January the barley and wheat are nearly a foot high and in March the plain is carpeted with wild-flowers, blue, scarlet, yellow and white, in such profusion that it resembles one vast garden. The grain harvest usually begins with the barley at the end of April, followed by wheat in May. Threshing and winnowing operations are prolonged till August. Beginning with the loquot in May the rest of the year provides a succession of delicious fruits' (Flinn).

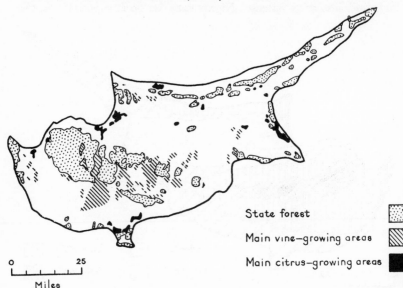

State forest

Main vine-growing areas

Main citrus-growing areas

0   25

Miles

Fig. 50.—Cyprus—forests and crops

Some 60 per cent. of the area of Cyprus is classed as arable. The forests cover a little less than one-fifth of the island, but of that less than 20 per cent. is fully stocked, scrub vegetation and sparse forest trees making up the rest. In very recent years forests have been protected from grazing and destruction which went on from ancient days. The main forest is made up of coniferous trees, the Aleppo pine being by far the most numerous.

Owing to a great variety of physical and biotic conditions, Cyprus produces a very great variety of crops and fruit. Water is the limiting factor and even with recent developments the area perennially irrigated does not exceed 60,000 acres (or 5 per cent. of the agricultural land), while another 110,000 acres are irrigated from streams after rain. Cereals account for nearly one-third of the agricultural land and in a good year 75,000 tons of wheat and as much of barley are produced. Wheat production at best covers two-thirds of the needs of the island, but about one-third of the barley is exported. Cereals are grown especially in the central lowlands. On coastal slopes the most numerous tree of Cyprus grows—the carob, the bean of which has been a staple export for many centuries. Britain is the main customer, using it for cattle feed. The olive tree is more nearly ubiquitous but less numerous. It grows everywhere below the 3,500-foot contour. Grape vines cover an area of 90,000 acres, being only second to cereals in extent. The vines, which are of ancient fame, grow on the limestone slopes above the carobs south of the Massif and in the Massif (see map). Vine products, which include wines, spirits, raisins and fresh grapes, provide an important income and a valuable export.

Fruit trees range from the tropical in sheltered coastal localities to the cool climate types in the higher parts of the Massif. They include bananas, pomegranates, figs, plums, apples, pears, cherries, almonds, apricots, but above all citrus. Citrus cultivation started expanding in the early nineteen-twenties. It is still expanding. In 1963 Cyprus exported oranges alone worth nearly £2 m. with lemons and grapefruit approaching another £1 m. Market gardening is also expanding. Potatoes in some areas are well-nigh a monoculture. They form an important export (£2·2 m. in 1963) as do carrots.

Agriculture is very largely in the hands of small peasant proprietors, who only since the last war managed to free themselves from heavy indebtedness and a vicious usury system. Today a co-operative movement is bringing new life into the countryside. The population engaged in agriculture has tended to decrease since the last war (143,426 in 1946; 124,400 in 1957). Regular paid agricultural employees in 1958 numbered only 4,000, having been drawn away by higher wages in the towns but their loss has been offset by mechanization and improved efficiency due to use of fertilizers, insecticides and better irrigation.

Mechanization has resulted also in the decline of the number of draught animals, especially oxen. The increase of non-food-producing population has resulted in a meat shortage accentuated by the decline of the goat population owing to legislation against this enemy of young trees. The number of goats now stands below the 150,000 mark but sheep exceed 350,000. Cyprus exports considerable quantities of cheese from sheep's milk. Because of the scorching summers there are no good all-the-year-round pastures but of recent years efforts have been made to develop a crop-rotation including a fodder crop and to develop dairy farming.

The mineral resources of Cyprus are of ancient renown; the name 'copper' is derived from *cyprium aes* (Cyprus metal). Since the Second World War there has been a striking revival of the mining industry in the Troödos Mountains, and its products—chiefly iron pyrites, copper

A.—5

pyrites, copper concentrates, asbestos, chrome iron ore and gypsum —have become the most valuable of the island's exports; in 1961–4 they accounted for over half the total value of £20 million.

The industries, which employ some 30,000 people, include the old but much expanded wine and spirits industries, textiles, tanning, plasterboard making, cement manufacture, canning, button and false teeth manufactures. Agricultural and pastoral industries provide most of the exports apart from minerals, though several manufactures of minor value contribute to the total, including two of an unusual character—artificial teeth, which are made in millions, and buttons

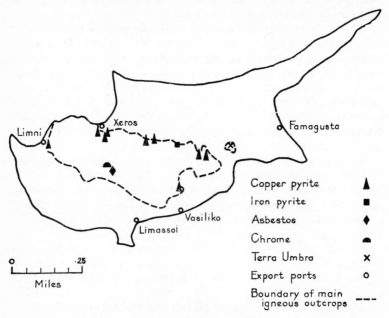

FIG. 51.—Cyprus—minerals

made from dom nuts by the hundred million. Since the war large sums have been sunk in Cyprus on Colonial Development and Welfare Schemes, Imperial defence, and business investments, with the result that imports have largely exceeded exports. In 1960–4 they averaged some £42 million, including a considerable sum for foodstuffs but mainly made up of manufactures, especially textiles, iron and steel goods, and machinery of all kinds.

The narrow-gauge railway which since 1905 had crossed the Mesaoria from the port of Famagusta through Nicosia was closed at the end of 1951, and Cyprus is now without railway transport. There is a good road system, comprising over 1,000 miles of asphalted main roads and 2,500 miles of secondary roads. Already, before the railway was closed, Cyprus had 8,500 motor vehicles and this total was doubled within three years.

Development has not been confined to material progress. An intensive campaign against malaria resulted in 1949 in the complete eradication of the malaria-bearing mosquito.

The population of Cyprus is increasing rapidly, the birth-rate being 25 per thousand and the death-rate only about 6. For many years there has been a steady emigration, recently 2,500 per annum, many going to Britain. The majority of the population live in clustered villages numbering 627 of which about one-sixth have more than 1,500 people. People travel to their holdings which are scattered and fragmented. There is a marked tendency to urbanization, but owing to acute shortage of working-class housing many villages are largely dormitory centres for urban, mining or defence works labourers. The largest town is the capital, Nicosia, with over 103,000 population including suburbs (1964). Other towns are Limassol with 47,000, Famagusta 38,000 and Larnaca 20,000, being also the main ports. Famagusta on the east coast is the chief port, and is being steadily improved. Owing to geologically recent uplift coastal waters are shallow and the bays tend to silt. Limassol on the south coast and Larnaca on the south-east are little more than open roadsteads. Cyprus has many attractions as a tourist resort—its mild winter and lovely spring climate, its natural scenery ranging from tropical strands to snow-capped winter-sports mountain resorts, and its historic monuments. Kyrenia, for example, has many retired people.

The strategic importance of Cyprus was emphasized when the British withdrew from Egypt and it became the Headquarters of the Middle East Command. Previously its strategic value was negative rather than positive—it was important to prevent it from falling into the hands of a prospective enemy. When independence was achieved in 1960, agreement was reached whereby Britain retains certain bases. The Air Age has brought Cyprus out of its old isolation: it has become readily accessible to tourists from Britain who seek winter warmth or residents from the hot countries of the Middle East who seek its snow-capped heights. In 1963 foreign visitors spent £4·5 m. in Cyprus.

An old but useful account of Cyprus will be found in W. H. Flinn's *Cyprus, a Brief Survey of its History and Development*, 1924. Up-to-date editions are available of the Handbook of Cyprus. Statistics are well summarized in the *Statesman's Year-Book*. See also D. Christodoulou, *The Evolution of the Rural Land Use Pattern in Cyprus*, 1959.

ARAB ASIA

A RAB Asia is a convenient term to include that part of south-western Asia where the Arab race is predominant, and where the common language is Arabic.[1] This includes roughly the whole of the continent lying south of the main mountain belt of Armenia and west of the Zagros. Until the First World War practically the whole of Arab Asia formed part, at least nominally, of the Ottoman Empire. After that war it was divided between the French mandated territory of Syria, the British mandated territories of Palestine and Trans-jordania, the Kingdom of Iraq, and the various Arab kingdoms and sheikhdoms of Arabia proper. In due course Syria and Lebanon became independent republics (1944), Transjordan an independent kingdom (1946) and the Arab kingdoms were consolidated as indicated on page 147. The British withdrew from Palestine in 1948 and the inde-pendent Jewish State of Israel was set up over part of the area.

Apart from the linguistic homogeneity of the area, there are other features from certain aspects which render it convenient to consider the area as a whole. Through Arab Asia lie the routes between Asia and Africa, between Europe and the Far East, and the land routes between Europe and Africa. The vast stretches of desert have resulted in the routes lying in the narrowly circumscribed area of the 'fertile crescent' from the Mediterranean to the head of the Persian Gulf, with the result that the countries controlling this area have had, from time immemorial, a strategic importance out of all proportion to their inherent wealth. This fertile crescent includes within its borders the birthplace and home of some of the earliest civilizations of which history has any records, and has witnessed the rise and fall of the capital cities of at least three mighty empires—Assyria, Sumer and Babylon.

Physical Features. Arab Asia is clearly demarcated on the north by the mountainous rim of the plateaus of Asia Minor and Iran—the Taurus and its eastward continuation as the Kurdistan scarp. Except for the narrow isthmus east of Sinai which separates it from Africa, Arab Asia is defined on all other sides by the sea—the Mediterranean to the north-west, the Red Sea to the south-west, the Arabian Sea to the south-east, the Persian Gulf and the Gulf of Oman to the east.

The dominant orographical feature of the whole area is the great plateau of Arabia with its high south-western edge overlooking the Red Sea and its long gentle slope to the north-east towards the plains of Mesopotamia and the depths of the Persian Gulf. At both its eastern

[1] It is only part of the Arab world in which Egypt assumed a leading role in 1958 and which is almost co-extensive with what is now commonly called the Middle East.

and western ends the Arabian Plateau is flanked by orographical features of a different character. To the east, occupying Oman, are fold ranges structurally connected with those of southern Persia. To the west are the mountain systems of Syria and Palestine, which are sufficiently important to merit careful note. Along the Mediterranean there is locally—especially throughout Palestine—a coastal plain. This is succeeded inland by a belt of upland country running from north to south, forming the range known as Lebanon in Syria and the hill-country of Israel and Jordan farther south. This is succeeded by a deep trench, also with a north-south trend, occupied by the Orontes in the

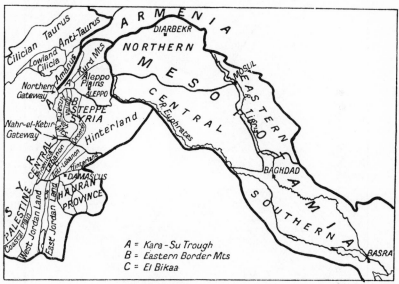

FIG. 52.—Banse's natural regions of Syria and Mesopotamia

north and the Jordan with the Dead Sea in the south. This trench is succeeded in turn by another range comprising the Anti-Lebanon of Syria and the hills of Moab or Transjordan farther south. On the land-ward side stretches the plateau. Mention must also be made of the mountain range in the Hatay with a north-east to south-west trend, reaching the coast south of Iskenderun (Alexandretta), which is prob-ably an offshoot of the Taurus Chain and is known as Amanus. This lofty range separates the Plains of Cilicia from northern Syria.

It is difficult, in south-western Asia, to separate the effects of climate and relief. The even north-easterly slope of the Arabian Plateau, so contrasted with the dissected slope of the Indian Plateau, is the result of the aridity of the climate and the absence of permanent streams. The great barriers of the region are not mountain chains—excepting of course the bounding heights on the north—but the broad waterless tracts of desert.

The rivers are naturally restricted to the damper fringes. The great twin rivers, the Tigris and Euphrates, the life of Iraq, rise amongst the snowy heights of the Armenian Knot. In the west the Orontes and the Jordan are the only two large streams.

Geology.[1] In its broad lines the geology of Arab Asia is relatively simple. Excluding Oman,[2] the geology and tectonics of which are con-

FIG. 53.—The structural units of south-western Asia

nected with those of Persia on the opposite side of the Persian Gulf, there is, underlying the whole of the peninsula, a great complex of Archean crystalline rocks. These are exposed over large areas in Hejaz, along the Red Sea tract and in the heart of the continent. Towards the north and north-east—that is, over much of northern Arabia, the Syrian Desert, Palestine and Syria—great spreads of Cretaceous lime-

[1] M. Blanckenhorn, 'Syrien, Arabien und Mesopotamien', *Handb. d. reg. Geol.*, V Band 4 abt. (Heidelberg, 1914); *Geology of Mesopotamia and its Borderlands* (His Majesty's Stationery Office, c. 1916).
[2] G. M. Lees, *Quart. Jour. Geol. Soc.*, **34,** 1928.

stones, but slightly folded, hide the underlying Archean. Northwards these give place to Tertiary rocks which persist till the fold ranges of the Persian-Turkish border are reached. The oilfield belt which trends along the southern shores of the Persian Gulf is parallel to the bounding range of northern Persia. Over all parts of the plateau there are huge spreads of lava, mainly of Tertiary age. The Mesopotamian lowland is largely alluvial and the delta of the Tigris-Euphrates is spreading rapidly seawards. In the fourth century B.C. the site of Basra was some distance out to sea.

Climate. The parallel of 34° which passes through the centre of the Eastern Mediterranean passes slightly to the north of Beirut, Damascus and Baghdad. By way of contrast the Tropic of Cancer passes across the middle of the Red Sea and through the heart of the Arabian Plateau to Muscat on the Gulf of Oman. Broadly speaking, therefore, Palestine, Syria and Iraq lie in the continuation of the Mediterranean belt; Arabia in the continuation of the extra-tropical high-pressure belt of the Sahara. In winter the continual cyclones which characterize the westerly wind belt deposit their moisture on Lebanon and the hills of Palestine, or on the second rampart formed by Anti-Lebanon. By the time they have crossed these two ramparts the winds are dry, hence the Syrian Desert and the northern part of the Arabian Desert. Slightly farther north the cyclones work their way along the 'piedmont zone' below the Kurdistan scarp into the Mesopotamian Plains. The moisture deposited along this zone, together with the water available from the rivers, is sufficient to give rise to the well-known 'fertile crescent' already mentioned. The whole tract farther south is rainless and suffers great extremes of heat in summer.

Arabia owes its rainlessness to its position in the high-pressure belt, and the lofty encircling rim which intercepts any moisture which might reach the interior. In summer, Arabia lies within the world zone of maximum heat; July average temperatures in places certainly exceed 95°. The heat on the coasts of Arabia is often even more trying than in the interior because of the humidity of the air caused by evaporation from the land-locked Red Sea or Persian Gulf. The notoriety of the Red Sea in this respect, a notoriety resulting from the inevitable four days by steamer *en route* for India, leaves one unprepared for the bitter cold which is possible in winter. In northern Arabia occasional frosts occur in winter; Lebanon and Anti-Lebanon are usually snow-capped, and Jerusalem under a fall of snow is by no means unknown.

Vegetation. The natural vegetation of most of south-western Asia is the evergreen Mediterranean woodland, passing gradually into desert as the rainfall decreases. The variations in altitude which characterize many parts of Arab Asia result in corresponding variations in vegetation. Thus bananas and oranges characterize the coasts of

Palestine; olive groves and vineyards occur at higher levels; pine forests would naturally clothe the higher slopes of Lebanon.

Some further details will be given later of certain deserts of Arabia, which are sometimes referred to as 'tame' deserts by contrast with unmitigated 'true' desert such as the heart of the Tarim Basin. The wide oases which lie in the heart of the 'tame' deserts support large numbers of men and animals, and only a succession of adverse seasons drives them forth to seek sustenance elsewhere.

Considering products common to much of Arab Asia, the fine quality of the wheat and barley of Syria and Mesopotamia is noteworthy. Palestine and Syria, the typical Mediterranean countries, are famous for their oranges, olives, figs and other fruits; silk is important in Syria; cotton in northern Syria and Iraq; whilst dates are associated with Arabia and Iraq, and coffee with south-western Arabia.

The large Oriental donkey is the commonest beast of burden throughout Arab Asia, and can do much of the work which it is popularly supposed can only be allotted to that ship of the desert, the camel. The famous Arab horses are raised by nomads along the borders of the Syrian Desert and bear witness to the fertility of the 'tame' desert. On the edge of the deserts, in the oases, amongst the mountains and indeed wherever pasturage can be obtained, even if only at certain seasons of the year, cattle, sheep and goats are raised by the nomadic pastoral tribes. The cattle are small; the sheep are commonly of the fat-tailed variety; whilst black goats are the most usual.

Population. Although Arabic is the common language of Arab Asia, it is very far from the truth to suppose that the Arab race is the sole race of the region. The geographical position of Palestine, Syria and Iraq on the great routeways of the ancient world is, in itself, sufficient to have caused a great diversity of races. Peoples from outside, such as the Egyptians, Greeks and Turks, who from time to time have dominated the lands, have frequently left a permanent impress of their rule.

The *Arabs* are the natives of Arabia, and, bearing in mind the aridity and poverty of their land, they are remarkably numerous. Normally they are organized as small tribes ruled by a chief or sheikh, and it was only in the early days of Islam that they moved as a nation and placed nearly all the lands between India and the Atlantic under their sway. At the present day the Arabs are found all along the southern borders of the Mediterranean and throughout Arabia and Syria. Their language, being the language of the Koran, tends to be co-extensive with the Mahommedan religion at least as far east as Persia and India.

The Arabs fall readily into two classes—the settled, or Hadarouin, and the nomadic, or Bedouin. The settled Arabs include the Syrians, but the Syrians are actually of very mixed blood. They may be defined as including all those peoples, except Jews, who spoke Aramaic at the beginning of the Christian era. They now speak Arabic, and from time to time there have been fresh infusions of Arab blood. Indeed, it is common among higher-class Syrians to claim descent from definite Arab tribes. Many Syrians, especially in Lebanon, are Christians.

The Bedouin Arabs are still almost entirely nomadic, though amongst the northern tribes a few practise agriculture, pitching their long black tents amongst the fields and migrating to mud villages in winter. The pure Bedouin Arabs are fine, tall, well-built men with dark skins, dark piercing eyes and black hair. They are brave, hardy and hospitable, but simple in their habits and food. The latter consists chiefly of bread, milk, dates and a little goat's flesh.

A few *Turks* are found in northern Syria and Mesopotamia and the Kurds are closely related to them. *Armenians* are scattered through the cities of Syria as traders, and during the First World War large numbers came to Mesopotamia as refugees. The *Jews* are in the main restricted to Israel and will be considered in detail later. The name *Frank* or *Frangy* has come to be applied to any European—most of the Europeans are but temporary residents—whereas the *Levantines* are those of mixed European and Eastern blood.

Communications. Excluding the northern routes through Russia, the possible lines of communication between Europe or Egypt on the one hand and India and the Far East on the other, which were available to the ancients, are not numerous. The passage through the complex of mountains of Armenia was extremely difficult, and we may concentrate attention on two groups of routes—(*a*) the Red Sea Routes, (*b*) the Persian Gulf Routes.

(*a*) The Red Sea Routes. Glancing at the map, one would say that one obvious route to India, available to the ancients, was across the narrow Isthmus of Suez and via the Red Sea—exactly the route followed today to India via the Suez Canal. Curiously enough, the Suez Route was dangerous in ancient times and traffic went up the Nile to Thebes, east across the desert to a port on the northern Red Sea coast. It will be noted that the Suez Route to India is today controlled by the nation which commands Suez on the one hand (Egypt) and the nation commanding the southern entrance to the Red Sea on the other. Here Great Britain holds Perim Island in the Straits of Bab-el-Mandeb and the Aden coast; France the opposite coast of Africa.

(*b*) The Persian Gulf Routes.[1] Because of the mountains on the north and the desert on the south, the routes from the Mediterranean to Mesopotamia and the Persian Gulf had of necessity to pass by the 'Syrian Saddle', otherwise referred to as the 'fertile crescent' or the 'piedmont', since it lies at the foot of the mountains. From the Mediterranean three lines of approach converged on Aleppo:

[1] Reference should be made, for example, to papers such as E. C. Semple, 'The Ancient Piedmont Route of Northern Mesopotamia', *Geog. Rev.*, **9,** September 1919.

(1) From Cilicia across the Bogtche Pass to Sendjeik and Aleppo.
(2) Alexandretta (Iskenderun) across the Beilan Pass to Aleppo
      (Alexander's route after the Battle of Issus in 332 B.C.).
(3) Mediterranean coast via Orontes Gorge to the plains of Antioch
      and Aleppo.

From Aleppo the route went across to Zeugma on the Euphrates
(from which there was a certain amount of river traffic) and thence to
Mosul (Nineveh) and Babylon. Whilst emphasizing the importance of
these routes, for the control of which Egypt, Babylon, Assyria, Persia
and Greece struggled in the past, one must not ignore the caravan
trade across the desert country farther south (see p. 149 and Fig. 59).
    Turning to modern times, we find Britain and France in control
of the Red Sea Route; hence the bold bid of Germany for the control
of the Syrian Saddle and the Persian Gulf route. There is no need
to retell the well-known story of the 'Berlin-Baghdad' Railway. The
actual Baghdad Railway was to run from Konya on the Anatolian
Plateau (where it joins the Anatolian Railway from Istanbul) to
Baghdad and the Persian Gulf. It threads its way by a series of tunnels
and along the sides of a precipitous limestone gorge through the
Taurus Range just east of the Cilician Gates, and passes across the rich
Cilician Plains through Adana, across the Bogtche Pass of the Amanus
to Haleb (Aleppo). From Aleppo it follows the old Syrian Saddle Route
to Nisibin, and from a little north of Aleppo to Nisibin forms the
boundary between Turkey and Syria. About 150 miles of tribal
country separated Nisibin from the head of the Mesopotamian Railways
and so far as German enterprise is concerned the Baghdad Railway
ended thus short of its goal. Eventually the gap was closed when the
line from Baghdad through Mosul was completed in 1940. There was
for long a note of tragedy in the unfinished Baghdad Railway—the
rolling stock was all marked in indelible letters of cast-iron 'Baghdad'
—and the marvellous engineering work of the Taurus tunnels makes
one realize the immense amount of energy directed by the Germans
towards the completion of the railway.
    Aleppo has a broad-gauge railway running to the port of Tripoli
and this has been continued along the coast to the larger port of
Beirut. Between Beirut and Damascus is a narrow-gauge rack-railway.
    The mention of Damascus brings us to the modern land routes from
the Mediterranean to Iraq and the Persian Gulf. The Syrian Saddle
route is comparatively neglected. It is easily possible for motor-cars,
but the local tribesmen for some years did not observe a close season
for motors. Instead a direct trans-desert route from Damascus to
Baghdad by six-wheeler motors became the regular means of communication. The motor conquest of the Syrian Desert is unique in
many ways, and the history of the scheme is worth noting. During the

First World War the British Army, forced by necessity, sent a convoy of lorries from Mesopotamia to Palestine across the desert. Several had to be abandoned, and the experiment was never repeated. After the Armistice several old Army cars were run by Arabs over the old Saddle Route between Baghdad and Aleppo, following the course of the Euphrates. In the spring of 1923 two young New Zealanders of Scottish extraction—the brothers Nairn, one of whom had served with the R.A.S.C. Mechanical Transport in the Palestine Campaign—grasped the possibilities of a desert route to Baghdad which would halve the time required for mails and passengers between Baghdad and London—at

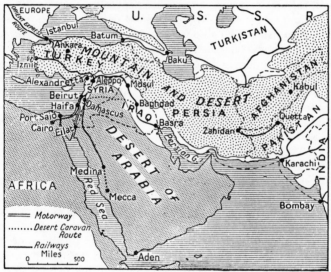

FIG. 54.—Routeways from the Mediterranean to the Indian Ocean.
The motor road, entirely in Israeli territory from Eilat on the
Gulf of Aqaba to Haifa, is an addition of great importance.

that time twenty-four days. In April, with two Buick and two Dodge cars, the desert crossing was made in four days. By the end of October a regular service was inaugurated, and ran almost continuously for many years. The usual route was from Beirut to Damascus (65 miles), then for 25 miles through the cultivated lands around Damascus, followed by a further 513 miles of desert to Baghdad. The journey can easily be accomplished in fourteen hours. The desert track is formed solely by the wheels of preceding cars. There is little soft sand, the surface is hard and stony, often, however, strewn with boulders. After a few low ranges, about 700 feet above the general level of the plateau, the ground slopes towards the valley of the Euphrates; the gravel surface gives place to dry alluvial mud, sometimes covered with camel-thorn, sometimes cracked and uneven, forming a very bad surface, and yet sometimes as smooth as the finest road. The valley of the

Euphrates is merely an enormous dry mud-flat and after rain the going is very difficult. A speed of 40–45 miles per hour can be regularly maintained over good stretches. During the Druse rebellion of 1926 an alternative route from Jerusalem via Amman to Rutba was used, but the surface is bad and the route 200 miles longer. In the latter part of 1926, therefore, a northern route from Tripoli via Homs and Palmyra was substituted. The company reverted to the direct route after the rebellion. In addition to six-wheeler passenger cars, freight cars were put into service. The opening of the through-railway in 1940 as well as the rendering safe of motor traffic following the fertile Saddle has made these desert routes to some extent out of date. The goods carried—at £15 per ton in 1928, lowered to £7 by 1934—were those of high value such as cocoons from Persia, caviare and, of course, mails. Airways now take such traffic but land routes have retaliated by putting on fine pullman motor services. Beirut is now a very busy air junction, the airports of Amman, Damascus and Aleppo are extensively used. An early morning start from Baghdad brings the traveller to London by evening.

The Political Geography of the Mediterranean Coastlands— Syria and Palestine. Prior to the First World War these lands, lying between Turkey on the north and Egypt (Sinai) on the south, formed part of the Ottoman Empire. The whole was often called Syria, thus the British Admiralty *Handbook of Syria* published in 1920 covered also Palestine which is the southern portion. When Palestine was captured from the Turks by British Forces under General Allenby in 1917–18 it passed under British military administration until July 1, 1920. Syria proper, the much larger area lying to the north, came on the other hand under French administration. The position was clarified in 1920 by the League of Nations, Palestine being defined as a mandated territory under British administration, Syria as a mandated territory under French administration. The boundaries of Palestine were so drawn as to include all the Jewish colonies which had been established in the preceding decades and in fact corresponded fairly closely with the ancient limits of the Promised Land of the Jews. The famous Balfour Declaration of November 2, 1917, had pledged the British Government to support Jewish claims to establish there a national home for the Jews, but at the time of the Armistice (1918) there were only 55,000 Jews in the country out of a total—Moslem Arabs, Christian Syrians and others—of about 750,000. The task of dealing with the inevitable problems was not an easy one nor an enviable one for Britain, and she resigned her mandate in May 1948. Simultaneously the Republic of Israel was proclaimed but its right to the mandated territory was disputed by the neighbouring Arab states. Fighting ensued and when an armistice (still in force in 1966) was agreed in 1949 Israel was confined to the predominantly Jewish areas while the Hashemite Kingdom of Jordan had extended west of the Jordan up to and including the old Arab city of Jerusalem, bordering the modern Jewish city. Meanwhile France had concluded a Treaty of Friendship and Alliance with Syria in 1936, and during the Second World War the Free French promised Syria independence. The government was handed over to the two Republics of Syria and Lebanon on January 1, 1944; in 1946 all foreign troops were withdrawn. A small part (including the Amanus Range) of the mandated territory in the north around Alexandretta had become the Republic of Hatay in 1938 but joined Turkey in 1939 by agreement with France. On February 1, 1958, Syria joined Egypt as the United Arab Republic, but this union broke up in 1961 and Syria again became independent.

The Republic of Israel [1]

Palestine as defined in 1920 had an area of about 10,429 square miles—rather larger than Wales or about the same as the State of New Hampshire or Vermont. With independence in 1948 Israel lost a considerable enclave of the hill country (around Nablus and Hebron) to Jordan and its total area is now 7,993 square miles. The southern half is a triangular wedge of desert known as the Negev which gives the country an outlet to the Gulf of Aqaba and so to the Red Sea. Though the Negev is the scene of much activity most of the population—which exceeded 2,500,000 in 1965—is crowded into the northern half of the country. There the land falls into three parallel strips:

(a) The *Coastal Plain* lies along the Mediterranean. Broad in the south, and known as the Plain of Philistia, it narrows northwards as the famous Plain of Sharon, till the projecting mass of Mount Carmel reaches the coast. A further stretch of plain lies round the Bay of Acre, but the coastal plain comes to an end at the northern border. The climate is genial and marked by comparatively small variations in temperature. At Gaza (now occupied by Egypt) the average temperature ranges from 56·5° in January to 79° in August; at Jaffa from 56° to 78°. Frost and snow are both practically unknown. [2] The rainfall is almost entirely between October and April, and there is a gradual increase in total amount from south to north. Thus Gaza has forty-one rainy days and a fall of 15·3 inches; Jaffa has sixty-three rainy days and 21 inches; Haifa has sixty-seven rainy days and 29 inches, whilst Beirut in Syria has eighty-two rainy days and 35·7 inches. Although the distinction between the cool wet season and the hot dry season is the well-marked one, local custom still refers to the 'early' rains of

---

[1] I am greatly indebted to Professor David H. K. Amiran of the Hebrew University, Jerusalem, for much help including the organization of a study-tour for me in December 1957 and to Mr. N. Gil for invaluable guidance in 1961.

[2] On February 6, 1950 Tel Aviv had its first day-long snow-cover since its foundation in 1911.

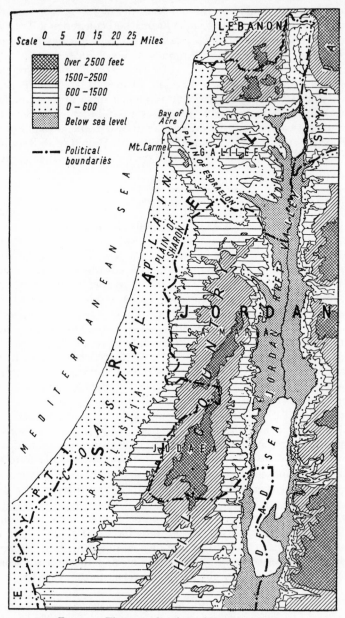

FIG. 55.—The natural regions of Israel and Jordan
In the south-west is the Beersheba Basin, between the Hills of Judaea and the Negev.

October and November (the 'former rains' of the Bible) contrasted with the spring rains (the 'latter rains' of the Bible) which are of fundamentally greater importance in agriculture. Both the early and spring rains are additional to the main fall which occurs from December to March. This is true of all Palestine and Syria. The maritime plain is thus climatically favoured; soils include light fertile loams with sub-surface water and the whole plain is proverbially fertile. It is this fertile plain which most qualifies the country for the title of 'land of plenty'; it is this plain which has supplied the needs of warring armies from Rameses to Allenby. Around Ramle and Lydda the plain is flat; elsewhere are low ridges up to 250 feet in height, and the whole plain is cut by innumerable transverse valleys or 'wādis'. The famous Jaffa oranges were grown mainly round Jaffa, which also served as the port of Jerusalem until the development of Haifa. Modern Jewish colonies have brought most parts of this previously under-populated fertile region into cultivation. In the south much is still devoted to grain (wheat and some barley as winter crops, maize and lately sorghum as summer crops) but intensity of cultivation increases northwards with citrus, bananas, vegetables and many other crops.

(b) The *Hill Country* forms a strip from 25 to 40 miles wide, roughly parallel to the Mediterranean coast. A spur of the hill country forms Mount Carmel and in the north of Israel the hill belt approaches the coast. The hill country is divided into two quite separate and distinct blocks by the broad fertile Plain of Esdraelon (or Jezreel), which is part of a belt of lowland connecting the coastal plain of Haifa and Acre with the Jordan Valley. The block of hill country to the north is the 'Galilee' of New Testament times, and Nazareth lies towards the centre, overlooking the Plain of Esdraelon. The larger block to the south is the Samaria and Judaea of the Bible, with Jerusalem occupying a central position in Judaea. It is not always realized that the places in Palestine which are of interest because of their association with incidents in the life of Jesus Christ lie in two separate regions—with 60 miles of country (Samaria) between the two groups. Nazareth, Cana and the cities of Galilee lie in the north; Jerusalem, Bethany, Bethlehem and Jericho are in the south. The hill country is built up of a succession of hard impervious limestones and softer flinty chalk of Cretaceous-Eocene age. The beds are nearly horizontal over the centre of a broad anticlinal upwarp and the individual bands of limestone vary from a few inches to several feet in thickness. Where the limestone prevails there are barren stony hills hemmed in and divided by innumerable valleys, mostly narrow and nearly all dry; the horizontal beds give a tame outline to the hills, and their summits are flat and covered with stones. Where the chalk appears, the outlines are softer and broad white patches and bands run over the mountains; here the water has worn down the hills, and plains result from the softer formation. Eocene chalk and limestone build up the foothill belt known as the Shephelah west of the Judaean hills. In the north the hills of Galilee are less arid in appearance, the hills often sharper and more pleasing to the eye. In south-eastern Galilee basalt flows are frequent. The change from south to north in the hill belt is mainly the result of increasing rainfall. The rainfall is heaviest on the crest of the hill country (Hebron, 24 inches; Jerusalem, 26; Nazareth, 27) and rapidly decreases eastwards towards the Dead Sea and the Jordan rift. As a result the eastern slopes of the plateau from Hebron to the Dead Sea and Jerusalem to Jericho are practically desert—the 'Desert of Judaea'. The hill country as a whole experiences considerably greater extremes of temperature than the coastal tracts. Jerusalem ranges from 48° in January to 75° in August, Nazareth from 49° to 79°. Frosts are usual in the winter months, and snow is by no means unknown. The Mediterranean forest which once clothed the Judaean Plateau has degenerated to a rough scrub with thorny bushes and a few dwarf oaks. The richer character of the Galilean Plateau is to some extent due to the heavy dewfall, especially in the late summer, more reliable rainfall and better soil. There is little doubt that the hill country was formerly far more extensively forested than it is now, and deforestation is held by some to be responsible for the present aridity of the country. Reafforestation (Aleppo pine) is one of the great aims in Israel and is already changing the landscape. Olive groves are important in Samaria and especially in Galilee, arable farming on the basaltic plateaus of eastern lower Galilee, and locally there are vines and figs, but large areas are quite uncultivated and support but a few sheep or goats. It is roughly the old Samaria which now forms the northern enclave of Jordan territory.

(c) The *Jordan Rift Valley* (El Ghor) is one of the most remarkable depressions on the surface of the globe. Both sides of this long straight valley, which averages 10 to 15 miles in width, are very steep, in places almost precipitous; the floor is almost level and from north of the Sea of Galilee to far south of the Dead Sea its surface is far below sea-level. It is drained by the Jordan, flowing first through a small lake-bed [1] and then through the Sea of Galilee (682 feet below sea-level) and then for 70 miles before emptying itself into the Dead Sea (1,292 feet below sea-level). The Dead Sea itself has a depth in the north of over a thousand feet, and its floor actually lies over 2,600 feet below sea-level. The drop from Jerusalem (+ 3,000 feet) to the Dead Sea (− 1,300) in a distance of 15 miles as the crow flies is remarkable. Except where the breezes from the Mediterranean penetrate, as they do along the Plain of Esdraelon and, to some extent, to the Sea of Galilee, the Jordan Valley is a very dry tract. Thus Tiberias, on the shores of the Sea of Galilee, has 18 inches, but around the Dead Sea the rainfall is very slight. As a result the vegetation in the southern

[1] Lake Hula or Huleh (waters of Merom), drained in 1955-8 for farmland.

portion is that of a desert; aridity is accentuated by the quantity of salt in the soil. This is one of the great difficulties in the way of proposed irrigation schemes. The high atmospheric pressure and absence of wind make the climate curiously oppressive: temperatures are high, Tiberias, for example, ranging from 57° in January to 87° in August; Jericho from 59° to 88°. Frost is almost unknown, the lowest recorded temperature at Jericho being 34°. Thus the crops possible are those of the subtropics, and if irrigation could be carried out this would form a valuable tract of land. This was, in fact, done at Beit ha-Arava.

(d) The *Negev* as the southern desert triangle is called is still largely the domain of semi-nomadic Bedouin. There are extensive limestone plateaus cut up by deep ravines and only limited tracts could be cultivated even if adequate water were available. However, the Beersheba Basin at the northern end of the region is a considerable plain with valuable loess soils and is currently the scene of remarkable activity. In July 1955 the first of two concrete pipelines to bring water to this arid country south of Beersheba was opened. It brings half the water of the little Yarkon River of Judaea to irrigate land on which a new agricultural settlement for immigrants is established almost weekly. The irrigation water is sparingly used—to supplement rainfall and local supplies when those are inadequate. This remarkable work pales into insignificance beside the gigantic work, started in 1960, to bring the waters of the Upper Jordan or from the Sea of Galilee through giant pipes to the south of the country. Beersheba is being planned and built on a grand scale as the metropolis of this pioneer land. In the southernmost Negev, the mountains around Eilat consist of the crystalline rocks of the basement complex of the Arabian peninsula. At Timma there are copper ores, and phosphates occur in several parts of the Negev. In September 1955 a well struck oil near Askalon and this Heletz field yields about 150,000 tons annually. Natural gas occurs near the Dead Sea.

Population. The peculiar problems of Palestine when it was a mandated territory were bound up with the varied population and their religious interests. According to the official Census of November 18, 1931, the population was made up as follows:

Moslems (mainly Arabs)	.	.	.	.	759,712 or 73 per cent.
Jews	.	.	.	.	175,031 ,, 17 ,, ,,
Christians	.	.	.	.	91,938 ,, 9 ,, ,,
Druses, Samaritans, Bahais, etc.	.	.	.	9,680 ,, 1 ,, ,,
	Total	.	.	.	1,035,821

In December 1946 the population was estimated at 1,912,110 of whom Jews numbered 608,230 or 32 per cent., compared with 83,790 or 11 per cent. in 1922.

The Balfour Declaration had laid down that 'His Majesty's
Government view with favour the establishment in Palestine of a
national home for the Jewish people, and will use their best endeavours
to facilitate the achievement of that object, it being clearly understood
that nothing shall be done which may prejudice the civil and religious
rights of existing non-Jewish communities in Palestine.' As the above
figures show, the Moslems formed the majority of the population, and
they naturally viewed with fear and apprehension the flooding of their
country with Jewish immigrants, and they were supported by their
neighbouring Arab states in demanding a limitation of immigration.
Palestine remained full of insoluble problems. It is the Promised Land,
the ancestral home of the Jews; but it is also the birthplace of Christianity and contains the spots most sacred to Christians; further, Jerusalem, after Mecca, is the holiest of Moslem cities, and the Moslems
have the rights of centuries of ownership. Jerusalem was in Moslem
hands from 1244 to 1917. The problems extend to minutiae. The
famous 'wailing wall' of the Jews in Jerusalem (now in Jordan) is a
fragment of the old Temple foundations; the pious offered up supplica-
tions for its restoration, but they stood on Moslem ground to do so, and
the rebuilding of the Temple would necessitate the destruction of one
of the famous Mahommedan mosques. The Church of the Holy
Sepulchre is shared by the various Christian sects, but a Moslem held
the key to prevent friction.

Although Palestine was then relatively underpopulated and vacant
land was available for settlement, a difficulty rested with the Bedouin
Arabs, who for centuries had wandered over hills and plains alike
with their destructive sheep and goats, and who resented the new
fences which trespassed upon their grazing grounds.

Some details of Jewish settlement may be of interest. There had
long been considerable colonies of Jews in the cities—especially Jerusalem—but the post-1920 schemes of settlement aimed not at increasing the Jewish population of the cities but at developing the land.
Jewish population at the Armistice was estimated at 55,000; in thirteen
years it had increased according to the official Census taken on
November 18, 1931, to 175,000; in January 1935 it was estimated at
300,000 or roughly 2 per cent. of the 15,500,000 Jews estimated to
exist. The Jewish immigrants were mainly from eastern Europe—
from Russia, the Baltic States and Poland—and the diversity of tongues
resulted in the reviving of the almost dead tongue, Hebrew (not
Yiddish), formerly only used in religious services. The immigrants
went at first mainly to the land settlements which were begun in 1878
when seven Jerusalem Jews acquired land for cultivation near Petah
Tiqva. The Jewish settlements by 1927 were over 220. They were
grouped along the fertile Maritime Plain but it is in reclaiming the
fertile but formerly marshy malarial Plain of Esdraelon that the Jews

made such remarkable progress. Many of the settlements were on land belonging to the Jewish National Fund (J.N.F.) which was established by the Zionist Organization for the purpose of acquiring land to remain the property of the Jewish people for ever, and were founded with the assistance of the Keren Hayesod (Jewish Foundation Fund), also created by the Zionist Organization. The Palestine Jewish

Fig. 56.—The State of Israel

Colonization Association (P.I.C.A.) on the other hand sold its land to settlers on the instalment system over forty to sixty years.

Although immigration varied from year to year the total of Jews grew and clashes with Arabs were inevitable. In 1937 a Royal Commission recommended a partition of the country but this found no favour with the Arabs. After the Second World War there was a flood of refugees. An attempt by Britain as the Mandatory Power to limit the flow by establishing a quota led to many unhappy incidents and failed. The creation of the independent state of Israel in May 1948 and the withdrawal of British troops, police and administrators was the signal for the invasion of Palestine by its neighbours. Hostilities continued until early 1949 when an armistice was concluded with Lebanon, Syria, Jordan and Egypt, but Israel lost a bite of 2,350 square miles to Jordan. Moslem Arab refugees to the number of some 600,000 fled from Israel but were soon counter-balanced by Jewish immigrants at the rate of 200,000 a year—themselves refugees from eastern Europe. The population, 90 per cent. Jewish now, reached 1,400,000 in 1951 and 2,200,000 by 1961 of whom 900,000 had arrived in the ten years to May 1958 from over a hundred different countries.

The absorption of this vast number of immigrants presents a great problem. Rural settlement has been by complete village units—over 500 new ones since 1948—which fall into two main types, the fully collective type or *kibbutz* and the individual smallholders' *moshav*. There is naturally an increasing reliance on urbanization and industrialization. Indeed half the total population is now in the three chief towns, Tel Aviv-Jaffa, Haifa and the modern city of Jerusalem (the old city is occupied by Jordan). A number of completely new towns have been established.

Prior to the recent influx of people, Israel was still mainly agricultural. The various small industries included the extraction of olive oil at Acre and elsewhere; soap-boiling at Haifa; wine-making in the older Jewish colonies of Rishon le Zīyōn (near Jaffa) and Zikhron Ya'aqov (Zichron Jacob). The orange production for export was almost entirely around Jaffa, but the acreage under oranges, grapefruit and lemons was increased fourfold between 1926 and 1933 and was spread more widely.

In the first ten years of independence 1948–58 land under cultivation grew from 400,000 acres to 950,000 and farming population from 90,000 to 350,000 persons. Nearly a third of the farm land is irrigated. The country produces 70 per cent. of the food consumed, nearly all milk, eggs, poultry and vegetables. In addition to old staples such as wheat and barley many new crops such as cotton, maize, rice, sugar cane, groundnuts and coffee are proving successful. Much fodder is grown for the dairy herds whilst Jaffa oranges form the leading export.

Large numbers of recent immigrants are absorbed in small industries, such as diamond polishing, sugar refining, light electrical and other engineering, drug and chemical including fertilizer manufacture, but heavy industry has also been started including iron and steel at Acre. Copper ore deposits are being worked near Eilat. Some of the most important natural resources of the country are the potash-bromine salts of the Dead Sea. A company, Palestine Potash Ltd., which was granted a concession to exploit them in 1930 had to suspend operations after the Israeli-Arab War of 1948. Renamed Dead Sea Works, it reopened its works in 1952 at the southern end of the Dead Sea by agreement with the Israeli Government, which has acquired a controlling interest (51 per cent.). Another major industry centres in large oil refineries at the port of Haifa. These were put out of action by the troubles between Israel and its Arab neighbours, as a result of which Iraq would not allow the crude oil to be pumped through the pipeline connecting Haifa with the Kirkuk oilfields. Arrangements were made in 1950 to keep the plant partly working on supplies by tankers. Since 1957 crude oil has come by pipeline from Eilat. Haifa has a modern harbour with a depth of 30 feet alongside the main quay, and is the chief shipping centre in Israel, as well as the second largest town. Easily the largest conurbation is Tel Aviv-Jaffa; Tel Aviv, the modern Jewish seaside town of phenomenal growth, now incorporating the ancient Jaffa (Joppa) had a population of 400,000 in 1961. But as a port Tel Aviv-Jaffa is merely an open roadstead, with two basins—one for the lighters by which vessels anchored outside are loaded and unloaded, and the other for fishing vessels and other small craft. A deep-water port is under construction at Ashdod, south of Tel-Aviv. In line with its general policy of planned economy, Israel has its own mercantile marine, including passenger ships plying in the Mediterranean, cargo-passenger liners for the North American trade, several large tankers and a fleet of fruit carriers for the citrus trade. Apart from its Mediterranean coast, it borders the head of the Gulf of Akaba (Aqaba) for some eight miles, at the southern tip of the Negev, and there Eilat has been opened up as a small port with plans for extensive development.

Communications. Palestine had a system of fine metalled roads, delightfully placed for the tourist, but abominably placed for the commercial development of the country. They were the descendants of tracks made when the hill ridges were the safest routes from robbers and their ambushes. They climbed amongst the limestone hills to the best viewpoints, but avoided the fertile plains. Motor transport became important but goods from the port of Jaffa destined for Amman in Transjordan had first to climb 3,000 feet to Jerusalem, then drop 4,300 feet to the Allenby Bridge over the Jordan and climb again 4,000 feet to Amman. The distance is about 75 miles in a straight line, and a road from Haifa could avoid all hills save the final climb from the Jordan Valley to the plateau. So the road system has been reconstructed so as to tap the rich agricultural lands and to converge on Haifa. Jaffa was supplanted as the chief port of the country by the completion in 1933 of the fine harbour at Haifa—the natural outlet of the country. Haifa (180,000 in 1961) has become the focus of road and rail transport and the chief manufacturing centre of the country. In one year alone it increased by 10,000 and the city has spread over the slopes of Carmel.

A standard-gauge (4 feet 8½ inches) railway traverses the Mediterranean coastal plain and was formerly linked up with the railways of Lebanon and Syria as part of the through route between Europe and Cairo. From Lydda (or Lod)—whose airport is Israel's aviation centre —branch railways connect with Tel Aviv-Jaffa and inland, through the hill country, with Jerusalem (2,600 feet). A line was opened in 1954 from Tel Aviv-Jaffa along the coast to give more direct connection with Haifa. Another line has been constructed to Beersheba. The old narrow-gauge lines are no longer being operated. There is an extensive network of good roads, totalling about 2,000 miles. Due largely to the short distances road transport is now more important than rail. The frontiers with Israel's Arab neighbours are closed and this has added greatly to the importance of direct access by El Al (Israeli) and other airlines.

Trade is based at present on an aided economy, the value of the imports being several times that of the exports. The Israeli pound (£I) enjoyed parity with the sterling £ until 1952, when it was devalued and again in 1962 to £18·40 = £1. In 1963 exports were valued at £125,000,000 sterling. Citrus fruit accounted for nearly half and polished diamonds 33 per cent.

THE HASHEMITE KINGDOM OF THE JORDAN

On the break-up of the Ottoman Empire after the First World War, the status of the 'Transjordan' territories—i.e. the territories east of the Jordan—'across the Jordan' from Palestine—was for a time indeterminate. In 1922 the League of Nations appointed the United Kingdom as the mandatory Power for Palestine and Transjordan, and recognized a British arrangement to erect Transjordan into an emirate under a son of the ex-King of the Hejaz. Development in the emirate proceeded along the lines of constitutional self-government, and when the mandate was relinquished after the Second World War the British concluded a treaty (1946; revised 1948) with Transjordan as a sovereign independent State; the Emir took the title of King, and the country was later proclaimed the Hashemite Kingdom of the Jordan. It extends eastward to the borders of Iraq and Saudi Arabia, and is also neighboured by Saudi Arabia on the south. Northward it is bounded by Syria.

Up to the time of the foregoing change of status, the western frontier followed the River Jordan down to and through the Dead Sea, and continued south along the Wadi Araba to the Gulf of Aqaba— the north-east arm of the Red Sea. The fighting between Israel and her Arab neighbours in 1948 carried the Jordanian forces west of the River Jordan, and when an armistice was concluded in 1949 they remained in occupation of a tract of over 2,000 square miles of Arab Palestine (see under Israel). This tract was incorporated in the Hashemite

Kingdom in 1950, and is known as West Jordan to distinguish it from the former emirate—East Jordan. In the same year the Hashemite Kingdom, which had previously used Palestinian currency, issued its own currency, having for unit the Jordan dinar, maintained at par with the £ sterling.

East Jordan is many times the size of the added territory; with an area of some 35,000 square miles, it is rather larger than Scotland. Here are the ancient lands of Gilead, Ammon, Moab and Edom, dividing into cross-sections the narrow strip along the eastern floor of the deep rift valley (below sea-level) which carries the River Jordan and the Dead Sea, and mounting the eastern escarpment to a narrow belt of hill country with peaks of 3,000 feet to 5,000 feet, merging into a bare plateau which forms by far the largest part of Transjordan. Bedouin range the plateau with their flocks of sheep and goats; cultivation is confined to the hill country and the valley floor, and even there it is only in the north that settled villages are found. Elsewhere in the cultivable zone, semi-nomadic tribes settle temporarily and raise crops in season as need arises. In the hill country an average rainfall of 20 inches is spread over the months October to May, and is followed by a rainless summer. On the plateau, the annual rainfall is no more than a few inches.

All the productive land is barely one-eighth of the whole, the total classed as arable being 1,200,000 acres, pastoral 1,500,000 acres, and forest or woodland 85,000 acres. Further development is dependent on the possibilities of irrigation notably from the East Ghor Canal. About 100,000 tons of wheat are grown, and half that weight of barley, as well as smaller but substantial crops of sorghum and olives, and grapes in the extreme north. Other products are on a very small scale. Sheep and goats, mostly the latter, are by far the most numerous live-stock—nearly half a million in 1948–9, after a big decline from the numbers in earlier years. There are about 60,000 cattle, and smaller numbers of other livestock include a few thousand camels.

No similar analysis of the agricultural economy of West Jordan is yet available.[1] The population of both territories is estimated at 1,500,000; East and West Jordan have each normally only about 450,000, but the troubles between Israel and her Arab neighbours have resulted, according to Jordan's reckoning, in an influx of 600,000 refugees from Israel. At best, Jordan is not on a self-supporting basis, and the maintenance of so many refugees, mostly lodged in camps, has been made possible only by financial aid from United Nations funds. In addition, Jordan has had interest-free British loans of £1 million in 1949 and £1·5 million in 1952 for the development of housing, roads, and irrigation. In good years Jordan has a surplus of foodstuffs and

[1] According to FAO the whole country in 1954 had 2,200,000 acres of arable and 1,830,000 acres of pasture.

livestock for export—chiefly wheat, also barley, sheep, wool and fresh vegetables. Imports, as usual in an aided country without a balanced economy, are several times the value of exports. Foodstuffs, building materials and textiles are the chief imports.

The known mineral wealth is small. Some phosphate deposits are worked, and the potash salts of the Dead Sea invite attention. There has been prospecting for oil in southern Jordan. The Trans-Arabian pipeline carrying oil from the Persian Gulf to the Mediterranean at Sidon (Lebanon) traverses Jordan, and a local oil refinery has been planned. Other industrial enterprises projected include a cement works.

The Hejaz Railway, which at one time connected with Medina but does not now even reach the Hejaz, runs through the eastern borders of the Jordanian hill country as far as Ma'an, serving *en route* the capital, Amman. It is a narrow-gauge line (105 cm.; 3 feet 5½ inches). There are over 400 miles of all-weather roads, and Amman is linked with the outside world by air. The capital has grown rapidly; not long ago a smallish country town, it now embraces an estimated population of 300,000 (1963). Irbid, in the settled country of the extreme north, is a town of growing commercial importance; and in the extreme south, where Jordan touches the Red Sea, important improvements are being made in the Hashemite Kingdom's sole port, Aqaba. In 1958 Jordan announced its union with Iraq as a United Arab Kingdom, but in July the King and royal household of Iraq were assassinated and Iraq declared a republic.

REFERENCES

The literature on Palestine is considerable, owing to its historical associations. Sir. G. A. Smith's *Historical Geography of the Holy Land* is the standard work. In 1958 a valuable National Atlas (in Hebrew) was issued covering all aspects of the geography of Israel. The changes since 1948 have been so spectacular that earlier geographical works have little relevance but a useful summary of natural resources is given by A. Bonné, *Geog. Jour.*, **92**, 1938, 259–66. See also the Report of the Anglo-American Commission, 1946, and N. Bentwich, 'Developments in the Negev', *Roy. Cent. Asian Journ.*, **42**, 1955, 176–83. The Israeli Ministry of Foreign Affairs issues numerous information booklets. See also J. S. Haupert, 'Israel', *Focus*, **14**, 7, 1964, and E. Orni and E. Efrat, *Geography of Israel*, Jerusalem, 1964.

SYRIA AND LEBANON

Although geographically the name Syria has been applied to the whole tract bordering the Mediterranean Sea and lying between Egypt on the south and Turkey on the north, popular usage tended to restrict the name to the part of this tract lying north of the Holy Land. Thus the French mandate from the League of Nations was broadly co-extensive with Syria as popularly defined. With the establishment of the separate republics of Lebanon and Syria in 1944 the 76,000 square miles of the old French mandate were split into two unequal parts—Lebanon of only 3,400 square miles (but with 1·75 million people and the great port of Beirut) and Syria of 71,210 square miles and 5·5 million people. Lebanon is clearly defined: the eastern boundary of Syria consists of arbitrary lines drawn across the desert with Jordan lying to the south-east, Iraq to the east.

Physical Features. The orography of Syria and Lebanon is of fundamental importance. As in the Holy Land to the south, four belts roughly parallel to the coastline may be distinguished, but they lack that precision of definition by which they are characterized in the southern areas. The four strips may be termed the coastal plains, the western ranges, the great central depression and the eastern ranges. Beyond the latter lie the eastern desert plateaus.

(a) The *Coastal Plains* are scarcely worthy of separation as a distinct unit. Cruising along the coast—a particularly delightful occupation, by the way, when the afternoon sun of early spring lights up the white limestone crags and throws them into relief against the bright green of nascent vegetation—one forms the impression that the mountains, lightly cloud tipped, rise directly from the blue Mediterranean. Actually however there is usually a narrow though fertile and valuable coastal plain which broadens out locally, especially in the vicinity of the ports of Tripoli and Beirut. Climatic conditions are similar to those farther south, except that the rainfall is usually somewhat heavier. The crops of the coastal plains supply the coast cities; in addition the Plains of Tripoli and Sidon have world-famous orange groves, growing fruit for export. The Plain of Beirut has huge olive groves, and the Plain of Latakia is famed for tobacco. The chief towns of the coastal strip are the ports, of which the largest and the only one with a harbour is Beirut in Lebanon (about 500,000). The other ports—Latakia or Lattakieh in Syria (68,500), Tripoli (100,000) and Sidon, both in Lebanon—have only open roadsteads.

(b) The *Western Mountain Ranges* in Syria vary considerably in character, and are divided by gorges or cols into three blocks from north to south:

1. The Amanus Range (Giaour Dagh of the French, from the Turkish Gavur Daghi) in the Hatay district of Turkey.
   The Gorge of the lower Orontes.
2. Jebel en Nuseirīye:
   The Homs-Tripoli Pass.
3. Lebanon in the Republic of Lebanon.

The Amanus Range may be regarded as a spur from the Taurus Ranges with a trend from north-north-east to south-south-west. It separates the Plains of Cilicia from the Plains of Antioch and reaches the sea in a marked promontory. The Baghdad Railway sweeps far

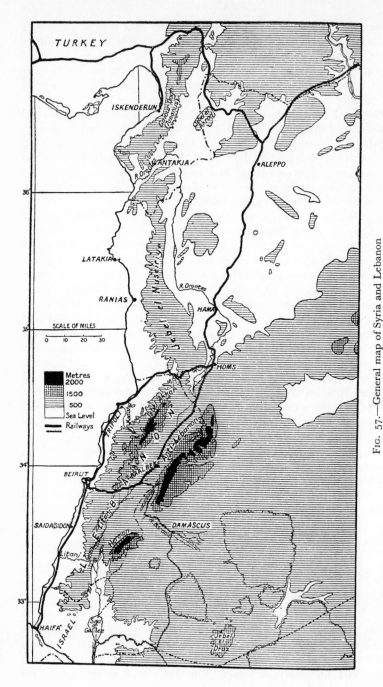

FIG. 57.—General map of Syria and Lebanon

The irregularly outlined areas in the south are areas of recent lava, giving rise to desert of harrah type. Note: Antakia = Antioch. The Hatay (Sanjak of Alexandretta now Iskenderun) has been part of Turkey since 1939. For Gaiour read Giaour.

to the north to take advantage of the central pass long known as the Amanus Gates or the Pillars of Jonas and now often as the Bogtche Pass (in Turkish territory). The railway tunnels through the range a little to the south of the Pass. In the extreme north an easier pass is formed by the valley of the Pyramus River (also in Turkish territory); in the south there is the Pass of Baylan or the Syrian Gates.

The great central block begins south of the Orontes mouth with a group of hills known in Roman times as Mons Cassius (Jebel el Akrād), but the main mass, farther south, is known as the Jebel en Nuseirīye and extends as far as the Syrian-Lebanon border in the pass utilized by the railway from Tripoli to Homs. The Nuseirīye Mountains are so called from the name of an heretical sect of Islam (also called Ansariyeh) who have amidst their mountain fastnesses maintained religious and to some extent political independence. The main ridge has an average elevation of about 3,000 feet, and on the east overlooks the Orontes Valley, towards which the slopes are almost precipitous. The slopes to the west, towards the sea, are gentler, steep slopes and rocky ridges alternating with small plateaus and cultivated areas. The mass is for the most part built up of limestone, bare peaks are seen in the higher slopes, but the lower slopes are wooded or forested. The climate is agreeable, for elevation tempers the summer heat; winter is comparatively short and there is a good rainfall. But the whole tract is the preserve of the Ansariyeh and remains comparatively little known.

South of the Tripoli-Homs railway in Lebanon, the southernmost of the three blocks of mountains begins as a thickly wooded chain known as Jebel 'Akkār, which passes southwards into the most famous of all Syrian ranges—Lebanon. Several of the peaks of Lebanon are over 10,000 feet: from December to April the upper heights are swept by furious winds, snowstorms, and torrential rains. The peaks are snow-covered and avalanches are common on the precipitous slopes. The mountains are of limestone and goat-tracks seam the mountain sides, but most of the inhabitants live in villages in irrigated valleys where luxuriant growth fringes the streams. Wherever soil is found the rocky slopes have been reclaimed and terraces have been made to great heights, and on the otherwise bare mountain sides luxuriant gardens of mulberry and vine flourish. The once famous 'Cedars of Lebanon' are now found in a few places, such as the head of the Kadisha Valley, where the ancient trees owe their preservation to the fact that from time immemorial the grove has been regarded as sacred.

Lebanon really extends as far south as the Leontes Gorge (or gorge of the Nahr el Lītanī), beyond which are the hills of Galilee.

(c) The *Great Central Depression* is not so well marked as in Palestine, nor does it sink below sea-level. In the north it is formed by the fertile Plain of Antakya (Antioch) in Turkey round the Lake of Antioch, southward it is formed by the valley of the Orontes, which rises where the floor of the valley reaches its highest level, between Lebanon and Anti-Lebanon. Southwards the valley is drained by the Lītanī.

The middle or Syrian part of the Orontes Valley lies in the country of the Nuseirīye, and though fertile is apt to be marshy and unhealthy.

Not so the upper course of the Orontes between its source and the town of Hama. Here the delightful valley known as the Plain of El Buqei'a or Bek-ka is about 10 miles wide. South of Homs this is in the State of Lebanon. Though hot in summer, owing to its comparatively low elevation, it is very fertile, and presents a pleasant picture in the spring of wide cultivated fields with poplar and fruit trees and vines. The railway from Aleppo to Beirut threads its way along the valley and affords the traveller glimpses of a charming though still-under-populated land. A curious system of irrigation is practised: the force of the stream is made to revolve great wooden water-wheels which carry water up in little buckets and tip it into an irrigation channel.

There is a scarcely appreciable divide between the headwaters of the Orontes and those of the Litani, which has a narrower, less important valley. Near the divide are the famous ruins of Ba'albek (Heliopolis).

(d) The *Eastern Mountain Ranges* do not form a continuous series; sometimes they are merely the edge of the undulating plateau. In the north the plateau is in general bare, treeless and waterless, becoming more and more arid as it approaches the desert. Except in the districts of Aleppo and where it approaches the Orontes high plains near Hama and Homs—where there is a comparatively small difference in elevation between the plateau and the Plain of El Buqei'a—the rainfall is generally low. Except where recent lava flows cover the country with a stretch of barren boulders, much of the land is cultivable and can support considerable crops. It is in this country that one sees villages of beehive-shaped huts—often the first dwellings of Bedouin who have forsaken their tents and taken to the plough.

Aleppo (496,000 in 1962) remains today, as it always has been, the great centre of the northern part of this area; the converging-point for the routes from the Mediterranean and the starting-point for the Syrian Saddle route to Mesopotamia. The picturesque citadel built on a high mound in the heart of the city, the old walled city with its narrow vaulted alleyways, its ceaseless streams of donkeys and camels, its throngs of Arabs in their picturesque flowing robes, its dim restful khans (wholesale warehouses), its flat-topped dwelling-houses, brilliant in the glaring sunlight, its occasional domed mosques with their slender minarets, form a nearer approach to the Westerner's idea of the East than the visitor to Eastern towns can usually dare to hope for.

The eastern range, as distinct from merely the edge of the plateau, begins opposite Homs and is known as Anti-Lebanon—separated from Lebanon by the upper valley of the Orontes. Many of the crestlines are over 6,000 feet; Anti-Lebanon is wilder and grander than Lebanon, largely on account of the lower rainfall and sparseness of vegetation. The frontier between the Republics of Lebanon and Syria lies along the crest of Anti-Lebanon. Towards the southern end of Anti-Lebanon the massif is cut through by the narrow rocky gorge of the Barada, a gorge whose tortuous windings are followed by the metre-gauge railway from Beirut to Damascus. Damascus, to which reference will be made later, lies at the eastern foot of Anti-Lebanon where the Barada disgorges on to the plain. South of the Barada Gorge the range rises again to the noble snowy heights of Mount Hermon—the summit of which is about 10,000 feet.

South of Hermon the eastern mountain ranges as such disappear and are again replaced by the edge of the plateau, the southern portion of which, lying in Jordan, has already been mentioned.

(e) The *Eastern Plateau* and the Syrian Desert. It has been pointed out that sometimes there is a range of mountains bounding the plateau on the west, sometimes there is not. When the mountains do not exist, the rain-bearing winds penetrate far to the east—as they do via Aleppo and along the Syrian Saddle. In the lee of Anti-Lebanon, on the other hand, the desert stretches right to the almost stark slopes of the mountains themselves. Motoring from Damascus along the eastern flanks of Mount Hermon towards Haifa, it is of the greatest interest to notice the gradual increase in the richness of the vegetation as one rounds the hill belt and comes to the plateau edge before dropping down into the Jordan Valley by the Sea of Galilee; from the desert wastes beyond Damascus it is a wonderful experience in springtime, when the slopes to the Jordan Valley are ablaze with wild flowers.

We have seen that Damascus lies at the foot of—indeed, climbs the lower slopes of—the easternmost range of Anti-Lebanon just where the Barada emerges from its gorge. It is the Barada which is responsible for the very existence of Damascus. Its waters are made to supply the fountains and water the land of what is a vast garden on the edge of the desert. The irrigated Damascus Plain has an area of about 150 square miles. The luxuriant gardens and green fields produce fruit of all kinds (especially apricots and grapes), as well as vegetables and grain in abundance. Groups of silver poplars—the wood of which is much used in Damascus—line the watercourses and are scattered over the whole area. As well as the city of Damascus with its 508,000 inhabitants (1962), over a hundred villages lie clustered in the plain. Damascus, as a result of its situation, cut off from maritime influences, has a climate of marked continentality—with temperatures ranging from an average of 43° in January to 83° in July. Frosts are frequent; temperatures as low as 26° have been recorded. The rainfall, naturally,

is low. Damascus, locally known as Esh Sham, is a city more modern
in appearance than, and lacking the charm of, Aleppo.

South of Damascus, where Mount Hermon no longer cuts off the
breezes from the ocean, lies the great Plateau of Hauran—'a vast treeless prairie, noted specially for its wonderful wheat crops' and capable

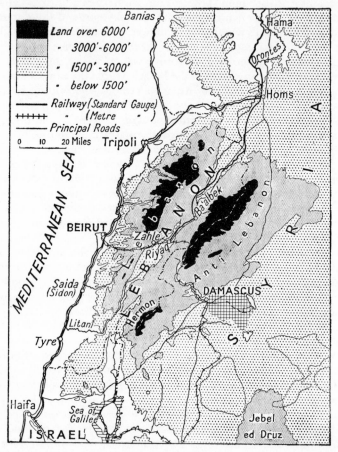

FIG. 58.—The position of Damascus (Esh Sham) and the State of Lebanon

The cross-hatched area shows the approximate limits of the irrigated area. This map shows the rival ports
for Damascus—Haifa and Beirut.

of becoming a great granary not only for Syria, but with a surplus for
export.

South of Hauran is the elevated, isolated Plateau of Jebel ed Drūz
—the home of the Druse sect of Moslems.

But sooner or later all parts of Syria—except in the extreme north—
pass eastwards into desert.

Population of the Republic of Syria. Six-sevenths of the inhabitants of Syria are Mahommedans. The remaining seventh are nearly all Syrian Christians. Of the Moslems the majority are Sunni Moslems; Alawites number 410,000 and Druses 118,000. The bulk of the population is of Arab origin, but there has been a large influx of foreign elements, including Turks, Kurds, Circassians, Armenians, Jews and Persians. It is largely as a result of the religious differences among the Moslem sects that the French organized Syria into four territories (*états*). The first has now become the Republic of Lebanon. The second was the Latakia State including Latakia and the Nuseirīye country; the State of Jebel ed Drūz is the land of the Druses, south of the Plateau of Hauran; whilst the remainder was the State of Syria proper—including Aleppo, Damascus, Hama and Homs.

Production and Industries. Syria is essentially an agricultural country. In 1962 FAO recorded nearly 15,500,000 acres as cultivated and a further 30,000,000 as cultivable. Wheat occupies over 4·2 million acres yielding 1·0 to 1·5 million tons of wheat; other leading crops were barley, maize, millet, oats, sesamum, chickpeas and lentils. More than half the wheat is grown in the Damascus Plain and the Hauran Plateau. The cultivation of cotton has been considerably extended in recent years. It is mostly of the short-stapled 'baladi' variety, for which the demand is decreasing, and it is being replaced by 'Texas' seed. Around Latakia, Aleppo and Damascus much tobacco is grown.

The silk-rearing industry is an old and important one. The white mulberry is extensively grown in northern Syria and around Damascus for feeding the worms, and Latakia, Damascus and Aleppo are the centres of the industry; but Canary bananas are replacing mulberries.

Syria has large numbers of sheep and goats, and there are over 2,000,000 sheep in the Aleppo district alone. Syria is, however, poor in minerals and the search for oil was abandoned in 1951.

Communications. Something has already been said of the railways of Syria. The mixture of gauges is unfortunate and so is the existence of frontiers: the broad gauge runs from Aleppo to Tripoli, and now on to the better port of Beirut: the slow narrow-gauge trains on the rack-railway between Damascus and Beirut now have a serious competitor in the motor and are used for goods only. Syria has over 2,500 miles of first-class road. The trans-desert motor traffic has been considered above.

Several oil pipelines cross Syrian territory: in particular the Iraq Petroleum Company constructed a line from Kirkuk to the small Syrian fishing port of Banias south of Latakia (1952), paralleling till near the coast older pipelines to Tripoli (Lebanon).

Foreign Trade. Syria has had a favourable trade balance since the Syria–Lebanon customs union was dissolved in 1950. Cotton and cotton thread, cereals, raw wool, olive oil, raw silk and cocoons, fruits and nuts are the chief exports; textiles (cotton, wool and silk) account for a third of the imports, followed by machinery and metal goods.

LEBANON

When, after the First World War, the French took over under mandate the administration of the Turkish territories comprised in Syria, they united various districts in the mountainous south-west corner of the country to form the State of Great Lebanon. When the mandate was relinquished during the Second World War, Lebanon as well as Syria was proclaimed an independent republic. It is a small country, about half the size of Wales, supporting a population of 1·75 million. It has a coast some 125 miles long and has a general width of about 30 miles, and the greater part is occupied by the Lebanon mountain mass, rising in the north to 10,000 feet. The height drops farther south, but the railway from Beirut (about half-way along the coast) to Damascus (see under Syria) crosses the mountains by a pass which even there is nearly 5,000 feet above sea-level. An excellent motor road, well graded, follows roughly the same route.

Lebanon, the main range, from which the country takes its name, rises in cultivated terraces from a fringe of coastal plains, and on the other side drops more abruptly, under more sterile conditions, to the Bekaa (El Buqei'a) Valley, which divides Lebanon from Anti-Lebanon —a smaller edition of the range, traversed by the Syrian-Lebanese frontier. In the Bekaa rise two rivers of classical fame: the Leontes (modern Litani), flowing southwards to empty itself into the Mediterranean after a comparatively short course, and the Orontes (Nahr el Asi, or 'rebellious river'), which flows north through Syria (q.v.) and has a course of over 200 miles.

The area of the Lebanese Republic is about 3,400 square miles. Nearly half is classed as built-on or waste, and nearly half as suitable for cultivation or grazing in roughly equal proportions. The balance of 8 per cent., some 280 square miles, ranks as forest and woodland, and, as in neighbouring countries, has been sadly depleted by indiscriminate felling and the ravages of goats, though there is still a cluster of the 'cedars of Lebanon' to recall one of the ancient glories of the country. It is estimated that goats number nearly half a million— vastly more than all the other four-footed domestic livestock put together. In recent years, however, there has been a very rapid increase in the number of cattle and a development of dairying and also an increase in the number of sheep and especially of poultry. Some 2,000 camels are employed, and there are only about as many pigs.

The narrow coastal plain and the very remarkable terraced hill slopes produce a wide variety of crops. Cereals are the most widely cultivated, covering nearly a quarter of a million acres out of about

700,000 acres of arable land (120,000 irrigated). Wheat tops the list with 175,000 acres, but averages only about 10 bushels to the acre, so that the yield is barely 60,000 tons. It is followed by barley (50,000 acres; 27,000 tons), and maize (17,000 acres; 13,000 tons). Potatoes provide 40,000 tons from 12,000 acres, and pulses are grown on a smaller scale. But the outstanding crops after cereals are grapes, olives and citrus fruits. The grape harvest amounts to as much as 90,000 tons from 50,000 acres, and 11,000 tons of olive oil are extracted from a crop of 35,000 tons. Oranges yield 140,000 tons, and lemons and other citrus fruits 25,000 tons. Bananas (14,000 tons), sugar cane (5,000 tons), groundnuts (1,000 tons), rice (1,000 tons) and sesame seed (1,000 tons) are other cultivations testifying to the sub-tropical character of the Lebanese climate, at least in part.

Lebanon, like Syria, has a legacy of good roads from the Second World War, and a sufficient railway service from pre-war days, as well as an excellent port in Beirut and a secondary port in Tripoli. Modern Beirut, with its well-equipped and busy international airport, its numerous luxury hotels, and blocks of flats spreading far out in the outskirts and linking with resort-suburbs on the slopes of Lebanon, is a remarkable phenomenon. It shares with other parts of the country and Syria the problem of refugees from Israel. Imports and exports are of the traditional character of countries engaged in primary production, with little industrial development. But the commercial importance of Lebanon is not limited to its own supplies and needs. It is a flourishing *entrepôt* of trade not only with Syria, with which it still has an economic agreement, but with Jordan and Iraq; and it has on its coast the terminals of oil pipelines—of 12-inch and 16-inch diameter at Tripoli, coming from Iraq, and one of 30 inches near Saida (the ancient Sidon), coming over 1,000 miles across Arabia from Ras al Mishaab, on the Persian Gulf.

See F. P. Vouras and Alice Taylor, 'Lebanon', *Focus*, **15**, 10, 1965.

ARABIA

Arabia proper is a great peninsula with an average breadth of 700 miles and a length of 1,200 miles, having thus a total area of about 1,000,000 square miles, or considerably greater than that of the Indian peninsula. The Arabs usually refer to their home as the 'Isle of the Arabs', emphasizing thus the geographical isolation of the peninsula. With the Red Sea on the west, the Arabian Sea on the south-east, the Gulf of Oman and the Persian Gulf on the north-east, Arabia is cut off from the rest of Continental Asia on the remaining side by a great desert barrier, the desert of the northern Nefud.

Arabia, properly speaking, extends roughly as far north as latitude 30° or 31°, though the great triangle of the Syrian Desert or the Hamad,

A.—6

which the ancient geographers included in Arabia, lies to the north of this line.

The broad physical features of the peninsula are already familiar—the plateau with its high western edge overlooking the Red Sea and its long, gentle slope to the Persian Gulf. Actually the edge of the plateau is higher than its function merely as an edge of an elevated block would warrant. Peaks in Midian and Yemen rise to over 8,000 and even 10,000 feet and the western and southern edges of the plateau appear as mountain ranges, not only from the sea, but also from the interior. This is due in part to the presence of volcanic piles, or of lava-flows resistant to denudation which have protected the underlying sandstones, and in part to the different nature of denudation at high levels producing jagged outlines which contrast with the sand-strewn plateau slopes. The explorations of H. St. J. B. Philby showed that the general eastern slope is not as simple as was supposed; a great ridge of highland 4,000–5,000 feet high, and with granite peaks rising to over 6,000 feet, crosses the heart of the peninsula from northern Yemen to Sedeir. Most of the sand of the plateau is derived from the disintegration—largely due to the alternate heating by the sun's rays and the cooling at night of the rocks—of mesozoic sandstones which were deposited over the ancient crystalline massif. Although it was realized that the mountainous part of Arabia bordering the Gulf of Oman was structurally allied to Persia and Baluchistan to the north,[1] it was not appreciated till the nineteen-thirties that conditions along the shores of the Persian Gulf were suitable for the occurrence of great oilfields.

There are no really perennial rivers in Arabia; their place is taken by countless river-valleys (wādis), which carry water after rainstorms. The high western edge of the plateau is naturally the main water-parting. The wādis which descend to the Red Sea have deeply eroded beds which form a great obstacle to communication from north to south; at the same time the waters are useless for navigation or irrigation. The wādis which descend towards the Persian Gulf (though often never reaching it), on the other hand, are long and shallow, their floors are often so slightly depressed below the general level that the traveller may cross them without being aware of their existence. Whereas the western wādis to the Red Sea are obstacles to communication, the wādis to the east are of distinct value. Though they may not carry permanent surface water, water is at all times present below their beds and may be reached by wells, and where the water level rises sufficiently near the surface strings of oases are found. These broad, shallow valleys are characteristic of Arabia; the 'badland' type of desert scenery so common in many deserts—as in parts of central Asia—is rarely seen.

[1] G. M. Lees, 'The Physical Geography of South-eastern Arabia', *Geog. Jour.*, **71**, 1928, 41–70.

Climatically, the great feature of Arabian conditions is dryness. Intense dryness makes the heat of the day comparatively bearable and, generally speaking, conduces to cool nights. The healing virtues of dry desert air have become proverbial, but when one visits the fringes of dry areas and sees the effect of clouds of dusty, germ-laden air in the diseased eyes, nose and mouth of dwellers near by one wonders why. It is in the heart of a vast, dry tract such as Arabia that the familiar statement is justified; conditions seem quite unsuited to germ life: human fertility is great, mortality is low, and longevity is the rule. The limiting factor in the multiplication of the human race is food and the advantages of the healthy climate tend to be outweighed by the shortage of food. Much of Arabia may be described as truly rainless. Yemen profits by the summer monsoon, heavy storms penetrate along the western watershed to beyond Mecca. Northern Arabia, not being shut in by mountains from the Mediterranean, gets slight winter and spring rains from that region. The heights of Oman in the south-east also attract a slight rainfall. It is the heart of the plateau which is rainless.

Arabia lies in the world belt of greatest heat in summer; the hottest regions are naturally the littoral tracts of Oman, Yemen, the Red Sea and Gulf coasts. In winter, snow usually appears on the highest crests of the northern heights, and occasionally on the surface of the plateau in the extreme north. The heights of Yemen and the western ridge have frost but not snow.

The dweller in more favoured lands might be tempted to regard the whole of Arabia as desert, with a few scattered oases. Actually, however, one should distinguish:

(1) True deserts.
(2) Dry steppes or steppe-deserts.
(3) Oases and cultivated land.

True deserts, wherein vegetation is absent, and where all fodder and water necessary for the journey from oasis to oasis must be carried, are of four kinds:

1. *Dahanah* is comparatively hard gravel plain, covered at intervals with sand belts of varying width. Ground water may be present at depth, but dahanah may elsewhere form a complete barrier.
2. *Nefūd* is a continuous area of deep gravel or sand, formed by wind action into high dunes.
3. *Ahqāf* is very soft dune country and cannot be crossed except in narrow belts, owing to the extreme physical labour involved. It is rare in Arabia.
4. *Harrah* is the name given to tracts of rough lava surface which cuts the feet of man and animals to pieces.

Fig. 59 shows roughly the areas occupied by true desert in Arabia. In the south there is the huge Ruba'el-Khāli ('The Abode of Emptiness' or the 'Empty Quarter'), termed also in the vulgar tongue Er-Raml, 'The Sand' *par excellence*. This vast stretch, 400 to 500 miles wide— dahanah and nefūd in the east, ahqāf in the west—completely cuts off the southern coasts from the heart of Arabia. The desert was crossed for the first time in 1931 by Mr. Bertram Thomas. A tongue of this

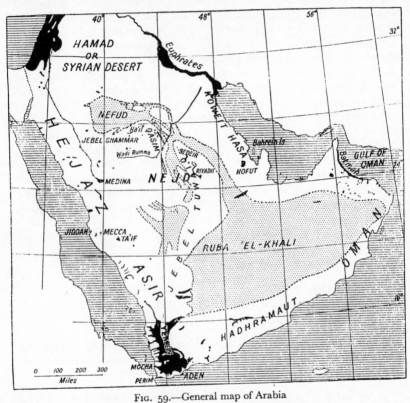

FIG. 59.—General map of Arabia

In black, cultivated land; dotted, deserts; blank, steppes and steppe-deserts.
Koweit and Bahrein are now more usually spelt Kuwait and Bahrain.

great desert stretches northwards and cuts off Nejd in the centre from the Persian Gulf. It is mainly of dahanah type and northward passes into *the* nefūd which separates the Syrian steppe-desert from central Arabia. The important point to notice is that the deserts stretch as a great semicircle around the heart of the peninsula.

Dry Steppes or Steppe-deserts, which may be likened to what we have elsewhere called by Sir Aurel Stein's term of 'tame deserts', occupy most of the rest of Arabia. They are vast tracts, with a hard or dusty surface, level or undulating, which justify the use of the designation steppe by having occasional natural water-holes and permanent coarse vegetation in hollows. The inhabitants include camel-breeding nomads and what to a European would seem useless desert supplies sufficient sustenance to maintain life amongst these frugal folk.

The *Oases and Cultivated Lands* of Arabia lie in two tracts:

(*a*) The heart of Arabia, surrounded by a ring of deserts.
(*b*) The tracts along the coasts and margins.

In the heart of Arabia, in the region sometimes designated Nejd, lie three groups of more or less connected oases. Jebel Shammar receives the drainage from two ranges and includes the towns of Hā-il and Feid and a score of villages—a real oasis surrounded by desert. Qasīm owes its fertility to constant ground water from the great Wādi Rummah and includes the large settlements of Aneizah and Boreidah—the largest and most commercial towns of the group—and about fifty other settlements. Nejd is by far the most extensive group and hence the frequent use of this name to cover the whole of central Arabia. The chief town, Riyādh, lies in the central oasis, but there is a large series of settlements.

The outer ring of fertile tracts reaches its greatest importance in the Yemen. On the east are the settled tracts of Hasa (Qatif oasis); along the shores of the Gulf of Oman is the fertile littoral of the Bātinah district of Oman. The south coast is almost entirely desert except west of longitude 50°. There the coastal tract becomes fertile in patches and vegetation runs inland up the valleys towards the plateau. In Yemen, along the shores of the southern Red Sea, there is a low coastal strip, fertile where the wādis reach the shore, and behind it are towering slopes rendered fertile by the monsoon rains. Even over the crest, the rainfall is sufficient to give good steppe land. This was the part of Arabia known to the ancients as 'Arabia Felix', the home of the celebrated Mocha coffee. The excellence of the coffee, grown on the slopes, is said to owe a great deal to the rising mists which protect the trees from the heat of the day. Northwards along the Red Sea, fertile tracts become fewer and the interest of the Hejaz lies in the celebrated Moslem sacred cities of Mecca and Medina—both utterly different from other Arabian cities in that they depend for their existence on pilgrims. Hejaz, as a whole, is divided into northern and southern halves by a huge uninhabited stretch of harrah, lying between Medina and Mecca and stretching to a point on the Red Sea. Of great importance to Mecca is the nearby oasis of Ta'if.

Before the First World War much of Arabia was, at least nominally, under Turkish influence or constituted part of the Ottoman Empire. Since 1913 the Arabs have really been working out their own salvation unchecked by foreign control.

The consolidation of Arabia owes much to Abdul Aziz Ibn Sa'ud who held firmly to his Hasa province (see Fig. 59) and Nejd and added thereto Jebel Shammar, thus creating the great central kingdom of Sa'udi Arabia. He assumed the title of King of Sa'udi Arabia in 1934, in which year he also made treaties with Britain and India. Along the Indian Ocean coast the Hadramaut includes a number of sultanates and sheikhdoms loosely under the British protectorate of Aden; Aden itself being, until 1963, a British Colony. The Persian Gulf coast has a string of sheikhdoms, grown wealthy from oil, which once relied largely on piracy to make up for the poverty-stricken character of their lands. These sheikhdoms remain outside the kingdom of Sa'udi Arabia: Kuwait (until 1961) and the island sheikhdom of Bahrain developed under British influence and so too have Qatar, Muscat and Oman. When piracy along the coasts was lessened, if not brought to an end, by the Maritime Truces imposed by Britain early in the nineteenth century, the coast became known as the 'Trucial Coast'—a name still used. Bahrain is the centre of the famous pearl fisheries of the Persian Gulf. Much of the trade with Nejd goes through Manama, Bahrain's capital and commercial centre.

The population of Arabia is not known with any precision. The estimates of area and population given in the annexed table are those relating to 1963 published by the United Nations. The least satisfactory are those of Sa'udi Arabia, but out of the total given there are probably a million nomads, two million in the Hejaz and two million in the Nejd oases. It is the population of the oases and the nomadic folk who have influenced the history, not only of Arabia, but of the whole of the world, out of all proportion to their numbers. There is a virtual impossibility of increasing the food-producing area in the oases; climatic conditions favour the growth of a virile and fertile race. With a high birth-rate and low death-rate there are two possibilities, emigration or death from starvation. The surplus population usually remains for some time within the peninsula gradually accumulating and tending to form new nomadic groups, which try to establish rights to wells and pasturage already occupied. At last the action of some tribe or tribes, or sheer want, forces them out with all their predatory habits and defective experience of settled life, towards the borders of Egypt, Syria or Mesopotamia. In ancient times the Semitic invasions of Babylonia, the Canaanite invasion of Syria, the Hyksos invasions of Egypt, and the Hebrew invasion of Palestine are all to be explained in this way: in more recent times the settlement of north-western Africa. Hardly any part of the peninsula is unaffected by the features of life on steppe and desert, agriculture is impossible in three-quarters of the area; even the single family must keep on the move in order to live. Yet it is these wandering folk, with their fierce struggle against nature, their distrust of their fellow-man, who may rob them of their

	Area, square miles	Population
Sa'udi Arabia	597,000	6,000,000
Yemen	75,000	4,500,000
South Arabia	112,000	1,000,000
Muscat and Oman . . .	82,000	750,000
Trucial States	32,300	110,000
Qatar	4,000	60,000
Bahrain	230	150,000
Kuwait	9,375 ⎱	322,000
Neutral Zone	3,560 ⎰	
	915,465	12,892,000

mess of pottage, who have given the world the great philosophic religions of Judaism and Mahommedanism and, obviously to some extent, Christianity.

Among the products of the oases, the chief food is the date, though grain is grown in considerable quantities in the larger oases. The fine Mocha coffee is exported in small quantities, the cheaper Brazilian or Javanese being imported for home use. Gums, hides and wool are produced and exported in small quantities. The breeding of camels is carried on by the nomads and camels are sold to surrounding settled peoples; the breeding of the famous Arab horses (chiefly in Nejd) is less important. Asses are only of slightly less value as means of transport than camels and are bred in large numbers in Hejaz, Yemen and Nejd.

Nearly all the inhabitants of Arabia are Moslems, but adhere to several sects. The great annual pilgrimage to Mecca (and, to a less extent, to Medina) is a feature of the greatest importance. The annual influx is estimated at between 100,000 and 500,000 and the passage of pilgrims is the occasion of much trading and also, until recently, unfortunately, the great cause of the spread of epidemic diseases. A piped water supply at Mecca and Jiddah has improved this. The pilgrims follow four chief routes:

(1) From Damascus to Medina and Mecca. The railway from Damascus to Medina was constructed in 1901–8 but the Arabian portion (530 miles) was ruined as a workable concern by T. E. Lawrence and his saboteurs in 1916–17 and functioned only as far as Ma'an in Jordan until reopened with international aid in 1964–6. The Medina–Mecca section was surveyed but never built. With Arabia's new-found wealth in oil the whole may now be constructed.

(2) From Cairo via Sinai and Yambo' to Medina or Mecca.

(3) From Baghdad through the heart of the peninsula via Riyadh and the oasis of Ha'il. A motor route from Najaf (near Baghdad) to Medina was opened in 1935.

(4) By sea to the port of Jiddah (Jedda) whence there is an excellent motor road (45 miles)—this is by far the most

important route now. In 1951 a standard-gauge railway,
constructed with oil profits, was opened from Damman, the
Persian Gulf port for the oilfield, to Riyadh, the capital of
Sa'udi Arabia, and it is planned to extend it through Mecca
across the peninsula to the Red Sea coast at Jiddah. There
is a deep-water pier (1950) and also a good airport at Jiddah.

Since 1932 the whole economic position as well as the world importance of eastern Arabia has been completely changed. It was in
that year that oil was struck in the centre of Bahrain island. Following
the great oil strike in northern Iraq in 1927 the Shell Company drilled
unsuccessfully in the Farsan Islands and British interests rejected as
valueless concessions in Bahrain island. The successful strike was made
by the Bahrain Oil Company, or 'Bapco', a subsidiary of Standard Oil
of California. The Kuwait Oil Company formed in 1933, however, is
half British capital, half American; in the same year American interests
(Arabian-American Oil Co. or Aramco) secured rights in eastern
Sa'udi Arabia from King Ibn Sa'ud, whilst in 1935 the Sheikh of
Qatar gave the concession in his territory to the British Anglo-Iranian
Company. The oil belt thus stretches from Kuwait at the head of the
Persian Gulf along the mainland of eastern Arabia and through the
Bahrain islands and is shared by American and British interests. The
first oil on the mainland was struck in 1936 at Damman in al Hasa
(Sa'udi Arabia); in 1938 the Kuwait Company discovered the Burghan
field—amongst the richest in the world; in 1939 the Dukhan field
in Qatar was added to the list, followed by Abu Hadriyah (1940),
Abqaiq (1941), Qatif (1944), Buqqah (1947) and Aby Dar (1948), all
in al Hasa. Pipelines were constructed from Damman to Ras Tanura
(which has a large refinery) and extended in 1945 (17 miles under
water) to the Bahrain refineries. Kuwait oil is piped to Fahahil.
Aramco sends much oil through the 1,068 mile long Trans-Arabian
pipeline to Sidon on the Mediterranean (completed 1950). Aramco's
main centre is Dhahran. Eastern Sa'udi Arabia and Kuwait are
amongst the world's half-dozen great producing areas; Qatar has a
large and Bahrain a smaller output; other parts of the coast are all lands
of great promise. In 1953 oil was found in the 'neutral zone' between
Kuwait and Sa'udi Arabia. By 1954 the Middle East as a whole was
exporting 122,000,000 tons of oil—far more than Venezuela or the
United States, the next great exporters.

Almost overnight these poverty-stricken sheikhdoms of the Trucial
or Persian Gulf coast have become rich—as well as highly significant
in world affairs. Hundreds of Europeans and Americans live in well-
planned modern towns and many thousands of local employees as well
as labourers from India and elsewhere enjoy riches and living conditions previously unknown in the whole sub-continent. Fragments of

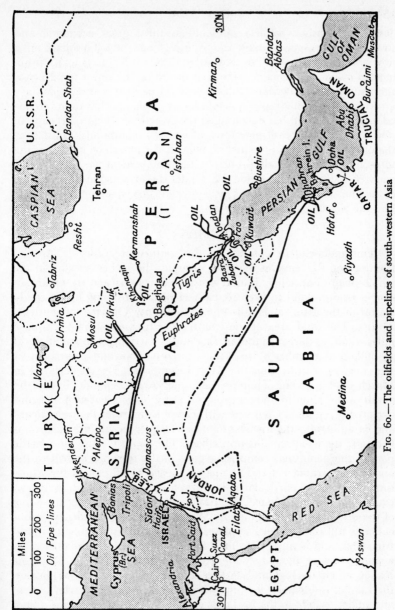

FIG. 60.—The oilfields and pipelines of south-western Asia

Since 1954 oil has also been produced in the neutral zone between Kuwait
and Sa'udi Arabia shown above. The vast Ghawar field, west of Dhahran, is probably the richest in the world. So strong is nationalist feeling however that the
countries are either seeking to control their own oil industry, as Iran has done,
or demanding a larger share of profits. In December 1957 Sa'udi Arabia concluded
an agreement with a Japanese group covering its share of possible oil offshore of
the neutral zone south of Kuwait on the latter principle; shipment of oil to
Japan began in 1961. Abu Dhabi is a later development (1964).

desert previously worthless suddenly assumed great economic and strategic importance (notably the 'Neutral Zone' of 3,560 square miles now administered jointly by Kuwait and Sa'udi Arabia): many problems of ownership remain unresolved including the rights to oil below the waters of the Persian Gulf. Towns on or near the oilfields have grown with amazing rapidity. Hofu for example now has over 100,000 people. King Sa'ud has encouraged the growth of Riyadh, his capital, now a sprawling, brash new town of 350,000 inhabitants. Until 1957 the oilfields had been operated on what had come to be known as the fifty-fifty principle—half profits to the government or ruler of the country, half to the concessionaire. Under this arrangement the income of the Sheikh of Kuwait in 1957 was £93,600,000 which probably made him the richest man in the world.

YEMEN

This independent country in the south-west corner of Arabia, fronting the Red Sea on the west, occupies the highest ground in the whole peninsula; a hot, humid coastal plain is backed by mountain ranges rising inland to over 10,000 feet before dropping to the sandy wastes of the Rub' al Khali—the vast 'Empty Quarter' of southern Arabia. The total area of the country is estimated at 75,000 square miles (half as large again as England), carrying a population of 4½ million. A member State of the United Nations and a signatory of the covenant constituting the Arab League, the Yemen declared in March 1958 in favour of joining the United Arab Republic. But on the death of the King in 1962 a group of army officers seized power and declared a republic. Civil war with Egypt supporting the republicans and Sa'udi Arabia the royalists followed. Despite a cease-fire in November 1964 the issue remains unresolved. The Yemen is the most fertile part of the peninsula, comprising most of the territory known to the ancients as Arabia Felix. The meteorological conditions in the Maritime Range are particularly favourable to coffee, which is grown extensively above 4,500 feet and has long been famous under the name of the original port of shipment, Mocha. That port has decayed, but coffee is still the Yemen's staple export; the crop is at its best around Menakha, and is shipped from Hodeida (now the premier port, with a population of about 30,000). At higher altitudes in the Maritime Range, and in the highlands farther east, as well as on a central plateau, the rainfall is adequate for the growing of grain crops—barley, wheat and millet—while in the lowlands grapes are grown for raisins. Hides are also exported, but the Yemen, unlike other countries in the Middle East, is better suited for agricultural than for pastoral industry. Hillsides are carefully terraced and cultivated on intensive lines, and normally the crops are more than sufficient for local needs. Aden normally draws grain supplies from the Yemen, and an Anglo-Yemeni Agreement in 1951 provided not only for demarcation of the frontier but also for British co-operation in economic development, education and hygiene in the Yemen.

Sana, the capital, a town of 20,000–25,000 inhabitants, is in the eastern highlands at a height of over 7,000 feet, and most of the other chief towns lie among the mountains at altitudes of 5,000–8,000 feet.

ADEN AND SOUTH ARABIA

Until 1959 the southern coastlands of the Arabian peninsula were occupied by Aden, a British colony, with a protectorate stretching for 740 miles from the Straits of Bab el Mandeb, at the southern end of the Red Sea, eastward to the borders of Muscat and Oman. Inland the protectorate extended to the confines of Yemen and to the 'Empty Quarter' (Rub' al Khali) of Sa'udi Arabia. The colony comprised a mainland area of 75 square miles around the port of Aden, about 100 miles east of the Straits; the rocky island of Perim (5 square miles), rising some 200 feet above the waters in the Straits; and far to the east, off the coast of Muscat and Oman, the Kuria Muria Islands, a small

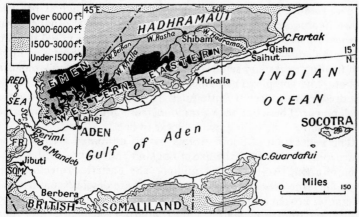

FIG. 61.—Aden and the entrance to the Red Sea

group (30 square miles) ceded to Britain in 1854 as a landing place for a telegraph cable. Formerly administered from India, Aden became a separate colony on April 1, 1937. In February 1959 the six western protectorate states (roughly the 'Western' area of Fig. 61) formed the Federation of South Arabia with its capital at Al Ittihad. In January 1963 a new constitution for Aden came into effect so that it became a State and joined the Federation, the British crown retaining sovereignty and certain powers. The naval base was given up in 1966–7.

The port of Aden is a large natural inlet lying between two rocky peninsulas—extinct volcanoes—linked by a low-lying sandy coast. The eastern peninsula, rising to 1,800 feet, is Aden proper; the western is known as Little Aden. Offering the only good harbour on the main trade route between Egypt and India, Aden was known to Arab

traders long before the Roman era. In the Middle Ages with the
eclipse of Arab influence it decayed till the East India Company
realized its value and, after abortive treaties with local sultans, annexed
it in 1839. Its early fame as an *entrepôt* was re-established, and the
opening of the Suez Canal brought it into fresh prominence as a port
of call and trans-shipment. Today it is comparable with Liverpool in
respect of the tonnage of the shipping entering the port; in 1963 nearly
6,000 deep-sea vessels of 29 million tons, in addition to coasters, called
at Aden. It can take vessels drawing up to 34 feet, and is visited primarily as a refuelling station, both for coal and for oil.

The trans-shipment of cargo provides a main occupation of the
population of the colony—estimated at mid-1964 at over 225,000, a
quarter of them in the old town whose proper name, Crater, is self-
explanatory. It is also called Camp. It was a good defensive site: the
modern town has grown up near the deep-water anchorage and is
known as Steamer Point or Tawahi. The population is very mixed with
numerous Arabs, Yemenis, Indians, Somalis, Jews and others.

The rainfall is negligible, in some years nil, though it has been
known to amount to 8 inches in a year. The only local product is salt,
obtained by solar evaporation from sea-water, which is raised by wind-
mills into shallow pans at the back of the harbour. The port is equipped
with floating docks and some ship-repairing as well as dhow-repairing
goes on. The completion in 1954 of a great oil refinery with its own
port dredged to 40 feet at Little Aden marked a new stage in economic
development. There has been a rapid increase in population and much
building activity including many blocks of flats.

The Federation of South Arabia has an estimated area of 60,000
square miles—more than the size of England and Wales—with a population of about two-thirds of a million. The Eastern Protectorate has
about the same area but fewer people. Both are desolate countries, the
Federation broken and rugged, rising to over 8,000 feet on the Yemen
border, and the three states of the Eastern Protectorate also much
accidented, with peaks of 5,000–7,000 feet near the coast, and inland
a flat-topped steppe, the Hadramaut, traversed from west to east by a
great wādi of the same name. In the past the Hadramaut has been
largely dependent on funds sent home and brought home by the large
proportion of the population who emigrated to Malaya and there
accumulated fortunes. When the Second World War stopped the free
movement of funds, famine ensued in the Eastern Protectorate. Areas
cropped by the Arabs amount to only 120,000 acres, of which sorghum
millet accounts for two-thirds; and livestock number about a million,
of which two-thirds are goats, the balance being made up of sheep,
cattle and camels. The British Government, as a Development and
Welfare Scheme, opened up by irrigation and settlement about 100
square miles in the Abyan district some 30 miles east of Aden port.
Here, among other crops, a very high-grade cotton of the Sudan type

has done well; in 1954 cotton to the value of nearly £2,500,000 was grown on 46,000 acres. At present a little tobacco is exported from South Arabia but there is a considerable import of dates and other foods. Aden port is the natural gateway for the Federation; in the Eastern Protectorate the chief port is Mukalla.[1]

With all their limitations it would be a mistake to think of South Arabia as primitive desert. The habitations of the people range from the crude goat-hair shelters of the nomad tribes to mud-brick buildings of five to seven storeys in the cities of the Hadramaut and to the veritable palaces of the Sultans and wealthy Seiyids, remarkable not only for their size but for their grace and beauty of form.

The island of Perim has an interesting strategic position right in the Straits of Bab-el-Mandeb and served as a coaling station from 1883 to 1935. The cable station was rendered redundant by the development of radio and was closed after the Second World War.

MUSCAT AND OMAN

This independent sultanate occupies the eastern corner of Arabia, with a coastline of a thousand miles lying partly along the Gulf of Oman, where it is skirted by high mountainous country, and partly along the Arabian Sea, where the land is mostly low-lying. The interior stretches back to the borders of the Rub' al Khali, and it is calculated that the sultanate has an area of 82,000 square miles (equal to that of England and Scotland) with a population of rather more than three-quarters of a million. A treaty of friendship, commerce and navigation concluded with Great Britain in 1939 reaffirmed the close ties which had existed between the two countries for nearly 150 years. At the capital, Muscat, in recognition of the Sultan's independence, Britain is represented by a Consul-General.

The two chief centres, Muscat and Mattrah, lie within a mile or so of one another on the Gulf of Oman, where the mountains come down to the sea. Muscat lies at the head of a cove dominated by rocky heights crowned by old forts, and exposed to *shamels* (the violent north-west winds of the Gulf region). Commercially it has lost ground to Mattrah, which has a larger harbour, is the terminus of caravan routes to and from the interior, and now has a bigger population, though both towns are small (between 5,000 and 10,000 inhabitants). Beyond them, for over 150 miles in the direction of the Persian Gulf, a narrow coastal plain carries date gardens, noted for the flavour and early maturity of their fruit. At the back, where the mountains rise to over 9,000 feet, the general aridity of the country is relieved by the green fertility of cultivated areas with sufficient rainfall for grain and other crops. Along the Arabian Sea the coast is mostly barren, but at the far western end the upland province of Dhofar is another

[1] The island of Socotra or Soqotra (Fig. 61) with about 8,000 people is included in the Eastern Protectorate. See D. Botting, *Geog. Jour.*, **124**, 1958, 200–9.

productive area, served by the small port of Murbat. Camels are extensively bred in the interior. Oil has been proved and production was planned to start in 1967.

A curious survival of the former wider extent of the sultanate was the territory of Gwadar, on the opposite (north) side of the Gulf of Oman, forming an enclave about 40 miles long and 15 miles deep, embedded in Pakistan near the Persian border. Two-thirds of the 15,000 people are congregated in Gwadar town and port. The Sultan of Muscat and Oman ceded the territory to Pakistan on September 8, 1958 'as a gesture of good will'.

TRUCIAL STATES AND QATAR[1]

From Muscat and Oman to the borders of Sa'udi Arabia, about half-way along the western shores of the Persian Gulf, stretch some 600 miles of coastal territory divided into seven independent sheikhdoms having long-standing treaty engagements with Britain to preserve the peace, suppress slavery, and abstain from entering into agreements with foreign States. They have a population of perhaps 110,000 but the failure to find oil has resulted in a mass migration of half for such places as Qatar, Bahrain and Kuwait with resulting decay of the old settlements. In 1955–6 a border oasis, Buraimi, was claimed by Sa'udi Arabia and came temporarily in the news. Slavery existed till 1962 and the British Political Agent exercised his right to free slaves who clutch the Union Jack flagpole though they invariably returned afterwards to their master's house. Because of the discovery of oil Qatar is quite different. The first shipment was made at the end of 1949. Five years later, in 1954, output was 4,700,000 tons—over 6,000,000 in 1957. The field is known as the Dukhan field, the oil port is Umm Said. The state occupies the whole of the Qatar peninsula and the capital is Doha or Dauha (45,000).

BAHRAIN ISLANDS

This group of islands lies along the Arabian coast of the Persian Gulf, in a large bay cutting deeply into the land. They are about 20 miles from the mainland (the Sa'udi Arabian province of El Hasa), and constitute an independent sheikhdom having treaty relations with Britain dating back to 1880. Their total area is a little over 200 square miles and they were renowned as the headquarters of the Persian Gulf pearl fisheries; now they have gained new fame as a source of oil.

The main island, Bahrain or Bahrein, is 27 miles long by 10 wide. It is linked to Muharraq Island (4 miles by 1 mile) by a causeway carrying a motor road and a swing bridge spanning the deep-water channel. These islands enfold two harbours, and from a third island, Sitra, another causeway and a pipeline project eastward for three miles to a deep-water anchorage. Dates, citrus fruits and lucerne are

[1] A. Melamid, 'Political Geography of Trucial Oman and Qatar', *Geog. Rev.*, **43**, 1953, 194–206.

successfully grown on the main island, and it is there also that oil was found in 1932 near the highest point, a rocky crater rising some 450 feet. Production increased by 1950 to nearly 1·5 m. tons and in 1963 was 2·3 m. This is small compared with the output in Sa'udi Arabia, but Bahrain also possesses a well-equipped refinery, with a throughput of 11·3 m. tons in 1963. An asphalt plant has been added to the refinery, which is situated on the main island at Manama, the chief town of the group.

KUWAIT

This sheikhdom under British protection until June 1961 at the head of the Persian Gulf, with an area of about 8,000 square miles (rather larger than Wales), has a population of 322,000 (Census of 1961, 400,000 in 1964). Until a few years ago it was typical of the smaller Arabian States—largely desert. It had an extensive harbour on which stood the capital, around it numerous date gardens and some cultivation of cereals and other foodstuffs for home consumption, a reputation for dhow-building, and a certain amount of general trade; but chiefly notable as a pivotal point in the political geography of the Middle East. Now its meteoric rise as one of the chief sources of oil supply in the Middle East has added to the political factor a 'big business' interest. Production for export did not start till the middle of 1946. In 1947 it was over 2 million tons; in 1950, 17 million tons. In March 1951 it was averaging 375,000 barrels a day, which (at 7·4 barrels to the ton) was at the rate of 18½ million tons a year. Then, following the nationalization of the Persian oil industry, Kuwait's production again went up by leaps and bounds, doubling the rate in six months, till in October it was over 3 million tons a month. By 1963 production exceeded 100 million tons, mainly from the Burgan oilfield at the back of Kuwait town and harbour. Ahmadi is the oil town and administrative headquarters of the British-American Kuwait Oil Company. It lies about six miles inland at an elevation of 400 feet, and is connected by a pipeline with Mina-al-Ahmadi, where a six-berthed loading jetty is constantly employed. The loading terminal started functioning in 1946; by 1955 it was handling over 1,000,000 barrels daily. Four-fifths of the oil is shipped crude, though the existing refinery has been expanded to handle 25,000 tons a day.

At the end of 1951 the oil company entered into a new agreement with the Sheikh of Kuwait, under which he became entitled to a half-share of the profits. Extensive development and welfare schemes were undertaken, including a water distillation plant with a capacity of a million gallons a day. A modern motor road connects Kuwait with Basra and most of the Company employees are Iraqis who travel in daily. In June 1961 when Britain made a new treaty with the Sheikh, Iraq laid claim to Kuwait on the ground it was once part of the Turkish province of Basra.

IRAQ [1]

For centuries part of the Ottoman Empire, Iraq was freed from the domination of Turkey during the First World War, during which 'Mesopotamia'—strictly the country between the rivers (Gk. *meso* = between and *potamos* = river)—familiarly Mespot to the troops, had

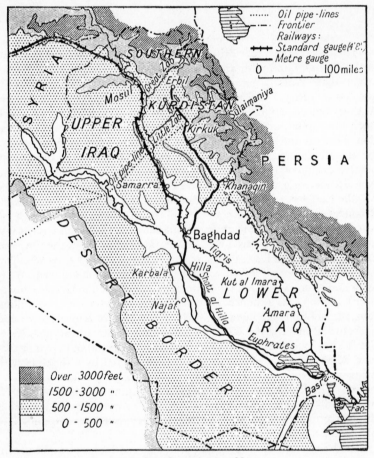

FIG. 62.—General map of Iraq

become a battleground between Britain and Turkey. A provisional Arab Government was set up in November 1920, and the Emir Faisal (third son of ex-King Hussein of the Hejaz) was elected King Faisal I

[1] I am grateful to the many friends who gave me so much first-hand information and showed me so much of the country when I was one of a Commission of four in 1953 advising the Government on the establishment of the University of Baghdad.

of Iraq. Turkey formally renounced any claim to the country by the Treaty of Lausanne (1923) and Britain recognized the complete independence of Iraq in 1927. King Faisal I was succeeded by King Ghazi, who died as the result of an accident, and was followed by his infant son (shortly before his fourth birthday) in 1939. In due course King Faisal II received his education in Britain. Both he and the Crown Prince (his maternal uncle who had been Regent until 1953) were assassinated in July 1958, when the King was twenty-three, and the country became a Republic.

The whole of Iraq is watered and drained by the two great rivers, the Tigris and Euphrates and their tributaries. As shown in Fig. 63 Iraq does not occupy as much as one half of the whole basin, especially if one includes that of the Iranian River, the Karun, which discharges its waters into the Shatt-el-Arab below Basra. In the north Iraq includes a large section of the mountainous country of Kurdistan along its frontiers with Iran and Turkey; in the west, arbitrary lines across the desert mark the frontiers with Syria and Jordan, and the same is true of the southern border with Arabia and Kuwait.

The whole Tigris-Euphrates valley-plain is not infrequently referred to as the 'Cradle of Humanity', or better as the 'Cradle of Civilization', a reference to the ancient civilizations which flourished in the region from 4000 B.C. onwards. The ancient Kingdom of 'Akkad, later and better known as Assyria, occupied the northern parts of the plain with its capital at Nineveh, near the modern Mosul. The Kingdom of Sumer or Babylonia occupied a more southern region, with its capital, Babylon, near the present Hilla, on the then course of the Euphrates.

The country has an area of 438,446 square kilometres, or 169,240 square miles, or nearly 50 per cent. larger than the whole British Isles. The population of 6,803,153 (1962) is however almost entirely restricted to those parts of the country which are organized in 14 liwas or provinces, and which exclude the 210,000 square kilometres of desert. The density over the settled areas of 90,000 square miles is thus about 75.

Physically Iraq falls into four divisions:[1]

    (a) The mountains of the north-east (Kurdistan).
    (b) Upper Iraq.
    (c) Lower Iraq.
    (d) The desert fringe.

Kurdistan. The wildest and least accessible part of Iraq is central Kurdistan—a highland region lying on the borders of Turkey and Persia. Peaks on or near the Persian frontier rise to over 10,000 feet. The successive ranges decrease in elevation towards the plains: the

---

[1] E. Banse (*Die Turkei*) divides Mesopotamia into four divisions—Northern, Eastern, Central and Southern. Central corresponds roughly with what is here called Upper Iraq, Southern with Lower Iraq and Northern (in which Banse includes a large area of Turkey proper) and Eastern with the mountain fringe.

mountains are generally barren or but sparsely wooded, but good pasture and cultivable land occur on the lower slopes and in the valleys. The inhabitants of this tract are mainly the lawless Kurds who continue to demand independence. Included in this tract are the fertile upland plains of es-Sulaimaniya.[1]

Upper Iraq corresponds roughly with the Assyria of old, embracing a large portion of 'Mesopotamia'—the land between the rivers—as well as the country between the Tigris and the foothills of Kurdistan. Upper Mesopotamia consists chiefly of an open, undulating, treeless plain with level areas in places and ranges of low hills in others. West of Mosul the Sinjar Hills even rise to 3,000 feet. South-east of Mosul, that is, between the Tigris and the frontier range, are rolling valleys which have much grass in spring, separated by sandstone ridges. Cultivated land in Upper Iraq is largely restricted to the deep broad valleys of the Euphrates and Tigris and the tributaries of the latter, the Great and Little Zab. In the Mesopotamian doab much of the land is arid and the soil often ruined by saline or alkaline deposits.

Lower Iraq begins a little above Baghdad and offers a great contrast to Upper Iraq. Practically the whole area is level and slopes but very gradually to the Persian Gulf. Baghdad, for example, is only 107 feet above sea-level. The Tigris and the Euphrates are raised slightly above the general level of the plain and in many places may be traced the high banks of ancient canals. Here and there are mounds which mark the sites of ancient cities, and near Basra is an isolated, extinct volcano rising to a height of 300 feet—but these are the only elevations which break the monotony of the level surface. The soil of Lower Iraq is a fine fertile alluvium—a powdery dust when dry, a tenacious mud when wet—which is still being added to by the annual overflow of the Tigris and Euphrates. In the days of the Babylonian Empire a great system of inundation canals utilized and controlled the annual overflow and Iraq was a land of amazing fertility. Now much of this fertile land lies waste; a large proportion of the flood-waters find their way into huge swamps which form the breeding-ground of countless myriads of malarial mosquitoes. Nevertheless, there are large stretches of rice and cornfields and enormous groves of date-palms.

The *Desert Fringe* needs but little description. The borders are hard, gravelly plains with patches of sand and there is frequently a scarp of 50 or 100 feet in height which marks clearly the junction with the Euphrates-Tigris plains.

The climate of Iraq is characterized by extreme heat in summer (Baghdad has an average of 92·5° F. in August) and a winter unexpectedly cold for the latitude (Baghdad 49° in January). The scanty

---

[1] The great dam at Dokan on the Lesser Zab, constructed 1955–6, is completely changing the region. See J. H. G. Lebon, 'The new Irrigation Era in Iraq', *Econ. Geog.*, 1955, **31**, 47–59.

rainfall, almost entirely in winter, averages about 10 inches in Lower
Iraq, but is curiously variable from year to year—and definitely insufficient for agriculture. One wonders why the great ancient civilizations flourished in a climate seemingly so far from ideal. There is no
doubt, however, that the climate (apart from swampy areas) is healthy,
whilst the flood-waters induce amazing returns from the very fertile
soil

FIG. 63.—The Basin of the Tigris-Euphrates

The stippled area is the alluvial delta-plain. This map shows that nearly the whole of Iraq lies within th
basin of the twin rivers, the basin also embracing large areas of Syria, Turkey and Iran.

Geologically it is probable that the river-plains of Iraq occupy a
geosynclinal trough trending north-west to south-east between the
Tertiary fold mountains on the northern side, and the gently folded or
tilted Tertiary sediments on the desert margin. The scarp referred to
above is where the Tertiaries give place to the Recent or Pleistocene
alluvium, which fills the heart of the basin. In a sense Iraq of the rivers
below Ramadi or Hit on the Euphrates and Samarra on the Tigris is

a 'delta' and is recognized as such when the term Rafidain is used, and the 'desert plateau' on the south and foothills on the north are separately distinguished. Economically the separation of the alluvial plain is of great importance: the great river control barrages on the main rivers are where they emerge from their narrow, bluff-bounded valleys on to the open plain.

The Euphrates is a slower river than the Tigris. It receives no tributary apart from intermittent wādis from the desert in its plains course through Iraq, and it is there too tortuous and interrupted by shallows to be of much use for navigation. It has, in the past, changed its course repeatedly; the old Hilla channel past the ruins of Babylon became almost dry until Turkish irrigation works sent some of the water back into the old channel.

The Tigris is about 1,150 miles long, and is navigable for steam craft for over 450 miles from above Baghdad to its entry into the Shatt-el-Arab. Below this point water is lost in the distributaries, and navigation suffers until Basra is reached—at the head of the artificially deepened estuary. The Tigris is extensively used by Arab craft, including the curious bowl-shaped coracles peculiar to Iraq, of plaited reeds covered with pitch. During the First World War it regained something of its ancient importance: by the end of 1918 nearly 2,000 steamers collected from all over the world were plying on the Tigris. The Tigris has several important tributaries from the mountains to the north—especially the Great Zab, Little Zab, Adhaim and Diyala. Each is liable to sudden floods, each has spread out an alluvial fan. In the case of the Adhaim and the Diyala this has forced the main course of the Tigris south-westwards. A similar extensive fan is associated with the Karun. Fortunately both the Adhaim and Diyala cut through a foothill fold range, the Jebel Hamrin, in gorges which afford excellent dam sites.

Both rivers are at their lowest at the end of the dry summer—about September or October. They then begin to rise and reach their maximum in April or May—the result of the melting of snows in the mountains of Turkey, from which they rise.

Irrigation. Like most alluvial plains, those of Iraq afford naturally fertile soils provided sufficient moisture is available. Rainfall is inadequate since it ranges from a precarious 3 inches on the desert margins to a fall rather more regular and coming mainly in the winter of about 16 inches in the Kurdistan foothills. Over the Mesopotamian plains it averages about 4 inches, over Upper Iraq about the same. From time immemorial water from the Tigris and Euphrates has been literally the life blood of the country. In common with rivers of varying volume elsewhere—for example, the Hwang Ho—in the low water season the river tends to choke its own bed by deposition of silt to a level above that of the surrounding plains, so that when succeeding flood waters break through the low natural levees, the river frequently abandons its old course for a new one, and abandoned channels are numerous, marshy areas frequent and of large extent. From earliest times circumstances have forced men to band themselves together to control and utilize the vital waters, and in this many see the origin of the urban civilizations associated with Babylon, Nineveh and other great cities now in ruins.

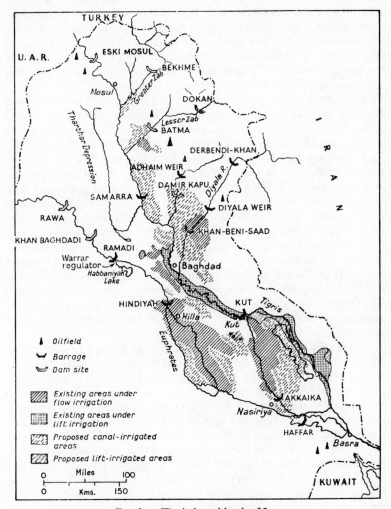

FIG. 64.—The irrigated lands of Iraq

Apart from the known fortunes of war, why, in so many cases, were these old cities, settlements of great size and magnificence, abandoned? Irrigation in Iraq is undoubtedly as old as settlement itself: some (as in large areas at the present day) was by simple lifting of water from the rivers, but elsewhere great canals were dug. It is probable, however, that these early canals were inundation canals only—they were filled with water at the flood season when the rivers spilled over into them. In years when the river waters failed to reach the requisite level they must have remained dry, and famine conditions would result. In other cases abnormal flows would result in disastrous flooding and abandonment of land, especially where permanent or semi-permanent marshy tracts were created. There can be little doubt too that the early irrigated land of the Tigris–Euphrates basin suffered from the trouble which is the greatest worry of irrigation engineers at the present day—the accumulation of salts in the soil through evaporation.

In contrast to its ancient prestige and glory there is no doubt that the land of Iraq passed through many centuries of decadence and decay. When the country was part of the Ottoman Empire, great works were planned by Sir William Wilcocks for the Ottoman Government. As a result the first of the great modern works, the Hindiya Barrage, was constructed across a channel excavated at the side of the Euphrates and, when complete, the Euphrates was diverted into the channel. The ordinary low or summer level of the river was raised by about 16 feet 6 inches, and the water conducted through the old Hilla channel to water an extensive tract of rich agricultural land. Some other works were constructed and a number of ambitious schemes proposed. But in the early years of the independence of Iraq after the First World War there were (as earlier editions of this book pointed out) neither funds available nor a sufficient population. Both these circumstances have changed with wealth from oil and a rapidly increasing population (believed to have more than doubled since independence) naturally demanding a higher standard of living.

A Development Board was created in 1950 and a Ministry of Development in 1953. The Board drew up a first 5-year plan (1951–6) followed by a second (1955–60). It dispenses 70 per cent. of the Government oil royalties as well as other funds and is concerned through seven sections with irrigation; roads, bridges and buildings; industry; agriculture and forests; housing; tourism; and land distribution. Of these duties the first for irrigation, flood control, artesian wells and drainage, absorbs nearly a third of the total budget. What may be called a comprehensive national scheme for the full utilization of water resources involves a number of distinct though interrelated aspects. There is first the construction of dams on the mountain courses of feeder streams designed for control of sudden floods and for irrigation of new lands, especially in the foothill belt, together ultimately with the generation of power. Under the second 5-year plan there is the Dokan Dam on the Lesser Zab, the Derbendi-Khan Dam on the Adhaim River and the Diyala Dam on the Diyala River.

In the second place there is the need for flood control on the two main rivers. On the Euphrates the Great Hindiya Barrage was the earliest of the great modern works. Higher up the river is the remarkable Habbaniyah Project, completed in 1956. This project consists primarily of the Ramadi Dam across the main river which holds back flood water which is allowed to flow, under control of the Warrar Regulator, into a natural depression where it forms Lake Habbaniyah. From this lake there are two outfalls, Dhiban and Majawa, which enable the water to be used for irrigation in the following summer. On the River Tigris the somewhat similar Tharthar scheme was completed

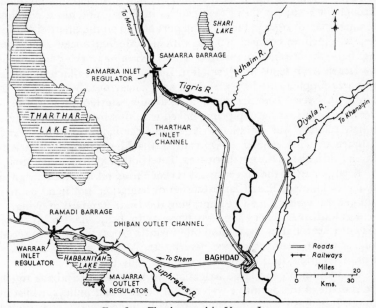

FIG. 65.—Flood control in Upper Iraq

in 1958. The great barrage across the main river at Samarra diverts flood water into a canal 65 kilometres long into the natural depression of the Wadi Tharthar, now converted into a huge lake. The full use of this water is in hand, so is the generation of power at the Samarra barrage, but Baghdad is safe from the disastrous floods of the past. Previously it was only protected by an earth wall and by deliberately breaching the levees, so that Baghdad became an island in the midst of floods. In the third place are the drainage projects designed not only to drain marshy areas (some caused by the rise of the water table consequent upon perennial irrigation) but also to wash accumulated salts out of irrigated areas. In places the concentration of salt had become so high that cultivation was rendered impossible. Usually a network of dams is involved from which the salty or stagnant water is lifted by electric pumps and discharged into the main rivers.

Oil. The first oil developments were at Khanaqin near the Persian frontier (Anglo-Iranian Oil Company) and the strike by the Iraq Petroleum Company at Baba Gurgur near Kirkuk (October 14, 1927). By 1950 the annual output was between 5 and 6 million tons, mostly from Kirkuk but other fields were becoming important. The companies concerned then guaranteed an output of 30 million tons a year and half the profits to the Iraq Government including supplies from the later fields near Mosul and the Basra field which came into production in 1951. Khanaqin has a local refinery which distributes its products throughout Iraq; the Basra field centres in Zubair and has a pipeline 72 miles long to storage tanks at the port of Fao on the Shatt el-'Arab. Several pipelines connect Kirkuk with the Mediterranean coast (see Fig. 60)—the original one went to Haifa (not now working because of the Israeli-Arab feud) and Tripoli in Lebanon. This 12-inch diameter pipe was supplemented by a 16-inch and, since 1952, by a 30-inch to Banias in Syria. Another field, at Rumaila, started production in December 1954. It has a pipeline linked with that from Zubair to Fao. A new refinery was completed at Daura near Baghdad in 1955 and bitumen is being refined at Quiyara in the Mosul district. The Ain Zalah field is also in the northern area. Total output 55·6 m. tons in 1963.

A large part of the Government revenue from oil has been assigned to a Development Board for extension of irrigation and flood control and general works aimed at improving the Iraqi standard of living.

Agriculture. There are two harvests in Iraq—one in April or May of wheat, barley, beans and other winter crops; the other between August and November of rice, maize, etc. At present only the most primitive agricultural implements are generally used.[1]

In addition to the large irrigation works mentioned above much use is made of the primitive water lift of buckets and pulleys, whilst in Lower Iraq fresh water is sent twice daily into specially constructed channels by the rise of the tide in the Shatt el-'Arab.

The most important crop in Iraq is the date-crop,[2] and it is in Iraq and Upper Egypt that the date-palm attains perfection. In southern Iraq there is one continuous date-plantation on either side of the rivers, those on each side of the Shatt el-'Arab being especially fine. Iraqi production varies greatly from year to year – for example from 445,000 tons in 1954 to only 252,000 in 1956—but is about a third of the world's total. Exports alone may exceed 150,000 tons. Later in this book we shall have occasion to refer to the extreme usefulness of all parts of the

[1] J. H. G. Lebon, 'Population Distribution and the Agricultural Regions of Iraq', *Geog. Rev.*, **43**, 1953, 223–8.
[2] V. H. W. Dowson, *Dates and Date Cultivation of the Iraq* (Cambridge: Heffer, 1921); bid., 'The Date and the Arab', *Jour. Royal Central Asian Soc.*, **36**, 1949, 34–41.

coconut palm in regions like southern India and Ceylon: in Iraq the same is true of the date-palm. The dates themselves are the staple food of the Arabs and may be prepared for food in a great variety of ways.

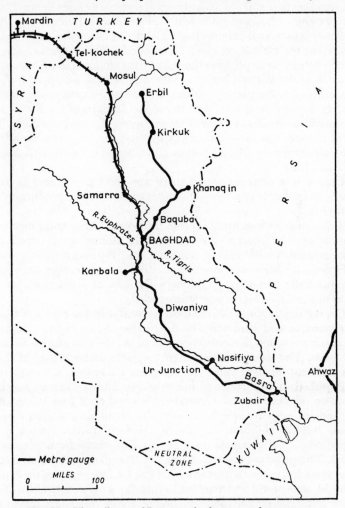

FIG. 66.—The railways of Iraq, standard gauge and metre gauge
A standard gauge line, using Russian equipment, was completed between Baghdad and Basra in 1964.

Syrup and vinegar are made from old dates and also a strong spirit ('arak), whilst the date-stones are ground for cattle and sheep food. The terminal bud of the stem is not unlike an almond in flavour but much larger and is eaten as a table delicacy. The fronds or leaves are woven into matting and half the population of southern Iraq lives in date-mat houses. A fibre from the outer trunk makes strong rope, whilst the light porous timber is much used in bridge-building and construction work. Basra is the centre of the date trade; only certain varieties are suitable for general export and are packed for shipment in wooden boxes. Poorer varieties enter into local trade and into trade with India.

Rice ranks second in importance to dates in Lower Iraq; the quality is poor but the yield is very large. The paddy fields are usually on the lowest parts of the slopes from the raised river channels to the surrounding swamps. Wheat and barley are the main cereals of Upper Iraq. In area sown (3 million acres) barley was the leading crop of the country but has recently been overtaken by wheat. In parts of the Mosul area the rainfall is sufficient for wheat grown by 'dry-farming' methods. The wheat is hard, red and of excellent quality, but is grown mainly for home consumption. Maize, millets and sesame are cultivated mainly in Lower Iraq.

Cotton is a crop for which there are great possibilities in Iraq, especially for the better types of American cotton, but production has fluctuated.

Tobacco is an important crop of the north. Other crops especially important in the Shatt el-'Arab region are opium, hemp, lentils and liquorice root. In the hills of northern Iraq European fruits grow to perfection; farther south oranges, mulberries and lemons grow well. Iraq has little or no timber, though the hills of Kurdistan and the banks of the Tigris were once well wooded.

On the desert fringes of the south-west and in the plains of Upper Iraq nomadic and semi-nomadic Arabs rear camels, horses, donkeys, sheep and goats, and the settled population usually own numerous sheep and goats. The wool obtained from the 7–8 million fat-tailed sheep is of excellent quality, whilst Angora goats are reared in Kurdistan.

Population. Apart from the Persians, Kurds, Turcomans and others on the borders and a considerable number of Jews in the cities and Indians who are recent arrivals, the population of Iraq consists almost entirely of Sunni and Shi'ah Moslems of Arab stock (over 90 per cent. of the population). Syrian Christians are numerous in Mosul. The principal town is, of course, Baghdad, of Arabian Nights fame. Founded in the eighth century, it was for five centuries the capital of the Moslem world and remains to this day a very sacred city of the Sunni sect. The famous pontoon bridge across the Tigris linked old Baghdad with new Baghdad on the east of the river but fine modern bridges have replaced it. Baghdad has for centuries been the meeting-place of caravan routes from Syria and Arabia on the one hand and Persia on the other, and, apart from its fame as a mart, manufactures silks, woollens, cottons, rugs, pottery, etc. Its expansion in recent years has been rapid, the population exceeding 552,000 at the census of 1947. Just as Baghdad is the city *par excellence* of the heart of Iraq, so is Basra *par excellence* the port—indeed the only one possible for ocean-going steamers, being situated some 60 miles up the Shatt el-'Arab. The Date City has a trying climate and was rendered unhealthy by nearby marshes, but is growing rapidly in population and prosperity. Its airport like that of Baghdad is now of great international importance.

Mosul is the second city of Iraq in size (341,000 in 1947), the metropolis of the north. Others of note are Hilla (near the ruins of Babylon), the holy cities of Kerbelan (Karbala) and Najaf; Amarah (Kurnah 'Amara) and Kūt-al-Imāra of war fame, likely to become a great wheat centre. Kirkuk had already grown to 148,000 in 1947.

Communications. The river traffic has already been noted and the railway system has been greatly developed in recent years. Basra

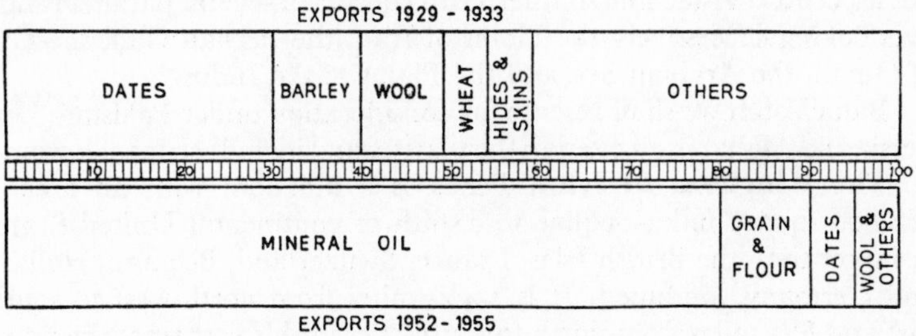

EXPORTS 1929 - 1933

DATES	BARLEY	WOOL	WHEAT	HIDES & SKINS	OTHERS

10	20	30	40	50	60	70	80	90	100

MINERAL OIL	GRAIN & FLOUR	DATES	WOOL & OTHERS

EXPORTS 1952- 1955

Fig. 67.—The pre-war and post-war exports of Iraq

This diagram is only approximate because royalties on oil are paid to the Government but the oil is sent by pipeline or shipped by the companies and total value is not shown in export figures.

and Baghdad were linked by metre-gauge rail in 1920, but not till 1936 did the Government decide to build the long-projected line from Baghdad through Mosul to join the Turkish system. Through running from Iraq to Turkey was established in 1940. The line is on standard gauge and follows the right bank of the Tigris. The line northwards from Baghdad to Kirkuk and Khanaqin is metre gauge. Iraq has a considerable mileage of earth roads: the system of all-weather metalled roads is being steadily expanded.

Foreign Trade. Apart from oil, grains (chiefly barley) and dates provide the bulk of the exports. Other items include wool, cotton and livestock. Iron and steel, machinery, metal goods, motor-cars, cotton and woollen piece goods, tea and sugar constitute the bulk of the imports, nearly a third of which come from the United Kingdom.

REFERENCES

Fisher, W. B., *The Middle East* (London: Methuen, 1950).
Lebon, J. H. G., 'Population Distribution and the Agricultural Regions of Iraq', *Geog. Rev.*, **43,** 1953, 223–8.
S. Van Valkenburg, 'Iraq', *Focus, Amer. Geog. Soc.*, 1954.
Govt. of Iraq Board of Development, *Development of Iraq*, March 1957.
Cressey, G. B., *Crossroads of Asia* (New York, 1960).

IRAN (PERSIA)

The Iranian Plateau. Between the Armenian Knot on the west and the Pamirs on the east there stretches a great plateau occupied by the States of Persia, Afghanistan and Baluchistan. The high northern rim is formed by the Elburz Mountains, overlooking the Caspian Sea, passing eastwards into Alla Dagh, flanked on the north by the Kopet Dagh, then into the Paropamisus Mountains of Afghanistan and the main mass of the Hindu Kush Chain, all overlooking the plains of Soviet central Asia. The southern rim consists of several parallel ranges overlooking successively the Plains of Iraq, the Persian Gulf, the Gulf of Oman, the Arabian Sea and the Plains of the Indus.

Baluchistan we shall reserve for consideration under Pakistan; both Persia and Afghanistan overlap the plateau and include strips of lowland.

The Kingdom of Iran. Persia is a kingdom with an area of 628,000 square miles—equal to a fifth of continental United States, or larger than the British Isles, France, Switzerland, Belgium, Holland and Germany combined. It is 1,400 miles from north-west to south-east and 875 miles from north to south. Yet in this vast tract the population was revealed by the Census of 1956 to be only 18,945,000 though previously estimated officially in 1955 at 21,794,000. Until recently Persia was an absolute monarchy, but in 1906 the Shah gave his consent to a Parliament, or Majlis. By 1925 the Majlis had become sufficiently forceful to depose the reigning Shah and his dynasty and to erect a new dynastic house. Since then the Prime Minister and the Majlis have exercised a dominant influence. The old familiar name Persia applies properly to a part only of the country and was changed officially to Iran. Confusion amongst foreigners between Iraq and Iran led the British Government to revert to Persia in all official references.

The heart of Persia is a great tableland, most of it with an elevation of from 3,000 to 5,000 feet. Except on the east, where the plateau merges imperceptibly into that of Afghanistan and Baluchistan, it is surrounded by walls of mountains, and every route to the heart of Persia involves an arduous mountain journey. The tableland of the interior, besides being walled in by mountains, is itself cut up by lines of mountains with a general trend parallel to that of the boundary ranges. It is only in eastern Persia that great desert plains are the predominant relief feature. The plains and valleys which lie between the ranges of the plateau would be utterly sterile were it not for the water derived from the snows of the mountains.

Along the southern borders of Persia the mountains in general approach close to the sea; the coastal strip is narrow, dry and barren except in a few areas where sufficient water is available to make irrigation of crops possible. The mountains of the northern border are loftier and more imposing, especially the Elburz. Most of the numerous ranges of north-western Persia have peaks rising to 8,000 or 10,000 feet, which dominate the upland valleys whose floors stand 4,000 or 5,000 feet above sea-level. The mountains of Persia culminate in the extinct volcano of Damavand, 19,000 feet. The narrow strip of plain along the shores of the Caspian presents a great contrast to the bleak, sterile mountains and plains of the interior. The rainfall is good, so that the mountain slopes are forested; the humidity is high, and the alluvial soils washed down from the mountains are rich, so that dense vegetation stretches right down to the Caspian. The forests have been cleared over large areas; fruits and field crops thrive, and it is in this region, the most favoured of all Persia, that the mulberry tree and sericulture flourish.

More than half Persia lies in the main basin of inland drainage; in addition the Seistan basin of Afghanistan and Baluchistan drains a considerable tract in the east and Lake Urmia a large area in the west. The north drains to the Caspian, mainly by the Aras or Araxes, Sefid Rud, Gargan and Artrek Rivers. Only about one-fifth of Persia drains to the Persian Gulf or the Arabian Sea, but of special importance is the Karun, which flows through a fertile plain at the head of the Persian Gulf.

The climate of the interior of Persia is sufficiently distinctive to have given the name 'Iran type' to a widely distributed type of climate—the climate of interior basins at considerable elevations in warm temperate latitudes. In winter the cold is intense, the mean January temperature being but slightly above freezing-point. There are sharp frosts at night, and the temperature may even drop below zero. In summer the skies are cloudless, the air dry and clear, so that the sun's rays are exceedingly powerful. Consequently the plateau, despite its elevation, is very little cooler than the Plains of Iraq. Tehran, for example, has a July average of $85°$, and the thermometer may rise to $110°$. The scanty rainfall, which rarely, if ever, exceeds an average of 13 or 14 inches on the plateau, falls almost entirely in the winter months. But even in winter the weather is normally fine and clear, only slightly less so than in summer. The precipitation, mainly in the form of snow, is naturally greatest on the mountains, and the snow provides water for irrigation when it melts in spring. Places in the valleys even near mountains have only a very low rainfall (Tehran, 9·0 inches; Isfahan, 3·6), and on the open plains the aridity is extreme. 'The salt swamps, in which the few streams that succeed in travelling so far from the mountains lose themselves, are frozen in winter, but in summer the heat in the neighbourhood is intolerable. Very violent winds, carrying clouds of salt dust, complete the picture of irremediable desert' (Kendrew).

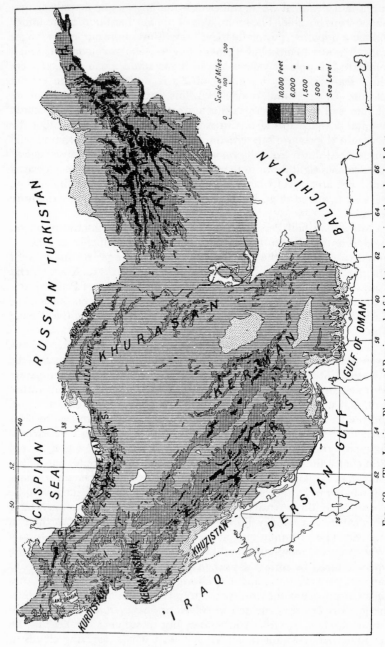

FIG. 68.—The Iranian Plateau of Persia and Afghanistan, showing the physical features

A very different state of affairs is found on the northern slopes of the Elburz, where the heavy rainfall, mainly in winter from the depressions which develop over the Caspian Sea, entirely changes the character of the climate.

Of the population of Persia probably 3,000,000 are nomadic. The nomads include Arabs, Turks, Kurds, Leks, Baluchis and Lurs. Of the settled population the vast majority are Mahommedans of the Shi'ah sect. There are important minorities of Sunni Moslems, Armenians, Jews, Nestorians and Parsis. The influence of relief on the distribution of population is very marked; the lines of towns and villages follow the trend of the mountains, their position actually being determined by the availability of water from the mountain streams. The largest towns are the capital Tehran, now exceeding 2·3 million, Tabriz (388,000 in 1964), Isfahan (340,000), Abadan–Khorramshahr (201,000), Meshed, Hamadan, Shiraz, Resht and Kermanshah (all exceeding 100,000). There is little doubt however that the population of Persia today is below what it has been in times past. The decrease, in face of a trying but healthy climate, is attributed to war and pestilence, as well as to social customs, such as early marriage. Above all, Persia needs man-power for development, and an increase in population is a prime national need. Parts are subject to disastrous earthquakes.

More than half the total area of Persia is desert and mountain 'waste', 12 per cent. forest, 6 per cent. pasture, 10 per cent. arable and 20 per cent. unused, though potentially productive. Only a third of the arable is at any one time under cultivation—about 3 per cent. of the surface. Nevertheless agriculture is, broadly speaking, the mainstay of Persian life. But with the exception of the Caspian provinces practically the whole country depends on irrigation. Hence to the traveller Persia appears as a land of small gardens or farms separated by vast tracts which, except in spring, present an aspect of unrelieved brown desolation. The system of irrigation in general use is an interesting but very expensive one. A well is sunk at the foot of the mountains until water is reached; the water is then conducted by a tunnel or canal ('qanats', or 'karez' as they are called in Baluchistan) to the area of level land to be irrigated. There is little doubt that modern irrigation works, storing the flood-waters of spring, could transform many of the tracts at present completely arid and sterile into flourishing cultivated land.[1] It is interesting to note that under Persian law any person who brings barren land under cultivation is legally the owner of it. The farming community of Persia works mainly in village-units, with the village headman supervising the work of all. A three-field system is adopted: one field being planted with wheat, rye, opium or other crops sown in autumn and harvested in summer; another field with maize, peas, rice or other crops sown in spring and harvested in autumn; the third field is left fallow.

[1] An important development is the Latian Dam, near Tehran, begun in 1964.

Wheat, barley and millets are grown throughout the country, but not oats or rye and only a little maize. Wheat is produced considerably in excess of the needs of the populace and is exported; the barley is grown mainly for horses. Rice is a very important crop in the provinces of Gilan (producing about 80 per cent. of the whole) and all along the Caspian littoral. Probably 750,000 acres are under rice; the grain enters into every meal throughout Persia, and there is still a surplus available for export, especially to Russia. Sugarcane could be grown in Persia in the same regions as the rice, and beet elsewhere, but actually Persia imports most of her sugar requirements. Beet sugar is however made in increasing quantities as a Government monopoly. Tobacco is widely cultivated along the shores of the Caspian and is of excellent quality; domestic consumption is high. The whole crop is purchased by the Government. Opium is a crop which merits special attention; for home consumption it has been cultivated since very early times but it is only within the present century that it became a staple article of export. The exports reached record levels between the wars, e.g. in 1926–7 of 96,000,000 krans, or roughly £2,000,000, but have dropped greatly since. Much used to find its way to China, though the finest was exported to London.[1] Tea is an important crop. Cotton grows in most parts of Persia up to 5,000 feet, and even before 1914 Persia supplied up to 200,000 bales to Russia. But the Persian cotton is coarse and short stapled. At present Persia imports yarn largely from India for her carpet industry, and cotton goods and yarn stand at the head of Persian imports. Whilst it is doubtful whether the plateau could grow good long-stapled cotton, Persia has excellent land suitable for American and possibly for Egyptian in the fragment of the Tigris low-land (Khuzistan) which lies within her borders. Persia has a climate well suited to fruits, both Mediterranean and tropical—including the dates of the Persian Gulf littoral. The vine grows well; wine and strong spirits are manufactured. As in India, the cultivation of indigo, henna and madder has suffered from the competition of aniline dyes.

Transport animals — horses, mules, donkeys and camels — are numerous in Persia, for they still form the chief means of transport over much of the country. The dry hill pastures are suitable for sheep and goats rather than cattle, and there is a considerable export of wool, in addition to the large quantities used in the local manufactures of cloths, carpets and shawls. There is a considerable export of hides and skins, roughly tanned at Hamadan and other centres.

Sericulture in Persia is interesting in that it was the silk industry of Persia which attracted most attention in Europe. The industry was virtually killed by disease in the latter part of the eighteenth century. The import of eggs from Turkey and Russia resulted in a revival from

[1] In 1955 the Senate adopted a Bill prohibiting the culture and production of opium throughout Persia.

1890 onwards and the production reached 1,200,000 lb. of raw silk before the First World War, which again crippled the industry. Eighty-eight per cent. was produced in Gilan, and three-quarters went to France, Italy, Russia and Turkey. Average production 1948–57 was 340,000 lb.

The Caspian fisheries are important, and before the last War much fish was exported to Russia. The produce, including sturgeon and caviare, was also exported to Europe via Russia—a procedure necessitated by the need of labelling caviare as 'genuine Russian'. The strained relations between the Soviet and Persia killed the fishing industry for a time and Russian concessions in Persian Caspian waters were terminated in 1953.

The forest wealth of timber lies mainly in the forests on the slopes of the Elburz in the provinces of Mazanderan and Gilan. The trees are mainly deciduous hardwoods. Timber also occurs in the province of Fars and in the Kurdistan section. Gum tragacanth is collected from a thorny bush which grows especially in the hill country between Kerman and Kermanshah. Gum arabic, gum ammoniac, and other gums, including that known as asafoetida (extracted from a desert plant growing in Khurasan), are also obtained, and liquorice root grows wild almost everywhere.

Geologically [1] Persia lies in the great Alpine fold belt. In the plains horizontal or slightly folded sandstones, limestones, and chalks of Tertiary and Cretaceous age predominate; the border ranges are highly folded, often over-folded, and have cores of old rocks, gneisses and granites. There is much igneous material, especially in the north-west. In the deserts the solid geology is masked by sands and other superficial deposits. Although numerous minerals are known to occur in Persia, they are scarcely touched owing to transport difficulties, and their real value is unknown. Coal and iron occur in the north-west, especially in Tehran Province, but proposals to make steel for rails were abandoned and a State-owned colliery did not prove successful. The one mineral which has been developed is oil. Surface shows had long been known, but it was only after seven years of experimental drilling by modern machinery that W. K. D'Arcy was rewarded by striking the Maidan-i-Naphtun (Maidan-i-Sulaiman) field in 1908.

The Anglo-Persian Oil Company was formed in 1909 and production began in 1913. There was a steady expansion till production was running at over 10,000,000 tons a year in the years before the opening of the Second World War. Following the declaration by the Government in 1925 that the official name of the country was to be Iran, the name of the oil company was changed to Anglo-Iranian and the oil-field from Maidan-i-Naphtun to Maidan-i-Sulaiman. The British

[1] F. G. Clapp, 'Geology of Eastern Iran', *Bull. Geol. Soc. America*, **51**, 1940, 1–101; *Geog. Rev.*, **20**, 1930, 69–85.

A.—7

Government held shares to the extent of £2,000,000 in the company—Persia had become an important source of fuel oil for the British Navy. In his book *The Economic Position of Persia* published in 1926 Moustafa Khan Fatch was able to record that 'the Persian oil industry has brought blessings on two nations, i.e. the British and the Persian'. The oil royalties furnished between 10 and 30 per cent. of the total revenue of the Persian Government; the company was spending several million pounds sterling a year in Persia, building roads, railways and well-equipped towns in a part of the country previously almost uninhabited. A pipeline 145 miles long was constructed to the great refinery on the island of Abadan. After the Second World War the output continued to expand—to 19·2 million tons in 1946; 20·2 in 1947; 24·9 in 1948; 26·8 in 1949 and 31·8 in 1950. On May 1, 1951, the Shah signed two decrees passed by parliament to nationalize the oil industry. Oil exports ceased in June; the National Iranian Oil Company took over the Anglo-Iranian properties but production almost ceased. A new government in 1954 reached agreement for a consortium of companies—American, British, Dutch and French interests —to reorganize the industry but they do not own either the oil or the installations. B.P. (British Petroleum) owns 40 per cent. of the shares. Production had climbed back to 25·9 m. tons in 1956. Outside the consortium area some promising localities, including some in the north near the Russian border, have proved disappointing, but a gusher was struck at Qum in the central plateau in 1956 and the N.I.O.C. have granted development rights to the Italian A.G.I.P. over the areas, including part of the Persian Gulf.

Persia is one of those countries to which factory industries—apart from oil—have scarcely yet penetrated. Industry remains a village industry: it is 'local, not national, and the various craftsmen transfer their knowledge to apprentices from one generation to another. These craftsmen manufacture goods for their livelihood, but many of them develop remarkable skill in handicraft, and show an intuitive love of beauty and achievement. The trade is greatly localized, because of the cheapness in the particular neighbourhood of the primary substance, and the traditional craftsmanship which generally remains in one district; in consequence every town or district can boast its speciality.'

Persian carpets are world famous; the men buy the wool and get it dyed, the women and children do the work. Even a skilled woman can work only one square foot in thirty hours; hence the high cost. The carpets have suffered from the introduction of aniline dyes; colours and patterns have become standardized. The industry has however gained from improved communications with Europe, but suffers from Indian, Turkish and Greek competition. The beautiful old silk carpets are now rarely made except to order. In the inter-war years carpets formed Persia's second export (14 per cent. of the total in 1923–4;

7 per cent. in 1941–2). In addition to carpets, woollen felts, woollen shawls and silks are made but the industries, especially the latter, have suffered extremely from the competition of imported factory-made goods. Home factory industries which have been attempted did not prove successful except for some spinning works at Tabriz. A seven-year economic development programme approved by the Majlis in 1949 was designed to change this.

Communications are first of all Persia's great need. Turning to this all-important question, there exist in Persia less than 2,000 miles of railways. A line runs from the Russian frontier from Julfa to Tabriz, 96 miles, with a branch from Sofian to Lake Urmia; it was built by

FIG. 69.—The main routes of Persia

Russia during the occupation of 1909–18. A new line from Tehran to Tabriz is well advanced. In the south-east a line was built from the Baluchistan frontier to Zahidan, 51 miles inside the Persian frontier, but is disused. Persia's great ambition had long been a main north to south line from the Gulf port of Bandar Shahpur on the inlet of Khur Musa, via Hamadan to Tehran and the Caspian at Bandar Shah. Construction was carried out by German, American, British and other firms. The section from the Caspian to Tehran was opened in 1937, and the completion in 1938, making 870 miles in all. There are branches, including a short one to Khorramshahr where the navigable Karun joins the Shatt el-'Arab, and a long one towards Meshed. Iran has actively pursued a road-making policy, and some 5,000 miles are motorable for most of the year. Sometimes the surface is poor, but not-withstanding the road conditions, the motor lorry is replacing the expensive, uncertain and slow caravan on all possible routes.[1]

It will be seen that there are four main lines of entry into Iran by land at present:

(1) From Russia to Tabriz.
(2) From Baluchistan to Zahidan.
(3) From Baghdad to railhead on the frontier and thence by regular motor service to Tehran, the capital. Through rates are quoted for passengers from Haifa to Tehran by Damascus and Baghdad.
(4) From Bandar Shahpur by rail.

Great use is made of air transport. Iranian Airways run inter-national services; at least five international airlines serve Tehran.

Persia's economic development in the near future is dependent on three main factors: transport, the improvement and extension of irrigation, and capital. In fact, capital is the prime necessity, but the fate of the Anglo-Iranian Oil Company (since renamed British Petro-leum) has shaken faith in Persian goodwill.

In the foreign trade of Persia the high place taken by sugar and tea amongst the imports should be noted, since both these commodities might be produced within the country. Cotton tissues account for a considerable proportion of the imports; Lancashire occupies first place as a supplier of bleached and prints, but India of the grey and also thread. Russia is an important supplier also. Machinery is now much in demand. Leading exports apart from oil include fruit, wool and hair, skins, raw cotton, carpets and gum tragacanth.

REFERENCES

There are numerous books of travel on Persia but few geographical works. Moustafa Khan Fatch's book quoted above is especially valuable; the informa-tion may be supplemented from the Reports published from time to time by H.M.S.O. or the Reports published by the United States Department of Commerce and Industries in the journal *Commerce Reports*. A more recent book is W. S. Haas, *Iran* (New York: Columbia University Press, 1946).

For a description of south-western Persia see C. J. Edmonds, 'Luristan', *Geog. Jour.*, **59**, 1922, 335–6 and 437–53; for the Caspian border, J. B. L. Noel, 'A Reconnaissance in the Caspian Province of Persia', *Geog. Jour.*, **57**, 1921, 401–18; and L. S. Fortescue, 'The Western Elburz and Persian Azerbaijan', *Geog. Jour.*, **63**, 1924, 301–18. See also A. Gabriel, 'Southern Lut and Iranian Baluchistan', *Geog. Jour.*, **92**, 1938, 193–210.

For a useful summary of later developments see Clarmont Skrine, 'New Trends in Iran', *Roy. Cent. Asian Jour.*, **42**, 1955, 100–15. In German there is Hans Bobek, *Iran* (Frankfurt, 1962) and in English *Iran* edited by H. H. Vreeland (New Haven, Conn., 1957).

---

[1] A caravan travels 15 to 25 miles a day.

AFGHANISTAN

JUST in the region where India's mountain rampart is weakest, it happens that the territory of Asiatic Russia approaches most closely the borders of India. In the latter half of the nineteenth century, when Imperial Russia was pushing her influence and extending her territorial rights farther and farther southwards towards the borders of India, only the territory of Afghanistan intervened to prevent the clash with the British spheres of influence. At the present time the proud, independent kingdom lies between Soviet Russia and Pakistan, and may be destined to play an important part in preserving the peace of Asia. The position of Afghanistan may be broadly indicated by saying that it is perched high up on the broad top of India's mountain wall, overlooking the rich fertile plains of India on the one hand and the important plains of Asiatic Russia on the other. The history of Afghanistan is the history of a typical buffer State; of the numerous invaders who have attacked India by land the majority have struck from the northwest by way of Afghanistan. Although Alexander the Great did not use the Khyber Pass route, he included Afghanistan in his sweeping conquests between 334 B.C. and 323 B.C.

Afghanistan has an area variously estimated at between 243,000 and 270,000 square miles, or more than twice the size of the whole of the British Isles. The boundaries of the country have been defined by a series of treaties: that between Afghanistan and India in 1893; that with Persia was demarcated in 1903–5; that with Russia dates from 1895. The treaty between Great Britain and Afghanistan signed at Kabul on November 22, 1921, marked the commencement of a new era. It closed the phase of Afghanistan as a hermit nation, entirely forbidden to foreigners unless specially bidden to carry out some work where technical knowledge was required. It recognizes the complete independence of Afghanistan, and agrees to an interchange of diplomatic representatives. The recognition of Afghanistan by Germany, France, Italy, Soviet Russia, Turkey and Persia quickly followed, and Britain now has an Embassy at Kabul.

Except for a strip of the Plain of Turkistan on the north, the whole of Afghanistan is occupied by lofty mountains and elevated plateaus. M. Raymond Furon, to whom is due the best account of the geography of the country,[1] distinguishes six physiographic regions:

(1) Afghan Turkistan, or rather Bactria, is a low plain situated between the valley of the Oxus and the mountain massif to the south. The rivers which rise in these mountains lose themselves in the sand

[1] *L'Afghanistan* (Paris: Blanchard, 1926).

before reaching the Oxus. Former irrigation works have been deserted and the tract is unhealthy and very sparsely inhabited, with Mazar-i-Sharif as the principal town.

(2) The Hindu Kush constitute a mountain complex, difficult of access, entirely barren and uninhabited. The average height of the mountains is over 15,000 feet and the peaks, which are always snow-covered, exceed 18,000 feet. The Passes of Nuksan and Khawak afford communication with Badakhshan; the Passes of Ak-Robat and Dendan-Shikan are used by the routes between Kabul and Mazar-i-Sharif.

(3) Badakhshan occupies the north-east of Afghanistan, to the east of Turkistan. It is a beautiful region, including the Little Pamirs, limited on the north by the Upper Oxus (or Amu-Darya) and completely isolated on the south by the main chain of the Hindu Kush. Except in the low-lying regions of the west the climate is healthy.

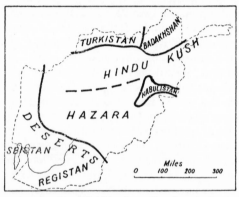

Fig. 70.—The natural regions of Afghanistan (*based on the descriptions of* Furon)

Some parts are forested, the valleys are cultivated or inhabited by shepherds with their flocks.

(4) Kabulistan is a convenient name for the series of alluvial plains which occupy the region round the capital, south of the Hindu Kush. Lying between 5,000 and 6,000 feet above sea-level, the plains are watered by the Kabul River and its tributaries, and constitute the richest and most densely populated part of Afghanistan. It is an agricultural region, surrounded by wild lofty mountains, with a healthy climate except where there are marshes.

(5) Hazara is a mountainous region occupying the whole of the centre of Afghanistan. It is comparatively well watered, but sparsely populated. Inhabited by immigrant Mongols, this region is still little known.

(6) The deserts of the south and west cover nearly a quarter of the country. The valley of the Helmand forms a green ribbon of fertile

land separating Seistan on the west from Registan on the east. These torrid sand-covered wastes are traversed with difficulty by nomadic Baluchis with their camel caravans, otherwise the regions are almost uninhabitable. Formerly the south-west was irrigated and prosperous, but drifting sand has completed the work of invading armies of the Middle Ages. It would seem that Seistan is becoming drier, for the great lakes Hamun-i-Helmand and Gaud-i-Zirreh are becoming smaller.

With the exception of water collected by the river Kabul and its tributaries, which belong to the Indus system, all the rain falling in Afghanistan drains into inland basins. The most important water-courses are the Amu-Darya (or Oxus), which for 480 miles forms the northern frontier; the Murghab, which after a course of 360 miles loses itself in the Oasis of Merv; the Hari-Rud, which waters the fertile plain of Herat before disappearing in the Oasis of Tejend. The Helmand is the longest river entirely in Afghanistan. After a course of over 600 miles across Hazara and the south-western deserts it empties into the marshy lake known as Hamun-i-Helmand, in the centre of the Seistan Basin. The upper valley of the Murghab and the Hari-Rud, as well as nearly the whole of the Helmand Valley, are in general cultivated; but most important of all are the plains of Kabul irrigated by the waters of the Kabul River. Nearly all the smaller rivers of Afghanistan are dry watercourses for three-quarters of the year.

Little is known of the mineral resources of Afghanistan.[1] Deposits of salt of Tertiary age, sufficient for the home consumption, occur in Badakhshan, Turkistan and Herat; iron ore exists in Kaffiristan, copper in the Hindu Kush, and lead in Hazara. Lapis lazuli and rubies are found in Badakhshan.

In general the climate of Afghanistan is very dry, sunny and characterized by great extremes of temperature. The higher regions, above 3,000 feet and including Kabul and Ghazni and most of Hazara, have very cold winters, when the thermometer drops below zero, and hot summers with day temperatures reaching over 100° F. Snow falls in January and February, followed by rain in March and April, the rest of the year being almost rainless. The total precipitation rarely exceeds 20 inches, 75 per cent. falling between January and April, when rain and melting snow give rise to numerous short-lived torrents. Habitations and cultivation cease at about 8,000 feet, though barley will ripen up to about 9,000 feet. The regions below 3,000 feet, which include Turkistan in the north, the area round Jelalabad in the east and the deserts of the south and west, have milder winters and very hot summers. For three months the day temperature is liable to exceed 110°. The rainfall, which comes in winter, does not normally exceed 2 or

---

[1] The best summary of the geology is given by Trinkler, with a geological map. See note on p. 184.

3 inches, and cultivation is limited to oases and the larger river valleys, where dates, pomegranates and sugarcane are the leading crops.

The population of Afghanistan is estimated to be about 12,000,000, mostly Sunni Moslems. There are five main racial stocks:

The *Pathans* are a white race calling themselves 'Beni Israel', since they claim descent from the ten lost tribes of Israel who were taken into captivity by Nebuchadnezzar. They occupy the tract along the Indian frontier, and are divided into numerous tribes, such as Waziris, Afridis and Mangals, notorious for their turbulence.

The *Hazaras*, who occupy the heart of the country, are Mongols with yellow skin and sparse beards, and are relics of the invasion of Ghengis Khan. They are peaceful, courageous agriculturists and

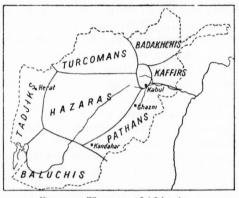

FIG. 71.—The races of Afghanistan

pastoralists. The ranks of servants and labourers throughout the country are largely recruited from the Hazaras.

The *Turcomans*, of Turkish origin, inhabit Turkistan. Many of them are camel drivers and vendors of horses.

The *Tadjiks*, of Persian origin, occupy the west of the country, including Herat.

The *Kaffirs* inhabit the mountains north-east of Kabul, and are a pale-skinned, blond-haired race only recently converted to Islam.

In addition to these five races, nomadic Baluchis wander over the southern deserts, and Badakchis occupy the north-east. The population in the Kabul Plains is very mixed, and now includes several thousand Indian traders. Nearly all Afghans, except Pathans, speak Persian in addition to their own language. The population of Afghanistan, apart from the nomadic groups, is concentrated in the valleys, where the alluvial stretches are sufficiently large and well enough watered for the cultivation of the staple crops—wheat and barley at higher levels, those noted above at lower. Isolated houses or farms are rare; they are grouped together in high-walled villages for safety. Few of the valleys are rich enough to support a town of any size, the principal exceptions being Kabul (400,000), Ghazni (15,000), Kandahar (115,000), Mazar-i-Sharif (42,000) and Herat. This last, situated in a fertile plain, with formerly over 100,000 inhabitants, has been several times ravaged by invaders and fell into decay, but has recovered to have 62,000 people. These figures are 1964 estimates.

The history of Afghanistan is pre-eminently the history of a typical buffer State. Dominated by Persia under Cyrus in the fifth century before Christ and afterwards by Alexander the Great, in the two thousand years which followed Afghanistan at various times formed part of the domains of the Chinese, Huns, Turks, Mongols and Persians, as well as being warred against by other nations, such as Russia in the nineteenth century. The modern period may be said to begin with the Anglo-Afghan War of 1879. In September of that year an English mission was assassinated and a month later an English army occupied Kabul. The throne was given to Abdour Ahman Khan, who reigned until 1901, occupying his life in consolidating his kingdom and pacifying it. He was certainly a great king, and he may be said to have founded the unity of Afghanistan. Twice attacked by Russia, some territory on the north was lost to that nation during his reign. From 1901 to 1919 his son Habib Ullah Khan held the throne. Though Afghanistan remained a hermit kingdom, foreigners were introduced from time to time to carry out the construction of certain works. During the First World War, despite the overtures of Germany and the action of Turkey, then a great Mahommedan nation, Afghanistan remained neutral and loyal to her promises to Great Britain. The accession of Aman Ullah Khan in 1919 was followed by a temporary rupture with Great Britain before the new era, already mentioned, was inaugurated. Until 1922 an absolute monarchy, Afghanistan is now a constitutional monarchy with Legislative and State Assemblies, and a Cabinet presided over by the King himself. The title of King was adopted by the Amir in 1926. Free primary and secondary education has been arranged, and the University of Kabul was established in 1932. There is a small standing army, but the King can call upon large numbers of well-armed tribesmen in time of war.

So rapid are the changes now taking place in Afghanistan that it is difficult to write a general account of the people which shall be generally applicable. The attempts of King Aman Ullah Khan to westernize his people in face of hostility resulted in his deposition, followed by the assassination of his successor (1933). The present King Mohammed Zahir Shah has held the reins firmly since: perhaps it is true to say that westernization has proceeded more gradually. Certainly in the time of Aman Ullah Khan one immediate result was a country suffering from severe indigestion. The words of M. Furon, penned in 1926, remain largely true today: 'On trouve actuellement un pays en retard, où se heurtent deux civilizations l'orientale et l'occidentale; pas encore de routes et déjà des camions de sept tonnes, des avions et pas de techniciens, un Emir aux ideés très modernes gouvernant une population indifférente ou rétive, un grand nombre d'étrangers attirés brusquement dans un pays totalement interdite il y a cinq ans.'

The national dress of the Afghan men comprises baggy trousers, a loose shirt worn outside, a vest, a girdle and shoes with turned-up toes. The usual head-dress is a turban, white or black, but a low fez cap is worn in the towns. Many of the older men wear a full beard—especially the mullahs or priests—which is not infrequently dyed red with henna. No good Mahommedan completely shaves the upper lip and a small moustache is left by all. Indoors, the Afghan women wear loose trousers, a mantle with long sleeves, stockings and sandals, whilst a veil covers the hair. When going out a sack-like garment—white or black or blue—is thrown over the head and reaches to the ankles. A small lace-covered window enables the wearer to see but not to be seen. In the country the women are often unveiled, and in Kabul European fashions are beginning to appear. The Afghans, like all Mahommedans, are permitted more than one wife, but the privilege is only exercised by the rich. Afghan houses exhibit to a remarkable degree the influence of geographical and social factors. As in most dry countries each man's house is his water-butt, and on the flat roof the precious rainfall is collected. Of recent years the ubiquitous corrugated iron has appeared and penthouse roofs are increasing in number. Mud and crude bricks are the building materials. The influence of religion is seen in the separation of each house into the men's quarters and the women's quarters, often on opposite sides of a small central court; and in the absence of windows except those opening out on the court. In the poorer houses—that is, in the majority—the men's and women's quarters are each reduced to a single room. Except for a prayer rug, of furniture there is none except in the houses of the rich, who sleep on a low table over a charcoal stove in winter.

The food of the Afghans consists of thin, flat cakes of wheat and barley; fruit; some rice amongst the rich, and occasionally well-cooked meat (beef or mutton). Over-indulgence in fruit results in various diseases. Alcoholic liquors are strictly forbidden and water is the usual drink, though green tea is widely used.

The flocks of sheep constitute the principal wealth of Afghanistan. The nomads drive their sheep from pasture to pasture, moving northwards into the mountains with the approach of summer. The fat-tailed sheep is a native of Afghanistan, and is characterized by the immense weight and size of its tail, caused by a development of masses of fat, forming stores of nourishment which are drawn upon in winter or when fodder is scarce. These sheep furnish the principal animal foodstuffs, the grease of the tail being used as a substitute for butter. The wool and skins provide material for the native clothing, and also furnish one of the chief exports. The manufacture of 'postins', or sheepskin-coats, is an important industry.

Mention has already been made of the concentration of agriculture

FIG. 72.—The routes of Afghanistan

The plain lines are motor roads or roads on which wheeled traffic is possible; the lightly dotted lines are mountain tracks. Passes across the Hindu Kush: **1** = Dendan-Shikan; **2** = Ak-Robat; **3** = Nuksan; **4** = Khawak. It will be noticed that railways approach the frontiers of Afghanistan in three points— one from Russian Turkistan, one from Baluchistan, one from Pakistan via Peshawar.

in the irrigated valleys. Irrigation is by means of wells, small streams and 'karez'. Two harvests are usual: wheat, barley and some peas form a winter crop grown in autumn and reaped in early summer; millet, maize and sometimes rice are summer crops. In the rich plains of Kabul a great variety of fruit is grown. In the lower regions (below 2,000 feet) one meets such characteristic Mediterranean fruits as oranges, figs and grenadines, as well as date-palms and sugarcane.

In Kabul are several State-owned factories for the manufacture of cloth, soap, arms and boots, especially for the army. Recent developments include a hydroelectric plant at Sarobi on the Kabul River, cotton mills with modern machinery at Pul-i-Khumri and Gul Behar, wool and sugar factories. Native arts and crafts are not very noteworthy.

The camel and the ass, to a less extent the pack-horse and ox, are the normal means for the transport of goods. A feature of the country is the walled caravanserai, found at intervals along the main routes, with a guardian who provides food for man and beast. Bullock-carts and motors can use certain roads, at least in summer—Peshawar to Kabul; Kabul to Ghazni, Kandahar and Herat, and Kabul to Bamian.

The foreign trade of Afghanistan is almost entirely with India via

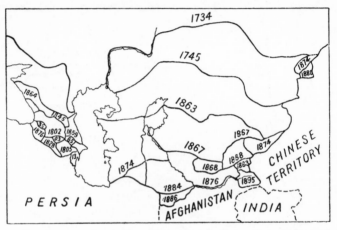

FIG. 73.—Russian expansion in the eighteenth and nineteenth centuries against the northern frontier of Afghanistan

Peshawar and with Russian Turkistan. No statistics exist of the total trade. Imports include cotton goods, dyes, hardware and various small manufactured goods, motor-cars and sewing-machines, tea, sugar, paper and cement. Persian lamb skins (Karakulis) are one of the chief exports; other skins, wool, fruits, spices, cotton and carpets are sent to Pakistan and India whilst considerable quantities of raw cotton are believed to go to U.S.S.R.

In addition to the works already quoted, an interesting and well-illustrated account of Afghanistan is given by Emil Trinkler: *Quer durch Afghanistan nach Indien* (Berlin: 1925). This has been translated into English by B. K. Featherstone: *Through the Heart of Afghanistan* (London: Faber & Gwyer, 1928). Dr. Trinkler has also given his scientific observations in an excellent summary of the geography of the country in *Afghanistan: eine Landeskundliche Studie, Ergänzungsheft nr*

196 zu Petermanns Mitteilungen, 1928. The latter work has a good bibliography; it is quite different in treatment from M. Furon's book, to which it is complementary. More modern are J. Ahmad and M. A. Aziz, *Afghanistan: a brief survey* (London: Longmans, 1936) and W. K. Fraser-Tytler, *Afghanistan* (London and New York, 1950).

A summary of the geography has been given by E. Reiner and Alice Taylor, 'Afghanistan', *Focus*, **15**, 5, 1965.

There is a certain amount of feeling in Afghanistan that the parts of the old North-West Frontier Province of India, now in Pakistan, inhabited by Pathans and allied peoples should be united with Afghanistan or to form a state to which the name Pakhtunistan is being applied.

THE INDO-PAKISTAN SUB-CONTINENT [1]

Introduction. There is perhaps no part of the world better marked off by nature as a region or a 'realm' by itself than the Indian sub-continent, now comprising the Republic of India and the Islamic Republic of Pakistan, two independent countries within the general framework of the British Commonwealth of Nations. Although there is great diversity within the sub-continent—from scorching deserts to steaming evergreen forests and from seemingly endless plains to the loftiest mountain chains in the world—the features which divide it as a whole from surrounding regions are too clear to be overlooked. On the north it is bounded by the great mountain wall of the Himalayas; on the west it is bounded by mountains and deserts; on the east by a whole series of lofty forested mountains separated by deep valleys. Elsewhere the boundary is the sea.

Within the mountains is a vast plain varying from about 150 to 300 miles in width which sweeps in a great arc from the delta of the Indus in the west to that of the Ganges and Brahmaputra in the east. The peninsular portion to the south of these plains is made up of a series of tablelands of varying elevation, crossed in places by mountain ridges and with coastal plains narrow on the western side but broader on the east.

The dense population rightly associated with Indo-Pakistan is for the most part concentrated on the plains: factors of relief, climate and soil have limited population densities on mountain and plateau.

It will be convenient first to consider the sub-continent as a whole. Strictly speaking the whole has never been under one ruler or formed a single political unit. The nearest approach to such unity was from 1858 to 1947 under the British Indian Empire. Though the fundamental division into 'India' and 'Pakistan' dates only from the partition of 1947 its roots lie deep in the past and call for a very brief reference to the history of the sub-continent.

Historical Outline. Little is known of the aboriginal inhabitants of India though pre-historians are gradually piecing together the story of early cultures of the peoples commonly grouped as pre-Dravidian. The generally accepted view is that India was later invaded by the Dravidians—dark-skinned, broad-headed peoples with broad, flat noses in some respects recalling the negro type. As the Dravidians spread they drove the pre-Dravidians to the hills and the dense forests where some tribes may represent their present-day descendants. After

[1] I am greatly indebted to my good friend Professor George Kuriyan for going through with me the sections on India and Pakistan.

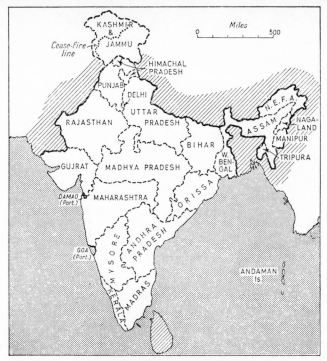

The States of the Indian Union.

On November 1, 1956 the reorganization of Indian States as shown in the above map came into being. In 1960 Bombay was divided into Gujrat and Maharashtra and Nagaland was created.

This map should be compared with Figs. 74 and 75 which show the pre-Partition provinces and princely states and also the position in 1953 after the smaller princely states had been absorbed. The above map should also be compared with Fig. 108 and it then becomes clear that the new division is primarily on a linguistic basis.

State	Capital	Language
Punjab	Chandigarh	Punjabi
Uttar Pradesh	Lucknow	Hindi
Bihar	Patna	Hindi
West Bengal	Calcutta	Bengali
Assam	Shillong	Assamese
Orissa	Cuttack	Oriya
Madhya Pradesh	Bhopal	Hindi
Rajasthan	Jaipur	Rajasthani
Gujrat	Ahmadabad	Gujarati
Maharashtra	Bombay	Marathi
Mysore	Bangalore	Kanarese
Andhra Pradesh	Hyderabad	Telugu
Madras	Madras	Tamil
Kerala	Trivandrum	Malayalam
Jammu and Kashmir	Srinagar	Kashmiri

Territories (centrally administered):

Delhi	Delhi
Himachal Pradesh .	. Simla
Sikkim (Protectorate).	. Gangtok
Manipur	Imphal
Tripura	Agartala
Andaman and Nicobar Is. .	Port Blair
Laccadive Islands	

The map also shows part of Assam is administered under special conditions as the North East Frontier Agency (NEFA). The Nagas who live in the tangle of hills on the Assam–Burma border agitated for a separate recognition, and so Nagaland was created in 1960 as a State of the Union though the population is only 400,000.

In 1965–6 agreement was reached that a separate Sikh state should be carved out of the Punjab but difficulties arose over the capital, Chandiganh.

Note on spelling of Place Names. Many place names in India, as well as names of natural features, have long been known by their conventional English spellings, often established when the transliteration of the vernacular was little understood. Since independence India has adopted an official spelling in English and in some cases has resuscitated old names. Thus Ganges is now Ganga, Jumna is Jamuna, Cawnpore is Kanpur and so on. Some changes are difficult for foreigners such as Tiruchchirappalli (Trichinopoly).

the Dravidians India was invaded again and again by successive waves of people, usually from the north-west.

The first great invasion or, better, mass-migration was that of the Aryans from across the Hindu Kush: peoples of the great Indo-European group speaking Sanskrit, a language allied to Persian and to many of the languages of Europe. The oldest Sanskrit books date from about 1500 B.C. and in the *Vedas* and *Upanishads* may be found the tenets of the Aryan religion, whilst in the *Code of Manu* is a picture of the ideal society. It was the Aryans who introduced the caste system as defining the position of the conquerors (already divided into Brahmins or priesthood and the Kshatriyas or warriors) to the conquered Mongols and Dravidians. Brahmanism established itself firmly till the sixth century B.C. when Gautama, a prince of the soldier caste, founded Buddhism, taking to himself the title of 'Buddha' or the enlightened. Buddhism is in the main a strict ethical code which represents a revolt against the caste system and Brahmanism. The rise of Buddhism is associated with the Ganges Valley—it was at Buddh Gaya in Bihar State that the Buddha received his enlightenment and after his death about 487 B.C. the religion spread steadily. It was widespread throughout India from about 250 B.C. to A.D. 350 but was destined to be virtually extinguished by the revival of Brahmanism or Hinduism, though it survives in strength in Ceylon, Tibet, south-east Asia and farther east.

Parts of northern India came within the Greek conquests of Alexander the Great, but Greek influence was swept away by the Scythians who poured in many waves over northern India between about 165 B.C. and A.D. 300. A long period of confused history followed till the first Moslem conquests. Moslem Arabs conquered Persia about the middle of the seventh century and made incursions into India but not till A.D. 999 did the Mahmud of Ghazni invade the country in earnest and initiate 500 years of Moslem Afghan rule in northern India. Afghan advance was gradual, Delhi not being taken till 1286 and the Deccan invaded in 1294.

Then came the invasions and conquests of the Moslem Mongolians or Moguls from central Asia. Although incursions started in 1219 it was not till the vast army under Tamerlane burst into India, sacked Delhi in 1398 and laid waste much of northern India that the foundations of Mogul power in India were established. It was not in fact until Babar in 1526 overthrew the last of the Afghan kings that the great Mogul Empire in India was established. Babar's grandson, Akbar the Great (1556–1605), extended the empire over the whole of northern India and south to the Narbada and absorbed parts of the Deccan. He was an enlightened man, tolerant in religion, who surrounded himself with just and able administrators. His son, Jahangir (1605–27), in 1616 received Sir Thomas Roe as Ambassador of James I and the rise of the Mogul power to its zenith in the inland heart of India was paralleled by the increase of European influence on the coasts (see above, p. 63). Under Shah Jahan (1627–58) the Mogul power reached its zenith. Of all the Mogul monuments none exceeds in beauty and magnificence the tomb which Shah Jahan built in honour of his wife—the Taj Mahal at Agra. Aurangzeb (1658–1707) extended the bounds of empire south to the Cauvery, but his intolerance was responsible for the cracking of the whole empire. The Moslem-Mogul Empire has given to the northern half of India its greatest monuments. Akbar's great capitals at Agra and the incredible palace-city of Fatehpur Sikri (abandoned after a few years because of difficulties in water supply: the elephants used to draw water from deep wells are said to have drunk more in their efforts than they supplied to the palaces!) are two outstanding examples. But it was an alien culture spread over the homeland of Hinduism: it is not difficult to see the origin of the partition of 1947 into Moslem Pakistan and Hindu India.

In the Western Ghats of Poona a minor Hindu nobleman was destined to found another empire. He was Sivaji who before his death in 1680 had conquered fortress after fortress in the wild Ghats country and established the Maratha power. It was a Hindu revival, at first almost missionary in character, which swept over India, now disrupted by Moslem warlords, reaching and conquering Delhi in 1719. But the Marathas suffered a severe defeat in 1761 and the struggle between Moslems and Marathas was the opportunity of the rise to power of the Sikhs. The Sikhs were a Hindu sect, believing in one God and fired by a great mission to reform Hinduism. Under Ranjit Singh (1780–1839) they came to dominate the Punjab from their sacred capital of Amritsar.

This glimpse of a divided India is needed to understand the expansion of European influence which falls into several periodst From the visit of Vasco da Gama to Calicut in 1498 to the establishment of the British East India Company in 1600 was a period of Portuguese monopoly. From 1600 onwards Dutch, French, British and other European powers struggled for supremacy for a century and a half— some account of which has been given above, pp. 62–5. In the mid-eighteenth century the British and French clashed in India—at first to the advantage of the French. Had it not been for Clive's victories over the French there might well have been French domination over the whole of India. The tragic incident of the Black Hole of Calcutta (1756) which resulted in Clive taking up the sword against the Nawab of Bengal and the victory at Plassey (1757) really began the great expansion of the East India Company as a territorial power. That phase lasted exactly a century—till the mutiny of 1857 and the establishment of the British Indian Empire under the British Crown in 1858.

The office of Governor-General had been created in 1774 and

successive Governors-General pursued the general policy of establishing peace, law and order. Wherever possible treaties guaranteeing these conditions of life for the people under their own accepted rulers were entered into—as with Nepal in 1616. Where, as in the fragmented Maratha State, warring bands disrupted normal life annexation of territory and its direct control by British administrators was the policy followed. Misrule came under the same heading.

So there grew up that separation of 'British India', divided into provinces of varying size and importance, and 'Indian India', or the Princes' India of 'Native States', varying from a few square miles to a vast territory of the size of Hyderabad. At the time of partition in 1947 British India covered 865,000 square miles with 296,000,000 people in 1941, Indian India 715,000 square miles with 93,000,000 people.

The consolidation of India under the British Crown proceeded steadily from 1858 onwards. There were wars on the north-west frontier and in Burma but the Indian sub-continent as a whole enjoyed peace perhaps for the first time in history. Population increased by leaps and bounds and rendered more intense the incidence of famines and epidemics. Attention was directed to irrigation and to the amelioration of rural conditions. The minutely detailed work which was carried out by the British administrators such as Settlement Officers is often not appreciated at the present day, but it is probably true to say that they knew more intimately every inch of ground under their control than was the case in any country in the world. 'Honoured Sir, you are my father and my mother' was not an empty form of address often received by a District Officer, it expressed a happy relationship, widespread but not universal, which persisted for decades.

But the rise of nationalism was natural and inevitable. Curiously enough it was the partition of Bengal in 1905, splitting a compact linguistic group, which really led to the first serious unrest. Queen Victoria had been proclaimed Empress of India in 1878: in 1911 at the great Coronation Durbar of King George V the King-Emperor announced great changes including the transfer of the capital from Calcutta to Delhi; the reconstitution of Bengal and the setting up of a new Province of Bihar and Orissa. The outbreak of World War I was the signal for a remarkable and spontaneous outburst of loyalty and devotion to the King-Emperor on the part of the princes and peoples throughout India, but Indians who served abroad brought back ideas of self-government. Thenceforward the country moved steadily towards self-government, not always at the pace demanded by some. Both Britain and India owe much to the influence of Mahatma Gandhi and his advocacy of peaceful means to attain India's aims. The story is a long and complex one but there can be no doubt that the handing over of power as a voluntary act by the British Government, backed by the goodwill of the British people, came at the right time. Whilst many who had served India in the past would have been happier to have seen a united India, the reasons behind the partition of 1947, as we have already seen, are deep-seated. On August 15, 1947, the Dominions of India and Pakistan came into existence. On January 26, 1950, the Indian Union (Bharat) declared itself a Republic within the British Commonwealth and in March 1956 the Dominion of Pakistan became the Islamic Republic of Pakistan, also within the British Commonwealth.

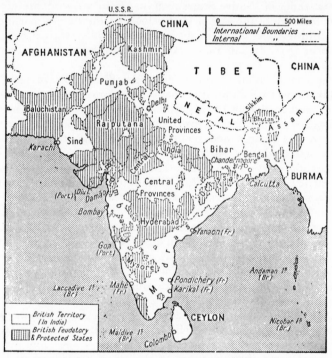

FIG. 74.—India before Partition in 1947

Future historians will surely name the first Prime Minister of India, Pandit Jawaharlal Nehru, as one of the great statesmen of all time. Imprisoned for sedition on more than one occasion under the later years of the British Raj, only a really great man would have named an Englishman, Lord Mountbatten, as the first Governor-General of a free India. The territorial reorganization of the Republic of India will be described below: in general terms the old provinces of British India were retained as units known as States. The smaller princely states of Indian India were first united into groups whilst the larger were made separate 'states'. In all cases the princes were granted pensions and the old distinction between British India and Indian India thus disappeared. In November 1956 came the great reorganization, largely on a linguistic basis, of the states shown in the map facing p. 188. Persuasion rather than coercion has been the general rule but mass migrations of Moslems from India and Hindus from Pakistan were not accomplished without much hardship and some bloodshed. The major unresolved problem has remained the State of Jammu and Kashmir, with a strong Moslem majority but a Hindu upper class and a country where rise the rivers whose water is the life-blood of Punjab's irrigation colonies.

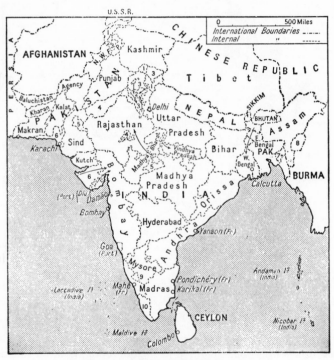

FIG. 75.—India and Pakistan in 1953

India: **1** = Himachal Pradesh; **2** = Patiala and East Punjab States Union (PEPSU); **3** = East Punjab; **4** = Ajmer; **5** = Bhopal; **6** = Saurashtra; **7** = Tripura; **8** = Manipur; **9** = Coorg; **10** = Travancore-Cochin.

Pakistan: **1** = Chitral; **2** = Dir; **3** = Swat; **4** = Bahawalpur; **5** = Khairpur; **6** = Las Bela.

Note. The places marked (Fr) are the *former* French possessions; Chandernagore (north of Calcutta) is not shown.

Pakistan has many problems to overcome and the establishment of the country has called for the exercise of statesmanship of a high order. There is first the division of the country into two parts separated by a thousand miles of Indian territory. Secondly there is a natural jealousy between the larger but less populous western part where the capital

Karachi (now superseded by Islamabad) was established and the smaller but more populous eastern part with a solid Bengali-speaking population racially and linguistically very different from the west.

In the pages which follow we shall first deal with the Indo-Pakistan sub-continent as a whole and its economic development up to the time of partition. Then follow separate treatments of the Republic of India and the Islamic Republic of Pakistan, assessing their resources and present economic development and considering the States and natural regions which they comprise.

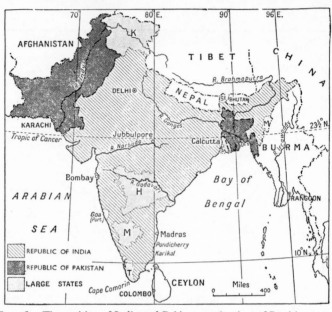

FIG. 76.—The position of India and Pakistan at the time of Partition, 1947

K = Kashmir; M = Manipur; M (South India) = Mysore; H = Hyderabad; T = Travancore.

For convenience and brevity in this section we shall use the word 'India' unless otherwise qualified to include both India and Pakistan.

India lies entirely to the north of the Equator. The southernmost point of the mainland, Cape Comorin, is in 8° N., the northern frontier reaches 36° N. Thus the Tropic of Cancer passes through the heart of India, so that roughly half of India lies outside the Tropics, in the Temperate Zone. It is perhaps but rarely that one realizes the whole of the Indus Plains and practically the whole of the Ganges Plains lie outside the Tropics. We always think of India as essentially a tropical country. And rightly so, for the whole area within the mountain wall must be considered as a unit; with a single major type of climate throughout, that of the tropical monsoon.

In longitude, India stretches from 61° E. to 97° E., with a central meridian of 80° E. passing almost through Jubbulpore and Madras and 90° E. through the Ganges Delta. India is 2,000 miles from north to south, 2,200 miles from west to east and has 4,000 miles of land frontier; 3,000 miles of sea frontier. The Republic of India takes its time (Standard or Railway time) from the meridian of 82° 30′, which is 5½ hours ahead of Greenwich time. East Pakistan takes its time from Dacca (6 hours); West Pakistan from Karachi (4½ hours).

There are two parts of India which lie outside the mountain barrier —the unimportant dry plateau of Baluchistan and the cold plateau of northern Kashmir (part of the plateau of Tibet). Burma, until 1937 an Indian province, is cut off from India by a mountain wall; in most ways Burma is not only distinct from India, but offers great contrasts. Two areas lying within the mountain barrier do not form part of India—the independent State of Nepal and the island of Ceylon.

Physical Features. It is scarcely necessary to repeat that India is divisible into three main parts:

1. A great mountain wall.
2. A great lowland plain, the Plain of Hindustan, through which flow the Indus, Ganges, Brahmaputra and their tributaries. It is now more often called the Plain of Northern India or the Indo-Gangetic Plain.
3. A great plateau, the Plateau of Peninsular India, using that term for the moment to embrace the whole of India south of the northern plains.

A fourth division may be added for the coastal strips which lie to the east and west of the peninsula.

The Mountain Wall. From the Pamir Knot in the extreme north-west the great chain of the Himalayas swings in an unbroken smooth curve south-eastwards for 1,500 miles. At first, in Kashmir, the chain is complex and it is possible to separate at least three main ranges— the Inner Himalayas, or Zanskar Range; the Middle Himalayas, or Pangi Range; and the Outer Himalayas, or Pir-Panjal Range. At the same time it is scarcely possible to regard as separate the great Muztagh or Karakoram Range which flanks the Himalayas on the north in Kashmir. Eastwards the Himalayan Chain becomes simpler and a twofold division into the Main or Inner Himalayas and the Outer Himalayas is sufficient. The main Himalayan Range includes Mount Everest [1] (29,028 feet), first climbed by the British expedition of 1953

---

[1] The attempts to 'conquer' Mount Everest have been recounted by many writers; see *inter alia* Sir Francis Younghusband, *The Epic of Mount Everest* (London: Arnold, 1926); H. Ruttledge, 'The Mount Everest Expedition, 1933', *Geog. Jour.*, **83**, 1934, 1–17; P. F. M. Fellowes and others, *First over Everest* (London: John Lane, 1933); H. Ruttledge, 'Everest', 1937; see also *Geog. Jour.*, **93**, 1939; Sir John Hunt, *The Conquest of Everest* (London, 1953). On the exact height see *Geog. Jour.*, **121**, 1955, 21–6.

after many previous attempts; Kinchinjunga (27,815 feet), first climbed by another British expedition in 1955, forms a spur from the main range. Makalu (27,790) and Dhaulagiri (26,795) are other giants. Mount K2 or Godwin-Austen (28,250) lies, not in the Himalayas, but in the Karakoram Range of Kashmir. It was conquered by an Italian expedition in 1954.

For some distance westwards from the Pamirs, the Hindu Kush forms the boundary between India and north-eastern Afghanistan; then follows the tangle of hills on the north-west frontier which merge into the Sulaiman Range between the Punjab and northern Baluchis-

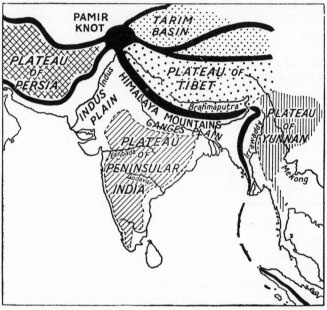

FIG. 77.—A simple physical map of India, showing the threefold division into the mountain wall, remarkably complete, the great plain, and the plateau

tan. A re-entrant in the wall, at the head of which lies the Bolan Pass, separates the Sulaiman Range and the Bugti Hills from the Kirthar Range, which lies between Sind and southern Baluchistan.

The mountains between India and Burma, though forming a continuous curve from north-eastern Assam to Cape Negrais, have received various names. In the north the comparatively simple and narrow divide is known as the Patkai or Patkoi Hills; then it broadens out into the Naga Hills and the Manipur Plateau, sending a broad branch westwards into Assam. This branch starts as the Barail Range, separated by a col from the Jaintia, Khasi and Garo Hills. Southwards from

Manipur are the Lushai Hills and Chin Hills, and then again a narrower wall known as the Arakan Yoma.

Geologists are not yet satisfied as to the structural relations between the Himalayas at their eastern end and the tangle of mountains which lie to the north-east of Assam and Burma. It is not clear whether the main folds continue eastwards as the Ta-shuch-shan or swing round into the Patkai-Arakan folds.

Emphasis must be laid on the completeness of India's mountain rampart, and hence the importance which attaches to the few possible passes.[1] Undoubtedly the weakest region is in the north-west, on the

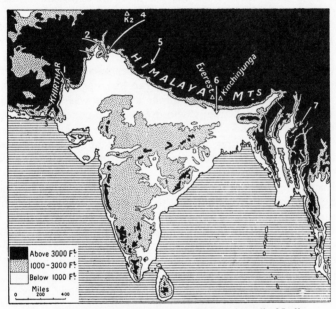

FIG. 78.—The chief routes across the mountain wall of India
The numbers refer to the explanation in the text.

Afghan frontier, and it is from this direction that India has been in; vaded again and again. Since—or even before—the days when Alexander the Great used this door into India, it has been a source of danger and remains so even to the present day. Here lies the most famous of all passes—the Khyber Pass—though Alexander did not himself use this route.

It may be useful at this stage to survey briefly the more important of the land routes into India, the approximate positions of which are indicated in Fig. 78. The chief routes in the north-west are the Bolan

[1] Kenneth Mason, 'The Himalaya as a Barrier to Modern Communications'' *Geog. Jour.*, **87,** 1936, 1–16.

Pass (1), the Khyber Pass (2), and the Gomal Pass (arrow only); whilst another route lies along the Makran coast (3). Ancient and medieval traders were accustomed to use routes corresponding closely to the Bolan Pass route from Kalat to Gandava and to the coast route via Sonmiani. Alexander arrived by a route rather north of the Khyber Pass and returned by the Bolan Pass. On the north the usual route into Kashmir is from Rawalpindi and Murree to Srinagar. From Srinagar there is a military road to Gilgit and through Hunza, whilst Tibet is reached from Srinagar across the Zoji-La to Leh and thence across the Karakoram Pass (4). From the Punjab to Tibet is the Shipki Pass (5). Thence for hundreds of miles there is no route across the Himalayas till Darjeeling (6) is reached.

From India to Burma there are half a dozen routes, none of them much used. The Hukawng Valley route, and the Tuzu Gap route a little to the south, lie in the north of Burma. A military road (the Stillwell Road) was constructed from Upper Assam into the Hukawng Valley during the Second World War but has fallen into disuse. An easier route is through Manipur and this was the main route followed by the Allied troops who drove the Japanese out of Burma in 1945. The An and Taungup Passes merely link central Burma and Arakan. These four routes are shown but not numbered on Fig. 78. The chief route from China to Burma is the Taping Valley route (7).

The Plain of Northern India. Inside the mountain wall, and forming a great curve from the Arabian Sea to the Bay of Bengal, is one of the most important plains in the world. It is more than 2,000 miles from end to end, and usually from 150 to 300 miles broad. There are several outstanding features of this amazing area. One is the dead flatness of the plain—not a hill, scarcely a mound to break the monotony of the level surface.[1] So gentle is the seaward slope that it is imperceptible to the eye. Nearly a thousand miles from its mouth, the Ganges is only 900 feet above sea-level. Another feature is the sudden rise of the Himalayas from the level plain. True, there are foothills, such as the Siwaliks, in places, but they occupy, if present at all, a zone which is inconspicuous in its width. The explanation of this is believed to be in the truth of the supposition that the stable ancient massif of the plateau underlies the plain and that the Himalayas were folded against the edge of it. The third feature of note is the immense thickness, enormous width and uniform character of the alluvium which forms the subsoil of the plain. A distinction is made between the 'older alluvium', in which certain salts have been segregated by circulating waters and form hard calcareous nodules (kankar), and the 'newer alluvium', in

---

[1] Note, however, that the sluggish rivers tend to silt up and raise their beds; when they overflow they deposit their silt near their main courses, building up low ridges higher than the intervening land.

which such concretions are absent. But otherwise the uniformity is amazing. Not a rock, not even a pebble is present, to alter the uniform character of the alluvium. Geologists are agreed that the present rivers —the Indus, Ganges, Brahmaputra and tributaries—vast as they are, could not have been responsible for this huge spread of deposit. Even a condition when the Brahmaputra joined the Ganges to flow *up* the Ganges Valley to join the Indus (forming one gigantic river, the Indo-brahm) seems almost inadequate.

The Plateau. Nearly the whole of India south of the great plain is occupied by a plateau which may be referred to, broadly, as the Plateau of Peninsular India. Between latitudes 21° and 24° N., a very

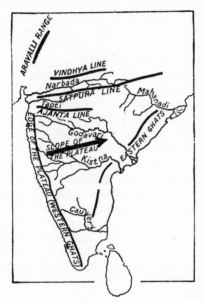

Fig. 79.—The essential features in the physical geography of the Indian plateau

important line of mountains runs across the plateau, roughly from west to east. This line is usually called the Satpura Line, from the name of the range which constitutes its western portion. Thence it passes into the Mahadeo Hills and Maikal Range of the 'Central Highlands', and then into the heights of the Chota Nagpur Plateau. The line is doubly reinforced in the west by the Vindhya Range on the north and the Ajanta Range on the south, and the whole has played a very important part in Indian history. It acted as a barrier against the spread of the Aryans, and it is to the south of this line that we find the Dravidian peoples and the Dravidian languages. The Satpura Line, therefore, is generally considered to mark the division between northern India on the one hand and Peninsular India or the Deccan Plateau, on the other. There is really no name which can safely be applied, without risk of misinterpretation, to the whole of India south of the plain, though geologically and in some respects geomorphologically it constitutes a single unit.

The plateau is highest in the south and west and slopes, on the whole, eastwards. Large parts of the south of the plateau, in Mysore, exceed 2,000 feet and even 3,000 feet above sea-level. The western edge of the plateau forms the Western Ghats, also known as the Sahyadri Mountains, the eastern edge (much more broken than the western) the Eastern Ghats. The crest of the Western Ghats usually exceeds 3,000 feet, the Eastern Ghats only do so in some areas. The Eastern and Western Ghats meet in the south of Mysore, and there, separated from them by a deep valley, is the small but lofty plateau of the Nilgiri Hills. Farther south, and separated from the Nilgiris by the Palghat Gap, the Cardamom Hills form the divide between the east and west coasts and terminate in Cape Comorin.

Running from south-west to north-east through Rajputana, in the north-west of the plateau, are the Aravalli Hills.

The surface of the plateau has been deeply dissected by river erosion. In the north-west, the Tapti occupies the trough between the Ajanta and Satpura Ranges; the Narbada the trough between the Satpura and Vindhya Ranges, and both rivers empty into the Arabian Sea. North of the Vindhya Range the drainage is almost entirely to the Ganges. South of the Ajanta Range and Central Highlands the general easterly slope of the plateau is reflected in the direction of the rivers. The main water-parting is formed by the Western Ghats. The Godavari, Kistna and Cauvery, with many of their tributaries, rise on the slopes of the Western Ghats, the Mahanadi has a more restricted course in the north-east of the plateau, but all find their way to the east coast. In general the course through the Eastern Ghats is marked by a stretch of rapids.

The plateau of Peninsular India is flanked by a narrow coastal strip on the west and a broader coastal area—not necessarily a plain—on the east. Details of these areas will be given later under the descriptions of the natural regions of India.

The Rivers of India. The rivers of India fall into two groups—those of northern India and those of Peninsular India. The differences between the two groups are fundamental and of the greatest importance. Those of northern India rise in the mountain wall or beyond it. They do not depend for their water entirely on the monsoon rains, they are fed also by the melting of the snows on the Himalayas. Although the volume fluctuates enormously, these rivers are never dry. They yield a supply of water which, though fluctuating, can be gauged and used for irrigation. Further they traverse, as broad slow rivers wandering lazily across the plains, areas of fertile alluvium, very suitable for irrigation. One might have added formerly that they afforded excellent highways; but on the principle that one cannot have one's cake and eat it too, the use of the water for irrigation has been at least one important factor in the decay of navigation. The three great river systems of northern India are:

1. The Indus River, with its tributaries the Jhelum, Chenab, Ravi, Bias and Sutlej (the five rivers of the Punjab), all joining to form the Panchnad before uniting with the Indus. Amongst tributaries received by the Indus on the opposite or right bank must be noted the Gilgit in Kashmir, the united Swat and Kabul, so important for irrigation in the Vale of Peshawar, and the Kurram Rivers.

2. The Ganga or Ganges, with its tributaries the Jumna (on the right bank, though it rises in the Himalayas), Gogra (with the Sarda), Rapti and Gandak. The tributaries of the Ganges which rise to the south naturally partake of the characteristics of the Peninsular rivers. The chief is the Son.

3. The Brahmaputra River, known through its long Tibetan course as the Tsanpo and in its gorge through the Himalayas as the Dihang, though longer than the Ganges, is less important to India because of its narrower valley and its course in a part of the plain already well watered by heavy rainfall.

The rivers of Peninsular India, rising as they do amongst the hills of the plateau, are fed only by the monsoon rains. In the dry season they often become almost dry—so nearly dry as to be all but useless for navigation. The inconstant supply of water renders them less suitable for permanent irrigation works, though reference will be made later to the well-known system of tank irrigation in the innumerable small valleys of their tributaries. Their valleys, too, are less suitable for irrigation, except in the broad, lower courses such as one finds in the deltas of the Kistna and Godavari. Failure to appreciate these important differences was responsible for a great waste of money in abortive irrigation schemes in Madras.

Finally it should be noted that whereas the rivers of northern India have a long upper course in the mountains, those of Peninsular India have not.

Geological Structure. In its broad lines the structure of India is very simple. There are but two distinct units:

(1) The very ancient stable massif of which the central portion forms the Deccan, together with the later rocks which mask much of its surface and especially its edges.

(2) The belt of fold mountains which wrap round the ancient block and which may perhaps be regarded as owing their existence to compression against its resistant edge.

The basal complex of the ancient block consists of highly metamorphosed rocks—gneisses and schists—of the Archean system. By far the larger part of the Peninsula—the central and southern portions—is occupied by this ancient crystalline complex, whilst to the north-east the rocks occupy wide areas in Chota Nagpur, Orissa and the Central Provinces and to the north-west in the Aravallis and other parts of Rajputana. Rocks of granitic type occur intruded into the complex, and special interest attaches to a group of intrusive rocks known as the

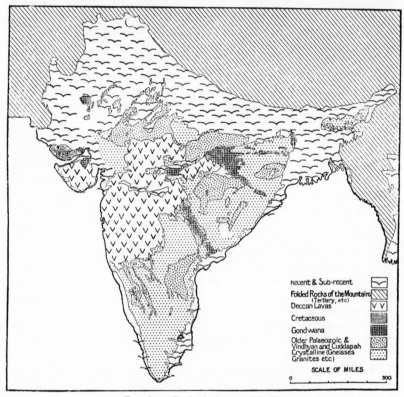

recent & Sub-recent
Folded Rocks of the Mountains
(Tertiary, etc)
Deccan Lavas
Cretaceous
Gondwana
Older Palaeozoic &
Vindhyan and Cuddapah
Crystalline (Gneisses
Granites etc)
SCALE OF MILES
0   500

FIG. 80.—Geological map of India

Charnockite series widespread in southern India. Occupying long troughs and hollows in the basal complex are the rocks of the Dharwar series—highly folded and highly metamorphosed sediments, now appearing as phyllites, slates, schists and marbles. They are often highly mineralized and economically important also as having yielded the famous Mekrana and Jodhpur marbles used by the Moguls for their great buildings in Agra and Delhi. The Cuddapah system is another group of highly folded and highly altered sediments—slates or schists. With the close of the period when the Cuddapah rocks were folded into the already complex mass of Archean and Dharwar rocks we are still in the pre-Cambrian era and no signs of life appear in any of these rocks. From that time onwards Peninsular India played its role as a stable block of the earth's surface.

The succeeding Vindhyan system of rocks consists of a vast thickness of sandstones, shales and limestones, which are probably also pre-Cambrian in age, but which rest in an almost undisturbed condition on the surface of the older rocks. The Vindhyan sandstones have provided the chief building stones of places like Agra and Delhi.

At a later date Peninsular India formed part of the great Gondwana Continent, and the next important series of deposits are sandstones and shales, most of them of fluviatile or freshwater origin, which were deposited in hollows on the surface of the continent. They are of great importance because they contain India's coal. From that remote time until the present the Deccan has remained for the most part a continental mass, but not one without history. Seas lapped round its margins and at times spread over some of the lower tracts round the margins. The Jurassic seas swept over much of Rajputana and have left traces in the form of sedimentary deposits. Cretaceous seas covered part, at least, of what is now the Narbada Valley and a large part of the Madras coastal area, where they laid down some well-known fossiliferous deposits known as the Trichinopoly Beds. But the most important episode of the Cretaceous Period was the pouring out of enormous stretches of basaltic lavas—the Deccan Traps of the older geologists—which cover an area today of 200,000 square miles in the north-west of the plateau. They give rise to the characteristic scenery of flat-topped hills of this region. The reappearance of Deccan rocks in the hills of Assam and their presence as small inliers near Delhi are two of the reasons which have led geologists to believe that the ancient massif of the Deccan underlies the great alluvial plains of the Indus and Ganges. Suess sees in this great depression a 'fore-deep' before the high crustal waves of the Himalayan uplift; Burrard, on the other hand, regarded the depression as a rift valley. The alluvial deposits cover 300,000 square miles; their thickness has never been ascertained, but borings have penetrated them to the depth of 1,300 feet without reaching a rocky bottom.[1]

It is impossible here to enter into detail regarding the structure of the great encircling belt of fold mountains.[2] There is little doubt that the area now occupied by the Himalayas was a broad deep sea—the Tethys—until well on in the Mesozoic era. The development of the 'Alpine storm' was a gradual process; much of the Himalayan tract

[1] For a summary of knowledge, see D. N. Wadia, *The Geology of India* (London: Macmillan, 3rd Edition, 1954).

[2] V. H. Boileau in 1951 emphasized the important role of tear-faults. See *Notes and News, Min. Met. Geol. Inst. India.*, **6**, 1951, 20–3.

was occupied by sea until late in the Tertiary. The mountain building movements culminated in the Miocene, but even the latest Tertiary beds are highly folded and the occasional earthquakes of the present day indicate that movement has not entirely ceased. In the Himalayan chain there is a central core of crystalline rocks, flanked by sedimentary rocks of all ages from Cambrian to late Tertiary. Rocks of later date play an important part in the foothills and in the more open folds of Baluchistan and the India-Burma divide. In the Himalayas the rocks are overfolded and overthrust towards the south—that is, against the Deccan stable block—as the representative section here reproduced in Fig. 81 will demonstrate (see also Figs. 11 and 12).

The Mineral Production of India and Pakistan. India, like so many Eastern countries, is still associated in the popular imagination with gold and precious stones. The association with gold is not unwarranted, for India had a capacity for importing and absorbing gold

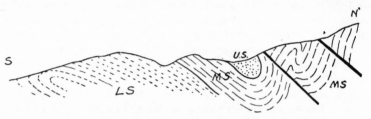

FIG. 81.—Section through the foothills of the Himalayas in the Punjab, showing overfolding and overthrusting even among the highest tertiary rocks (the rocks shown are Lower, Middle and Upper Siwaliks, Mio-Pliocene in age)

which was unparalleled by any country in the world, but as a producer India occupies but a minor position. This is in the main true also in the case of precious stones. As a whole, India has not been an important mineral-producing country, but is well endowed with iron ore, coal and ferrous alloy minerals. There are seven minerals of which the annual production exceeds £1,000,000 in value—coal, iron ore, manganese ore, gold, mica, oil and salt. It must be remembered that older statistics include Burma which is rich in certain minerals (see pp. 397-9). Less than one person per thousand of the population is employed in mining. It should be noted that the oil of the Punjab lies in Pakistan; most of the other minerals are in India.[1]

Coal. In the ten years 1916-25 India's production of coal fluctuated, somewhat narrowly, between 17·3 million tons (1916) and 22·6 million tons (1919), with an average rather below 20 million tons. In 1926-35 the average increased to 22·6 million (28·3 million in 1938). By 1947 output reached 29·3 million tons and in 1963 reached 66·9 m. metric

---

[1] For information on minerals see *Progress of the Mineral Industry of India, 1906-1955*, Golden Jubilee Volume of the Mining, Geological and Metallurgical Institute of India, 1956.

tons worth £116 m. Practically the whole of the coal comes from the Gondwana deposits, which occupy ancient depressions in the plateau. Roughly nine-tenths is produced by the group of coalfields (Raniganj, Jherria and Daltonganj) which lie in the Damodar Valley on the edge of the Chota Nagpur Plateau, partly in West Bengal and partly in Bihar. There is a useful production from Singareni in Hyderabad; rather more from Warora in the Wardha Valley of Madhya Pradesh

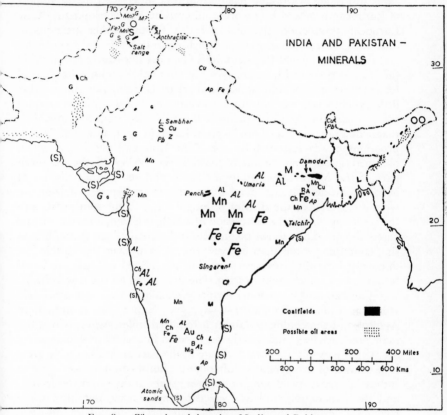

Fig. 82.—The mineral deposits of India and Pakistan

(Courtesy O. H. K. Spate)

Al, Bauxite (ore of aluminium); Ap, Apatite; Au, Gold; B, Barytes; Ch, Chromite; Cu, Copper; Fe, Iron ore; G, Gypsum; L, Lignite; M, Mica; Mg, Magnesite; Mn, Manganese; O, Oil; Pb, Lead; RA, Refractories and Abrasives; S, Salt (in parentheses, by evaporation of salt water); V, Vanadium; Z, Zinc. Italics indicate unexploited reserves; size of letters very roughly proportional to importance. 'Atomic sands' are thoria-bearing ilmenite and monazite. To this map should be added the important gas resources of Sui and Sylhet.

and some from Umaria east of Jubbulpore. There are some unimportant lignites and brown coals in Assam and the Punjab. The Gondwana coal is a bituminous coal usually of good quality.

Under the Second Five Year Plan, India set a target of 60,000,000

tons by 1960-1 since the expansion of coal production is basic
to the whole Plan. The development of lignite in South Arcot
should be noted, but production is hindered by water underlying the
deposit. Pakistan's total output averages half a million tons (1951-7).

Iron Ore. Iron ore is widely scattered over the mountainous and
hilly parts of the country and, with the profuse employment of charcoal
for smelting, Indian villagers made iron of excellent quality. But this
expensive mode of working has been almost superseded by the import
of European iron and iron wares, followed by the development of the
European production methods in India. Of the earlier attempts to
introduce the modern processes of smelting in India the most successful
was that of the Bengal Iron and Steel Co. near Barakar in the north of
the Raniganj coalfield, where ores are obtainable and a suitable coal
for smelting is procured at Karharbari or Giridhi. For many years
little progress was made, but in the early years of the present century
the company began to supplement the local clay ironstone ores with
magnetites obtained in Chota Nagpur. Later, in 1911, a more ambitious
programme was initiated by the Tata Iron and Steel Co. which
obtained leases over the rich massive ore bodies of the northern
part of the Mayurbhanj State of Orissa, and the Raipur district of
Madhya Pradesh. Later even more important deposits of iron ore
were discovered in the district of Singhbhum, to the south-east, and
the company obtained a concession in which, it is said, a ravine cutting
across the ore range shows a continuous thickness of 700 feet of hema-
tite, containing more than 60 per cent. of iron. Even before this last
discovery, blast-furnaces were started in 1911. Steel was first produced
from modern rolling mills in 1933. The site chosen for the new industry
was Jamshedpur where some formerly exploited ores were available.
Here the Calcutta–Bombay railway (via Nagpur) has a branch to
Asansol and the coalfields (about a hundred miles away), whilst the
main ore-fields lie 45 miles to the south-west. Limestone and manganese
are within easy reach. Thus a village in the barren scrub quickly grew
into a town of over 100,000 inhabitants. Jamshedpur is now a great
industrial centre, producing not only a great variety of articles in iron
and steel, including mill and electrical machinery, but also heavy
chemicals, fertilizers and explosives. The large demand for tin-plate
by the Burmah and Anglo-Persian Oil Companies led to the erection
of plant in Bengal capable of manufacturing about 30,000 tons of tin-
plate annually. The Tata Company had a monopoly of steel until
1934-5, when works were erected at Belur, north of Calcutta. Soon
after independence in 1947 three great new projects were initiated
with the help of German, Russian and British technicians for completion in 1956-61. Output of steel reached 4·3 m. metric tons in 1963-4
and 6 m. in 1964-5. (See p. 263.)

In the meantime it may be noted that the local indigenous iron-smelting industries had practically disappeared.[1] Sir Lewis Fermor has estimated that the reserves of iron ore in India probably total 10,000 million tons.

Petroleum. Mineral oil is an important resource in both the Union of India and Pakistan. In 1947 production exceeded 82,000,000 imperial gallons (330,000 metric tons). In 1962 India's output was 1,290,000 metric tons and that of Pakistan 534,000, a total of 1,824,000 metric tons. In West Punjab (Pakistan) the production is from the little Khaur field which dates from 1922 and from the more recently developed richer Dhulian field and Balkassar. That from Assam (India) is from the two small fields of Digboi (of which a considerable extension was recently proved) and Nahorkatiya. It may be noted, in passing, that there is little possibility of large new fields in the well-explored territory of Assam and the Punjab. Indeed the prospects for new fields are not bright, though Baluchistan holds out possibilities. Pakistan also has in the Punjab at Joya Mair some oil so heavy that it is really a natural bitumen valuable for road building. Since partition the whole position in Pakistan has been changed by the discovery of a rich *natural gas* sand at Sui north of Sukkur. The gas is piped to Karachi (1955) and also to Multan (1958) and Lahore. In the east a rich strike has been made in the Sylhet area which supplies Dacca and Chittagong.

Manganese Ore ranks high in value amongst India's minerals. The quantity produced annually has reflected world conditions and, taking the years 1916 to 1926 inclusive, showed a low total of 474,000 tons in 1922 and a record level of 1,015,000 in 1926. As a result of the depression production dropped rapidly to a low level of 213,000 tons in 1932, but rose to nearly a million tons in 1938. In 1947 it was 210,000 tons and since partition has been much higher—1,185,000 tons in 1963. The ores are fairly widely distributed in the Dharwar rocks of the plateau, but three-quarters of the production was from Madhya Pradesh (Central Provinces). Here the ore is worked in open quarries in the hillsides in the districts of Balaghat, Bhandara, Chhindwara, Jubbulpore and Nagpur. Sandur in Madras is a very big producer. Keonjhar in Bihar is also important. The chief use of manganese ore is in the manufacture of ferro-manganese and spiegeleisen—both of which are alloys of manganese and iron. It is also used in the chemical industries. The Indian production is exported entirely in the form of ore and export was helped by the opening of the railway to Vizagapatam. India is the second producer of manganese ore in the world, ranking after U.S.S.R. and having outstripped Ghana.

Gold occupies third place but the production is now practically

[1] See C. S. Fox, 'The Raw Materials for the Iron and Steel Industry of India', *Trans. Mining and Geol. Inst. India*, **20**, 1925, 87–194. In a review of the mineral resources of India presented to the Fourth Empire Mining Congress in July 1949, Dr. S. K. Chatterjee claimed that India had resources of four minerals in amounts which should be regarded as of world importance: iron ore, titanium ore, thorium ore and mica.

restricted to the Kolar goldfield of Mysore. The production for many years was comparatively steady, fluctuating between 380·8 and 393·5 thousand ounces of fine gold in the period 1921–6, but fell later, reaching 336,000 ounces in 1933. Profitability of mining and so the quantity and value have fluctuated with the price of gold. Some workings in the three mines, now nationalized, are over 9,000 feet deep. In 1947 the yield was 168,000 ounces and after partition climbed a little. Another mine at Ballara in Mysore has been opened and another at Hutti in Hyderabad reopened. Total production in 1956 was 206,000 ounces; in 1963 138,280 ounces.

Salt. The production of salt in India reached a value of nearly £2·5 million in 1947 and the total quantity is usually rather over 3,000,000 tons—very nearly 5,000,000 tons in 1963. There are five main sources—evaporation of seawater along the coasts of Madras, near Bombay and near Karachi, the mines of the Salt Range in the Punjab and the Sambhar Lake in Rajputana.

Saltpetre is produced in considerable quantities in the Punjab, Uttar Pradesh (U.P.) and Bihar, but the output has been decreasing in quantity and value since the use of artificial fertilizers became general. Saltpetre in India is a natural product formed in alluvial soils from animal and vegetable refuse in a climate with alternating dry and wet seasons. The efflorescence was collected from the soil and purified.

Mica is a characteristic Indian mineral, and India is one of the world's large producers. Since partition it has ranked third in value after coal and manganese ore. The supplies are from the Nellore mines of Madras and especially the Hazaribagh, Gaya and Monghyr districts of Bihar. Some of the Nellore sheets are said to be 9 feet in diameter and are of great purity. A use has been found in the manufacture of micanite, or mica boards, for the enormous mass of scrap-mica which was formerly wasted. The annual production of mica ranged between 1,600 and 2,800 tons in 1916–25. In 1926–35 it averaged 2,000 tons. Mica is a valuable insulating material in the ever-expanding electrical industries and it is not surprising to find the output has expanded towards a total of 33,500 tons in 1963.

Chromite is found in many parts of India and in 1947 30,000 tons were produced in Baluchistan, Mysore and especially at Singhbhum. In 1955 there was a record output of 28,000 tons from Pakistan and 89,000 from India, rather less in later years.

Copper Ore, though widespread, is mainly obtained from Singhbhum (Bihar). In 1947 330,000 tons of ore yielded 6,350 tons of copper; in 1956 output was 7,628 tons of copper; in 1963 nearly 10,000 tons.

Silver–Lead–Zinc Ores have been worked in Rajasthan since 1948.

Precious and Semi-Precious Stones. A few diamonds are still found in central India including the new Panna mines; emeralds in Rajasthan. India has some interesting examples of the fluctuating demands for minerals. *Monazite* from Travancore was once important in the gas-mantle industry but the demand disappeared about 1925. But thorium, obtained from monazite, has now new uses—in atomic plants, for tracer bullets and so on. Ilmenite, associated with monazite, has many new uses. Both monazite and ilmenite are found as sands on the Travancore shores, the heavy grains having been naturally concentrated by wave action. India has a carbo-electric aluminium smelter at Muri near Jamshedpur which has stimulated production of bauxite from the laterites of the Peninsula. In 1955, 7,225 tons of aluminium were produced; in 1963 it exceeded 54,000 tons.

Amongst the minerals not already mentioned may be noted the magnesite of Madras; the barytes of Madras; gypsum, china clay (Eastern Ghats and Bihar), kyanite and sillimanite (refractories). Building and ornamental stones are widely quarried in many parts of India; and so is limestone for the manufacture of lime and cement. Over 9,000,000 tons of cement are produced annually. As permanent buildings replace homes of mud, this industry is bound to grow.

Details of the minerals of India and their occurrence will be found in D. N. Wadia's *Geology of India* (Macmillan). Every year a Report on the Mineral Production of India is published in the *Records of the Geological Survey of India* and every five years a volume of the *Records* is devoted to a *Quinquennial Review of the Mineral Production*. In the long series of Memoirs and Records issued by the Geological Survey most of the important mineral deposits have been dealt with. India and Pakistan are gradually being surveyed and maps on the scale of one inch to one mile are available for many areas. They are hand-coloured and copies are prepared on request by the Geological Surveys. Since partition there have been separate Geological Surveys for India and Pakistan. The Indian Survey now publishes a semi-popular quarterly entitled *Indian Minerals*.

Soils. Elsewhere in this book the very large part played by climate in the formation of soils has been emphasized. Provided there is an approximate chemical similarity between the original rock types— e.g. alluvium and gneiss may have a composition roughly the same— the soils formed therefrom will probably be almost identical. This is particularly the case in regions of heavy rainfall where laterite forms. A large percentage of lime in the original rock may exercise a controlling influence on the resulting soil, but not always. Broadly speaking India has four main types of soil:

(1) The 'red' soils of the crystalline tracts—on the whole indifferent thin soils formed over regions of crystalline rocks where the rainfall is poor or moderate (southern Deccan).

(2) The black cotton or *regur* soils—formed over the Deccan lavas with poor or moderate rainfall.

(3) The alluvial soils, characteristic of the northern plains.
(4) The laterite soils, formed in regions of heavy rainfall with a dry season.

This may be called the 'traditional' classification of soils in India. For an attempt to equate it with the Russian scheme of Schokalsky see Spate's *India and Pakistan*, pp. 83–92.

Broadly speaking the soils are poor owing to leaching, termite action, lack of restorative crops and organic manure. Nitrogen content is often less than a third of that usual in England.

I have shown [1] that over limited areas soil and climate may counteract one another thus:

Very light soil + moderate rainfall ⎱ have vegetation cover same
Clayey soil   + light rainfall   ⎰ in both cases.

The Climate of India. We have already considered in broad outline the climate of India and it remains to recapitulate the main features and to consider the variations. We will ignore those areas lying outside the mountain wall—in particular Baluchistan—where the climate is of an entirely different type. It must then be emphasized, in the first place, that the climate of India is essentially of one type— the tropical monsoon type. Too much is apt to be made of the local variations; important, for example, as the winter rains in the Punjab may be, they are a feature entirely subsidiary to the main summer rainfall régime. The seasonal rhythm is a feature of such importance that it may be said to dominate all phases of Indian life, and may conveniently form the basis for a general account of the climate.

There are three seasons in India:

(a) The Cold Weather, from October to the end of February.
(b) The Hot Weather, from the beginning of March to the beginning or middle of June.
(c) The Rains or Rainy Season, from the beginning or middle of June to the end of September or October.

The welcome breezes of the north-east monsoon are not, as a rule, felt until November, and October is really an unpleasant intermediate month when the rains are drying up but the cold weather has scarcely commenced. Hence there is considerable justification for the grouping of the seasons adopted by the Meteorological Department of the Government of India:

(a) The season of the north-east monsoon:
   i. January and February, cold-weather season.
   ii. March to mid-June, hot-weather season.

---

[1] L. D. Stamp and L. Lord, 'The Ecology of Part of the Riverine Tract of Burma', *Jour. of Ecology*, **11**, 1923, 129–59.

(*b*) The season of the south-west monsoon:
    i. Mid-June to mid-September, season of general rains.
    ii. Mid-September to December, season of retreating monsoon.

Conditions in the Cold-Weather Season. In January, which is the typical cold-weather month, there is, as one would expect, a steady increase of average temperature from north to south. At Peshawar it is below 50°; in the northern part of the Punjab Plains below 55°, and as far down the Ganges Valley as Benares below 60°. The days are warm as an English July, but the nights are distinctly cold and slight frost is common. Madras, on the other hand, has a January average of 75°; frost is quite unknown. Calicut has 78° and Colombo 79°. The January isotherms have, therefore, as shown in Fig. 83, a comparatively regular east-west trend. Relief plays such an important part in Indian climatic conditions that it seemed of value to give also a map showing the actual temperatures in January. This has been done in Fig. 84 and serves to emphasize the wall of cold air coinciding with the mountain wall of India.

Pressure conditions in January show a rather feeble high-pressure area developed over the cold plains of the north-west from which the winds blow outwards—making their way gradually towards the Equatorial belt of low pressure, gathering in force as they go. In modern terms there is an area of subsidence over northern India and a small mass of cP air. An isobar map of Asia really gives an entirely false impression in that it shows the low-pressure area of north-west India linked with that of central Asia. Actually there is no connection between the two: the Himalayas form an effective barrier, projecting well into the upper layers of the atmosphere. There is a twofold result of this: in the first place India does not suffer from the intensely cold winds which sweep across China in the winter, and in the second place the winds are generally but light, averaging only 2 or 3 miles per hour in northern India. It has been suggested that there is really a connection between these winds and the high-pressure system beyond the Himalayas, and it is pointed out that strong winds blow down the gorges of the Himalayas by which the great rivers of India reach the plains. But these winds are night winds: during the day there is actually a breeze *up* the gorges.

The outward-blowing winds of India in the cold season are controlled in their direction by the topography—they are westerly or north-westerly down the Ganges Valley, northerly in the Delta, becoming north-easterly (the direction of the normal Trade Winds) over the Bay of Bengal. These off-shore winds are naturally dry, and January and February are delightfully fine, rainless and cloudless months over most of India. Except in the north-west and the extreme south the cloud-covering rarely exceeds two-tenths. Ceylon and the

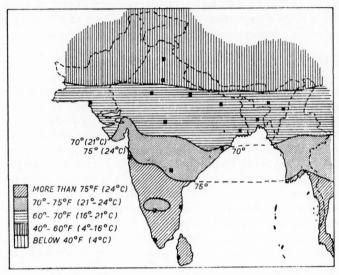

FIG. 83.—The climate of India. January sea-level isotherms

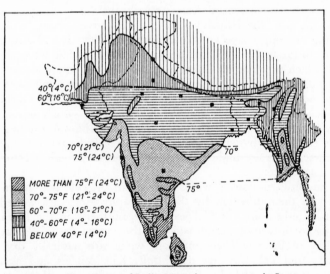

FIG. 84.—The climate of India—actual temperatures in January

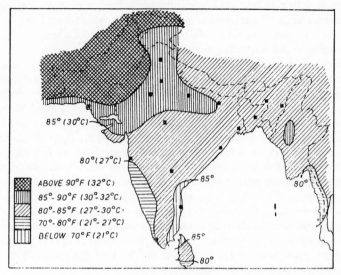

FIG. 85.—The climate of India—July sea-level isotherms

ABOVE 90°F (32°C)
85°-90°F (30°-32°C)
80°-85°F (27°-30°C)
70°-80°F (21°-27°C)
BELOW 70°F (21°C)

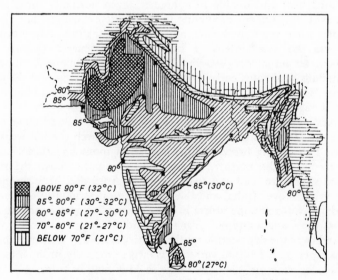

ABOVE 90°F (32°C)
85°-90°F (30°-32°C)
80°-85°F (27°-30°C)
70°-80°F (21°-27°C)
BELOW 70°F (21°C)

FIG. 86.—The climate of India—actual temperatures in July

extreme south, being within 10° of the Equator, are within the influence of the Equatorial belt and are influenced by temporary northward migrations of the Equatorial low-pressure belt. Madras and the south-east have a considerable rainfall in November and December during the period of the retreating monsoon.

Mention must be made of the cold-weather storms which are an important exception to the generally fine weather in the north-west. From December to March cyclones, originating over the Mediterranean, travel slowly eastwards across Persia and Baluchistan or Afghanistan and down over the plains of the Punjab. They are only shallow depressions and are accompanied usually by light winds only, but they provide an appreciable rainfall, especially in the northern Punjab (see graph for Lahore, Fig. 93). They usually die out before reaching the lower part of the Ganges Valley. These rains are of special importance to the winter crops of wheat and barley, and their absence in Burma explains the failure of wheat in districts otherwise suitable. Although of considerable importance, the amount of rain is small, even in the Punjab, in comparison with the monsoonal fall. It is probable, however, that these cyclones deposit the bulk of the snowfall on the mountains of Kashmir and the north-west.

The cold weather is a season much appreciated by Europeans in India. In the north, the Indian population finds the nights and early mornings unpleasantly cold, and activity is often deferred until the sun has warmed the air. It is curious how one becomes accustomed to continued heat and unable to appreciate even normally stimulating coldness. I well remember staying in the United Provinces one January after some years in Burma, and thinking that the early morning cold was the most intense I had ever experienced, though the thermometer actually registered 39° F. In Assam and Bengal, moisture is abundant in the air, early morning mists are common and the cold weather is less bracing. Farther south one still appreciates a blanket at night, though the thermometer may rarely drop below 65°.

Conditions in the Hot-Weather Season. With the northward movement of the sun, temperatures rise rapidly and in March the hot weather begins. The cooling breezes of the north-east monsoon are no longer felt—except in the northern plains—and along the coasts the most marked winds are land and sea breezes. In April and May the noon sun is vertical over India, and these are the hottest months over most of India. Average temperatures in May exceed 85° even in the humid delta of the Ganges and 90° over the Middle Ganges. The air is very dry, and over the dry north-west the relative humidity may even be as low as 1 per cent. Diurnal variation is large, especially in the interior. In Sind, for example, the daily range in May may be from 75° or 80° to 105° or 110°. In most of the drier regions of India the thermometer rises above 100° for some hours during the day in April and May. The effects of temperatures greater than blood-heat are curious until one gets accustomed to them. Everything feels warm to the touch—one is so used in the ordinary way to finding something cool to touch that this is at first very curious. Personally I used to find that temperatures above 105° produced a curious lethargic condition. One normally rests during the heat of the day, but it is often too hot to sleep or read, and it is possible to reach at times a curious state of coma when the mind is a perfect blank. This is said by some to be an impossible state of affairs, but it only needs to be experienced to be believed. Air-conditioning of buildings, still rare, has a great future in India.

By April or May a feeble but definite low-pressure area has developed over India and the winds are in-shore, bringing considerable rain to southern India and south-eastern Ceylon. These are the well-known 'mango showers'. This rain falls mainly during violent thunderstorms,

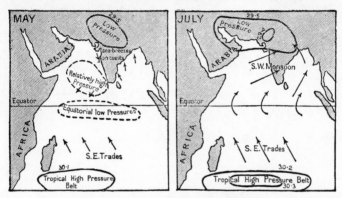

Fig. 87.—Diagram of monsoon conditions, showing Sir John Eliot's conception of the cause of the 'bursting' of the monsoon

which tend to develop late in the afternoon and may continue with intense flashes of lightning and tremendous thunderclaps until well into the evening. In the drier districts there is no rain, but violent dust storms are frequent. Sometimes the storms are in the form of tornadoes or whirlwinds of small diameter. I remember on many occasions, being camped in the deathly still, lifeless *indaing* in the Dry Belt of Burma with not a breath stirring, not a living thing moving during the heat of the afternoon, when suddenly a noise like the roar of an express train has arisen from apparently nowhere and a little tornado could be seen sweeping across the dry hill-sides, whirling dust, leaves, twigs and small branches in hopeless confusion. Rotten Euphorbia trees are uprooted as if by magic, when suddenly the storm dies down as quickly as it began. Such conditions are favourable for the development of tropical cyclones, which are especially dangerous at this season in the southern part of the Bay of Bengal.

Conditions during the Rainy Season. About the middle of June the monsoon bursts. The word 'bursts' aptly describes the suddenness of the change which is initiated, as a rule, by a great downpour of rain accompanied by violent thunder and lightning. Even in those regions where the mango showers and the afternoon thunderstorms have, as it were, heralded the change, there is nevertheless a sudden and unmistakable difference from the day the monsoon actually breaks. The strong, steady south-westerly winds, for one thing, mark the difference. The goal of the winds is, of course, the low-pressure area over north-western India. Two things must be emphasized. India is quite cut off

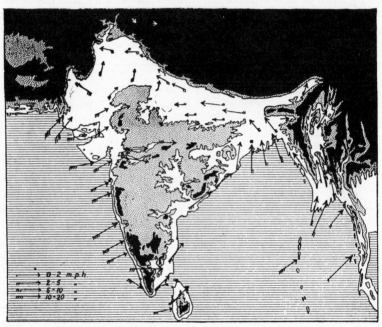

Fig. 88.—Map of India showing the average direction and strength of the monsoon winds in July

The length of the arrow is in proportion to the steadiness of the wind; strength is shown by the number of barbs.

from central Asia, there is no connection between the Punjab low-pressure centre and that over the heart of the continent. In the second place, the low-pressure area has already been in existence for a month or two before the monsoon arrives. Why the sudden change, which is no mere intensification of the previous light sea-breeze? Sir John Eliot, late Government Meteorologist of India, believed that during India's hot weather there existed still the normal Equatorial low pressure towards which the south-east trades were drawn and which was separated from the northern Indian area by a ridge of higher pressure. The Equatorial low pressure (Inter-Tropical Convergence Zone, ITCZ) and the ridge of high pressure to the north act as barriers, suddenly they are overcome and the south-east Trade Winds are drawn across to the north Indian area. In other words a main mass of mT (maritime tropical) air overwhelms the cP which formerly existed to the north.

It is certain that the rain-bearing wind is one of much greater strength than the light cold-season monsoon—in general at least twice the strength. At Bombay its average speed is 20 miles per hour, in other parts of India rather less. The actual direction of the winds is controlled to a marked degree by the relief of the country. There are two main streams, separated by the land mass of Peninsular India. The influence of that over the Arabian Sea scarcely extends north of the Gulf of Cambay. The Bengal stream blows up the Ganges as an east wind, reaching the Punjab from the south-east. Naturally the burst of the monsoon is experienced first on the west coast and arrives rather later elsewhere:

	Mean date of commencement	Mean date of ending
Bombay	June 5	October 15
Bengal	June 15	October 15–30
Punjab	July 1	September 14–21

With the exception of the Madras coast all India derives the bulk of its rainfall from the south-west monsoon. Even in the wettest parts, however, it must not be supposed that it rains continuously. Heavy downpours are interspersed with fine intervals, though in the wetter parts it is rarely that one sees the sun. In the drier regions—up the Ganges Valley, for example—sunny periods are usual, and the rains fall during the passage of series of depressions not unlike those of the Westerly wind belt in Europe. Nearly everywhere the rains result in a welcome drop in atmospheric temperature; hence in most parts of India, June, July, August and September are cooler than March and April. Only in the driest regions of the Punjab and Sind are the extremely high temperatures continued in June and July. This is a point not always appreciated by dwellers in other parts of the Northern Hemisphere who are apt to think of July and August as the warmest months. The rains are not generally unpleasant; the dried-up ground, where before not a particle of green was to be seen, appears to live once more, and nature revives as it does in the spring of more northern latitudes. The most unpleasant feature of the rainy season is usually the high humidity. Nothing will dry. Despite the temperature of over 80°, European residents in such places as Bombay or Chittagong have charcoal fires in order to get some semblance of dryness to their bedclothes and undergarments. Doors swell and refuse to shut; drawers do the same and refuse to open; boots and shoes have an unpleasant habit of growing green whiskers in the night; anything which has been stuck together with gum or glue promptly crumbles into fragments.

There is little difference in a rainfall map of India for the whole year and a rainfall map for the rainy season. Fig. 89 is a rainfall map for the whole year. Certain isohyets only have been selected—those of 80 inches, 40 inches and 20 inches. These lines are extremely important, and their position should be borne in mind when considering the distribution of natural vegetation, forests, agriculture and irrigation in India. They serve to distinguish four rainfall areas:

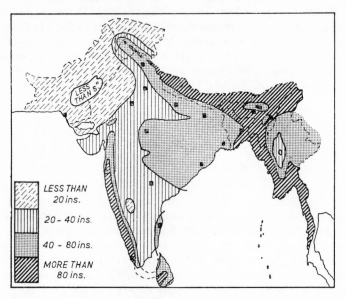

FIG. 89.—A rainfall map of India for the whole year

(a) The rainfall division with more than 80 inches a year. The natural vegetation is normally evergreen forest and the great food crop is rice. There is rarely danger of famine through drought, but considerable danger of destruction of crops by floods. Earthworks are frequently undertaken, as in the Ganges Delta, as a protection against floods.

(b) The rainfall division with between 40 and 80 inches a year may be called the region of moderate rainfall. Monsoon forest, in which the trees are leafless in the hot weather, is the natural vegetation; there is a mixture of dry-zone and wet-zone crops, but rice usually predominates. Irrigation is normally unnecessary, but irrigation works may be undertaken as a protective measure against years of drought.

(c) The rainfall division with between 20 and 40 inches may be called the region of poor rainfall. The natural vegetation is usually scrubland; forests only grow in favoured localities. This is the region of the typical dry-zone crops such as millet; wet-zone crops (such as rice) can only be grown with the help of irrigation. India's great famine zones lie in regions with less than 40 inches of rain. Not only does the rainfall tend to be inadequate, but it falls, as we have seen, during the passage of depressions. It is apt to vary considerably in amount from year to year, hence the danger of famine which is only obviated by large irrigation works.

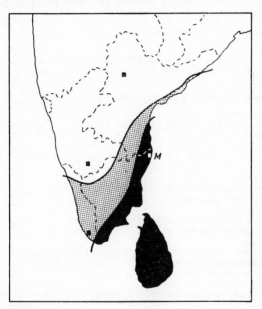

FIG. 90.—The cold-weather rainfall of southern India

The area shown black receives more than 10 inches of rain in the months of November and December, the dotted area more than 5 inches. It must be emphasized that this cold-season rain falls during the period of the retreating monsoon and not when the north-east monsoon is blowing.

(d) The rainfall division with less than 20 inches of rain is desert and semi-desert. Permanent cultivation is almost impossible without irrigation.

Conditions during the Period of the Retreating Monsoon. In October the rains become much less intense, the skies clear and the sun appears, causing the temperature to rise. The land is water-logged, the atmosphere humid and the temperature over the whole of India is remarkably uniform—a few degrees above or below 80°. The month is unhealthy and unpleasant—'sticky' is the usual adjective applied to the weather. In November and December the temperature drops considerably in the north. Over the sea and land the south-westerly current of air practically ceases and the air becomes stagnant. Local variations in heat and moisture give rise to tropical cyclones. A large number of these seem to originate in the neighbourhood of the Andaman Islands and travel towards the west or north-west over the Bay of Bengal. These cyclones normally bring much rain to the coasts of Madras, where November and December are the wettest months, whilst the remainder of India is almost rainless. These tropical cyclones are sometimes very destructive to life and property.

The Climatic Regions of India. The simplest climatic regions of India are those based primarily on rainfall and may be arranged thus:

Climatic regions	Natural regions
(a) Regions with more than 80 inches:	
(1) West Coast:	
i. North—long dry season. Example: Bombay	Same
ii. South—short dry season. Example: Trivandrum	Same
(2) Bengal and Assam. Example: Chittagong	Deltas. E. Hills. Assam Valley
(b) Regions with 40 to 80 inches:	
North-east plateau and Middle Ganges Valley. Example: Nagpur	N.E. Plateau. Middle Ganges
(c) Regions with 20 to 40 inches:	
(1) Carnatic or Tamil Region in which the wettest months are November and December. Example: Madura	Same
(2) Southern and north-western Deccan with mean January temperatures of 65°–75°. Example: Hyderabad	S. Deccan N.W. Deccan
(3) Upper Ganges Plain with lower January temperatures and higher July ones. Example: Delhi	U Ganges Plain Central Indian Foreland
(4) Northern Punjab Plains where winter rainfall is important. Example: Lahore	Punjab Plains (Northern)
(d) Regions with less than 20 inches:	
(1) North-west lowland. Example: Karachi	Punjab Plains (South) Sind. Thar. Rajput Upland
(2) North-west plateau. Example: Quetta	Baluchistan. N.W. Hills

The Himalayan region should be considered separately (Examples: Simla and Darjeeling). Later in this section we shall describe India under natural regions; we have indicated by the side of the climatic regions the correspondence with the natural regions distinguished later on.[1]

[1] Of the very greatest importance to India is the variation in the monsoon from year to year. In fact it is not too much to say that this is the biggest single factor influencing life in India. It would be of immense advantage to be able to predict the character of the monsoon weather even just before the rains break, and to this end research has been directed and attempts made to correlate the Indian weather sequence with weather in other parts of the world. The results have not been very decisive. See R. C. Mossman, 'On Indian Monsoon Rainfall in relation to South American Weather, 1875–1914', *Mem. Indian Meteor. Dept.*, **23**, Part VI, 157–242 (Calcutta, 1923), and A. V. Williamson, *Geog. Rev.*, **21**, 1931.

Irrigation in India. From the account of the rainfall of India, it is clear that large areas suffer naturally from a deficiency of moisture. A large part of the Punjab Plains and the Lower Indus Valley in Sind, to take the outstanding case, have a rainfall of less than 20 inches a year, parts as low as 5 inches, and though their soil is naturally a fertile alluvium, such a rainfall is totally inadequate for agriculture in a tropical country like India. Moreover, in those regions with normally

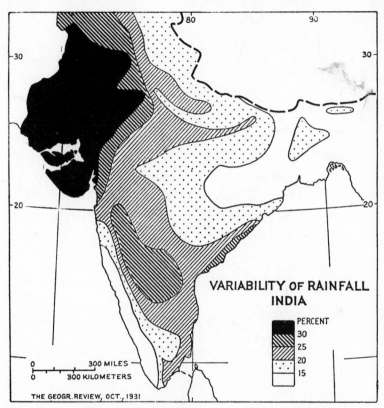

VARIABILITY OF RAINFALL
INDIA

PERCENT
30
25
20
15

300 MILES
300 KILOMETERS

THE GEOGR. REVIEW, OCT., 1931

FIG. 91.—The variability of rainfall in India (*after* A. V. Williamson)

a better rainfall and where 'dry crops' are the mainstays of agriculture, wide fluctuations from year to year have resulted in the past in terrible famines. It is to be noted that the 'famine areas' of India are not the driest parts, but those parts with an intermediate rainfall. From very early times the inhabitants of India have sought to take advantage of the richness of the soil in such dry areas as the Punjab by irrigating the land, and have attempted to insure against drought by the construction of wells and tanks in those areas with a moderate rainfall.

But the vast irrigation works now so characteristic of India are mainly a product of the last hundred years—since 1865. Modern engineering skill is only a partial explanation of this. Comprehensive

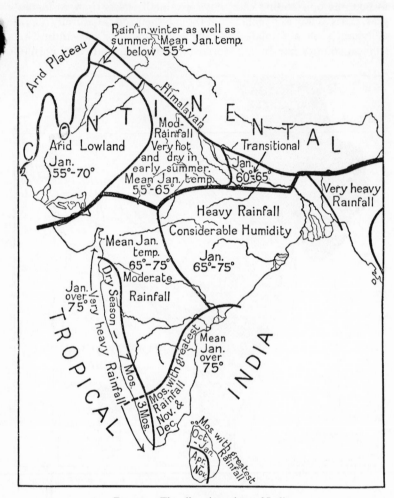

FIG. 92.—The climatic regions of India

The divisions shown on this map are modified from those drawn up by Kendrew. In particular the fundamental separation of 'Continental India' and 'Tropical India' was suggested to me by Professor Kazi Saied Ahmad.

irrigation schemes involve, in the first place, the complete control of the sources of water; where a river basin is occupied by a number of independent powers, the attempt of any one of the riverine nations to utilize the water of the river for its own benefit is apt to result in continuous strife. Difficulties arise, as they did in Australia over the river Murray, even with friendly groups of the same race. Finally, only a wealthy central authority can undertake the initial cost. Thus the British Indian Government, the first to control the whole of the

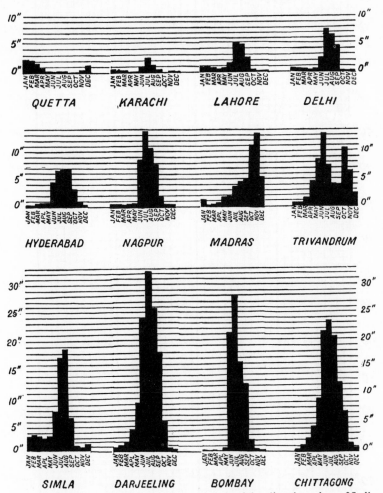

FIG. 93.—Rainfall graphs for towns characteristic of the climatic regions of India

sub-continent, was able to carry out irrigation schemes on a scale which would have been impossible to a group of smaller authorities, however well inclined. Since partition one of the major difficulties has been the cutting of main irrigation canals by the boundary between Western Pakistan and India; further, Pakistan's vital supplies of river water originate in Kashmir (see Fig. 133 and notes, p. 296).

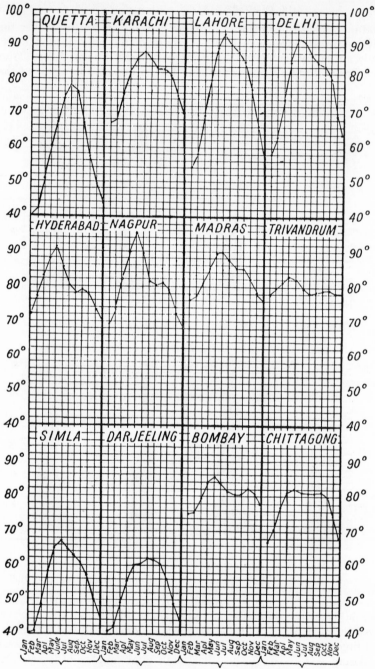

FIG. 94.—Temperature graphs for towns characteristic of the climatic regions of India

It is difficult to realize the huge extent of irrigation works in India and Pakistan. Taking the Republic of India alone, out of 236,000,000 acres actually under crops in 1950-1, 49,000,000 acres were irrigated —over a fifth of the whole. In Pakistan, out of 57,000,000 acres under crops, 21,500,000 were irrigated—over a third of the whole. Expressed in another way, the area irrigated in India is roughly ten times the total area of cultivated land in the most famous of all irrigated countries, Egypt. One scheme alone, the Sukkur Barrage Scheme in Sind, added to the permanently irrigated land of Pakistan an area greater than the total cultivated land of Egypt. It has been said, with some approach to truth, that India adds an Egypt to her area every year and the world takes no notice.

The above figures refer *only* to those parts of India and Pakistan for which figures are available—broadly the area of pre-partition British India and some of the major States. Returns made to FAO give for India in 1960-1 60,200,000 acres irrigated out of 328,000,000 acres of arable land actually sown (excluding 56,300,000 fallow) and for Pakistan 25,000,000 acres out of 52,000,000 sown. In Indo-Pakistan as a whole the irrigated area expanded from 30,000,000 acres in 1900 to 70,000,000 at the time of partition. With China about the same Asia has still 70 per cent. of the world's irrigated land.

Four types of irrigation are distinguished. At the time of partition about 42 per cent. of the land irrigated in the Republic of India was by canals, 25 per cent. by wells, 19 per cent. by tanks, 14 per cent. by other means. Government works accounted for 85 per cent. of the canal irrigation, private works for only 15. Government is responsible for about 35 per cent. of other types of irrigation. Recent developments (see p. 265) aim to combine irrigation and power.

A very serious problem which has arisen in recent years, especially in West Pakistan, is that of waterlogging (see p. 297). It is not sufficient to water the land; surplus water must be drawn off by adequate drainage. Another problem is the accumulation of salts in the soil in hot, dry lands where evaporation is very strong.

Perennial Canal Irrigation is by far the most important type of irrigation in India. Up to the time of partition the British Indian Government had spent 160 crores of rupees—roughly £120,000,000—on irrigation works in India. The most important works are in the drier parts of the great plain—in the Punjab, the former United Provinces and Sind —and will be considered in detail later. Twenty-two per cent. of the expenditure had been on the Punjab; 16 per cent. in the United Provinces; 20 per cent. in Sind; 7 per cent. in Bombay Deccan; and 9 in Madras. The Government canals in India, at the time of partition, included 25,000 miles of main and branch canals, and 60,000 miles of distributaries; they irrigated 40,000,000 acres. The percentage return on the capital outlay varies enormously; on the whole it has averaged some 5 per cent. net.

Inundation Canals are fed by the rivers, from which they take their water, in the flood season only. In the past they have been very important, especially in Sind, but they have been replaced by perennial canals. They had the double disadvantage that just in those seasons when water was most needed they were liable to be but partly

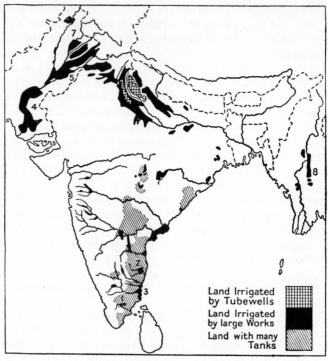

FIG. 95.—Irrigation map of India

1, Perivar system; **2,** Cheyyar, Poini and Palar system; **3,** Cauvery Delta system; **4,** Sind; **5,** Punjab systems; **6,** Ganges-Jumna systems; **7,** Vale of Peshawar; **8,** Burma; **9,** Sarda system.

filled, and that they could not take full advantage of the river supplies, and dried up in the hot season.

Tanks. In most of the drier parts, especially of the southern and south-eastern parts of Peninsular India, mud walls or 'bunds' are built across the valleys of small streams, so that water collects and forms a pond or lake during the wet season. Such ponds or lakes are designated by the rather misleading title of 'tanks'. The water is utilized at the close of the rainy season, but in the hot season the tanks dry up completley. In years of scarce rainfall, when water is most needed, the danger is that the tanks may never be filled owing to the insufficient rainfall. Tank irrigation is of prime importance in Hyderabad, Mysore and Madras.

Wells. Although the surface of the land may be dry in the drier regions, there is often water at a short distance below the surface. This is particularly the case in the great alluvial areas where the permanent water table is only a few feet below the surface. This water can be reached by wells and brought to the surface.

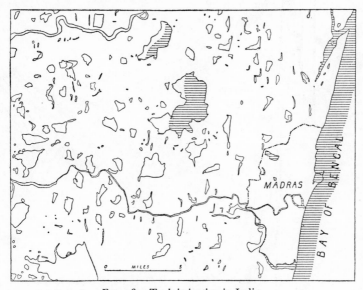

FIG. 96.—Tank irrigation in India

Sketch-map showing the immense number of, and huge area occupied by, tanks in the vicinity of Madras City. Only those lined have permanent water.

Tube Wells. In the northern parts of the U.P., not yet served by canals, electrically pumped deep tube wells have been developed. The success of tube-well irrigation depends upon cheap hydro-electric power.

Other Types of Irrigation. Large areas—over 10 per cent. of the whole area irrigated in India—are still watered by such primitive means as bucket lifts, including the 'shaduf', from streams.

The Natural Vegetation of India. Some reference has already been made, in dividing India into climatic regions, to the controlling influence which rainfall exerts upon the distribution of natural vegetation. Excluding for the moment the mountainous areas, India falls naturally into four rainfall-vegetation regions:[1]

[1] I elaborated these divisions for Burma: Stamp, *The Vegetation of Burma* (Calcutta: Thacker, Spink & Co., 1924). The same division is used by Troup (*Silviculture of Indian*

The Wet Zone, with a rainfall of over 80 inches (Evergreen Forests).

The Intermediate Zone, with a rainfall of 40 to 80 inches (Deciduous or Monsoon Forests).

The Dry Zone, with a rainfall of 20 to 40 inches (Dry Forest and Scrubland).

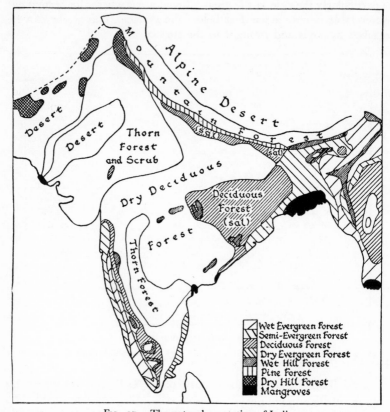

FIG. 97.—The natural vegetation of India

This map is based on the one given by H. G. Champion in his important work on Indian Vegetation (*Indian Forest Records*, New Series, Vol. I, 1936).

The Arid Zone, with a rainfall of less than 20 inches (Desert and Semi-Desert).

Trees), Schlich and others (*Manual of Forestry*, Vol. I), but they adopt rather lower rainfall limits thus:

> Wet Zone: over 75 inches.
> Intermediate Zone: 30 to 75 inches.
> Dry Zone: 15 to 30 inches.
> Arid Zone: less than 15 inches.

These would seem to be the minimum amounts necessary for each type of forest: worked on the optimum or characteristic amount for each type.

Additional types are Hill and Alpine Forests in the mountains, Tidal and Riparian Forests.

The Evergreen Forests are found chiefly on the west coast of the Peninsula, on the lower slopes of the Eastern Himalayas, in Assam, eastern Bengal, the wetter parts of Burma and the Andaman Islands. The forests are of Equatorial type; high humidity and even temperature favour vigorous growth and many of the trees reach a height of 200 feet and over. As in the true Equatorial forests, the number of species is very large and often only one of a species will be found in an acre of forest. This is a serious disadvantage in exploitation, where it is usual to work only one or two types of timber. In addition many of the trees have wood which is extremely hard, in other cases of little value. Hence the evergreen forests are comparatively unimportant. Even within 50 miles of such a thoroughfare as the Brahmaputra in Assam they remain liane-choked, fever-stricken haunts of wild elephants. Some species of trees occur in all three areas (West Coast, Bengal-Assam and Burma-Malaya), and examples are *Mesua ferrea*, *Michelia*, *Eugenia*, *Calophyllum*; others are more restricted. Bengal-Assam is rich in *Castanopsis*, whilst in Burma-Malaya more than half the trees belong to the family of the Dipterocarps.

The Deciduous or Monsoon Forests are the characteristic forests of India, and occur over nearly half the area of the country, but especially in three tracts—a strip along the wetter, western side of the plateau; a great block in the north-east of the plateau; and the sub-Himalayan tract. The forests are mostly very mixed, but three species stand out because of their economic importance. *Teak* (*Tectona grandis*) grows through most of the Peninsula proper, but not on the east coast. It is rarely found as pure stands. The *Sal* (*Shorea robusta*), in contrast to teak, is gregarious and grows in two main areas—the north-eastern plateau and the submontane tract of the Eastern Himalayas. The *Sandalwood* (*Santalum album*), though evergreen, occurs in the deciduous forests of southern India.

The Dry Forests or Thorn Forests and Scrubland occur in the drier parts of the Deccan, north-western India and the Dry Zone of Burma. The small trees often develop enormously long roots and are often armed with sharp spines—as a protection against destruction by animals. Various species of *Acacia* are characteristic. This is really a savanna.

The Semi-Deserts and Deserts are marked by the occurrence of stunted bushes, often of species found elsewhere as forest trees. *Acacia catechu* is a good example. Plants with succulent stems or leaves, notably *Euphorbia*, are also characteristic.

The Hill Forests or Mountain Forests are usually found above the 'frost line', except that in the dry north-west frosts occur also on the plains. Frosts do not usually occur below 5,000 feet in southern India; in Assam, below 3,000 feet. The mountain forests include evergreen oaks, succeeded, generally at higher levels, by conifers. Details will be given later under the description of the Himalayan regions. The Deodar (Himalayan cedar, *Cedrus deodara*), blue pine (*Pinus excelsa*), chir pine (*P. longifolia*), silver fir (*Abies Webbiana*) and spruce (*Picea morinda*) are economically the most important trees.

The Tidal Forests occur along the sea coast and in the estuaries of rivers; especially in the Sundarbans, and around the Andamans. The mangrove swamps, though the most familiar type, are not as important as the lofty forests of *Heritiera*.

The Riparian Forests are of minor importance.

It will be gathered from this description that the natural vegetation of India is essentially forest, and that even the desert tracts are really very dry types of forest. Patches of grassland occur interrupting the monsoon forests on the hills, and much of the open thorn forest has a carpet of grass, but otherwise grassland is not characteristic of India. It is a popular fallacy that forest when cleared and then deserted returns to forest. Such is usually not the case: the deserted clearings become covered with forest 'weeds', especially bamboo. Enormous areas of India are occupied by useless, waste jungle which has originated in this way.

It must be borne in mind that in a thickly populated country such as India the natural vegetation has been cleared over enormous areas.

The older statistics are deceptive because they include Burma. Thus in 1918–19 out of a grand total of 1,101,356 square miles for British India, State forests covered 266,019 square miles or 24·2 per cent. and other forests 85,000 square miles or 7·8 per cent., so that nearly a third of the country was forested. But half the total was in Burma. It should be noted that these figures, though from official sources, are quite different from those recorded in the agricultural returns. In the latter only land legally administered as forest is recognized as such—13·4 per cent. of the area of British India, including Burma, in 1935–6. Other forest land, including State 'reserved' forests which may be reserved for prevention of soil erosion and other reasons besides timber production, may thus come into the categories of 'waste' or 'not available for cultivation'.

Bearing these points in mind we may use the figures now published annually by Food and Agriculture Organization of United Nations. In 1955 India records 50,089,000 hectares (124,719,000 acres) of forest or 15·2 per cent. of the surface; Pakistan 2,501,000 hectares (6,177,000 acres) of forest or 2·7 per cent. of the surface.

The exploitation of 'reserved forests' is carefully regulated by Government, and is carried out either by Government agents or by lessees under supervision. The method of working the timber of the forests is interesting. It is cut in the dry season and dragged to the small streams by elephants or buffaloes. With the advent of the rains the streams rise and the logs are floated down to the main river. There they are joined together to form rafts—in the case of heavier timbers provided with bamboo floats—and floated down to the saw-mills. It may take two or three seasons for logs to 'come out' of the area in which they have been felled and in the Himalayas many areas remain unworked because of the difficulty of floating out the timber.

The principal timbers extracted have already been mentioned. In addition enormous quantities of firewood are obtained, and many of the so-called 'forests' are areas of scrubland reserved for the sake of economizing fuel-wood. Amongst other forest produce may be noted resin (especially from *Pinus longifolia*); bamboo; grasses for fodder—in ordinary years enormous numbers of cattle graze in the forests; in times of scarcity the grass is cut and the hay sent to threatened districts; tanning materials; essential oils (mainly from sandalwood and planted eucalypts); wood oils; cutch (a dye obtained from *Acacia catechu*); and finally lac. India has practically a monopoly of the lac industry and the export is of great value. Lac is the sticky secretion caused by a small insect which is now artificially propagated on a small scale.

Agriculture. India and Pakistan are both essentially agricultural countries. Three-quarters of their vast populations depend on agricultural pursuits for their existence.

Fairly complete agricultural statistics,[1] prior to partition, are available for British India (except Baluchistan), but for only certain of the Indian States. Of necessity many general statements were based on the position as it was in British India, i.e. the provinces. For example in 1930-1 in British India 230,000,000 acres supported a population of 272,000,000—representing about 0·85 of an acre per head of population (compare figures given for China). Even allowing for double cropping, the acreage per head was well under one acre. It is in fact difficult to make an accurate allowance for double cropping, because India normally has two harvests—the *kharif* harvest in October and November for crops sown in the early weeks of the monsoon, and the *rabi* harvest in February or March for crops sown at the end of the monsoon, about November. These harvests often alternate on the same piece of land;

---

[1] *Agricultural Statistics of India* (annual); Vol. I, British India; Vol. II, Native States (Calcutta: Published by Government of India). After 1920-1 the acreage and yields were only published for the provinces and states; they were formerly given for each district, and it is from the district statistics that some of the details for each natural region, given later, were originally worked out. For a general account of agriculture, including some details since partition, see Sir E. John Russell, *The World's Agriculture* (1954). For an earlier account see J. Mackenna, *Agriculture in India*. An indispensable and convenient work of reference on all matters relating to agriculture is the Abridged Report of the *Royal Commission on Agriculture in India* (London: His Majesty's Stationery Office, 1928), though much of the detail in this has been incorporated in the general descriptions of Sir John Russell. Agricultural statistics are now published annually and summarized in the *Yearbook of Food and Agricultural Statistics* published by FAO.

double cropping upsets this rotation. The alternation also partly accounts for the large area of current fallows, typical of Indian agriculture. To take an example from northern India, rice might be sown in June, reaped in October–November (*kharif* crop) and the land then lie fallow till the following October or November when wheat would be sown for reaping in February or March (*rabi* crop), the ground then being prepared for rice sowing again in June. Apart from this, land is commonly allowed to rest and in the old statistics for British India current fallows were about 20 per cent. of the total arable land.

Since partition agricultural statistics have covered a steadily increasing proportion of both countries, and the distinction between provinces and native states has disappeared. First there is the general picture of land use in the two countries. Since India now plans to change to the metric system entirely the figures may be given in thousands of hectares (1 hectare = 2·47 acres and 100 hectares = one square kilometre).

Land Use in India and Pakistan, 1955

	India	Pakistan	Sub-Continent
Arable land and tree crops . .	158,341 (48·1%)	24,404 (25·8%)	182,745 (43·2%)
Permanent pasture and meadows .	11,155 (3·4%)	— —	11,155 (2·6%)
Forest . . .	50,089 (15·2%)	2,501 (2·7%)	52,590 (12·4%)
Unused, potentially productive . .	22,872 (7·0%)	67,577 (71·5%)	176,880 (41·8%)
Waste (including urban areas) .	86,431 (26·3%)		
Total Area . .	328,888	94,482	423,370

The land classed as 'unused, potentially productive' for the Republic of India in this table (comparable figures are not available for Pakistan) is 7 per cent. of the land area. This is much more realistic than the 17–18 per cent. of 'cultivable waste' in the old figures for British India. Since the diagrams given for most of the natural regions (pp. 283–357) are based on the old returns, the proportion shown as 'waste' is probably too high in all cases.

Turning now to the crops grown, the table given opposite is based on the statistics for 1956 published by FAO and the figures given are a percentage of the total area of arable land, including current fallows, and land under tree crops.

This table emphasizes certain contrasts between Pakistan and India. East Pakistan is very wet rice–jute country with few other crops; West Pakistan relies largely on irrigation, so there is but a small area devoted to the dry zone millets and oil-seeds. The Indian Republic on the other hand, with vast areas on the Plateau of poor soils, low and precarious

	India	Pakistan	Sub-Continent
Food-grains . . .	65·5	71·4	66·2
Rice	20·0	37·2	22·3
Wheat	7·8	18·7	9·3
Barley	2·1	1·0	2·0
Sorghum (jowar) millet .	10·5	2·3	9·4
Other millets (bajra, ragi)	12·2	3·8	10·9
Maize	2·4	1·8	2·3
Dry beans . . .	3·7	1·0	3·3
Gram and other peas .	6·8	5·6	6·7
Sugarcane . . .	1·3	1·7	1·4
Other food crops (est.) .	2·5	2·0	2·5
Total food crops . .	69·3	75·1	70·1
Cotton	5·1	5·9	5·2
Oil-seeds	7·4	3·6	6·7
Jute	0·7	2·7	0·8
Tea	0·2	0·1	0·2
Tobacco	0·2	0·3	0·2
Other non-food crops, fodder and fallow . . .	17·1	12·3	16·8
	100·0	100·0	100·0

rainfall and with no facilities for irrigation, has nearly a quarter of the farmed land (22·7 per cent.) under millets.

Although the position is gradually improving, it is well known that the yield of crops in India is low. A delayed monsoon may cause almost complete failure of crops, especially millets, which are not protected by irrigation. Using again the figures published by FAO, the total production of food grains in the year 1956 was as follows (in thousands of metric tons):

(1964 figures in brackets)

	India		Pakistan	
Rice	42,890	(36,489)	13,718	(11,815)
Wheat	8,707	(9,708)	3,368	(10,174)
Barley	2,793		130	
Sorghum (jowar) . .	7,546	} (12,963)	250	
Other millets . . .	6,960		373	
Maize	3,068	(4,527)	461	(584)
Total cereals . . .	71,964	(69,555)	18,319	

Presuming that all the cereals are eaten as human food, there was available for each Indian almost exactly 500 grams a day, or a little over 1 lb. of 'raw' cereal, and for each Pakistani 600 grams. If an allowance is made for seed and a 10 per cent. loss in preparation (husking, grinding, cooking) the net amounts available are reduced to about 420 and 500 grams respectively—equivalent to a daily intake of 1,512 and 1,800 calories. This is insufficient to support life, and even adding all the pulses does not bring it up to a minimum of 2,000 calories a day. In a careful study of 12 sample villages in U.P. Dr. Muhammed Shafi has shown how the people are compelled to make up the deficiencies in diet by drinking sugar-water, and in other ways.[1] In fact the whole of India and Pakistan lives at or near starvation level.

Rice.[2] Rice is easily the most important food-grain in India and Pakistan, occupying, as the above table shows, a third of the area devoted to food-grains and over a quarter of the total cropped area. It is the staple food-grain in all the wetter parts of India; almost the sole grain where the rainfall is more than 80 inches; still the most important with

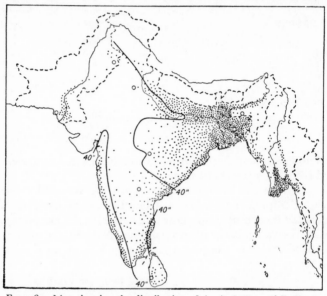

Fig. 98.—Map showing the distribution of rice in India and Pakistan

Each dot represents 50,000 acres sown. The circles show, for purposes of reference, the positions of some major towns. The lines shown are the 40-inch annual isohyets and demonstrate that rice is unimportant where the rainfall drops below 40 inches. This distribution map, like those for other crops in this section, has been constructed from figures given in *Agricultural Statistics*, 1920–1, for reasons explained in the footnote on p. 229, but may be taken to show the average inter-war and present position.

a rainfall of between 40 and 80 inches. Where the rainfall is less than 40 inches it can only be grown, generally speaking, with irrigation. Although considered botanically as a single species, there are many hundred varieties of rice, differing in the colour, size and shape of the grain, in the height of the stalks and in the climatic and edaphic requirements of the plant. The existence of numerous varieties in India is due, in some measure, to the conservatism and ignorance of the cultivators,

[1] Quoted in L. D. Stamp, 'The Measurement of Land Resources', *Geog. Rev.*, **48**, 1958, 1–15. 1,000,000 calories a year produced by the farmer, or 900,000 available for consumption (roughly 2,460 a day) is there taken as a Standard Nutrition Unit, adequate to support one human being.

[2] See D. H. Grist, *Rice* (London: Longmans, 1953; 2nd Ed., 1955).

who go on growing a particular, often inferior, variety merely because their forefathers did before them. Incidentally the conservatism of the consumers, who demand a particular variety, is equally marked. The numerous varieties fall into two main classes, of which the second is by far the more important.

(1) Upland or hill rice (which can be grown on hill slopes).

(2) Lowland or swamp rice (which requires level, flooded fields).

Practically the whole crop is grown for local consumption. Rice in the husk is known as paddy (sometimes written padi); indeed in

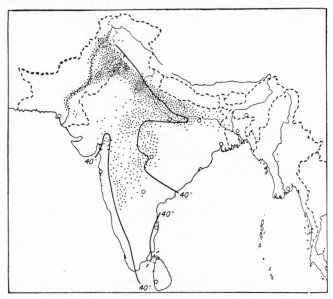

Fig. 99.—The distribution of wheat in India and Pakistan, showing the concentration in the Punjab and U.P.

Nearly all the wheat-growing regions have less than 40 inches of rain per year, but it should be noted that the crop is important mainly in the temperate parts of northern India which have a marked cool season. In the north of the Punjab the wheat benefits considerably from the winter rainfall which comes at a time when it is required to 'swell' the grain. Each dot represents 20,000 acres. There has been a recent extension in the irrigated area of Sind.

Eastern lands generally the word rice is little used, and one invariably refers to paddy fields and paddy cultivation. The polished rice so familiar in Western lands is rarely seen in the East, where rice is merely husked and skinned. The paddy grain is sown under water and for the first few weeks of its existence the young rice plant grows under standing water. As the time of ripening approaches, gradually less and less water is required. The great river deltas and alluvial plains thus form ideal rice-lands. The presence of an impervious layer just below the surface is important for retention of the water. In hilly country the slopes must be carefully terraced before the necessary flat fields are obtained. On the whole crop yields in India are low, those for rice far below many other countries. In recent years the introduction of intensive Japanese methods of cultivation has started to improve local yields. Whether in hilly or flat country, the cultivators choose one small field as a 'nursery', from which the tiny plants when about 6 inches high are transplanted, by hand, in small bundles in rows in the flooded fields. The labour involved is obviously enormous, more especially when one remembers that the ploughing is done by a small wooden plough drawn by a couple of slow-moving oxen or water buffaloes.[1] Reaping is also by hand. The growth of the rice plant when flooded is

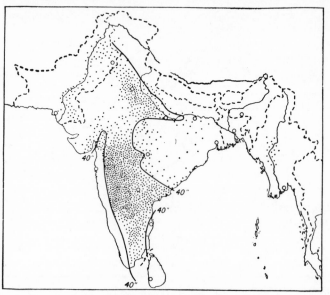

FIG. 100.—The distribution of millet in India and Pakistan

Each dot represents 50,000 acres. The lines shown are the 40-inch isohyets and demonstrate that millet is essentially a 'dry zone' crop. This diagram refers to the two chief millets, jowar and bajra.

extraordinarily rapid—even 6 or 9 inches in twenty-four hours—and given great heat ripening is so rapid that as many as five crops from one area can be obtained, though in India, owing to the marked seasonal rhythm, a single crop is the rule except in the deltas. Rice in India is mainly a summer crop; it is planted towards the end of the rains and is ready for reaping, according to the locality, between November and February.

Wheat has become the favourite food in the drier parts of northern India. It is there a winter crop, so that the land can often be used for

[1] One advantage of the nursery system is, however, often overlooked. The rice can be planted in a nursery *before* the harvest is gathered of other crops on land which the rice will later occupy.

other purposes during the rest of the year. It is sown after the rains and ripens before the great heat commences. Wheat is especially important on the irrigated land of the Punjab, and disappears with increasing heat, moisture and rainfall down the Ganges Valley, but has spread a considerable distance southwards on the plateau—as far as the Dharwar district of Bombay. For many years there was a large surplus of Punjab wheat exported from the Punjab via Karachi to the United Kingdom, elsewhere in Europe, and Egypt. It reached a peak value of Rs 190,000,000 (then £13,000,000) in 1917–18 but later dwindled to very small totals, even when flour is included. During the Second World War the position changed completely. For various reasons, including the huge population increase, India has become a large importer of wheat, especially from Australia. Pakistan itself had to import 800,000 tons in 1952–3, though normally there is a surplus in the west for export to the east. Indian wheat is a hard wheat and was formerly much appreciated by the Italians for macaroni making.

Barley is almost co-extensive in its distribution with wheat, but grows on lighter soils.

Millet constitutes the staple food in nearly all the drier parts of India, occupying a fifth of the total cultivated area and more than a quarter of the area devoted to food-grains. It thus ranks an easy second to rice among Indian crops. There are three principal kinds—*cholum* or *jowar* (great millet), *cumbu* or *bajra* (spiked millet) and *ragi* or *marua*. Where the rainfall is less than 40 inches millet is everywhere important, and it can be grown without irrigation even when the rainfall is as low as 20 inches. When the rainfall exceeds 40 inches it rapidly decreases in importance. Fig. 100 clearly illustrates this. Millet is grown entirely for home consumption; there has been a considerable tendency in recent years for it to be replaced by wheat wherever soil conditions will allow. The stubble left in the millet fields is important as cattle grazing.

Maize flourishes both on the plains and in the hills where the rainfall is moderate. It is grown as a subsidiary food-grain and for fodder in many parts of India, but only among certain hill tribes is it the chief grain. It grows with millet in fairly dry regions and with rice in somewhat damper regions, but it ceases to be important in such areas as the Lower Ganges Valley, where the rainfall exceeds 60 inches.

Gram (Chickpea) is the most important of the pulses and affords good human food as well as fodder for cattle and horses.

Pulse is used as a general term to include the edible seeds of various plants of the pea and bean family (Leguminoseae), just as cereal is used to include the edible seeds obtained mainly from various members of the *Gramineae*. Various pulses are grown in India; they afford nutritious food and a valuable variant to rice or millet, but are apt to be indigestible and to cause flatulence if eaten in excess. It will be seen that they cover a large area, and if miscellaneous grain is included the 'various grains and pulses' occupy third place after rice and millet.

Sugarcane is grown in nearly all parts of India, but most comes from the irrigated lands of the Upper Ganges Plains and the Punjab. India was in a very curious position with regard to sugar. The climate is eminently suitable, and India has a huge agricultural population, to whom the labour attending sugar cultivation is nothing new. The sugar industry was once one of the flourishing industries and until 1890 practically none was imported. Then for many years India produced but a fraction of her requirements and imported huge quantities from Java. In recent years that position has been changed. There are numerous modern mills, especially in Uttar Pradesh, and the bulk of the requirement is now home-produced.

Other Food Crops. Many of the most interesting and in some ways one might say the most characteristic of India's foodstuffs are cultivated on areas insufficiently important to be shown on a general table. The early traders sought especially the spices of India, and if there are two things which will ever remain in the present-day visitor's mind it will be his first Hindu dinner with its succession of hot curries and highly spiced foods and the galaxy of smells, spicy and otherwise, which greeted his nostrils from his first bazaar. Fields of *chillies* with the blood-red pods are a picturesque sight, but perhaps fail to excite admiration as much as the contemplation of a Madrassi cook abstractedly chewing chillies as he prepares dinner. The best *pepper* in the world still grows on the rich, damp soil of the Malabar coast; the plant is a climber and is trained up tree-trunks. *Ginger* is obtained from the rhizomes or underground stems of *Zingiber officinale*, and grows especially in the rich, damp soil of Bombay and Madras. *Nutmegs* and *cloves* also grow in India.

Numerous fruits are grown in India for local consumption; the *mango* is perhaps the most delicious of all fruits when one has learnt to eat it respectably; it is the fruit of a large evergreen tree, and is ready just before the rains break (hence mango showers). The *Jack fruit* also grows on a huge evergreen tree in wetter regions; the *durian* is celebrated for its appalling smell. *Bananas* or *plantains* grow almost everywhere—a few plants near every hut or village; *papayas* (paw-paws), with the consistency of soft soap but a pleasant mild flavour, are almost equally widespread. *Custard apples* and *mangosteens* deserve mention, but, apart from mangoes, the fruits of India lack the acidity which renders temperate fruits so refreshing. An exception must be made for the delicious small sweet *limes*, used fresh for making the most popular of soft drinks. Oranges, apples, pears and plums belong to the hills but there has been a remarkable development of citrus orchards on irrigated land in the Punjab in recent decades.

Among root crops *potatoes* are usually obtainable in Indian villages, so are *onions* and *sweet potatoes*, and various other vegetables such as brinjals, tomatoes, cabbages and turnips. *Coconuts*, to be mentioned later, are widely used as a flavouring matter in curries.

Oil-seeds. Turning to crops which are mainly 'non-food' crops, oil-seeds vie with cotton for pride of place as the most important. Formerly between a quarter and half the crop was exported. *Sesamum* is a plant of the dry zone or intermediate areas; linseed and rape do not flourish in the wettest parts. The oil obtained from rape is known as colza oil, which, before the extended use of mineral oil, was a favourite lamp oil. It is also used as a lubricant and for a variety of other purposes. The oil from sesame or sesamum is widely used in India for cooking and for anointing the body; it is also used in soap manufacture and the best kinds for margarine. *Linseed*, the seed of the flax plant which is grown in India, as in other tropical countries, not for its fibre but for its seed, is used for oil which is of especial importance in the manufacture of paints and varnishes. Special interest attaches to *ground-nuts*. The ground-nut, also known as the monkey-nut or pea-nut, is a small leguminous plant which grows about a foot high. The nuts are borne on shoots which after flowering bury themselves in the soil. The 'nuts' are nutritious and furnish a pale yellow oil closely resembling olive oil. It can be used as a substitute for olive oil as a salad oil, in the manufacture of margarine and especially in the manufacture of soap. But the real importance of the plant to India is that it thrives in very light sandy soils in dry regions—often where practically nothing else will grow. In 1911–12 it was not sufficiently important to be separately recorded in India; in 1912–13 it occupied only 394,000 acres. In 1930–1 it occupied 5,310,000 acres in British India alone—a larger area than any other oil-seed crop in India. This was one of the great triumphs of the Agritural Department of the British Indian Government. Its growth in importance continues. In 1963–4 16,800,000 acres yielding 5,290,000 tons of nuts were harvested in India alone, not including Pakistan.

The importance of the coconut is not adequately indicated by the relatively small area it occupies. It is a denizen of the sandy shores of tropical lands, though it will grow in plantations some distance from the sea. Of all palms it is, perhaps, the most graceful, and is the one indissolubly associated with tropical scenery in the imagination of dwellers in temperate lands. The palm bears for a considerable part of the year, and 200 nuts per palm is not an unusual average. The thick outer covering of the nut is rarely seen abroad; it is stripped off by striking the nut sharply on an iron-pointed stake set up in the ground. The husks so obtained are left to ret in water for about six months—the lagoons behind the sandy seashores of Malabar and Ceylon are ideal for the purpose and the local residents seem born immune to smells—and the fibre or 'coir' beaten out by sticks or by machinery in modern plantations. Coir is very strong and is used for ropes, as matting, floor coverings and the stiffer parts for brushes and brooms.

Copra is the dried white flesh of the nut. The nuts are cleft in two with a hatchet and exposed for a short while to the sun, when the flesh curls and separates from the shell. It is then dried either in the sun or in a special drying house. Coconut oil is now usually obtained by compression of copra; the residue forms the cattle food known as poonac. The oil is used in cooking and by many Indians for the anointing of the body or hair. That exported is used, as are the other oils, in the manufacture of soap, margarine and candles. The kernel is also prepared in another way as desiccated coconut, for use in confectionery.

Mention must be made of cotton-seed oil, an important by-product in the cotton areas.

The residue from all the oil-seeds, after the expression of the oil, is valuable as cattle food.

The one important oil not yet mentioned is castor oil. It is especially valuable as a lubricant at low temperatures, as it does not solidify even with 30° of frost. This is one of the properties which make it valuable as a lubricant for aircraft. The medicinal oil—a great favourite with nearly all peoples in India—is obtained from smaller seeds, there being two varieties of seeds, large and small.

Cotton. India with Pakistan ranks second to U.S.A. as a producer of cotton. The average output for the five years preceding World War I (1909–13) was over three-quarters of a million tons—nearly 4,000,000 bales of 400 lb. gross or 3,400,000 United States' bales of 500 lb. This was rather more than a quarter of the United States' production. In 1956 yield in India was about 840,000 metric tons and in Pakistan a further 309,000 tons. Cotton in India is a 'dry zone' crop, and is very largely restricted to the area with less than 40 inches of rainfall. There are three leading areas of production:

(a) The black cotton soil of the north-western part of Peninsular India, forming the hinterland of Bombay. The high plains of Berar are especially important. The sticky, moisture-retaining soil is suited to the growth of native cottons of short staple. The yield is generally low—less than 100 lb. per acre.

(b) The fertile alluvium of the Indus and Ganges plains. When irrigated the American cottons, greatly superior to the native varieties, grow well.

(c) The ferruginous soils of the south of India which, in parts of Madras, grow cotton of excellent quality.

An increasing proportion of India's cotton is being consumed by home mills, at many centres, but there was before 1939 a large export to Japan and China and continental Europe (Italy, Belgium, Germany, France). Indian cotton is not, as a rule, sufficiently good to meet the requirements of Lancashire manufacturers. The acreage under cotton fluctuated somewhat more widely than was the case with other crops.

This reflected very largely conditions in the world's cotton markets. Thus the acreage in the former British India dropped to a low average of 13·6 million acres in 1931–5 compared with a high average of 14·6 million acres in 1916–21. Just before the outbreak of the Second World War the total for the whole of India was estimated to be 25·9 million acres. This total dropped during the war but since partition has been recovering. Figures for 1963–4 were 19·8 million acres in the Republic of India and 3·6 million acres in Pakistan. Cotton continues to be a major export from Pakistan (Karachi).

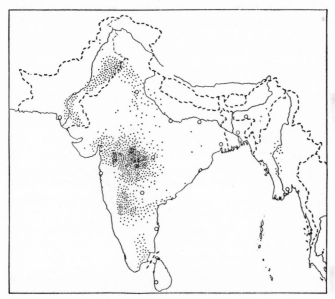

Fig. 101.—The distribution of cotton in India and Pakistan, showing the three principal areas mentioned in the text

Each dot represents 20,000 acres.

Much attention has been given to the improvement of Indian cotton. Though Cambodia cotton is firmly established in Madras and Egyptian cotton grows well in Sind, repeated experiments have proved the difficulty of establishing exotic varieties on the great cotton soil areas and research has therefore been directed to the improvement of existing Indian varieties. Rapid degeneration of varieties improved by selection has caused the already conservative farmer to lose faith; the conservatism already noted in connection with paddy-farming and carelessness in the mixing of seed are other potent factors.

Jute. Jute is the cheapest of the common fibres, and from its use in the manufacture of cheap wrapping canvas, bags, etc., is often referred to as the 'brown paper of the wholesale trade'. The fibre is weaker and less durable than flax or hemp, and is somewhat easily rotted by water. It does not bleach but is easily dyed. The jute plant (*Corchorus capsularis* and *C. olitorius*) is raised from seed, and grows to a height of 10 or 14 feet. It grows best in well-drained soil; in muddy swamps the plants are taller, but the fibre is coarser. In the Ganges Delta, which yields over nine-tenths of the world's jute, the seeds are sown in March or April; in August or September the plant is ready for cutting. The first process in the preparation of the fibre is retting in stagnant water, after which the fibre is stripped from the stem by hand, washed and dried in the shade before being sorted, graded and baled. A good yield is 3·5 bales or 1,400 lb. per acre.

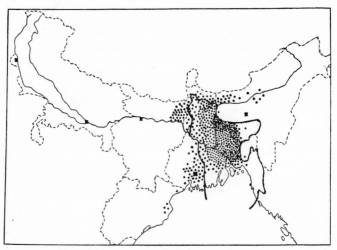

Fig. 102.—The pre-partition distribution of jute in India, showing the remarkable concentration of the bulk of the world's acreage in Bengal and the neighbouring parts of Assam, Bihar and Orissa. Pakistan is demarcated by a plain line

The area of heaviest production is in eastern Bengal on the 'new delta' some distance from the jute-mill towns north of Calcutta (shown by a square dot). Each dot represents 5,000 acres.

Originally the preparation of jute was a peasant industry in Bengal and the fibre was used for making clothes. Its 'discovery' as a substitute for hemp dates from 1832, and was made by a Dundee merchant. The jute trade developed along with the international trade in grain, since one of the principal uses of the fibre is in making sacks for grain. About half of India's jute is now manufactured into 'gunny cloth' locally in mill towns north of Calcutta; the other half is exported, mainly to Great Britain—where hessian canvas and other jute fabrics are made at Dundee and Barnsley—to the United States and elsewhere.

Fig. 102 shows the area of production as it was before partition. Partition has seriously upset the jute trade; most of the production was in eastern Bengal (now Pakistan), but the jute mills were on the Hooghly, now in the Indian Republic. The Indians have tried to stimulate production, often on unsuitable land; the Pakistanis have sought to limit cultivation and to establish their own mills. There is now, for example, a huge mill with very modern equipment at Narayanganj near Dacca. It was feared at one time that bulk handling of grain would kill the demand for jute and during the slump of 1931-2 acreage dropped to below 2,000,000. In 1951-2, however, it was 3,376,000 acres in Pakistan alone. By 1955 Pakistan had reduced the acreage to 1,650,000, whilst in India proper it reached 1,758,000.

Other fibres obtained in India include mesta (*Hibiscus*), hemp and kapok.

Indigo. From time immemorial the art of dyeing has been practised in India, and it has been ascertained that some of the mummy cloths of the ancient Egyptians are embroidered with blue threads—dyed with indigo undoubtedly brought by Arab merchants from India. Indigo is, *par excellence*, the Indian dye. The indigo plant is a small shrub, but is usually grown as an annual from seed in very carefully prepared soil. Sowing, in Bengal and Bihar, takes place early in March, and the precarious crop, easily spoilt by too much or too little rain, is normally ready for cutting in the middle of June. The plants are stacked in steeping vats and covered with water. After about ten hours the water, now bright orange, is run off into the beating vats and beaten by hand or churned by machinery. During this process it changes in colour, at first to green, then to dark blue. The indigo is allowed to settle, the water is run off and the colouring matter is boiled and finally the pulpy mass is pressed, cut into cubes and dried.

Broadly speaking, modern coal-tar dyes have killed the indigo industry. During World War I, when German dyes were difficult to obtain, the area under indigo rose temporarily to 765,000 acres (1916-17), but in general has since steadily decreased. It may now be called almost a dead industry.

Opium. Opium is the dried juice of the opium poppy (*Papaver somniferum*). Incisions are made at sunset in the unripe capsules of the poppies and by morning the milky juice has hardened to a brown substance—the opium of commerce. Morphia is an extract of opium and is, of course, a very valuable drug, producing sleep and insensibility to pain. In the public mind opium is associated with its abuse in China, and India with its share in supplying this harmful drug to Chinese markets. The history of the opium traffic is a happy hunting-ground for politicians of all creeds. The present position, at any rate, is that Indian exports of opium have ceased, except as is consistent with legitimate medical requirements vouched for by the Governments of the importing countries. In the interests of human progress the British Indian Government voluntarily gave up a vast revenue. Unfortunately the Indian agriculturist was robbed of a lucrative crop. From 615,000 acres in 1906–7, the area occupied by the opium poppy declined steadily, reaching the low levels of 43,000 acres in 1930–1 and 4,812 acres in 1938–9. Official war-time needs sent up the acreage to 36,415 in 1943–4. The old Indian centres were the Ganges Valley (Ghazipur and Patna) and the Malwa Plateau. Since partition the policy of restriction has continued. Cultivation is now almost entirely restricted to Uttar Pradesh near Ghazipur where 19,000 acres were permitted in 1947–8. Opium smoking is forbidden in India except on medical certificate.

Coffee. The once lucrative and extensive coffee-planting industry of Mysore and southern India was virtually annihilated by disease, but has been resuscitated so that coffee covers over 200,000 acres, especially in Mysore and the Nilgiri Hills and in the former little province of Coorg. Production in 1963 was 42,000 tons.

Tea. The tea of commerce is obtained by drying the leaves of a small evergreen shrub, *Thea camellia*, a native of south-eastern Asia. The shrub requires a deep, fertile soil very well drained, as stagnant water in the soil is particularly harmful. Soils of recently cleared forest land are excellent, but provided the drainage is good, tea grows well on valley lands, as in Assam. The tea shrub may be classed as a sub-tropical plant, but is a very hardy plant and, provided the growing season is long, warm and moist, is not injured by winter frost. Left to itself, it grows to the size of a small tree, but when grown for tea it is pruned every year in the spring to form a bush 3 or 4 feet high. Some weeks after pruning young shoots appear, and when the leaves reach a certain size they are picked. Another crop of leaves, or 'flush', occurs later, and others at intervals of a week or ten days during the season. There are three or four pickings in China, sixteen in Assam, and even more in Ceylon during the season. An abundance of cheap but skilled labour is obviously essential for the picking of the leaves the moment they are ready, especially as the various flushes afford tea of differing quality and a delay in picking affects quality. After gathering, the leaves are withered (by being spread out on wire trays and dried), rolled, partly fermented, dried and sifted.

Until after 1850 China supplied the entire commercial crop of the world. About that date Assamese supplies began to be important, and Assam came to supply nearly half the world's export. Assam is believed by many to be the original home of the tea plant, and it was discovered there growing wild when the first attempts to make plantations were made over a century ago. The plantations are situated on the hilly slopes on either side of the Brahmaputra Valley and, of recent years, have extended in the valley itself. They stretch westwards into Bengal around Darjeeling, and beyond even to the Punjab, and another important area is on the southern slopes of the Garo and Khasi Hills in Assam near Sylhet. The other tea-growing area of India is in the extreme south. Amongst the Nilgiri Hills and the hills of Travancore the delicately flavoured aromatic 'China' teas can be, and are now, grown in India. Despite production of tea in many other countries, demand has at times outstripped supplies with consequent rise in prices.

Tobacco. Although India ranks next to the United States and China as a producer, its tobacco cannot be described as a cash crop. Indian methods of curing do not suit European tastes, and, further, the production is only sufficient to satisfy home demand. The tobacco plant is widely distributed; the quality and character tend to vary according to soil. Heavy soils produce strong tobacco and light ones mild. Tobacco (*Nicotiana tabacum*) is a handsome annual with large, broad leaves, covered with tiny hairs, and grows to a height of several feet. The flower shoot is nipped off in order that the strength may go to the leaves. Much of the Indian tobacco is grown on alluvial soil; often on the banks of mud and silt left by the river after the flood season is over. Bombay, Madras and the Punjab rank among the great producing areas.

Fodder. The enormous numbers of cattle in India consume huge quantities of food and in nearly all the dry parts this has to be specially grown. Hence fodder occupies 3·75 per cent. of the total area of cultivated land. Various leguminous plants are the favourite fodder plants as well as millet and other grain. Fodder crops are especially typical of the Punjab irrigation colonies and are the basis of the growing dairy industry there and in U.P.

Other Crops. Other non-food crops in India include cinchona (quinine), of which there are plantations in Sikkim and southern India; rubber, of which there are plantations in Travancore and the extreme south of Madras—always in wet regions.

The Position of Agriculture in India. It is undoubtedly a fact that the position of agriculture in India is far from satisfactory.[1]

The yield per unit area of almost every crop in India is exceedingly low—in nearly every case far below the world averages (figures in tons per hectare):[2]

Crop	India	World	Typical country with good yield
Wheat	0·71	1·16	United Kingdom, 3·12; Denmark, 4·03
Barley	0·84	1·30	Japan, 2·46
Maize	0·82	1·72	United States, 2·87
Rice	1·36	1·86	Italy, 4·93; Japan, 4·22
Sugarcane	33	40	Hawaii, 209

[1] Sir John Russell, *op. cit. sup.*
[2] See the summary published in L. D. Stamp, *Our Developing World* (London: Faber & Faber, 1963). Figures are from FAO sources and refer to 1956.

What are the causes of the admittedly low yield of Indian crops? India is richly endowed by Nature in the matter of soil and climate— vast areas of fertile, alluvial land and a comparatively small area of useless mountain land (contrast China). Among the causes are:

(1) Soil exhaustion. The land is being continuously impoverished owing to the lack of manure and the uninterrupted cultivation of heavy and exhausting crops. Despite the huge number of cattle, it is well known that the Indian agriculturist does not use cow-dung as manure, but as fuel. The dung is picked up and plastered in cakes on the walls of the houses so that it may dry in the sun.[1] What a contrast to China!

(2) Export of natural manures—mainly in the form of oil-seeds, which contain a large proportion of the nitrogenous fraction of the soil.

(3) Uneconomic farming due to subdivision and fragmentation of holdings. Excessive subdivision is a common feature of village life throughout India: it is mainly the result of Hindu and Mahommedan laws of inheritance causing the division of land among the heirs. Fragmentation refers to the land held by any one owner being in a number of small fragments. There are many areas where a field of half an acre is divided between twenty separate owners.[2]

(4) Agricultural indebtedness and consequent poverty. Probably only about one-fifth of the Indian agriculturists are free from debt, a third or more so heavily involved that escape is absolutely impossible.

Broadly, it seems that the whole thing works in a vicious circle. Small holdings result in uneconomic farming,[3] which leads to extreme poverty, indebtedness and the sale of food commodities and oil-seeds; sale of food and oil-seeds is impoverishing the soil and keeping the farmer undernourished; poor and undernourished, he cannot purchase manure, modern farming apparatus, or increase his land-holding to a size which permits economic farming. Yet India's progress depends upon an increase in the standard of living and an increase in the purchasing power of the masses. We have mentioned once or twice the conservatism of the Indian agriculturist. Actually he has little chance

---

[1] The late Professor M. N. Saha calculated (*Nature*, **177**, 1956, 923–4) that cow-dung contributed the equivalent of 40,000,000 tons of coal annually or 32 per cent. of India's total fuel, compared with wood 34 per cent., oil and H.E. 6 and coal 28.

[2] It must, however, be explained that there are two types of land tenure in India. In Bengal, Bihar, U.P., Punjab and Madhya Pradesh zamindari tenure prevails. Single proprietors or proprietary brotherhoods possess large estates of several hundreds or thousands of acres and the State land revenue is payable on each estate as a whole, being assessed at about one-half of the rental. In Bombay, Madras and Assam raiyatwari (or ryotwari) tenure prevails. Each petty proprietor holds directly from the State, and, as a rule, cultivates his own piece of land.

[3] In Bengal, to take a typical state, there are 11,000,000 cultivators (actual workers) to farm 24,500,000 acres—less than 2¼ acres per cultivator. In England before the days of mechanical appliances there were 17 acres per cultivator (1851). Now the average English full-time farm is 99 acres of crops and grass.

to be anything else. He cannot improve his lands and increase his yield by manuring—he has not the initial wherewithal.[1]

Much emphasis is laid by some Indian economic writers on the iniquity of India's export of foodstuffs and raw materials.

It is held that export of grain, oil-seeds and raw materials should cease, that much of the land devoted to such raw materials as cotton and jute should be released for foodstuffs, that the cotton and jute actually produced should be consumed entirely in Indian mills which would therefore increase the industrial population in the towns and relieve the pressure on the land. The relief of the pressure on the land would permit increase of holdings, adoption of modern economic methods of farming, and thus increase the wealth and purchasing power of the agricultural masses.

Unfortunately food production in India and Pakistan has not been keeping pace with population increase. In 1930–1 the people of India were consuming about 1½ lb. or 680 grams of grain and pulse per head per day or nearly 2,500 calories, which is about a world average. As detailed above, calorie intake is probably now less than 2,000 per day.

Livestock. According to the returns made to FAO (Food and Agriculture Organization of United Nations), the domestic animals in India and Pakistan include (in millions):

India (1955–6): Cattle 158·9, buffaloes 44·8, sheep 38·7, goats 56·6, horses 1·5, mules 0·06, donkeys 1·3, camels 0·6, pigs 4·7, poultry 97·4.

Pakistan (1953–4): Cattle 31·1, buffaloes 7·1, sheep 6·15, goats 10·07, horses 0·47, mules 0·04, donkeys 0·91, camels 0·45, pigs 0·10, poultry 14·0.

This is equivalent to 50 cattle per 100 of population, compared with 62 per 100 in British India twenty years earlier. Broadly there are two bullocks or male buffaloes for every plough and for every 10 or 12 acres to be ploughed. This again is less than formerly—an advantage.

The bullock or buffalo is primarily the motive force for the plough and the draught animal. The honours of the plough or cart are frequently shared by the cow. The essential equipment of the peasant farmer includes a pair of bullocks or buffaloes to do the ploughing and draw the cart; a cow to propagate the species (services of a bull are shared) and quite secondarily to give milk.

---

[1] This is the gloomy side of the picture, and the vastness of the problem is apt to blind one as to what can be accomplished. Educational propaganda of the right type could achieve marvels, and of this a proof is afforded by the record contained in that remarkable and stimulating book, *The Remaking of Village India*, by F. L. Brayne (Oxford University Press). In recent years much has been accomplished by broadcasting with communal listening to the village receiving set. Much is also being achieved by the spread of higher-yielding varieties and use of artificial manures, especially ammonium sulphate, is spreading.

Oxen. The characteristic cattle of India are the large white, humped bullocks—Zebu cattle, often known abroad as Brahman cattle. In the U.P. and near some large towns such as Bombay dairying is important. Otherwise, although Indians use milk, the yield of milk is very small. The bull is sacred to the Hindu—a position which is little to be wondered at seeing the importance of the ox in his everyday life.

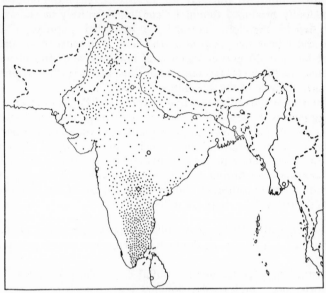

Fig. 103.—The distribution of sheep in India
Each dot represents 50,000 sheep (based on 1930–1 figures).

Hindus do not therefore eat beef, and the consumption of meat in the whole of India is but slight. The dish of delicacy amongst Europeans, by way of contrast to the cold shoulder of mutton, is cold hump. The hide is a valuable part of the animal.

Buffaloes. The buffalo is heavier and stronger than the ox, but slower. Although at home in wet lands—whence the name water-buffalo—and never so happy as when wallowing in a mud pool, or standing in water with his long horns floating on the surface of the water and keeping just the nostrils above the stream—the buffalo is found in numbers in the drier parts of India—where the horns, having lost their original purpose as floats, are curled—as well as in the wetter. The young buffaloes are covered with brown hair which they lose as they grow old, and the adult buffalo is an ugly pig-like animal with a doubtful temper and a rooted objection to Europeans. The milk is rich and better than that from Indian cattle.

Sheep. Comparatively speaking, sheep are not very numerous in

India. They live mainly on the dry hills, where the pasture is insufficiently good for cattle. Over half the total are in Madras and southern Deccan and they are fairly numerous in the Punjab. The sheep of India are poor and yield neither good wool nor good mutton, and the skin is often the most important part.

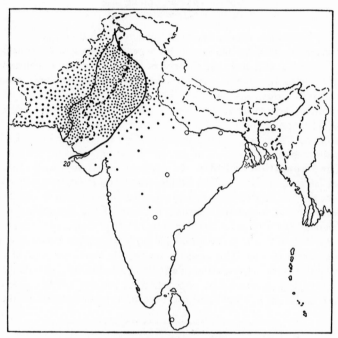

FIG. 104.—The distribution of camels in India

Each dot represents 1,000 camels. The line shown is the 20-inch annual isohyet and demonstrates the concentration of camels in the very dry regions. As irrigation extends so the numbers of camels drop—they do not take kindly to work on the wet irrigated land.

Goats. Goats are to be found everywhere in India, for they live on the poorest pasture and seem to find sufficient to sustain life even in the driest parts. There is a large export trade in goat skins.

Horses and Ponies. There are less than 1,500,000 horses and ponies, including young stock, in the Republic of India. Obviously they are not used as plough animals. They are most numerous in the U.P., and are used specially for small carts.

Mules and Donkeys. Mules and donkeys are very valuable in hilly regions, being sure-footed, and are almost as valuable as camels in very dry regions. More than half the donkeys are in the dry regions of the north-west.

Camels. The camels in India and Pakistan afford a most interesting example of climatic control of distribution. Fig. 104 needs no further comment.

Elephants. It is easy to exaggerate the importance of the elephant whose main use in India today is in the forests and timber yards. One of the joys of India is to

> See the elephants piling teak
> In the sludgy-wudgy creek;

and they have their uses as beasts of burden in forest country.

Fisheries. Fishing has long been a peasant occupation round the coasts of India and some of the rivers but two recent developments call for mention. One is the introduction of trawlers and modern apparatus for deep-sea fisheries. The other is the cultivation of the fast-growing vegetable-feeder *Catala catala* in ponds and irrigation tanks. The spawn or young fish are sold at two or three rupees a thousand and in 8 or 9 months grow into fish weighing $5\frac{1}{2}$ to 6 lb. The importance of such a source of protein is very great.

The Population of India. A Census of the whole Indian Empire, British India as well as Indian States, was taken every ten years from 1871–2, the last having been in 1941. Care must be taken in comparing figures given in successive censuses because of the variation in area considered. The total area considered by the 1941 Census was 1,581,410 square miles, with a population of 388,997,955, giving a mean density for the whole of 246. The area of the British Provinces was 865,446 square miles, with a population of 295,808,722 (density 342); of Native States, 715,964 square miles, population 93,189,233 (density 130).

As constituted in 1947 Pakistan (with states) had an area of 364,737

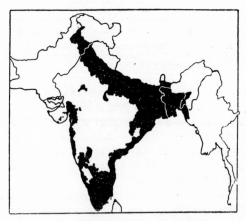

FIG. 105.—The distribution of population

All parts shown in black have a population density exceeding the average for the whole of India of 276 per square mile in 1951. This map demonstrates the concentration in the lowlands, especially in the great alluvial plains.

square miles and included 70,000,000 of the 1941 Census (density 194). Excluding Kashmir (82,258 square miles, 4,000,000 people), Indian Union was left with 1,134,415 square miles (315,000,000).

Both countries took a census in 1951. The total for the Indian Union was 356,891,624 excluding Jammu and Kashmir (4,370,000)

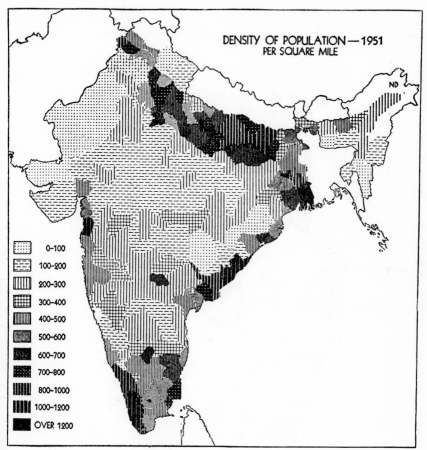

DENSITY OF POPULATION — 1951
PER SQUARE MILE

0–100
100–200
200–300
300–400
400–500
500–600
600–700
700–800
800–1000
1000–1200
OVER 1200

Fig. 106.—The population of the Republic of India—density in 1951

and the tribal areas of Assam (550,000). The total for Pakistan was 75,842,165—giving a grand total of about 437,654,000. The total for the 1961 Census for India alone is 439,235,000; Pakistan, 93,721,000.

The distribution illustrates extraordinarily well the influence of geographical factors.

(a) Physiographic influence: the population is densest in the low-lands and high plains.

(b) Geological or edaphic control: the population tends to be concentrated on the great tracts of alluvium.

(c) Climatic control: the effect is obvious in the desert regions and Baluchistan but is obscured elsewhere by the extensive use of irrigation.

The chief anomaly is the low density in the Assam Valley.

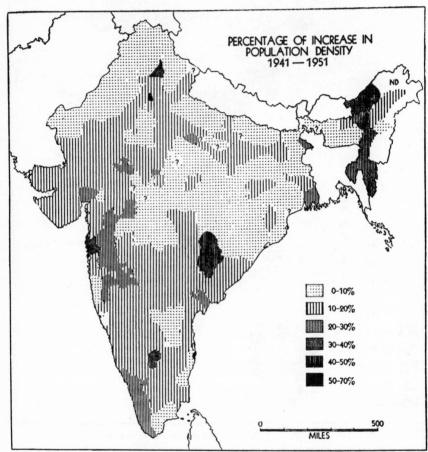

PERCENTAGE OF INCREASE IN
POPULATION DENSITY
1941 — 1951

	0-10%
	10-20%
	20-30%
	30-40%
	40-50%
	50-70%

FIG. 107.—The population of the Republic of India—increase 1941–51

Highest densities are reached in eastern Bengal (Pakistan) of over 800. In a few districts of eastern Bengal and elsewhere—excluding urban areas—the density may exceed 2,000. Three-quarters of the Indian population are agricultural, hence the pressure on the soil is very great; but India, generally speaking, has nothing to compare with the dense agricultural populations of many parts of China.

The Indian population is increasing. Eliminating territorial changes the rate per cent. of real increase has been

	Per cent.		Per cent.
1872–1881	1·5	1921–1931	10·6
1881–1891	9·6	1931–1941	15·0
1891–1901	1·4	1941–1951	12·5
1901–1911	6·4	1951–1961	21·7
1911–1921	1·2		

In the decade 1921–31 the increase was from 318,942,480 to 352,837,778—an almost incredible increase of nearly 34,000,000; but this was eclipsed by the change in 1931–41 from 338,119,154 in India, excluding Burma, to 388,997,955—a jump of over 50 million. The increase 1941–51 was almost as large—48·6 million; 1951–61, 95 million.

The influenza epidemic of 1918–19, which accounted for between 12,000,000 and 13,000,000 victims, was probably worse than any plague India has known and more than equal to the mortality from plague from 1898 to 1918. This explains the low percentage increase in the decade 1911–21.

The population of both India and Pakistan is still predominantly rural and only about 10 per cent. of the people live in towns of 5,000 persons or over. Nevertheless urbanization is proceeding apace. It was hindered by the influenza epidemic which hit the towns worse and resulted in many towns decreasing in population in the decade 1911–21. In 1931 India as a whole had only 38 towns with over 100,000 inhabitants and only 65 with between 50,000 and 100,000. By 1941 the number with over 100,000 had increased to 58. By 1951 Bombay and Calcutta both exceeded 2½ millions, Madras, Delhi, Hyderabad and Karachi had become million cities. Partition in 1947 brought about great mass movements of Hindus and Moslems but perhaps the most serious recent development is the growth of the landless labourer class —80,000,000 in India alone.[1]

The Races of India. It is impossible, in the space available, to deal even in the most cursory manner with the races of India, and no attempt will be made to do so. In the words of Lord Ronaldshay:[2] 'Imagine a region the size of all Europe exclusive only of Russia, with a population of 320,000,000 practising nine great religions and speaking 130 different dialects [3] belonging to six distinct families of speech. That is India looked at from the point of view of the statistician. But statistics are dry bones. If their meaning is to be grasped they must be seen clothed with flesh and blood. And that means hard and extensive travelling. When within the space of a few months, for instance, one has been brought into contact with the business-like Parsi of Bombay, the

---

[1] George Kuriyan, 'India's Population Problem', *Focus*, **5**, No. 2, 1954.
[2] *India: a Bird's-eye View.*
[3] The Census Report of 1921 gives 222 Indian vernacular languages.

indolent and easy-going Burman, the courtly and cultured Brahman of southern India, the primitive Kohl or Bhil of the jungles of central India, the emotional and subtle-minded inhabitant of the towns of Bengal, the cheery hill-man of the Eastern Himalayas, the great land-owners of the United Provinces and the Punjab, the proud aristocracy of Rajputana, the wild Afridi of the North-West Frontier and the picturesque chieftain of Baluchistan, then it is that statistics as to race and language begin to assume definite meaning and reality.'

Perhaps the most fundamental of all difficulties in trying to get a simplified conception of the peoples of India is the difficulty of dis-entangling differences due to race, language, religion and culture. One finds oneself talking or thinking in one sentence of Dravidians, Bengalis, Parsis, Brahmans and Tamils as if they were comparable divisions of the people.

Race. In the dim and unchronicled past, it is legitimate to suppose that India was inhabited by wild, uncivilized tribes, which we may call the pre-Dravidian peoples. Then India was invaded by the Dravidians —dark-skinned, broad-headed peoples with broad, flat noses in some respects reminiscent of negro races. As the Dravidians spread in India they drove the pre-Dravidians to the hills and the forests, where a few still survive. After the Dravidians, India was invaded again and again by waves of people from the north-west, by clever cultured peoples who closely resemble the well-bred European in type and are scarcely darker than the average South European. They are represented today by the Rajputs, Jats and others. They took possession of the best lands, such as the fertile plain of the north, and drove the Dravidians into Peninsular India, south of the Satpura line. Pressing on the heels of the Indo-Aryans, but never penetrating far into India, were the Turko-Iranians—the Baluchis, Brahuis and Afghans. Then India has been influenced from the north-east by purely Mongolian peoples—the present inhabitants of Burma, parts of Assam and Nepal. Eight racial types may be distinguished at the present day:[1]

(*a*) Pre-Dravidians—such as the Veddas of Ceylon.

(*b*) Dravidians—confined to southern India.

(*c*) Aryo-Dravidians due to the mixture of Indo-Aryans and Dravidians—typical of the United Provinces.

(*d*) Indo-Aryans or Indo-Europeans—the 'aristocracy' of the in-vaders who remained pure.

(*e*) Scytho-Dravidians—a Turko-Iranian-Dravidian mixture, e.g. many Marathis.

(*f*) Turko-Iranians of the north-west borders.

[1] This scheme is far from being universally accepted as expressing the racial origins of India, especially as regards the Marathis and Bengalis. For a different view, see B. S. Guha, in 'An Outline of the Field Sciences of India', Indian Science Congress Assoc., 1937.

(g) Mongoloids such as Nepalese, Burmans, etc.

(h) Bengalis or Mongolo-Dravidians where Aryan blood has mixed in the upper strata of a Mongoloid-Dravidian fusion.

Language. The racial divisions just mentioned are not recognized in India; they do not exactly correspond to any established division of the people and are determined mainly on anthropometric grounds. A clear-cut division of the country on the basis of language is possible,

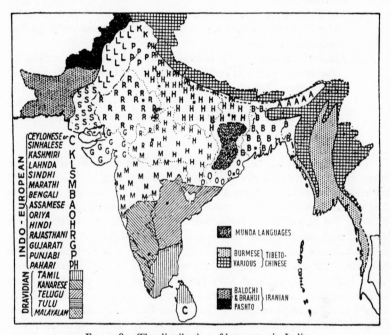

FIG. 108.—The distribution of languages in India

Those listed under the heading 'Indo-European' all belong to the Indo-Aryan branch of that family (except Kashmiri), whilst the Iranian languages form another branch of the same family. The linguistic boundaries now coincide closely with state boundaries. See also *Focus, Amer. Geog. Soc.*, Feb. 1956.

but it must be remembered that certain languages have become wide-spread and are spoken by people of varied race, origin and religion, whilst some of the indigenous and most interesting languages are almost extinct. We may distinguish four main groups of languages:

(a) *The Austric family* includes Malay in one group and the Talaing language of Lower Burma in another. It is interesting as including also the Munda languages spoken by the hill tribes (Santali, Kherwari, etc.) in the Chota Nagpur Plateau and elsewhere in India. They are simple agglutinative languages and probably represent the speech of the earliest inhabitants of India.

(b) *The Dravidian family* of languages is mainly confined to the south of India. Those who hold that the Dravidians are the aboriginal inhabitants of India regard the Dravidian tongues as descended from the language of its original people. The Dravidian languages include Telugu, Tamil, Kanarese (Kannada) and Malayalam, and are spoken by over 90,000,000 people. The whole family of languages is restricted to India.

(c) *The Tibeto-Chinese family* of languages includes those spoken by the Mongoloid inhabitants of Burma (Burmese) and India's northern borders.

(d) *The Indo-European family* of languages includes those spoken by the vast majority of Indians, except in the south. The Iranian languages (Balochi and Pashto), shown separately on Fig. 108, form one branch of the family, the other branch (Indo-Aryan) including all the remainder shown on the map except Kashmiri.

It must, of course, be realized that the languages of India are no mere dialects but are entirely distinct languages. English has conferred on educated India the boon of a common tongue, and the use of this lingua franca has played an important part in the unification of India. Neither the Republic of India nor the Republic of Pakistan has a natural national language and to give any one language official status as *the* national language is very liable to cause serious jealousy. The educated Indians are bilingual or multilingual in English and one or more Indian languages. A very large proportion of the uneducated masses are also bilingual, but not in English. All over northern India Hindustani (an impure form of Hindi) has been adopted as a common language and is spoken or understood in nearly all the bazaars. Tamil takes its place in southern India and Ceylon. Spoken Urdu is closely akin to Hindi but is written in Persian script. Most of the languages of northern India as distinct from Pakistan are written in characters derived originally from Sanskrit; in the same way Pali is the parent of the Dravidian languages.

Notwithstanding the difficulties Hindi has been made the official language of the Union of India but English is still used for all official purposes. Fourteen languages are 'recognized'—Assamese, Bengali, Gujarati, Hindi, Kannada (Kanarese), Kashmiri, Malayalam, Marathi, Oriya, Punjabi, Sanskrit (a dead classical language), Tamil, Telugu and Urdu. Urdu, Bengali and English are the languages of Pakistan.

Religion. More important than race or even language, there is religion. In India the lives of the people are often entirely controlled by the dictates of their religion. It determines their upbringing, education, customs and habits, diet, occupations, dwelling-place, type of home and in fact their whole social environment. Hence we may refer to religions also as cultures.

According to the Censuses of 1961 the numbers professing the various religions are given as follows:

	Indian Union		Pakistan	
	Millions	Per cent.	Millions	Per cent.
Hindus	366·5	83·8	10·9	11·6
Sikhs	7·8	1·8	—	—
Jains	2·0	0·4	—	—
Buddhists	3·3	0·8	0·7	0·8
Zoroastrians	0·1	—	—	—
Muslims	46·9	10·7	82·6	88·1
Christians	10·7	2·4	0·7	0·8
Jews	0·03	—	—	—

Hinduism may be described as the national religion of the Union of India. It is difficult to define Hinduism, and a prominent Hindu, asked for a definition, could only reply that a Hindu is (1) one born in India of Indian parents and (2) accepts and obeys the rules of caste. It has been truly said that language divides the people of India into geographical groups; religion divides them into horizontal strata. A caste may be described as a very rigidly delineated stratum of society. 'Roughly a caste is a group of human beings who may not intermarry, or (usually) eat, with members of any other caste. Very frequently a caste has allotted to it a profession or occupation.' A plausible origin for what is now almost a unique system was propounded in the now famous theory of Dr. Hoernle. He supposed that 'a swarm of Aryan-speaking people entered India through the high and difficult passes of Gilgit and Chitral and established themselves in the fertile plains between the Ganges and the Jumna.[1] They followed a route which made it impossible for their women to accompany them. They took to themselves wives from the daughters of dusky pre-Dravidian aborigines. Here by contact with a different, and in their sentiment, inferior race, caste came into being.'[2] Perhaps the most famous book in all the religious literature of India is the Institutes of Manu. Here we are told that Brahma, the creator of the known universe, from his mouth, arms, thighs and feet respectively created the four great leading castes, the Brahman or priests, the Kshatriya or warriors and gentlefolk, the Vaiçya or traders, and the Sūdra or servile classes. Other castes were

[1] The Hinduism of the aristocratic Rajputs is believed to have arrived earlier.
[2] J. D. Anderson, *The Peoples of India* (Cambridge, 1913).

gradually formed by intermarriage. A man might marry a woman of the caste next below his own, but a woman might not marry a man of a lower caste. The most disgraceful union of all was that between a Brahman woman and a Sūdra man, the resulting offspring being relegated to the lowest caste of all, the Chandāl.

Western nations may rant at the present-day development of the caste system, but the underlying ideas are firmly rooted in mankind. How many Americans, to take an example from a thoroughly democratic race, view with equanimity the mating of one of their white womenfolk with a negro? The Jim-Crow car suggests the untouchables. Or even to details: the rich young screen hero, scion of a noble family, marries the pretty flower-girl who ain't got no grammar and lives happily ever after. But even the most venturesome scenario writer rarely makes a successful match of the noble lady and the dago dustman.

The present multitude of castes in India has been classified in a variety of ways. Occupational or functional castes are hereditary trade unions with strict rules; tribal castes have arisen by the conversion of border tribes; sectarian castes are of the religious revival order; castes have also been formed by migration, changes of custom as well as by intermarriage, as already explained.

Hinduism, as a religion, recognizes a Supreme Being and a host of minor deities. 'Superimposed on a heterogeneous people differing widely from one another in race, language and political and social traditions and interests, the vagueness and elasticity of its system and the protean form of its mythology, its ceremonies and its ordinances, have enabled it to absorb and overlap the various animistic systems which it encountered. But its very adaptability goes far to deprive it of synthesis and cohesion and the inherently disruptive tendency of its caste system, unrestrained by any paramount central authority, places it largely at the mercy of local and sectional interests.' [1]

Very great importance attaches to certain of the customs associated with Hinduism. One is the custom of pilgrimages to sacred spots—particularly to Hardwar [2] or Banaras on the Ganges. These movements have been responsible for the spread of culture, language and trade, and have done much to bring about the contact between races which is so important a factor in economic and social progress. Another is the custom of infant or child marriage. Eleven per cent. of Hindu girls

[1] An educated Brahman once told the writer that he could see no difference between his religion, which recognized one Supreme Being as Creator of the Universe and which taught a moral and ethical code by sanctifying or deifying (for the benefit of ignorant masses) great teachers or leaders, and the Unitarian form of Christianity. Further, he saw no reason why Christianity should not be absorbed as a sect of Hinduism, a sect whose followers were devotees of and believers in the deity of Jesus Christ. Jones's *The Christ of the Indian Road* deserves study in this connection.

[2] Some linguistic scholars insist the spelling should be Haridwar.

under 10 are already married, 44 per cent. are married by the age of 15 and 81 per cent. by the age of 20. Eugenically, the tragedy is not in child marriage, but in the effective cohabitation which commences usually at the first signs of puberty. The effect on infant and maternal mortality is obvious. Further, the prejudice against the re-marriage of widows is deep-seated in Hindu social opinion, with the result that many women are condemned in infancy to lifelong widowhood. Despite efforts for reform by individuals and governments, change of view is slow with the masses.

Sikhs. Sikhism was an attempt to reconcile the ancient Hindu beliefs with a purer creed, which rejected polytheism, image worship and pilgrimages. It remained a pacific cult till the political tyranny of the Muslims and the social tyranny of the Hindus converted it into a military creed. Two of the fundamental rules required of a Sikh are that he should wear long hair and refrain from smoking. The Sikhs include over 6,000,000 of the fine stalwart people around their sacred city of Amritsar in East Punjab. At the time of partition there was some doubt whether they would join Hindu India or Muslim Pakistan. They chose the former. In 1965-6 it was agreed to form a Sikh state.

Jains. The Jain religion is held to have been an offshoot from Hinduism and many Jains still consider themselves Hindus. They are traders and widely distributed in India.

Buddhists. Buddhism arose as an offshoot of Hinduism, and Gautama Buddha, founder of this atheistic, highly moral religion, preached in the Ganges Valley. Buddhism is now, however, practically extinct in India proper, but is the religion of many hill peoples to the north.

Parsis. The Parsis, or Zoroastrians, are Sun-worshippers and follow the ancient creed of Persia. The Parsis are a well-to-do community, almost entirely restricted to Bombay City. Their custom of delivering up their dead to the fowls of the air is one which has always attracted attention—perhaps far less nauseating than appears at first sight.

Muslims. Mahommedanism, or Islam, is the second great religion of India. Brought by invaders from the north-west, its stronghold remained in the north-west of India, but it penetrated right down the Ganges Valley and became firmly established in Bengal. Islam has never, however, penetrated to the same extent in Peninsular India, and in most of southern India the Muslims never numbered more than 10, or possibly 15, per cent. of the population. Islam in India has been strongly affected by Hinduism: some Muslims—especially converts from Hinduism—retain caste and observe Hindu festivals as well as their own. Nevertheless there is a great gulf between Hindus and Muslims; the deep-rooted antagonism between them was ever ready to flare up, and resulted in partition in 1947 and to continued strained relations between India and Pakistan. Until the Second World War purdah was still rigidly observed among the majority of Muslim women (as well as among high-caste Hindus), and this custom has been the controlling influence in domestic architecture. Amongst the intelligentsia women are now enjoying rapid emancipation.

Christians. Christianity now claims nearly 9,000,000 of the people of India. The Syrian Christians, who from the early centuries of the Christian era have formed the bulk of the population of Travancore, form a group quite distinct from the proselytes of the Christian missions in India. The Roman Catholic, Anglican and Baptist are the most numerous sects. Christians of many Protestant sects joined together in 1947 to form the Church of South India. Christianity has made great progress among the Animistic hill tribes and the lower-caste Hindus.

Animists. Under the comprehensive title of Animism are grouped the primitive faiths of the hill peoples, usually involving some form of spirit worship.

The great religions of India tend to be associated with definite 'religious centres'—famous places of pilgrimage or seats of learning connected with one of the religions. Thus Varanasi (Benares), with its thousands of Hindu temples and its Hindu colleges, is a centre of both the Hindu religion and the culture connected with it. The influence of such a cultural centre spreads through all grades of society: the establishment within recent decades of the great Benares Hindu University bears witness to the vitality of the influence of Varanasi amongst the educated, just as the countless crowds who throng to its bathing ghats do to its influence amongst the masses. To the Hindus the Ganges (Ganga) is the most sacred river: to die or to be cremated on its banks is to gain everlasting peace. Hardwar, where the Ganges leaves the mountains, and Allahabad, where the Ganges and Jumna join, are especially sacred. The Muslim Universities of Aligarh and Hyderabad (Deccan) (where Urdu is the medium of instruction) and the religious colleges of Deoband (U.P.) form the modern cultural centres of Islam in Hindu India, whilst the Sikhs, Jains and Parsis are grouped about their cultural centres in the Punjab, Rajasthan and Bombay respectively. Buddh Gaya, where the Buddha received his enlightenment, is a place of pilgrimage in Bihar; another is Sarnath near Banaras.

Religion controls the food requirements of the Indian populace. The Hindus are for the most part vegetarians; the Muslims eschew alcohol and pork, regarding the pig as an unclean animal. It is forbidden for a Buddhist to take life and he will not kill an animal for food.[1] To a less extent religion controls clothing, though it is impossible here to detail the numerous types of costume found in India.

---

[1] It should be observed that in fishing one does not take life; out of the water the fish dies. Meat which someone else has killed is permissible food to most Buddhists.

Manufacturing Industry.[1] Great changes have taken place in recent years in the status of India as a manufacturing country. Factory industries have not only been established to supply the needs of the huge local market, but there are indications in many cases that supply will exceed the home demand and that India's manufactured goods will seek an entry into the world's markets—especially in the Far East and in competition with Japan. Indian cotton goods are even entering Britain, in defiance of Lancashire.

Although the development of power industries has profoundly affected Indian life in many of the larger towns, village industries and handicrafts are still important. It is true that the old craftsmen are dying out and that the influx of workers to the mills scarcely balances, in numbers, the loss of workers in the old native industries. This explains the decrease in the numbers employed in many industries shown in Census reports. Amongst the handicrafts which still exist, most villages have their weaver, dyer, potter, carpenter and blacksmith. In certain centres are more specialized handicrafts—wood and ivory carving, the working of brass, silver and gold, the making of rugs and carpets, the weaving of silk and hand-printing of cotton cloths and the making of lacquer goods. The skill of the workers is such as to excite the admiration of western nations and to create a limited 'luxury' market for the goods. In sum the output of these traditional but unorganized crafts must be very large.

In the new India there is something of a conflict between the Gandhian ideal which sought to resuscitate village crafts whilst mistrusting centralized factories and the reliance on large-scale urban industrialization envisaged under the Five Year Plans.

Power industries are mainly the product of the present century. Although the first jute-mill near Calcutta dates from 1834 and the first cotton-mill near Bombay from 1851, the extension beyond these two towns and these two industries was slow. Labour had to be trained—as well as to be brought from rural environments—and coal had to be imported and the products of the mills had to overcome the competition of goods from Britain and other countries with a long tradition of factory work. 'Cheap' labour is not cheap unless it is also efficient, and efficiency involves training and practice. But recent progress has been phenomenal. In 1893 there were only 700 factories coming under the Factory Acts; in 1929 there were 7,000. In 1949 in India alone there were 7,000 factories using power and each employ-

[1] On all that concerns the economic position of India, reference should be made to that invaluable volume by Dr. V. Anstey, *The Economic Development of India* (Longmans, 1930, and later editions). Recent developments are summarized in *India at a Glance* (Longmans, 1955). A good summary of the Second Five Year Plan (1956–61) is *The New India* (Macmillan, 1958). See also George Kuriyan, 'Spatial Distribution of Industry in India', *Indian Geog. Jour.*, Jan.–Mch., 1962.

ing more than 20 persons. In 1960 there were 8,704 factories using power and employing over 50—in all just under 3,000,000 persons.

Iron and Steel. The smelting of iron is a very old village industry and traces of old workings can be found in very many areas. But the native industry was almost killed by cheap imported iron before a modern

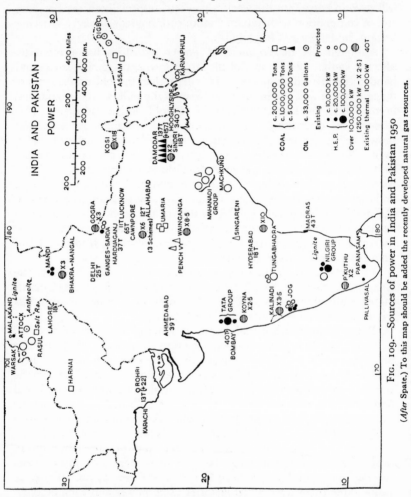

FIG. 109.—Sources of power in India and Pakistan 1950

(*After* Spate.) To this map should be added the recently developed natural gas resources.

large-scale industry was established under a system of protection. India owes its modern industry to the courage and determination of a Bombay merchant—Mr. Jamsetji Tata. By his sons the Tata Iron and Steel Company was formed, and the first blast-furnaces were started in 1911. The Company's output of pig-iron reached 842,000 tons and of crude steel 721,000 tons in 1933–4 (record figures to that date). This represented three-quarters of India's consumption of rails, sections, bars, plates, etc. The focus of the industry is the Eastern Bengal–Bihar Coalfield region; Jamshedpur (near the Singhbhum iron-field) has been changed from a village to an industrial town of over 100,000 inhabitants within the space of a few years. Other companies include the Steel Corporation of Bengal, the Indian Iron and Steel Company, and there are smelting works on the coalfields at Burnpur and Kulti. Pig-iron

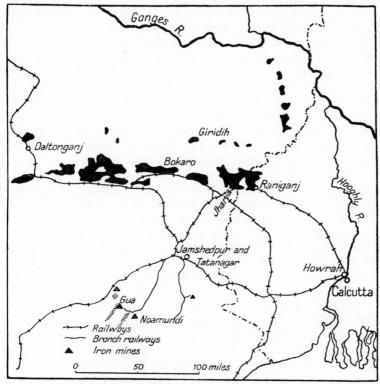

Fig. 110.—Map showing the position of Jamshedpur
Coalfields are shown in black.

production rose steadily to 1,644,000 tons in 1937–8 and after partition was maintained at slightly above this total, rising to 1,958,000 tons in 1956. Steel likewise increased slowly to 1,737,900 tons in 1956. Government policy under the Second Five Year Plan (1956–61) was greatly to expand the industry by building new works with German, British and Soviet help in different parts of the country—Rourkela (Orissa—German), Durgapur (West Bengal—British), and Bhilai (M.P.—Russian)—and extending Jamshedpur.

The Cotton Industry. Cotton is one of the native plants of India, and although enormous quantities are produced for export (especially from Pakistan) more than half the total raw cotton produced is used in the two countries as a whole. Taking the first thirty years of the present century, the consumption of piece goods increased by 35 per cent. per head of population—consequent upon the rising standard of living—and the total consumption by nearly double that percentage. To meet these new demands the village industry as well as the factory industry increased its output—the village industry from 850 to 1,300 million yards; the mill industry from under 500 to about 2,500 million yards. In the same period imports dropped by 300 million yards. The modern mill industry includes nearly 600 spinning and weaving factories in India alone (1949) (apart from 2,000 ginning factories), employing 660,000 workmen. The capacity is now 5,000 million yards a year so that India is second only to the United States. Unlike the jute industry, which was founded by Europeans with European capital, the cotton-mills have been almost entirely Indian owned and financed. The most important centre is Bombay which enjoys the advantages of hydro-electric power; others are Ahmadabad, Nagpur, Kanpur and several places in Madras. Bombay also exports raw cotton.

The Jute Industry. Raw jute and jute manufactures account for more than a fifth of the exports of India and Pakistan but the manufactures are worth twice the raw material. Of the world's production of 2,000,000 tons practically all is from the former province of Bengal. Now as noted above the output of the raw material is shared between Eastern Bengal (Pakistan) and Western Bengal (India), but the output from the old-established Indian mills on the Hooghly (Hugli) north of Calcutta is still several times that of the newer mills in Pakistan.

The Silk Industry. India has long been famous for its beautiful silks and many of the old towns are still noted for special types. There are only a few modern mills though India alone had 489 factories using power and employed a total of 300,000 in 1949. Brocaded silks are made in Bengal, the Punjab and southern India; striped silks and the famous gold brocades all over northern India at such centres as Agra, Banaras, Amritsar, Ahmadabad and Surat.

The Woollen Industry. India has long been celebrated for carpets and shawls. The weaving of shawls is a typical industry of Kashmir. Carpet-making is carried on in many parts of India but especially in the Punjab, Kashmir and in Madhya Pradesh, various towns producing distinctive types. Coarse blankets are made in many parts of northern India, where the winters are cold. It is notable that in all the textile industries cheap imported dyes have almost completely replaced the old vegetable dyes.

Metal Working. Many castes in India use brass for all cooking utensils and brass working is an important industry in many towns of northern India—as Banaras. Bombay and Poona are centres of silver working, Jaipur and Delhi of gold.

Cement. Apart from an abortive attempt in Madras in 1902 the establishment of the cement industry in India dates from 1912 when works were opened in Porbandar. The First World War cut off imports and gave a fillip to the industry so that by 1930 it had become a major enterprise. In 1947 before partition there were 23 works with an output of 2,700,000 tons and plans were laid to double this in a few years. In fact output reached 6 m. tons in 1955 and 9 m. in 1964. Cement is heavy and bulky in proportion to value and it is important to minimize transport costs by establishing cement works as widely distributed as the raw materials—limestone and clay—will permit. Madras and Bihar lead in output, followed by Madhya Pradesh, Hyderabad, East Punjab, Rajasthan and the original centres in Saurashtra.

Other Manufactures. Remarkable developments in varied manufacturing industries took place during the Second World War. Such new industries as the making of scientific instruments at Banaras drew naturally on the skill of older workers in metal. Such places as Kanpur became great centres of new factories. In addition to industries already mentioned there are oil refineries in Assam and the Punjab for local oil and at Bombay for imported crude; many flour-mills; tobacco factories in Madras; tea-packing establishments in Assam and Madras; lac factories; as well as general engineering, railway, motor and electrical engineering and shipbuilding works. The manufacture of sugar has spread rapidly. In 1940 there were 500 mills employing 100,000; in 1934 there were only 130 and 30 in 1931. Most of them are in Uttar Pradesh. Production of sugar and gur is over 6 million tons.

An important recent development is the manufacture of fertilizers especially of ammonium sulphate (using gypsum from Rajasthan but local coal) at Sindhri in the Damodar Valley. Production began in 1951, output exceeded 290,000 tons in 1954-5. There are other fertilizer plants in South India, and in Travancore. This is bound up with the drive to improve agriculture. By 1956 a quarter of all villages had been brought into the National Extension Service and C.D.P. (Community Development Projects) are playing a large part.

The priorities given to industrial development under the Second Five Year Plan are interesting. First come iron and steel, heavy chemicals including fertilizers and engineering. Second are aluminium, cement, pulp, phosphatic manures and drugs. Third is the modernization of textile works.

India's development is being co-ordinated by a series of Five Year Plans. The first covered 1951-6; the second 1956-61; the third 1961-6.

Hydro-electric Power.[1] Development of water power is playing a major

[1] George Kuriyan, 'Hydro-Electric Power in India—A Geographical Analysis', *Indian Geographical Society, Monograph 1*, 1945.

part in Indian industrial development. By 1952 there were in the Republic of India 22 generating stations which generated nearly three million million Kwh. Four great new schemes in progress were:

(1) The Damodar Valley (Damodar Valley Authority—D.V.A.), begun 1948.

(2) Hirakud on the Mahanadi. The world's largest earth dam, completed 1957.

(3) Bhakra-Nangal on the Sutlej. Nangal headworks, opened 1954, irrigate 1,200,000 acres out of total planned of 3,600,000.

(4) Tunga Bhadra in Andhra and Mysore. Power station opened January 1957.

(5) Kosi River, Nepal and Bihar.

It should be noted that the bulk of the manufacturing industry described above lies in the Indian Republic. Pakistan is not so well situated. Amongst the publications issued by the Pakistan Government is an annual review and that for the Sixth Year (1953) refers to the basic fact that the new country 'inherited an economy which, being wholly agricultural, was not dependable on account of her underdeveloped system of irrigation, lack of industrialization and widely fluctuating world market prices'. Jute is the main cash crop, followed by cotton. Other exports are tea, hides and skins. A poor monsoon results in insufficient wheat for home needs in West Pakistan and there is no surplus of rice in East Pakistan. So policy has been 'to develop such essential industries as will make Pakistan self-sufficient at least in essential consumer goods'. Stimulation of industry falls mainly on the Government and the *Industrial Development Corporation* is required by law to give particular attention to the following basic industries: jute, paper, iron and steel, shipbuilding, heavy chemicals, fertilizers, sugar, cement and textiles.

As noted already Pakistan has some oil in the Jhelum and Rawalpindi districts of the Punjab and one refinery at Attock, but little coal. The recent discoveries of natural gas at Sui in the west and Sylhet in the east are therefore very important. Attention is being paid to hydroelectric projects. Among minerals rock salt is abundant, and there is plenty of limestone for cement; a large modern factory is Zeal-Pak at Hyderabad. A lack of both iron ore and metallurgical coal makes the establishment of heavy industry extremely difficult but a wide range of light industry is possible and indeed is in course of being established.

The Communications of India. Railways have played a major role in the development of modern India. The first line to be completed was 21 miles between Victoria Station, Bombay and Thana. Amid great ceremony and before huge crowds the first train made the journey on the afternoon of April 16, 1853, in 57 minutes. The following year a line was opened between Howrah (Calcutta) and Hooghly and by early 1855 had been extended to Raniganj, the coalfield centre. In 1856 the first section of a line in Madras was completed. The story really begins in 1843 when an engineer of the Great Western Railway of England was invited by the Governor of Bombay to study the need for railways. At that time the G.W.R. was using a broad gauge and so was established the broad Indian gauge of 5 feet 3 inches which is the 'standard' gauge of India. A number of companies incorporated in England received contracts and guarantees, at first with the East India Company but after 1858 with the Secretary of State for India. Construction proceeded apace but it was long before railways were financially self-supporting. The railways were at first designed to open up the more productive parts of the country to trade, and to link strategically important places for defence. After the great famine of 1878 the Famine Commission made it clear that only the increase of railway mileage to 20,000 could save the country from the ravages of future famines so that other new companies were formed and many new lines constructed. By 1900 mileage had reached 24,752 and that was the first year in which Indian railways made a profit. A rapid expansion to 34,656 miles in 1913–14 followed, but during the First World War there was a heavy strain on Indian railways and no replacements, whilst locomotives and rolling stock were sent to the Middle East— some lines were even dismantled to provide rails. Following the advice of the Acworth Committee the Government began to take over both ownership and management of more and more of the railways though some not till as late as 1944. In 1928 a start was made with electrification—local lines from Bombay. The Second World War again resulted in the release of locomotives, wagons, track from branch lines and other material for military use. At the time of partition route mileage of Government-owned lines had fallen to 31,533, of which 24,830 were in India, 6,703 in Pakistan.

After partition in 1947 the railways were regrouped and many small units incorporated in the major systems. In the *Republic of India* these comprise:

(1) *The Central Railway* (5,428 miles) including the old G.I.P.R. (Great Indian Peninsular), Nizam's State and some small lines. Headquarters: Bombay.

(2) *The Western Railway* (5,631 miles) including the old Bombay, Baroda and Central India Railway with the Saurashtra and other small lines. Headquarters: Bombay.

(3) *The Eastern Railway* (5,667) including the old Bengal-Nagpur Railway and much of the East Indian Railway. Headquarters: Calcutta.

(4) *The Northern Railway* (6,006) including those parts of the North-Western Railway lying in India (Eastern Punjab) and parts of the E.I.R. Headquarters: Delhi.

(5) *The Southern Railway* (6,016) including the old South Indian Railway (S.I.R.), Madras and Southern Mahratta Railway (M. and S.M.R.) and Mysore Railways. H.Q.: Madras.

(6) *The North Eastern Railway* (5,557) including the former metre gauge north of the Ganges. Headquarters: Gorakhpur.

Later the *North East Frontier Zone* (H.Q.: Pandu) and *South Eastern* (Calcutta) were separated.

The total mileage in the Republic of India is now over 34,000 and

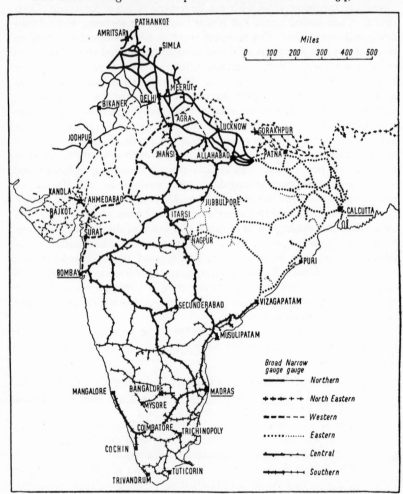

Fig. 111.—The principal railways of the Republic of India, showing the way in which the main lines radiate from the three great ports

The railway network of the old Indian Empire has been cut severely by the India–Pakistan boundaries both in the east and the west. Many connecting lengths of line have actually been torn up. Railway headquarters underlined.

the distribution of broad gauge (about 15,000 miles) and metre gauge (about 15,000 miles) is shown in Fig. 111.

Under the first Five Year Plan nearly 80 per cent. of the expenditure for transport was earmarked for railways. The Assam rail link has been constructed to connect the Assam Railways across the difficult Tista and Torsa rivers with those north of Western Bengal so as to avoid crossing East Pakistan. Another important project is the Kandla–Deesa line to open up the parts of Rajasthan formerly served from Karachi. Locomotive works have been established at Tatanagar (Bihar) and at Chittaranjan in West Bengal. The first locomotive from the latter was completed in 1950 and a steadily increasing output is planned. Coaches are made at Bangalore and elsewhere. In 1953 when Indian Railways celebrated their centenary, they had become the nation's largest industrial undertaking. Just as the old lines were described in earlier editions of this book as radiating from the chief ports, so it will be noticed do the eight new groupings emphasize the focal importance of Bombay (Central and Western), Calcutta–Howrah (Eastern and South Eastern) and Madras (Southern).

The *railways of Pakistan* fall naturally into two systems. Those of West Pakistan form the North Western Railway (comprising most of the lines of the old company with the same name) with a network in West Punjab and two main lines southwards to Hyderabad (Sind) and thence to Karachi. The route mileage is 5,362 miles of which 4,562 is broad gauge. Nothing makes the visitor realize the reality of partition between Pakistan and the Republic of India more than the dismemberment of the railway systems. Only one line—the old main line between Lahore and Amritsar—was allowed to remain and even on that it was seven years after partition (in 1954) that limited through running was restored. The other lines are either obstructed by frontier works or actually torn up where they formerly crossed what is now the border—as at Ferozepur.

The railways of East Pakistan form the Eastern Bengal Railway with 7,682 miles of route (544 miles broad gauge, mainly south of the Ganges crossing at Sara). The different sections of the system are isolated by navigable waterways, but Dacca and Chittagong form two focal points.

When compared with other civilized countries India has still few metalled *roads*. There are a few 'trunk roads', such as the one from Calcutta to Peshawar, which antedate the motor era, but the majority have been built to accommodate the rapidly increasing motor traffic. Very great strides were made during the Second World War. A large proportion of the metalled roads of India are still found round the larger towns, or acting as 'feeders' to the railways. A powerful, well-sprung car can go almost anywhere in the dry season, and over-crowded, ill-treated motor-buses now serve a large proportion of village India. The inevitable dust of dry-season India is everywhere a curse.

A.—10

Away from the railways and metalled roads one is usually restricted to the maximum of 15 or 20 miles a day which bullock-cart travel will allow, especially in the wet season.

The *rivers* of India are much less important than formerly, as already explained, owing to the growth of the railways and the use of river water for irrigation. The largest system of river transport is found

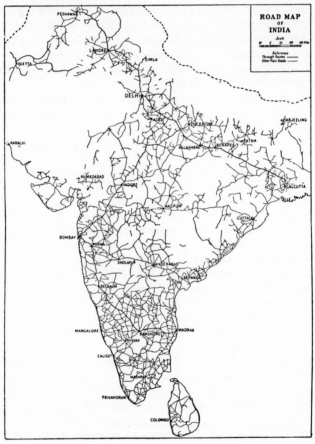

FIG. 112.—The motor roads of India

Very great progress in road construction was made during the Second World War.

in the Ganges Delta in Eastern Pakistan. Except for the Calcutta and Eastern Canals, the salt-water Buckingham Canal of Madras and the canals of the southern West Coast, the canals of India are little used for navigation—they are for irrigation.

Air. European mail now reaches India by air—in a day from London. Air services link all important cities.

Both India and Pakistan have become remarkably 'air-minded'. Both countries have important international lines (Air India and Pakistan International Airways). For Pakistan the only easy link between the East and West halves of the country is by air—either direct from Lahore to Dacca or touching down at Delhi. Whereas movement from the one country to the other by rail or road is beset by many difficulties, air travel such as from Bombay to Karachi or Calcutta to Dacca is simple. For India, air transport has revolutionized the control exercised by the Central Government at Delhi.

The Foreign Trade of India and Pakistan. The great bulk of the foreign trade is sea-borne—over 95 per cent. Before partition in 1947 nearly all the sea-borne trade passed through the four great ports of Bombay, Calcutta, Karachi and Madras, and the whole country could be considered as divided into the hinterlands of those four ports. Since partition there has been little change in the hinterlands served by Bombay and Madras. Karachi now serves West Pakistan only, so that the Government of India has developed Kandla on the Rann of Cutch to serve the country between Cutch and Delhi, which formerly lay in the hinterland of Karachi. Calcutta serves the rich coalfield area and the Ganges Valley as well as, by a tortuous railway route, the tea gardens of Assam, but has lost the jute and rice lands of most of the Delta. East Pakistan was left without a modern port, hence the strenuous efforts to develop Chittagong, now provided with deep water wharves, and the stimulus given to the delta ports Chalna, Khulna and Narayanganj. Turning to Peninsular India, since the deepening of the approaches Cochin has enjoyed a large expansion of trade; in aggregate a considerable volume is handled by Vizagapatam, Tuticorin, Calicut, Dhanushkodi, Cocanada, Trivandrum, Surat and Okha. Often the trade of the smaller ports is predominantly an export trade. It pays a tramp steamer to call and pick up a complete cargo, but not to unload small quantities of a miscellaneous nature. India's first five ports—Bombay, Calcutta, Madras, Cochin and Vizagapatam, together with Kandla, are controlled by the Central Government. Much use is now made of Mormugao.

The first two figures below show for comparative purposes the trade of the old Indian Empire, including Burma, for some inter-war years. Though the total trade was large, it was comparatively small on a per capita basis—well under £1 or five dollars a head. It was typically an exchange of Indian raw materials (the rice was from Burma) for European, especially British, manufactured goods. It will be noticed however that jute manufactures from the Hugliside mills bulked largely among exports, that Japanese goods were conspicuous among imports. Until recently the Indian peasant knew nothing of banks and distrusted paper money. His savings, if any, often his capital, temporary or permanent, took the form of gold and silver jewellery worn by his wife. There was an apparently insatiable demand for gold and silver. With the very marked rise in the price of gold in terms of rupees this demand slackened, disappeared, and was replaced by a release of gold and silver. No details, however, were made public of the import or export of treasure after 1940.

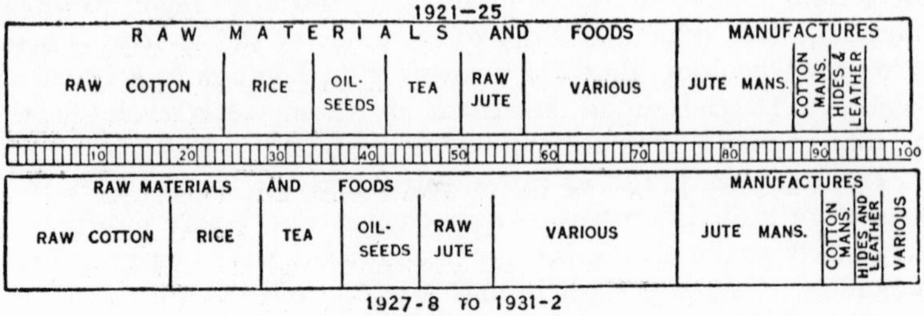
1921–25
RAW MATERIALS AND FOODS
MANUFACTURES
RAW COTTON
RICE
OIL-SEEDS
TEA
RAW JUTE
VARIOUS
JUTE MANS.
COTTON MANS.
HIDES & LEATHER
10
20
30
40
50
60
70
80
90
100
RAW MATERIALS AND FOODS
MANUFACTURES
RAW COTTON
RICE
TEA
OIL-SEEDS
RAW JUTE
VARIOUS
JUTE MANS.
COTTON MANS.
HIDES AND LEATHER
VARIOUS
1927-8 TO 1931-2

FIG. 113.—The exports of the old Indian Empire, including Burma

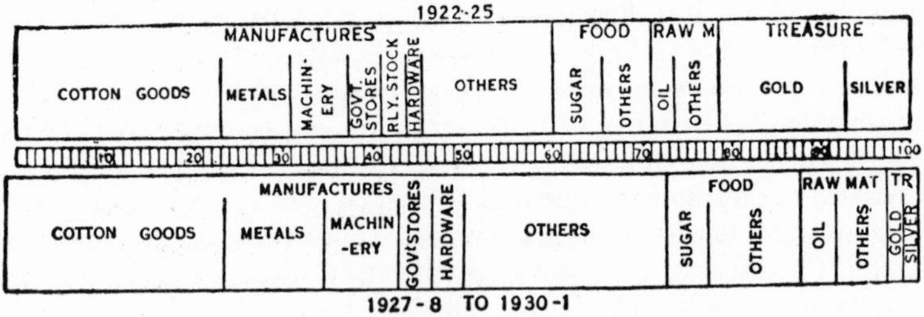
1922-25
MANUFACTURES
FOOD
RAW M
TREASURE
COTTON GOODS
METALS
MACHIN-ERY
GOVT. STORES
RLY. STOCK
HARDWARE
OTHERS
SUGAR
OTHERS
OIL
OTHERS
GOLD
SILVER
10
20
30
40
50
60
70
80
90
100
MANUFACTURES
FOOD
RAW MAT
TR
COTTON GOODS
METALS
MACHIN-ERY
GOVT. STORES
HARDWARE
OTHERS
SUGAR
OTHERS
OIL
OTHERS
GOLD
SILVER
1927-8 TO 1930-1

FIG. 114.—The imports of the old Indian Empire, including Burma

The Foreign Trade of Pakistan since Partition. The foreign trade of Pakistan shows very clearly the contribution which the Deltas region of Bengal, with its large output of jute, and the irrigated plain of the Punjab with its production of cotton had made to the exports of

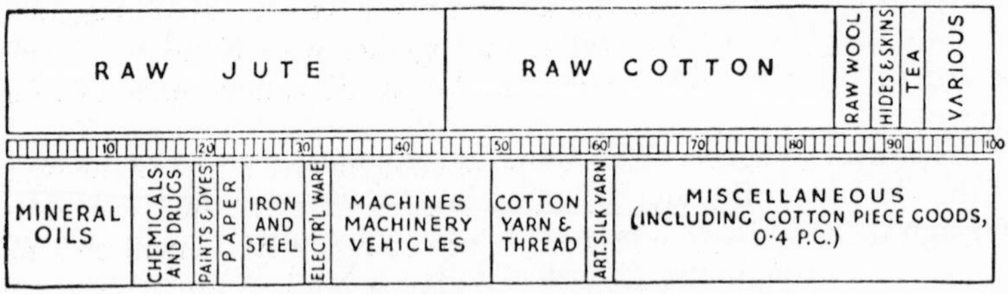
RAW JUTE
RAW COTTON
RAW WOOL
HIDES & SKINS
TEA
VARIOUS
10
20
30
40
50
60
70
80
90
100
MINERAL OILS
CHEMICALS AND DRUGS
PAINTS & DYES
PAPER
IRON AND STEEL
ELECTR'L WARE
MACHINES MACHINERY VEHICLES
COTTON YARN & THREAD
ART. SILK YARN
MISCELLANEOUS (INCLUDING COTTON PIECE GOODS, 0·4 P.C.)

FIG. 115.—The foreign trade of Pakistan in 1953–4

In 1963–4 raw jute (38 per cent.), raw cotton (10) and jute manufactures (10) led. Food represented 15 per cent. of imports.

India as a whole before partition. There is obviously now the excessive reliance of Pakistan on these two commodities, shown in Fig. 115. Fig. 115 also shows the varied needs of Pakistan in its imports. There is a remarkable absence of cotton goods, formerly the leading import.

A not inconsiderable proportion of the imports of machinery is in fact of cotton-mill machinery for Pakistan's own new factories. Fig. 116 shows how widespread is Pakistan's foreign trade. The high place taken by Japan is noteworthy.

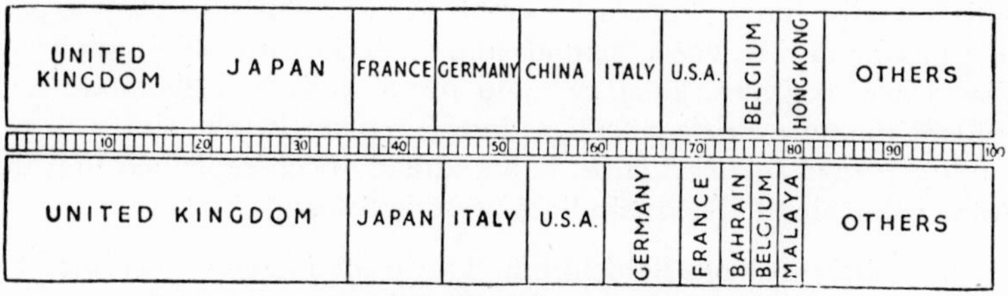

UNITED KINGDOM	JAPAN	FRANCE	GERMANY	CHINA	ITALY	U.S.A.	BELGIUM	HONG KONG	OTHERS

UNITED KINGDOM	JAPAN	ITALY	U.S.A.	GERMANY	FRANCE	BAHRAIN	BELGIUM	MALAYA	OTHERS

Fig. 116.—The direction of Pakistan's foreign trade in 1953–4
(Exports above, imports below)

The Foreign Trade of the Republic of India since Partition.

The exports of India since partition show the importance in the economy of the tea of Assam—a quarter of the whole—and the high

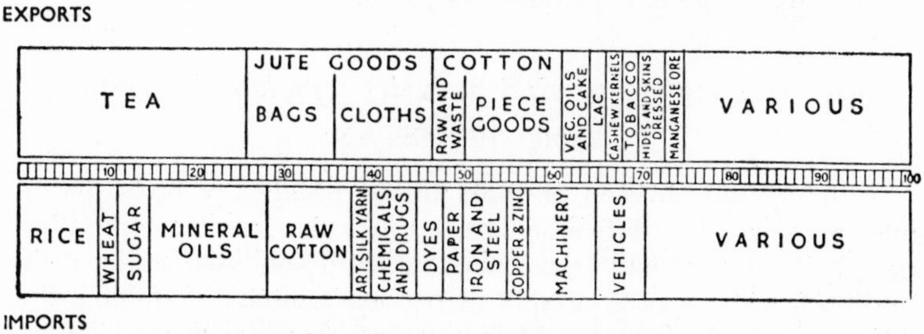

EXPORTS

TEA	JUTE GOODS		COTTON		VEG. OILS AND CAKE	CASHEW KERNELS	LAC	TOBACCO	HIDES AND SKINS DRESSED	MANGANESE ORE	VARIOUS
	BAGS	CLOTHS	RAW AND WASTE	PIECE GOODS							

RICE	WHEAT	SUGAR	MINERAL OILS	RAW COTTON	ART.SILK YARN	CHEMICALS AND DRUGS	DYES	PAPER	IRON AND STEEL	COPPER & ZINC	MACHINERY	VEHICLES	VARIOUS

IMPORTS

Fig. 117.—The foreign trade of India (excluding Pakistan) after partition
Wheat has now replaced rice as the leading food import.

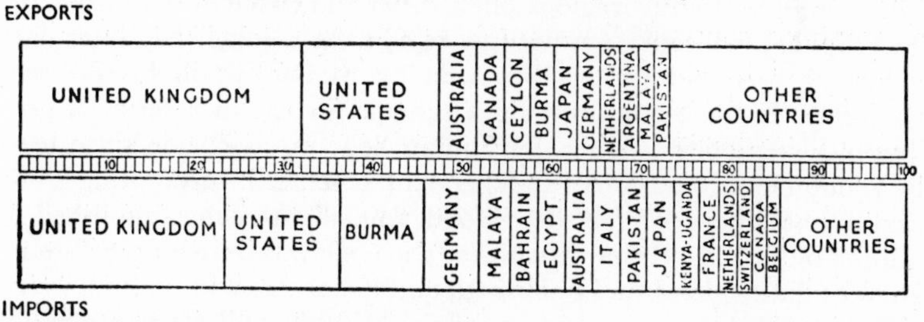

EXPORTS

UNITED KINGDOM	UNITED STATES	AUSTRALIA	CANADA	CEYLON	BURMA	JAPAN	GERMANY	NETHERLANDS	ARGENTINA	MALAYA	PAKISTAN	OTHER COUNTRIES

UNITED KINGDOM	UNITED STATES	BURMA	GERMANY	MALAYA	BAHRAIN	EGYPT	AUSTRALIA	ITALY	PAKISTAN	JAPAN	KENYA-UGANDA	NETHERLANDS	FRANCE	SWITZERLAND	CANADA	BELGIUM	OTHER COUNTRIES

IMPORTS

Fig. 118.—The direction of the foreign trade of India (excluding Pakistan) after partition

In 1963 the exports went to the U.K., U.S.A., Japan and U.S.S.R.; imports came from U.K., U.S.A., Germany, Japan and U.S.S.R.

place now taken by manufactures of cotton and jute. On the import side India's present inability to grow enough food at home is seen in the import of rice, wheat and sugar. It is interesting to note the dominant position which the United Kingdom still occupies.

A reform which has been undertaken by the Indian Government has an important bearing on foreign trade, as well as being of profound significance internally. It is the whole-hearted change to the decimal system. The rupee remains as the monetary unit, but is now divided into 100 paise (naye paisa, or new money) instead of into 16 annas each of 4 pice or 12 pies. Seers, maunds and other measures of weight are to give place to grams, kilograms and metric tons; the kilometre is to replace the mile, degrees centigrade will replace fahrenheit.

The Foreign Overland Trade. It has already been explained that this trade is but small. The main lines are as follows:

(a) Persia through Baluchistan. This trade increased considerably after the construction of the railway.

(b) Afghanistan, mainly through the Khyber Pass. There has been a sharp rise in this trade.

(c) Tibet and central Asia through Kashmir.

(d) Nepal.

(e) Tibet, especially through Darjeeling.

THE NATURAL REGIONS AND STATES OF INDIA AND PAKISTAN

Although the division of India into a number of broad natural units presents little difficulty, it is curious that until comparatively recently no attempt had been made to draw up and to describe a comprehensive scheme of geographical regions. Climatic or rainfall divisions had been made by the Meteorological Department in India, and most of the provinces had been divided into natural regions for Census purposes. The Census regions often differ somewhat widely from the geographer's concept of a natural region. At a somewhat later date a scheme of broad regions was used by McFarlane in his *Economic Geography*. In 1922-4 I drew up a scheme for use in a series of geographical textbooks written for Indian Schools, a scheme since used in a number of books. An independent scheme, incorporating some unpublished ideas of W. Arden Wood, was, slightly later, published in outline by J. N. L. Baker. Mr. Baker's scheme was drawn up before he knew of that which I had published, and it is satisfactory to find a very close agreement between the two. The publication of Professor O. H. K. Spate's *India and Pakistan* (London: Methuen, 1954) affords for the first time a comprehensive regional treatment. He distinguishes the three macro-regions of the Mountain Rim, Indo-Gangetic Plains, and Peninsula, and finds 25 regions of the first order coinciding in general with those used in this book. In the pages which follow I have adhered to my original arrangement of regions since, on the whole, they have been confirmed by Spate's detailed work. The factors concerned in the delineation of regions are primarily physiography and structure, secondly climate. By constant reference to the correlation between the natural regions and the States and former provinces of India and Pakistan an attempt has been made to obviate the repetition which would result were the States described separately.

A primary division of India on the basis of physiography and structure has already been made. A further subdivision on a climatic basis is necessary and it is found that the regions so determined are, in the

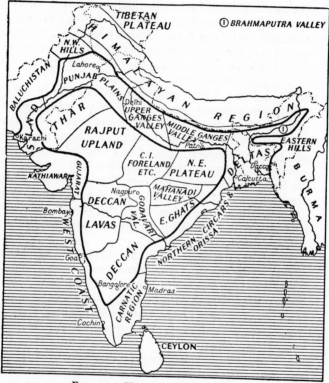

FIG. 119.—The natural regions of India

main, remarkably homogeneous. The natural regions of India thus fall primarily into three groups:

(a) The natural regions of the Mountain Wall.
(b) The natural regions of the Northern Plain.
(c) The natural regions of the Indian Plateau.

The Natural Regions of the Mountain Wall. The barrier of mountains by which India is hemmed in on the north-east, north and north-west varies enormously from end to end, especially so far as climatic conditions are concerned. Some localities in Assam can claim rainfalls which rank amongst the highest recorded in the world; some localities in the north-west are almost rainless. Elevation also plays an important part in the differentiation of the mountain wall into distinct regions. The mountain wall of India may therefore be considered as comprising six units:

(1) The Eastern Hills Region—or the North-East Hills—comprises the eastern parts of India's mountain rampart, the hills which separate India from Burma and the hills which occupy a considerable portion of Assam. Broadly speaking, the region is one of very heavy rainfall and was originally covered except at higher levels with thick evergreen forest of Equatorial type. The population, naturally, is but sparse.

(2) The Himalayan Region comprises the Himalayan Mountain Chain approximately from the level of 5,000 feet upwards. It is at that level that marked changes in vegetation occur and the notoriously unhealthy sub-tropical forests give place to the healthy invigorating heights associated in the popular mind with India's famous hill stations.

(3) The Sub-Himalayan Region comprises the foothills between the plains and the mountains as well as the lower slopes of the Himalayas themselves. Both the Himalayan and Sub-Himalayan Regions fall naturally into a wetter eastern half and a drier western half.

(4) The Tibetan Plateau lies on the far side of the Himalayas, but a part comes within the borders of the State of Kashmir.

(5) The North-Western Dry Hills or the North-West Frontier Region comprises the north-western portion of the mountain wall. By contrast with the north-east it is a very dry region but agrees with all parts of the mountain wall in being but sparsely populated.

(6) The Baluchistan Plateau, like the Tibetan Plateau, lies outside the mountain rim and is a dry plateau scarcely affected by the monsoon which plays such a dominant part in India proper.

The Natural Regions of the Northern Plain. The subdivision of the great alluvial plain of northern India is again based on climatic variations. True, there is a distinction between the older alluvium of the Punjab and Uttar Pradesh and the younger alluvium of the deltas, but the resulting regional differences are but slight when compared with the regional variations caused by climate.

(7) The Lower Indus Valley or Sind is the alluvial plain of the

Lower Indus, lying in a region of very low and irregular rainfall and depending for its supply of moisture on water from the Indus.

(8) The Punjab Plains occupy the larger and more important part of the States of West Punjab (Pakistan) and East Punjab (India) and comprise a still more extensive plain in a region of low rainfall—depending very largely for water on the five tributaries of the Indus. This region is sometimes called the Indo-Gangetic Plain west.

(9) The Upper Ganges Plain comprises that portion of the Gangetic Plain which has an annual rainfall of less than 40 inches —corresponding to the western two-thirds of Uttar Pradesh, formerly the United Provinces.

(10) The Middle Ganges Plain may be described as an intermediate region with a mixture of wet zone and dry zone crops. The Upper and Middle Ganges Plain are linked together in Baker's scheme as the Indo-Gangetic Plain east.

(11) The Lower Ganges Plain or the Deltas Region is the wet region of newer alluvium corresponding roughly with the former province of Bengal—now comprising much of West Bengal (India) and the greater part of East Bengal or East Pakistan.

(12) The Brahmaputra Valley or Assam Valley is narrow compared with the Ganges Valley. It is, like the Deltas, a region of heavy rainfall.

The Natural Regions of the Indian Plateau. The whole of India south of the Northern Plain may be called the Indian Plateau. One might use the term Peninsular India, but more frequently that designation is reserved for the land south of the Satpura Range. At the same time it is unwise to refer to the Deccan without qualification because of the multiplicity of meanings which has been given to that name. Ten natural regions grouped as follows may be distinguished:

(a) Coastal Regions round the plateau proper.

(13) Cutch, Kathiawar and Gujarat, forming the transition between the dry Indus Valley and Thar Desert on the one hand and the very humid West Coast on the other.

(14) The West Coast Region lies between the crest of the Western Ghats and the Arabian Sea and comprises a narrow coastal plain and the slopes of the Western Ghats. It falls into northern and southern halves lying respectively in Bombay and Mysore-Kerala and separated by the Portuguese territory of Goa. The

whole region is very wet, but the dry season becomes progressively longer as one goes northwards, away from the almost Equatorial climatic conditions of southern Kerala (Travancore).

(15) The Carnatic or Tamil Region, also referred to as the East Coast south, comprises a broad coastal plain and an inland hilly part. The region differs from the remainder of India in the incidence of the rainfall; October, November and December being the rainiest months.

(16) The Northern Circars Region, including Orissa, also referred to as the East Coast north, lies between the Eastern Ghats and the Bay of Bengal.

(b) Regions of the Plateau (Peninsular India proper).

(17) The Deccan Region, using the word Deccan in the strict sense, is the high southern portion of the plateau.

(18) The Deccan Lavas Region is the north-western part of the plateau, lying mainly in Bombay State, with a dry climate and the sticky black cotton soil.

(19) The north-eastern part of the plateau is a complex region comprising five subdivisions—the Central Indian Highlands, Chota Nagpur Plateau, Eastern Ghats, Chhattisgarh Plain or Mahanadi Valley and the Godavari Valley. The region as a whole has a moderate rainfall (40 to 60 inches) and is thinly populated and still largely covered with forest. The population is concentrated mainly in the two valley regions.

(c) Regions north of the Satpura mountain line and sloping down towards the Northern Plain. The mountain belt itself is often treated as a distinct region.

(20) The Central Indian Foreland lies between the Ganges Plain and the Narbada-Son trough.

(21) The Rajput Upland Region is a complex region of hills and plateaus bounded on the south by the Vindhya Mountains and on the north-west by the Aravalli Hills.

(22) The Thar or Great Indian Desert lies between the Aravalli Hills on the south-east and the Indus-Punjab Plains on the north and west.

PAKISTAN AND ITS NATURAL REGIONS [1]

IN the years which preceded the grant of independence it was the firm hope of many leaders in India and all over the world that the reins of government would be handed over to a United Indian government. But the antagonism between Moslem and Hindu is very old, strong and deep-rooted and the ideal of an independent Moslem-Indian state took firm hold. In his book *Pakistan: the Fatherland of the Pak Nation* (published by the Pakistan National Liberation Movement from Cambridge, England, first in 1935) Choudhary Rahmat Ali says he first formally used the name Pakistan on January 28, 1933, though it was invented earlier. It can be interpreted as meaning the land (*-stan*) of the pure (*pak*) but is said to have suggested itself to a group of students at Cambridge from the initial letters of *P*unjab, *A*fghania (i.e. North-West Frontier Province), *K*ashmir and *S*ind, with the termination from Baluchi*stan*. Compared with its actual present limits, the theoretical Pakistan of Ali included also Kutch, Kathiawar (Saurashtra), East Punjab and a large part of the United Provinces. The movement stood also for the creation of separate Moslem states in Bengal and Assam (Bangistan) and Hyderabad Deccan (Osmanistan) but did not visualize Bengal as an integral part of Pakistan itself.

The actual boundaries of Pakistan were decided on the principle of Moslem-Hindu majorities by Sir Cyril Radcliffe since the Moslem and Hindu members of the Commission of which he was chairman failed to agree. The Radcliffe award followed existing minor administrative boundaries rather than physical features (whether natural or man-made) so that difficulties created by the cutting of roads, railways and especially canals tended in some cases to be accentuated especially in north Bengal and near Ferozepur.[2]

The major difficulty of Pakistan is obviously its separation into two parts which are virtually linked only by religion and contrasted in almost every other way. With a thousand miles of alien territory between, Pakistan faces a problem shared by no other major country in the world.

West Pakistan is extensive, on the whole sparsely populated by

[1] In my travels in Pakistan in 1955 I received unstinted help and lavish hospitality from so many friends, including many former students, that it is difficult to particularize. I derived much benefit from the invitation of the Pakistan Association for the Advancement of Science meeting at Bahawalpur City, and appreciated especially discussions at Karachi with Professor M. B. Pithawalla who has done so much by his writing to spread a knowledge of Pakistan and with Dr. S. Z. Ahsan and Dr. S. I. Siddiqi. At Lahore I owe a great deal to Professor Kazi S. Ahmad and his colleagues, and at Dacca to Professor Nafis Ahmad and his colleagues.

[2] See especially O. H. K. Spate, 'The Partition of India and the Prospects of Pakistan', *Geog. Rev.*, 38, 1948, 5–29.

stalwart peoples used to life in an arid environment. Its more populous parts depend essentially on irrigation: there is still land in plenty where water can be made available. Though its peoples speak Punjabi, Sindhi and other languages Urdu was long a court language and is familiar to and used by many. For West Pakistan is not a 'new' country but rather the re-incarnation of the Moslem state which had lasted for more than a thousand years.

East Pakistan is a small area, one of the most densely populated in the world, so that its population exceeds in total that of the spacious lands of the west. The population is homogeneous, living in the wet environment of rice-growing delta lands and speaking Bengali.

Pakistanis from West and East each have a sense of superiority; each regards service (such as government service) in the other half as something approaching exile.

The division of material resources between Pakistan and the Republic of India will have become apparent from the preceding pages. But developments in Pakistan have been remarkable—in both West and East. India has the coal but the rich strikes of gas at Sui (West) and Sylhet (East) have altered the power position. India had the factories but Pakistan is developing her own (see p. 266).

Where enmity is so old and deep, it would be too much to expect close friendship between the new countries. Partition gave rise to the greatest mass migrations of peoples in the whole history of the world— probably involving eight to ten million. Pakistan confidently expected to include the east Punjab with the Sikh 'capital' of Amritsar so that when the Sikhs decided to throw in their lot with the Hindus the Moslem feeling against the Sikhs was very bitter and resulted in much bloodshed. I was in Lahore in January 1955, when the frontier was opened to Sikhs for the first time since partition—the occasion being the Indian-Pakistan cricket test: enmity seemed to have vanished.

Whilst many Pakistani leaders consider they are being subjected to undue pressure by their big neighbour India, the Hindu attitude towards their erstwhile conquerors and rulers is understandable. To them the Moslems have made the task of ruling and developing the sub-continent much more difficult. The water position on the borders of East and West Punjab may be cited. Where canals are cut an impartial judge might say the water should be shared in the same proportion as before partition. Both countries have a pressure of population on land and water and India may well say we must save our own people from starvation before we give away any water at all.

There is clearly an element of impermanence in the present position and with that in mind we may turn to a consideration of the natural regions—remaining obviously permanent divisions despite changes in political frontiers, though the uses man is making of the natural resources show some remarkable changes.

WEST PAKISTAN

West Pakistan, shown in Fig. 120, when compared with the map of natural regions shown in Fig. 119 is seen to comprise

(*a*) the whole of the North-West Dry Hills (North-Western Hills and Sub-Montane Indus of Spate);

(*b*) the Plateau of Baluchistan;

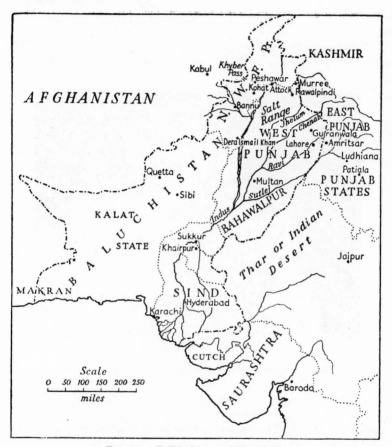

FIG. 120.—Political map of West Pakistan

In 1955 the States and Provinces of West Pakistan were integrated into 'one unit' with its administrative centre at Lahore.

(*c*) small parts of the Western Himalayan and Western Sub-Himalayan Regions;

(*d*) Sind;

(*e*) nearly all the Punjab Plain proper, i.e. excluding what I have

previously called the South-Eastern Punjab Plain and which
Spate calls the Indo-Gangetic Divide;

(*f*) the fringe of the Thar Desert.

East Pakistan as shown in Fig. 136 lies almost wholly in my
'Delta Region' and covers most of it except the 'Old Delta' of western
Bengal.

The North-West Dry Hills Region

This natural region, also known as the North-West Frontier Region,
coincides very roughly with the former North-West Frontier Province

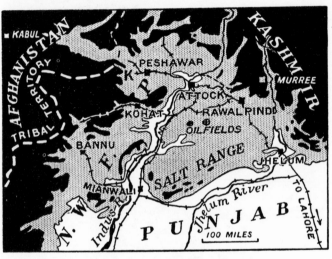

FIG. 121.—The Dry Hills Region of the north-west

K = Khyber Pass. Land over 1,000 feet, dotted; over 3,000 feet, black.

(excepting the northern part which lies amongst the Himalayan
tangle) together with the West Punjab Districts of Jhelum, Rawalpindi and Attock. The region is thus divided into two parts by the
river Indus.

The *Cis-Indus Tract* of the Punjab, or the part of the region to the
east of the Indus, consists of a dry sandy plateau bounded by the
Lesser Himalayas on the north and terminated abruptly by the Salt
Range, which overlooks the fertile Punjab Plains, on the south. Only
dry crops are possible, and millet is the staple food of this tract. Almost
in the centre lies the little oilfield of Khaur with that of Dhulian
nearby.

The *Indus Valley* is a tract of land with considerable possibilities, but the harvests vary greatly with the extent of the floods from the river. The difficulty of finding a suitable site for a dam has hindered large-scale irrigation.

The *Trans-Indus Tract*, lying between the Indus and the hills of the frontier, consists of a series of three plains—Peshawar, Bannu and Dera Ismail Khan—separated from one another by the low hills of Kohat and offshoots of the frontier range. The Vale of Peshawar is extensively irrigated and well wooded, presenting in spring and autumn a picture of waving cornland and smiling orchards framed by rugged hills. Adjoining Peshawar is the District of Kohat, a rough hilly tract inter- sected by narrow valleys. The southern spurs of the Kohat Hills fade away into the Bannu Plain. Where it is irrigated from the Kurram River, the Bannu Plain is very fertile, especially round Bannu itself. Where not irrigated, there are broad stretches of rough stony ground

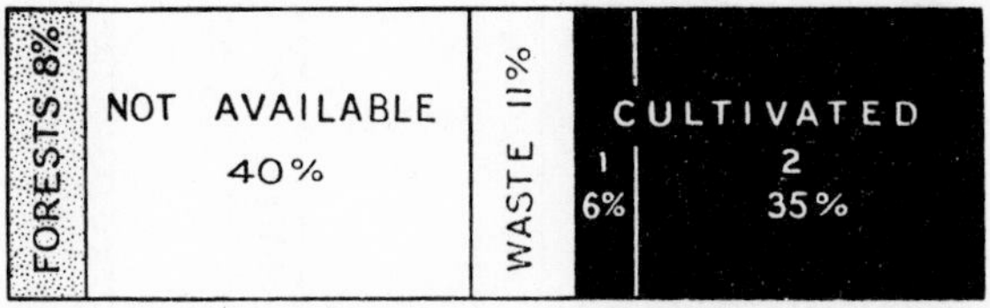

FORESTS 8%	NOT AVAILABLE 40%	WASTE 11%	CULTIVATED	
			1 6%	2 35%

FIG. 122.—The classification of the land in the North-West Dry Hills Region

See explanation in the text. As in all similar diagrams 'cultivated land' includes current fallows (marked 1, 6 per cent.) and land sown (2, 35 per cent.).

broken up by deep gullies cut by flood-water from the hills. Nearer the Indus River the plain becomes more fertile again, but its crops depend on the rainfall, which varies widely from year to year. A broken range of sandstone hills divides the Bannu Plain from the Daman or plain land of Dera Ismail Khan. This plain is a clay desert, but the soil is naturally fertile and in good rainfall years there is an abundant crop of grass. In these plains of Peshawar, Bannu and Dera Ismail Khan the summers are very hot and the winters very cold—frost occurs nearly every year. The plains, where fertile, are densely populated.

The Frontier Hills. To the west of the three plains just described lie the barren, treeless hills, inhabited by the warlike tribes of the frontier —Waziris, Afridis and Orakzais—all belonging to the group of people known as the Pathans. Here and there are fertile valleys, such as the upper part of the Kurram Valley, and in them are little hamlets and sometimes forests of stately pine trees. Some of the hillsides in the valleys are clothed with grass and the people of Kohat keep large numbers of sheep. Elsewhere the hills of the frontier are inhospitable in the extreme. This tract is almost outside the influence of the monsoon, and most of the scanty rain falls in the cold season.

Agriculture. Fig. 122, which has been drawn to show the proportion of cultivated land in the region, does not include the hills and
mountains of the tribal tracts, but refers simply to the Districts of
Jhelum, Rawalpindi, Attock, Peshawar, Kohat, Bannu and Dera
Ismail Khan. It may seem surprising, in so dry a region, that forests are
indicated as covering 8 per cent. of the area. This is largely a question
of classification: most of the 'forests' are merely scrubland, but valuable
because even the poorest timber and firewood have a value in such a
dry country. In addition a covering even of scrub protects the land
from soil erosion and the 'forests' are protected accordingly. The woodland is mainly in the north where the rainfall is slightly more than in
the south. Nearly half the region, bearing in mind that we are dealing
only with the more fertile parts, is occupied by hills, mountains and
useless ground. The proportion of waste land which might be utilized
is but small. Most of this 'waste land' is found in the plain of Dera

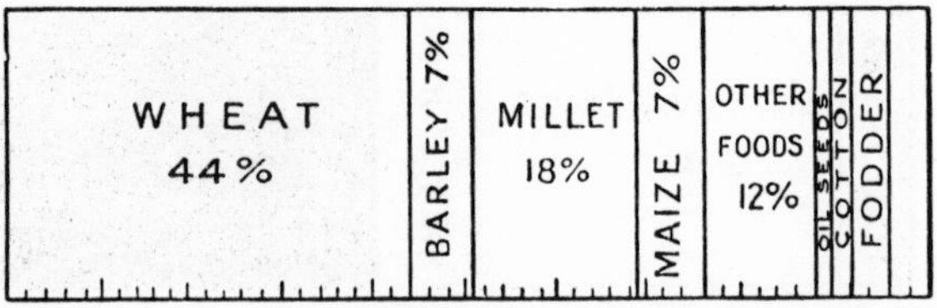

FIG. 123.—The crops of the settled parts of the North-West Dry Hills

Most of the wheat is grown on irrigated land; the millet on land dependent on rainfall. This diagram,
like all the others of a similar character in the section on India, has been constructed by taking the figures
for all townships or tahsils lying within the natural regions concerned. For reason of economy, the
Government of India ceased the publication of such detailed statistics and hence the diagrams are based
on those for the latest year available, 1920–1 (*Agricultural Statistics for India*), due allowance being made
where that season was an exceptional one. Where extensive changes have taken place since that time, the
facts are noted.

Ismail Khan, as yet unirrigated. The cultivated land comprises both
irrigated land and land with dry crops. The most important irrigated
areas are in the Vale of Peshawar, watered by the Government Canals
known as the Upper Swat Canal, Lower Swat Canal and Kabul River
Canal. Many of the crops of the Bannu Plains are also irrigated, but
on the sandy plateau of Jhelum and Attock mainly dry crops (millets)
are grown. In the region as a whole wheat is easily the leading crop.
Seen in the spring after a few showers of rain, the irrigated plains of
Bannu or Peshawar present to the eye a vast waving sea of wheat, with
here and there streaks or patches of darker coloured gram. After the
harvest the same area has been described as 'a bleak, howling wilderness, fit home for the whistling heat-laden dust storm which often
sweeps across its surface'. Millet is the chief dry crop. As in other parts
of north-western India there are two harvests, the Rabi and Kharif.

Population and Communications. One of the great railway
highways of old British India—from Calcutta to Delhi and Peshawar—
runs right across the northern part of this area. It crosses the Jhelum

at Jhelum and the Indus near Attock, where that mighty river flows through a narrow gorge. Since 1925 the railway has been continued right through the Khyber Pass to the Afghan frontier. It was preceded through the gorge by a military road, a continuation of the Calcutta-Peshawar Trunk Road, one of the few metalled roads to antedate the motor era. Care should be taken to notice also the railway along the east bank of the Indus which serves to link up the strategic railways which begin on the west bank and run into the valleys of Kohat and the Kurram Valley (this railway runs to the frontier and is also connected directly with Peshawar) and into the Bannu Plain.

Enough has been said to indicate the marked difference between the settled valley agriculturists and the frontier tribesmen. The enlistment of the latter in the British Army did something to curb their natural desire for raiding—a time-honoured custom not yet dead.

In the region large hydro-electric projects are in hand, notably the Warsak dam on the Kabul River where it enters the Peshawar Plain.

Peshawar (151,776 in 1951) is the former capital of the old North-West Frontier Province. It controls the Khyber Pass and thus nearly all the trade between India and Afghanistan. Peshawar stands at one end of the route, Kabul at the other. *Kohat, Bannu* and *Dera Ismail Khan* are the natural centres of their respective plains and are military as well as trade centres. *Rawalpindi* (340,175 in 1961) is the chief town of the Cis-Indus tract and is the starting-point for the principal routes into Kashmir and hence the centre for Pakistan-Kashmiri trade. The building of the new capital of Pakistan, *Islamabad*, near Rawalpindi was begun in 1961.[1]

The Plateau of Baluchistan

Baluchistan lies outside the mountain wall of India and consequently outside the influence of the monsoon. It comprises several Districts—in general the most fertile parts were those under direct British administration now known as Pak-Baluchistan—and the large States of Kalat and Las Bela. Physically Baluchistan comprises an arid plateau surrounded by a ring of mountains and forming a region of inland drainage; the arid Makran coast in the south; a tract of tangled mountainous country in the north-east continuous with the mountain frontier tracts of Waziristan and Afghanistan. South of the Bolan Pass Baluchistan also includes a fragment of the Indus Plains, but a portion not draining directly to the Indus. The total area of this huge tract is nearly 135,000 square miles—considerably more than the whole of the British Isles—but it has a total population of a little over a million. As elsewhere since Partition the old distinction between the districts and states has gone but population and development tend to be concentrated in the east in what were the districts assigned to the British Government by treaty in 1879.

[1] See *Geography*, **51**, 1966, pp. 58–61.

The Plateau of Baluchistan varies from 1,000 to 3,000 feet above sea-level; most of the surrounding mountains reach over 6,000 feet. The country as a whole has been aptly described as consisting 'largely of barren mountains, deserts and stony plains; its climate is subject

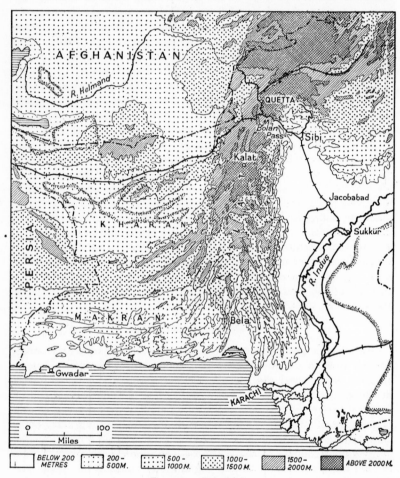

FIG. 124.—Baluchistan
For Gwadar see p. 156.

to the extremes of heat and cold, and the rainfall is uncertain and scanty'. On the plateau in Kalat State the average rainfall nowhere exceeds 10 inches, and some idea of its precarious nature may be gained by stating that taking a year at random three stations out of twenty-five recorded no rainfall at all, and four others less than an inch, although the 'averages' for these places ranged from 3 to 6 inches. The old British districts especially the country over 5,000 feet in the north-east enjoy heavier falls, ranging up to 20 inches in exposed stations. The rainfall curve for such stations as Quetta (9·7 inches) is distinctly Mediterranean in type, with an insignificant secondary maximum in summer. Stations among the hills in the north-eastern extension of Baluchistan have both summer and winter maxima. Snow is usual in the higher parts in winter.

There are no large rivers which can be used for irrigation as there are in those parts of India where the rivers flow from the Himalayas; the rivers are short, rushing torrents which flow after rain, but are often dry for many months of the year. For the most part they drain into shallow lakes in the midst of the plateau—lakes which often dry up entirely in the hot weather.

With the lack of water and the extremes of heat and cold and the difficulty of cultivating sufficient crops to sustain life, Baluchistan is far from being an ideal country, and it is not difficult to explain the flow density—nine per square mile. The majority of the people are nomadic and belong to three principal races—the Brahuis, Balochi (or Biluchi) and Pathans—speaking different languages. The Brahuis in particular hate the scorching heat of summer and migrate to the mountains, driving before them their thousands of sheep and goats, their horses, cattle and camels. In the cold weather they return to the alluvial plains to find pasture for their flocks and herds there. In bad seasons, and often for every winter, many Brahui families march to Sind, returning in the spring. There are thus two main factors which have determined the retention of nomadic habits in Baluchistan—one is the great extremes of heat and cold, the other is the lack of land which can be cultivated or irrigated and the consequent necessity of wandering from place to place to find food for man and beast. In summer the nomads live in 'jhuggi', shelters made of branches, or 'kizhdi', tents made of goat's hair matting or of blankets. In winter they may live in villages, in huts having walls of straw and mud, the roofs made with rafters of wood (when available), covered with matting of dried palm leaves or tamarisk. It is only in the towns that one finds buildings made of mud bricks dried in the sun.

The soil in some of the valleys and plains of Baluchistan is naturally very fertile, and in many areas the most has been made of the scanty water supplies available. The water from the mountain streams sinks into the ground at the foot of the hills some distance from where it might be of use in watering good alluvial soils. Long tunnels, known as karez, have been constructed to tap these underground supplies. Karez are not found elsewhere in India, but are common in Persia. Land irrigated in this way is only found in a few parts of Baluchistan, but especially near Quetta, in the district known as Quetta-Pishin.

Here the people are Pathans. A few of the level tracts of alluvium in Baluchistan are irrigated by flood-water from the streams. Indeed, in good seasons as many as three crops may be grown on the same piece of land. This is done by the Jatts, who live in the District of Kachhi. The most important crop in Baluchistan is *jowar* (millet); other crops include wheat, barley and rice, whilst fodder (lucerne, etc.) is grown for the cattle and sheep. Fruits, such as grapes, apricots, peaches, apples and melons, grow well. Along the Makran coast dates, for which Panjgur is especially famous, provide food for man and beast. A little fishing is carried on along the coast itself.

Reference has already been made to the diversity of language in Baluchistan. Balochi, Brahui, Pashto and Dehwari are the chief languages, but Jatki is growing in importance. They are all Iranian languages, and thus different from the majority of Indian languages. Most of the inhabitants of Baluchistan are Mahommedans.

There are really no indigenous towns in Baluchistan. Quetta, which has only been partly rebuilt after the destruction by earthquake in 1935, and Sibi are both of British origin. The strategic position of Quetta at the head of the Bolan Pass—by far the easiest route from India to Baluchistan—is obvious.

Across the deserts of Baluchistan there are numbers of old camel caravan routes. One of the most important of these routes, running along the north of the country and far into Persia, was replaced by a railway on the broad gauge (5 ft. 6 in.), which was completed in 1919 to the village of Zahidan in Persia. It is now, however, disused in part, and the remainder has only one train a week. Many routes are motorable.

Baluchistan is a fascinating country, and a wealth of information on the country and its people is to be found in the Reports on the Census of India, especially for the Census Years of 1911 and 1921. Slavery in Kalat was only abolished in 1926. But now there is development in various directions. The Sui Gasfield (Fig. 125) is actually in Baluchistan and there are possibilities of oil and other minerals.

Sind

With the exclusion of a strip of desert on the east, the natural region of Sind or the Lower Indus Valley corresponds closely with the administrative Province of Sind of the old British Indian Government.

Sind has often been called the 'Unhappy Valley'. In the days of old, when India was invaded by the Greeks and the Arabs, the invaders had marched for long, weary days and weeks through the desert wastes of Persia and Baluchistan, and the Valley of the Indus seemed a shining promised land. But the epithet reflects the uncertainty of life in a land of deficient and irregular rainfall, formerly dependent for water on the extent of river floods. Sind consists of a broad, dry, alluvial plain stretching from the edge of the Baluchistan Plateau (the Kirthar Hills) on the west to the Thar Desert on the east. Running through the centre of the plain is its life and soul—the Indus River. Just as Egypt is the 'Gift of the Nile', so may Sind be described as the 'Gift of the Indus'.

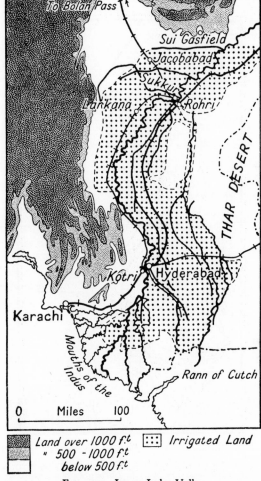

FIG. 125.—Lower Indus Valley

Some distance below the point where the Indus leaves the Punjab it flows through a rocky gorge which is important in several ways. It separates the Punjab Plains from the Plains of Sind; it affords a good foundation for the railway bridge of Rohri and for one of the largest irrigation dams in the world. North of Rohri in the hills of Baluchistan is the great Sui gasfield now with pipelines to Karachi and the Punjab.

A considerable part of Sind has an average rainfall of less than 5 inches a year, and even the coast has but little more. It follows that agriculture depends almost entirely upon irrigation, but until recently the irrigation was by means of inundation canals. Water spilt over from the river Indus into the canals when the river was in flood, but

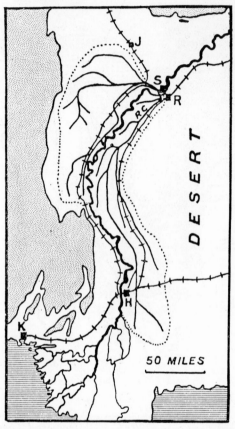

FIG. 126.—The Sukkur or Lloyd Irrigation Scheme, as completed in 1932

S = Sukkur; R = Rohri; J = Jacobabad; H = Hyderabad; K = Karachi. The canals are shown by plain lines; the approximate boundaries of the land to be irrigated are dotted. Land over 500 feet stippled. This map should be compared carefully with Fig. 125 which shows the area actually irrigated by this and other systems.

later in the year they became dry. Moreover, there was great danger of deficiency of supply in those years when the river failed to reach its normal flood level. For many years a great scheme was under consideration to replace the inundation canals of Sind by a system of perennial canals. The barrage, known as the Lloyd or Sukkur Barrage, was completed in 1932 but not all the canals are yet complete. A huge dam has been built across the river Indus below the town of Sukkur and an area of 7,500,000 acres will be irrigated (5,500,000 annually)—equal to considerably more than the total cultivated area of Egypt. The whole was planned for completion in 1962–3.

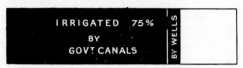

IRRIGATED 75%
BY
GOVᵀ CANALS
BY WELLS

Fɪɢ. 127.—Diagram showing the proportion of the cultivated land of Sind which is irrigated. Seventy-five per cent. of the whole, including current fallows, is irrigated, the bulk by Government canals. The continuous cropping of irrigated land results in it producing nine-tenths of the crops

Away from the irrigated land, Sind is a lonely barren desert. Here and there are the remains of canals no longer used and of cities long since deserted. There are deep, dry valleys which were once occupied by branches of the Indus. Probably the main stream of the Indus once

Fɪɢ. 128.—Position of Karachi

Land over 1,000 feet shown black; the desert, dotted. The principal sea routes serving Karachi are those along the Makran coast (also a land-caravan route) marked 1 above; from Basra and the Persian Gulf (2); from Aden and the Red Sea (3); from Bombay (4). The main routes from the hinterland to the port are those from the Punjab by railway (B); that from Baluchistan via Quetta and the Bolan Pass (A); and that from Delhi and Agra via Hyderabad and the desert (C). The last has not operated since partition.

flowed much farther to the east than it does now, and emptied itself into the Great Rann of Cutch. The old course is marked by a broad valley, but is quite dry. The Rann of Cutch is an interesting region. It was once an inland sea, but was gradually filled up by mud and sand brought down by rivers. It is no longer an arm of the sea, but merely a marshy area, almost completely dry in the hot season. It is still being filled up by sand blown from the Thar Desert, and soon it will be dry, barren desert.

It is interesting to notice that the Delta of the Indus has long remained unirrigated—a curious contrast to the rich rice-growing deltas of the Ganges, Irrawaddy, Mahanadi, Godavari and Kistna Rivers. There is excellent pasture in parts of the Indus Delta, but much of it is a useless, waste region, almost uninhabited. Near the coast it is flooded by the waters of the river and the sea in the hot season and in the cold season is a waste inhabited only by wild birds. Farther inland is a strip of desert where once flourished cities and ports. All this is now being changed, for the Lower Sind Barrage across the Indus near Kotri-Hyderabad, started 1950, was completed in 1955. From it four canals lead off and command a vast area.

Agriculture. About nine-tenths of the crops of Sind are irrigated. The former high proportion of fallow resulted from the dependence on inundation canals and has been steadily decreasing. The area under wheat has increased from 480,000 acres in pre-Barrage days to 1,265,000 acres in 1950-1, and cotton from 253,000 to 812,000. Lower down the Indus the Kotri Barrage irrigates 2,792,000 acres, mainly for rice.

Population. Formerly the ports of Sind were small towns in the delta, but they are now entirely replaced by the great port of Karachi which is west of the delta and was based originally on a natural rock-girt harbour. It serves as the outlet not only of Sind but of most of Western Pakistan, and has grown very rapidly in size and importance in recent years since it became the capital of Pakistan. The communication between Karachi and its hinterland is by railway; the direction of the main lines should be carefully noted. Karachi has become a great airport—the front door into the Indian sub-continent from Europe and there is a network of inland lines. By contrast with Bombay the dry climate of Karachi was in the main responsible for the absence of modern cotton-mills, but this dry climate favours the handling of grain which can be stored without damage from damp. Pakistan is developing many factories now at Karachi. In some years Karachi is now an importer of wheat instead of the chief exporter. Hyderabad, the lowest point where the Indus has been bridged, and Sukkur are the other two towns of note in Sind.

One of the consequences of partition has been the phenomenal growth of Karachi, first capital of Pakistan. It had only 216,883 people at the Census of 1921 and 359,492 in 1941, but by 1951 the total population exceeded 1,009,000. Since then refugees from India have continued to pour into the city. Huge extensions to the city itself, and a number of well-designed satellite towns, each with its own industries, have struggled to keep pace with the influx but huge numbers live by squatting on the pavements or on any piece of waste ground, building huts out of any material available and having their cattle, water-buffalo and goats roaming all round. It has proved difficult to settle these strangers on the land: they tend to drift back to Karachi which had 1,912,598 at the 1961 Census. Perhaps never before was a city set such a problem.

West Punjab or the Punjab Plains Proper

The word 'punjab' or 'panjab' is a Persian word meaning 'five waters' or 'five rivers'. The Punjab Plains are really the valley plains of the five rivers—Jhelum, Chenab, Ravi, Bias and Sutlej. These five

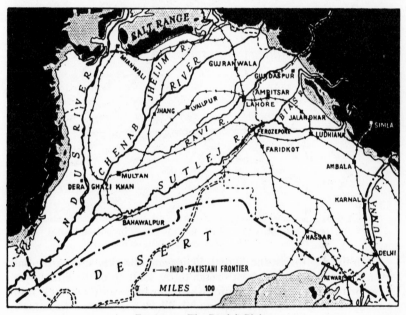

FIG. 129.—The Punjab Plains

The heavy dot-and-dash line indicates the limit of the natural region, the lighter broken line the limit of the old province. Land over 1,000 feet, dotted; over 3,000 feet, black.

The Indo-Pakistan frontier reaches across these open plains between Lahore and Amritsar

rivers all rise among the snow-clad heights of the Himalayas and flow broadly in a south-westerly direction before joining to form the Panch-nad, which eventually joins the Indus near the south-western border of the old province. The Indus itself, though flowing for some distance through the west and south-west of the province, plays an insignificant part in its economy. In the dry season the rivers of the Punjab Plains are shallow and sluggish, occupying but a small portion of their wide beds, but in the rainy season, when the warm sun of April and May has melted the Himalayan snows and the monsoon rains are pouring down on the mountain slopes, the rivers become rushing torrents often miles wide. The rush of water does not always follow the same channel. The river may leave its old bed, and in a single night destroy miles of fertile fields, cutting for itself a new channel. Between the rivers (the doab) there is usually a flat, alluvial plain covered with cultivated fields, but where the land rises even a little between the rivers the water-table is lowered, irrigation becomes difficult and a scrub-covered waste takes the place of fertile fields.

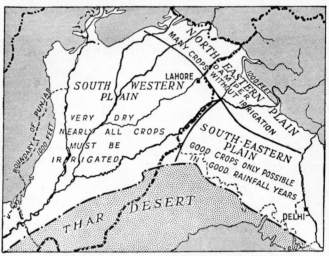

FIG. 130.—Map showing the threefold division of the Punjab Plains
The heavy interrupted line is the India–Pakistan boundary.

On the north-west the Punjab Plains end abruptly against the Salt Range and on the north-east stretch to the foothills of the Himalayas. It is the tracts near the mountains which sometimes suffer severely from earthquakes. On the east the Punjab Plains fade across the almost imperceptible divide into the Gangetic Plains; the area shown on Fig. 130 as the 'South Eastern Plain' is the Indo-Gangetic Divide of Spate. It is now the [East] Punjab State of the Indian Union which has absorbed the former princely state of Patiala. To the south of the Sutlej River, the land begins to rise very gradually and becomes drier and drier till it passes into the barren waste of the Great Indian Desert. In the south-west the desert approaches close to the Indus on the one hand as the southern end of the Sulaiman Range does on the other, and the constriction naturally separates the Punjab Plains from Sind. Throughout the whole of the Punjab Plains hills are completely absent. The soil is everywhere alluvial; the 'kankar' nodules are the only stones available.

Climate. From their northerly position the Punjab Plains become cold in winter—with an average temperature of less than 60° in January—but, as already noted, become the hottest part of India in June and July. Frost is frequent at night in winter. The region of greatest heat (with the highest recorded summer temperatures in the world) lies in the south-west and forms the heart of the low-pressure centre towards which the monsoon winds flow. The south-western parts of the plains have a very small and irregular rainfall, averaging in some stations even less than 5 inches. Towards the north and east the rainfall increases and a characteristic feature of the northern part of the plains is the considerable fall from winter cyclones. It is mainly on a climatic basis that the Punjab Plains can be divided into three separate areas or sub-regions. The first two lie mainly now in Pakistan, the third in India.

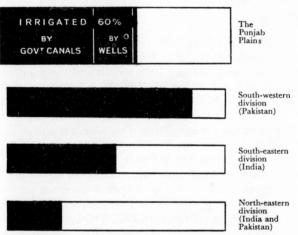

FIG. 131.—Diagrams illustrating the proportion of cropped land which is irrigated in the Punjab Plains as a whole and in the three divisions

    (*a*) The North-Eastern or North Central Plain. This is the wettest part of the plains (along the foot of the mountains) and has a rainfall of between 20 and 30 inches. A very large number of wells are found in this region and it is possible to grow many crops without canal irrigation.

    (*b*) The Western Plain. This includes the driest parts, with a usual rainfall of only 5 or 10 inches. It is almost impossible to grow any crops without irrigation.

    (*c*) The South-Eastern Plain (India). Here again the rainfall averages between 20 and 30 inches, but varies very much from year to year. In good years many dry crops can be grown, but in bad years none.

Despite the low average rainfall sudden heavy rainstorms are apt to occur towards the end of the rains in September and October, especially on the barren foothills. Disastrous flooding may occur (as in October 1955) and good agricultural land is often overwhelmed by masses of sand and shingle.

Irrigation. It will be gathered that irrigation is absolutely necessary over a very large part of the plains. Without it much of the Punjab would be as barren as the Great Indian Desert. Indeed, it is not always realized that over much of the now productive land of the Punjab Plains the rainfall is actually less than in the barren wastes of the desert. Irrigation is carried on in four principal ways—by wells, by tanks, by inundation canals and by permanent canals. Some of the irrigation works date from very early times, but the large modern works were all initiated by the former British Indian Government.

Canal Systems. In the Punjab Plains there are six main canal systems:

(a) The Western Jumna Canal takes its water from the Jumna, near where that river leaves the Himalayas. This is an old canal which has now been rebuilt and much improved. This system is in East Punjab (India).

(b) The Sirhind Canal takes its water from the Sutlej River and, like the Western Jumna Canal, it waters the south-eastern part of the Punjab Plains. This system is also in East Punjab (India).

(c) The Upper Bari Doab Canal takes its water from the Ravi River near Madhapur, where the river leaves the Himalaya Mountains. It waters the upper or northern part of the Bari Doab or the region between the *Bia*s and *Rav*i Rivers. Notice the derivation of the word Bari. This system is in East Punjab (India).

(d) The Lower Chenab Canal ranked at the time of its construction amongst the largest irrigation works in the world. It derives its water from that impounded by a great weir across the river Chenab at Khanki. It waters nearly 2½ million acres in the lower part of the Rech Doab or the region between the *Rav*i and *Ch*enab Rivers.

(e) The Lower Jhelum Canal takes its water from the Jhelum at Rasul and waters part of the Jech Doab (between the *Jh*elum and *Ch*enab Rivers).

(f) The Upper Chenab—Lower Bari Doab Canal System—is also known as 'The Triple Project', and is one of the cleverest examples of irrigation in the world. The Upper Chenab Canal takes its water from the Chenab at Merala, at the foot of the Himalayas. It waters the upper part of the Rech Doab, but the main canal is carried by an aqueduct across the Ravi River and becomes the Lower Bari Doab Canal, watering the lower part of the Bari Doab. But when this scheme was arranged it was found that so much water would be taken from the Chenab River by the Upper Chenab Canal that insufficient would be left in the river to fill the existing Lower Chenab Canal. And so the Upper Jhelum Canal was built to bring water from the Jhelum to the Chenab at Khanki and to help supply the Lower Chenab Canal. The Upper Jhelum Canal also waters part of the Jech Doab.

In addition to these areas in the Punjab proper are the large works in the former State of Bahawalpur, south of the Sutlej. Part of the state is watered from the Ferozepur dam (F of Fig. 132) but more

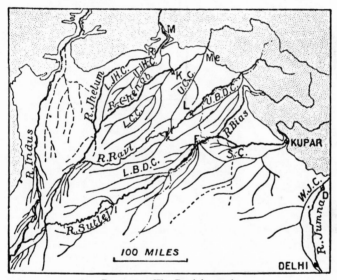

Fig. 132.—The Punjab canals

For explanation, see the text.
Part of the system between the Indus and Jhelum is complete and functioning (Thal scheme).

from Sulemanki Weir. Lower down is Islam Weir (I of Fig. 132). Where the Sutlej and Chenab join is the great Panchnad Weir, completed 1932.

The Thal area (Sagar Doab) between the Indus and the Jhelum-Chenab long remained without modern canal irrigation. This was due mainly to the relief of the ground, which rises slightly above the general level of the plains and renders irrigation difficult. In addition there was the difficulty of finding a good dam and storage site on the Indus, but the problem is being tackled. It is important to notice

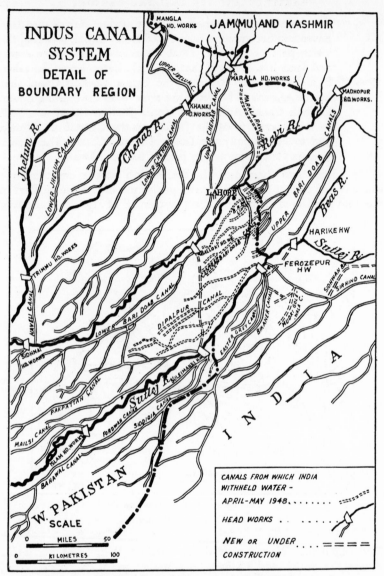

FIG. 133.—The Punjab canal systems on the Indo-Pakistan border

This map shows that the Jhelum, Chenab, Ravi, Beas and Sutlej Rivers, on the waters of which the Western Punjab (Pakistan) relies for its existence, all rise beyond the Pakistan existing borders—in Kashmir or India. From headworks at Madhopur on the Ravi and those under construction at Harike on the Sutlej, India could withdraw practically all the water of those rivers. A particularly difficult problem is presented by the Ferozepur headworks on the river Sutlej. Although the river there is the boundary the headworks are controlled entirely by India despite the dependence of a large area of Pakistan on water from this dam. Farther north, although Pakistan has constructed the Link Canal shown south-east of Lahore, it may not receive enough water from the Ravi to supply the canals (formerly served direct from India) dependent upon it. Note: Recent usage favours the spelling Beas as in this map.
A waters agreement between India and Pakistan was reached early in 1961.

the arrangement of canals in a great irrigation system and a map (Fig. 148) has been included to illustrate the point. It may be remarked, in passing, that a large proportion of the water distributed over the land eventually soaks back into the river courses; thus, although the Upper Jhelum Canal may take nearly all the water in the Jhelum at Mangla, there is sufficient lower down to supply the Lower Jhelum Canal. A major difficulty is to maintain an exact balance between water supplied to the land and water drained off. In some areas land has been ruined by accumulation of salts resulting from evaporation. In other areas waterlogging has caused the abandonment of large tracts. Attention is being paid to afforestation as an aid to drainage.

Agriculture. The most important crop of the Punjab Plains is wheat—occupying between one-quarter and one-third of the whole

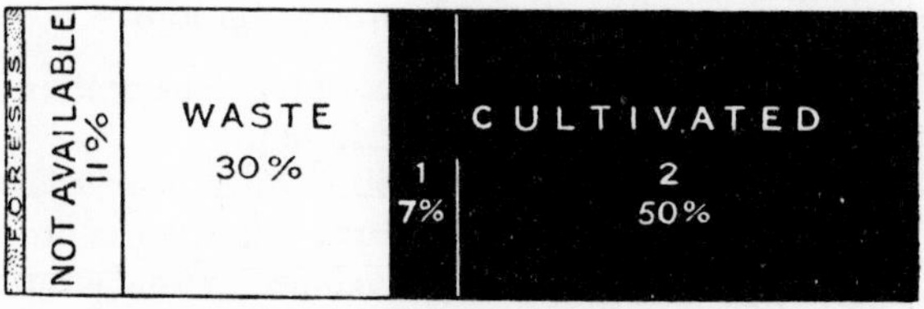

FIG. 134.—The classification of the land in the Punjab Plains

1 = current fallows; 2 = area sown.

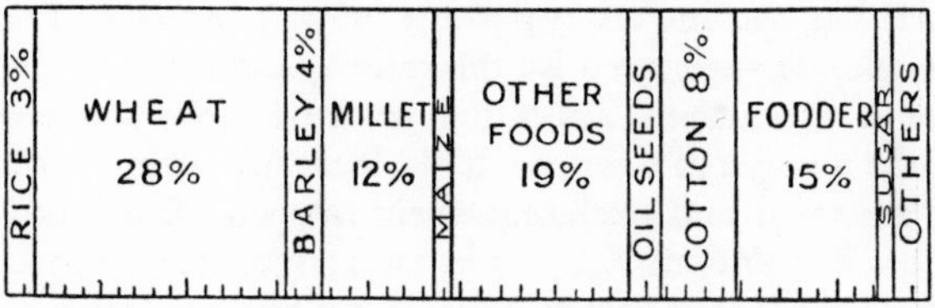

FIG. 135.—The crops of the Plains of the Punjab

cultivated area. Another important crop is millet, often grown on the same ground as wheat, the wheat being grown as a winter crop and reaped in the spring; the millet utilizes the monsoon rainfall and is ready for reaping in the autumn. Much millet is also grown as a 'dry' crop where wheat cannot be grown. Wheat and millet, together with maize, form the staple food of the people. Barley is another important crop. Other crops include oil-seeds. Sugar occupies a considerable acreage in the north-eastern part of the plains, but is less important than in U.P. By far the most important crop not grown for food is cotton, and it is on the irrigated land of the Punjab that most of the American cotton of India is grown. The large acreage under fodder is explained by the need, in such a dry region, of supplementing food naturally available for cattle which are needed in large numbers for ploughing. There has been a large recent development of citrus fruit.

Population. Agriculture affords subsistence to more than 60 per cent. of the population of the Punjab. The people live mainly in small villages scattered over the plains. The huts are built of mud or mud and wattle—a direct result of the absence of stone in the great alluvial plain. The flat roofs of the huts, made of rough branches coated with mud, reflect the dryness of the climate. In days gone by the peaceful cultivators of the Punjab suffered much from robbers who swept down upon them from the hills, and this resulted in their herding together in villages for greater safety. Though the cause is removed the result remains; there are few of the isolated farms so common in the Ganges Delta. A distinctive feature of the Punjab is the neatly planned irrigation settlements—prosperous villages where none existed before. The cities of the Punjab Plains can be divided into two groups:

(a) The great cities of the past,[1] famous religious centres or ancient capitals, such as Lahore and Multan.

(b) Cities of modern origin or old cities which have adapted themselves to modern needs and form collecting centres for agricultural produce or have developed manufactures of their own. Examples are Lyallpur and Gujranwala.

Lahore (429,747 in 1931, but 849,476 in 1951 and 1,296,477 in 1961) is the largest town, and now the seat of government of the unified West Pakistan. It has become an important railway centre and no less than 30,000 people are supported by the railway industry.

Multan is the natural collecting centre for the south-west of the Punjab. It is a very old town, with old local industries. Afghan traders still visit the town and exchange their raw silk, fruits and spices for piece goods. Population: 142,768 in 1941; 190,122 in 1951.

Lyallpur has modern cotton-mills; it is a fine new town with a large wheat trade. Population: 179,144 in 1951.

Gujranwala (120,860 in 1951) is an active trade centre. *Sialkot* (167,543 in 1951) in the Rech Doab is near the Himalayan foothills.

EAST PAKISTAN
The Lower Ganges Valley or the Deltas Region

This natural region corresponds very closely with the old Province of Bengal, as constituted in 1912. In 1947 the province was divided into West Bengal (the western third, including Calcutta, forming

[1] As with similar towns in many parts of India and Pakistan, several of these decreased in size in the decade 1911–21. But this was partly due to the terrible influenza epidemic of 1918–19, and in the decades 1921–31, 1931–41, 1941–51 and 1951–61 there has been a rapid increase in urban population almost throughout Pakistan.

part of India) and East Bengal (the eastern two-thirds forming East Pakistan). The region consists almost entirely of a vast alluvial plain— the deltas of those mighty rivers, the Ganges and Brahmaputra. In the north, Bengal includes a small strip of Terai country (known in Bengal as the Duars) and the District of Darjeeling lies in the Himalayan Region. In the east the Chittagong Hill Tracts and Chittagong

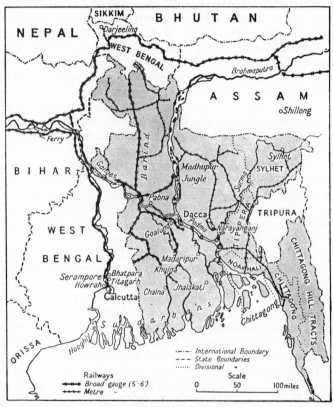

FIG. 136.—East Pakistan (stippled)

In 1956 the boundaries of the Indian State of West Bengal were adjusted so that a narrow strip o state territory links the former isolated section in the north with the main area in the south.

Dursim belong to the Eastern Hills Region and give Pakistan a share in the water-power and forest resources of these hills. East Pakistan also includes the Sylhet District or Surma Valley transferred from Assam in 1947.

The heavy rainfall makes the Delta very different from the Upper and Middle Ganges Plain; instead of being dry and brown in the hot season, the countryside is always green. The climate is equable when compared with the Middle or Upper parts of the Ganges Plain. Everywhere the rainfall is sufficient for the growth of a rich and luxuriant vegetation and for the cultivation of paddy. The rainfall increases from west to east. Calcutta has 60 inches, Dacca 73 and Sylhet 160.

The region falls naturally into three sub-regions:

(a) *The Ganges-Brahmaputra Doab or North Bengal.* This area stretches from the Terai country on the north to the Ganges River on the south. To the north-east is the narrow Brahmaputra or Assam Valley, to the west is the broad Ganges Valley. It is watered by streams flowing down from the Himalaya Mountains. They are torrents in the wet season and frequently change their courses, as the Tista has done, but in the dry season are almost dry. The usual flat surface is broken near the centre by a stretch of low hills, called the Barind, covered with brushwood jungle—the remains of a former forest.

(b) *The Old Delta or Central and Western Bengal.* Owing to several causes the great delta of the Ganges and Brahmaputra has moved gradually from west to east. Central Bengal is a land of 'dead and dying rivers'. The waters of the Ganges, with their load of fertile silt, no longer pass through the numerous channels. The place of flowing waters is taken by large swamps or 'bhils', many of which have been drained and form valuable rice land. Near the sea are the Sundarbans —extensive swamp forests which furnish useful timber, and especially firewood, to the towns farther inland. In central Bengal the country is not, as a rule, more than 50 feet above sea-level.

(c) *The New Delta and the Surma Valley.* Here the great rivers are still actively building up their deltas, and every year huge quantities of silt are brought down by the Ganges and Brahmaputra. In the high-water season a great part of the area is flooded and a rich deposit of silt spread over the country. It is a typical delta region, covered by a network of rivers, streams and creeks. Boats take the place of carts, there are few roads and few railways. In the rains only the river banks and the artificial mounds on which stand the houses appear above the water. It is impossible to go from one village to the next, or even from one house to another, without a boat or a raft or something which will float. Yet it is a fertile region, producing enormous quantities of rice and jute, as well as, except in places, a healthy region inhabited by a dense population. In the north-east is a small area of low hills—having an average height of only 40 feet above sea-level—but still important enough to prevent the Brahmaputra-Ganges from changing its channel to even farther east. This region is called the Madhupur Jungle and is still covered with grass or forest.

Agriculture. There is a somewhat larger percentage of waste land and land 'not available' for cultivation in the deltas than in the Middle or Upper Ganges Plains. This is due to the large area still occupied by swamps, as well as to the waste lands of the Barind, Madhupur Jungle and Western Bengal. In this connection the huge multi-purpose scheme based on a dam and power-house at Bheramara on the Ganges just below the Sara or Hardinge Bridge aims to extend the cultivation season throughout the year by irrigation in the dry months (only 9 per cent. of the rainfall comes between November and March), to drain the old permanent marshes, and to eliminate the salinity which affects the soil south of Khulna through seepage of sea water (see *Geography*, **43,** 1958, 206–8). The 'forests', which cover 6 per cent. of the region, are the Sundarbans—found in the Districts of Backergunge, 24-Parganas and Khulna. Even with these excisions well over half the region is cultivated. Rice is by far the most important crop—it occupies practically three-quarters of the whole cultivated area. The dry-zone crops of the Upper and Middle Ganges have disappeared; the area occupied by wheat, barley, millet and maize is so small that it cannot be shown separately on Fig. 152. A very important new crop appears—jute. Another crop is the oil-seed crop.

Population. There is a marked uniformity of population in this natural region. The inhabitants are nearly all Bengalis, and 95 per cent. speak Bengali as their native language. But the Bengalis are divided into two well-marked groups by their religion—about half are Mahommedans and slightly less than half Hindus. It is not surprising that the demarcation between East Bengal (Pakistan) and West Bengal (India) proved extremely difficult though the movement of refugees was not on

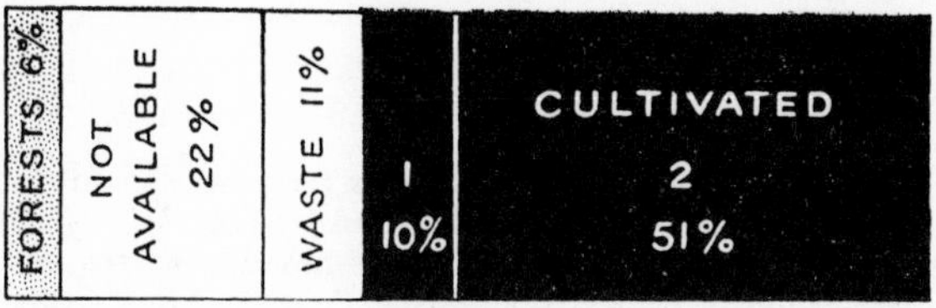

FIG. 137.—The classification of the land in the Ganges Delta Region

The forests are the Sundarbans. The high proportion of land not available is due to the presence of waterways, marshes, etc.

the scale of West Pakistan. Agriculture occupies 75 out of every hundred, industry 8 and trade 5. In some parts there are scarcely any villages, properly speaking, but isolated farms scattered over the fields. In the New Delta it is necessary first to construct an artificial mound on which the huts can be built above the level of floods.

Dacca (213,218 in 1941 but 556,712 in 1961) is the largest city and capital of East Pakistan and serves as the centre for the rich agricultural regions of the New Delta. Unlike Calcutta, Dacca is an old capital of Bengal and was an important city 300 years ago.

Narayanganj and *Madaripur* are examples of collecting and distributing centres which act as clearing-houses for the jute and rice.

Jhalakati is the centre of the betel-nut trade. *Sylhet,* the chief town of the fertile Surma Valley formerly in Assam, has only 21,000 people.

The completeness of the separation between India and Pakistan since partition in 1947 is not always realized. There is little trade or traffic across the border; except at a few selected spots most roads and rails are blocked and usually any goods must be man-handled across. East Pakistan has set out to become independent of the surrounding tracts of India. The railways, consolidated as the Eastern Bengal Railway, mainly narrow gauge, do not provide for through running between the two countries. Even the air services between Dacca and Calcutta are relatively restricted. The development of the jute industry has been noted (p. 243) and Pakistan is proud of the great new mill at Adamji. The need for a Pakistani town in the west has led to the growth of Rajshahi but the spectacular development has been that of Chittagong and its hilly hinterland with resources of water-power (one of the greatest dams in the world has been built at Kaptoi, creating a lake stretching into several valleys and over 50 miles in length), timber and hill-land suitable for such crops as tea. Chittagong has been developed into a first-class ocean port with deep-water wharves. Here transshipment can take place between the railway or the innumerable country boats of the Deltas Region or the 350,000-ton flotilla of the East Bengal Government and ocean-going steamers. For similar reasons the loss of Calcutta has stimulated the growth of such delta ports as Khulna and Chalna.

REFERENCES

For all aspects of the geography of Pakistan reference should be made to the two standard works: Nafis Ahmad, *An Economic Geography of East Pakistan,* O.U.P., second edition 1966, and Kazi S. Ahmad, *Pakistan,* 1965. See also F. J. E. Tearle, 'Industrial Developments in Pakistan', *Roy. Central Asian Soc.,* **52,** 1965, 224–37.

THE INDIAN REPUBLIC AND ITS
REGIONS

REFERENCE has already been made to the origin of the name Pakistan. There is no equivalent name in common use to cover the remainder of the sub-continent. Officially the Republic of India is known also as Bharat, but that name seems to have received but limited use in ordinary speech. Pakistanis sometimes talk of the continent of India being occupied by Pakistan and Bania or Hindoostan, but just as 'India' has been and still commonly is applied to the whole sub-continent so is Hindustan or Hindoostan.

The descriptions in the preceding pages will have made it clear that the Republic of India apart from its superiority in size and population retains many of the natural resources of the sub-continent. These include practically all the coal, much of the oil and water power, most of the iron ore and metallic minerals. The great cities, manufacturing towns and ports fell mainly to India. Pre-partition, as shown by the Census of 1941, Pakistan only had the two centres of Lahore and Karachi with more than a quarter of a million, India had fourteen.

Since partition the Republic of India has shown many remarkable developments. Perhaps the greatest change of all has been the disappearance of the princely states: glamour has gone as Demos has risen to power.

When India became independent in 1947 the Government inherited a curious hierarchy of administrative divisions. In the first place there were the old British provinces which became, with certain modifications Part A States, 10 in number. The larger 'native states' or groups of smaller ones became Part B States (8 in number), the minor provinces and other native states became Part C States (10), whilst the Andaman and Nicobar Islands became a Part D Territory. Such was the Union of India. With the States Reorganization Bill submitted to the Union Parliament in March 1956, and made law and operative on November 1, 1956, all this became of historic interest. The new divisions are those shown in the map facing p. 188. As explained there the division is primarily on a linguistic basis, and it is argued by some that this will lead to a cleavage between states speaking different languages rather than a closer union.

Some of the new states have awkward shapes, and access from all parts to the state capital is not always easy. It may be that adjustments will later be made. For these and other reasons the descriptions which follow are based on natural regions.

305

The Eastern Hills Region

The hills which lie along the borders of India and Burma sweep in a long curve from the far north-eastern corner of Assam to Cape Negrais on the south-west of Burma. Various names are applied to different parts of the hill belt; in the north the comparatively narrow

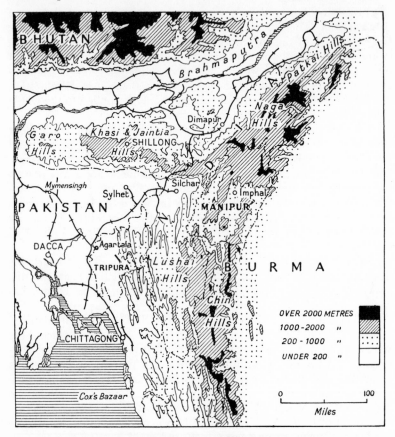

FIG. 138.—The Eastern Hills Region

belt is known as the Patkoi or Patkai Hills. These broaden out to form the Naga Hills and to enclose the Manipur Plateau. Southwards the Lushai Hills, Chittagong Hills and Chin Hills are remarkable in that they consist of a succession of long parallel ranges separated by deep valleys. Still farther south the hill belt gradually narrows, forming the Arakan Yomas. Between latitudes 25° and 26° N. a broad arm of the hill belt runs westwards through Assam to the border of Bengal, forming the Khasi, Jaintia and Garo Hills and including the broad plateau on which Shillong stands. In physical and geological structure this tract differs considerably from the main belt—it is in fact a detached portion of the Indian plateau.

Taking first the main hill belt, by contrast with the other parts of the mountain wall, the ranges of the Eastern Hills are low; the highest peaks scarcely reach 10,000 feet, whilst the majority of the ranges do not exceed 6,000 feet in height. The region as a whole lies in the track of the main Bengal current of the monsoon and the ridges lie athwart or, except in the north, slightly oblique to the normal direction of the winds. The rainfall is consequently very heavy, but there are marked contrasts in a short distance between valley bottom and ridge top.[1] The parallel arrangement of the long unbroken ridges is responsible for the inaccessibility of most of the region and the difficulty of communication between one valley and another. Normally the hillsides are covered with dense evergreen forest—of tropical species in the lower parts, evergreen oaks in the higher parts—whilst the ridge-tops are grassed. The hill tribes have, however, destroyed vast areas of the forest by burning off to obtain small patches for their shifting cultivation; useless bamboo thickets now occupy the deserted clearings. Consequently the total area of useful forest is comparatively small. The physical controls which have resulted in the existing sparse population of small hill tribes are sufficiently obvious. The difficulty of communication between one valley and another, to be effected only by toiling up and down tortuous tracks,[2] often not wide enough even for a pony or mule, explains the multiplicity of languages and the variety of customs found amongst such peoples as the Nagas, Chins and Chinboks. Except where Christianity has been carried by the indefatigable mis sionaries, Animism is the prevailing religion. Slavery, human sacrifice and head-hunting survived until a late date, but rapid progress led to the demand for the recognition of a separate Nagaland in 1960. The chief settlement, Kohima, is on the road from Dimapur to Imphal (Manipur). The small Naga villages are usually placed on spurs, near a spring in the hillside, but well situated in case of attack. On the nearby patches of cultivated land hill rice is the chief crop; only some of the more advanced tribes terrace the hillsides. The torrential downpours which characterize much of the region in the wet season are apt to strip the clearings bare of both crops and soil. The little plateau which is occupied by the State of Manipur has a fertile soil and a good quantity of rice is grown—a little is even exported.

The Assam Plateau lies directly in the path of the monsoon, with the result that the southern slopes are credited with some of the heaviest

---

[1] Compare also Manipur, on a plateau surrounded by hills, with an annual fall of a little over 60 inches only.
[2] It was over this incredibly difficult country that Burma was successfully re-entered by the Allied Armies in 1944–5.

rainfalls in the world. Cherrapunji has nearly 500 inches a year, and in one year nearly a thousand inches fell. Over the crest, on the surface of the plateau, the rainfall rapidly decreases. Shillong, though only 30 miles from Cherrapunji, has only 83 inches. Although no railway yet climbs to the surface of the plateau, the Assam hills are far more accessible, less rugged and far more cultivated than the main part of the Eastern Hills Region. On the northern slopes towards the Brahmaputra are some of the numerous tea gardens for which Assam is famous; a coarse kind of cotton is grown on the Garo Hills (and also on the Lushai and Chittagong Hills). Fruit trees such as oranges do well in the Garo Hills. Cultivation and settlement is spreading, for the population is still sparse and many of the Biharis who have worked as coolies in the tea gardens settle year by year in these tracts.[1]

Taken as a whole, the population of the Eastern Hills Region is between 50 and 60 to the square mile. The diagram (Fig. 139) on this

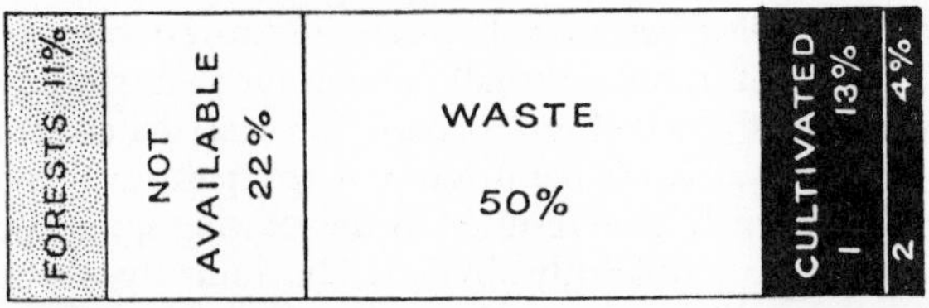

FIG. 139.—The classification of the land in the Eastern Hills Region

As in all similar diagrams 'cultivated land' includes current fallows (marked 1, 13 per cent.) and land sown (2, 4 per cent.). The relative proportions of these two are especially noteworthy.

page shows the apportionment of the land. The small percentage (about 4 per cent.) of cultivated land should be noted as well as the comparatively large proportion of fallow.

It is worth emphasizing once more that no railway connects India with Burma across this region. Of the through routes possible for bullock-carts, the Hukawng Valley Route and the Manipur Route from Dimapur are the chief and were converted into motor roads for the invasion of Burma by Allied forces in 1944–5. The famous Stillwell Road from Ledo in Assam into the Hukawng Valley is however disused. There is a railway which joins the upper part of the Assam Valley with the Bengal Plains, running as far as the port of Chittagong. It crosses the hills as shown in Fig. 138. Branches run from this railway to Sylhet, whence the rainy southern slopes of the Assam hills can be reached, and to the mouth of the Ganges-Brahmaputra. Shillong, the administrative centre of Assam, is reached by motor road from the north from the railway running along the Brahmaputra. The tortuous

[1] This region has been studied by S. P. Chatterjee in one of the first comprehensive monographs by an Indian, 'Le Plateau de Meghalaya' (Garo-Khasi-Jaintia). Paris, 1936.

ascent of this narrow road on to the plateau made it necessary to institute one-way traffic—up for half the day and down for the other half. Latterly the road has been greatly improved and there is now a road from Shillong to Sylhet. Politically the whole of the natural region lies in the Republic of India except for the southern part—the Chittagong Hill Tracts. The Sylhet district, formerly part of the province of Assam, is geographically part of the Deltas Region and is now an integral part of Eastern Pakistan. Chittagong as the port of the Pakistan part of the region has increased greatly since partition.

The Eastern Himalayan Region

The great curve of the Himalayas may be divided into two parts, an eastern and a western, mainly on a climatic basis. The eastern region may be taken as extending as far west as the western boundary of Nepal or to the Ganges River. Structurally it is simpler than the western tract and is characterized by a heavy monsoon rainfall.

It is characteristic of the Eastern Himalayas that they rise very

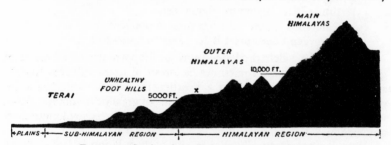

FIG. 140.—Section through the Eastern Himalayas

The cross marks the approximate position of the Himalayan hill stations—as accessible from the plains as possible but beyond the belt of comparatively unhealthy hills of the Sub-Himalayan Region.

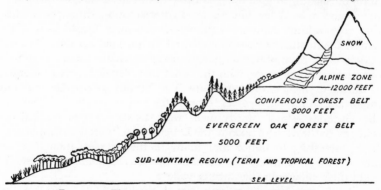

FIG. 141.—The vegetation belts of the Eastern Himalayas

rapidly from the plains. The zone of unhealthy foothills is comparatively narrow. Excluding the foothills and the Terai, the Himalayas in the east fall simply into two parts—the main Himalayan Range and the Lower or Outer Himalayas. Nearly everywhere the main ridge is 18,000 or 19,000 feet, and Everest, despite its height of 29,000 feet, seems to be only one of a chain of peaks. It falls to the lot of Kinchin-junga, especially when viewed from the hill station of Darjeeling, to achieve fame as the most magnificent mountain in the world. The third highest, its beauty is largely the result of its isolated position.

Darjeeling has a rainfall of rather over 100 inches, and may be considered characteristic of the eastern half of the Himalayas. It is an interesting experience, just before the break of the monsoon, to stand on one of the heights near Darjeeling and watch the clouds rolling up from the Bay of Bengal below the level of one's feet, obscuring the view across the plains below. A little later and Darjeeling is enveloped in the clouds—a state of affairs which lasts nearly half the year.

Excluding the Sub-Himalayan strip below 5,000 feet, three vegetation zones may be distinguished:

(4) Snow: above 16,000 feet.
(3) Alpine Belt: 12,000 to 16,000 feet.
(2) Coniferous Forest Belt: 9,000 to 12,000 feet.
(1) Evergreen Oak Forest Belt: 5,000 to 9,000 feet.

In the Alpine Belt rhododendrons are important; sometimes they grow in dense thickets, sometimes as forests of trees with red, twisted stems, at higher levels merely a heather-like carpet. Just below the snow-line the only vegetation may be tufts of grass or mountain plants with a 'cushion habit'. Inaccessibility prevents forest exploitation to any extent.

Population. Naturally the density of population is low—almost everywhere less than 100 to the square mile and usually far less. The State of Sikkim, to give one example, has as a whole sixty people to the square mile. A few villages are scattered amongst the mountains; they are not large and consist simply of a few huts. Nearby is usually a patch of cultivated land—forest cleared by burning and used for a few seasons only. Most of the hill people are Mongolians; there are numerous races and languages, with the result that Nepali has been adopted as the *lingua franca* of the mountains. The Nepalis are perhaps the most important of the hill peoples, though the ruling people in Nepal are the Gurkhas—small, sturdy men, well known for their qualities as soldiers. In the State of Sikkim, the Lepchas and Bhutias are important. It is interesting to notice that many of the peoples, though living amongst the mountains, hate the cold. The Lepchas, especially, usually build their villages in the warmer valleys.

The Eastern Himalayas lie in Nepal, the little State of Sikkim, the Indian District of Darjeeling and Bhutan.[1] *Katmandu* is the capital of

[1] Sikkim is an Indian Protectorate; Bhutan (winter capital, Punakha) is an independent state, ruled by a Maharajah, having close treaty relationships with India.

Nepal and most of the population of Nepal is found in its vicinity (see pp. 359–60). *Darjeeling* is an important hill station—under British rule it was the hot-weather capital of Bengal and the centre of numerous tea gardens. It commands also the principal route to Lhasa. Farther east is *Kalimpong*, through which town wool is imported from Tibet.

The Eastern Sub-Himalayan Region

Like the Himalayan Region, the Sub-Himalayan is divisible into eastern and western halves on a climatic basis. Lying between the level Gangetic Plains and the Himalayas, it is usually possible to divide the Sub-Himalayan Region into two parallel strips. The strip nearer the plains is level or undulating land only slightly raised above their level. It is, or was, swampy and usually covered with coarse, tall grass and is known as the 'Terai', or as the 'Duars' in northern Bengal. Nearer the Himalayas the second strip consists of a belt of hills, including such groups as the Churia Ghati Hills of Nepal, the Dun Hills of northern Bihar and the Sinchula Hills of northern Bengal, as well as the lower slopes of the Outer Himalayas. These ranges of foothills do not generally exceed 4,000 feet in height, and are usually covered with damp and unhealthy forest. Indeed, the whole of the Sub-Himalayan tract was an unhealthy, malarial region shunned by men and had the additional disadvantage of frequent earthquakes. Gradually, however, drainage and cultivation have been pushed into the Terai, and in some areas the hillsides are elaborately terraced. Along the northern fringe of the Ganges Plains there is a long line of towns—Saharanpur, Pilibhit, Kheri, Bahraich, Motihari, Jalpaiguri, etc., connected by railway, which may be regarded as 'frontier towns' and the bases of agricultural operations against the Terai. In the eastern half now under consideration the rainfall of the Terai varies from over 100 inches in the east to 40 inches in the west, so that it is ample for cultivation. Among the foothills there are naturally large local variations.

The characteristic vegetation of the hilly parts is a monsoon forest of the valuable sal. The sal flourishes especially on the cones of coarse gravel brought down from the hills and known as bhavar. The forest is interrupted over large areas by patches of coarse grass such as occur in the Terai. In the west there are numerous patches of dry thorn forest; in the wet east it is found that the sal forest occurs mainly on the ridges, rich wet tropical evergreen forest in the valleys.

In some parts the population in the Terai is still scanty, though tea gardens are well established in northern Bengal and in the District of Jalpaiguri the density reaches 300. In Uttar Pradesh much of the Terai is now cultivated, and in places the population reaches 500 to the square mile. The sal forests are an important source of timber.

The large area of the Sub-Himalayas and Himalayas lying north of the Brahmaputra in Assam is occupied by various tribes and is loosely administered by India as the North East Frontier Agency (NEFA), though also claimed by China (see Fig. 153).

The Western Himalayan Region and Kashmir

The Western Himalayan Region includes Kashmir, and not only is the mountain chain itself far more complex than in the east, but the greater complexity is reflected in the vegetation and it is more difficult to separate vegetation zones. Broadly, five great parallel ranges of mountains can be distinguished:

The Karakoram or Muztagh Ranges.
The Ladakh Range.
The Zaskar Range or Inner Himalayas.
The Great or Middle Himalayas or Pangi Range.
The Lesser or Outer Himalayas or Pir Panjal Range.

The Karakoram Ranges are the highest of all, and there are many peaks more than 25,000 feet high, of which K2 or Mount Godwin Austen is the loftiest, and probably ranks second in height amongst the mountains of the world. This great chain completely shuts off the bleak Tibetan Plateau beyond. The Karakoram Pass is the chief of the difficult passes and is followed by the path from Leh to Tibet.

The Ladakh and Zaskar Ranges also form great walls, with many peaks more than 20,000 feet high.

The Great Himalayas are also very high, and many peaks exceed 15,000 feet.

The Lesser Himalayas have an average height of 10,000 to 12,000 feet. Though the peaks are not much more than half the height of those

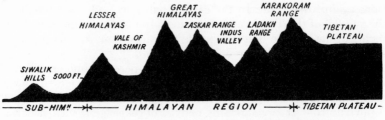

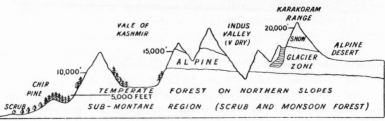

FIGS. 142 and 143.—Sections through the Western Himalayas, showing the disposition of the ranges and the vegetation belts

in the Karakoram Range, it is this range, with its snowy crest, which occupies the horizon as a beautiful vision to the dweller in the Punjab Plains.

The Indus River rises in the Tibetan Plateau, and for a long distance flows between the great Ladakh and Zaskar Ranges. The Upper Indus Valley is very dry (Leh has but a few inches of rain and snow a year), for the lofty Great Himalayas allow but little of the monsoonal influences to penetrate beyond. Below the town of Skardu the Indus

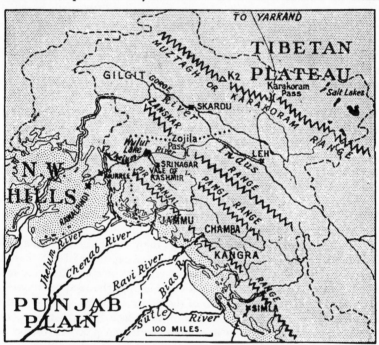

Fig. 144.—The western part of the Himalayan Region and Kashmir

India claims the whole state but the provisional cease-fire line is dotted.
Land over 3,000 feet, closely dotted; land between 1,000 and 3,000 feet, lightly dotted.
Zanskar is now more commonly written Zaskar as in the text.

passes through a tremendous gorge, is joined by the Gilgit, and turns southward, then west again and finally south until it cuts its way right through the mountains to the plains.

Between the Great and Lesser Himalayas is a valley different from most of the mountain valleys. In the first place, it is much broader, with a valley floor sufficiently wide to include the extensive Wulur Lake. This valley is the world-famed Vale of Kashmir. Through the vale wanders the Jhelum River, here broad and navigable and unlike most Himalayan rivers. If there is one thing the world traveller learns, it is that few places on the earth's surface really live up to their reputation.

Perhaps Kashmir is one of the exceptions. This is not the place to enlarge upon the charm of a leisurely journey by houseboat from Wulur Lake to Srinagar, but it is one of those rare pleasures which is not overrated. The hillsides owe much of their beauty to the wonderfully rich carpet of mountain flowers—especially at Gulmarg—whilst the more accessible hill-slopes are covered with terraced fields of fine fruit trees—apples, pears and oranges. The land near the river suitable for cropping is very valuable, and it is in Kashmir that one finds floating islands. Rafts are made and covered with a little earth in which seeds are then sown. Not infrequently a man's land may aptly be described as lost, stolen, or strayed.

In popular parlance Kashmir is often used as if synonymous with the little Vale of Kashmir, which occupies but a very small part of the otherwise bare, rugged, mountainous State. (Compare the Vale with a density of over 200 and the Indus Valley with a density of 10.) *Srinagar* (over 200,000), the capital, lies in the Vale and is famed for its wood-carving industry and the weaving of shawls. The former road from Rawalpindi (Pakistan) to Srinagar is closed; there is now an all-Indian motor road from Pathankot and Jammu through the Banihal tunnel. Northwards from Srinagar a new motor road to Leh crosses the Zaskar Range by the Zoji La.

Out of the five rivers of the Punjab only the Sutlej rises beyond the Himalayas in Tibet and cuts right through. The others rise amongst the Zaskar or Great Himalayas, but all cut through the Lesser.

The Western Himalayas are drier than the Eastern. Simla, the famous hill station and former 'hot-weather capital' of India, has 62 inches; the total gradually decreases westwards and is often very low indeed in the deeper mountain valleys. Fig. 143 shows approximately the vegetation zones. The scrub of the plains begins to change in the Sub-Himalayan Region at a height of 3,000 feet. Rather below 5,000 feet the Himalayan Region is entered, and from 5,000 to 10,000 or 12,000 feet is found the temperate mountain forest. In the drier parts the forests usually clothe the northern sides of the mountains, where they have more shade, so that the snow lies longer and the moisture is not evaporated by the sun. The southern sides are often bare, stony slopes or covered with short grass and bushes. It is a little difficult to separate the mountain forest into two zones as in the Eastern Himalayas. It consists of a mixture of broad-leaved oaks and the needle-leaved pines and deodars. Broadly speaking, the chir pine (*Pinus longifolia*) of the lower slopes gives place upwards to the deodar (*Cedrus deodara*) and blue pine (*Pinus excelsa*), whilst above 8,000 feet spruce, silver fir and beech are found. Some of the forests of Kashmir are more accessible than those of the Eastern Himalayas. Logs of deodar and blue pine are floated down to the saw-mills on the plains.

The Kashmiris are the principal people of the Western Himalayas and naturally live in the more sheltered valleys. Rice is grown in tiny fields carefully levelled and irrigated at the bottoms of the valleys, other crops in minute fields on the hillsides. Below 8,000 feet the most important crop is maize, but wheat can be grown up to this level. Buckwheat is grown in the poorer, stony soils. In the wilder parts, such as the Indus Valley, the only inhabitants are a few wandering shepherds. Most of the people of the State of Jammu and Kashmir are Muslims who, on partition in 1947, naturally favoured joining Pakistan. But the ruling family was Hindu favouring union with India. Fighting broke out and a cease-fire line was demarcated by U.N. in January 1949 (see Fig. 144). Eighteen years after partition the problem was still unsolved; in January 1966 the Russians arranged a conference in Tashkent.[1]

The hill States now grouped as Himachal Pradesh are similar to Kashmir in general features. On convenient spurs are found such hill stations as Naini Tal (U.P.) and Mussoorie, as well as Simla, already mentioned.

The Western Sub-Himalayan Region

The western part of the region is much drier than the eastern, though it has a heavier rainfall than the adjoining plains. Again a division into two strips can be made. The Terai is absent and the outer and lower strip includes the foothills such as the Siwalik Hills north of Delhi and the slopes of the mountains up to 3,000 feet. This strip is usually covered with a poor monsoon forest or scrub. The most interesting tree in the forest is *Butea*, known otherwise by various native names, such as chichra, dhak and palah, and in English as 'Flame of the Forest' from its red flowers. Probably much of the Sub-Himalayan Region was once dhak forest. It yields good firewood; gives a useful gum; dye can be made from the beautiful flowers, whilst the dried leaves form fodder for cattle. But the dry forests of this strip are still more useful for their yield of bamboo—of importance as a building material in the plains. With the removal of the forest cover the foothills have become more liable to damage by torrents from the mountains with the result that much good land has been lost. The second strip extends from 3,000 to 5,000 feet above sea-level, and in it the chir pine is very common. This strip might, indeed, be considered the lowest zone of the Himalayan Region. Turpentine can be obtained from the resin of this tree.

The western part of the Sub-Himalayan Region is not so unhealthy as the wetter, eastern part. With a rainfall generally between 30 and 40 inches dry crops can be grown. Wheat and maize are the chief, but gram and millet are also grown and, in addition, much fodder. Cultivation is gradually being extended and the scrub forests are disappearing, with the result that the population density is, in both the western and eastern Punjab, now as high as 300 to the square mile.

It must also be remembered that the great irrigation canals of the

[1] For an excellent summary see Ram Nandan, 'Jammu and Kashmir', *Focus*, **13**, 1, Sept. 1962.

Punjab Plains and Uttar Pradesh take their water from the rivers just where those rivers leave the hills; hence there is a line of important irrigation works within the borders of the Sub-Himalayan Region. Other small towns serve as exchange centres where the dwellers in the hills meet, and exchange produce with, merchants from the plains. Special interest attaches to Hardwar, where the sacred Ganges emerges from the mountain gorges and which is hence a very important centre of pilgrimage.

The Tibetan Plateau

It must be mentioned, in passing, that within the confines of the State of Kashmir a small portion of the Tibetan Plateau, described elsewhere, is included.

The East Punjab [1]

Under the reorganization of 1956 the Punjab has now absorbed the former princely state of Patiala and other smaller states. The whole coincides with the south-eastern plain of Fig. 130 and part of the north-eastern plain. In fact the great part lies outside the 'land of the five rivers' or Punjab proper and there is considerable justification in Spate's separate region of the 'Indo-Gangetic Divide', except that the word 'divide' scarcely conveys the general idea of a featureless plain of indeterminate drainage.

With an area of about 47,205 square miles (population 20·31 million in 1961) the Punjab is a relatively small state of the Indian Union. The general features have been described on pp. 293–6.

With the partition of the old province of the Punjab between Pakistan and India, the provincial capital Lahore went to Pakistan. India has seized the opportunity boldly by designing and building an entirely new town, *Chandigarh*, as the state capital. It was formally inaugurated on October 7, 1953.

Amritsar (264,840 in 1931, but 391,010 in 1941 and 376,295 in 1961) is less ancient than Lahore, but is famous as the stronghold of the Sikhs who stood out against the Mahommedans in the eighteenth century. It suffered badly from fever, due largely to the stagnant water which soaked into surrounding hollows from the Upper Bari Doab Canal. The old manufacture of carpets remains and there are many modern developments. It is the sacred city of the Sikhs whose religious life centres round the Golden Temple. *Ludhiana* has modern cotton-mills. *Ambala* is a modern town of British origin, and a railway junction, *Patiala*, deserves mention as one of the largest towns in a former native state and a trade centre for the south-eastern Punjab.

The whole is an area much disturbed by partition. The boundary

---

[1] Officially in the Indian Union called simply Punjab. In 1966 the Sikhs were promised a separate state.

was a matter of great difficulty: mass migrations of Hindus and Moslems upset the social structure and economic life of the region. From 1947 to 1954 no trains ran across the border despite the few miles of featureless plain which separate Lahore and Amritsar.

Delhi

When Delhi was made the capital of India in 1912, the district around was separated from the Punjab and at the same time made independent of the United Provinces on the east. The little state of Delhi lies almost on the divide between the Indus drainage basin and the Ganges drainage basin—to be precise the city itself lies on the west bank of the Jumna River and hence in the Ganges Basin, but it is convenient to deal with Delhi before considering the Ganges Plain. Delhi, which had a Census population of 2,061,758 in 1961 compared with 521,849 in 1941, is the third city of India in size and growing very rapidly. It owes its importance in the main to its strategic position.

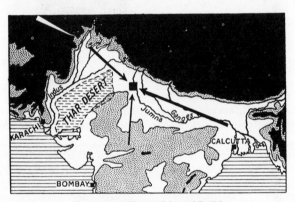

FIG. 145.—The position of Delhi

Land over 1,000 feet, dotted; over 3,000 feet, black. A red sandstone spur of higher ground stretches northwards to Delhi itself.

It stands at the head of both the great divisions of the Hindustan Plain —the great fertile plain of the Ganges and the great plains of the Punjab. From Delhi any place in the plains is easily accessible. Further, Delhi lies where the great desert and the hills of the plateau on the south approach somewhat closely to the Himalayan chain. As shown in Fig. 145 it was inevitable that the invaders of India from the north-west would avoid crossing the desert and be compelled to pass near the site of Delhi before they could reach the fertile plains of the Ganges. So in the past Delhi has often been the capital of India. Standing on the Jumna, Delhi was at the 'head of navigation' of that great river and boats could go all the way from Delhi to Calcutta. The land routes from the north-west there joined the water routes of the north-east. In modern times railways have largely replaced land and river routes, and Delhi has become a great railway centre, easily accessible from all parts of India. Irrigation has increased the fertility of the surrounding lands; much cotton is grown and sent to Delhi, where there are now modern cotton-mills. The capital, New Delhi, dating from 1912, with its magnificent buildings, stands a short distance from the old city. At a convenient distance, to the north of Delhi, on the healthy heights of the Himalayas, is Simla, the hot-weather seat of Government, whither the Government used to migrate annually from Delhi.

The Upper Ganges Plain

The Punjab Plains fade imperceptibly eastwards into the Ganges Plains. From Delhi which has a rainfall of 25 inches, there is a gradual increase in precipitation as one goes down the Ganges Valley. The

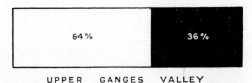

FIG. 146.—Diagram showing the proportion of the cropped land in the Upper Ganges Valley which is irrigated (irrigated land in black)

40-inch rainfall line passes through Allahabad and may be taken as roughly the limit, except for a strip along the northern part near the Himalayas, of the natural region which we have called the Upper

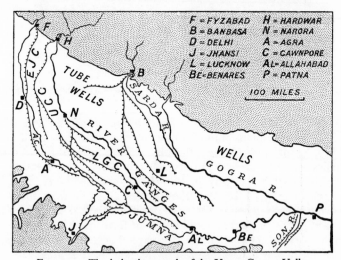

FIG. 147.—The irrigation canals of the Upper Ganges Valley

EJC = Eastern Jumna Canal; AC = Agra Canal; UGC = Upper Ganges Canal; LGC = Lower Ganges Canal. See also Fig. 148.

Ganges Plain. The climate is thus damper and at the same time less extreme than in the Punjab. The region lies between the Sub-Himalayan strip in the north and the slopes of the Central Indian Foreland, which begin just to the south of the Jumna River, in the south. Delhi is only 700 feet above sea-level and the hill-less plain

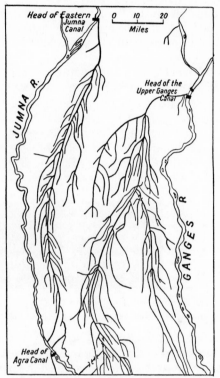

FIG. 148.—Fragment of a canal map of the northern part of the Ganges-Jumna Doab, showing the arrangement of main canals, branch canals and distributaries. The arrangement is roughly the *reverse* of that of a river and its tributaries.

slopes imperceptibly towards the east (Allahabad, 400 feet). Obliquely across it from north-west to south-east flows the Ganges; near the western and southern boundary is the Jumna. Nearly half the region lies therefore in the Doab between the Ganges and Jumna.

Irrigation. Taking the region as a whole, 36 per cent. of the crops are grown on irrigated land. In the Doab the proportion rises to 50 per cent., in the District of Meerut reaching 57 per cent. There are at present five chief canal systems:

    (*a*) The Eastern Jumna Canal (originally constructed between 1718 and 1748, but later abandoned) takes its water from the

Jumna River near Fyzabad, just where the river leaves the mountains.

(b) The Agra Canal takes its water from the Jumna River just below Delhi.

(c) The Upper Ganges Canal takes its water from the Ganges near the sacred spot of Hardwar, where the river leaves the mountains. Begun by Sir P. T. Cautley in 1839, now with 8 hydro-electric stations completed 1956.

(d) The Lower Ganges Canal takes its water from the Ganges at Narora.

(e) The Sarda Canal (constructed between 1920 and 1930) takes its water from the Sarda River at Banbasa (1928).

The areas not irrigated by canals get their water from wells. The old masonry wells are operated by the shaduf (orderkli), the Persian wheel, and by direct bullock lift. Many years ago deeper tube-wells pumped by oil-engines were tried but were not very successful. Then in 1929 was initiated the Ganges Canal Electric Grid Scheme. Small falls (fortunately made when the Upper Ganges Canal was con-

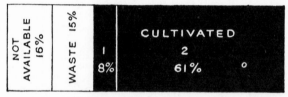

FIG. 149.—The classification of the land in the Upper Ganges Plain
Notice the complete absence of forests and the very high proportion of cultivated land.

structed) have been used to generate electricity which is used both for village and town supply and for pumping tube-wells.

Wells previously constructed were electrified in 1931, and later the Government carried out a tube-well scheme with 1,500 wells irrigating 2,000,000 acres east and west of the Upper Ganges, and also supplying water to the Upper Ganges Canal in times of deficiency.

Agriculture. Largely as a result of irrigation, the proportion of cultivated land in this region reaches the high figure of 69 per cent. Double-cropping is usual on the irrigated land, wheat being a leading winter crop. Fig. 152 has been drawn to show comparatively the crops in the three regions of the Ganges Plain. Everywhere in the Upper Ganges Plain wheat and barley together occupy a larger area than rice. Some of the driest districts grow no rice at all. In common with other dry regions millet is an important crop, here ranking second only to wheat. Other food crops include maize, gram and various pulses. Sugarcane is grown in most parts of India and, although it occupies only a small area when compared with other crops, the region now under consideration is the most important for sugarcane in India. By far the most important crop not grown for food is cotton. Agra and Delhi are the two chief centres of modern cotton manufacturing. Fodder is an important crop because, for its size, the Upper Ganges

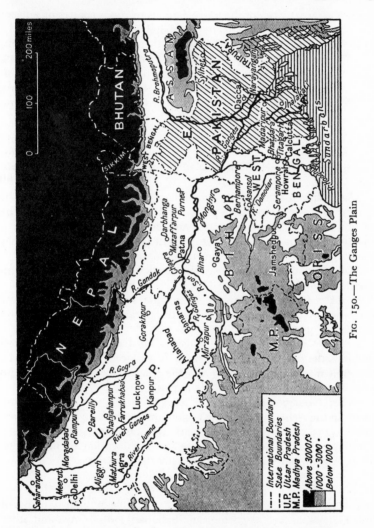

Fig. 150.—The Ganges Plain

Plain has more cattle than any other region of India. Dairy farming—generally so unimportant in India—is an industry of importance in certain districts, Aligarh in particular being well known for its butter. By contrast with cattle, sheep and goats are not numerous as there is little waste land on which they can be pastured.

Population. The region compares closely with the Punjab Plains in that 88 per cent. of the population live in villages of less than 5,000 inhabitants, and in which the huts are of mud or mud and wattle. Again the towns fall into:

(a) The great cities of the past—famous religious centres or ancient capitals such as Lucknow, Allahabad and Muttra.

(b) The cities which have adapted themselves to modern needs, forming collecting stations for agricultural produce or having modern factory industries. Examples are Kanpur (Cawnpore), Meerut and Moradabad. Included in this group are the 'frontier' towns on the border of the Sub-Himalayan Region, such as Saharanpur.

Lucknow (595,440 in 1961) is the capital and the second largest city of Uttar Pradesh. It is an important railway centre and has manufacturing industries which developed greatly during the Second World War.

Allahabad, situated at the junction of the Jumna and the sacred Ganges, is a very important place of pilgrimage. Its position at the junction of these two waterways, and latterly its development as a railway centre, has made it an important collecting centre, but it has no manufactures of note of its own. Population 411,955 in 1961.

Muttra, on the Jumna, near the head of the Agra Canal, is an important religious centre.

Farrukhabad, on the Ganges, is an interesting example of a river port whose former importance has disappeared since the railways became the great arteries of trade.

Kanpur (*Cawnpore*), on the Ganges, with a population of 895,106 in 1961 is the largest city in the state. It is a great railway centre, an important manufacturing town and the chief collecting centre for the agricultural products of the whole region.

Meerut (200,470 in 1961) and *Moradabad* (180,100) are growing centres in the richest parts of the region, and with them may be linked Bareilly (254,409), Aligarh (185,020), Rampur (135,407) and Shahjahanpur. *Agra* (462,029), celebrated as the location of the world-famous Taj Mahal, has also modern factory industries.

The Middle Ganges Plain

This natural region comprises nearly the whole of Bihar lying north of the Ganges, as well as portions of Shahabad, Patna, Gaya and other districts lying immediately to the south of the river, together with that part of Uttar Pradesh lying east of Allahabad and north of the Ganges. The region is intermediate in character between the dry Upper Ganges Plain and the very wet Deltas Region of Bengal. The rainfall varies from 40 inches in the west to just over 60 inches in the northern part of the

Purnea district. The climate is less extreme than in the Upper Ganges Plain or the Punjab, but it is still cold enough in January (average of 61° F.) for fires to be used in some better houses. In the hot season the scorching winds blowing down the Ganges Valley are still felt, but

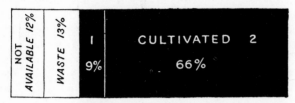

FIG. 151.—The classification of the land in the Middle Ganges Plain

Again the absence of forests should be noted.

the heat is less intense than in the Punjab or the Upper Ganges. Except in the narrow strip south of the Ganges, where the climate is drier and the Son and other streams are used for irrigation, the irrigation works are protective measures against years of poor rainfall rather than indispensable necessities. Most of the region is an extensive plain

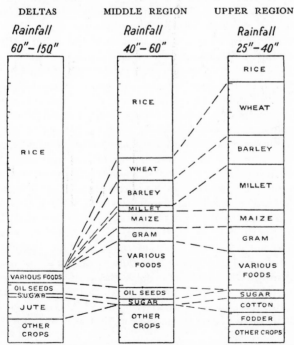

FIG. 152.—The crops of the Ganges Valley—the three main natural regions compared

This diagram illustrates extremely well the remarkable influence of rainfall on the crops of India.

watered by tributaries flowing down from the Himalayas. All the streams bring down quantities of mud and silt and have built up for themselves banks which are higher than the surrounding land, whilst the deposit of silt in the bed itself raises the water-level above that of the plains on either side. Consequently the rivers frequently overflow and cause widespread floods in the rainy season.[1] Shallow lakes and marshes scattered over the surface of the region represent old deserted courses of such rivers or low-lying areas between them. As far as possible, however, the marshes have been drained and the land cultivated, with the result that no less than 75 per cent. of the whole area is under crops.

Agriculture. Fig. 152 demonstrates the intermediate character of the crops. Rice has now become more important than wheat and barley, and it is interesting to note that the change in relative importance actually takes place along the 40-inch isohyet. Millet, the staple grain in so many of the drier parts of India, has almost completely disappeared; cotton is of very little importance, but a considerable area is sown with oil-seeds—linseed, rape or mustard and sesamum. This natural region used to be the principal indigo-growing area of India, but the vegetable dye industry has been almost killed by the use of coal-tar dyes. This was also one of the great opium-growing regions.

Population. The inhabitants of the greater part of this natural region—that is, of Bihar—are the Biharis. On the whole, they are men of quiet thoughts but long memories, vigorous and disciplined, and are thus somewhat different from their neighbours, the quicker but less vigorous Bengalis. Like the Bengalis, the Biharis live in the midst of their fields rather than in villages like the people of the Upper Ganges Plain and the Punjab. The population is dense and the pressure on the land so severe that there is a large annual emigration. Many of the Baharis go every year in the cold season to work in the mills of Bengali or the docks of Calcutta, returning to their homes after four or five months in time to cultivate their land during the rains. Others go to the tea gardens of Assam, and afterwards settle permanently there.

Again, there are few large towns in this predominantly agricultural region. Again, there are the famous old towns such as Banaras (Benares) and Monghyr and more modernized towns such as Patna. In U.P., on the banks of the Ganges, lies Banaras, the largest town in the region.[2] Banaras is an ancient as well as a modern centre of Hindu culture and a very sacred place of pilgrimage. The railway bridge across the Ganges is the first above Sara in Bengal. *Gorakhpur* is now a great collecting centre and railway junction for the north-eastern part of U.P. and contrasts with the now neglected river ports of *Mirzapur* and *Fyzabad*. Eastwards in Bihar, *Patna* is the state capital and an important col-

---

[1] The worst offender was the Kosi River now, by agreement with Nepal, controlled by a great dam.

[2] In April 1956 the old name Varanasi was officially substituted for Banaras.

lecting centre for agricultural produce. The town has given its name to 'Patna rice', a very fine type well known in Europe. Patna stretches for a long distance along the south bank of the Ganges and is connected directly with Calcutta (Howrah) by the Eastern Railway. *Bhagalpur* and the famous old town of *Monghyr* also lie to the south of the Ganges; *Darbhanga* and *Muzaffarpur*—the latter the centre of the now dying indigo industry—are collecting centres north of the river. *Chapra*, situated at the junction of the Gogra and Ganges Rivers, used for that reason to be an important river port with numerous factories, but is now less significant.

West Bengal

This province or state of the Indian Union comprises only 30,000 square miles of the old Province of Bengal but includes Calcutta and the Hooghly-side jute-mill towns. The character of the country has been described on pp. 300–3 and the area is shown on Fig. 136.

Calcutta (1,729,599 in 1941, including Howrah, 2,108,891; in 1961 2,927,289) is the largest city, and, although having less than half the population of Greater London, ranks third, after Bombay, in the British Commonwealth. A little more than a hundred and fifty years ago the site of Calcutta was an unhealthy swamp; it has been made into one of the healthiest cities of India by the labours of man and the activities of the British Government in India. Although over 70 miles from the sea up the river Hooghly, its wharves are accessible to the largest ocean steamers plying in Indian waters. Dangerous as it is to small craft, the bore which rushes up the river at high tide helps to keep the waterway clear. Very little, if any, water from the Ganges now flows through the Hooghly, but Calcutta has water communication with the east and north of the delta. The Calcutta and Eastern Canal plays an important part in this respect and enables raw jute to be sent cheaply to Calcutta's mills when the political relations between Pakistan and India permit. The Hooghly is the westernmost of the important delta channels, consequently railways from the west have no extensive waterways to cross. Hence it is Howrah, on the opposite side of the Hooghly, that is the main terminus of railways from Delhi, Bombay and Madras. Howrah was connected with Calcutta across the Hooghly by the famous 'bridge of boats' of which the central boats could be removed, now replaced by a new bridge.

Outside Calcutta there are really no big cities or towns. Amongst the largest of the jute-mill or rice-mill towns are *Bhatpara*, *Titagarh* and *Serampore*, all on the Hooghly above Calcutta.

The Brahmaputra or Assam Valley

The Assam Valley, occupied by the middle course of the Brahmaputra, is very different from the broad alluvial plains of the Ganges. The valley, from its western end where it merges into the plains of

Bengal to the eastern end where it is closed round by mountains, is about 500 miles long, but has an average breadth of only about 50 miles. The river itself is broad, it divides and unites again many times. The broad 'braided' area includes gravel terraces, and waste marshy tracts liable to flooding, but there are also rich alluvial lands given over to rice-growing. Palm trees and villages are dotted about amongst the paddy fields; farther away from the river are found the gentle slopes covered with tea gardens.

Most of the Assam Valley has a rainfall of over 80 inches, but the centre, lying in the lee of the Garo, Khasi and Jaintia Hills, is somewhat drier. Although colder in winter than the Deltas, owing to its more northerly position, cloudy skies tend to temper the heat of the hot season. Winter fogs are common.

Population. The population density is only about 170 to the square mile, compared with 600 and over in the Deltas and Ganges

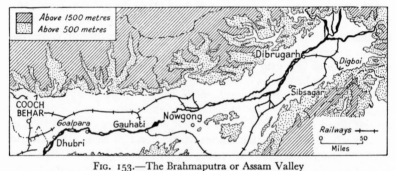

FIG. 153.—The Brahmaputra or Assam Valley

The hill country north of the valley is the North-East Frontier Agency (p. 311).

Plains and there is a marked tendency for the population to be concentrated at the western end of the valley, in the Districts of Goalpara and Kamrup which adjoin Bengal. The comparative sparseness of population accounts for the large proportion of waste land—48 per cent., or roughly half the whole. Every year, until partition, large numbers of Bengalis came from the more crowded parts of Bengal and settled in Assam. Nepalis come from the Himalayas and find in the Assam Valley more fertile land than in the mountains. There are large numbers of Biharis employed as coolies in the tea gardens, and every year numbers of them settle on the land, their place in the tea gardens being taken by fresh arrivals from Bihar. The population of the Assam Valley has thus been rapidly increasing and the waste land brought under cultivation. Only a fifth of the inhabitants of Assam now speak Assamese, the language of the natives. Formerly large areas were considered unhealthy, but medical science has done much to make possible the spread of settlement. Rice, entirely for home consumption, is the chief crop; tea and oil-seeds rank next. The distribution of tea has already been considered; the increasing tendency for the tea gardens to spread from the hillsides to the flat lands of the valley, which are equally suitable provided the drainage is good, should be noted. Jute is important in the west. At the eastern end of the Assam Valley, on the borders of the hills, are two small oilfields, including the field of Digboi. There is a small coalfield nearby also. The Brahmaputra River is used

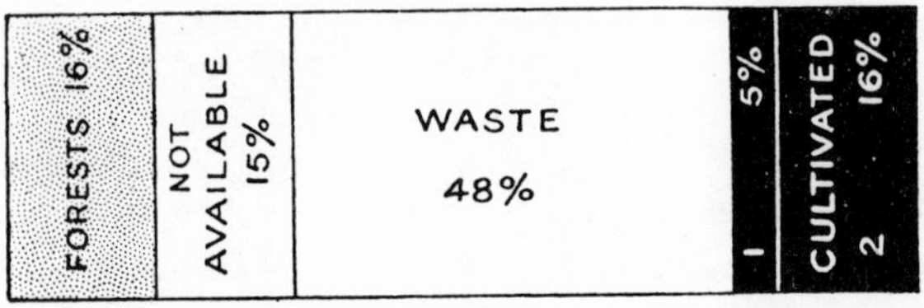

FIG. 154.—The classification of the land in the Brahmaputra Valley

The very large area of land awaiting development is noteworthy.

by country boats for the greater part of its length and interrupts railway communication. The western end of the valley is connected through Bengal with Calcutta by a branch of the former Eastern Bengal Railway, whilst running along the eastern part of the valley, south of the river, is the former Assam-Bengal Railway. But the two lines are separated by the river at Gauhati. However, since partition communication between Assam and Calcutta through Eastern Bengal (Pakistan)

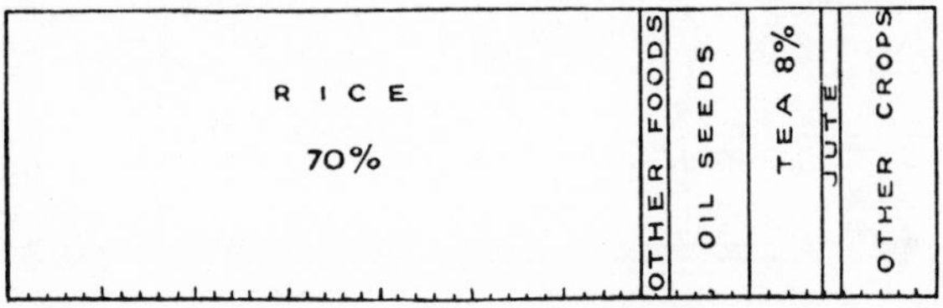

FIG. 155.—The crops of the Brahmaputra Valley

has been interrupted. Instead, a long rail haul by a circuitous route round the north through wholly Indian territory has been made possible by the construction of a short railway link there, as shown in Fig. 136. From Gauhati to Shillong there is a good motor road; from Dimapur a motor road which carried immense traffic in 1943–5 runs into Manipur State.

Ledo, at the head of the valley, was the starting point for the war-time traffic by a specially constructed road into North Burma and China and for the air traffic which flew over 'The Hump'.

Kutch, Kathiawar (Saurashtra) and Gujarat

Strictly speaking, Kutch, Kathiawar and Gujarat do not constitute a natural region. They form together rather a transition belt between

the desert on the north, or the very dry valley of Sind, and the very wet
West Coast on the south. On the whole the region is a lowland one,
less than 1,000 feet above sea-level, but there are numerous small hills.
It lies on the seaward side of the Rajput Uplands and the northern
extension of the Western Ghats. It is simplest to consider the whole
area as divided into five parts—Kutch, Kathiawar, Northern, Central
and Southern Gujarat.

   Kutch or *Cutch* is bounded on three sides by the great marshy useless

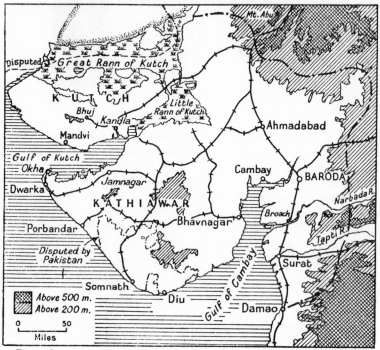

FIG. 156.—Cutch, Kathiawar and Gujrat; almost exactly the same as Gujrat
State, 1960

Land over 500 feet, dotted; over 2,000 feet, black.

   In recent years there has been a remarkable expansion in trade of the small Kathiawar ports—
especially Bhavnagar which has a deep-water port and Okha, a few miles from Dwarka, which was the
best-equipped port between Karachi and Bombay till the recent development of Kandla.

tract known as the Rann of Cutch, and on the remaining sides by the
sea. It is for the most part a barren, rocky, treeless and almost useless
country and might be counted as part of the Thar Desert which lies
to the north. In 1949 the Government selected Kandla, near the
eastern end of the Gulf of Cutch, as the site for a new major port
which was completed in 1955.

   Kathiawar is a large peninsula suffering from a precarious rainfall.
In the centre is a group of forest-covered hills—the Gir Forest—famous
as the haunt of the only lions found in India and among which most of

the rivers have their source. The forests yield some good timber. A large part of the remainder of Kathiawar is a barren land of very little use. Over large areas the bare rocks are exposed at the surface, and are not covered by any soil; between the rocky ridges are barren, sandy valleys. Here and there are a few more favoured spots, almost like oases in the desert. The people and their villages are concentrated in these richer areas, such as around Damnagar, or in the cotton-growing tracts near Dhari. Wherever irrigation is possible in Kathiawar, wheat becomes an important crop. Porbandar stone, a limestone much used for building in Bombay, is quarried along the coast. There are also salt deposits along the coast and lime may become a source of wealth. Politically Kathiawar consisted of a large number of small Native States and the principal towns are the capitals of the states. They were grouped as Saurashtra, now part of Gujrat State established in 1960.

Northern Gujarat is still a dry region and may, on the whole, be described as a flat region with a poor sandy soil. It may be remarked that the greater part of Gujarat was in Bombay, including the several scattered areas which formed the rich and progressive Native State of Baroda. Wherever the soil is richer in Northern Gujarat the population is dense and much millet is grown; the poorer, sandy parts are inhabited by primitive peoples such as the Kolis, who in times past used to plunder their richer neighbours. Irrigation is not very important, since few of the streams flow all the year, but cultivation is protected by tanks.

Central Gujarat is wetter, and the 40-inch isohyet intersects it. Rice can be grown on the low-lying stretches of alluvium bordering the rivers, but millet and cotton are more important. The black cotton soil is found in the south. The eastern parts are more hilly and largely covered with scrub. The climate of this part of Gujarat is healthy and the population is denser than farther south.

Southern Gujarat is the wettest part of the region and adjoins the West Coast Region on the south. Along the coast the climate is equable and healthy; there one finds a narrow strip where the soil is salt and poor and the water brackish; behind this is a broad strip of rich black soil very suitable for rice and the best kinds of Indian cotton, sugar-cane and many other crops. Here the land is thickly populated, the people rich and flourishing. Farther inland hills appear, covered with forest and thick jungle. In these inland parts the soil is poorer, cotton and rice of indifferent quality are the most important crops. The eastern parts of Southern Gujarat are still wilder; more than half is covered with dense unhealthy forests inhabited by primitive tribes, and the whole is only thinly peopled. There is thus a remarkable change as one goes inland from the coast.

Towns of Gujarat. Running through Gujarat from south to north is the main line of the old Bombay, Baroda and Central Indian Railway, now the Western Railway. The chief towns of the region—

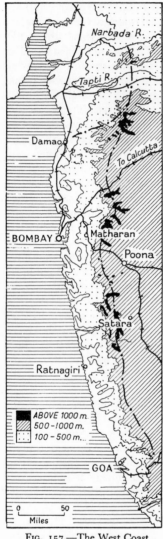

FIG. 157.—The West Coast
Region (North)

The heavy line indicates the approximate limits of the natural region, coinciding with the crest of the Western Ghats. The numerous hills along the coast south of Bombay suggest a contrast with the southern part of the West Coast.

Daman, Surat, Broach, Baroda and Ahmadabad—lie along this line. From north of Ahmadabad a branch runs into Kathiawar, another to the new port of Kandla.

Daman or Damaõ, in Southern Gujarat, was a Portuguese possession, as was Diu on the south coast of Kathiawar.

Surat (117,434 in 1921, only 99,000 in 1931, and 288,026 in 1961) is in Southern Gujarat, near the mouth of the Tapti River, but it has now nothing like its old importance. Before the rise of Bombay it was the leading town of the West Coast, and the first factory of the East India Company. Its former importance is symbolized in the use of the name 'Surat' (like that of its neighbour, Broach) for a certain quality of Indian raw cotton.

Baroda (295,144 in 1961), capital of the former State of Baroda, has modern cotton-mills and is a large railway junction.

Cambay and other towns round the Gulf of Cambay are less important than formerly. The great cotton-mills of towns such as Bombay have replaced the small local industries and there is no longer an export trade from the small seaports of the fast-shallowing Gulf. Instead all the trade is through the great port of Bombay.

Ahmadabad (1,149,918 in 1961) is the great collecting centre of Northern Gujarat and stands high among the important cities of India. In 1960 when the state of Bombay was divided into Gujrat (north) and Maharashtra (south), Ahmadabad became the capital of Gujrat.

The West Coast (North) or Konkan

The West Coast Region is the narrow strip between the crest of the

Western Ghats or Sahyadri Mountains—that is, the edge of the plateau
—and the Arabian Sea. The strip of plain between the mountains and
the sea is very narrow, much narrower than in the north, in the Gujarat
Region already considered, near the Narbada and Tapti Rivers. The
northern part of the West Coast may be considered as extending as far
south as the Portuguese territory of Goa and lies wholly in Bombay
State. Except north of Bombay the rainfall is everywhere over 80 inches,
but the dry season is slightly longer than in the southern part of the
West Coast and the annual range of temperature, though only 10° at
Bombay, slightly greater.

The numerous short, swift streams which flow down from the
Ghats have each formed its alluvial fan, whilst the waves which beat
against the shore during the period of the south-west monsoon have
piled up sand-dunes along the coast. In the northern part of the West
Coast, however, spurs from the hills reach the coast and the strip of
alluvium is not continuous. Although the coastal strip is so narrow—
only 30 or 40 miles wide—three parallel strips may be distinguished:

(*a*) The steep slopes of the Western Ghats.
(*b*) The flat alluvial land.
(*c*) The sand-dunes along the coast.

The steep slopes of the Western Ghats—here composed of Deccan lavas
—and the smaller foothills are usually clothed with luxuriant tropical
forest or monsoon forest in which teak is important. Some of the forests
are evergreen, for the climate is always hot and steamy and the species
of trees are numerous. One of the most important, however, is teak,
and the working of the teak is an important industry from Bombay to
Travancore. The teak flourishes where the rainfall is not too heavy

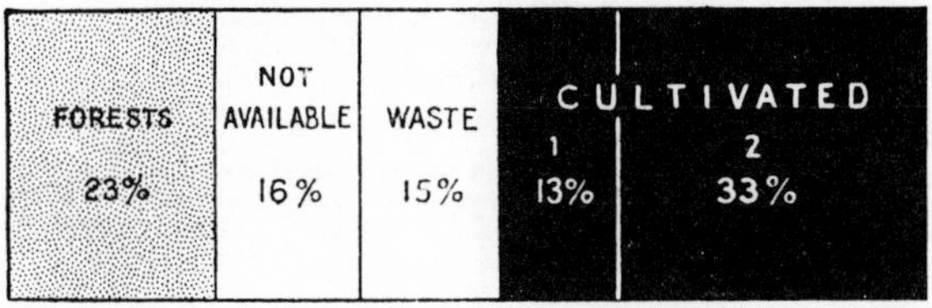

| FORESTS 23% | NOT AVAILABLE 16% | WASTE 15% | CULTIVATED | |
| | | | 1 13% | 2 33% |

FIG. 158.—The classification of the land in the West Coast Region (North and South

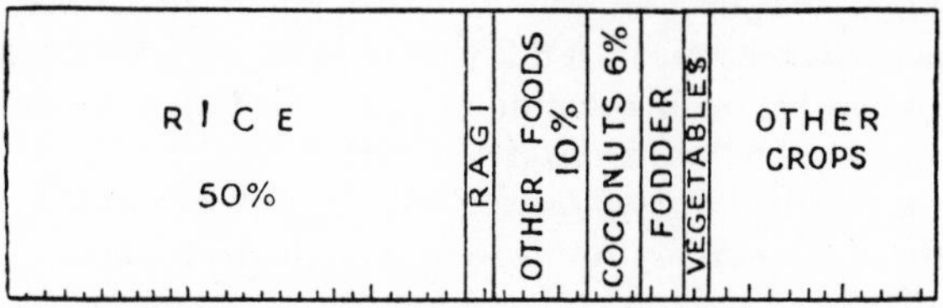

| RICE 50% | RAGI | OTHER FOODS 10% | COCONUTS 6% | FODDER | VEGETABLES | OTHER CROPS |

FIG. 159.—The crops of the West Coast Region

rather than in the wettest parts. The many short rivers on the West Coast are of little use in navigation, but can be used for floating logs. The rivers near Bombay have been harnessed and supply electric power to the Bombay cotton-mills. From about latitude 21° southwards, the Ghats present an almost uninterrupted face except for the two gaps which have done much to determine the rise to importance of Bombay.

The flat alluvial land forms the most important part of the West Coast Region. The water of the small streams from the hills is prevented from reaching the sea by the sand-dunes and frequently spreads out to form shallow lagoons, though these are not so marked as in the

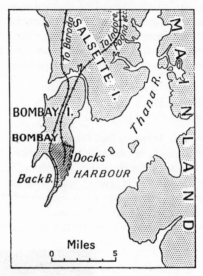

FIG. 160.—The position of Bombay

This sketch-map demonstrates the magnificent harbour but emphasizes the restricted area of the island on which Bombay is built and the consequent difficulty in expansion. Back Bay is being partly reclaimed to provide more land.

southern part of the West Coast. The banks of the lagoons are often lined with coconut plantations; here lie the numerous villages, and every possible piece of land is sown with paddy, interrupted at intervals by groves of areca nuts. In this part of India each hut in the villages has its own garden with coconut or areca (betel) nut trees and the separate huts may be some distance apart.

The coast itself is largely covered with groves of coconut palms. At intervals there are marshy tracts with mangrove swamps.

Agriculture. Figs. 158 and 159 have been drawn for the whole of the West Coast, including both the northern and southern portions.

The first, however, serves to show the considerable area, nearly a quarter, which is forested and also the large proportion occupied by marshes, swamps, lagoons, etc., and so 'not available'. Rice is by far the most important food crop and occupies about half the cropped area. The importance of coconuts is worthy of special note.

Population. The region is densely populated; the average density is over 200 to the square mile and hence actually much higher on the cultivable tracts. The language of the region is Marathi and it is interesting to note that the lascars who man the Eastern merchant service and whose ancestors were the Maratha pirates are from this West Coast. The only town of any size or importance is Bombay. The absence of other centres is explained by the difficulties not only of communication with the interior, but also along the coast itself. So real is the latter difficulty that to this day there is no railway running along the West Coast. Openings suitable for harbours are few—in fact, scarcely exist between Bombay and Marmagao—and, in the absence of communication with the interior, any port would have but a very small hinterland.

Bombay (1,489,883 in 1941, but 4,152,056 in 1961) is now the first city of India and has overtaken Calcutta for supremacy as a port. Bombay owes its eminence to several factors. There is, first, its magnificent natural harbour; second, its command of two gates through the Ghats; third, its situation on that side of India which faces Europe; and fourth, the richness of its hinterland, including as it does the great cotton lands of the Bombay Deccan. There are other factors which have proved favourable to its rise: the suitability of the climate for cotton spinning and weaving; the presence of water-power resources in the Ghats nearby. Like New York Bombay is built on an island and feels the difficulty of expansion on its island site. A large part of the old misnamed Back Bay (which faces the Indian Ocean and the south-west monsoon and hence was 'back' from the sheltered harbour) has been reclaimed and a magnificent line of residential flats has been built along the sweep of the Marine Drive. Further reclamation southwards has proved very expensive. With its phenomenal growth the character of Bombay has changed. Many cotton-mills have gone and given place to miscellaneous industries, including an Indian Hollywood. Industry has spread across the rail and road bridges to Salsette Island and beyond. There is a great refinery; on the way to Thana is a colossal Government dairy, with stall-fed buffaloes producing rich milk which is bottled and distributed as a monopoly throughout the city. Modern Bombay has not forgotten the need to provide amenities: there are numerous clubs and playing fields and the remarkable Hanging Gardens of Malabar Hill and numerous bathing beaches and swimming pools. The great harbour is thronged with craft of all kinds, though the modern deep-sea fishing industry is still in its infancy. At a later stage a mainland port—perhaps Mandva—to the south-east across the harbour may be developed.

Bombay is mainly a Hindu city. Though 70–80,000 Parsees out of a world total of 125,000 live there they are numerically over-shadowed. Ninety per cent. of men in Bombay wear European dress so that old distinctions by dress have been lost but there is rivalry between the Gujarati-speaking and the Marathi-speaking inhabitants.

The West Coast (South)

This region is broadly similar to the northern part already described. Under the state rearrangement of 1956 the northern third is now part of the enlarged State of Mysore,[1] the south coincides with the State of Kerala formerly Travancore-Cochin. The tract has long been recognized as a region distinct from the remainder of India under the name of the 'Malabar Coast'. Climatically the dry season is shorter and the annual range of temperature (for example, 5° at Trivandrum) less than in the northern part of the West Coast. The difference may seem slight, but is sufficient to affect vegetation—the planting of rubber is restricted to the south. The whole region tends to be broader and is divisible, still more distinctly, into three strips:

(a) The slopes of the Western Ghats are covered with dense ever-green forests, and forests cover nearly a quarter of the whole region. The Ghats here consist of Archean rocks.

(b) The flat alluvial land behind the sand-dunes, where the water of the streams from the hills is prevented from reaching the sea and so spreads out to form shallow lagoons. The lagoons have been connected by canals and it is possible to travel for hundreds of miles—almost the entire length of the region— by these waterways. This delightful region is only too little known even to the seasoned resident of India. Many of the lagoons open to the sea, and are deep enough to form harbours for native craft. One, the harbour of Cochin, has been dredged to form a modern ocean port. The banks of the lagoons are often lined with coconut plantations, whilst every suitable piece of land is planted with paddy. Here and there are groves of the areca-nut palm, and the pepper plant, for which this coast has so long been famous, is still grown, together with other condiments and spices such as cardamom.

(c) The sand-dunes along the coast, largely covered by coconut plantations.

Population. The region is densely populated, and in Travancore-Cochin the density actually exceeds 1,000 to the square mile. The

[1] Spate treats this Goa-Kanara, now the coastal section of Mysore, as distinct both from Konkan to the north and Kerala to the south.

staple food is, of course, rice, and some of the rice cultivators are
backward jungle tribes. The coconut palm is of great importance to the
inhabitants. Their huts are thatched with its leaves, and the wood is
used for building and for firewood. The preparation of the fibre of the
husks or 'coir-picking' is an important industry and so is the drying

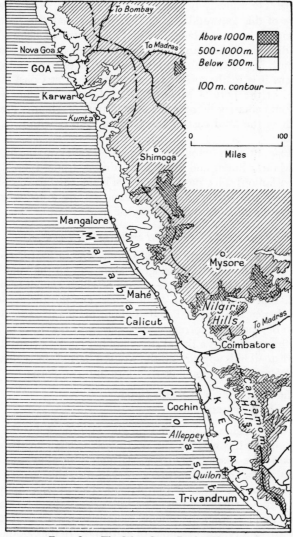

FIG. 161.—The West Coast Region (South)

The heavy line indicates the approximate limits of the natural region. Mahé was given up by the
French in 1954 (see p. 359) and Goa by the Portuguese in 1961.

of the kernel for export as copra. Coconut oil is also obtained from the latter, whilst the milk of the nut is made into a potent liquor. Rubber-planting has become a noteworthy industry in Travancore. Fishing is a common occupation along the coast.

The Western Ghats really terminate in the Nilgiri Hills, which are separated by the Palghat Gap, as shown in Fig. 161, from the Cardamom Hills. The railway between Madras and the West Coast takes advantage of this gap, and it should be noted that one branch runs north along the coast to Mangalore and one south to Cochin. The line from Madras to Quilon and Trivandrum takes advantage of a gap farther south in the Cardamom Hills. By virtue of these railway communications it is really correct to say that the West Coast lay in the hinterland of the port of Madras. When Cochin harbour was completed, it immediately became the second port of Madras Presidency, and much of the land east of the Palghat Gap is within its normal hinterland.

Kozhikode or *Calicut* (population 195,521 in 1961) was the fifth largest town in Madras State, and has a small timber trade. Like Cochin, it was once a famous spice port. *Trivandrum* is the chief town of Travancore; *Alleppey* and *Quilon*, also in Travancore, are growing industrial centres, where coir rope and matting are made.

The Carnatic Region or Tamil Region (Tamilnad)

Either of these designations seems preferable to East Coast South, since the region now to be considered embraces all the land between the plateau and the Bay of Bengal—much of which cannot be described as coastal. This is the region of India where Tamil is the predominant language, hence the name 'Tamil Region' or 'Tamilnad'. Since the separation of Andhra it corresponds closely with the State of Madras.

Near the sea there is a broad stretch of flat land—a coastal plain—but inland small hills appear and the western part of the region is quite hilly. The Carnatic Region falls therefore into two parts:

(a) The coastal plain of South India.
(b) The hilly western parts.

The whole region is bounded on the south-west by the crest of the Cardamom Hills and on the north-west extends to the slopes of the plateau. The coastal plain consists mainly of alluvium, together with certain younger sedimentary rocks; the hills are of ancient crystalline rocks like those of the plateau. The physiography of this region is particularly interesting. The hills of crystalline rock are often steep-sided and rise from the alluvial plains like islands from a smooth sea. They are thus typical examples of '*inselberge*'. In the Cuddapah area to the north the Cuddapah system of rocks (late pre-Cambrian) is little folded and gives rise to flat-topped hills.

Climatically the region is quite distinct from the remainder of India. During the period of the south-west monsoon the area lies in the lee of the Cardamom Hills and the plateau, so that during India's normal rainy season from May to September no part receives more than 20 inches of rain. In October, during the change of the monsoons,

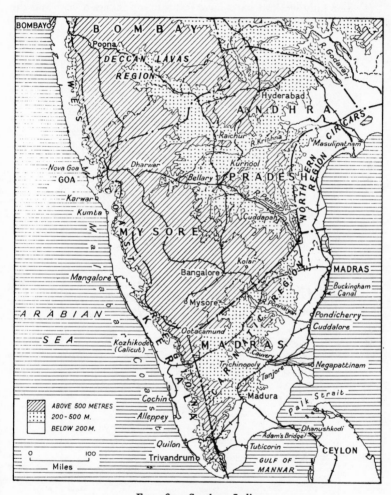

FIG. 162.—Southern India

The broken lines are the state boundaries; the heavy lines the boundaries between natural regions.
State boundaries are pre-1956.

severe storms occur along the Madras coast and heavy rain falls, with the result that October is a very wet month over much of the region. In November and December similar storms bring rain (compare Figs.

90, 92), and the coastal plain is wetter than the hilly regions to the west. The two parts differ somewhat climatically:

(a) The coastal plain has a rainfall of just over or just under 40 inches a year, falling mainly in October, November and December.

(b) The hilly western parts have less than 40 inches a year and the régime is nearer the normal.

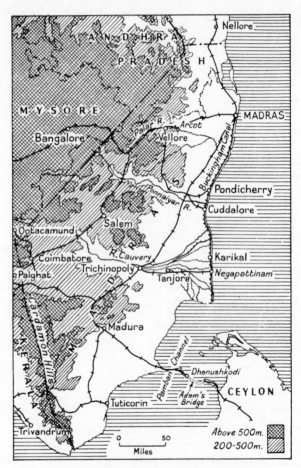

FIG. 163.—The Carnatic or Tamil Region

The broken line indicates the approximate limits of the natural region as a whole and the map at once suggests its twofold division into coastal plain and hilly west.

The cloudless skies which prevail from January to June result in high temperatures, and the East Coast has, therefore, a bigger annual range than the West Coast, but less than the plateau (compare Madras, 14°; Nagpur, 27°).

Irrigation. Nearly two-thirds of the coastal plain are cultivated and the percentage of forests and waste land is small in each case. Of the hilly western parts forests occupy a quarter and nearly half is cultivated, whilst the percentage of waste ground is again small. The percentage of cultivated land in each case is high when one remembers that the rainfall over a large part of the region is less than 40 inches and the soils in the interior are often indifferent. In good or normal rainfall years the land is easily able to support the dense population, but the rainfall is apt to vary within wide limits. Despite the many thousands of irrigation tanks (see Fig. 96) this has been one of the great famine areas of India. The famine menace still exists, but has been largely overcome by improvements in communication, whereby foodstuffs can be rushed from other parts of India into the stricken area. Modern canal irrigation works have done much to mitigate the danger of famine. Amongst the more important works may be noted:

(*a*) The Periyar Project. The Periyar River rises in the Cardamom Hills and flows westward through Travancore to the Arabian Sea. It flows, therefore, through a well-watered region where its water is not required for irrigation. The valley was therefore dammed and a tunnel made through the hills and the water diverted to the dry eastern side of the hills. There it is conducted by canals and waters thousands of acres in the neighbourhood of Madura.

(*b*) The Poini, Palar and Cheyyar Systems. South of the town of Arcot, these three rivers have been dammed and their waters irrigate a large tract of country west of Madras.

(*c*) The Cauvery Delta System. One of the oldest irrigation works in India is the large system of canals which now covers the whole of the delta of the Cauvery River. The system was reconstructed by the British nearly a hundred years ago and greatly improved by the Mettur Dam—then the largest in the Empire—opened in 1934. 1,300,000 acres are now irrigated; there are 1,500 miles of main and branch canals and 2,000 miles of distributaries.

Agriculture. There is, not unnaturally, a considerable difference between the crops grown on the coastal tracts and those grown amongst the hills. On the coastal plain rice is the chief crop and is mostly grown on irrigated land, millet on land which is not irrigated. In the hills where flat land suitable for irrigation is scarcer and rainfall is less, millet replaces rice as the chief crop. Taking the region as a whole, about equal quantities of rice and millet are grown and both together form the staple foodstuffs. The contrast with the West Coast is interesting and, by comparison with northern India, the absence of wheat is noteworthy—the warmer winter is unsuited to the varieties of wheat at present cultivated. Some years ago, during a severe famine in Madras, supplies of wheat were rushed into the stricken area from the north. Yet such is variation in custom consequent upon the vastness of India and such the inherent conservatism of the ignorant masses that

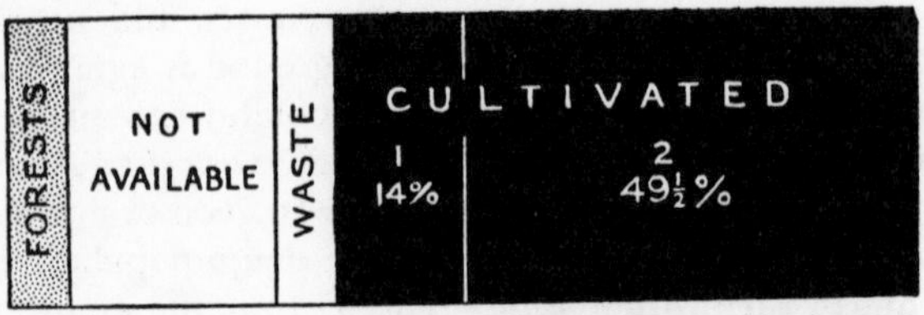

FIG. 164.—The classification of the land in the coastal parts of the Carnatic Region

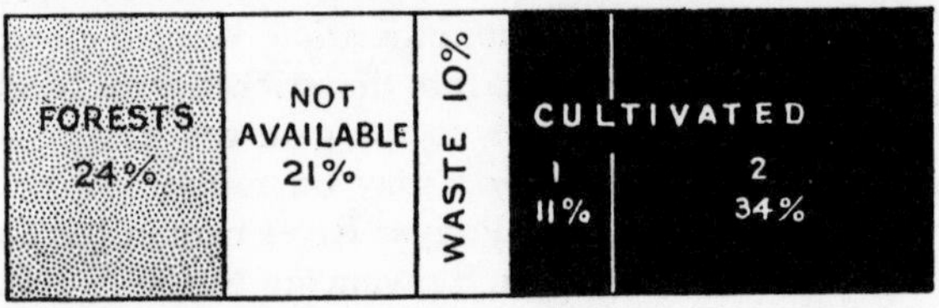

FIG. 165.—The classification of the land in the hilly western parts of the Carnatic Region

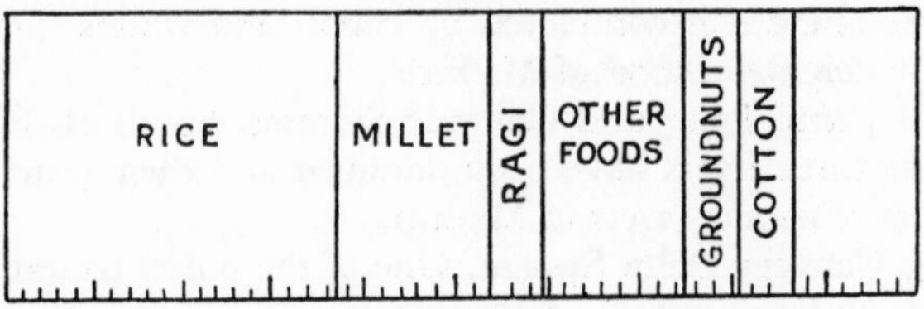

FIG. 166.—The crops of the coastal parts of the Carnatic Region—where there is much flat land available for rice, and water for irrigation is obtained from the rivers, so that rice covers 37 per cent. of the cropped area

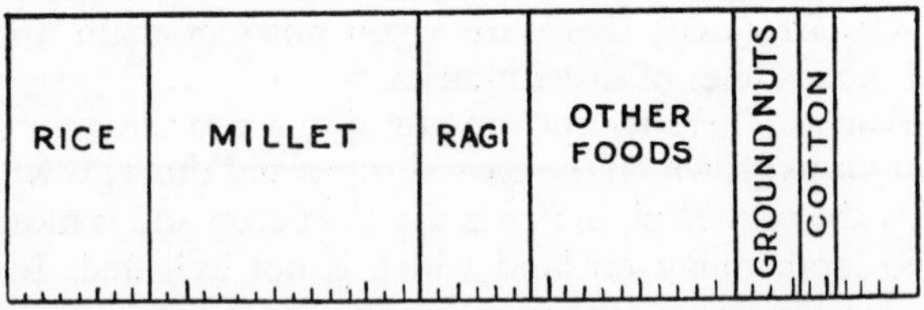

FIG. 167.—The crops of the hilly western parts of the Carnatic Region—where far less flat, irrigable land is available for rice, and millets (including ragi) cover 42 per cent. of the cropped area

thousands died of starvation in sight of the untouched wagons of wheat. The poor, light dry soils of many parts of the region favour the growth of ground-nuts. On the hilly lands the short-stapled Indian cotton is grown, but on the irrigated land it is possible to grow American upland. Sugarcane and tobacco are cultivated over most of the area. All along the coast itself on the sandy dunes are coconut plantations. On the slopes of the Nilgiri Hills—that is, really on the slopes of the edge of the plateau—there are important tea gardens. On the dry hill pastures of this region sheep are more numerous than in any other part of India.

The forests, which are shown in Fig. 165 as occupying a very considerable area, grow on the hill-slopes wherever there is sufficient moisture. The most important trees are teak (especially in Coimbatore and on the slopes of the Nilgiri Hills) and sandalwood. Timber trees are planted in many parts of the region.

The minerals of the region are not very important, but the lignite of South Arcot is proving important and much salt is obtained from the sea along the coast.

Important industries, also along the coast, are fishing and pearl-fishing.

Population. The population over the region as a whole is dense—over 400 people to the square mile. In a few areas it almost reaches 2,000. The region corresponds closely with the area in which the Tamil language is spoken, and the people are nearly all Dravidians, if one excepts the hill tribes such as live in the Nilgiris.

Madras (777,481 in 1941, but 1,729,141 in 1961) is the fourth largest city in India and, in value of trade, the third of the Union's great ports. Madras has not the same extent of rich hinterland as Bombay, Calcutta and Karachi, which share the trade of the huge Indo-Gangetic Plain. On the east coast of India there are no natural inlets which are suitable for harbours, yet there are many small ports along the coast. At nearly all of them—except Madras—steamers have to anchor some distance off shore and land goods and passengers in small boats or 'mussoola'. The landing is often dangerous, owing to the line of surf, and in the past there has been much loss of life and damage to merchandise. Madras is the only port which has a modern artificial harbour, built at great cost and only finished in 1909. The principal export is leather, and the tanning of hides and skins is an important local industry. There are also numbers of cotton-mills in Madras and both cotton goods and raw cotton are exported. Madras is well served by railways, the principal of which have already been noticed. Running north and south through Madras is the Buckingham Navigation Canal, a salt-water canal nearly 250 miles long, which obviates a passage for small craft along the stormy coast.

Tuticorin is also a cotton centre and famous for the produce of the pearl fisheries in the shallow Gulf of Mannar. It is the port for the southern part of the region and has a regular service of steamers to Colombo. The mail route between India and Ceylon is, however, via Dhanushkodi and Talaimannar, where the intervening 22 miles is very shallow and it has been proposed to build a causeway. Owing to the shallowness of the sea there is very little steamer traffic through the Palk Strait between India and Ceylon, but it is now proposed to deepen the Pamban Channel. *Cuddalore* and *Negapatam* are other small ports; *Tiruchirapalli* (Trichinopoly; population 249,862 in 1961), *Salem* (249,145), *Madurai* (Madura, 424,810) and *Tanjore* are the chief inland centres. Madura has a dyeing industry and lies in the heart of rich irrigated land. *Pondicherry*, which was the chief town of the scattered French possessions in India, lies on the coast south of Madras.

The Northern Circars Region

This region, which may also be called East Coast North, is a narrow coastal strip lying between the Eastern Ghats and the Bay of

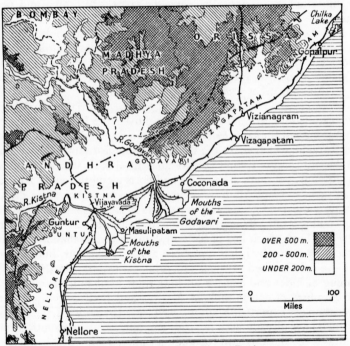

FIG. 168.—The Northern Circars Region

Bengal. It comprises those northern districts of Madras Presidency (from north to south, Vizagapatam, Godavari, Kistna, Guntur and Nellore) which have been incorporated in the new State of Andhra (where Telugu is spoken, not Tamil) and parts of Orissa along the coast. The region corresponds roughly with the old kingdom of Kalinga.

It is not a continuous coastal plain. Towards the south the deltas of the Godavari and Kistna Rivers occupy a large area; farther north there is a coastal plain interrupted by many small hills—consisting of the same ancient rocks as the plateau—some of which reach the sea coast. In the north is the delta of the Mahanadi River, including the large shallow Chilka Lake—an arm of the sea, which has been cut off by the growth of the delta. Throughout the region there is a marked contrast between the level tracts of alluvium and younger sedimentary rocks which afford a fertile soil and the small hills or inselbergs of old crystalline rocks which afford but a poor soil and on which but little will grow. Amongst the minerals obtained from the old rocks may be noted the manganese ore near Vizagapatam. Along the shore there is usually a sandy strip and at times wind-blown sand does considerable

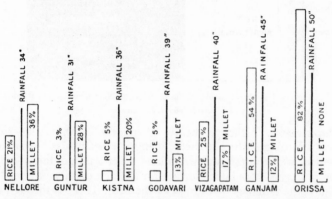

Fig. 169.—The crops of the Northern Circars Region showing the variation in the relative importance of rice and millet according to rainfall. Irrigated crops are not included. Ganjam was transferred from Madras to Orissa in 1936

damage to the agricultural tracts inland. Mangrove swamps occur around the deltas and salt impregnation may ruin the soil of considerable tracts. The winning of salt is important in Orissa. The slopes of the Eastern Ghats, which bound the region on the west, are usually forested, and the sal is an important tree.

Climatically the region becomes progressively drier from Orissa southwards until Nellore is reached, where there is a slight increase. The 40-inch isohyet passes through the District of Vizagapatam. In contrast with the Carnatic Region, however, the rainfall régime is that of the greater part of India. It should be noted that the south-west monsoon blows parallel to the coast of the region, otherwise the rainfall would be much heavier.

Agriculture. This region affords a fascinating example of the climatic control of crops in India. The importance of the 40-inch isohyet has already been emphasized as forming the dividing line between 'Dry Zone' and 'Wet Zone' crops. Around Cuttack, with an average rainfall of 50 inches, rice occupies 82 per cent. of the cropped area, whereas millet is practically absent. In Ganjam, with an average fall of 45 inches, rice occupies 54 per cent. and millet 12 per cent. Going southwards along the coast there is, as shown in Fig. 169, a progressive diminution of rainfall, accompanied by a diminution in rice acreage and an increase in millet acreage. In Guntur, with a rainfall of 31 inches, millet occupies nine times the area of rice on the non-irrigated area. In Nellore with more rain there is again more rice. In the irrigated areas of the Kistna and Godavari deltas large quantities of rice are grown. Spices form an important crop in this region.

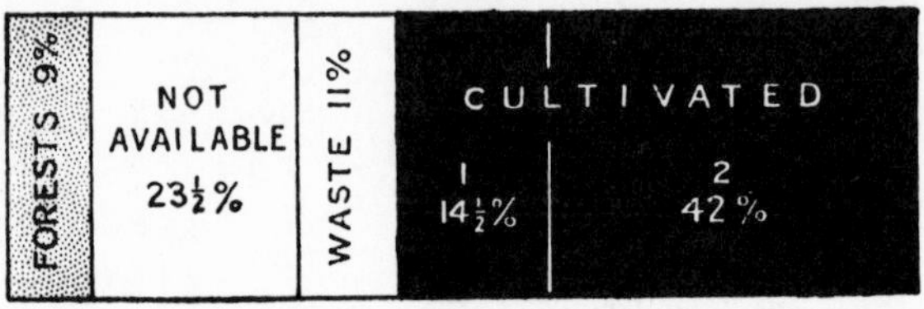

FIG. 170.—The classification of the land in the Northern Circars Region
1 = current fallows; 2 = area sown.

Population. Although nearly a quarter of the area—rugged hillocks affording pasture to sheep, mangrove swamps, etc.—cannot be cultivated, whilst forests and waste land cover a fifth of the whole, this region is thickly populated, having an average density of about 400. Telugu is the language over most of the area. There is through communication in this area between Calcutta on the one hand and Madras on the other, but it is a feature of special importance that only a single railway cuts through the ramparts of the Eastern Ghats. Consequently the small ports along the coast—Cocanada, Masulipatam, Calingapatam and Gopalpur—have but very limited hinterlands. A railway was completed in 1932 between Raipur in the Central Provinces, now Madhya Pradesh, and Vizagapatam. The latter town was already one of the best ports along a coast of indifferent harbours, being partly sheltered by a headland known as the Dolphin's Nose. A modern harbour was finished in 1933, and *Visakhapatnam* (with Waltair), to use the correct modern name for Vizagapatam, has become the main outlet for a large and important tract of the north-eastern part of the plateau. It has now a shipbuilding industry. *Vizianagram* is the only inland town of note in the Northern Circars. In Orissa there is a canal running to the Hooghly River near Calcutta and on it lies the once important port of Balasore, where formerly English, Dutch and French factories existed. A new state capital Bhubaneswar has been built 18 miles from *Cuttack*, the old capital of the kings of Orissa. Puri, pleasantly situated on the coast, is a famous place of pilgrimage.

The Southern Deccan or Deccan Proper [1]

Although the term Deccan is often applied to the whole of Peninsular India south of the Satpura line, it is more properly restricted to the southern and south-eastern parts of the plateau. Thus delineated

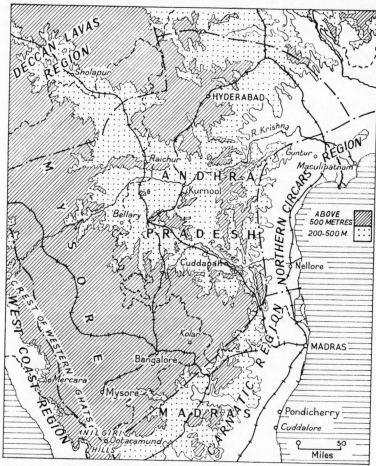

FIG. 171.—The Southern Deccan or Deccan proper

the Deccan embraces nearly the whole of Mysore, the Deccan Districts of Andhra (eastern Bellary, Kurnool, Anantapur, Cuddapah), part of Chittoor and those northern districts of Andhra which previously

[1] Spate calls the southern elevated parts Karnataka (South Deccan Plateaus) and the north-eastern part Telangana—approximating now to the parts lying in Mysore and Andhra respectively.

formed eastern Hyderabad. As shown in Fig. 171 practically the whole is more than 200 metres or 650 feet above sea-level and the greater part of the south over 500 metres or 1,650 feet. The lower ground is occupied by the broad valleys of the Kistna (Krishna) and its tributaries and that of the Penner. The greatest heights are reached on the southern borders. Here, separated by a deep trough from the Deccan proper, is the lofty little massif of undulating grassland, the home of the Kota and Toda tribes, known as the Nilgiri Hills, where one dome (Dodabetta) reaches

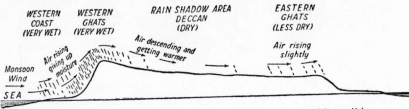

Fig. 172.—Section across the Deccan Plateau, illustrating rainfall conditions

8,760 feet. The rolling plains of the plateau itself are broken by granitic or gneissose masses that rise abruptly and form dome-shaped hills and boulder-covered inselbergs.

Climatically the region lies in the 'rain-shadow' area of its own western edge—the Western Ghats; and, except for a strip along the Ghats themselves, the rainfall is less than 40 inches. In some parts the annual fall actually drops below 20 inches. Further, the rainfall is irregular from year to year, and famine is a severe menace. The reddish

FORESTS 16%	NOT AVAILABLE 16%	WASTE 14%	CULTIVATED	
			1 11%	2 43%

Fig. 173.—Classification of land in the Southern Deccan. A large proportion of the forested land is found in the damper, western part of the region on the slopes of the Ghats

soils are suitable for irrigation and cultivation is protected by tanks, but in bad years the tanks remain unfilled even in the height of the rainy season. The temperatures are naturally more extreme than on the coasts and elevation results in temperatures below 50° on the hills in winter.

Manganese ore, iron ore and chromite are mined in small quantities, but the gold of Kolar in Mysore is the chief mineral product. In the inter-war years the Kolar goldfield has produced annually between

300,000 and 400,000 ounces of fine gold, and in later years about half that amount. A little gold is also found farther north.

Agriculture. Forests cover 16 per cent. of the surface of the Deccan, a rather surprisingly large percentage for a rather dry region. The forests are concentrated, however, in the west of the region—on the slopes of the Western Ghats—and on the damper slopes of hills in other parts, where aspect is an important factor. In Mysore the largely forest-clad western half of the state is called the malnad; the drier, flatter, eastern half the maidan. Broadly speaking, the old crystalline rocks yield but a poor soil (generally reddish in colour and hence contrasting with the North-Western Deccan), so that, although more than half the region is cultivated, the yield of the individual crops is but poor. Over most of the region there is insufficient rainfall and a scarcity of suitable flat land for the cultivation of rice. Most of the rice cultivation is, therefore, concentrated on the level surface of the plateau in parts of Mysore and in the irrigated valley lands of the Kurnool and

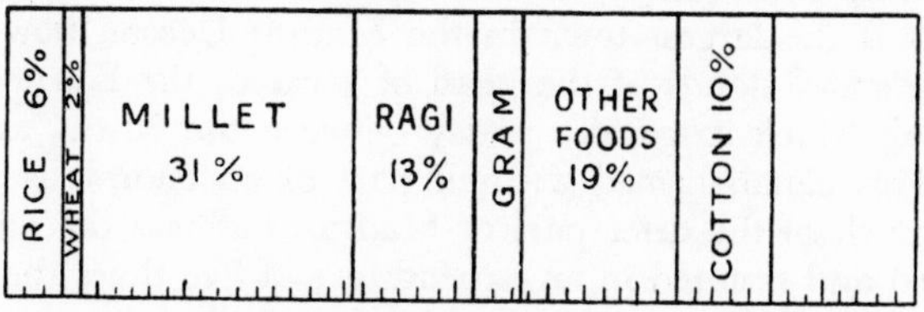

FIG. 174.—The crops of the Deccan Plateau (Southern Deccan)
For explanation, see the text.

Cuddapah Districts of Andhra. Fig. 174 shows that a small area—2 per cent. of the cropped surface—is occupied by wheat. Nearly all this wheat is grown in the Dharwar District of Mysore, which is distinct in several respects from other parts of the Deccan. Nearly everywhere, as in all the drier, hilly regions of India, millet is the staple food of the people and the most important crop. Cotton is another noteworthy crop, but it does not occupy the dominant position that it does in the Bombay Deccan. A very large proportion of India's tobacco is grown in Andhra.

Coffee-planting was formerly an important industry in Mysore, but disease wiped out many plantations. It later showed a marked recovery. Tea gardens are important on the well-drained slopes of the Nilgiri Hills.

Sheep flourish on the dry grasslands of the hillsides (compare the Carnatic Region), and the Deccan has nearly a quarter of all the sheep of India. Cattle are numerous and in the drier parts large quantities of fodder are grown for their food.

Population. When compared with the coastal tracts and the great northern plains, the Deccan is not thickly populated. Around

Hyderabad there are only about 225 people to the square mile, in southern Mysore 300 and elsewhere about 200. In the south-west of the region—that is, in Mysore—nearly all the people speak Kanarese (or Kannada); in the remainder of the region Telugu is the principal language. It is for this reason that the eastern half of the former state of Hyderabad, which falls in the Deccan Region, was called Telingana (Telangana), or the land of the Telugu language, and has now been made part of Andhra.

Mysore (253,865 in 1961) was the capital of the former princely state and the principal palace of the Maharajah was there. *Bangalore* (905,134 in 1961) is a larger city and though excentrally placed has been made the new State capital—with vast parliament buildings and many new industries, including telephones. Both Mysore and Bangalore have old-established silk factories. High up in the Nilgiri Hills, in Madras, is the hill station of Ootacamund—the familiar Ooty to which the Madras Government formerly migrated in the hot weather —reached by a hill railway from the plains below, now by fine roads.

Bellary is the largest town in the Madras Deccan now added to Mysore. *Kurnool* stands at the head of a canal, the Kurnool-Cuddapah Canal, which irrigates a valley between the Kistna and Penner Rivers. This canal formed a small part of an enormous scheme to irrigate much of the drier part of Madras, but was the only part to be finished and resulted in an expenditure of five times the estimated cost. The authorities were deceived by the wonderful success of irrigation in the northern plains and failed to realize the entirely different conditions, not only in the water available, but in the nature of the soil, which was such that it was in places ruined rather than improved by irrigation. Profiting by past experience, post-Partition India attacked the problem anew and has built a great dam across the Tunga Bhadra with power works.

Hyderabad (1,118,553 in 1961), the sixth largest city in India and the capital of the former great State of Hyderabad or the Nizam's Dominions, lies in the north-east of this region and has been made the capital of Andhra Pradesh.

The Deccan Lavas Region

More than one name exists for this natural region. The term Deccan Trap Region should at least be dropped, since the term 'trap' is a relic of the days when geologists lacked sufficient faith to endorse their opinions by calling an ancient lava a lava. Perhaps a better term would be the Black Cotton Soil Region, since it is the area covered by the cotton soil which matters, and not the area of the Deccan Lavas—not always exactly the same. The term Bombay Deccan may be used, since the region concerned lies essentially in the hinterland of Bombay, but it oversteps the bounds of the former Bombay State. Much may be said for the simple name the North-Western Deccan. The name Maharashtra is a reminder of the connection with the Marathi language and the old Mahratta empire. Roughly the area under consideration is the area covered by the well-known black cotton soil, as far north as the Satpura line and westwards to the crest of the Ghats. So defined it embraces the whole of Maharashtra which lies on the plateau and the north-western districts of the enlarged Mysore State.

The North-Western Deccan is a land of bare, undulating plains from which rise flat-topped ranges of hills, conspicuously terraced owing to the sheets of lava of which they are composed. The scenery is thus at once contrasted with that of the Southern Deccan. The soils

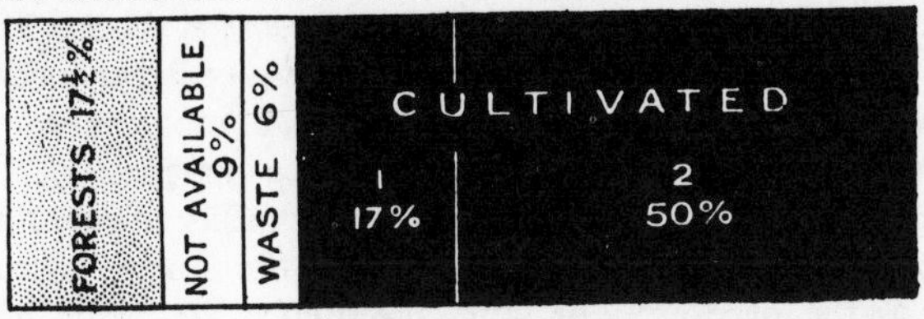

FIG. 175.—Classification of the land in the Deccan Lavas Region

Special interest attaches to the small proportion of waste land and the high percentage of cultivated land —67 per cent., including 17 per cent. of fallows—compared with the other plateau regions.

are generally dark in colour and thus contrast with the usually reddish soils of the south; they are retentive of moisture and suitable for crop not requiring irrigation. Thus, although the climate, including rainfall, is roughly comparable with that of the Southern Deccan, there is a relative absence of tanks. The land is lower than farther south; con-

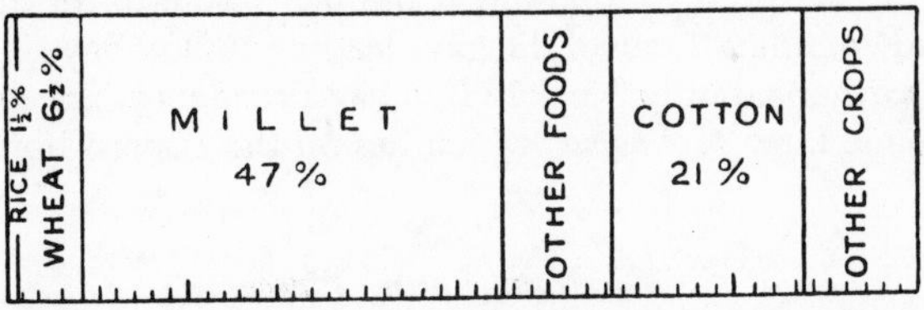

FIG. 176.—The crops of the Deccan Lavas Region (Bombay Deccan)

This diagram illustrates extraordinarily well that the black cotton soil does not lend itself to irrigation and the cultivation of rice. The acreage devoted to non-food crops is exceptionally high.

siderable and important areas, such as the broad valley of the Purna in Berar and the upper part of the Tapti and of the Wardha, lie below or but slightly above the 1,000-foot contour. The tableland proper really rises south of these high plains of Berar and Nagpur, and the Ajanta Range lies on its threshold.

Agriculture. The apparently large percentage of forest in this predominantly unforested region is explained by the extensive tracts along the western margins—that is, on the slopes of the Western Ghats and the damper hill-slopes elsewhere. The remarkably low percentage of waste land is worthy of comment; no less than two-thirds of the whole region are cultivated. With a low rainfall and a soil unsuitable for irrigation rice is of very little importance. Conditions favour the growth of millets as the chief food crops, especially the Great Millet. The spread of wheat from the north is important. A great contrast between this region and the Southern Deccan is not immediately apparent from a comparison of Figs. 176 and 174. In the North-Western Deccan commercial or cash crops, mainly cotton and oil-seeds, grown for export or sale, are the outstanding feature of the rural economy; in the Southern Deccan food crops for home consumption are of predominant importance. The region at present under consideration is, of course, the cotton-producing region of India *par excellence*, though the cotton is almost entirely native Indian. The high plains of Berar form the foci of cultivation—well situated for supplying the Bombay mills.

Population. Although such a large proportion of the North-Western Deccan is cultivated, the average density of population is low —about 200. The region is the home of the sturdy Marathas, and Marathi is the predominant language, hence the name Marathwara long used for the western half of the former state of Hyderabad. Over the heart of the Indian plateau there is little difference in density of population. This is the result of rich black soil unsuitable for irrigation plus low rainfall on the west, balancing poorer soil suitable for irrigation plus better rainfall on the east. The towns of this region are, in the main, collecting centres. *Sholapur* in Bombay and *Gulbarga* in northern Mysore have this function and so, still more markedly, have *Akola* and *Amraoti* in the heart of the cotton lands of Berar. *Poona* (258,197 in 1941, but 597,562 in 1961) is different; it lies near the crest of the Western Ghats and commands one of the gaps leading to Bombay. It was made the hot-weather capital of the old Bombay Presidency. Special mention will be made later of *Nagpur*, which lies on the eastern borders of the region.

The North-Eastern Plateau

The north-eastern part of the plateau is not a single entity in the same way as the Southern or North-Western Deccan. Its plateau character has been more masked by the effects of river erosion, and there are marked contrasts between the broad river plains of the Mahanadi and Godavari and the wild fastnesses of the Eastern Ghats and the Central Highlands. There are, however, certain features common to the whole:

(a) Practically the whole is more than 500 feet above sea-level and the line of the Eastern Ghats still forms the boundary of the plateau area. Where the rivers pass this boundary there are falls and rapids.

(b) The basal system of rocks is everywhere the pre-Cambrian complex, though masked in some of the valleys by alluvium and older sediments.

(c) The rainfall is more than 40 inches and hence greater than in other parts of the plateau.

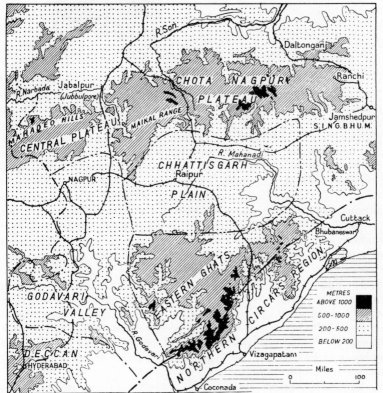

Fig. 177.—The north-eastern part of the Indian Plateau, showing an approximate division into natural regions

It is convenient to consider the north-east of the plateau as bounded on the north by the Narbada-Son trough and thus including as its edge the Satpura-Mahadeo-Maikal line of hills and the northern rim of the Chota Nagpur Plateau. Five sub-regions may then be distinguished.

(a) The Chota Nagpur Plateau.

(b) The Central Plateau or Central Highlands, embracing the western continuation of the Chota Nagpur Plateau.

(c) The northern part of the Eastern Ghats, perhaps better termed the Bastar-Orissa Highlands.

(d) The Chhattisgarh Plain or Valley-plain of the Upper Mahanadi.
(e) The Godavari Valley and the Nagpur high plains.

FIG. 178.—The classification of the land in the Chota Nagpur Plateau

The Chota Nagpur Plateau is one of the wildest and least developed parts of India and is partly inhabited by primitive tribes. A large proportion of the surface is forest-covered and the valuable gregarious sal tree is an important constituent of the forests. On the flatter parts of the plateau there are extensive open grassy stretches or areas of scrubland. Many of the river valleys are rocky, but where they are broader paddy can be grown in small fields. The region has been termed, not inappropriately, the 'Wales' of India. The central core has formed the refuge for many of the early inhabitants of India. Peaceful penetration is fast altering the character of the margins: on the eastern margins is the principal coalfield region of India; in other parts are the principal iron ore and mica mines of India; in other parts forests are the source of attraction. A great scheme was begun in 1948 for the economic development of the Damodar Valley after the manner of the Tennessee Valley in the United States. The Damodar drains eastwards from the heart of the region but is an irregular stream, almost dry for part of the year but liable to floods stretching over a broad area at others. The scheme includes seven multi-purpose dams and a great central power station at Bokharo. In addition to the great iron and steel industry at Jamshedpur, large quantities of fertilizer are being manufactured at Sindhri.

Until very recently, at least, some of the forest tribes used bows and arrows, lived principally on wild animals (including monkeys) and fruits and wore no clothing but a few leaves. Small of stature, honest and brave, they possess many of the qualities lacking in so-called civilized peoples. The most numerous tribes are the Santals, who have so far been brought into touch with civilization that three out of every hundred perform at least one journey by railway in a year. The collection of lac is an industry of importance amongst the forest-dwellers. Their agriculture is limited to the cultivation of maize, millets, oil-seed and pulses for their own use.

The Central Plateau or the *Central Highlands* may be described as generally similar to the Chota Nagpur Plateau, but less extensive. The western portion (Mahadeo Hills) is separated from the eastern (Maikal

Hills) by an important pass, guarded by Jabalpur (Jubbulpore) in the Narbada Valley to the north.

The Eastern Ghats in this part of India, with which may be linked the Bastar Highlands, are divided into two unequal portions by the Mahanadi Valley. The larger southern portion lies largely in what used to be called the 'Agency Division' of Madras because it was not organized into districts, but was administered by Agents. The ordinary law of the land was not enforced and the primitive tribes who inhabit this thickly forested country are still left to follow their own customs as far as possible. As yet no railway penetrates this backward part of India. The population is less than 40 to the square mile.

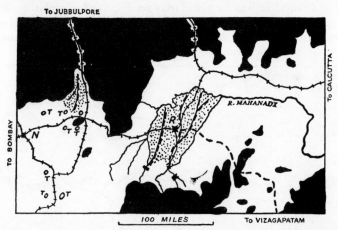

FIG. 179.—The irrigated area of the Chhattisgarh Plain around Raipur (**R**)

N = Nagpur; T = Important tanks. The dotted line shows the direction taken by the railway direct to Vizagapatam. Land over 1,500 feet, black.

The Chhattisgarh Plain lies between the three areas of highland just described. It is a broad valley-plain drained by the upper course of the Mahanadi and its tributaries. The natural vegetation of mixed deciduous forest, in which sal was an important tree, has been largely cleared and large areas are given over to rice cultivation. For the latter purpose much land has been irrigated around the natural centre of the region, Raipur. There is little doubt that this area is one capable of further development and there was good reason for the construction of the line from Raipur to the port of Vizagapatam. The great dam of Hirakud (see p. 266) is modern evidence of faith in the area.

The Valley of the Godavari and its tributaries includes the wetter, eastern parts of the Wardha Valley and also the Wainganga Valley-plain. It is physically continuous with the high plains of cotton-growing Berar, but the soil is no longer of the black cotton soil type, the rainfall is heavier (over 40 inches) and rice replaces millet. *Nagpur*

(301,957 in 1941, but 643,659 in 1961) lies to the north-west, almost midway between Bombay and Calcutta and on the borders of two great natural regions—the north-western and north-eastern plateaus. Formerly the administrative centre of the old Central Provinces, it has now been included in the eastern part of Bombay State. It has cotton-mills. In the south, stretches of the Godavari are navigable for at least part of the year. Where the river cuts through the Ghats by a series of rapids, a tramway has been made.

The Central Indian Foreland [1]

The Central Indian Foreland may be described as a plateau which rises gradually from the Ganges Plain and terminates southwards in an escarpment overlooking the valley of the Son River in the east and the

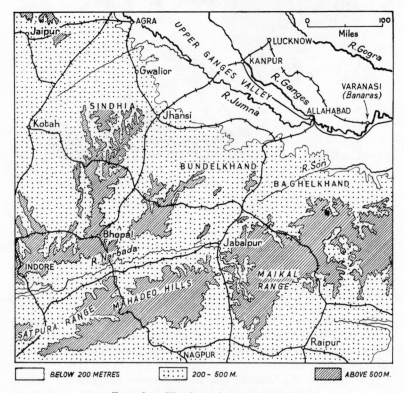

FIG. 180.—The Central Indian Foreland

[1] The Central Vindhyan Country of Spate.

Narbada River in the west. To this escarpment the name Kaimur Range has been applied in the east, Bhanrer Range in the centre and Vindhya Range in the west. The drainage north of the crest of the scarp is entirely to the Ganges, thus the region lies in the Ganges Basin. Although a plateau, it is separated from the Great Deccan Plateau by the Narbada-Son trough, across which it faces the heights of the Mahadeo and Maikal. Thus it is a typical 'foreland' to the great plateau when approaching from the plains of the north. There is no real western limit; the Central Indian Foreland fades into that complex region which has here been called the Rajput Uplands. The chief difference between this eastern half (of which the most typical parts are the areas known as Baghelkand and Bundelkhand) and the Rajput Upland Region is that most of this region has a rainfall of more than 40 inches and the underlying rocks are ancient crystalline. In the Rajput Uplands wheat, millet and cotton are the staple crops; in this region rice assumes more importance (especially if one includes the Son Valley) and cotton almost disappears. *Jhansi* is the town which commands the principal approach to the Foreland from the Ganges Valley. The position of *Jabalpur* (Jubbulpore, 295,375 in 1961) at the head of the Narbada Valley is interesting. It commands a gap through the Central Highlands to the south and the natural route down the Narbada Valley to Bombay on the west and, indeed, the easiest through route from the West Coast to the Ganges Valley. This is the line followed by the railway from Bombay to Calcutta, and *vice versa*, via Jabalpur and Allahabad; although the distance is greater, the gradients are less severe and the time shorter than straight across the plateau from Bombay to Calcutta via Nagpur. Jabalpur has important cotton manufactures. The important town of Gwalior (300,587 in 1961) has varied manufactures; it lies in the north near the Upper Ganges Valley.

The Rajput Upland Region

The name Rajput Upland has been chosen to designate this somewhat complex region because it is the home of the Rajputs of colourful and legendary fame and because it lies largely in the group of former Native States now grouped as Rajasthan. It is, on the whole, a plateau sloping towards the Ganges Valley on the north-east and drained by tributaries of the Ganges. Running across the region from south-west to north-east is the Aravalli Range which rises in Mt. Abu to 5,646 feet. To the north-west the country becomes lower and fades into the Thar Desert, now included in the State of Rajasthan. Southwards the plateau stretches into Madhya Pradesh as far as the scarp of the Vindhya Range overlooking the Narbada trough. To the north of the Vindhyas lies a tract of Deccan lava forming the well-known Malwa Plateau; farther north and north-west are the old crystalline rocks. For the sake of

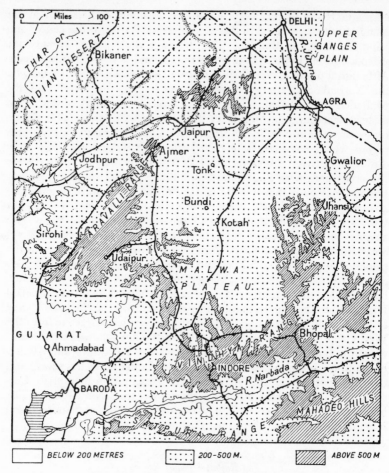

FIG. 181.—The Rajput Uplands (Rajasthan)

FORESTS 8%	NOT AVAILABLE 30%	WASTE 21%	CULTIVATED	
			1 11%	2 30%

FIG. 182.—The classification of the land in the Rajput Upland Region

The somewhat low percentage of cultivated and the high percentage of waste land when compared with the Deccan Lavas Region to the south reflect the uncertainty of the rainfall.

convenience we will consider with this region the Narbada Valley and the following five units may be distinguished:

(a) The Aravalli Range and its north-eastern extension.
(b) The network of forested hills of southern Rajputana.
(c) The valleys of eastern Rajputana.
(d) The Malwa Plateau built up of Deccan lavas and its southern edge, the Vindhya Range.
(e) The Narbada Valley.

Climatically the whole region is a dry one, with an average rainfall of less than 40 inches. The rain falls mainly during severe storms and the total amount fluctuates widely from year to year. Irrigation is almost impossible owing to the configuration of the surface and crops depend mainly on rainfall. Hence in good years the crop yields may be excellent; in bad years the crops may fail entirely. Fortunately there are two harvests (rabi and kharif), and the failure of one does not necessarily mean the failure of the other.

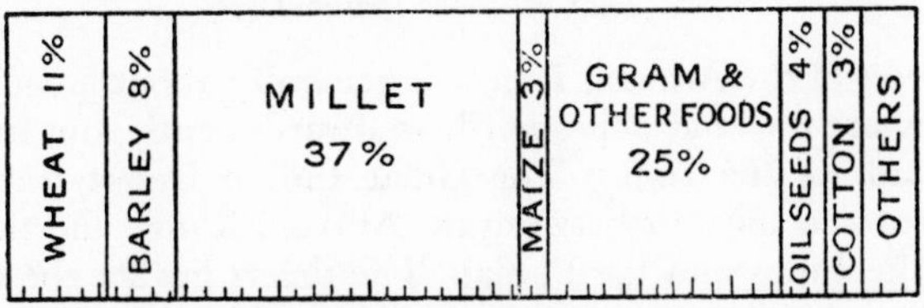

FIG. 183.—The crops of the Rajput Uplands
The large proportion devoted to gram, mainly for fodder, should be noted, and the very small percentage of non-food crops.

The sparse population reflects in the main the precarious rainfall. In good years the region could support a much larger population. The staple food is millet, with wheat and barley in smaller quantities. Large quantities of gram are grown for fodder. Considerable areas are forested, but the forests are of a dry type, merging into scrubland.

Population. In the hilly forested parts of this region live the Bhils, a primitive forest tribe. In other parts of the region the people are mainly Hindus, with Rajasthani as their language. Rajputana is also the great centre of the Jains. It is interesting to notice that an unusually large percentage of the population is engaged in industry. Many native industries still survive, e.g. the making of cotton goods, whilst woollen goods, especially blankets, are made in most parts of Rajputana from the wool of local sheep and goats. In the drier regions camel-hair is used in the manufacture of carpets, blankets, clothes, etc.

Several important routes run through the region. That along the Narbada Valley has already been mentioned; through the heart of the region runs the route from Agra to Bombay; along the northern slopes of the Aravalli Range is the main line from Delhi via Ahmadabad to Bombay.

Ajmer in the heart of Rajasthan was formerly the principal town of the tiny State of Ajmer. It is a flourishing town of 231,240 inhabitants (1961); increasing in size, it has food and textile industries and railway workshops.

Jaipur (403,444 in 1961) is larger than Ajmer, and with its textile and railway industries showed a 60 per cent. increase in 1941–51. It has been made the capital of Rajasthan.

Abu is a small hill station at the southern end of the Aravalli Range, 5,000 feet above sea-level. As a result of its elevation there is a rainfall of 60 inches, though the nearby plains have but 20.

Udaipur is a beautiful little town once the capital of the proud State of Mewar, occupying a hilly plateau at the southern end of the Aravalli Hills. Most of the Malwa Plateau has been included in Madhya Pradesh, the capital town of which, Bhopal, is on the southern margin.

The Thar or Great Indian Desert

The crest of the Aravalli Range is generally about 3,000 feet high and from there the land slopes north-westwards gently, but irregularly, to the plains of the Indus. The Great Indian Desert occupies this sloping area and thus lies between the Aravalli Range and the alluvial plains of the Indus and the Punjab. The desert lies for the most part in Rajasthan, but stretches into West Pakistan, into the Punjab, Bahawalpur and Sind.

It consists of a sandy waste, interrupted by rocky hills and waterless valleys. The ground is often entirely bare; in some places there may be a few shrubs or plants with thick, fleshy leaves and stems which can store up water, or with very long roots which can reach the moisture far below the surface. The rainfall of the desert is generally less than 10 inches annually, and even this amount is very irregular and falls mainly during storms. In some years no rain at all falls. It should be noted, however, that the rainfall is greater than in many parts of the rich Indus Valley. The Thar Desert remains a desert because of the absence of water for irrigation and the absence of level land which could be irrigated.

Naturally the desert is but very thinly populated. The former state of Jaisalmer, in the heart of the desert, has only 4 people to the square mile. Some of the people live in villages which spring up wherever there is a little water and some handfuls of millet and fodder can be grown. Frequently the water in the wells fails or becomes salt and the village must needs be abandoned. Camel traders across the desert are numerous, and the little town of Jaisalmer is a centre of camel routes. *Bikanir* is a small town towards the north-east which is noted for its manufacture of camel-hair goods and carpets. It is a flourishing town, increasing in size.

The importance of the desert as a barrier to man's movements has already been noted in reference to the strategic position of Delhi. To this day there is neither road nor railway through the heart of the desert, though the line from Karachi to Delhi goes across the south and that from Bikanir to Lahore across the north. Neither has functioned as a through route since partition.

THE ANDAMAN AND NICOBAR ISLANDS

The Andaman and Nicobar Islands formed one of the 'minor' provinces of India under the charge of a Chief Commissioner resident at Port Blair. In the Nicobar Islands he is represented by an Assistant Commissioner. Under the constitution of the Republic of India they form a centrally-administered Territory.

Both groups of islands are very interesting and may in the future play an important part in Indian economy, since there are tracts which may be suitable for settlement.

The Andaman Islands

The Andaman Islands lie in the Bay of Bengal, about 120 miles from Cape Negrais in Burma, which is the nearest point on the mainland. The principal islands form a long line running north and south between Latitude 10° 30′ and 13° 30′ N. Five of the largest islands lie close together, and are called the Great Andaman; to the south lies the island of Little Andaman. There are, in addition, about 200 small isles in the group, including the Ritchie Archipelago, lying to the east of the main line. The total area is estimated to be 2,508 square miles. The Great Andaman group, though over 200 miles long, is only 32 miles wide at the broadest part.

Geologically the chain forms a continuation of the Tertiary fold mountains of the Arakan Yoma in Burma. The rocks are believed to be mainly Eocene in age. There are small areas of older sedimentary rocks with large masses of serpentine and areas of limestone believed to be Miocene. To the east of the group, in the Gulf of Martaban, lie the tiny volcanic islands of Narcondam and Barren Island. Coral reefs fringe all the coasts.

The Great Andaman consists of a range of hills of which the highest point is about 2,400 feet above sea-level. The higher hills are usually nearer the east coast, and in general the eastern slopes are steeper than the western. The coastline is exceedingly indented, especially on the east, and creeks run many miles into the islands. Mangrove swamps fringe all the coasts except in the most exposed localities.

The climate may be described as intermediate in character between that of the tropical monsoon lands of India and the Equatorial climate of the East Indies. The temperature varies but a few degrees throughout the year and averages about 85° F. The rainfall is heavy over the whole group and probably averages well over 100 inches (Port Blair, 138 inches). The rainfall reaches its maximum from June to September during the south-west monsoon, but the rest of the year is far from rainless. Many of the dangerous cyclones which are common in the Gulf of Martaban seem to originate in the Andaman Islands.

Except in the neighbourhood of Port Blair and a few other localities where clearing has been carried out, the islands are densely forest-clad from the seashore to the summit of the highest hills. The forest is evergreen and contains many valuable timber trees, the best known of which is the padauk or Andaman red-wood (*Pterocarpus dalbergioides*). The only large mammals are a pig and a civet-cat.

The total population according to the Census of 1951 was 18,939, which may be compared with that of 1921 of 19,223 (14,258 males and 4,965 females). The islands were used from 1858 to 1942 by the Government of India as a penal settlement for life and long-term convicts, but the practice has been discontinued since the islands were reoccupied in 1945 after the Japanese occupation. The aborigines only numbered 474 (255 males and 219 females) in 1933; but particular interest attaches to them. They are savages of a low type, belonging to the Negrito race and therefore allied to the Semang of the Malay Peninsula and the Negritos of the Philippine Islands. The Andamanese have been fully studied by A. R. Brown. He estimates that they numbered about 5,500 in 1858.[1] They are short of stature, the men averaging 58½ inches and the women 54 inches. Intensely black in colour, they have the tightly curled hair of the negro but only a slightly prognathous face. The normal costume of the men is a belt or a belt and necklace, but on ceremonial occasions a number of ornaments is worn. The women wear one or more belts of pandanus leaf, which vary in pattern according to whether the woman is married or unmarried. Suspended from the front of the belt is a small apron of leaves. Children are carried in a sling thrown across the body. The Andamanese are organized into tribes and have an elaborate social organization. They believe in 'spirits', and when an Andamanese man or woman dies he or she becomes a spirit.

The Government of India is now encouraging immigration and settlement of the islands (it has settled some displaced families from East Bengal) and it is hoped that they will afford an outlet for some of the over-populated parts of India. The coconut and rubber tree grow well, and the fibre plants, Manila hemp and sisal hemp, can also be

---

[1] They are still rapidly decreasing in numbers. In 1921 there were 786 compared with 474 in 1933. Present numbers are not known.

cultivated. Clearings amount to about 75,000 acres out of a total area of 1,600,000 acres. In 1953 there were 7,000 head of cattle and 3,000 goats. The bulk of the population is concentrated in and around Port Blair. Port Blair is in wireless communication with Burma and a weekly mail steamer connects the port with Calcutta and Madras. Port Blair lies on the eastern side of South Andaman, the large southern island of the Great Andaman group. It has a fine natural harbour, well sheltered from the south-west monsoons. Other safe anchorages include Port Cornwallis and Stewart Sound, the latter being conveniently situated for the forest trade.

The Nicobar Islands

The Nicobar Islands lie to the south of the Andamans, about 75 miles of sea separating the two groups. They were formally annexed by Britain in 1869. There are twenty-one islands, with a total of 635 square miles. The islands fall into the three groups of Northern (with Car Nicobar as the largest island), Central (with Camorta and Nancowry) and Southern (with Great Nicobar). Geologically the islands form a continuation of the chain of the Arakan Yoma and the Andaman Islands, and consist mainly of Tertiary rocks with intrusive masses of gabbro, serpentine, etc., probably of Cretaceous age.

At the Census of 1961 the inhabitants numbered about 14,500; 12,009 in 1951: in 1931 the number was 9,481. The staple product of the islands is the coconut. The islanders have traded in coconuts for at least 1,500 years, and the production is estimated at 15,000,000 nuts per annum. Nearly half are sold by barter—there being no coinage—and exported in the form of copra in native craft and Chinese junks. The Nicobarese are immigrants to the islands, where they arrived from Indo-China some time before the Christian era. They are an offshoot of the Mongoloid race, which includes the Burmese, Shans and Malays. The Nicobarese men average $63\frac{3}{4}$ inches in height; the women 60 inches. The skin is yellowish or reddish brown and the hair dark, rusty brown, coarse and straight. They are not naturally prognathous, but the adults are repulsive in appearance, owing to the dilation of the lips by constant sucking of green coconuts and chewing of betel-nuts. Their food is first the coconut and secondly pandanus pulp, fish and imported rice. They are intelligent but lazy, truthful and honest, fond of sport and very just. Democratic in their organization, their headmen are naturally chosen and disputes settled by a committee of elders. The Nicobarese wear but little clothing, except on ceremonial occasions.

The Nicobar Islands have a fine harbour (Nancowry Harbour) between the islands of Camorta and Nicobar. During the Japanese occupation of 1942–5 some small jetties were constructed here and elsewhere. A good general account of the two groups is to be found in the *Report on the Census of India*, 1901, Vol. III. A popular account is given by C. B. Kloss, *In the Andamans and Nicobars* (London, 1903). Details of Anthropology will be found in A. R. Brown's *The Andaman Islanders* (Cambridge, 1922), and G. Whitehead's *In the Nicobar Islands* (London, 1924). See also G. West, *Car Nicobar* (London, 1950).

THE FORMER FRENCH SETTLEMENTS IN INDIA
(Etablissements Français de l'Inde)

No place typifies more strongly the old struggle between the European rivals for Eastern trade than does Pondichéry, until 1954 the chief French settlement remaining in India. It was founded by the French in 1674, taken by the Dutch in 1693 but restored in 1699. The English captured it in 1761 but restored it four years later, only to retake it in 1778. It was restored a second time in 1785 but again taken in 1793. The final stage came with the Treaties of 1814–15, which closed the struggle between Britain and Napoleon's France. They recognized French rights to five separate settlements in India— Pondichéry (Pondicherry), Karikal, Mahé and Yanaon, all on the coast, and Chandernagor on the Hooghly north of Calcutta, with a total area of about 196 square miles. In 1949 Chandernagor voted for union with India and was transferred the next year; in 1954 the transfer of the remaining four settlements (with 318,000 people in 1952) was agreed. So ended, quietly and amicably, three centuries of French rule over fragments of Indian territory.

THE FORMER PORTUGUESE SETTLEMENTS IN INDIA
(Estado da India)

The main territory of Portuguese India was the considerable territory of Goa with the capital Goa or Pangrim and valuable port of Mormugao and three islands on the Malabar Coast. It also included Daman (with two small territories) on the Gulf of Cambay and Diu (also with two other small territories) on the coast of Gujarat. The total area of Portuguese India was 1,537 square miles with a population in 1950 of 637,846. Portuguese India stood in rather a peculiar position. Goa is sufficiently large to have developed in the course of three centuries of contact with Roman Catholic Portugal a quiet cultural life of its own. A large proportion of Goanese have some Portuguese blood, the majority are Christians; they are proud to be distinguished as 'Goans' or 'Goanese' and of the fact that they have achieved a distinctive reputation—for example in the culinary arts—far outside their small territory. Whilst Indian ambition was to bring the Portuguese territories into the Indian Union, demonstrations made it clear in 1953–5 that many Goanese did not take the same view. However, the territories were occupied in December 1961 and became a Union Territory in 1962.

NEPAL

The independent Kingdom of Nepal stretches for 500 miles along the curve of the Himalayas, being bounded by the Sarda River on the west and by the Singalela Ridge (which separates it from Sikkim) on the east. It stretches from the tropical jungles of the Terai on the south to the eternal snows of the main Himalayan Range which in general forms the northern frontier. The total area is about 54,000 square miles and the population estimated in 1964 at about 9,500,000. The country was closed until recently to Europeans and was one of the least known parts of Asia. It was only in 1924 that the Prime Minister asked for help from the Survey of India in undertaking a detailed survey of the country, and the first accurate skeleton map, contoured, was published as a frontispiece to the General Report of the Survey of India, 1926-7.

The country falls into four drainage regions—from east to west the Kosi system of the Kosi and its seven tributaries; the valley of Nepal drained principally by the sacred Bagh Mati; the Sapt Gandakis system (or the seven rivers which unite to form the Gandak), and the Karnali system.

The name Nepal is properly restricted to the valley of Nepal— known in Nepal itself as 'the country contained within the Four Passes'—to the east the Saga Pass, to the south the Phar Ping, to the west the Panch Mané, to the north the Pati Pass. This valley, 'the historic heart of the whole country, the ancient centre of culture in a sea of mountains, is the one considerable piece of flattish ground to be found on the southern slopes of the Himalaya until the far greater western valley of Kashmir is reached'. The valley is only about 15 miles long and 7 miles wide, thickly populated and includes the capital, Katmandu (195,000; surrounding valley 450,000).

The ruling race in Nepal is that of the Gurkhas, one of the most famous of the world's military races, whose warlike energies find an outlet in the organization of the Government on military lines—even the judges have military titles—and formerly in voluntary service in the British Indian Army. The reigning family are Hindu Rajputs, but the chief power was in the hands of the Prime Minister (an hereditary office), to whom it was permanently delegated by the King in 1867. Indeed the country was virtually ruled by the Rana family. This came to an end in 1951 when constitutional reforms were announced by the King. The coronation of his son as King Mahendra in May 1956 was made the occasion of inviting many diplomats and foreign dignitaries to the country. The march of progress is apparent elsewhere in Nepal: slavery was abolished in 1924-6, the capital connected with the outside world by telephone and the first railway opened in 1926. This railway penetrates 25 miles into the country, and the journey to the capital can now, since 1954, be completed by motor road or by the daily air service. The life of the country centres round Katmandu; the great feature of village life in the mountains is the weekly fair. The first organized party of tourists arrived in 1955, in 1956 a Five Year Plan of modernization was announced—covering communications, irrigation, education, health services, hydro-electric schemes, industries such as cement and pulp, and tourist facilities. India has now built a great dam on the Kosi River inside the Nepalese border.

A recent brief account of the geography of Nepal is given by P. P. Karan and A. Taylor in *Focus, Amer. Geog. Soc.*, **6,** 1956, 10.

CEYLON[1]

GEOGRAPHICALLY Ceylon is closely allied to Peninsular India, from which it is separated merely by the narrow and shallow Palk Strait. The coastal settlements have formed part of the British

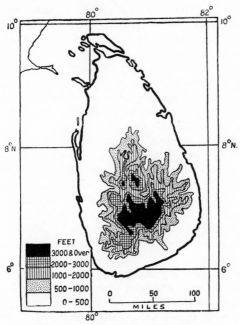

FIG. 184.—Physical map of Ceylon

Empire since 1796, being constituted a Crown Colony in 1802, and from 1815 to 1948 the whole island was British territory. On February 4, 1948, Ceylon became a self-governing member of the British Commonwealth.

The island is shaped roughly like a pear, and lies between 5° 55′ and 9° 50′ of North Latitude; it is this southerly situation combined with an insular position which gives Ceylon a climate approaching the Equatorial, and renders it climatically distinct from the neighbouring parts of India. The longest diameter of the island is from north to south and is roughly 270 miles. The area is 25,332 square miles (65,630 sq. km.)—a little smaller than Scotland.

[1] I am much indebted to Mr. B. H. Farmer for comments on this section.

Physical Features and Geology. The island consists of a central mass of mountains, surrounded by broad coastal plains. Many of the central mountains are high, rising to over 6,000 feet, and include such famous peaks as Pidurutalagala (8,292 feet), overlooking the well-known hill station of Nuwara Eliya; Kirigalpotta (7,857 feet); the lower but still more famous Adam's Peak (7,360 feet) and Namunukula (6,679 feet). In the north the coastal plain is almost flat, elsewhere its surface is somewhat irregular. The rivers are all short and radiate from the central mass of mountains. They are not of very great importance, though in the drier parts of the island innumerable streams are dammed to form tanks; whilst round the coasts many rivers empty into shallow coconut-girt lagoons, to which reference will be made later.

The mountains of Ceylon consist of crystalline rock of pre-Cambrian age, closely allied to and originally forming part of the great massif of Peninsular India. These old rocks in Ceylon are noted for the beautiful gemstones, especially sapphires, obtained from them. The gems are mainly obtained from pockets of weathered rock and from alluvial deposits along the western slope of the mountain mass, and are worked in hundreds of little quarries. Besides sapphires, rubies, moonstones, cat's-eyes and other stones are obtained. The best stones are sent to Europe and America, the poorer to India. Another important mineral obtained in the old rocks is graphite or plumbago. Phlogopite mica also occurs in economically workable deposits and ilmenite, zircon and monazite are found in beach sands. The pre-Cambrian rocks also underlie the coastal plain, but there they are covered by a thick coat of laterite ('kabouk'). The formation of laterite is seen to perfection in the south-west. Laterite is formed in the humid tropics which enjoy an alternation of wet and dry seasons. In the wet season the rain-water acts chemically on the superficial layers of the rocks and many salts pass into solution. In the dry season the surface dries and a deposit of iron and aluminium salts is left. As the surface waters evaporate, fresh supplies are drawn up from below by capillary action. The resulting laterite has a cellular or sponge-like texture, the network consisting mainly of oxides of iron, the spaces being filled with residual matter, largely quartz grains. The laterite hardens on exposure to the atmosphere, and the residual matter is washed out of the pores by the mechanical action of rain, resulting in a porous rock much used in Ceylon for building and for road metal. Where the rainfall is sufficient, the laterite affords a deep red soil. The surface of the underlying crystalline rocks is irregular, and at intervals around the coastal plain the old rocks appear at the surface through the coating of laterite. In the north the old rocks have been covered by soft miocene limestone (cement industry). Along much of the coast are sand-dunes thrown up by the sea, and very frequently extensive fresh-water or brackish-water lagoons lie behind the sand-dunes or sandy beaches. In the north of the island are certain sandy peninsulas, notably that of Jaffna. The end of the Mannar Peninsula is only 22 miles from the nearest point of India (the port of Dhanushkodi). Ceylon is nearly joined between these two points by a line of rocks and sandbanks called Adam's Bridge. Fringed as it is by sandbanks, the coast of Ceylon is for the most part low, but at intervals the old rocks appear at the surface, and give rise to rocky headlands, as, for example, the Point de Galle, at the entrance to the old port of Galle. Some of the larger lagoons, already mentioned, are open to the sea and form deep indentations along the coast. Coral flourishes round the island; coral reefs are numerous and much of the sand consists of comminuted coral.

Climate. For a tropical country, the climate of Ceylon is comparatively healthy. Nearness to the Equator results in the temperature being high throughout the year, but heat is less oppressive than in many parts of India. The presence of the sea keeps the climate equable, and everywhere along the coast land and sea breezes are felt. There is little difference between the temperature of day and night—the daily range at Colombo is only 12° F. The annual range is also small. January is usually the coldest month, and May the hottest, but around

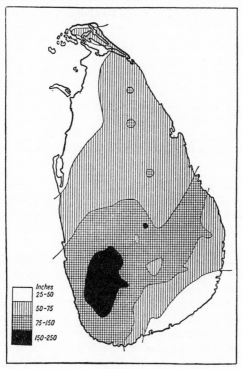

Fig. 185.—The average annual rainfall of Ceylon

the coast there is only a difference of about 5° between the mean temperatures for the two months. The mean annual temperature for the coastal districts is about 81° F. In the interior there are several hill stations, notably Nuwara Eliya (pronounced Nuralia), which are delightfully cool throughout the year.

Although Ceylon is a comparatively small island, the rainfall varies greatly—from less than 40 inches in the dry regions to over 200 in exposed situations. Ceylon gets its rain both from the south-west and the north-east monsoons. There is a heavy rainfall on the west and on the south-west coasts and on the mountains from the south-west monsoon, the rain falling mainly between June and October. On the north-east coast and the eastern slopes of the mountains the heavy rainfall is later in the year—mainly in November and December—and is derived from the north-east monsoon. Amongst the hills the constant mists of the rainy season are apt to be unpleasant. The northern part of the island has no hills to intercept the winds, and is a dry region. So also is the south-eastern part of the island. The following figures illustrate the varying types of climate found in the island:

	Alt., ft.		Jan.	Feb.	Mar.	Apr.	May	June	July	Aug.	Sept.	Oct.	Nov.	Dec.	Year
Colombo	24	Temp. °F.	79	80	81	81·5	82	80	80	80·5	80	79	79	79	80
		Rain, in.	3·2	1·9	4·7	11·4	12·1	8·4	4·5	3·8	5·0	14·1	12·5	6·4	88·3
Jaffna	20	Temp. °F.	77·5	79	83	86	85	84	83	83	83	82	79·5	78	81·8
		Rain, in.	2·7	1·3	1·2	2·0	1·7	0·7	0·9	1·5	2·9	9·4	14·4	10·3	48·8
Trin-comalee	99	Temp. °F.	78	79	80	83	85	84	83	83·5	83	81	79	78	81
		Rain, in.	5·7	2·2	1·4	2·1	2·4	1·4	2·1	4·5	4·2	8·0	13·6	15·3	62·9
Nuwara Eliya	6,200	Temp. °F.	57·5	57·5	59	60	62	60	59	60	59·5	60	59	58	59·3
		Rain, in.	5·9	2·0	3·5	5·6	6·9	12·7	12·0	8·0	8·5	11·0	9·1	8·4	93·3

Vegetation. Just as the climate of Ceylon varies greatly from place to place, so does the natural vegetation. The lower slopes of the mountains used to be covered with thick evergreen rain-forest. Now much of the forest has been cleared to make room for rubber plantations and tea gardens, and there is little timber of value left. The wetter parts of the lowlands were also covered with wet evergreen forests, but the Dry Zone was occupied by forests of a much drier type. The forests remaining are carefully controlled by Government and yield a valuable supply of firewood for the railways and general purposes, as well as timber in the log which is used by the saw-mills of Colombo. The production of sleepers is decreasing, also that of firewood (which is being replaced by coal). The trees are mostly native hardwoods, but fast-growing eucalypts as well as conifers are being used in plantations. The famous satinwood and ebony of Ceylon are slow-growing trees of the drier forests. A great part of the wetter land is now used for rice and coconuts, but the drier parts are still largely untouched. Taking the whole of Ceylon, about one-fifth is cultivated; about 'one-fifth is covered with thick forest. 'Chena' or 'hena' (i.e. shifting) cultivation is practised in many parts, especially of the hills (cf. *taung-ya* in Burma) and the Dry Zone, but there remains a considerable area of waste land which might be utilized.

Population. According to the Census of July 1963 the population of Ceylon was 10,624,507, exclusive of military, naval, air force and shipping personnel who happened to be in Ceylon at the time when the Census was taken. The population shows an increase of over two and a half million since 1953. The principal group is the Sinhalese (formerly known as Cingalese or Cingalees), who, in the sixth century B.C., came from the north, and conquered the island. There are now two main groups of Sinhalese—the low-country Sinhalese and the Kandyan Sinhalese. The Sinhalese are Buddhists by religion, Buddhism having been introduced from India in the third century B.C. The natural centre of Buddhism in Ceylon is Kandy, the old hill capital. At Kandy is the so-called Temple of the Tooth, where a supposed tooth of the Buddha is preserved. The north of Ceylon is inhabited mainly by Tamils, who are Hindus by religion, and who came over from India either as conquerors in past ages, or in recent times as labourers in the tea gardens and on the rubber and coffee estates. The two groups of Tamils are often separated as the Ceylon Tamils and the Indian Tamils. The Tamils number nearly $2\frac{1}{4}$ million—21 per cent. of the total population. The Moors, who number over half a million, are traders, boatmen or fishermen, who came originally from Arabia. They are Mahommedans by religion. The descendants of the old Portuguese and Dutch settlers, though considerably mixed with Sinhalese blood, form a well-marked community and are known as Burghers. Europeans in 1963 numbered 7,000. In the wilder parts of the Dry Zone there are still a few thousand Veddas—members of a very primitive hill tribe, of great ethnological interest—but they are decreasing in numbers. The people of Ceylon live mainly on the wetter parts of the plains, and in the hills; on the dry infertile soils of the northern region, and in the east, there are very few inhabitants. The occupation of 62 per cent. of the population is agriculture, 12 per cent. are engaged in industrial occupations, and 8 per cent. in trade. The urban population is 15 per cent. of the whole, the principal towns (1963) being: Colombo, 510,947; Galle, 64,942; Jaffna, 94,248; Kandy, 67,768.

In 1953 the adherents to the principal religions were: Buddhists, 5,217,143; Hindus, 1,614,004; Mahommedans, 541,812; Christians, 714,874. The total population in 1921 was only 4,497,853, so that it doubled in less than 40 years.

The two principal vernacular languages are Sinhalese and Tamil; English is the principal commercial and official language. In 1962 there were 8,765 government and assisted schools attended by over 2,351,000 children so that literacy is now almost universal. There are also technical and industrial schools, and a University College was opened in 1921, and the University established in 1942.

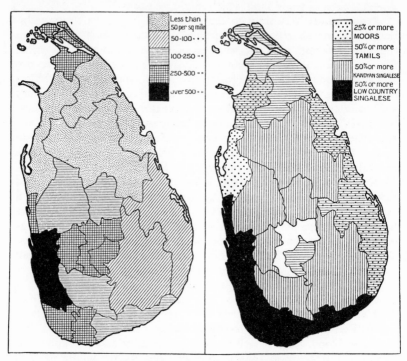

FIG. 186.—The population of Ceylon

The first map shows its density and illustrates the comparative sparseness in the northern plain and in the eastern coastal areas. The second map shows the composition of the population and stresses the concentration of the Tamils in the north and of the old seafaring Moors along the coasts. It may be surprising to see that in the heart of the island, around Kandy itself, the Kandyan Sinhalese drop below 50 per cent. This is due to the large numbers of Tamil coolies employed on the tea estates. (Based on the census of 1921.)

The Sinhalese have a characteristic native dress. Both sexes wear a cylindrical skirt, like the Burmese lungyi (see Burma). The women wear a tight cotton bodice and a loose jacket of some thin and light material. The better class Sinhalese men wear a white jacket, cut on European lines, with a high collar. The older generation of Sinhalese men wear the hair long and knotted at the back, whilst the crown of the head is surrounded by a curious comb, consisting of a piece of tortoiseshell bent to form three-quarters of a circle, a remnant of the days when Dutch settlers demanded tidy hair among their servants.

It has very short teeth and the ends are finished off into points. It is placed on the head as a crown would be with the points forward. The present generation favours short hair, and the use of the comb is becoming rare. The Tamils in Ceylon tend to retain their native dress.

Government. The first Europeans to settle in Ceylon were the Portuguese in 1505, who formed settlements along the south and west coasts. About the middle of the next century the settlements were wrested from them by the Dutch. The old Dutch forts are still to be seen in Galle and other places, and, though the fort itself has disappeared, the heart of Colombo retains the name and is still known as The Fort. In 1796, the foreign settlements of Ceylon were annexed by the British Government to the Presidency of Madras, but in 1802 Ceylon was separated from India to form a separate Crown Colony. In 1815 the interior districts of the island—the domains of the King of Kandy—were absorbed. Attaining self-government on Dominion lines on February 4, 1948, the U.K. handed over naval and air bases in 1957.

For purposes of Government the island is divided into nine provinces—Western, Central, Northern, Southern, Eastern, North-Western, North Central, Uva, and Sabaragamuwa—shown in Fig. 192.

Natural Regions. A simple division of Ceylon may be made into three: (*a*) the hills of the centre; (*b*) the belt of lowland of varying topography lying between the hill country and the sea; (*c*) the Jaffna Peninsula and the limestone region of the north. The lowland or Maritime Belt varies, however, greatly in character according to variations in climate (especially rainfall) and a subdivision is desirable.

The late Miss E. K. Cook suggested the division of the island into the regions shown in Fig. 187. This may be compared with the scheme proposed by B. H. Farmer in O. H. K. Spate's *India and Pakistan* (1954). He also has a threefold division—the Hills, the Lowland Wet Zone (South-West Lowlands) and Lowland Dry Zone.

The Hill Country, formed by the mountainous centre of the island, falls into a main mass and a south-western extension (No. 13 of Fig. 187)—the Sabaragamuwa hill country. The region as a whole consists of ridges separated by deep valleys, or occasional broad marshy or grassy plains surrounded by mountains. Comparatively little is now left of the vast forests which covered the region before the days of European planting. The trees are nearly all evergreen and get smaller the higher one goes, so that above 5,000 feet the trees are too small to be of any use as timber. The rainfall of most of the region is heavy; the rain does not fall so heavily as on the plains, but is more continuous, and for days or even weeks together the sun may be hidden by dense clouds of mist. The greater part of the rain falls from June to October during the period of the south-west monsoon. Nearly all the tea gardens are found in this region as well as many of the rubber plantations. Cacao is grown north and north-east of Kandy, the old capital of

Ceylon, which is 1,650 feet above sea-level and 72 miles from Colombo by rail. A few miles from Kandy is Peradeniya, famous for its Botanical Gardens. The native inhabitants of the hill country are the Kandyan Sinhalese, who have carefully terraced for rice cultivation many of the steep hillsides. A large amount of coffee used to be grown in Ceylon, but, still more than in southern India, the trees were swept away by disease.

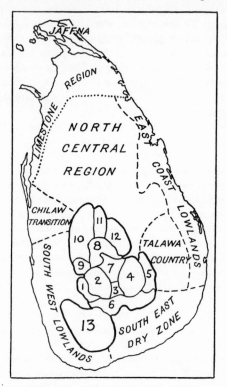

FIG. 187.—The natural regions of Ceylon (*after* E. K. Cook)

For explanation, see text. The limit of the limestone after E. J. Wayland, *Quart. Jour. Geol. Soc.*, 79, 1923.

The minor regions of the hill country shown on Fig. 187 (numbered as in the text) are:

(1) *The Adam's Peak Ridges* enjoy—or suffer from—the heaviest rainfall in the island and the continuously moist atmosphere causes much inconvenience. The shrine on Adam's Peak attracts many pilgrims in the driest months, but the region was almost uninhabited until its suitability for tea was realized.

(2) *The Hatton Plateau* is slightly drier (150 inches) and the area has become almost one vast and continuous tea garden. The principal inhabitants are English tea-planters and their Tamil labourers.

(3) *The High Plains* form a grassy plateau with few people, though the climate is healthy and bracing.

(4) *The Uva Basin* is surrounded by mountain ranges and so is comparatively dry and bracing. It is a grass-covered area—the 'Uva Downs' and former rice lands of the valley floors are less important than the tea gardens of the hillsides. The chief town is Badulla.

(5) *The Lunugala Region* is a long wall-like ridge with a flanking eastern platform bounding the Uva Basin on the east. Formerly scantily peopled, the clearings for tea and rubber are comparatively recent.

(6) *The Southern Platform* 'is like an immense natural step, with a rapid rise from the flat low country to the 1,000-foot level and lies in

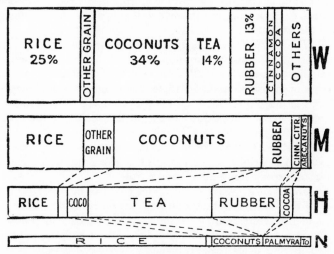

FIG. 188.—The crops of the whole of Ceylon (**W**) and of the three natural regions

M. Maritime Belt; **H.** Hill Region; **N.** Northern Region. (Note.—Cinn. Citr. = Cinnamon and Citronella; To = Tobacco.)

front of the steep southern wall of the hill country proper. It is intermediate in character between the low country and the hills and seems to offer considerable possibilities of development.'

(7) *The Piduru Ridges* comprise a central knot with many of the highest peaks in the island from which radiate steep ridges and deep valleys. It is naturally the coolest part of the island, forested and inaccessible, with rhododendron predominating in the higher parts. The delightful hill station of Nuwara Eliya has been established in a beautiful mountain basin in the shadow of Pidurutalagala. Here many temperate crops can be grown, including most of the fruits and vegetables of England.

(8) *The Kandy Plateau* has for long been the most populous and well-developed part of the hill country. Its inaccessibility rendered it a suitable area for the siting of a capital (it became the hill capital in the sixteenth century). Buddhist pilgrimages to the Temple of the Tooth are an important feature of the life of Kandy.

(9) *The Dolosbage Group* is a block of hills cut off from the main mass by the valley of the Mahaweli Ganga. The forests have been cleared comparatively recently for planting—especially of rubber.

(10) *The North-Western Uplands* form a transitional region with rubber, coconuts and cacao.

(11) *The Matale Valley* is a 'stuffy' enclosed valley, opening out into the northern plains in the north and affording a route to Kandy on the south. Tea and rubber are the leading crops, but there is a considerable cultivation of cacao and an extensive series of paddy terraces along the floor of the valley.

(12) *The Knuckles Group* lies to the east of the Matale Valley and is the part of the hill country most influenced by the north-east monsoon.

(13) *The Sabaragamuwa Hill Country* is one of the most lonely and wild parts of the island and still a haunt of numbers of wild elephants. It consists of a series of ridges trending from north-west to south-east, separated by deep valleys. Ratnapura, in this region, is the centre of the gem-mining industry.

The Lowland Belt for the most part is rolling country, not exceeding 1,000 feet in height and in most of the Wet Zone with a thick red lateritic soil except along the coastal strips.

The South-West Lowlands, or low, wet country, come under the influence of the south-west monsoon and have a rainfall of between 75 and 100 inches. There is often too much water: floods are common and drainage is a leading problem. The level lands and the valleys are occupied by rice fields (usually yielding two crops a year, one after each monsoon). The higher lands towards the hills are covered by the peculiar mixed tree cultivation of the Sinhalese. Each farmer has coconuts, areca-nuts, mangoes, jaks and bread-fruit, together with yams and small plants like pepper. On the borders of the hill country are rubber plantations and tea gardens. All along the sandy coasts are groves of coconuts. The husks are allowed to soak and rot in the shallow lagoons and so the fibre (coir) is obtained. Industries connected with the coconut find employment for large numbers of people. The kernels are roughly dried for export as copra. Even more important is the export of carefully dried or 'desiccated' coconut prepared in factories. There are also factories for the preparation of coconut oil. The preparation of coir is mainly a cottage industry. Areca-nuts (betel-nuts) are also grown for export. Of the spices for which Ceylon has long been famous, cinnamon is the most important. The cinnamon tree likes a light sandy soil, and grows in those parts of the coastal regions where such a soil is available. The cinnamon of commerce is obtained from the inner bark of young shoots. The industry is less important than formerly. Other spices include cardamoms and cloves. Citronella oil, prepared from a grass, is also obtained mainly in the south-west. This is the most densely populated part of the island, villages and isolated human habitations being very evenly spread over the whole area. The larger towns are near the mouths of the more important rivers or lagoons and include Colombo, Negombo and Matara. Except in such towns, most of the people are Low-Country Sinhalese, though along the coast are many Moors. The fishing-boats are the well-known catamarans and outrigger canoes, made from coconut palm logs or jak trees and having a log attached to one side by two connecting wooden poles.

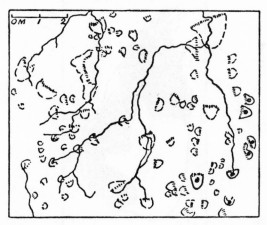

Fig. 189.—Tanks along the stream courses of the North Central Lowland

Only those marked with a dot were being used prior to the recent resuscitation of the area.

The capital of Ceylon, Colombo, is on the west coast. It has now a fine artificial harbour and is a port of call at the junction of many ocean routes as well as being the commercial centre of the island. Before the harbour of Colombo was finished, Galle in the south-west used to be the principal port of call. The entrance to the rock-girt harbour is still guarded by an old Dutch fort.

The Hambantota or South-East Dry Zone is characterized by a deficiency of rainfall and has less than 50 inches a year, whilst evaporation is strong. Thorn scrub predominates, but small trees of the interior include ebony and satinwood. Today there are few inhabitants, but in the past there were 'tanks' and more people. Dry Zone crops such as cotton and ground-nuts may help in the salvation of this area but irrigated paddy is the first hope.

The East Coast Lowlands form a flat strip 10 to 30 miles wide with an almost continuous succession of lagoons and marshes cut off from the ocean by coconut-clad sandbanks. Mangrove swamps fringe most of the lagoons: the coast is lined by a succession of villages facing away from the stormy sea and paddy land occupies all flat stretches. The rainy season is that of the north-east monsoon and the coast is hot during the period of the south-west monsoon. Batticaloa lies at the exit of a long series of connected lagoons; Trincomalee, on a large bay with a protected deep-water harbour, was, until 1957, a British naval base and recently a naval oil fuel depot. It is in the East Coast Lowlands that the great Gal Oya irrigation scheme was undertaken after the Second World War.

Fig. 190.—The worst malarial districts of Ceylon (shown in black) before the use of D.D.T.

(*After* E. K. Cook)

The North-Central Region occupying a large area in the northern half of the island was once a fertile, thickly populated tract with innumerable 'tanks' or storage reservoirs on every river. But the region was deserted—probably as a result of the ravages of malaria or other diseases—and most of the tanks fell into disuse and are marked today only by unhealthy swamps. Dense jungle now stretches like a sea over hundreds of square miles and hides the poor remnants of the former tank villages and the wonderful ruined cities such as Anuradhapura— a capital city as long ago as the fifth century B.C. The modern Anuradhapura has been made a focus of rail and road routes. Vast schemes for the restoration of irrigated lands are now in progress.

The Talawa Country is a distinctive tract, isolated and consisting of savanna (grassland dotted with trees—the 'talawa' of the Sinhalese). Here live most of the very primitive Veddas—the aboriginals of Ceylon.

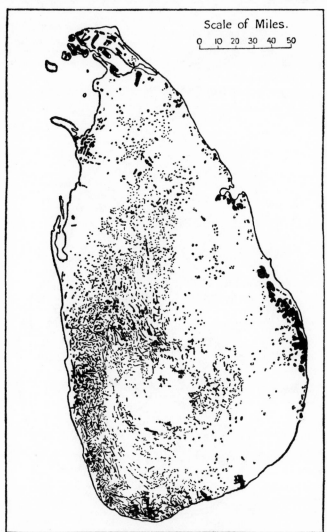

Scale of Miles.

0 10 20 30 40 50

FIG. 191.—The rice lands of Ceylon
(Map constructed by A. Ginigé, M.A.)

These last three regions are the present scene of great activity in promoting irrigation and new settlement. In particular the Gal Oya has been dammed and very large areas rendered fit for development.

The Chilaw Transition Zone lies between the South-West Lowlands and the North Central Lowlands.

The Jaffna Limestone Region as indicated on Fig. 187 has been

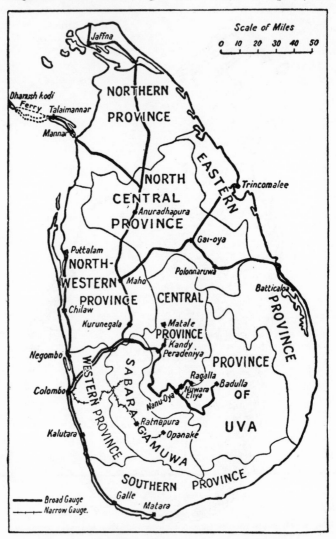

FIG. 192.—The railways, towns and provinces of Ceylon

demarcated according to the extent of the almost horizontal beds of limestone, partly of Miocene Age. The most distinctive part of this very interesting region is the Jaffna Peninsula itself, densely peopled almost exclusively by 'Ceylon Tamils', who cultivate every available acre. In the east are many salt pans and tracts of saline soil on which little will grow and a thorny scrub covers much of the mainland limestone area. The once important Palmyra palm is giving way to the coconut.

The mail route from Ceylon to India is through the port of Talaimannar, at the end of the sandy Peninsula of Mannar and the terminus of the Ceylon Government Railways. From Talaimannar daily steamers cover the 22 miles of shallow sea to Dhanushkodi, the terminus of the South Indian Railway. South of the Mannar Peninsula is the shallow Gulf of Mannar, famous for its pearl fisheries.

Communications. The railways of Ceylon are broad gauge (5 feet 6 inches) and are State-owned. Colombo is the natural centre of the railway system. One line runs southwards along the coast to Galle and Matara, whilst the main line runs northwards through the old historical town of Anuradhapura to Jaffna, with branches to Talaimannar and to Trincomalee and Batticaloa. Another line, constructed at great expense and running for a considerable distance high up on the sides of a deep valley, runs from Colombo to Kandy, and winds about amongst the hill country to Badulla. The journey from Colombo to Badulla is one of great interest. Ceylon is better served by roads than India, and there are many excellent motor roads now used by enormous numbers of motor-buses. Outside Colombo and Galle there are few hotels, but there is a series of excellent Rest Houses, constructed by Government primarily for the use of officials, at which travellers may secure shelter, and, in many cases, food. Perhaps these little details are out of place here, but they mean a great deal to the European resident or visitor. There are few countries which approach more closely the Western idea of the Tropics than does Ceylon, few journeys in the world to surpass for quiet beauty an afternoon train ride to Matara, with the sun setting over the sea within a frame of coconut palms and golden sand, or few memories which will last as vividly as that of exploring the Temple of the Tooth by the light of a flickering candle or of watching the moonbeams amidst the ghostly shadows of the old Dutch Fort at Galle.

Production and Industry. Out of about 4·5 million acres under cultivation in 1963, the areas occupied by the principal crops were:

	Acres
Coconuts	1,071,000
Rice	1,562,000
Other grains	105,000
Tea	587,000
Rubber	676,000
Cacao	20,000
Cinnamon (1951—now less)	30,000
Citronella (1951—now less)	34,000

Cattle number over 1½ millions and buffaloes 850,000; goats over half a million, but there are few sheep. There are now Government dairies and cattle farms.

The distribution of coconuts is shown in Fig. 193, and reference has been made above to associated industries. The value of coconut products exported in 1926, 1952 and 1963 will give some idea of changing relative importance:

	Value, million rupees		
	1926	1952	1963
Coconuts, fresh	1·4	3·0	c. 1·7
Copra	39·8	33·2	39·2
Desiccated coconut	17·3	65·3	60·1
Coconut oil	15·5	133·1	99·0
Poonac	0·9	—	—
Fibre-bristles	1·2		
Fibre-matting	0·9 }	21·8	c. 40·0
Coir yarn	1·8		
	78·8	256·4	c. 240·0

This table makes clear the increasing importance of oil extraction in the country of origin.

As shown in Fig. 195, the tea gardens of Ceylon are found in the hills, mainly between Kandy and Nuwara Eliya. The quantity of black tea exported normally reaches over 450,000,000 lb. (annually) in addition to a little green tea. By contrast to the coconuts, tea is produced on large estates, many of which are owned by large companies. The same is true of the rubber plantations. As shown in Fig. 196, the rubber plantations are found on the lowlands and lower slopes of the hills, mainly in the south-west. It is necessary to realize the extremely hilly nature of much of this country, and many of the Ceylonese rubber estates are on steep valley sides—well seen in the train journey from Colombo to Kandy. In this respect Ceylon offers a considerable contrast to Malaya.

The cacao of Ceylon is restricted to the region of the hills, north-west, north, and east of Kandy. There are two crops—spring and autumn. The acreage under cacao tended to decline and the replacement of cacao by rubber was a marked feature of the boom years. Of recent years acreage has increased. It is difficult to realize that Ceylon was once famous for its coffee, for the crop has practically disappeared, the competition of Brazilian and Javanese preventing a recovery from the epidemic which destroyed the original plantations.

Paddy is the principal food grain of Ceylon, but is not produced in sufficient quantities to satisfy home requirements. There are two har-

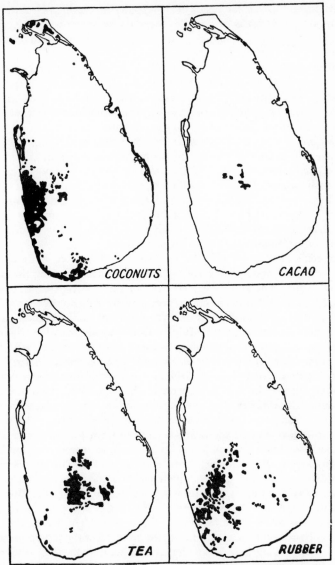

Figs. 193–6.—The distribution of four leading cash crops of Ceylon

vests, corresponding to the two monsoons, on the vagaries of which the crops depend. In the south-west are seen numerous examples of the elaborate hill-terracing so characteristic of the more fertile hill-slopes of Java; in the east and north paddy depends largely on the irrigation from tanks. Special attention is being paid to the extension of irrigation to meet the needs of the rapidly increasing population. In addition to large areas irrigated by large Government works—over 200 in number—there are also 200,000 acres of paddy irrigated by nearly 3,000 village tanks.

Reference has already been made to the cinnamon and citronella of Ceylon, both essentially characteristic of the island; cardamoms, papais, areca-nuts and tobacco are worthy of note, as well as three fibres—sisal hemp, kapok and cotton, the latter almost entirely from the Hambantota district of the dry south-east.

Manufactures on a large scale are restricted to the preparation of agricultural products—connected with the tea, coconut, rubber and cocoa plantations. Native manufactures are of minor importance commercially, and include the working of tortoise-shell (mainly at Galle), carving, weaving, basket-work, and the cutting of gems. Especially since the creation of a Ministry of Industries in 1947 many new industries have been encouraged—for plywood, leather, boots and shoes, coir goods, cement, textiles, paper and others.

Special interest attaches to the fisheries of Ceylon. Although the inshore waters abound in both surface and bottom-feeding fishes, the native catamarans and outriggers are not the best type of fishermen's boats; they are too small to carry large lengths of line or net. As a result there is a considerable import of dried fish from southern India as well as the famous (for its smell) Maldive fish from the Maldive Islands. A trawling company started modern fishing operations on the Pedro Bank (off Point Pedro) and Wadge Bank (off Cape Comorin) in 1927. The pearl fisheries of the Gulf of Mannar are under Government control. A 'fishery' is held in certain years only, when it is ascertained that there are sufficient numbers of mature oysters to warrant it. The oysters are retrieved from 5 to 10 fathoms by skilled Tamil divers. The oysters are allowed to rot and the pearls recovered from the washings. There is also a pearl fishery of a different character in the shallow almost land-locked Bay at Trincomalee, known as Lake Tamblegam. Here the 'window-pane oyster' occurs which yields small irregular pearls, in considerable demand locally, though not good enough for the European market. When oysters are present in the lake it is the practice of the Government to lease the fishery for three years. The water does not exceed about 12 feet in depth; in depths up to 5 feet the natives from the surrounding villages pick up the oysters with their toes, diving for them in the deeper parts. According to the usual custom the divers retain one-third in lieu of pay. Another interesting fishery is the chank fishery of the Palk Strait. Chanks are univalve shells in great demand in India for the purpose of manufacturing bangles, etc., and the huge number of nearly 2½ million have been fished annually.

Foreign Trade. Figs. 197 and 198 illustrate the foreign trade of Ceylon. The trade is carried on mainly by British vessels.

Taking a later year, 1963, of the exports 30 per cent. went to the United Kingdom, 8 per cent. to the United States, 6 per cent. to China. Ceylon has three staple exports—tea, rubber and coconut products. Between a third and a half of the tea goes to the United Kingdom, other customers being Iraq, United States, Australia and South Africa.

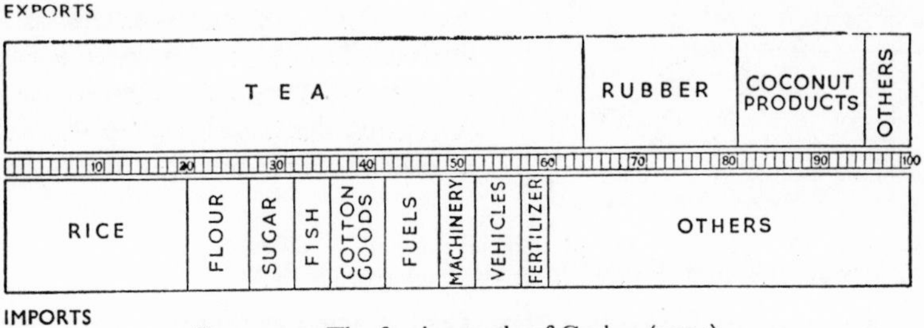

EXPORTS

TEA		RUBBER	COCONUT PRODUCTS	OTHERS

RICE	FLOUR	SUGAR	FISH	COTTON GOODS	FUELS	MACHINERY	VEHICLES	FERTILIZER	OTHERS

IMPORTS

FIG. 197.—The foreign trade of Ceylon (1954)

In 1963 tea represented 67 per cent., rubber 15 and coconut products 13.

The United States and the United Kingdom purchase most of the rubber. Desiccated coconut goes mainly to the United Kingdom; copra to India, Italy and Australia, and oil to India, the United Kingdom and the Netherlands.

The bulk of Ceylon's imports come from the United Kingdom, India, China, and Burma, these four areas supplying nearly half of the

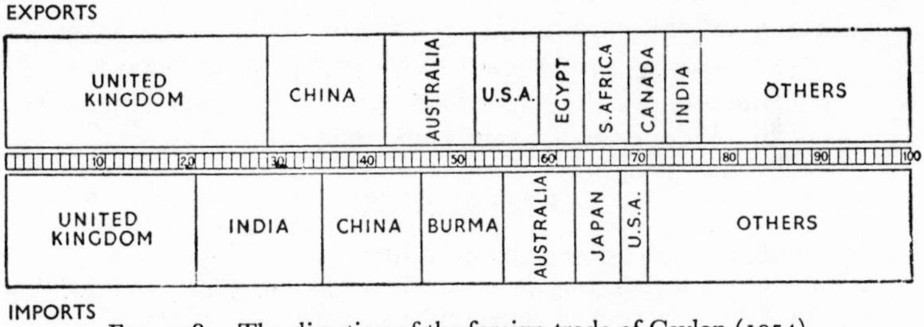

EXPORTS

UNITED KINGDOM	CHINA	AUSTRALIA	U.S.A.	EGYPT	S.AFRICA	CANADA	INDIA	OTHERS

UNITED KINGDOM	INDIA	CHINA	BURMA	AUSTRALIA	JAPAN	U.S.A.	OTHERS

IMPORTS

FIG. 198.—The direction of the foreign trade of Ceylon (1954)

In recent years the position is very similar.

whole. Burma supplies much of the rice; Australia most of the wheat; the United Kingdom, China, Japan and India most of the cotton and other textile goods and general manufactures.

Nearly all the foreign trade of Ceylon now passes through the port of Colombo. Before the building of Colombo harbour, Galle was the principal port of call. Galle is a fine but small natural harbour and has a dangerous rocky entrance, facing into the teeth of the south-west monsoon. Trincomalee was a British naval base, and benefited by the

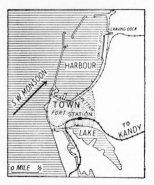

coming of the railway, whilst mails for South India go by Talaimannar pier. Otherwise Colombo has almost a monopoly of foreign trade; no less than five berths are available for vessels drawing up to 33 feet and ocean liners which previously anchored in the harbour are able to come alongside the wharves completed in 1955. A graving dock and patent slip and an oil-fuel depot are also available.

FIG. 199.—A sketch-map of the artificial harbour of Colombo, showing how it is sheltered from the south-west monsoon

Note on the Colombo Plan. Ceylon acted as host to a conference of the Prime Ministers of India, Pakistan, Burma, Indonesia and Ceylon out of which grew in 1950 the Colombo Plan for Cooperative Economic Development of South and South-East Asia. It is primarily for self-help among members of the British Commonwealth.

The Maldive Islands were formerly a dependency of Ceylon, being situated about 400 miles to the south-west. They are ruled by a Sultan. The group consists of twelve coral atolls, but a vast number of islands (200 inhabited) 115 square miles in area, richly clothed with coconut palms. The people number 82,000; they are Mohammedans and are great fishermen and traders. During the Second World War an important airfield was established on Gan island in the Addu atoll and in 1957 it was re-established as a staging post. In 1960 the Maldivian government gave the island to Britain for 30 years. The Maldive Islands became independent on July 26, 1965.

REFERENCES

Census Publications. Decennially since 1871.

Ceylon is fortunate in having an active Survey Department which publishes not only an excellent series of topographical maps, but others of a special nature.

An important geographical work on *Ceylon*, by Miss E. K. Cook, was published by Macmillan & Co. Ltd. (London) in 1931, and revised 1939 and 1951 by K. Kularatnam. See also B. H. Farmer, *op. cit. sup.* The Ceylon Year Book has recent information.

Jennings, Sir W. Ivor, *The Economy of Ceylon*, Oxford Univ. Press, 1951.

MacFadden, C. H., 'The Gal Oya Valley: Ceylon's Little TVA', *Geog. Rev.*, **44**, 1954, 271–81.

MacFadden, C. H., 'Ceylon and the Colombo Plan', *Focus, Amer. Geog. Soc.*, 1955.

Pakeman, S. A., *Ceylon*, New York, 1964.

Farmer, B. H., 'Recent Developments in Ceylon', *Roy. Central Asian Soc.*, **52**, 1965, 238–248.

BURMA[1]

THE Union of Burma, as a sovereign independent state with a republican form of government, came into existence on January 4, 1948. On that day the last British Governor handed over authority to the first President of the Burmese Republic in accordance with the treaty which had been signed in London on October 17, 1947. Burma elected to sever all formal connections with the British Commonwealth and was admitted an independent member of the United Nations later in 1948.

The present inhabitants of Burma are descendants of various Mongolian tribes which migrated southwards into the basin of the Irrawaddy in remote times. More than 2,000 years ago the people accepted Buddhism and since that time its monastic system has dominated the life of the country. The great Pagan dynasty of 1084–1287 gave place to some centuries of Shan rule before Burmese Kingdoms of varying extent and power were re-established. The earliest European contacts with Burma were by the Portuguese, followed about 1612 by the British and Dutch East India Companies. When internal dissensions threatened the peace of neighbouring parts of India, Britain was compelled to take action and the First Burmese War of 1824 followed. By the peace of Yandabu (1826) Arakan and Tenasserim were ceded to Britain and to these Pegu was added after the Second Burmese War of 1852. The notorious King Thibaw ruled Upper Burma from 1876 to 1885 when again Britain was compelled to take action. Annexation of Upper Burma was proclaimed on January 1, 1886, and Burma, despite its differences in population and indeed in almost every respect, became a province, the largest province, of India. For long it was considered by many the 'Cinderella province' and was finally separated from India in 1937. In December 1941 the Japanese invaded the country, which suffered severely during the British retreat as well as from the occupation and from the battles fought during the re-conquest in 1945. The liberating troops performed the almost incredible feat of crossing the mountain barriers from India and driving the Japanese southwards. Britain acceded to the demand for independence but it was a severely disorganized country which the Burmese leaders took over. The Union of Burma comprises Burma proper (the former British territories of Upper and Lower Burma) and five states: Kayah State (formerly Karenni), Kanthoolei (Karen State) in the south, the former Federated Shan States and Wa States reorganized as the 'Shan State',

---

[1] I am greatly indebted to Professor Daw Thin Kyi for invaluable help during my re-visits to Burma in February 1955 and January 1960.

a new 'Kachin State' in the north and a Chin Territory (see Fig. 211). War between the Burmese and the Karens and later with insurgent groups hindered the rehabilitation of the country until about 1959.

The country as a whole is cut off by mountain barriers and difficult hill country from its neighbours and so is remarkably isolated. It is geographically part of Indo-China rather than of India and was indeed

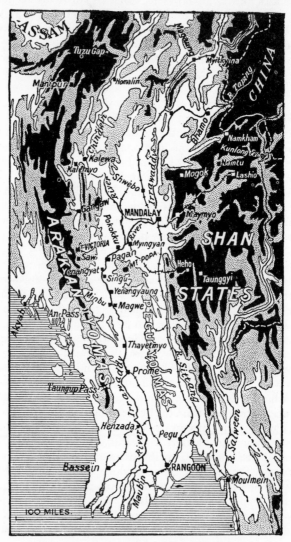

FIG. 200.—General map of the heart of Burma

Land over 1,000 feet, dotted; land over 3,000 feet, black. The north and south alignment of the physical features and the threefold division of the country are readily apparent.

long known to the French as 'Indo-Chine anglaise'. It stretches from 9° 55′ to about 28° 30′ of North Latitude and from Longitude 92° 10′ to 101° 9′ East of Greenwich. It thus has an extreme length from north to south of about 1,200 miles and an extreme width of 575 miles. The area is variously estimated: that given by United Nations Demographic Year Book 1957 is 677,980 km.[2] or 260,600 square miles. Of this Burma proper is about 184,000 square miles. With a total population of between 20 and 21 millions many parts are sparsely inhabited.

Roughly a third of Burma lies outside the Tropics, but the configuration of the country, like that of Indo-Pakistan, is such that the whole may be regarded as a tropical country.

Structure. Burma falls naturally into three great geomorphological units:

(a) The Arakan Yoma, a great series of fold ranges of Alpine age, which forms the barrier between Burma and India. The foothills of the Arakan Yoma stretch as far as the shores of the Bay of Bengal.

(b) The Shan Plateau massif, occupying the whole of the east of the country and extending southwards into Tenasserim. The massif forms part of what has been called the Indo-Malayan Mountain System and has existed as a geomorphological unit since the close of the Mesozoic.

(c) The Central Basin, lying between the Arakan Yoma and the Shan Plateau. Formerly a gulf of the early Tertiary Sea, open to the south, it is now occupied by a great spread of Tertiary rocks.

The great mountain range of the Arakan Yoma and its continuation northwards has a core of old crystalline rocks. On either side are hard, tightly-folded, sedimentary rocks, mainly Tertiary in age. A small part of Burma—the Division of Arakan—lies between the Arakan Yoma and the Bay of Bengal. Some of the peaks of the Arakan Yoma rise to over 10,000 feet and the highest is believed to be Mount Victoria. The whole range forms an effective barrier between Burma and India proper. Chromite and other useful minerals are known to occur, especially in association with serpentine intrusions, but are not at present exploited. The western edge of the Shan Plateau massif is well marked, both physically and geologically. It rises abruptly from the valley and for 400 or 500 miles the edge is formed by a long strip of granitic or gneissose rocks. The plateau averages 3,000 feet in height, but its surface has been much dissected and running through the centre from north to south is the deep trough occupied by the Salween River. Southwards the plateau passes through Kayah and the Karen State into Tenasserim and gradually loses its plateau character. The predominant rocks in the Shan Plateau are gneisses—which yield the

rubies and other gemstones for which Burma has so long been famous—
and a massive limestone of Devono-Carboniferous age. Rocks of all
ages from pre-Cambrian to Jurassic occur in the massif, whilst deposits
of late Tertiary and Pleistocene age occupy old lake-basins. In pre-
Cambrian rocks at Mogok occur the principal ruby 'mines'—the workings are open-cast—but the industry is now of minor importance. At
Bawdwin, associated with a group of ancient volcanic rocks, are very

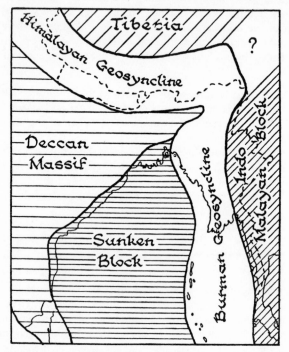

FIG. 201.—The structural units in eastern India and Burma, showing the relation of
the oil belts of Burma (Fig. 202) and Assam to the geosynclinal areas of early
Tertiary times

extensive deposits of silver-lead ore, mainly argentiferous galena,
smelted at the nearby works of Namtu. The refined silver and lead are
sent by rail to Rangoon for export. Other silver-lead deposits are known
in other parts of the Shan States and have been worked in the past by
the Chinese. Tenasserim forms a continuation of the tin-bearing belt
of Malaya and large quantities of tin and tungsten are obtained.
Geologically this portion of the Indo-Malayan Mountains consists of
large granitic intrusions, elongated in the north-south direction and
intruded into a series of ancient rocks of unknown age. The basin of the
Irrawaddy between the Arakan Yoma and the Shan Plateau consists

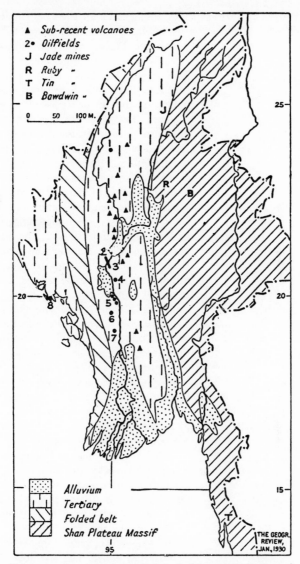

Legend on map:
▲ Sub-recent volcanoes
2• Oilfields
J Jade mines
R Ruby "
T Tin "
B Bawdwin "

0   50   100 M.

Alluvium
Tertiary
Folded belt
Shan Plateau Massif

THE GEOGR.
REVIEW,
JAN., 1930

FIG. 202.—An outline geological map of Burma (L. D. Stamp)

Showing the oilfields of Burma, lying in the old gulf between the Arakan Yoma on the west and the Shan plateau on the east.

The oilfields are numbered: **1**, Indaw; **2**, Yenangyat-Lanywa; **3**, Singu-Chauk; **4**, Yenangyaung; **5**, Minbu; **6**, Yenanma; **7**, Padaukbin; **8**, Arakan.

The Singu field (3) extends northwards under the river Irrawaddy. In the years 1925–30 a great wall was constructed enclosing a sandbank on the opposite shore of the river. The reclaimed area became the model oilfield of Lanywa, producing 30 million gallons a year. Of the fields shown above only Lanywa-Singu and Yenangyaung can be described as important. In addition to the oilfields the Pyaye gasfield is near 7 and tin ore has been mined at Mawchi in Kayah State to the south of the Shan State.

almost entirely of Tertiary rocks, remarkable for their enormous thickness. This is for the most part a lowland area, with ranges of hills—of which the Pegu Yoma are the most important—running from north to south. The Pegu Yoma in fact separate the southern part into a western part—the valley of the lower Irrawaddy—and an eastern, the valley of the Sittang. The northern part is drained entirely by the Irrawaddy and its tributaries, including the Chindwin. Forming a line down the centre of the western basin are the well-known oilfields of Burma. From north to south are the fields of Indaw, Yenangyat-Lanywa, Singu, Yenangyaung, Minbu and several minor fields. The most important fields are Yenangyaung and Singu. Brown coal also occurs in considerable quantities in the valley of the Chindwin (a semi-bituminous seam is being opened up near Kalewa) and elsewhere in the Tertiary rocks, but as yet has been little used. Along a line running roughly along the centre of the ancient Tertiary trough are numerous extinct volcanoes: some form small tuff cones with small crater lakes; others are plugs of rhyolitic matter, but the largest is the complex cone of Mount Popa, reaching a height of nearly 5,000 feet above sea-level.

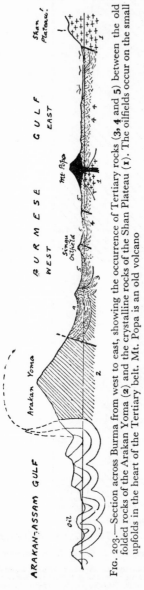

FIG. 203.—Section across Burma from west to east, showing the occurrence of Tertiary rocks (3, 4 and 5) between the old folded rocks of the Arakan Yoma (2) and the crystalline rocks of the Shan Plateau (1). The oilfields occur on the small upfolds in the heart of the Tertiary belt. Mt. Popa is an old volcano

The Arakan coast of Burma is Pacific in type; it is rocky and dangerous, backed by high mountains and fringed by islands. Of the islands, Ramree and Cheduba are the largest. The Tenasserim coast is similar, in the south is the Mergui Archipelago. Between the Arakan and Tenasserim coasts lies the low delta of the Irrawaddy and Sittang Rivers.

Most of the hilly and mountainous regions were formerly forest-covered and over large areas have good fertile forest soils. Where clearings have been made, temporary cultivation has destroyed the virgin richness of the soil. In the wetter regions the heavy rains often entirely wash away the soil from cleared hillsides and expose the bare rock. The limestone rocks of the Shan Plateau are usually covered by a thin red soil, from which the lime has been entirely leached out. The richest soils in the province are the alluvial soils of the flat Irrawaddy Delta and the broad river valleys. Excellent loamy soil is also afforded by the mixed clays and sands of the Peguan rocks, but the Irrawaddian and other sandy series give rise to extensive tracts of very light soil, almost pure sand. In the wetter parts of Burma, owing to the well-marked dry season, a thick mantle of lateritic soil stretches over most of the lowland tracts.

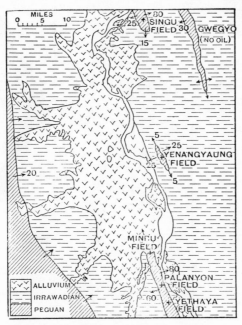

FIG. 204.—Sketch-map showing the position of the Yenangyaung Oilfield of Burma

The Peguan are the oil-bearing strata, and the richness of the field is associated with the isolation of the small upfold and the consequent wide 'gathering ground' for the oil.

Climate. The climate of Burma is closely comparable with that of India: the seasons are the same and no separate description is necessary. Burma has a marked 'dry belt' in the heart of the country which, in a minor degree, acts as a low-pressure area during the rainy season. Both monsoons tend to have a north-south direction, owing to the alignment of the mountains and valleys. The great variation in rainfall in Burma is noteworthy. Most of Arakan and Tenasserim have nearly 200 inches of rain; in the heart of the Dry Belt the rainfall is as low as 20 inches. Along the coast, and especially in the south (Tenasserim), both the daily and annual range of temperature are small. In Moulmein the annual range is 8°; in Rangoon it is 10°. Away from the moderating influence of the sea, the range of temperature increases greatly and is especially large in the Dry Belt. The annual range in Mandalay is 20°. The average temperature in the south of Burma is about 80°; it decreases as one goes northwards. In the extreme north sea-level temperature ranges from about 63° in January to 85° in May.

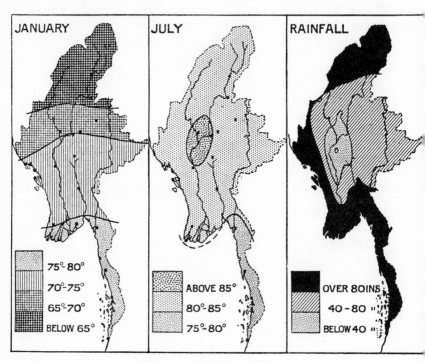

FIG. 205.—The climate of Burma

Vegetation. The wide range of rainfall in Burma is responsible for great variations in the natural vegetation. Frost never occurs in the lowlands, but roughly above 3,000 feet the occasional frosts have caused a great change in vegetation. Above that level, which may conveniently be called the frost line, evergreen oak forests, sporadic pine forests and wide areas of open land with bracken and grass are the rule. Rhododendron forests occur at higher levels. Below the frost line the natural vegetation depends mainly upon the rainfall, and the same divisions are distinguished as in India:

(a) With more than 80 inches of rain, evergreen tropical rain forests occur. The forests are of many species of trees, but

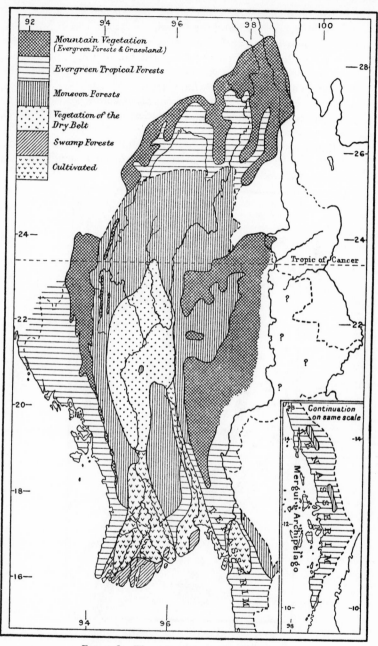

Fig. 206.—The natural vegetation of Burma

more than one-half belong to the Dipterocarpaceae. The
timbers are hard and little used.

(b) With between 40 and 80 inches of rain are the monsoon forests
which lose their leaves during the hot season. These forests
are the home of the valuable teak tree as well as of the pyinkado and other useful timber trees.

(c) With less than 40 inches the forest becomes very poor and
passes into scrubland and semi-desert. There is little or no
true grassland.

(d) Extensive areas of the Irrawaddy Delta are clothed with tidal
forests, in which some of the trees reach a height of over
100 feet and are of considerable value.

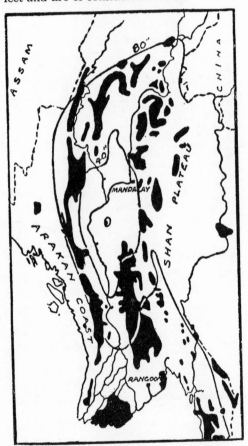

FIG. 207.—The reserved forests of Burma

The principal forests 'reserved' by the Government are those monsoon forests containing teak and
pyinkado and hence are found, as this map shows, mainly in those regions where the rainfall is between
40 and 80 inches annually. The principal exceptions are the tidal forests of the Delta.

The wasteful methods of the cultivator have, in the past, resulted in the destruction of vast areas of valuable forest. The practice was to cut down and burn a tract of virgin forest, cultivate the field (taung-ya) so formed for two or three years while the pristine freshness of the soil lasted and then to desert it for a fresh tract. It was but rarely that the forest established itself again over the deserted taung-ya, more often the area became covered with a tangled mass of bamboo, bracken or grass. For more than a century, however, the Forest Department has been at work, and all the valuable forest areas constituted into Government Reserves. Various privileges are accorded to those who live within the reserved area; the timber (mainly teak for constructional work and pyinkado—*Xylia dolabriformis*—for railway sleepers) is worked now by the State Timber Extraction Corporation under careful supervision. Extraction has long been so controlled that it shall not exceed regeneration. Timber is normally second or third in importance amongst the exports of Burma. As the annexed table shows more than half Burma is forested.

BURMA—LAND USE 1950

Arable	.	.	.	.	.	21·1 mn. acres	12·6 per cent.
Irrigated	.	.	.	.	.	1·3 ,, ,,	0·8 ,, ,,
Forest and Woodland	.	.	.	.	96·6 ,, ,,	57·7 ,, ,,
Unused, potentially productive	.	.	.	19·3 ,, ,,	11·5 ,, ,,
Other land	.	.	.	.	30·5 ,, ,,	18·2 ,, ,,
Total .	.	.	.	.	167·5 ,, ,,	100·0 ,, ,,

Excluding Shan State, Putao, Chin Hills, Naga Hills and Karenni. Not all the arable was actually cropped in 1950, hence the lower figures in the next table.

Products

Agriculture. Burma is essentially an agricultural country. Only 11 per cent. of the people were classed as urban in 1931, and despite the later growth of Rangoon the proportion has not greatly increased. The agriculture is concentrated on the alluvial lands of the Delta and the valleys of the Irrawaddy, Chindwin and Sittang. Rice is by far the most important crop and occupies two-thirds of the cropped area. The production of rice is steadily recovering to the pre-war total of 7,000,000 tons per year, or over a third of a ton per head of population. There is, in consequence, a large surplus available for export. As rice has to be transplanted as well as sown and irrigated, it needs a considerable amount of labour expended on it; and the Burman has the reputation of being a somewhat indolent cultivator. The Karens and Shans who settle in the plains expend more care in ploughing and weeding their crops. Where the rainfall is less than 40 inches rice cannot be grown without irrigation, and cultivation in the Dry Zone is largely concentrated on sesamum, millet, ground-nuts, cotton and beans. In the Dry Belt nearly 1½ million acres are irrigated. At the time of the British annexation of Burma there were some old irrigation systems in the Kyaukse and Minbu Districts, which had been allowed to fall into disrepair, and these were later renewed and extended. In addition to this the Mandalay Canal, 40 miles in length, with fourteen distributaries, was opened in 1902; the Shwebo Canal, 27 miles long, was opened in 1906, and later two branches 29 and 20 miles in length, and the Mon Canal, begun in 1904, 53 miles in length. Throughout the country, fruits, vegetables and tobacco with fodder where required are grown for home consumption. In comparison with India, there is room for considerable agricultural expansion in Burma. The old official returns of 1930–1 used to class 60,000,000 acres as cultivable waste, as against under 20,000,000 acres of 'occupied' land. The figures in the table given above from FAO sources are more realistic but still emphasize the large area potentially productive. The principal crops are shown in the following table:

AGRICULTURAL PRODUCTION

	Area (acres), 000		Production (metric tons), 000	
	1934–8	1962–3	1934–8	1962–3
Rice	12,327	11,953	6,971	7,289
Maize	210	c. 160	39	c. 30
Dry beans	365	1,709	71	204
Ground-nuts	765	1,530	176	422
Sugar	—	111	101	120
Sesamum	1,437	1,573	50	78
Cotton	495	551	ginned 21	52
Tobacco	100	120	45	48
Rubber	—	—	8	9

From FAO and other sources. Excluding Shan States and certain hill tracts.

In addition the millets of the Dry Zone occupy 606,000 acres (1962–3). The rubber plantations are in the south, mainly in Mergui and Tavoy.

LIVESTOCK

	1938	1952	1956
Horses	51,000	12,000	14,000
Mules	1,000	1,000	1,000
Cattle	5,194,000	4,575,000	4,798,000
Pigs	530,000	440,000	522,000
Sheep	82,000	28,000	37,000
Goats	293,000	190,000	239,000
Buffaloes . . .	1,018,000	765,000	874,000

These figures are for Burma proper. There are many more animals in the hills. They suggest the rather slow post-War recovery in contrast to rapid population growth.

Domestic Animals. Small humped oxen are kept everywhere as beasts of burden and for use in ploughing. They are replaced to a considerable extent in the Delta and wetter areas by the heavier water buffalo. The possession of a pair of bullocks or buffalo for dragging the simple wooden plough or the springless two-wheeled cart is essential to every cultivator, hence the large numbers involved. There is as yet little development of dairying but a drive to improve cattle is taking place and big cattle-farms have been established at Minbu and elsewhere in the Dry Belt. Herds of small goats are numerous in the Dry Belt and small numbers of very poor sheep are reared.

Fisheries. Fisheries and fish-curing exist both along the sea-coast of Burma and in inland tracts and as many as 100,000 persons may be classed as primarily fishermen. Salted fish and the strong-smelling fish-paste known as *ngapi* form important articles of food, lending variety to the basic diet of boiled rice. As population and purchasing power increase there are opportunities for expansion and more systematic development of fisheries. There are in addition some pearling grounds in the Mergui Archipelago, which have been worked spasmodically for mother-of-pearl.

Minerals. It must be understood that the working of minerals in Burma on modern lines was developed by companies with British capital and British executive personnel. The oil wells and other installations were deliberately put out of action to avoid their falling into the hands of the Japanese invaders. Since the liberation the process of restoring the mineral industries has been slow, especially because of the disturbed state of the country. In addition conditions laid down by the now independent Government of Burma require or may require reorganization of companies previously operating in the country. The table on p. 394 shows the general position.

By far the most important mineral produced was oil, known and worked in hand-dug wells at Yenangyaung for at least a couple of centuries and worked by modern methods since the eighteen-eighties. The largest of the oil companies, the Burmah Oil Company Limited, sent the oil from Singu and Yenangyaung by pipeline to refineries at Syriam near Rangoon: other companies used river barges. From 1909 to 1939 the annual production did not depart widely from a million metric tons a year (255,000,000 gallons), a policy of steady production and conservation of reserves being followed. Burmese oils are too rich in the valuable petrol for them to be used economically as crude. Since independence a refinery at Chauk (Singu) supplies much of the internal needs of the heart of the country; the refinery at Syriam has been reopened and the Government has reached a sharing agreement with the Burmah Oil Company.

A natural gasfield (Pyaye) which I had a share in discovering in 1924–5 was later developed to supply fuel to an important cement works—a new industry, now nationalized—on the Irrawaddy near Thayetmyo. In 1959 gas pressure dropped and a search was made for new supplies.

Little use has been made of the extensive deposits of brown coal or lignite found in the Chindwin Valley and in old lake basins in the Shan Plateau. Some of the latter also have oil shale. Rather better coal deposits near Kalewa in the Chindwin Valley still await development. Attention has been turned to the development of hydro-electric power and power from works in Kayah State reached Rangoon in 1960.

MINERAL PRODUCTION

	1935	1939	1960
Burma proper			
Tin concentrates, tons	4,268	5,441	1,790
Tungsten concentrates, tons	2,522	4,342	880
Antimony, tons	34	345	—
Rubies and sapphires, carats	107,915	222,102	2,247
Jadeite, cwt.	1,265	767	1,400
Gold, oz.	1,485	1,206	194
Shan State			
Silver, 000 oz.	5,279	6,175	1,888
Bawdwin			
Lead and concentrates, tons	72,060	77,180	576
Zinc, tons	78,590	59,347	17,010
Copper matte, tons	8,950	7,935	172
Nickel spiers, tons	4,850	2,896	706
Iron ore, tons	25,085	26,259	—
Karenni			
Tin and tungsten concentrates, tons	4,989	5,593	incl. above
Burma			
Petroleum, tons	970,421	1,064,376	530,000

The silver, lead, zinc, copper and nickel in the above table represent the output of the Bawdwin mines of the former Burma Corporation Limited—one of the companies reorganized under the laws of the Republic with the Government participating. The mines of Tenasserim first produced large quantities of tin and tungsten during the First World War but later the output fluctuated widely with the price of the metals.

In the Mogok or Ruby Mines area alluvial rubies, spinels and other precious stones were long obtained by washing superficial deposits. Under ancient laws and customs women enjoyed special privileges not accorded to men and most of the washing was done by them. Later systematic washing and rock mining were undertaken. The historic Burma Ruby Mines Limited after many vicissitudes went into liquidation in 1925-6. Changes in fashion and the development of artificial rubies dealt it the death blow.

The famous jade of China is found in the north of Burma and exported overland to China via Mogaung and Bhamo. The mines are situated beyond Kamaing, north of Mogaung, in the Myitkyina District. The miners are all Kachins. The value varies enormously according to colour, which should be a particular shade of dark green. Semi-transparency, brilliancy and hardness are, however, also essentials. The old river mines produced the best quality. The quarry mines produce larger quantities, but the quality is not good.

Gold is found in most of the rivers in Upper Burma, but the gold-washing industry is for the most part spasmodic in the intervals of agriculture.

Amber is extracted by Kachins in the Hukawng Valley, but the quality of the fossil resin is not very good.

Salt is manufactured at various places in Upper Burma, notably in the lower Chindwin, Sagaing, Shwebo, Myingyan and Yamethin Districts, as well as in the Shan States and at Bassein.

Iron ore is found in many parts of the hills, and was formerly worked for local smelting by inhabitants of the country.

Communications. From time immemorial the principal highway of Burma has been the Irrawaddy and its tributaries.[1] Most of the 600 steamers of the Irrawaddy Flotilla Company were sunk in a deep part of the upper Irrawaddy to prevent them from falling into the hands of the Japanese. The Government now has an Inland Water Transport Board to provide river transport. The railways have rather supplemented than replaced the rivers as highways of trade. The metre-gauge Burma Railways were taken over by the Government of India in January 1929, and now form a State system of over 2,000 miles, though reduced to half that total during the occupation. The main line runs from Rangoon to Mandalay, where it was formerly interrupted by the Irrawaddy, but is continued on the opposite bank of the river to Myitkyina. A magnificent rail and road bridge, three-quarters of a mile long, was opened in 1934, destroyed during the Japanese invasion, reopened 1954. There is no railway connection with India, nor with any neighbouring country. The centre of the oil-fields, Yenangyaung, is still inaccessible by railway. Until the nineteen-thirties Burma was virtually without roads, but over 5,000 miles of metalled road are now open, including a good motor road from Rangoon to Mandalay. The famous Burma Road runs from Lashio in Burma (and from Bhamo) 800 miles to Kunming in China. The

[1] See L. D. Stamp, 'The Irrawaddy River', *Geog. Jour.*, **95,** 1940, 329-56.

wartime Stillwell Road from Ledo in Assam to Myitkyina in Burma and the road through Manipur to Kalewa are now disused. Outside Rangoon and Mandalay hotels are almost unknown: away from the ·ailway, river or motor road much of the travel is still by bullock cart —in the hills by elephant or mule—covering about 15 miles a day. There are rest houses, built primarily for Government officials on our, where the traveller may obtain shelter for a nominal payment, hough he must make his own preparations for food and bedding. Most of the smaller villages of Burma consist of a collection of from a dozen to a hundred or more huts, built of timber uprights and bamboo and in the heart of the country surrounded by a stockade against wild animals and dacoits or robbers.[1] The civil head of the village is the thugyi or headman, chosen by the villagers and recognized by Government; the spiritual head of the village is the senior hpoongyi of the hpoongyi-kyaung. Larger villages or towns arise as collecting or distributing centres or have important bazaars. In many cases their importance has been enhanced by their having been made the administrative headquarters of a district or a division. A large number of the more important towns are river ports—Bhamo, Kalewa, Monywa, Sagaing, Mandalay, Pakokku, Myingyan, Salè, Yenangyaung, Magwe, Minbu, Allanmyo, Thayetmyo, Prome and Henzada afford examples. Much use is now made of air transport.

Manufactures and Art. The staple industry of Burma is agriculture, but many cultivators are also artisans in the by-season. In addition to rice-growing and the felling and extraction of timber, and the fisheries, the chief occupations are rice-husking, silk-weaving and dyeing. The introduction of cheap cottons and silk fabrics has dealt a blow to hand-weaving, while aniline dyes are driving out the native vegetable product; but both industries still linger in the rural tracts. The best silk-weavers are to be found at Amarapura (Mandalay) where there is a famous school. There large numbers of people follow this occupation as their sole means of livelihood, whereas silk and cotton weaving throughout the country generally is carried on by girls and women while unoccupied by other domestic duties. The Burmese are fond of bright colours, and pink and yellow harmonize well with their dark olive complexion, but even here the influence of Western civilization is being felt, and in the towns the tendency now is towards maroon, brown, olive and dark green for the women's skirts. The total number of persons engaged in the production of textile fabrics in Burma, according to the Census of 1931, was 284,800, against 419,007 in 1901. The chief dye-product of Burma is cutch, a yellow and brown dye obtained from the wood of the *sha* tree, used for dyeing the yellow robes of the Buddhist monks. Cutch-boiling formed the chief means of livelihood of a number of the poorer classes in the Prome and Thayet-

[1] See O. H. K. Spate, 'The Burmese Village', *Geog. Rev.*, **35,** 1945, 525–43.

myo districts of Lower Burma. Cheroot-making is widespread and smoking is universal among both sexes. The chief traditional arts of Burma are lacquer working (centred at Pagan), wood-carving and silver work.

Modern industry began with oil-working and refining, timber-working, rice milling, railway engineering and metalliferous mining. The Burmans took readily to motor transport and a demand for motor mechanics sprang up. Although industrialization has been hindered by the disturbed conditions following the Japanese occupation, there are now many small-scale works associated especially with the phenomenal growth of Rangoon. In addition there are textile mills, and the fine modern works of the State-owned Burma Pharmaceutical Industry pre-pare drugs for the whole country.

Population. The population of the Republic of Burma at the Census of 1953, partly estimated, was about 19,045,000. This compare with a Census total of 16,823,798 in 1941 (details were destroyed in the Japanese occupation), 14,667,146 in 1931 and 13,212,192 in 1921. In the latter year the density was only 57; it is still only about 90, or half that of India. It is still essentially a rural population. Rangoon even with its huge influx of refugees had only 688,000 in 1963 (with suburbs 1,530,000) and Mandalay 213,000. The only other town which touched 100,000 was Moulmein. Estimated total mid-1963, 23,735,000

The inhabitants of Burma belong to many races and speak many languages. The indigenous peoples are Mongolians; the Burmans are the most advanced and occupy the fertile lowlands; the other races are largely restricted to the hills. Large numbers of Indians have long been attracted to Burma by the higher rates of wages, the opportunities for trading and cultivation, and Rangoon in the inter-war years was said to be the largest immigration port in the world. Those who came as coolie labour to Rangoon were naturally men, with the result that males outnumbered females by up to 10 to 1, creating difficult social conditions. The relationship with the indigenous population was not always harmonious and when the British withdrew many Indians re-turned to India. Others had settled permanently and decided to remain, but the Indian population remains smaller than before.

It is believed that Burma has been populated by successive waves of migration from the north; indeed, the advance of the Kachin races was still in progress when Burma was annexed to the British Empire.

The Burmans, including the closely allied Arakanese of the Arakan coast, the Mons of the country around Moulmein and the Tavoyans around Tavoy, embrace 80 per cent. of the total population. They have the broad, flat Mongolian face, but not the almond-shaped eye, of the Chinese. Their skin varies in colour from a pale brown to a dark coffee brown. Some of the town-bred Burmese ladies are no darker than the average north European. The national dress consists of a cylindrical skirt, called a lungyi, worn folded over in a simple fold in the front and reaching to the ankles. All Burmese, of both sexes, prefer silks of bright but delicate shades and even the poorest possesses at least one silk lungyi. The distinctive Burmese silk, woven round Mandalay

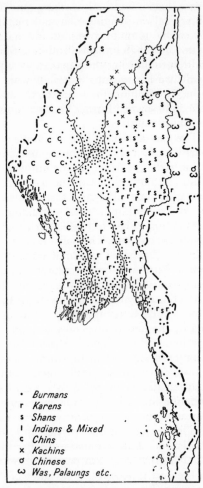

● Burmans
r Karens
s Shans
ı Indians & Mixed
c Chins
× Kachins
ơ Chinese
ꞷ Was, Palaungs etc.

FIG. 208.—The approximate distribution of the population of Burma

Each dot or other symbol represents 1,500 people. The concentration in the valleys of the Irrawaddy and Sittang and the deltas should be noted.

and Inlè Lake, is still in general use. The lungyi is worn by both sexes; the men wear also a single-breasted short jacket of sombre hue, called an 'aingyi'; the women's garment is similar but double-breasted and usually white. The older generation of Burmese men wear their straight black hair long, tied in a knot on one side of the head. It is now general to cut the hair in European style. The men's head-dress is the fast-disappearing gaungbaung—a strip of brightly coloured thin silk wound round the head. The women formerly oiled their long tresses with coconut oil and arranged them in a cylindrical coil on the top of the head. Now a quick knot at the back is more usual. Flowers are used to decorate the hair, but a head-dress is never used.

The Burmans are Buddhists and their religion occupies a large place in their life. The spiritual head of every village is the yellow-robed hpoongyi or monk. The monastery or hpoongyi-kyaung just outside the village walls is also the village school. Every village has its pagoda, a silent reminder of the precepts of Buddha, and whitewashed pagodas crown almost every hill, but there are no temples in the ordinary sense of the word. As a result of the numerous village schools, the percentage of wholly illiterate men is small. The women are more industrious and businesslike than the men, but their school education has been neglected. The Burmese women enjoy an amount of freedom unusual in non-European races. As a whole the Burmese are characterized by cleanliness, a sense of humour and a love of sport, but prefer a life of ease to one of sustained work.

The various hill tribes are in general less advanced than the Burmese. Perhaps the most advanced are the Karens, who inhabit the Pegu Yoma, the Karen and Kayah States (Fig. 211) and have settled also in the Delta. Strife between the Karens and Burmans has been one of the unhappy features of the post-war situation. The Shans occupy most of the Shan Plateau and are also found in the upper part of the Chindwin Valley. The Kachins belong mainly to the far north, the Chins to the western mountains, whilst on the Chinese borders are found the Palaungs, Was, etc. All the hill tribes of Burma are non-Buddhists; their religion is described by the general term Animism. Christianity has made rapid strides amongst them, especially amongst the Karens.

The Indians have settled mainly in the Rangoon area, in Arakan and along the rivers and railway lines. Except in the remoter districts, Indians formerly supplied much of the coolie labour, and the Indian moneylender was much in evidence. There were roughly a million Indians in pre-1941 Burma, comprising about equal numbers of Hindus and Mahommedans and drawn mainly from Madras, Bihar, Orissa and Bengal. The total is now probably about half that.

The Chinese form an important community. Except on the border in the north-east the Chinese belong essentially to the artisan and merchant classes and make excellent law-abiding citizens.

Commerce. The foreign trade of Burma for a recent year is shown in the table on p. 404. It is shown in kyats, the new currency introduced by the Government of the Republic, a kyat being equivalent to an Indian rupee (currently 1s. 6d.). The total trade had recovered, in 1962–3, to about K.2,370 m., nominally £180 million.

The development of Burma's trade in pre-war years is now mainly of historic interest. Rice was the staple export—two-thirds of the total by value, followed by petroleum products, teak, metals and concentrates, cotton, hides and skins.

The bulk of the foreign trade of Burma passes through Rangoon.[1] Other leading ports are Bassein, a rice port on the west of the Delta; Akyab, the outlet of Arakan; and Moulmein, Tavoy and Mergui, which serve Tenasserim. Government steamers (replacing the British India Steamship Company) link Rangoon with these outlying ports, but much travel is by air.

1963

Imports		Exports	
£ million			
Total	78·2		94·3
Textiles	19·1	Rice and products	59·6
Iron and steel	8·1	Oil seeds	6·4
Machinery	10·7	Teak and other	
Chemicals	8·2	hardwood	10·7
Vehicles	4·3	Rubber	2·2
Milk	3·8	Cotton	3·2
Coal and coke⎫		Metals and ores	3·2
Mineral oil ⎭	3·8		

Natural Regions. For an adequate study of this large and varied country, a division into at least seven natural regions is desirable:

1. *The Arakan Coastal Strip.* The Arakan coast is of the Pacific type and the folded foothills of the Arakan Yoma approach closely to the Bay of Bengal in many areas. The actual coastal strip, therefore, may be said to comprise those areas which are sufficiently level to permit of settlement and agricultural development but which are both small and scattered, though including a considerable and important tract of alluvium in the hinterland of Akyab, and also a number of large islands such as Ramree Island. The coast is much broken up, both by rocky headlands and islands and by stretches of mangrove swamps. As a result natural harbours are numerous, but the mountainous country of the hinterland and the difficulty of communication across the Arakan Yoma have prevented the development of any considerable ports, with the single exception of Akyab. The whole area has a heavy rainfall,

---

[1] The port and city of Rangoon form a most interesting study—both are virtually the product of the last century. The situation controlling both water and land routes into the heart of the country should be noted. See O. H. K. Spate and L. W. Trueblood, *Geog. Rev.*, **32**, 1942, 56–73.

often excessive, and soil erosion by heavy downpours is much to be feared. The remnants of a dense evergreen forest cover exist, but the forest cover has been largely replaced by dense bamboo thickets. Of the cropped land, rice occupies 90 per cent. of the area, whilst the sea

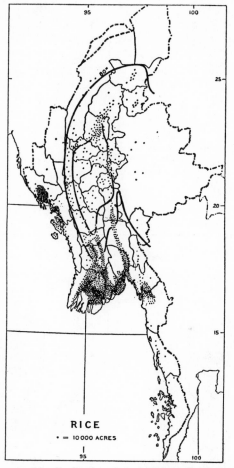

RICE

• = 10 000 ACRES

FIG. 209.—The distribution of rice in Burma (L. D. Stamp)

provides the second main product, fish. The cultivated land is mainly in the vicinity of Akyab, the chief town and port. Such is the isolation of the region that there is little communication with the rest of Burma except by sea, and the Arakanese speak a distinctive dialect. Some Arakanese even desire a separate state. Recently the port of Kyaukpyu has been developed and air services afford a ready link with Rangoon.

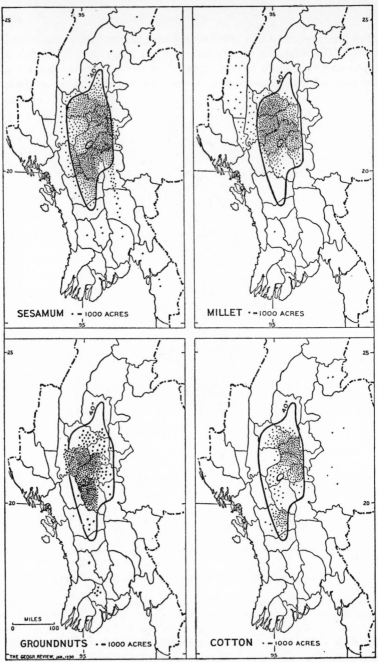

FIG. 210.—The distribution of the four chief 'Dry Zone' crops of Burma
(L. D. Stamp)

2. *Tenasserim.* This region resembles Arakan in many respects—in the north and south alignment of the physical features, in the broken coastline and the limited areas of cultivable land. Geologically there is a contrast—the complex of old sediments penetrated by large granite masses is associated with the occurrence of ores of tin and tungsten and a considerable mining development. Climatically the rainfall is heavy, as in Arakan, but, being nearer the Equator, the dry season is shorter and renders the area suitable for rubber planting. As in Arakan, fishing is important, but the pearling grounds of the Mergui Archipelago are less important than formerly. Many of the smaller islands are inhabited by primitive peoples, often called the sea gypsies. The coasts are sheltered by the outer fringe of islands, and fishing villages of bamboo huts built out over the water occur at frequent intervals. The chief tract of cultivable land—essentially for rice—is in the immediate hinterland of the chief town and port, Moulmein. It exports timber, including some teak from over the Thai border. A railway from Moulmein to Bangkok was long suggested and during the occupation the Japanese linked the Thai and Burmese systems by a line constructed with prisoner-of-war labour, at least a third of the prisoners dying during the work. The line has been abandoned.

3. *The Western Hills Region.* This region comprises the Arakan Yoma and its satellite hill ranges of folded sedimentary rocks, having nearly all a north and south alignment. Forest covers most of the hills from base to summit—valuable teak forests on the drier eastern side of the region. The region is the home of the Chins—and such is the isolation of individual valleys that almost every one had its own dialect. The villages are small, internecine strife was common, life difficult. The poor crops of maize, millet or hill rice are grown on small patches of shifting cultivation known as taungyas. The appallingly wasteful system of burning down the forest for these clearings resulted in the destruction of vast quantities of valuable timber. Passes across the region are few and difficult and the foothills are unhealthy and fever-ridden. The Second World War changed the position. Fort White and Tiddim became accessible by road and now the progressive Chin Territory is easily reached by air.

4. *The Shan Plateau.* This geographical region coincides closely in extent with the Shan State and is a continuation of the Yunnan Plateau of China and of northern Thailand. The word Shan is probably the same as Siam. The plateau has a rolling surface and the Burmese portion is generally between 3,000 and 4,000 feet above sea-level and terminates abruptly on the west in an almost continuous scarp edge 3,000 feet high overlooking the plains of central Burma. The edge has isolated the plateau; wheeled vehicles long remained unknown in the Shan States—even the familiar bullock-cart. The plateau is sparsely inhabited by hill peoples, of which the Shans are the chief, but which

include also Kachins, Palaungs and Was. Some of the last were, and possibly still are, head-hunters and the territory east of the Salween remained largely 'unadministered'. There are immense tracts of the plateau suitable for crops, including temperate fruits, and the rainfall is believed to average about 60 inches. The minerals are important—especially the silver-lead mines of Bawdwin. The Shan Plateau is penetrated by two railway lines and several good motor roads. Maymyo was the hot-weather seat of the Government in British days and is now an army training centre; Kalaw is another hill station. On the surface of the plateau are several lakes, decreasing in size, including Lake Inlé, where are found the famous 'leg-rowers'. The principal villages in the Shan States are those which form the capitals of the former little states which made up the Federation. The ruler of each state was a Sawbwa but the Sawbwas have now relinquished their powers. The State Council meets at Taunggyi. Southwards the Shan Plateau passes into deeply dissected country, drained by the Salween but reached more easily from the north or by road from Toungoo. It now forms the Kayah State with its capital at Pa-an. Southward the new Karen State is inhabited by the bulk of the Karens.

5. *The Northern Hills Region*. This region occupies the north of Burma and includes the source of the Irrawaddy and its principal tributary, the Chindwin. The whole territory slopes southwards from the mountain rim, and the forested mountains of the north—including much wild country sparsely inhabited by Kachins and Shans and still partly unadministered—give place gradually southwards to lower hills with fertile valleys occupied by Burmans. In the famous 'triangle' between the Mali Kha and the 'Nmai-Kha—the two headstreams of the Irrawaddy—strenuous efforts had to be made as late as the twenties to abolish slavery. The Chindwin is navigable by flat-bottomed steamers of small draught to about Lat. 24° N., the Irrawaddy regularly to Bhamo, whence there is a well-known trade route to Yunnan. The railway penetrates still farther north to Myitkyina, but it is still nearly 300 miles by jeep track to the northernmost administrative centre of Puta-O. From this northern region comes the jade so popular in China, as well as some inferior amber. Most of this region now lies in the Kachin State which comprises the districts of Puta-O, Myitkyina and Bhamo.

6. *The Dry Belt*. The Dry Belt occupies the heart of Burma. It is a flattish and fairly thickly populated region, extensively cultivated and having some irrigated areas. It is approximately delimited by the 40-inch isohyet and has large areas of light sandy soils. The characteristic 'Dry Zone' crops are well shown in the distribution diagrams. The Dry Belt is the natural heart of Burma, and so long as Burma remained an independent kingdom or land empire, it was natural that the capital of the country should be here. No less than seven former capitals do indeed

lie in the Dry Belt—including Mandalay and Ava. All parts are comparatively easily accessible from these centres—especially by river. In the heart of the Dry Belt are the major oilfields.

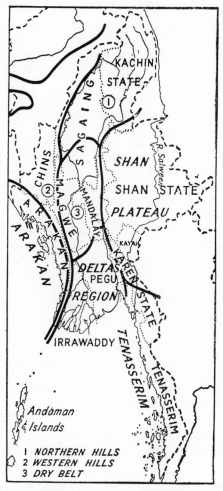

. 211.—The natural regions of Burma, showing their relation with the division of the country and the four states

7. *The Deltas Region*. This region really comprises three parts:

(a) The lower Irrawaddy Valley and the Irrawaddy Delta—a great alluvial rice-growing area in which communications are mainly by water.

(b) The forested Pegu Yoma, evergreen in the south deciduous teak in the north, yielding timber floated down to Rangoon and Pegu.

(c) The Sittang Valley and Delta—very much narrower and less extensive than the Irrawaddy Delta but providing no less than one-fifth of all the rice grown in Burma. At the outlet is the town of Pegu which gave its name to the former Province.

One result of the Japanese occupation was the disruption of the rice trade and much land in the delta was abandoned. The cultivators became refugees in Rangoon, squatting on any piece of vacant land and the subsequent strife between Burmans and Karens accentuated the refugee movement.

The capital and chief port, Rangoon, calls for special mention. It is sited where the southernmost spur of the Pegu Yoma affords firm ground near the Rangoon River from which there is water communication with the Irrawaddy on the west and the Pegu River from which there is communication with the Sittang on the east. It thus commands the chief routeways to the north and at the same time is accessible to ocean-going liners with wharves along the Rangoon River. Largely the creation of the British period, it was formerly more an Indian than a Burmese city with a Chinatown also. The population was swollen by refugees from the Delta and elsewhere during the troubled times which followed independence; many have remained and satellite residential towns have been built to the east across the Pegu River. The old industries of rice milling, with oil refining farther down the river and timber working, have given place to a more varied range, notably textiles, engineering and a modern government pharmaceutical factory. In 1960 hydroelectric power from the east became available.

REFERENCES

General: Scott, J. G., *Burma, a Handbook of Practical, Commercial and Political Information* (London, 1925).
Scott, J. G., *Burma from the Earliest Times io the Present Day* (London, 1924).
White, H. T., *Burma* (London, 1923).
French, F. G., and Stamp, L. D., *A Geography of Burma for Schools* (London, 1924).
Dautremer, J., *Burma under British Rule* (London, 1913).
Geology: Chhibber, H. L., *The Geology* and *The Mineral Resources of Burma* (London, 1934). (2 vols.)
Vegetation: Stamp, L. D., *The Vegetation of Burma* (Calcutta, 1925).
Population: Census of India, 1921, Vol. X, Report and Tables, and later Census Reports.
Fielding Hall, *The Soul of a People.*
Statistics, etc.: Publications issued by the Government include:
Economic Survey of Burma (annual).
Quarterly Bulletin of Statistics.
Season and Crop Report (annual).
The National Income of Burma.
Pyidawtha: The New Burma, 1954.
Grant, W. J., *The New Burma* (New York: Macmillan, 1941).
Christian, J. L., *Modern Burma* (Univ. of California Press, 1942).
Ma Mya Sein, *Burma* (Oxford, 2nd Edition, 1944).

SOUTH-EASTERN ASIA AND INDONESIA

THERE are two reasons why the peninsulas of south-eastern Asia and the islands of the East Indian Archipelago should be considered, in the first place, as a whole. The first is that there is structural continuity between the principal orographical features of the mainland and the islands; the second is that climatically both Malaya and the East Indies lie in the region of Equatorial climate, whilst the broader peninsula of Indo-China and the Philippine Islands agree in lying to the north of it and in having certain features in common.[1]

Between the populous lands of India and China lies the broad peninsula of Indo-China—divided between Burma, which we have already considered, Thailand or Siam, and the old French sphere of influence, Indo-China. From this broad peninsula a narrow subsidiary one extends southwards as Malaya. Grouped round these peninsular masses are the now familiar festoons of islands which make up the whole East Indian Archipelago.

Structurally Indo-China [2] has a core of older rocks—varying in age from pre-Cambrian to Middle Mesozoic, but which were certainly folded before the Tertiary period. This old core, which builds up the Shan States Plateau of Burma, occupies most or all of the Malay Peninsula; it is extended southwards to embrace the little islands of Singkep, Bangka and Belitung and a broad wedge of country in the island of Borneo. This old massif was folded, apparently in the main by Mesozoic earth movements, and long folds have a roughly north-south direction. The mountain system which builds up the massif is often known as the Indo-Malayan mountain system, to distinguish it from the later Tertiary or Alpine mountain systems. The country rocks of the Indo-Malayan Mountains include huge stretches of phyllites or slaty rocks believed to be pre-Cambrian in age, as well as considerable areas of massive limestone probably mainly Devono-Carboniferous. Rocks, especially reddish shales, shown by their fossils to be early Mesozoic in age, are included in the folding, which must therefore have been at least later than their deposition. Of very special interest are the numerous intrusions of granite, now generally

---

[1] Three full-scale geographical treatises in English covering this whole area are now available: E. H. G. Dobby, *Southeast Asia* (London: Univ. of London Press, 1950), Ch. Robequain, *Malaya, Indonesia, Borneo and the Philippines* (London: Longmans, 1954), C. A. Fisher, *South-east Asia* (London: Methuen, 1964).

[2] See J. W. and J. C. Gregory, 'The Alps of Chinese Tibet and their Geographical Relations', *Geog. Jour.*, **61**, 1923, 153–79; J. W. Gregory, 'The Banda Arc', *Geog. Jour.*, **62**, 1923, 30–2; H. A. Brouwer, *The Geology of the Netherlands East Indies* (New York, 1925).

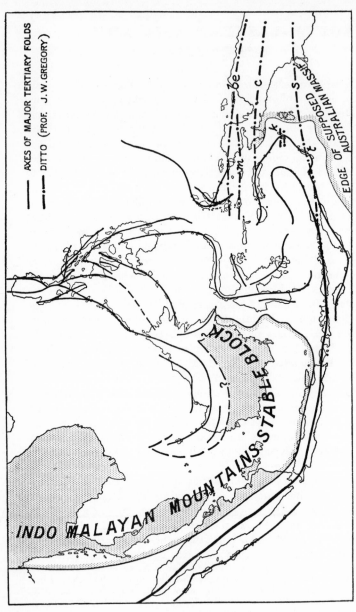

FIG. 212.—The major tectonic features of the East Indies

In the main after H. A. Brouwer; Philippines after Warren D. Smith. Brouwer and others believe that New Guinea forms part of the Australian massif and that the Tertiary folds end against it as the 'Banda Arc,' shown on the above diagram shaped as a fish-hook. Prof. J. W. Gregory considered, however (*Geog. Jour.*, 1923), that the main Tertiary folds pass on through New Guinea which is *not* therefore part of the Australian stable block. Gregory's main trend lines are marked : **s.** Sunda line; **c.** Buru-Ceram line; **m.** Sula-Misool line; **be.** Batanta-Jappen line. Obviously the critical areas in the discussion are the Kei Islands (**k**) and Tanimbar Islands (**t**). The lines shown on the above map are not actual anticlinal folds, but major trend lines. Minor folds occur round the edge of the stable block as in Java. Later research by Brouwer has almost completely disproved Gregory's ideas, and has shown that

believed to be early Cretaceous in age and therefore roughly contemporaneous with the Deccan lavas of India. The granites occur mainly in masses elongated in the direction of the grain of the country—the exposed areas often not exceeding a mile in width but a dozen or more miles from north to south. The importance of these granite masses lies in the association of the famous tin deposits of Siam, Burma, Malaya and Indonesia with their peripheries. Broadly speaking, the granites give rise to the higher hills, being more resistant to weathering than the sedimentary rocks. The more important of the younger rocks in the central core are the clays and shales found infilling old lake-basins and which carry sometimes lignite, sometimes oil shale. In Siam and elsewhere alluvium hides large areas of old rocks.

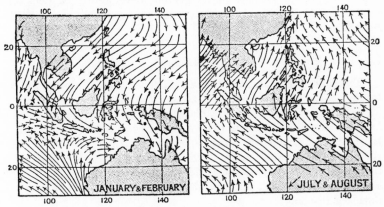

FIG. 213.—The prevailing winds of the East Indies; the length of the arrows is proportional to the constancy of the winds

The meeting of the arrows in the left-hand map indicates the inter-tropical front.

(*From Kendrew's 'Climates of the Continents', by permission of the Clarendon Press.*)

Flanking the central core are the fold ranges of Tertiary mountain systems. The mountain chains themselves are built up mainly of folded sedimentary rocks, in which Tertiary strata are included. Between the ranges and the old core or on the flanks of the ranges, are areas occupied mainly by slightly folded sediments of Tertiary Age. It is in these latter areas that are found the oilfields of Burma, Sumatra, Java and Borneo. The oilfields themselves are usually anticlinal puckers in the basins of Tertiary sediments. Although several of the mountain chains have central cores of ancient metamorphic rocks, the place of the granite intrusions of the Indo-Malayan Mountains is taken by rather minor intrusions—especially of serpentine and basic igneous rocks—and by extrusive masses. Indeed, volcanoes, both active and extinct, are characteristic of the Tertiary fold lines or their flanks throughout the archipelago. An excellent example is afforded by the stately succession of volcanic piles which render Java such an extraordinarily beautiful land. No one after a night trek from the hill station of Tosari could forget the thrill of watching the dawn gradually illumine the wonderful series of peaks which frown down upon the yawning, rumbling crater of Bromo; whilst only Fujiyama can be held to surpass in beauty the perfect symmetry of Meröe.

Although broadly the whole of Malaya and the East Indies lies in the Equatorial belt, the details of the climate vary with position relative to the Equator or with local physical conditions and will be considered under separate divisions.[1] Further, the community of physical structure in south-eastern Asia is not reflected in its human and economic geography: its constituent parts offer some extraordinary contrasts. The dense population and high economic development of Java contrast curiously with the undeveloped and almost unknown interior of Borneo and New Guinea.

MALAYA [2]

The Malay Peninsula, or Malaya, forms the south-eastern extremity of the mainland of the continent of Asia. The region south of Thailand, to which the term Malaya is commonly restricted, extends from the island of Singapore (Lat. 1° 20' N.) to a point to the north in Latitude 6° 40', where it abuts on Siamese territory. Geographically the peninsula extends farther to the north, embracing a considerable tract of Siam. The narrowest part of the isthmus, the Isthmus of Kra, is in Latitude 10° N., and it is here that the southernmost part of Burma is reached.

Physical Features. In general the relief is diversified and there are few large areas of flat land, though extensive tracts of low undulating land exist. The main mountain divide lies nearer the west coast than the east. Several parts rise to over 7,000 feet. Gunong Tahan is 7,184 feet, Mount Kerbau or Gunong Korbu reaches 7,160 and Mount Hulu Temengor 7,020 feet. Towards the north the main range is cut across by the valley of the Perak River and towards the Siamese border becomes indistinct. West of the Central Range the country is undulating, fertile and extensively developed. East of the range there is an extensive mass of wild, forested mountains and the country is less developed than on the western side. The contrast between the eastern

---

[1] The complexity of rainfall conditions in the archipelago may be gathered from the fact that Dr. Boerema, in a publication of the Meteorological Observatory at Batavia (*Verhandelinger*, No. 18), distinguishes sixty-nine rainfall 'types' in Java and Madura and eighty-six in the other islands. A very thorough study of the climate has been made by C. Braah, *Het Klimaat van Nederlandsch-Indië* (in English and Dutch) (Batavia, 1923), in 3 vols., and by I. E. M. Watts, *Equatorial Weather* (London, 1955).

[2] In the revision of this section I am greatly indebted to Professor R. Wikkramateleke at Singapore and Professor Robert Ho in Kuala Lumpur, my hosts during a re-visit to Malaya in 1960.

and western sides of the peninsula is reflected in the tracts of water on either side. On the east coast is the South China Sea, a tract of water so stormy in the period of the north-east monsoon that communication is difficult despite the existence of several river mouths as harbours. On the west coast lie the tranquil Straits of Malacca and, 60 to 100 miles

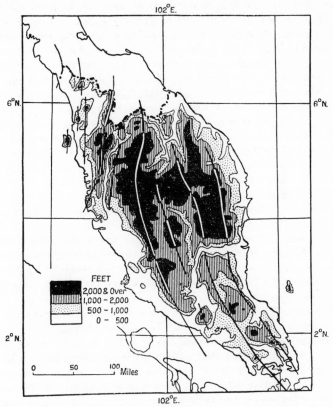

FIG. 214.—A physical map of Malaya showing the coulisses (in white or black lines) recognized by Scrivenor

away, the shores of Sumatra. In the past, just as is the case today, human life and movement have been concentrated on the western side of the peninsula.

Geologically Malaya belongs entirely to the central core of south-eastern Asia, to which reference has been made above, and so offers a marked contrast to Sumatra and Java. The large intrusive masses of Mesozoic granite form the mountains of the main ranges; certain of the very rugged mountains of the east are formed of quartzite and shales—the Pahang Quartzites—but on the east coast granite appears again. On the west of the peninsula are certain remarkable masses of limestone—remarkable because of their vertical sides rising to heights of many hundreds of feet. Many of these masses are riddled with fascinating natural caves. Most of the rocks of the valleys are shales of doubtful age, though including strata at least as young as Middle Mesozoic. There are ancient volcanic rocks—the Pahang Volcanic Series—but none of such recent date as there are in Java. Although only three or four small patches of Tertiary rocks, occupying basins, are known to occur, they are interesting as carrying seams of coal. The basin at Batu Arang in Selangor provided coal for the railways till they turned to oil and later for a cement works, but quality is poor and the one open-cast mine closed down in 1960. With no oil and only poor coal, Malaya undertook the elaborate Cameron Highlands hydro-electric scheme (opened 1963, see *Geography*, **51**, 1966, 61–4). The inland alluvial deposits of the valleys are the source of most of the tin ore found in the country; in places gold also is found, sometimes gold alone. On the east coast there are few stretches of flat land. On the west coast, sheltered by Sumatra, and not exposed to strong winds or heavy seas, there are considerable alluvial plains and extensive mangrove swamps. Some of these lowlands are formed by alluvial deposits washed down by the rivers, others are due to the denudation to base level of the softer tracts of shale.

Reference has been made above to the 'main mountain divide' of Malaya. Actually there are a number of ranges or 'coulisses' placed *en echelon*, as shown in Fig. 214. (See J. B. Scrivenor, 'The Physical Geography of the Southern Part of the Malay Peninsula', *Geographical Review*, **11**, 1921, 351–71.)

The climate of Malaya favours the formation of laterite, which consequently occurs over wide areas; bauxite is now quarried.

Climate and Vegetation. Malaya lies entirely north of the Equator, with the result that although the climate is Equatorial and the rainfall well distributed throughout the year, there is an increasing tendency as one goes northwards for a rainfall maximum to be marked and for a 'dry season' to develop. Really it is only possible to separate two seasons—a wet and a wetter. This is well seen by contrasting the figures for Singapore with those of Penang. On the west coast the 'wet season' corresponds with the period of the Indian monsoon. On the other hand, the east coast is under the influence of the north-east monsoon and has a definitely wet and stormy season between November and March. The average rainfall of Malaya may be said to be rather over 100 inches. In some exposed situations it rises to 270 inches; in some sheltered valleys it drops to 60 inches. Water-power is an important resource.

In general the climate of Malaya is hot and humid throughout the year. It is essentially monotonous—never cold, but never excessively hot, with scarcely any appreciable seasonal variations except perhaps on the east coast. It has been truly remarked that the climate of Malaya is a healthy and delightful one for those in good health, but it kills by its very monotony; it affords no chance of recuperation for those who are 'run down'. It is curious how susceptible to slight changes of temperature one can become after living in such an atmosphere. Owing to the high humidity thick, damp fog is common between six or seven and nine or ten in the morning, and the air seems chilly despite a temperature of about 75° or more. Later the sun breaks through and the heat may seem very intense, although the thermometer rarely registers any temperature over 90°. In the afternoon the formation of clouds and a downpour of convectional rain, sometimes with thunder, are common. The Cameron Highlands, about 25 miles south-east of Ipoh at about 5,000 feet, were developed as a hill station.

	Jan.	Feb.	Mar.	Apr.	May	June	July	Aug.	Sept.	Oct.	Nov.	Dec.	Year
Singapore:													
Temp., ° F.	78·3	79·0	80·2	80·8	**81·5**	81·1	81·0	80·6	80·4	80·1	79·3	78·6	—
Rainfall, in.	8·5	6·1	6·5	6·9	7·2	6·7	6·8	8·5	7·1	8·2	10·0	10·4	92·9
Penang:													
Temp., ° F.	79·7	80·1	81·3	**81·7**	81·5	80·6	80·2	79·9	79·5	79·7	79·2	78·8	—
Rainfall, in.	3·9	3·0	4·7	7·0	11·0	7·2	8·9	12·8	19·0	16·1	10·9	4·8	109·3

The natural vegetation of Malaya is essentially lofty evergreen forest. Forest in general extends from the top of the highest ranges—elevation does not seriously affect the character of the vegetation until the 5,000-foot contour [1] is passed—to the seashores. Here and there its continuity was—and still is—interrupted by special associations of plants. The most noticeable of these special associations are the mangrove swamps of the flat west coast—trees specially adapted to enable them to draw moisture from a soil impregnated with salt water and thus 'physiologically dry' to most plants. An essential characteristic of most mangroves is the presence of aerophores—vertical peg-like projections from the roots into the air which permit the breathing or aeration of the root tissues except during the two periods of the day when the tide covers the soil of the swamps. The common trees of the mangrove swamps number about half a dozen—*Bruguiera, Avicennia* and *Rhizophora* are the principal genera. On the sandy strands of the east coast a narrow band of the graceful feathery *Casuarina* trees is a common feature. On the higher ranges the forest becomes sparser and the quartzite ranges of the east are almost devoid of trees.

Elsewhere, where man has not interfered with it, the forest holds undisputed sway. Equatorial forests are frequently described as gloomy and vault-like, with a lifeless floor to which sunlight never penetrates. Not so the delightful forests of Malaya. True, the dense crowns of

[1] Above 2,000 feet there is, however, a change in the species, and the forest is lower.

foliage make a continuous canopy through which shafts of sunlight penetrate but occasionally, and are all the more fascinating because of their rarity. The trees are of many species, rarely gregarious, growing close together, tall, straight and unbranched, generally supported by plank buttresses at the base. Members of the great family of the Dipterocarpaceae predominate among the larger trees, averaging 150 feet in height, but the number of species of trees in Malaya alone exceeds that in the whole of India. Then there is a lower storey of shade-

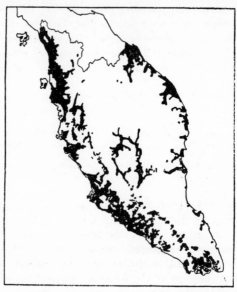

FIG. 215.—Cultivated land in Malaya (cultivated land in black)

This map emphasizes the concentration of cultivation towards the coasts and stresses the greater development of the western side of the peninsula.

loving trees, 20–50 feet in height, and a ground storey of shrubby-trees, bamboos, canes, large-leaved herbaceous plants, mosses and ferns. Far from being devoid of vegetation the ground is usually very well covered. On and among the trees are a host of epiphytes (especially ferns) and climbers, whilst a striking feature of the forests is the mass of fallen coils of the woody lianas. The atmosphere within the forest is humid and still, so quiet very often as to be sinister, for the animal life is concentrated in the tree-tops above. In such an atmosphere the leaves and fallen branches disintegrate quickly and form a deep rich mould— a perfect home for saprophytes of all kinds.

In its natural form the forest furnishes little which is of immediate use to man.[1] Few of the plants furnish fruits or roots which are nourish-

[1] The chief minor products are canes (rattan or rotan and malacca canes), gutta percha (from the tree *Palaguium oblongifolium*, now rare in the peninsula), damar

ing as food, and not a small number are poisonous; the trees are hard-wooded and difficult to clear with primitive implements; land which has been laboriously cleared soon becomes covered with a growth of rank grass (the 'lalang' of the Malays) and then by forest 'weeds'. Primitive man wages an unequal struggle against Nature; even though he succeed in keeping his little clearing free, a heavy downpour may wash his crops from the ground and the very soil from his plot. It is small wonder that the forests of Malaya are inhabited by the primitive backward Semang; the Malays have concentrated along the west coast valleys where paddy can be grown, but even there they have been forced by the climate to a position of cheerful but indolent *laissez-faire*; it is the vigorous new-comers with the richer blood engendered by a cooler climate who have effected the economic development of Malaya.

Agricultural Development. 'The country is extremely fertile, and fertility, though a bad master, makes a splendid servant for a wise and competent humanity. Not only is the forest a huge store of timber and other valuable products, but the soil won from it is admirable for all ordinary tropical crops. Tickle the fertile soil and it laughs.' [1] Modern agricultural studies have demonstrated many difficulties, however, and some have suggested that the laugh is a jeer.

The three chief agricultural crops in the peninsula are rubber, coconuts and rice or 'padi'. Rubber is the great plantation crop and the plantations are largely under European management; some progress has been made in the organization of coconut plantations along comparable lines, but to nothing like the same extent; the cultivation of padi is essentially in the hand of Asiatics. Agriculture, other than the cultivation of these three crops, consists of 'mixed farming', almost entirely in the hands of Chinese and Malays. Near all important centres of population Chinese market gardens are found which supply vegetables to the local markets. The Chinese have brought with them their own methods of agriculture—fully discussed in another chapter—and have been pioneers in the cultivation of several crops, notably pineapples, tapioca, gambier and pepper. The Malays lack the organizing power and the industry of the Chinese. Malayan native agriculture is restricted to the cultivation of rice, the production of native fruits—many of which are but the product of the local trees—and the careless rearing of a multitude of minor crops, including spices, tobacco, coconuts and fibres. In parts rural life is being changed by the building of new model villages (see *Geog. Mag.*, April 1955).

A factor which enters largely into agricultural practice is the danger of soil erosion. Flat land is comparatively free from this danger, but on

(obtained by tapping certain dipterocarps) and jelutong (an exudation product from trees of the genus *Dyera*, formerly in demand in the United States for the manufacture of chewing gum). Rotan and damar are the only minor products mentioned in the Annual Report for 1953.

[1] A. R. Wheeler, *The Modern Malay* (London: Allen & Unwin, 1928).

hill-slopes and undulating land it is ever present. Once the surface layer, rich in humus and plant food, is removed, it is doubtful whether anything can restore the original fertility of the soil. The ground must never be ploughed over large areas or completely cleared of weeds—so that European or American methods of agriculture are totally unsuitable. Perhaps the best method of preserving the soil is the growing of a 'cover crop', especially a leguminous crop which will add valuable nitrates to the soil. Weeding in strips or circles, digging of catch pits, bunding and terracing are other methods of nullifying the erosive action of the heavy rains.

Rubber is the chief agricultural product of Malaya. The romance of the introduction of rubber from South America to the East has often been told. 70,000 seeds were rushed by a specially chartered ocean liner from the Amazon to England in 1876 and 2,800 plants were successfully reared in the Botanical Gardens at Kew. A consignment of nearly 2,000 plants was sent to the Botanic Gardens at Peradeniya in Ceylon, but it was not until the next year that seedlings from Ceylon were successfully established in Malaya. The low price of rubber and the continuance of supplies from Equatorial Africa prevented any interest being taken in the new culture, and it was not until 1895 that any rubber was planted as an estate culture on a large scale. At first progress was slow and it was difficult to persuade planters of the value of the new crop. In 1905 rubber plantations occupied, in the four states of the Federated Malay States, about 40,000 acres; this was increased to 250,000 in 1910, 500,000 in 1915, and 780,000 in 1920. At the end of 1925 the total area under rubber in the whole of British Malaya was about 2,250,000 acres. But this is small compared with 1,997,000 acres of plantations in 1952 and 1,616,000 acres in smallholdings in 1952. The approximate net export of rubber from British Malaya including Penang and Singapore rose from about 6,500 tons in 1910 to 68,000 in 1915 and after as follows:

(in long tons)

1916 . . . 96,000	1931 . . . 518,000	1950 . . . 693,000
1917 . . . 127,000	1932 . . . 406,000	1951 . . . 692,000
1918 . . . 114,000	1933 . . . 445,000	1952 . . . 609,000
1919 . . . 204,000	1934 . . . 465,000	1953 . . . 554,000
1920 . . . 181,000	1935 . . . 422,000	1954 . . . 571,000
1921 . . . 151,000	1936 . . . 358,000	1955 . . . 637,000
1922 . . . 213,000	1937 . . . 476,000	1956 . . . 624,000
1923 . . . 201,000	1938 . . . 361,000	1957 . . . 655,000
1924 . . . 183,000	1939 . . . 361,000	1958 . . . 690,000
1925 . . . 210,000	1940 . . . 549,000	1959 . . . 783,000
1926 . . . 286,000	1941–1946 Japanese Occupation	1960 . . . 767,000
1927 . . . 242,000	1947 . . . 954,000	1961 . . . 791,000
1928 . . . 409,000	1948 . . . 731,000	1962 . . . 791,000
1929 . . . 577,000	1949 . . . 710,000	1963 . . . 841,000
1930 . . . 554,000		

The rubber 'boom' lasted till 1919. The effect of world-wide depression was first felt in the rubber industry in October 1920. Within a year prices had dropped to a quarter. At that time Malaya and Ceylon were producing three-quarters of the world's rubber and so were able to control prices by restricting output. The Stevenson Restriction Scheme was put into operation in November 1922 but (see Fig. 216) the Dutch East Indies were coming in as large producers. Rubber was freed in 1928 since when there have been other schemes to lower costs and maintain prices. On the whole increasing world demand has led to the general increase in output shown in the table opposite.

Rubber and tin made possible Malayan development. Immense areas of dense uninhabited forests were converted into flourishing plantations, a vast army of Tamils, Chinese and Malays employed on land previously useless. The revenue derived from the industry was wisely used in providing Malaya with a system of metalled roads and railways unrivalled in the East—solid assets which the depression could not touch.

1934-8

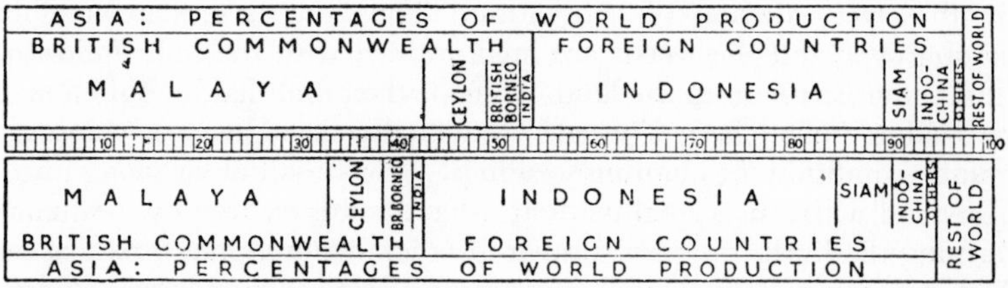

1951-3

Fig. 216.—The world production of rubber, which rose from 90,000 tons in 1909-13 (average) to 1,010,000 tons in 1934-8, over 1,500,000 tons in 1951-3, and 1,802,000 in 1954. It exceeded 2,140,000 tons in 1962.

The forest is cleared by felling the large timber trees and burning off all that remains. It seems a terrible waste of valuable firewood, but the value of that commodity does not at present warrant its removal. The extraction of the great stumps of the forest trees is a difficult and expensive matter; they are often left in the midst of the plantations to rot. As soon as the burnt area begins to recover, weeds spring up and grow with incredible rapidity. The use of cover crops to fight the weeds has taken the place of clean weeding for reasons already noted. More and more attention is being given to careful selection of trees for planting: 100 to the acre on ground completely cleared of stumps is a standard number, but thinning takes place later and half that number is the ideal in the twelfth year. In Malaya, owing to climatic conditions, there is a steady flow of latex throughout the year. The latex is in the bark of the tree; hence a thin slice is cut off the bark. Various systems of 'tapping' are adopted; the general one now is to cut half-way round the circumference of the tree every other day. The latex drains into a little glazed earthenware cup, and an hour or so after tapping the coolies collect the latex in pails. The coolies for this work are usually Tamils from South India; one coolie looks after 300–400 trees and is usually paid in proportion to the weight of the latex brought in. The latex is diluted with water at the 'Store', coagulated by the addition of acetic acid. The coagulated latex is then machined into 'sheet' rubber or long strips of crêpe, washed, drained and smoked or dried. It is exported mainly as 'smoked sheet' or crêpe. The great change of recent years has been the increased acreage of smallholdings (compare Sumatra, p. 447).

Other Crops. The space devoted to rubber in this section is justified by its paramount importance in Malaya. The chief cereal crop— indeed, the only cereal crop of importance—is rice. Rice is the staple diet of 99 per cent. of the population, yet Malaya produces only about a third of the total consumed and only 16 per cent. of the population are engaged in rice cultivation. Rather under 900,000 acres are under rice (compare rubber), equivalent to only 0·2 acre per head of population. The only self-supporting states are Kedah, Kelantan and Perlis— states in which Malays predominate. 95 per cent. of the rice is grown by the 'wet' method of cultivation: 'The land is either ploughed or dug over and the weeds are incorporated with the soil. Following this, water is run on to the land, which is then puddled by buffaloes or by rolling, raked free of weeds, and finally brought to a consistent muddy condition for planting seedlings.' In very soft areas ploughing is dispensed with. In dry cultivation, where land is cleared by frequently burning the bush, the seed is sown in holes or sometimes broadcasted. The crop depends on rainfall and the yield is lower than in wet cultivation. It seems curious to talk of 'irrigation' in a wet country such as Malaya, but rice cultivation is most successful with a carefully controlled water supply, such as is carried out in those areas of which Krian (70,000 acres) is the chief. Coconuts thrive well throughout Malaya, but especially in the coastal districts of the west. The African oil palm has been introduced into Malaya and over 100,000 acres planted. Amongst fruits, pineapples are important. In the island of Singapore the canning industry was in the hands of a strong Chinese combine, formed in 1926 by the union of the eight Chinese-owned canning factories, with the object of securing uniformity in grading, packing and quality. The exports of tinned pineapples in the inter-war years rose steadily from about 40,000 tons in 1925–7 to over 80,000 in 1936. The bulk went to Britain. The industry was killed by the Japanese occupation but has since been revived in Johore. Exports of canned pines climbed to 17,000 tons in 1953.

Pines thrive on poor soil—rich soils produce larger fruit but with a poorer flavour. The 'Queen' pines, grown for canning, are very small (3 to 5 lb.), but very sweet. The plants are propagated from suckers at the base of the fruit and are planted in rows 5 feet apart, the plants being 2½ feet apart in the rows. In Johore peat soils are used. Apart from fruits for local use, bananas and limes might be grown as cash crops. Several fibres are well suited to Malayan climatic conditions, but are little grown; the same is true of sugarcane, tapioca, coffee, tobacco and the spices for which Malacca was once famous. Tea has made some progress; cacao was planted in Trengganu in 1953 and Virginia tobacco in Kelantan.

Amongst animals water-buffalo are mainly used for padi cultivation; large numbers of cattle are imported from India and Siam for draught purposes.

In common with other countries in the East progress is being made in modernizing the fishing industry—especially by mechanization. Outboard motors can be fitted to traditional craft, others converted to motor-boats. The Malays are also taking to the cultivation of carp and other fish (*Tilapia*) in ponds and of prawns in brackish water.

Mining.[1] Mining in Malaya is virtually synonymous with tin-mining. Reference has been made to the former single coal mine at Batu Arang in Selangor and also to the occurrence of gold. Monazite is also found; phosphate or guano is obtained from the bat-infested caves of the limestone country (the most objectionable feature of exploring the fascinating caves of Malaya is the appalling stench, as one is often compelled to tramp ankle- or even knee-deep in bat-guano); whilst china-clay occurs in many places and is successfully exploited for the manufacture of the little cups used in the rubber plantations. Iron-ore mining (especially in Trengganu) produces 6 million tons; it is exported mainly to Japan as is also bauxite from Johore. Apart from these, tin is the great mineral. Chinese records show that it was known and worked in the fifteenth century; the Dutch in the seventeenth and eighteenth centuries attempted to monopolize the output of Kedah and Perak. Towards the end of the eighteenth century the annual output from Perak was estimated at 5,000 pikuls (300 tons), the bulk of which was won by Malays in Kinta and Batang Padang. 'The discovery of the rich tin fields of Lamt, however, was the main cause of the exploitation of Malaya for tin, and the faction fights which took place there between the various clans of Chinese in the 'seventies led to British interference, and so eventually was evolved the present administration' (Greig).

Nearly all the tin mined in Malaya is alluvial tin; lode mining for the mineral *in situ* is still relatively unimportant. The ore is the oxide, cassiterite. In the detrital gravels, derived from the disintegration of granite and the country rocks, the tin ore usually occurs as rounded fragments varying in size from that of a pea to the finest sand. The

[1] A technical treatise is J. B. Scrivenor's *Tin Mining in Malaya* (London: Macmillan, 1928) and a good geographical study is J. B. Ooi, 'Tin Mining Landscapes of Kinta', *Malayan Journal of Tropical Geography*, 1955.

richest deposits are found in the valleys of the west of Malaya, where the granites border the limestones and other rocks. In a valley filled with the gravel wash the heavy tin is usually found concentrated in the lower layers of the superficial deposits, often in pockets in the under-lying red rock. Frequently a great thickness of useless 'over-burden' has to be removed, and this is an important factor in the cost of mining. The tin-bearing gravel is then removed by hand labour with trucks and rails (as in most European-owned mines) or by coolies shovelling the gravel into baskets which are carried to the washing sheds (as in many Chinese-owned mines). The gravel may also be pumped out, together with large quantities of water, by means of gravel pumps, or a great jet of water may be turned on to the deposit and the soft gravel washed out of place ('hydraulic mining'). It will be noted that in all cases the tin is worked in open-cast workings and not in underground mines. Tin ore is very heavy and so can be removed from the light gravel by washing in 'concentrating sluices'. The 'tin concentrate' is sent to Singapore, Penang and U.K. for smelting. Another important method of working in flat alluvial valleys in Malaya is by dredges. A pit is excavated in which the dredge will float; it then eats away the rich ground in front of it, sorts out the tin and dumps the waste behind. It is important to note that ground which has been 'worked over' in this way is available for agriculture. Considerable quantities of tin ore —a few per cent. of the total—are won by the age-old method of panning. Most of the work of this kind is done by women, especially by Tamils. Whilst most of the tin of Malaya is alluvial tin from the west of the peninsula, tin ore is known to exist in lodes to the north and east, and development may be expected there in the future. Between the years 1900 and 1908 Malaya produced roughly 50,000 tons annually, representing between 50 and 56 per cent. of the world's total. A steadily increasing output from Bolivia forced down Malaya's share in the world's production. From 1909 to 1916 production ranged between 43,850 tons and 50,000 tons, representing between 36 and 46 per cent. of the world's total; from 1917 to 1922, with a production ranging from 34,500 tons to 40,000, Malaya's share was 30 to 33 per cent. A production of 53,000 tons in 1931 was followed by 28,000 in 1932, due to a quota agreement, but later expansion followed to a peak of 80,651 in 1940. In the years which followed the Japanese occupation and despite frequently hazardous conditions of life pro-duction again climbed to over 57,000 tons in 1951 and to about 60,000 tons in 1955–63. All these figures of tonnage are of tin content. The tin ore from the mines is bagged, sold to a local buyer (who may be a Chinese), or to one of the two great smelting companies. Most of the ore finds its way to the big smelteries of the two companies in Singapore and Penang. At Singapore it is smelted on the small island of Pulau Brani, just south of the harbour. 'Straits Tin' is refined to an average of 99·9 per cent. pure and has properties which render it the best of all tin in the tin-plate industry.

Political Divisions. Malaya was invaded by Japanese forces in 1941 and Singapore fell on February 16, 1942. On the defeat of Japan in 1945 preparations were made for a new constitution. On February 1, 1948, the Federation of Malaya came into being, consisting of the nine states of Perak, Selangor, Negri Sembilan, Pahang, Johore, Kedah, Perlis, Kelantan and Trengganu, and the two British settlements of Penang and Malacca, with a federal capital at Kuala Lumpur. Singa-

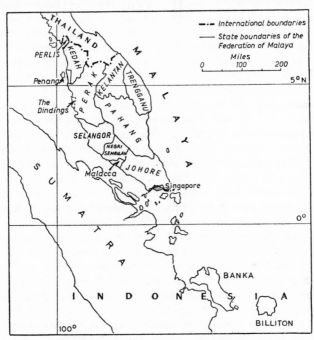

FIG. 217.—Political map of Malaya

pore became a separate Colony and Labuan was added to North Borneo. Up to 1941 the division was into:

(a) The Straits Settlements, a British Crown Colony.
(b) The Federated Malay States (F.M.S.) of Perak, Selangor, Negri Sembilan and Pahang.
(c) The Unfederated States of Johore, Kedah, Perlis, Kelantan and Trengganu.

The old Straits Settlements comprised the island of Singapore, the island of Penang and Province Wellesley on the mainland (another tract on the mainland, the Dindings, was retroceded to Perak on

February 16, 1935), the old settlement of Malacca as well as the more distant Cocos Islands, Christmas Island and Labuan off the coast of Borneo.

All the British areas in Malaya and the East Indies were occupied by the Japanese during the Second World War and when the countries were liberated in 1945 there was an obvious need for reorganization, including a greater co-ordination than in the past.

On August 31, 1957, the Federation of Malaya became the eleventh sovereign member-state of the Commonwealth of Nations. The Supreme Head of State is elected for five years from among the ruling sultans.

The colony of Singapore became a State in 1959. Moves for a wider union came from Malaya and on 16 September 1963 the Federation of Malaysia came into being—Malaya, Singapore, Sarawak and North Borneo (renamed Sabah) with its capital at Kuala Lumpur. Brunei refused to join at the last moment and Singapore withdrew two years later.

As usual, the story of the spread of British influence in the Malayan Peninsula is a long and complex one. Malacca is one of the oldest European settlements in the East, having been founded by the Portuguese in 1511, held by them from 1511 to 1641, by the Dutch from 1641 to 1824, when it passed into the hands of the English. Penang was a depot of the British East India Company, founded in 1786. Singapore was of little importance when it was obtained by the British from the ruler of Johore in 1819, though it is said to have been a place of note before its destruction by the Javanese in 1377. Malacca, Penang and Singapore were incorporated under one government in 1826 and under the control of the East India Company. In 1867 they were separated from India and made a Crown Colony, administered by the Secretary of State for the Colonies in London. The settlement of Penang was afterwards made to include a portion of the opposite mainland—only two miles distant—known as Province Wellesley, as well as the island of Pangkor, which, with the neighbouring strip of the mainland, is known as the Dindings. The Cocos Islands were placed under the Government of the Straits Settlements in 1886, Christmas Island in 1889 and Labuan in 1907. In 1955 the Cocos Islands were transferred to the Commonwealth of Australia; Christmas Island in 1958.

The separate Malay states are each ruled by a Sultan with the help of advisers. The Malays and their rulers are Mahommedans but the huge influx of Chinese into Malaya has presented many problems. On the whole the Malays are peasant cultivators and country-lovers; the Chinese populate the towns which they have largely created and run much of the industry and commerce of the whole area.

British protection dates from 1874 when Residents were appointed to Perak, Selangor and Sungai Ujong. Johore entered into a Treaty with Great Britain in 1885. Negri Sembilan is really a complex state formed by the union of nine small states in 1889, Sungai Ujong joining the Union in 1895. In 1896 a treaty was made between the British Government and the four states of Perak, Selangor, Negri Sembilan and Pahang which united to form the Federated Malay States (F.M.S.) with a capital at Kuala Lumpur, but the powerful State of Johore remained outside the Federation. The remaining four states (Perlis, Kedah, Trengganu and Kelantan) lie on or near the Siamese border and the rights of suzerainty and protection were handed over by Siam to Britain in accordance with the Anglo-Siamese Treaty of 1909.

Britain spent very large sums in building a great Naval Base on Singapore Island, along the Johore Strait which separates the island from the mainland. But the base proved vulnerable to the Japanese who used jungle warfare tactics in an assault from the north. The dense Equatorial forests of the heart of Malaya provided ideal country from which guerilla warfare could be maintained against the Japanese forces: unfortunately just as good for the communist and other subversive elements which have maintained a constant war against the forces of law and order since the end of the Japanese occupation. Singapore surrendered to the Japanese on February 15, 1942, was restored to British rule on September 5, 1945, passing back to civil administration on April 1, 1946. It became an independent state within the Commonwealth in 1959.

The annexed table shows the approximate areas of each of the states in the Federation and also changes in population over an approximate 25-year period. The states offer some sharp contrasts, reflecting the geography of the peninsula as a whole. The west has most of the plantations, much of the mining and has attracted most of the Chinese settlers and has also the main urbanization. Johore, Negri Sembilan, Selangor, Perak and Kedah all share in this belt as well as Malacca and the tiny State of Perlis on the Siamese border. The forested heart of the peninsula is sparsely populated and this accounts for the relatively low density of population in Pahang and much of Kelantan. The eastern coastlands and plains are mainly occupied by Malayan cultivators so that the proportion of Chinese is small.

In the early part of the inter-war years it was broadly true to say of Malaya as a whole, including Singapore and Penang, that the country districts were Malay but the towns were predominantly Chinese. In the F.M.S. the figures were: Malays 615,651; Chinese 644,120; Indians 310,752; others 27,247. Chinese were far less numerous in the other states. For the most part the Indians were temporary immigrants of the coolie class recruited by the rubber companies: males outnumbered females. The Chinese fall into two groups, the Malayan born Chinese who are, of course, British subjects and the recent immigrants, Chinese-born. The Malayan-Chinese play a large part in the life of the community, forming the greater part of the merchant, artisan and clerical classes, and many have risen to positions of great wealth and influence, though commonly content to leave politics and administration to others. The immigrant Chinese swarmed into

THE FEDERATION OF MALAYSIA

State	Area, sq. m.	Population		Capital
		1933	Census 1957	
Johore	7,330	490,000	925,919	Johore Bahru
Negri Sembilan	2,565	218,590	365,045	Seremban
Pahang	13,873	175,406	312,978	Kuala Lipis
Selangor	3,167	490,635	1,012,047	Kuala Lumpur
Perak	7,980	713,139	1,220,633	Ipoh
Kedah	3,660		701,486	Alor Star
Perlis	310		90,834	Kangar
Kelantan	5,750		505,171	Kota Bahru
Trengganu	5,027		278,147	Kuala Trengganu
Pulau Pinang (Penang)	110	183,000	571,923	George Town (Penang)
(Prov. Wellesley	288)			
Melaka (Malacca)	640		291,233	Malacca
Unlocated			1,499	
Total (Malaya)	50,700		6,276,915	

The State of Singapore

Singapore	224·5	515,000	1,800,000[1]	

[1] Estimate, mid-1966.

The total area of Malaya and Singapore Island is approximately 50,924·5 square miles (almost exactly the area of England). For Sarawak and Sabah see pp. 434–7. At end 1963 the total population of the Federation of Malaysia was estimated at 7,604,454 (3,810,388 Malaysians, 2,802,816 Chinese, 843,257 Indians and Pakistanis, 147,993 others).

Singapore in great numbers as coolie labour, usually arriving at first without their womenfolk. Unsettled conditions in China brought as many as 132,886 in 1923 alone; depression in the rubber industry and so in Malaya as a whole caused a net loss of 425,000 in 1930–3. In post-war years the influx has been renewed so that by 1956 Chinese in Malaya numbered 2,413,325 compared with 3,092,788 Malays and 759,753 Indians and Pakistanis. In Singapore Chinese numbered 987,201 out of a total population of 1,290,493 and compared with

157,121 Malayans. One reason for the separation of the State of Singapore from the Federation of Malaysia is the predominance of Chinese there. Taking the Chinese and Indians together it is not difficult to see why males outnumber females in the proportion of 5 to 3 in Malaya.

Singapore. The island of Singapore lies at the southern end of the peninsula, from the mainland of which it is separated by the narrow Johore Strait, only about a mile wide. The city and port of Singapore,

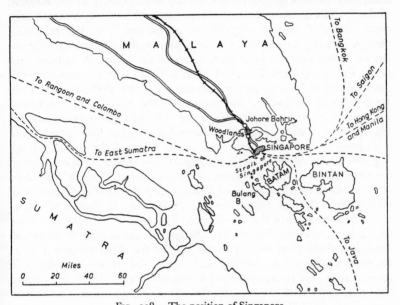

FIG. 218.—The position of Singapore

The railway and road are continuous between Woodlands and Johore by a causeway.

with three-quarters of the people, is on the south side of the island, separated from the Indonesian islands of Bintang, Batam and Bulang Besar by the Strait of Singapore. The island itself is 27 miles long, 14 miles wide from north to south. The south-west of the island is hilly, though fringed with mangrove swamps, but to the east is flat and sandy or marshy. Much of the island is cultivated, being occupied by rubber plantations and coconut groves (the latter on the more sandy ground) and by market gardens supplying vegetables for local consumption by the ever-expanding urban population. The cultivation of pineapples for canning assumed the position of a large-scale industry but is now dead; so is pepper cultivation. Tobacco is grown and blended with imported leaf. Four periods characterize Singapore agriculture —experimental 1819–1865; tapioca, gambier and pepper 1866–1895; rubber and pineapple 1896–1946; market gardening 1947 onwards.

A.—15

About 15,000 Chinese smallholders cultivate the 10,000 acres of market gardens in the fertile land of valley bottoms, whilst second growth scrub occupies the remainder of the island—giving place to gardens of residences.[1] But the emphasis is now on industrialization.

The British owe the possession of this valuable island to the genius of Sir Stamford Raffles, who purchased it in 1819 from the ruler of Johore for the sum of 30,000 dollars. At that time it was almost un-inhabited. It owes its importance mainly to its position at the meeting of the world's great trade routes from east and west, at the same time being favoured with a magnificent anchorage. The Johore Strait, though narrow, is deep in the eastern part, and the naval base for the British Admiralty was built on this side of the island. A railway runs across the island from Singapore to Woodlands and is connected with the railways of Malaya by a causeway across the shallow part of the Johore Strait. Adjoining the railway is the main road. Industrial activities include tin-smelting, rubber refining, saw-milling, leather-tanning and a wide range of minor industries, but Singapore's fame rests upon the vast commerce which centres round the port. Through it passes much of the trade, both import and export, of the Malayan Federation and of other countries nearby, notably Indonesia. Published statistics deal with the trade of Malaya as a whole, three-quarters of which passes through Singapore (Figs. 221, 222). If Singapore's trade could be shown (as in the old diagram Fig. 220) its entrepôt character would be very clear. The docks of Singapore are constantly being ex-tended and the civil airport to the east of the town became a great international junction; another and larger airport was completed in August 1955, five miles to the north-east of the city. There is no doubt that Singapore and Penang have benefited greatly through being free ports—free from Customs dues.

Penang is a pretty rocky island rising to over 2,000 feet in the centre. The central part is still forested, but on lower ground are numerous rubber and coconut plantations. The principal town, officially named George Town, though always known as 'Penang', faces the mainland and the narrow strait forms a sheltered harbour. On the mainland is Prai, a terminus of the Malayan Railway from which there is through communication with Singapore in less than twenty-four hours and with Bangkok in less than thirty-six hours. Though only metre gauge the railways are excellent. Penang island is now Pulau Pinang.

Malacca is now of small commercial importance, though of great historical interest. A number of old buildings remain to remind one of its former glories. The state is now known as Melaka.

Kuala Lumpur, the capital, is the largest town in the Federation and the centre of commercial activity. It is connected by rail and road with

[1] An excellent detailed map of the island is included in the Annual Report of the Colony of Singapore, 1953, and some sheets of a very detailed land use map have been published. The central steam power-station is now the largest in south-east Asia.

Port Swettenham. The staple products are rubber, rice, coconuts, sugar, tapioca and pepper. The exports, however, pass mainly through Singapore and Penang. *Ipoh* is important as a mining centre.

At the time when Malaya was deriving large revenues from rubber

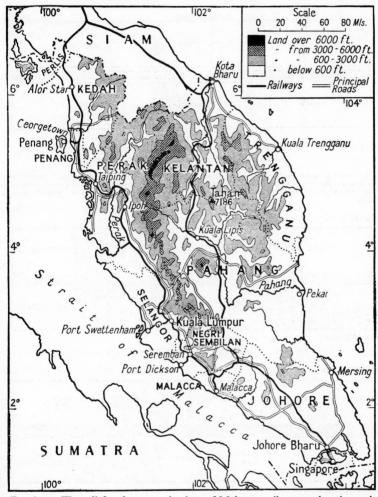

FIG. 219.—The relief and communications of Malaya—railways and main roads

Owing to the remarkable development of the tin and rubber country on the western side of the peninsula there is a very fine network of motor roads (not shown on this map) when compared with the eastern.

and tin, the governments concerned wisely spent much money on developing an excellent system of metalled and tarred motor roads. Malaya, at least in the populous valleys and plains of the west, had an excellent network long before most countries in the East.

Christmas Island lies in the Indian Ocean about 220 miles south of the western end of Java. It has an area of 64 square miles and a population in 1956 of 2,444. It is a densely wooded island rising to a plateau 1,000 feet above sea-level and is famous for its extensive de-

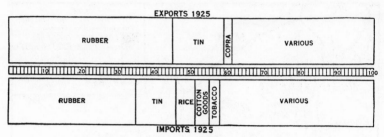

EXPORTS 1925
RUBBER
TIN
COPRA
VARIOUS
10 20 30 40 50 60 70 80 90 100
RUBBER
TIN
RICE
COTTON GOODS
TOBACCO
VARIOUS
IMPORTS 1925

FIG. 220.—The foreign trade of the Straits Settlements in the inter-war years, showing the entrepôt character of the trade

It should be noted that the tin and rubber, imported mainly from the Federated Malay States, represented a greater proportionate value of the exports and actually also a greater intrinsic value because of the treatment they undergo in Singapore. Note: In recent years no comparable figures have been published.

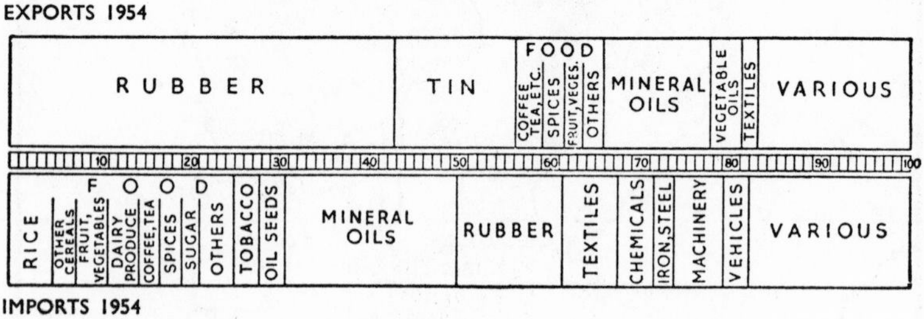

EXPORTS 1954
RUBBER
TIN
FOOD
COFFEE TEA, ETC.
SPICES
FRUIT, VEGES.
OTHERS
MINERAL OILS
VEGETABLE OILS
TEXTILES
VARIOUS
10 20 30 40 50 60 70 80 90 100
RICE
FOOD
OTHER CEREALS
FRUIT, VEGETABLES
DAIRY PRODUCE
COFFEE, TEA
SPICES
SUGAR
OTHERS
TOBACCO
OIL SEEDS
MINERAL OILS
RUBBER
TEXTILES
CHEMICALS
IRON, STEEL
MACHINERY
VEHICLES
VARIOUS
IMPORTS 1954

FIG. 221.—The foreign trade of Malaya as a whole

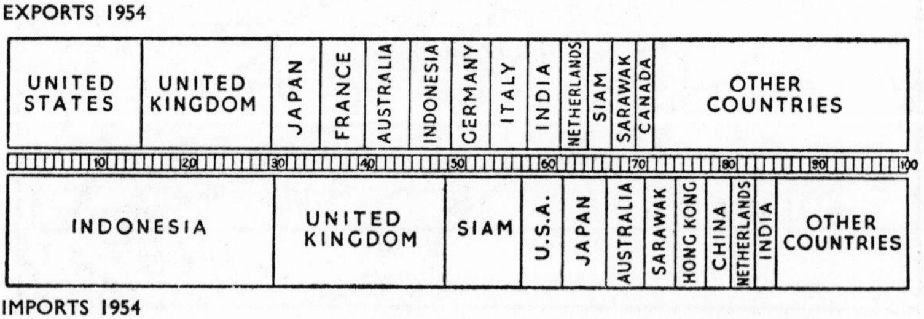

EXPORTS 1954
UNITED STATES
UNITED KINGDOM
JAPAN
FRANCE
AUSTRALIA
INDONESIA
GERMANY
ITALY
INDIA
NETHERLANDS
SIAM
SARAWAK
CANADA
OTHER COUNTRIES
10 20 30 40 50 60 70 80 90 100
INDONESIA
UNITED KINGDOM
SIAM
U.S.A.
JAPAN
AUSTRALIA
SARAWAK
HONG KONG
CHINA
NETHERLANDS
INDIA
OTHER COUNTRIES
IMPORTS 1954

FIG. 222.—The direction of the foreign trade of Malaya, including Singapore

posits of phosphate of lime worked by the Christmas Island Phosphate Company. Over 280,000 tons were exported in 1953. It was administered as part of Singapore until transferred to Australia in 1958.

The Cocos or Keeling Islands also lie in the Indian Ocean about 1,200 miles south-west of Singapore and 530 miles west of Christmas

Island. There are 27 small coral islands—the largest 5 miles long and a quarter of a mile wide—with fewer than 1,000 people (605 in 1953); but they have extensive groves of coconut palms yielding nuts, copra and oil for export. They were declared a British possession in 1857, placed under the Governor of Ceylon till transferred to the Straits Settlements in 1886. The main settlements are on Home and Direction islands—the latter with a Cable and Wireless Station. On West Island is an airstrip which played an important part in communications during the war with Japan and was later controlled by the Australian Department of Civil Aviation as a half-way halt between Australia and South Africa, before the islands became a dependency of Australia in 1955.

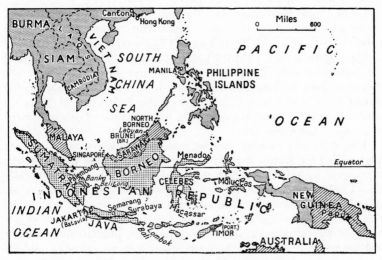

FIG. 223.—Political map of the East Indies

REFERENCES

Both the Federation of Malaysia and the State of Singapore publish an excellent *Annual Report*. The *Journal of Tropical Geography* has important papers, especially 'Padi Landscapes of Malaya' by Prof. E. H. G. Dobby, 1955. Professor Dobby first published his *Southeast Asia* (University of London Press) in 1950; the more elaborate volume by W. B. Fisher (Methuen) appeared in 1965. For Singapore see R. Wikkramatileke, *Journal of Tropical Geography*, **20,** 1965, 73–83.

BRITISH BORNEO

Though Indonesia has the major part of the great island of Borneo
—the third largest in the world excluding the continents—the northern
and north-western parts (between a quarter and a third of the whole
island) form part of the British Commonwealth. The territory under
British influence is organized in three political units:

(1) Sabah, formerly the Colony of North Borneo, part of Malaysia.
(2) The protected State of Brunei.
(3) The former Colony of Sarawak, now part of Malaysia.

The island of Labuan, lying off the coast of Brunei, formerly part
of the Straits Settlements, is now part of Sabah.

Sabah (North Borneo) occupies the northern part of the island and
has an area of about 29,387 square miles. The territory was under the
jurisdiction of the British North Borneo Chartered Company from 1888
to 1942, when it was occupied by the Japanese. This was the last of
the great chartered companies to administer British territory. On
liberation from the Japanese occupation it became (with Labuan) the
Crown Colony of North Borneo. When the Federation of Malaysia
came into being on September 16, 1963, it became one of the constituent
states under the name Sabah.

Physically the country can be divided into three fairly distinct
zones called by Rutter the plains, the downs and the hills. Though
interrupted by hill ridges which extend to the coast the plains generally
extend behind a coastal fringe of mangrove swamps from two to six
miles inland and consist of alluvial flats naturally covered with grass.
This tract is well suited to cultivation. On the west coast much of it is
occupied by native cultivators of rice, and the plantations of rubber
and coconuts; on the north and east coasts it forms valuable land for
the growth of tobacco. The downs consist of low hills rising like little
islands from the plains. Plantations and orchards cover the more fertile
of them, but in others the heavy rains have swept away the fertile soil
and they are bare but for coarse grass. The hill zone usually begins
with great abruptness, range after range densely forested rising steeper
and higher until they reach 6,000 feet. Most of the ranges run parallel
to the coast. The whole system culminates in the great granite mass of
Mount Kinabalu (13,455 feet), 25 miles from the coast, forming a
striking landmark from far and near. Geologically the downs and the
lower hill ranges consist mainly of Tertiary sediments, important
because of their content of mineral oil and coal.

Most of the rivers of North Borneo have a sandy bar at their mouth,
but many, especially those draining towards the east, are navigable by
launches, and from time immemorial have formed the chief highways
of the country. The Kinabatangan is 350 miles long and navigable for
over 200.

The climate of the coastal belts is typically Equatorial. The temperature of the coastal belts averages rather over 80°; the thermometer rarely rises above 95° or drops below 65°. The year falls roughly into two seasons, the season of the north-east monsoon and the season of the south-west monsoon. The north-east monsoon blows from the middle of October to the middle of April and is the principal rain-bearing wind. The south-west monsoon, blowing from April to October, is not so strong, but sudden squalls are frequent, the wind is

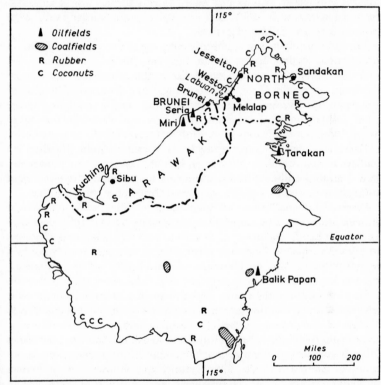

FIG. 224.—Borneo

drier than the north-east monsoon and the months when it is blowing tend therefore to be hotter. The rainfall is generally less in the interior (Tenom, 62 inches) than on the coasts, where it ranges up to 200 inches (Sandakan, 127 inches).

The natural vegetation of the greater part of North Borneo is luxuriant evergreen forest. It would seem that Borneo was cut off from the Asiatic mainland only at a comparatively late period geologically and a large number of the Asiatic mammals occur in Borneo. Of particular interest amongst the animals are the anthropoid apes, the well-known *orang-utan*.

The population of Sabah at the Census of 1960 was 454,421 compared with 277,476 in 1931. It consists mainly of Chinese and Mohammedan settlers on the coast and aboriginal tribes inland. The Europeans and Eurasians numbered 1,896; Chinese, 104,542; Malays, a few thousand. The most numerous of the native peoples are the Dusuns, Muruts and Bajaus. The chief towns are Jesselton, the capital, on the west coast (21,497) and Sandakan (29,291).

The British North Borneo Company held the land under grants from the Sultans of Brunei and Sulu. North Borneo was declared a British Protectorate in 1888, and in 1898 certain border lands were acquired from the Sultan of Brunei.

The chief products are rubber, timber, sago, rice, coconuts, Manila hemp, gums, coffee, fruits, spices, tobacco, tapioca and canes. In recent years there has been a rapid rise in the production and export of rubber, especially from smallholdings, and tobacco. The timber includes serayi (Borneo cedar) and camphor, and is a staple export, though rubber is easily the leading export. The trade is carried on mainly through Singapore and Hong Kong with Britain and the Commonwealth.

There is a metre-gauge railway (127 miles) from Jesselton to Melalap, with a branch to Weston on Brunei Bay. As yet there are only a few hundred miles of roads. Airstrips at Labuan, Jesselton and Sandakan are used by regular services to Singapore and elsewhere.

Brunei. This small state of 2,226 square miles is an enclave in Sarawak territory. The population, according to the 1963 estimate, numbered 98,438, including a few thousand Chinese, some Indians and a few Europeans. The remainder, over three-quarters, are Malays and native races. The development of the oilfields led to a great increase in population (only 40,657 in 1947). The chief town is Brunei, on the river of the same name. The old town was actually built over the water of the river, but the main new town is now on the mainland.

Most of the interior is heavily forested and there are numerous kinds of valuable timber. Agricultural products include sago; plantation rubber is increasing in importance. 'Cutch' is the name given to an extract of mangrove bark. The fortunes and importance of Brunei completely changed after the discovery (in 1929) and development of one of the most prolific oilfields in the British Commonwealth. The centre is the post-war town of Seria which by 1952 had over 11,000 people. The oilfield extends offshore and some wells have been drilled from jetties. Production reached 42,000,000 barrels in 1956 but has now passed its peak. The crude oil is shipped by tanker from the port of Kuala-Belait and accounts for over 95 per cent. of Brunei's exports. Some is refined at Lutong.

Sarawak has an area of 48,250 square miles and lies south of North Borneo along the north-west coast. Until 1942 it was a state ruled with pure autocracy by an English Rajah. In 1841 the Sultan of

Brunei granted control of part of the present area of Sarawak to the Englishman, Sir James Brooke, who thus became the first Rajah. The young state was nearly overthrown by a Chinese mutiny in 1857. Additions of territory were made in 1861 and 1905, and in 1888 Sarawak was acknowledged as an independent state under the protection of Great Britain. The third Rajah, His Highness Charles Vyner Brooke, succeeded in 1917, and in 1941 the centenary of Brooke family rule was celebrated throughout the territory. The Japanese took possession in 1942 and after liberation the fourth Rajah ceded the country to Britain on July 1, 1946. It became a state of the Federation of Malaysia in 1963.

As in North Borneo there is usually a flat coastal strip separated from the mountainous interior by a belt of downs or hills. Geologically the mountain ranges of Borneo, including Sarawak, belong to the great Tertiary or Alpine system of folds. The oilfields are situated on anticlines on the flanks of the main ranges.

Several of the larger rivers are navigable by large steamers for some distance into the interior and the rivers still form the principal highways of the country.

The climate on the whole resembles that of Sabah, but the rainfall régime varies and in some areas the wettest months are between April and October, as they are in India.

The population was estimated in 1962 at about 776,990, including 136,000 Malays and such native peoples as Dyaks, Kenyahs and Muruts, but there are large numbers of Chinese settlers. As in other parts of the East, there is a marked division of trades and professions amongst different nationalities. The Chinese supply the merchant and artisan (especially carpentry) classes as well as the best agriculturists, cooks and water-carriers; the Malays are fishermen and woodsmen and personal servants; the Indian 'dhobi' or washerman and the small Indian shopkeeper are also present. The Chinese, Malays and Indians preserve, in the main, their national costumes.

The chief towns of Sarawak are the capital, Kuching (50,679), about 23 miles from the mouth of the Sarawak River; Sibu, about 60 miles from the mouth of the Rejang River; and Miri, the headquarters of the Sarawak Oilfields Limited. Both town and oilfield were seriously damaged during the war but have been restored. The oilfields at Miri and Bakong, opened up in the twenties, adjoin, but are not as rich as, that of Brunei, and output is declining. Bauxite is exported.

The agricultural products include sago, rice and pepper; plantation rubber is increasing in importance. Fishing is an important industry.

REFERENCES

There are numerous books dealing with ethnography and with exploration and adventure in the interior of the great island of Borneo, but there are few works from the geographical standpoint. The following are the more important general works:

C. Bruce: *Twenty Years in Borneo* (London, 1924).
O. Rutter: *British North Borneo* (London, 1922).
S. Baring-Gould and C. A. Bampfylde: *History of Sarawak* (London, 1909).
A. Ireland: *The Far Eastern Tropics* (London, 1905).
I. H. N. Evans: *Among Primitive Peoples in Borneo* (London, 1922).
F. W. Roe: *The Natural Resources of Sarawak* (Kuching, 1953).
For recent developments see the *Annual Reports* (H.M.S.O.), also C. F. Preuss, 'Sabah', *Focus*, **14**, 3, 1963.

THE REPUBLIC OF INDONESIA

The former Dutch possessions in south-east Asia included the greater part of the East Indies or Indonesian Archipelago excepting only the northern and north-western parts of Borneo (British) and the eastern half of the island of Timor (Portuguese). The Dutch East India Company, formed in 1602, conquered successively and ruled the islands until 1798 when the administration was handed over to the Dutch Government. Under the Dutch remarkable developments took place notably in Java (with Madura) which became one of the most populous and highly developed countries in the Tropics. With an area of only 51,057 square miles Java and Madura came to have a population of about 65,000,000 (1966) or 1,270 persons to the square mile. The remainder of the vast area, some 682,000 square miles having a population of only about 40,000,000 or 60 per square mile, constituted for the Dutch the 'Outer Territories'. Development and settlement, notably of Sumatra, were proceeding apace up to the time of the Japanese invasion of 1941-2. The occupation lasted until 1945 and strong nationalist movements developed. Sporadic fighting occurred in many areas between Netherlanders and various groups of Indonesians, the position being complicated in some cases by the continued presence of Japanese troops. British and Indian forces were landed in Java and Sumatra to help in restoring order and twice the United Nations intervened. Eventually a Bill was passed in the Netherlands Parliament handing over sovereignty and formal transfer took place on December 27, 1949. At first the country was known as the United States of Indonesia, which recognized the fact that the Javanese leaders of the independence movement were representative of only a small part of the vast area. Next year, however, the name was changed to the Republic of Indonesia and union with the Netherlands was ended in 1954. The status of the western half of New Guinea (West Irian) remained unsettled: it was left in Dutch hands until 1963.

The Republic of Indonesia is divided into twenty provinces—many with a considerable degree of autonomy designed to satisfy separatist movements. During the general turmoil of its early existence several parts of the republic declared their 'independence'. In December 1957 about 60,000 Dutch nationals remained in Indonesia but by 1962 this total had been reduced to under 10,000. Many of the islands have been renamed and place-names with their Indonesian spelling may be difficult to recognize.

The Republic has a total area of nearly 576,000 square miles and a population of 97 million (1961) with its capital at Batavia, renamed Djakarta or Jakarta, in Java. Indonesia's share of Borneo (Kalimantan) is 208,000 square miles (almost as large as France), Sumatra is 164,000

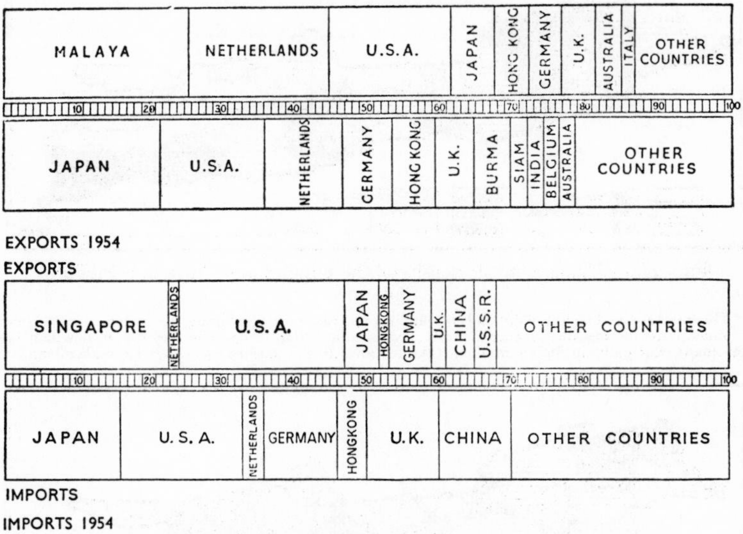

MALAYA	NETHERLANDS	U.S.A.	JAPAN	HONG KONG	GERMANY	U.K.	AUSTRALIA	ITALY	OTHER COUNTRIES

JAPAN	U.S.A.	NETHERLANDS	GERMANY	HONG KONG	U.K.	BURMA	SIAM	INDIA	BELGIUM	AUSTRALIA	OTHER COUNTRIES

EXPORTS 1954
EXPORTS

SINGAPORE	NETHERLANDS	U.S.A.	JAPAN	HONGKONG	GERMANY	U.K.	CHINA	U.S.S.R.	OTHER COUNTRIES

JAPAN	U.S.A.	NETHERLANDS	GERMANY	HONGKONG	U.K.	CHINA	OTHER COUNTRIES

IMPORTS
IMPORTS 1954

FIGS. 225–6.—The direction of the foreign trade of the Indonesian Republic in 1954 compared with 1960.

square miles, Celebes (Sulawesi) 73,000 and Java 51,000. The Lesser Sunda Islands include Bali, Lombok, Sumbawa, Sumba, Flores and Timor, whilst the Moluccas are the original Spice Islands.

The chief exports of Indonesia, with percentage of the total by value in 1962, are rubber (40), petroleum (32), tin ore (5), tea (3), palm oil (3), tobacco (2), copra (2) and coffee (2). Imports are mainly manufactured goods in great variety. The direction of foreign trade has undergone great changes: strained relations with Malaysia and Singapore have had a marked effect in recent years.

JAVA AND MADURA

Java, with its satellite island Madura, is in many ways unique. It is one of the most densely populated agricultural countries in the world, yet a very large proportion of the surface is over 3,000 feet above sea-level and of necessity the density drops to 300 to the square mile in certain of the more mountainous districts. The remarkable density of a thousand to the square mile has been attained in the last century: in 1800 the total population was estimated between 3 and 4 millions, in 1850 11 millions, in 1900 28 millions, in 1926 36·9 millions, and is now over 65 millions. A study of population changes seems to indicate

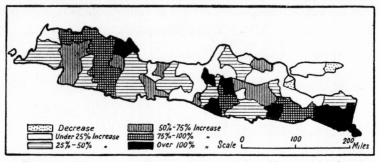

FIG. 227.—Changes in the density of the population of Java and Madura, 1895–1920

This map shows that the plainlands of Madura and the north, including the sugar country round Surabaya, must be regarded as already fully developed and that progress in opening up new land has been made principally in the mountainous country towards the south coast. (*After* van Valkenberg.)

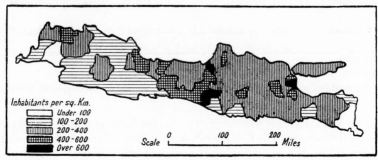

FIG. 228.—The population of Java: density in 1920
(*After* van Valkenberg.)

that saturation point has been reached in most areas. Indeed, in 1954 90,000 were settled in other parts of Indonesia. Javanese form the bulk of the population and furnish an almost unique example of an industrious Equatorial race. In contrast to Malaya, Java has less than a million other Orientals (chiefly Chinese).

Before the present régime there were about a quarter of a million Europeans, the great majority Dutch, living in Java. The Dutch had in fact made a success of settling in and colonizing an Equatorial island though it is true that they lived mainly in such towns as Batavia,

Semarang and Bandung. The Dutch attitude towards Java as a home was different from that of the English towards Malaya. It was not a question of waiting for the triennial home leave and of looking forward to retirement at fifty or fifty-five; the Dutchman evolved a bungalow residence with well-furnished 'stoep' or porch for permanent occupation and expected to pass all his days in the island, with holidays in the hill stations. In the nineteen-thirties medical men were saying that the thick sun-helmet then universally worn by the Englishman in India was as much nonsense as the red-flannel spine pad of a generation earlier. The Dutch in Java, or at any rate their golden-haired children who played freely in the open without hats, had already discarded it. It took the Second World War to prove that heat apoplexy is real enough but not sun-stroke through the skull, so that the old solar topee has disappeared.

The colour bar was less marked in Java than in most parts of the East; there was a considerable amount of intermarriage and the Eurasians instead of forming a distinct community mixed freely with the Europeans. The death-rate among the domiciled Europeans was

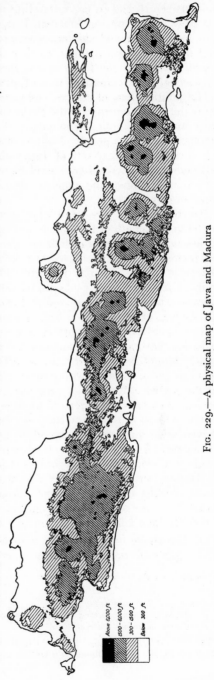

FIG. 229.—A physical map of Java and Madura

Reduced from the official maps.

Above 6,000 ft.
1,500 - 6,000 ft.
300 - 1,500 ft.
Below 300 ft.

low—between 16 and 19 per 1,000, thus approximating to that in the great cities of Europe and America. It is, perhaps, true that the weaklings—men, women and children—were repatriated if the climate was found not to agree with them, so that those who remained were of vigorous stock; but the fact remains that people of European stock were successfully acclimatized in an Equatorial climate.

The position has, of course, completely changed. Not only have most of the Dutch returned to the Netherlands but numbers of Javanese troops (and their families) who fought with them are now to be found in Holland as well as people of mixed blood.

It is common now to talk of 'Indonesians' as if one race inhabited the Republic. In fact the dominant element is the sturdy brown-skinned Mongolian Javanese, the majority Muslims, who control the vast empire of many races.

Structurally Java consists of a late Tertiary fold with its main axis parallel to the length of the island. The main ridge resulting from the fold lies nearer the south coast than the north and accounts for the more rugged nature of the south. The exposed rocks are almost entirely Tertiary in age; it is rarely that the older core is exposed. But the dominant feature in the geology and relief of Java is the numerous volcanoes which burst out along the line of weakness. A score or more reach heights exceeding 8,000 feet, many are over 10,000 feet and rise to those cloud-capped heights in a beautiful symmetrical concave-sided cone. Several of the volcanoes are still in the solfataric stage of activity; Mount Bromo in the east is still active, whilst lava eruptions from others have occurred within the last century.[1] The loftier volcanoes and the higher ridges are of necessity uncultivated waste land, but elsewhere a climate characterized by heavy rainfall and great heat has resulted as usual in rapid and deep weathering and the formation of a soil lateritic in character but exceptionally fertile, as soils derived from volcanic rocks frequently are. In the north of the island there are broad spreads of alluvium derived from this rich parent rock. Volcanic and soft Tertiary strata, combined with the climate, thus explain the amazing fertility of Java as a whole, despite the comparatively small area of flat land—an interesting contrast with Japan.[2]

Broadly Java falls into five parallel strips:

(a) The entire northern coast, with few exceptions, is an alluvial plain, forming some of the most fertile rice and sugar lands

---

[1] In March 1963 Mount Agung in Bali blew its top off and killed 1,500 people.
[2] The contrast may be expressed thus:

	Java	Japan
Percentage of surface below 600 feet	36	30
Percentage of surface formed by volcanic rock . .	36	32
Percentage of surface cultivated	80	20

The contrast is, in the main, due to the relative inability of the Japanese climate to form soil rapidly from comparable materials.

in the island. Here are found the chief towns and ports, though natural harbours do not exist.

(b) Inland there follows an undulating or hilly tract of Tertiary rocks which furnish a soil much less fertile than that of either the alluvium or the volcanic rocks. Here are found the oilfields of Java, the very important mineral wealth of the island (see Fig. 230), and most of the teak plantations.

(c) The volcanic belt consists of a complex string of volcanoes separated by high plains filled with volcanic ash of great fertility. Many of the smaller tuff-cones are terraced from base to summit, and it is in this part of Java that one sees the amazing panoramas of curvilinear paddy fields rising one above the other in a seemingly endless succession. The higher slopes of the volcanoes are often forested and attract a heavy

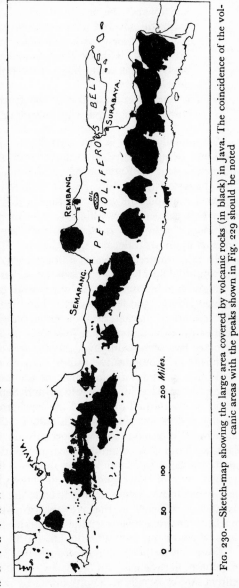

FIG. 230.—Sketch-map showing the large area covered by volcanic rocks (in black) in Java. The coincidence of the volcanic areas with the peaks shown in Fig. 229 should be noted

rainfall, which is stored sufficiently long to assist in the irrigation of paddy fields late in the season.

(d) The fold-mountain belt of Tertiary limestones and sandstones
lies towards the southern coast. Large areas are rugged and
wild, still covered with dense evergreen forest and forming a
barrier between north and south, which is broken in two main
areas only. Rubber plantations have replaced the forests in
parts of the west, but the east holds out less prospect of
development.

(e) The narrow coastal strip in the south consists largely of raised
coral reefs covered with laterite or hill-wash.

Climatically Java is just outside the Equatorial belt, properly
speaking, being situated between 6° and 9° S. Nevertheless, Java is
sufficiently near the Equator to have the small annual range of temperature characteristic of truly Equatorial stations. In Jakarta (Batavia),
a typical example, the yearly average is 78·6° F. (25·9° C.); the annual
range between January, which is curiously enough the coldest month,
and May, the hottest, is less than two degrees. In Java temperature
depends upon altitude, not upon season. The decrease in the average
yearly temperature is about 1° F. for every 310 feet of ascent. The snow-
line would lie far above the tops of the highest mountains, but frosts are
common on calm nights in the dry season, especially on high enclosed
plateaus, from 4,500 feet upwards. The high humidity throughout the
year is another characteristic of the climate; even in the driest month
the mean relative humidity at Jakarta is 78 per cent. Broadly speaking,
there are two seasons in Java, the dry season and the wet season, but
the terms are comparative rather than absolute. In the 'dry season'
the island is under the influence of the east or south-east monsoon
(especially marked in July, August and September), which naturally
brings heavy rainfall to most of the southern coastal strip, though it is
the dry season for most of the island. In the wet season the west or
north-west monsoon blows, especially in December, January and
February, and is the main rain-bearing wind except along the southern
coast. In fact the island lies for much of the year within the inter-
tropical zone of convergence. At all seasons local winds are important
and overshadow the monsoon currents; the mountainous nature of the
country is reflected in the irregularity of the rainfall, for there is a
marked coincidence between the mountains and areas of high precipitation. Much of the rain actually falls during thunderstorms.

Over the fertile lowlands of northern Java the annual rainfall is,
in general, between 40 and 80 inches, and it is very desirable to protect
cultivation, especially rice cultivation, by irrigation works which shall
insure a regular and constant supply of water and by protection works
against flooding. The strong surf along the southern coast has prevented

the formation of deltas, but all the little streams flowing northwards carry large quantities of silt and have built up considerable deltas, still rapidly increasing in size. The streams tend to raise their beds by silt deposition above the level of the surrounding plains and hence the danger of disastrous floods. Thus permanent works for irrigation and flood control now protect about 4,000,000 acres of cultivated land.

Agriculture in Java is divided naturally into subsistence agriculture

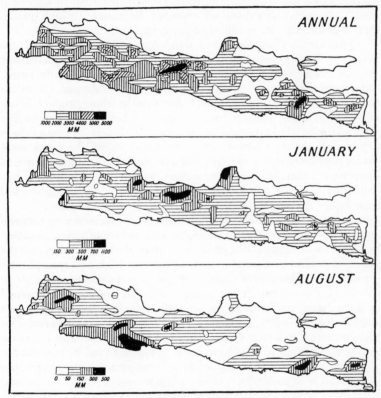

FIG. 231.—The rainfall of Java

and plantation agriculture, though the distinction is less marked than when privately-owned estates were held by Europeans or Chinese, especially in western Java.

The main product and the staple food of the people is rice. Nearly a quarter of the surface of the island is under wet paddy, a further 3½ per cent.—amongst the mountains—under dry or hill paddy. In the plains the young rice plants are planted out in the early part of the rains and harvested in the early part of the dry season, the land being used for secondary crops or left fallow for the remainder of the year, but in the little irrigated terraces which cling to the slopes of the mountains there is no set seed-time or harvest. Despite the huge production Java is not self-supporting and imports rice. Diet in Java is more varied than in most rice-eating countries; maize, cassava, sweet potatoes, ground-nuts, soya beans, other pulses, potatoes and chillies (capsicum) —all occupy large areas and the smallholdings (as distinct from plantations) also have sugarcane and tea. In addition are tobacco and rubber. From the smallholdings some cassava (from which tapioca is made), coconuts and rubber are exported. Because of its high quality there was formerly some export of Java rice.

Quite distinct are the plantation crops, which were developed mainly on European owned or managed estates for export. As in other tropical countries the plantation industry has suffered many vicissitudes—disease may sweep through the crops; economic conditions change the emphasis. At one time coffee was the staple product; it was displaced by sugar which in turn declined, rubber coming into leading place. During the Japanese occupation all owners of estates were deprived of their properties. After liberation, when the estate companies re-entered into possession, not only had the plantations suffered from neglect and damage, often deliberate, but the conditions of law and order made it difficult, sometimes impossible, to attain the old production. All foreign-owned estates have been nationalized.

In 1927–32 sugarcane easily came first in acreage, covering between 400,000 and 450,000 acres, yielding 2,800,000 tons of sugar, prepared by about 180 factories. The plantations were almost exclusively on the plains of central and eastern Java. Yield was high—40 tons of cane per acre—and Java after Cuba was the largest exporter of sugar in the world. But the export was mainly for India and India determined to foster home production (see pp. 238 and 265). By 1934–5 Java's acreage had dropped to 100,000 and production to 510,000 tons though there was a recovery in 1937–8 to 250,000 acres and 1,422,000 tons. Exports alone in 1938 were 1,196,500 metric tons. By contrast the export from the whole of Indonesia in 1949 was a mere 47,000 tons though it rose to 80,000 in 1952 and 281,000 tons in 1954. In 1963 total Indonesian production was 658,000 metric tons but exports were small.

The story with tea is somewhat similar. In the nineteen-thirties it occupied second place to sugar in acreage—90 per cent. of the production was from European or Chinese managed estates, mainly in western Java (though there were also estates in Sumatra). The plantations were on hill-slopes, terraced to encourage adequate drainage but to prevent soil erosion by rain, mainly between 1,000 and 4,500 feet above sea-level, the upper limit being set by night frost. Production reached an average of 220,000,000 lb. or 100,000 tons and in 1938 exports alone were 82,000 tons. In 1949 exports were only 27,000 tons— 45,000 in 1954 and 36,000 in 1963.

Coffee is one of the old-established plantation industries. As in

Ceylon and South India, the trees suffered from the coffee-leaf blight and the original *Coffea arabica* gave place to *Coffea robusta* introduced from Africa in 1901. A later trouble was another pest, the coffee beetle. The coffee plantations are mainly among the hills of eastern Java, where there is a more pronounced dry season of special value to coffee. The yield varies considerably from year to year. Exports in 1949 were only 5,000 tons compared with 70,000 tons in 1938 but had recovered to 38,000 in 1954 and 65,000 in 1963.

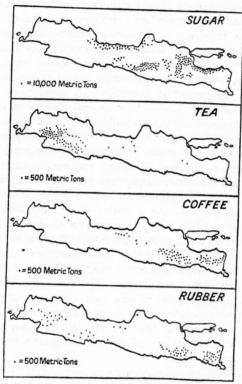

FIGS. 232-5.—The chief plantation crops of Java

The area under rubber in Java increased enormously in inter-war years, though the acreage is less than in Sumatra. In 1951 Indonesia as a whole took the lead from Malaya as first world producer with an output of 790,000 tons (573,000 in 1963). Java tobacco has a good reputation; the cultivation is especially important in central Java around Jogjakarta and Surakarta. Another plantation crop is cacao, but the annual output has never been large. Palm oil and sisal were other plantation products.

Of special interest is the cultivation of cinchona, for long practically a Government monopoly. Java came to supply nearly the entire world production of quinine and rendered the old name 'Peruvian bark' quite a misnomer. The yield of quinine from Javanese bark is double that of the original Peruvian bark. The estates are nearly all in Preanger, especially south of Bandung at elevations of 4,500 to 6,000 feet, but exports have declined greatly. Java also provides a major share of the world's cocaine, obtained from the leaves of the coca tree.

Livestock is relatively unimportant in Java and there was a decline over the period 1939–49. The 2 million buffaloes are needed in the rice-fields; so also are some of the 3 million cattle, though these include Australian and Friesian cows imported as dairy cattle and kept on the mountain pastures to maintain a milk supply. There are numerous goats and sheep, as well as 100,000 pigs kept mainly by the Chinese.

The forests, which cover large areas of the southern mountains, are economically less important than the teak plantations, which cover 1,800,000 acres of the lowlands of central and eastern Java, where there is a pronounced dry season and the rainfall is less than 80 inches.

Amongst native industries that of bamboo-hat plaiting and the famous batik work (for which Jogjakarta (Djokjakarta) is one of the chief centres) may be noted. Although imported cottons printed with the old batik patterns have largely killed the real batik industry, there is still a touch of racial pride in the desire of many Javanese to possess at least one sarong or some garment of genuine batik. It may be explained that batik working is a process of dyeing cotton cloths. Elaborate patterns are traced on the fabric, all parts *not* to be dyed are covered with wax on both sides (applied warm and allowed to cool). The cloth is then dipped a dozen or more times in the dyeing solution —blue or brown as the case may be. The wax is then cleaned off; the parts already dyed are covered with wax and other patterns traced on the undyed portions before the whole is dipped in the second dye. Elaborate patterns in dark blue, brown and white are thus produced in great variety and striking individuality. Copper working is another industry of interest.

Jakarta is another of the cities of Asia which has witnessed a phenomenal recent growth. It was credited with 3,000,000 people in 1961, whilst Surabaja and Jogjakarta have each over a million.

Java has an excellent road system with two main roads running east and west connected by a number of cross-roads. The railways centre on the three main ports of Jakarta, Semarang and Surabaja. They were seriously damaged during the Japanese occupation but are being restored. The old harbour of Jakarta is now used as a fishing port and the fine, well-equipped harbour of Tandjung Periak lies 5 or 6 miles to the east. Semarang has only an open roadstead, but Surabaja is well sheltered by the island of Madura and a harbour basin has been constructed. These three ports are respectively the main outlets of western, central and eastern Java. There are several other small ports: Tjilatjap on the south coast; Tjirebon (Cheribon), Pekalongan and Pasuruan on the north coast. Amongst inland centres, there is the fine city of Bogor (Buitenzorg) with its famous botanical gardens; Bandung, in the heart of the fertile high plains of west Java; Garut, a delightful hill station; and Jogjakarta and Surakarta, two towns with over 100,000 inhabitants in central Java. Java is fortunate in having a number of excellent hill stations.

The foreign trade of Java is an epitome of that of Indonesia as a whole. Jakarta, it should be noted, has a considerable entrepôt trade, but in this respect is overshadowed by Singapore, only 36 hours' steaming away.

Sumatra [1]

With an area of 164,000 square miles, Sumatra is one of the world's largest islands. Stretching from 6° N. to 6° S., Sumatra straddles the Equator and lies almost entirely in the Equatorial belt—1,060 miles from north to south, 250 miles wide at the widest part. Off the west coast is a line of islands separated from the mainland by a wide and deep channel: on

[1] A magnificent great volume of 560 pages, sumptuously illustrated, is O. J. A. Collet's *Terres et Peuples de Sumatra* (Amsterdam, 1925).

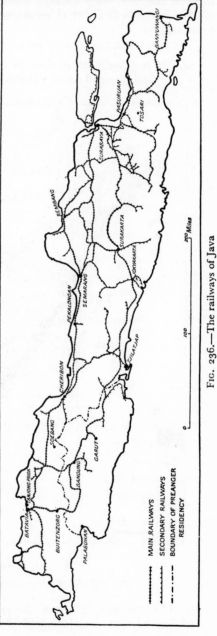

Fig. 236.—The railways of Java

MAIN RAILWAYS
SECONDARY RAILWAYS
BOUNDARY OF PREANGER RESIDENCY

the east the low, often swampy coastlands shelve gradually into the shallow Malacca Strait which separates the northern half of the island from Malaya.

The island consists of three parallel belts:

(a) The mountain belt in the west with large continuous areas over 3,000 feet and many volcanic peaks rising to over 8,000 feet.

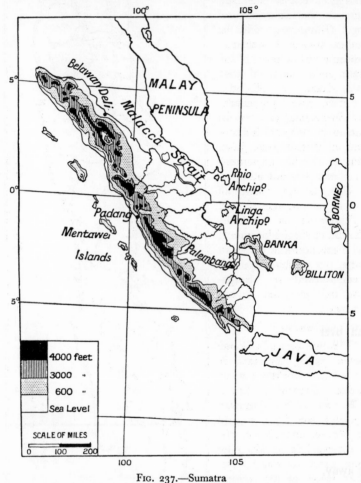

FIG. 237.—Sumatra

Note.—Billiton is an older alternative spelling of Belitung.

(b) The intermediate belt of hills and rolling country.

(c) The alluvial coastal lowland of the east.

The Mountain Belt consists of highly folded rocks of various ages up to and including the early Tertiary, together with large areas covered by volcanic lavas. There are at least ten giant volcanoes which have been active within the past 300 years, and Krakatau, in the Sunda Strait between Sumatra and Java, makes an eleventh. In the north the mountain belt is made up of the Atjeh Highlands and the waterparting is central. Farther south the Batak Highlands consist of a great plateau of volcanic tuff with a remarkable central lake, Lake Toba. From this area southwards the mountain backbone lies near the west coast and the resistant volcanic rocks present a steep forest-clad face to the westerly monsoon. Sometimes the mountains pass into headlands which drop shear into the ocean; in a few places are small swampy plains. In the south the mountain belt consists of two parallel ranges separated by a long, narrow, flat-bottomed trough. Volcanic rocks occupy very large areas in the south.

The Intermediate Belt comprises the foothills of the mountains spreading eastwards into undulating country and then into a wide plain. Much of the area is underlain by gently folded Tertiary rocks in which both coal of moderate quality and oil occur, but in places underlying Triassic rocks reach the surface. Oil occurs especially in the north—in the area behind Langsa and Aroe Bays, just north of the port of Belawan (Fig. 237)—and in the south in the hinterland of Palembang (Palembang-Djambi and other fields). There are important plantation areas in this intermediate belt, especially around Medan in the hinterland of Belawan. Over other areas, as between Palembang and the mountains, the intermediate belt is still clothed with dense Equatorial forest.

The Alluvial Coastal Lowland in places is very extensive. There are huge areas of useless mangrove swamp, notably in the area on either side of the Sungei Kampar, a stream which reaches the sea south-west from Singapore. The islands in the shallow Malacca Strait are also vast swamps and swamp forests. Between Palembang and Bangka Strait is another huge area of almost uninhabited swamp forest.

The great interest of Sumatra lies in the fact that it is still a pioneer land with huge areas which can be settled and developed. Javanese have been migrating from over-populated Java and there are also numerous Tamil immigrants and a few Chinese. Some of the native peoples made large sums of money from rubber, and amongst crops being developed are rubber, oil-palm, tea, tobacco and rice. Mineral oil has brought both wealth and a development of ports, roads, railways and social services. Belawan or Belawan-Deli on the Deli River is a modern port which has grown up where only mangroves flourished a few decades ago. It is the terminus of the railway from Medan. Palembang is the second port of Sumatra, and also is the terminus of a railway which runs through to the south-coast port of Telukbetung, and has oil refineries. Padang is the chief west-coast port and is situated where the mountains can be crossed both by railway and motor road.

The rapid development of Sumatra is indicated by the population growth. By the Census year of 1930 it had reached 7½ million, compared with under 6 million in 1920, and was 15·7 million in 1961.

Singkep, Bangka and Belitung (Billiton)

These little islands form a continuation of the Indo-Malayan mountains of Malaya, and, like the latter, are rich in tin. Singkep forms one of the islands of the Riau-Lingga Archipelago. It is from these islands that the tin ore of the Indonesian Republic is obtained.

Bali and Lombok

Bali, 'the jewel of the East', adjoins the eastern end of Java and shares the physical and some of the economic characters of the larger island, and is even known as 'Little Java'. With an area of rather over 4,000 square miles and a population of over 2 million, the population density in Bali and Lombok reaches over 500. Between Bali and Lombok is a deep channel, famous as the position of 'Wallace's Line', which the great naturalist held to separate the Asiatic and Australian fauna and flora.

Celebes (Sulawesi) and its Dependencies

Celebes, separated from Borneo on the west by the Strait of Macassar, ranks third in point of size amongst the islands of the archi-

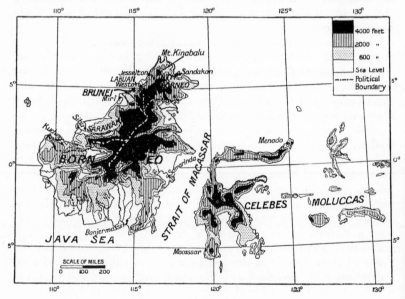

FIG. 238.—Borneo and Celebes

pelago. Its area is roughly 72,680 square miles, its population about 7,000,000. Celebes has been likened in shape to the hand of a gouty patient or to a scorpion, but perhaps the description of Tomlinson is better—'a handful of peninsulas tied in the middle and flung into the ocean'. Celebes has all the things needful to make it one of the most fortunate countries in the Indies; an exceptionally fertile soil, largely volcanic, an excellent climate, though one rather less equable than Java or Sumatra; numerous secure natural harbours, vigorous and intelligent inhabitants. The Portuguese settled in Macassar in 1625; in 1660 they were driven out by the Dutch. The people of Celebes have been in contact with Europeans thus for three centuries, but much of the island is still virtually under the control of native sultans. Makasar (Macassar), the chief port, has a considerable export of copra, rattan and macassar oil (derived from the seeds of *Schleichera trijuga* and used as a basis for cosmetics). Our Victorian ancestors used macassar oil as hair oil, hence the need to protect upholstered chairs by anti-macassars. Manado, in the north, is a clean, prosperous district, exporting copra, coffee and spices (nutmegs and mace).

The Molucca Islands (Spice Islands)

On the west the Moluccas are divided from Celebes by the Sea of Celebes, eastwards they are linked with New Guinea by a mass of islands, some inhabited, many uninhabited. The Southern Moluccas were the Spice Islands *par excellence* and in the early days of Dutch occupation were cruelly and unscrupulously exploited. They still provide, normally, a considerable part of the world's supplies of such spices as pepper, cloves and nutmegs. The name Sandalwood Island, sometimes applied to Sumba of the Lesser Sunda Islands, is indicative of another specialized product. In the Spice Islands the pepper vines were nearly all destroyed during the Japanese occupation, resulting in a shortage felt throughout the world. Both white pepper (40 per cent. of the whole) and black pepper were produced. The difference between the two is only one of preparation. The pepper berries grow in bunches and ripen irregularly. The bunches are picked, piled in heaps to induce fermentation before being dried in the sun. The berries are separated from the stems by simply trampling on them. When dry they are sorted and sifted and constitute black pepper ready for the market. For the preparation of white pepper the biggest and ripest berries are selected, put into bags or baskets and immersed in slowly running water. After about eight days the softened flesh can be removed by trampling, and the hard core washed in clean water, and dried in the sun.

In addition to the Spice Islands black pepper was produced in south Sumatra, white pepper in the island of Bangka; both in northern Sumatra and parts of Borneo.

Borneo (Kalimantan)

The Indonesian section of Borneo covers an area of some 205,000 square miles but the average density is low—about 20. In the main it is a thickly forested little-developed country with a mountainous core and numerous offshoots separating wide expanses of lowland. It has oilfields and refineries around Tarakan and Balik Papan. The principal field is that north of Balik Papan in eastern Borneo. A little oil is obtained from the island of Seram.

PORTUGUESE TIMOR

The island of Timor, at the south-eastern extremity of the archipelago, falls within the geographical range of Indonesia; but neither the Portuguese, who started its European occupation, nor the Dutch, who came after them, succeeded in ousting the other, and the island was divided between them till the Dutch handed over their part of it to Indonesia in 1949, leaving the Portuguese still in possession of the rest (see F. J. Ormeling, *The Timor Problem*, Groningen, 1956).

Timor is a long narrow island with a longitudinal axis of some 300 miles, lying north-east to south-west, and an area about half as large again as Wales. Portugal has the north-east part of the island, and, by a curious arrangement, an enclave on the north-west coast of the Indonesian section; altogether, some 7,300 square miles (rather less than Wales) supporting a population of 517,000 (1960). Dili (Dilly), the capital and chief port, on the north-west coast, has some 52,000 inhabitants.

The physical characteristics of Portuguese Timor are those of the whole island, which is traversed by a volcanic range—quiescent now except for a few mud geysers—with peaks up to nearly 10,000 feet. An interesting feature is a series of raised coral beaches at an elevation of 4,000–5,000 feet. Monsoon forest once covered most of the country, but stretches of dry savanna suitable for livestock now dominate. The arable land is not highly cultivated. Exports include sandalwood, coffee, copra and wax.

WESTERN NEW GUINEA OR WEST IRIAN

The western half of the wild undeveloped island of New Guinea which is usually considered as part of Australasia rather than an East Indian island, was part of the Dutch East Indies. It remained Dutch territory until 1963. It covers no less than 160,000 square miles but has fewer than a million people. Some small oilfields have been discovered —the first commercial production was in 1948 (see Fig. 239). See M. H. Khan and Alice Taylor, 'Western New Guinea', *Focus*, **12,** 5, 1962.

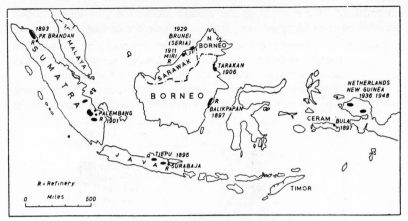

Fig. 239.—The oilfields of the East Indies

The dates of discovery are indicated. **R** = refinery.

THE REPUBLIC OF THE PHILIPPINES [1]

The Philippine Islands have an area of 114,834 square miles, distributed among no less than 7,083 islands and islets, but only 466 have areas of one square mile or over. By far the largest islands are Luzon, 40,422 square miles, and Mindanao, 36,538 square miles. Nine others, Samar (5,050 square miles), Negros, Palwan, Panay, Mindoro, Leyte, Cebu, Bohol and Masbate, have areas of over a thousand square miles. The islands were discovered in 1521 by the Portuguese navigator Magellan, who was slain by the natives of one of the small islands. In 1565 the Spaniards undertook the conquest of the islands, named in honour of a son of the Spanish King, and in 1571 they founded Manila. The Philippine Islands were ceded by Spain to the United States after the Spanish-American War in 1899. Under the United States the islands developed greatly and received a gradually increasing measure of self-government. In 1934 an Act of Congress signed by the President of the United States was accepted by the Philippine Legislature. For ten years the Commonwealth of the Philippines was to be governed by a President who must be a Filipino. The Japanese invaded the islands in December 1941, and occupied the whole by 1942, remaining until 1945. The independent Republic of the Philippines came into existence on July 4, 1946.

The Philippine Islands stretch from south of Taiwan in Latitude 20° N. southwards to the Sulu Islands in about Latitude 5° N. They thus lie almost entirely outside the Equatorial Belt and their climate is

[1] I am greatly indebted to Mr. D. Z. Rosell and Professor A. Cutshall for invaluable help and hospitality when I visited Manila in 1957.

determined in the main by the Asiatic monsoons. According to the rainfall régimes three or four climatic regions are distinguished:[1]

(a) All the western parts, in which the wet and dry seasons are sharply differentiated, the wet lasting from June 15 to December 1, i.e. during the period of the Indian monsoon.

(b) The eastern parts have a humid, cloudy climate with heavy rain throughout the year but with a marked maximum in

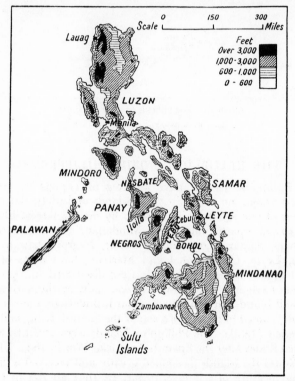

FIG. 240.—The Philippine Islands—physical map

winter when the rain is derived from the normal North-East Trade Winds (December to May). In the months from June to December, the rain is derived from the monsoon winds of which the direction, on the average, is roughly southerly and hence which bring rain to the east as well as to the west coast.

(c–d) The central belt of the islands has a climate which is transitional in character, either having a dry season restricted

[1] José Coronas, 'The Climate and Weather of the Philippines, 1903–1918' *Govt. Phil. Isl. Census of 1918* (Manila, 1920); E. B. Manalo, 'The Distribution of Rainfall in the Philippines', *Phil. Geog. Jour.*, 1956.

to March and April (especially in the north) or having no marked dry season but no marked period of maximum rainfall.

The majority of the typhoons for which the South China Sea and the East China Sea are notorious originate between Latitudes 8° and 15° N. to the east of the Philippines. They are most frequent from July to November, less frequent in May, June and December and rare in other months, being almost entirely absent in February. The Philippine

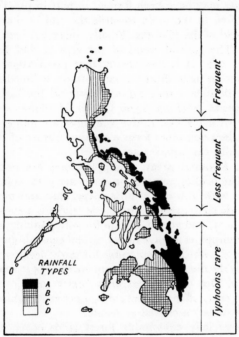

FIG. 241.—The climate of the Philippine Islands—rainfall types after José Coronas

A. East Coast climate, with rain throughout the year but with a winter maximum from the North-East Trades.
B. Transitional type with short dry season (March and April).
C. Transitional type with no marked dry season.
D. West Coast climate, with sharply differentiated wet and dry seasons.
    [*Note.*—**A** corresponds to (*b*) described in the text; **D** to (*a*) and **B C** to (*c–d*).]

Islands may be divided into three belts, the southern, central and northern. Typhoons are very rare in the southern belt and not very common in the central, but the northern part of the islands lies right in the track of the majority of the disturbances at their most violent stage. The frequency of typhoons is an important factor in the economic development of the islands.

Structurally [1] the islands consist of Tertiary fold ranges and may

[1] A full account of the geology and mineral resources was given in Warren D. Smith's *Geology and Mineral Resources of the Philippine Islands*. Manila: Government Printing Bureau, 1925 (dated 1924); information may be brought up to date from U. S. Zafra, *Philippine Economic Handbook*, Silver Spring, Maryland, 1960.

be considered as the crumpled edge of the Asiatic continental platform. Close to the eastern margin of the group is a great foredeep in which the deepest known part of the Pacific is located—only 50 miles from Mindanao. The China Sea to the west of the archipelago is probably a sunken block or *graben*. The land areas of the Philippines are merely the higher portions of the partly submerged mountain chains—in part folds involving Tertiary sediments, in part the summits of volcanoes. The fold ranges may have been formed in part in pre-Tertiary times, but were uplifted in the main towards the end of the Miocene and again at the end of the Pliocene. Finally, there has been considerable recent uplift. The general trend of the arcs or fold lines has been shown in Fig. 212. It is noteworthy that pre-Tertiary sedimentary rocks cover but an insignificant area; Tertiary sediments and igneous rocks are the dominant rock types. Nearly all the higher mountain ranges with peaks reaching 9,500 feet in Mindanao are built up of plutonic or extrusive rocks. Active volcanoes are numerous and both active and extinct volcanoes form a striking feature of the Philippine landscapes, whilst earthquakes are frequent.

Except in favoured areas, Philippine ores are not very highly productive. The leading mineral products are gold, copper and chromite, together with iron ore, a little silver, lead and mercury. Other minerals include coal, gypsum, limestone (there is a considerable production of cement) and guano. Except for gold panning, mining enterprises in the Philippines involve heavy capital expenditure, and it is this factor in the main which is responsible for tardy development. Interest was aroused by the discovery of uranium ore in 1954 in southern Luzon.

Land Use. Out of the total area forests cover over half; grass pastures, 3 per cent.; mangrove swamps, 2 per cent.; whilst 38 per cent. (44,000 square miles) is classed as arable.

The commercially exploitable forest lands cover 32,300 square miles. In the south the forests are of the Equatorial type [1] and furnish hardwoods for constructional and cabinet uses, as well as rattans, bamboos, tan and dye barks and dye woods. Other trees yield gums and resins and vegetable oils as well as gutta-percha. Large areas are covered with bamboo. Elsewhere in this book there has been occasion to lament the appalling destruction of fine forest by shifting aboriginal cultivation. The same is true of the Philippines. Sixty per cent. of the deforested area—40 per cent. of the area of the archipelago—is today covered with commercially worthless second-growth forest or giant grasses.

But agriculture is the mainstay of the archipelago's economy. The

---

[1] Valuable detailed studies of variation according to elevation have been made by W. H. Brown, 'Vegetation of Philippine Mountains', *Manila Bur. of Sci. Publ.*, No. 13 (1919). Another important paper, in connection with a study of Asiatic vegetation, is E. D. Merrill, 'Distribution of the Dipterocarpaceae', *Philippine Jour. of Sci.*, **23**, 1923, 1–33.

chief food crops are rice (nearly 8 million acres), maize (nearly 5 million acres), sweet potatoes, cassava and bananas. Three commercial crops are of outstanding importance—coconuts, sugar and Manila hemp.

The principal food crops are rice and maize and no comment is necessary except to point out that production is insufficient and that there is a large import of rice as well as of wheat and wheat flour. 'If the rice growers of the Philippines obtained as high acre yields as do the growers of Japan or the United States, instead of buying from India and Japan one-fourth the rice consumed in the islands, the Philippines would be the third largest rice-exporting country in the world.' [1] This was written fifty years ago but is still broadly true: rice yields in 1962 were only a quarter to a third those of Japan. Import of wheat is mainly from the United States.

The hemps are the great rope-making fibres and may be separated into the true or soft hemps and the hard hemps. One leading hard-fibred hemp is abaca or Manila hemp, in the production of which the Philippine Islands have practically a monopoly. It is obtained from the stems and huge leaves of *Musa textilis*, a plant of the banana family —indeed the plants so closely resemble bananas that the uninitiated cannot distinguish them. The plants require well-drained soil, hence are frequently grown on steep hillsides, an evenly distributed rainfall and constant high humidity. For long the industry was in native hands; nearly all stripping was done by hand and the quality of the fibre was largely a matter of good or bad stripping. In 1913 Manila hemp formed 45 per cent. by value of the exports of the islands, but the industry fell to a very low ebb during the Japanese occupation and in 1950 provided only 12 per cent. Output in 1963 had recovered to 128,000 out of a world total of all hard fibres (including sisal) of 800,000 tons.

Coconut products form the leading exports of the islands, and in the production of copra and coconut oil, the islands may be classed as the leading country in the world. There is a very large demand for coconut oil in the United States and the bulk of the requirements is obtained from the Philippines. Of all vegetable oils coconut is most highly esteemed in the States because of its readily saponifiable properties which render it suitable for cold process soaps, as well as because it is the only oil for the manufacture of soaps which will lather in salt water (marine soaps) and one of the few which form soft soap with caustic soda. The high percentage of glycerine also renders the oil of special value. Consequently coconut planting has been developed as a plantation industry in the island to a degree which is not found in Ceylon or Malaya, where the coconut groves are mainly in smallhold-ings. The distribution of the plantations is limited primarily by climatic

[1] H. J. Waters, 'The Development of the Philippine Islands', *Geog. Rev.*, **5**, 1918, 282–92. Power from the great Maria Christina hydro-electric plant (in Mindanao) is now used for the manufacture of ammonium sulphate.

factors—to the central and eastern regions because of the well-distributed rainfall, to the centre and south because of the typhoons of the north. In the south the coconuts come into competition with abaca. The plantations do best on plains sloping downwards to the sea, where the drainage is good but circulating waters renew the supplies of plant food; this is well seen on the slopes of Mount Banahao. When establishing a plantation the nuts are first germinated and then transplanted when the seedling is about a foot high. Experiments have shown that

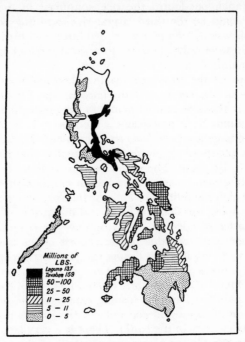

Fig. 242.—The production of copra in the Philippine Islands
(*After* L. J. Borga.) This map should be compared carefully with that showing climatic regions.

light and air in plenty are essential for a good yield, hence the trees are spaced 10 metres—33 feet—apart. They come into bearing at the age of six years and continue for thirty or forty years. Some idea of the spread of the industry may be gauged from the rise in production from roughly 125,000 metric tons of copra (oil converted to copra at 0·6 lb. oil = 1 lb. copra) in 1910–13 to 367,000 tons in 1921–4, and from 22 per cent. of the world's total in 1913 to 30 per cent. in 1922. In 1936, production was estimated at 615,000 tons of copra (export included 291,000 tons copra and 159,000 tons oil). In 1938 the Philippines took the lead over Indonesia as the world's leading exporter. Despite a recession during the war, export of copra exceeded a million tons in 1947 and has been maintained at such high figures since that time as to form up to 70 per cent. of the exports in some years. The best copra is obtained from very ripe nuts, just about to fall, and the elimination of unripe nuts is one of the several ways in which large, carefully controlled plantations can maintain the quality of the copra. The cloudy skies of the islands prevent sun-drying in many areas and have thus proved a blessing in disguise in that the installation of modern hot-air drying apparatus is general and is gradually eliminating the old smoke-drying.

The sugarcane cultivation has also entered upon a new phase. In 1913 Dean Worcester was able to record the fact that one modern central mill had been established, otherwise 'the machinery and methods employed might almost be called antediluvian, and it is a wonder that sugar could ever have been produced at a profit under

Percentages of total :	A S I A						NON – ASIA		
PHILIPPINES	INDONESIA	CEYLON	INDIA	MALAYA	OTHERS	OCEANIA	MEXICO	OTHERS

Fig. 243.—The position occupied by the Philippine Islands in the world's production of copra and coconut oil (converted to copra), 1954

In 1909–13 the Philippine Islands had a little over 20 per cent. of world exports, nearly all exported as copra. By 1922–5 the share had increased to nearly 30 per cent., but nearly half was exported as coconut oil.

such conditions . . . deep ploughing was unknown . . . there was not an irrigated field of cane in the islands'. Before the Japanese occupation output had reached 8½ million tons of cane, 1 million tons of raw sugar and 800,000 tons exported. Post-war production has recovered and now exceeds these figures: 1,244,000 tons were produced in 1954; 1,554,800 in 1963.

Another leading crop is tobacco, of which the domestic consumption is very large and the export considerable. Bananas form an important part of the food of the people but do not figure as an export. Rightly or wrongly it has been held that most of the tropical products imported by the United States might be produced in the Philippines, including rubber, coffee, cocoa and tea.

The leading animals in the Philippine Islands are the heavy water-buffalo (carabao), especially important in the rice-fields. There were 3·3 million in 1963, together with a million cattle, horses and mules, 6,200,000 pigs, 500,000 goats and 13,000 sheep.

Communications and Trade. There are railways in Luzon (735 miles), Panay and Cebu (132 miles), but destruction during the war was heavy and only 600 miles of track were in operation by 1952. There are some 35,000 miles of roads (1963)—very good in the main island of Luzon. Apart from inter-island trade, most of the commerce centres on Manila.

A.—16

Roughly 75 per cent. of the foreign trade is with the United States. The chief articles imported and exported are shown in Fig. 244.

Population. The total population, according to the Census of 1960, was 27,087,685, the bulk of whom are 'Filipinos', allied racially to the Malays with a considerable admixture of Chinese and Spanish blood in places, and converted to Roman Catholicism by the Spaniards. The Independent Filipino Church, with rituals resembling those of the Catholic Church but proclaiming that modern science is superior to

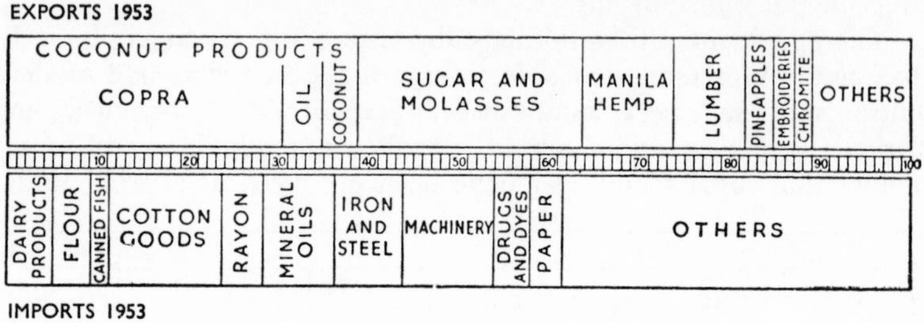

EXPORTS 1953

COCONUT PRODUCTS			SUGAR AND MOLASSES	MANILA HEMP	LUMBER	PINEAPPLES	EMBROIDERIES	CHROMITE	OTHERS
COPRA	OIL	COCONUT							

DAIRY PRODUCTS	FLOUR	CANNED FISH	COTTON GOODS	RAYON	MINERAL OILS	IRON AND STEEL	MACHINERY	DRUGS AND DYES	PAPER	OTHERS

IMPORTS 1953

FIG. 244.—The foreign trade of the Philippine Islands

The main changes to 1963: copra 22, oil 6, coconut 3, sugar 20, hemp 4, lumber 20, copper 4.

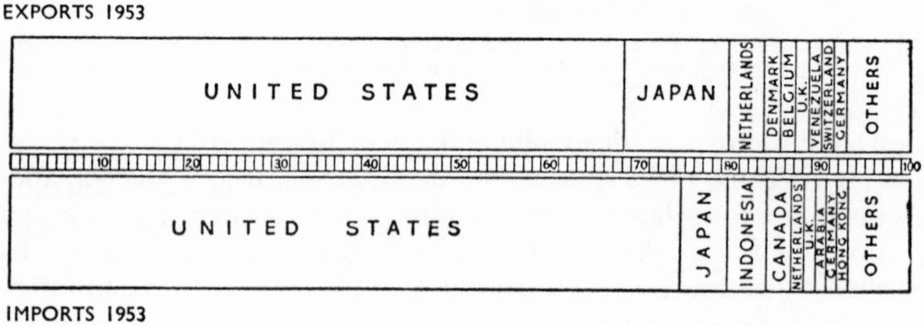

EXPORTS 1953

UNITED STATES	JAPAN	NETHERLANDS	DENMARK	BELGIUM	U.K.	VENEZUELA	SWITZERLAND	GERMANY	OTHERS

UNITED STATES	JAPAN	INDONESIA	CANADA	NETHERLANDS	U.K.	ARABIA	GERMANY	HONG KONG	OTHERS

IMPORTS 1953

FIG. 245.—The direction of the foreign trade of the Philippine Islands

It has recently become more widespread.

Biblical tradition, denying the possibility of miracles and conceiving God as a single invisible Father, is said to embrace about 10 per cent. of the people. Muslim Moors number half a million in Mindanao and Sulu, and there are numbers of pagans still in outlying tracts.

Manila is the chief industrial and commercial centre, with a population in 1960 of 1,138,600. The new capital Quezon City just to the north-east had 398,000. The Chinese community (110,000) is important in Manila. Other towns are Iloilo on Panay (151,000); Cebu on Cebu (251,000); Zamboango on Mindanao (131,000); Davao on Mindanao (226,000), Basilan (156,000), Bacolol (119,000) on Negros SanCarlos (125,000) and Rizal (133,000). The Philippines have a hot-weather capital in Baguio.

The Republic of the Philippines is a country of contrasts and unique in many ways. The only Christian country in Asia, nearly half its population of charming, handsome and talented people speak English which is the medium of instruction in schools, though nationalism has decreed that a new language based on Tagalog (allied to Malay) shall be the official national language. Only a small number (especially merchants in the tobacco business) still use Spanish. American influence is very strong—a large and modern American car is a *sine qua non* of membership of the upper classes, whose life in sophisticated Manila or Baguio is in marked contrast to the rural areas. The old walled city which is the core of Manila suffered badly during the Japanese occupation, but the main city has been rebuilt. As well as the modern buildings, its innumerable jeep-buses and Coca-Cola signs are constant reminders of American influence.

REFERENCES

There is an extensive general literature; the more serious works include W. C. Forbes, *The Philippine Islands*, 3 vols. (Harvard University Press, 1945), R. G. Hainsworth and R. T. Moyer, *Agricultural Geography of the Philippine Islands* (Washington, 1945), and J. E. Spencer, *Land and People in the Philippines* (University of California Press, 1952). See also R. E. Huke, 'Republic of the Philippines', *Focus*, **11**, 8, 1961.

THAILAND (SIAM)

The independent Kingdom of Thailand has an area of slightly under 198,000 square miles, but a population according to the Census of 1960 of only 26,257,916, giving a density of 132 per square mile. By comparison with India and China, Thailand is still sparsely populated but the population is increasing rapidly. It was estimated at only 8,357,000 in 1913 and at the Census of 1947 was 17,442,689. The great majority of the inhabitants are Siamese or Thai, and are closely akin to the Shans of Burma—indeed the words 'Siam' and 'Shan' are probably of identical origin.

The country is called by its inhabitants Thaï or Muang-Thaï— 'the Kingdom of the Free'—or alternatively Prades Thai. Since the European language mainly used in the country is English the Siamese Government announced officially in 1939 the change of the name Siam to Thailand. From 1942 to 1945 Siam became the unwilling ally of Japan in order to avoid the worse position of Japanese occupation. Britain reverted officially to the old name Siam, but after the renewed declaration in 1949 that the designation should be Thailand, that name came into general use.

The limits of the kingdom have varied considerably even within comparatively recent times, consequent especially upon the French sphere of influence to the east where the French held some territory west of the Mekong, the natural frontier, till 1941. In the south-east the Siamese claimed the greater part of the old Kingdom of Cambodia but after a dispute with France in 1907 the frontier gave most to be included in French Indo-China. In 1941–2 the Japanese, to secure

Thai collaboration, arranged the temporary restoration of this territory to Siam. In the south Thailand occupies the full width of the isthmus, the narrowest part of which is known as the Kra Isthmus, so that the country has a direct outlet to the Indian Ocean. The Thai, like the Burmese, are Buddhists and religion dominates their lives as it does their neighbours', but external manifestations are different and the ornate 'wats' contrast with the simpler pagodas of Burma. In the extreme south of the country the people are mainly Mahommedan Malays. By treaty in 1909 the Malay states of Perlis, Kedah, Trengganu and Kelantan transferred their allegiance from Siam to become states of British Malaya.

The full autonomy of Siam was recognized by Britain in 1926, and in 1932 reforms changed one of the few surviving absolute monarchies with a government in which most important offices were held by members of the Royal Family into a constitutional monarchy with a Council of State and a Legislative Assembly. There have been changes since, including more than one *coup d'état*, but Siam remains a constitutional monarchy. In 1934 local government was strengthened by the division of the country into ten 'circles', further divided into provinces, districts and communes.

Geographically Thailand falls naturally into four main divisions—Northern, Central, Eastern and Southern Thailand.

Northern Thailand embraces an area of some 60,000 square miles, and consists of a series of roughly parallel hill ranges and valleys trending north and south. The hills gradually increase in elevation towards the west and north, reaching heights of over 6,000 feet. They are all thickly forested, except where scarred by the clearings of hill tribes or interrupted by masses of bare rock. The hills are drained by numerous streams, of which those on the extreme west join the Salween; those on the extreme north the Mekong; but the remainder flow southwards into four streams which eventually join about latitude 16° N. to form the Menam.[1] The valleys range from broad, open cultivated tracts to narrow forested gorges. Naturally the valleys are broader towards the south, wide banks of rich alluvium fringe the streams and form some of the most valuable agricultural land in the kingdom. The town of Chieng-mai lies in the heart of this region and is connected with Bangkok by rail.

Central Thailand has an area estimated at 55,000 square miles and consists virtually of one vast plain stretching from the mountains on the borders of Thailand on the east, and for 300 miles from the north to the head of the Gulf of Siam in the south. Only here and there do small hills rise abruptly to interrupt the general dead level. The plain lies at a very slight elevation above sea-level, and is subject to regular annual floods. It is drained by sluggish streams—of which the Menam is the

[1] Menam = THE river; properly the Menam Chao Phaya.

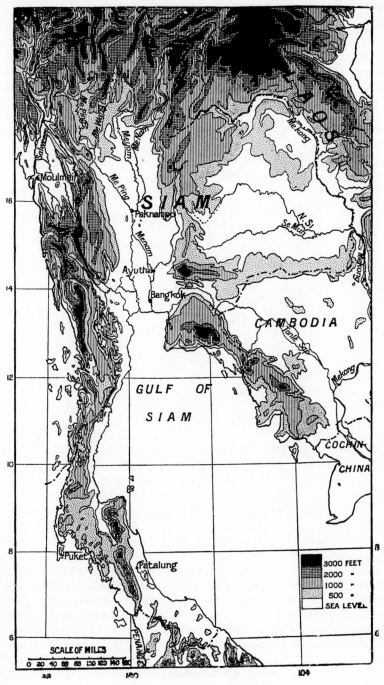

FIG. 246.—General map of Thailand

chief—whose beds have been raised slightly above the level of the plain by their own alluvial accumulations. 'Belts and patches of jungle occur to the northwards as well as in the east and west littoral districts, but the greater part of the plain consists of wide expanses, thinly clothed with tall Palmyra palms, dotted with the clumps of bamboo which

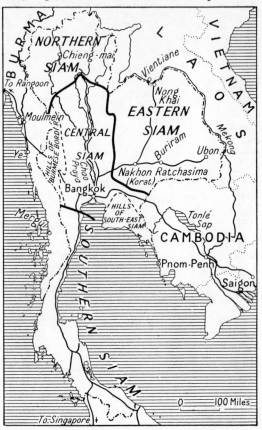

FIG. 247.—The natural regions of Thailand, showing also railways. The notorious Burma-Siam railway constructed by slave labour by the Japanese is shown linking Bangkok to a point north of Ye

mark the presence of villages, or absolutely treeless. The surface soil is heavy, clayey and entirely of alluvial formation, and about a quarter of the area is under cultivation, while the rest, covered in the main with grass and reeds, awaits a practicable scheme of irrigation and the coming of a population, which two factors alone are wanting to make Central Siam one of the greatest rice-producing districts of the world' (Graham, 1912). Since these words were written the Royal Irrigation Department has opened up considerable tracts north of Bangkok, connecting by a canal the Menam and Bang Pakawng Rivers and constructing numbers of smaller canals. In 1916 the Prasak South Canal Project, by which 250,000 acres are irrigated, was started. The great plain of Central Siam lies in the immediate hinterland of Bangkok.

To the east and south-east of Bangkok is a small area of hills, some rising to 3,000 feet, largely covered with a dry forest resembling the *indaing* of Burma, known to the Siamese as *pa-deng*. Through part runs the railway to the frontier, continued beyond by a good road to Siemreap with its modern French hotels and within six miles of the famous ruins of Angkor.

Eastern Thailand has an area of about 65,000 square miles and consists of a huge shallow basin, encircled by hills. The basin is drained eastwards by the Mun and the Shi, which unite before joining the Mekong. Included in Eastern Thailand is also a strip of country between the Mekong and the girdle of hills just mentioned, and the whole region is bounded on the north-east and east by the Mekong itself, forming also the boundary of the kingdom. Most of Eastern Thailand has an indifferent soil and an adverse climate. Thin scrub jungle covers the slopes of the hills, huge swamps much of the low ground, at least during the rains—or dried-up wastes of grass and reeds in the hot season. 'A population of some million and a quarter, Laos, Siamese and Kambodians, that is, about 20 people to the square mile, inhabits this inhospitable land, wresting from the reluctant soil crops barely sufficient to maintain an existence which, passed amidst damp and mud for one half of the year and in a dry, hot and dust-laden atmosphere for the other, is one of the most miserable imaginable, more especially since this whole neighbourhood is peculiarly liable to the visitation of epidemics of diseases affecting both men and cattle' (Graham).

Southern Thailand has an area of about 25,000 square miles and comprises all the narrower part of the Malay Peninsula, and farther north a strip between Lower Burma and the Gulf of Siam. In some places this strip is scarcely a dozen miles wide and rises steeply from the coast to the mountain divide on the Burma frontier. Farther south the region is sharply divided by the central range into an east coast and west coast tract. 'The natural scenery of this district is very beautiful, making a picture, constantly repeated with minor variations, of caerulean blue water, golden beaches, villages nestling among tall palmtrees, miles of rolling evergreen jungle behind these, and at the back of all the magnificent purple mountains towering into the sky. Though generally of a hilly character, the east coast district comprises several broad open plains of varying extent where, on a light but rich soil of clay and sand alluvium, crops of rice are annually grown and large herds of cattle are raised. Round about the towns of Lakon and Patalung the largest and most fertile plains are situated. In these open lands a considerable population lives and prospers exceedingly by agriculture and by fishing in the seas which are here alive with fish of many kinds. Far different from that of the people of Eastern Siam, their lot is of the happiest, for with plenty to eat, an equal climate and little or no disease, they scarce know the meaning of trouble' (Graham). The western coast of the peninsula is more indented than the eastern and resembles that of Tenasserim (Burma) to the north. On one of the islands lies the town of Puket, long famous for its tin mines, and with a large Chinese population. It is through the delightful east coast region of Southern Thailand that the railway between Malaya and Bangkok runs.

Thailand may be said to have one great river of its own—the Menam. Both the Salween and Mekong for considerable distances form the boundaries of Thailand, but the Menam and its tributaries lie completely within Thai territory. The Menam (or Menam Chao Phaya, to use the full name) is to Thailand what the Irrawaddy is to Burma. Of the four head streams the Meping and Mewang are rapid shallow streams liable to sudden floods; the Meyom and Menam to the east rise at lower elevations and flow quietly to the confluence at Paknam Po, being navigable for about 140 miles above that point. From there to the sea the waters of the Menam follow a number of tortuous courses. On one of the channels lies the old capital of Ayutia. The low banks are thickly fringed with bamboos and tall palms 'shading and half concealing an almost continuous succession of long straggling villages, interspersed with innumerable monasteries, temples and pagodas.' The river is thronged with craft of all kinds, a highway, a sewer, and the sole water supply for a large proportion of the country's people. Bangkok bestrides the Menam about 20 miles from its mouth and is remarkable for its size relative to the total population of the country. Its population is over 2,300,000 and it handles 85 per cent. of the foreign trade of Thailand. As elsewhere in the East there are many Chinese traders in Bangkok and the other towns.

Geologically the hills of Northern, Western and Southern Thailand form part of the great Indo-Malayan mountain system. The higher ridges are usually of granite; the other rocks are gneisses, schists, slates, sandstones and limestones varying in age from pre-Cambrian to early Mesozoic and including occasionally lake-basins of younger rocks, exactly as in Malaya and eastern Burma. The shallow basin of Eastern Thailand has a rim composed on the north and west mainly of limestone. The interior of the basin is covered with alluvium, in which lateritic soils prevail. Central Thailand is nearly all alluvium, the occasional hills being of limestone. Thailand naturally shares in the mineral riches of the surrounding countries; the minerals are numerous and varied. Tin is especially important in the island of Puket; tin and wolfram are also found in other parts of the Thai portion of the Malay Peninsula. Alluvial gold is widely distributed and has been spasmodically panned by natives and Chinese—especially in the slack seasons for agriculture. Coal and iron, zinc, manganese, antimony and other minerals also occur. Production in 1962 included over 20,300 tons of tin concentrates, also wolfram, antimony and lead ore. There was also an output of iron ore and a considerable tonnage of cement.

The climate and seasons in Thailand closely resemble those of India—the so-called cold season from the end of October to February, the hot season from March to May and the rains from June to October. Central Thailand benefits from the cooling winds from the Gulf of Siam from March to October; the basin of Eastern Thailand is cut off from these and suffers great extremes as well as a lower rainfall. The wet south of Thailand, in the peninsula, has a short dry season and a small annual range of temperature.

The classification of vegetation drawn up for Burma applies equally well to Thailand. The teak forests of the north-west are commercially important; the cutting of the timber is an important industry and is mainly in British hands. The logs are either floated down the Menam to Bangkok or, to a less extent, down the Salween to Moulmein in Burma.

Agriculture in Thailand was long almost synonymous with the cultivation of rice. Apart from small patches of vegetables grown for individual family use, the bulk of the cultivated land was occupied by rice. The area reached over 16,000,000 acres in 1963 compared with 8,400,000 in 1934–8 and the harvest 9,250,000 metric tons compared with 4,357,000. Nevertheless the years since the Second World War have been marked by a diversification—with marked increases in maize, coconuts, soya-beans, ground-nuts, sesamum, cotton, sugarcane and especially rubber and tobacco. Thailand has nearly 6 million cattle, nearly 7 million buffaloes, 187,000 horses and over 12,000 elephants. Fishing is important in Thailand, for just as every meal consists of rice, so every meal is flavoured with fish—roasted, fried, boiled or raw; fresh or 'preserved'. The Buddhist religion of the vast majority of the Thais deprecates the taking of animal life; that a fish, removed from the water, is foolish enough to die is a dispensation of Providence.

Kapi (the ngapi of the Burmese) is a fish-paste made of scraps, oddments, small fish, rare fish and doubtful fish, sand and salt, pounded and kneaded, often by bare feet, in a kapi trough and allowed to ferment before being dried into little cakes or stored in jars. Its use, and likewise its ineradicable odour, permeate the farthest corners of the country. Millions of fish are trapped in pools left after the monsoon.

In 1896 the Government took over both the construction and direction of the railways and the Royal State Railways of Siam became one of the largest commercial undertakings in the country. The railways are all metre gauge and four main lines radiate from Bangkok. Owing to the shortage of fuel and the expense of bringing bulky wood to the capital early use—in the thirties—was made of diesel locomotives. Through-running with Singapore began in 1918 and through-expresses since 1922, and by 1950 there were 2,030 miles of railway open. Construction of roads came later than railways and at first was concentrated on extensions of the railway system. As elsewhere the advent of motor-lorries and cars changed that and Thailand absorbed an immense number of bicycles. However, bullock and buffalo carts are still the rule over much of the country and three-quarters of commercial traffic is still carried by water.

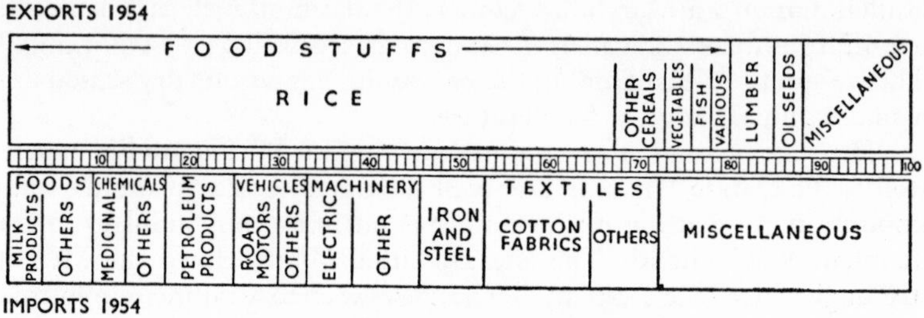

EXPORTS 1954

FOOD STUFFS						OTHER CEREALS	VEGETABLES	FISH	VARIOUS	LUMBER	OIL SEEDS	MISCELLANEOUS
	RICE											

FOODS		CHEMICALS		PETROLEUM PRODUCTS	VEHICLES			MACHINERY		IRON AND STEEL	TEXTILES		MISCELLANEOUS
MILK PRODUCTS	OTHERS	MEDICINAL	OTHERS	PETROLEUM PRODUCTS	ROAD MOTORS	OTHERS	ELECTRIC	OTHER		IRON AND STEEL	COTTON FABRICS	OTHERS	MISCELLANEOUS

IMPORTS 1954

FIG. 248.—The foreign trade of Thailand
The lumber is teak. Rubber should be added to the exports: now second in value to rice.

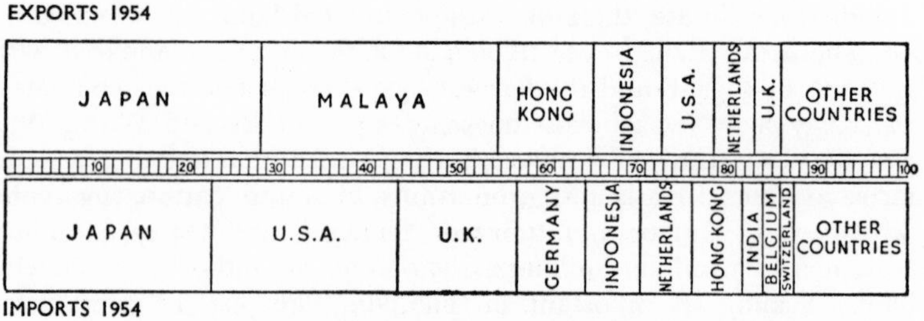

EXPORTS 1954

JAPAN	MALAYA	HONG KONG	INDONESIA	U.S.A.	NETHERLANDS	U.K.	OTHER COUNTRIES

JAPAN	U.S.A.	U.K.	GERMANY	INDONESIA	NETHERLANDS	HONG KONG	INDIA	BELGIUM	SWITZERLAND	OTHER COUNTRIES

IMPORTS 1954

FIG. 249.—The direction of the foreign trade of Thailand

Recent years have been marked by the phenomenal growth of Bangkok. The original site was a loop in the river, so that there was a natural water defence on the north, west and south, and a canal or klong, with reinforcing walls, formed the defence on the east. It is in that direction that the city expanded, early extensions being defended by further canals. Latterly, though these waterways are still numerous some have been filled in. One magnificent road bridge spans the Menan, and has permitted industrial and residential expansion to the south-west but immediately facing the old city is still a primitive Venice of the East, where shops face the innumerable waterways, and the houses on piles are only accessible by boat. The main river is really the port: the bar at the entrance to the Menam has been dredged so that vessels drawing up to 28 feet can use the reinforced concrete wharf of the new port. It is visited annually by over 1,800 vessels, with aggregate tonnage of 5·9 m.

The main features of Thailand's foreign trade are shown in Figs. 248-9. Amongst the exports the overwhelming importance of rice is noteworthy; the prosperity of the foreign trade and the existence of a favourable trade balance depend largely upon the rice harvest. A feature of interest was the rapid growth in the output of rubber from the Thai portion of the Malay Peninsula, but it is now of less importance.

REFERENCES

An excellent book, essential to supplement the inadequate account here given, is W. A. Graham's *Siam, a Handbook of Practical, Commercial and Political Information*, 2nd Edition, 2 vols., 1924 (London). Like Burma, the poetic charm of Siam has inspired a large number of books, such as E. Young's *The Kingdom of the Yellow Robe*, Le May's *An Asian Arcady*, P. A. Thompson's *Lotus Land*, and Pierre Loti's *Siam*. For details of trade and economic development, reference should be made to the *Statistical Year-Book of the Kingdom of Siam*, and the British Government's Commercial Reports. A very comprehensive work is W. Credner's *Siam: das Land der Tai*, Stuttgart, 1935. See also L. D. Stamp, 'Siam before the War', *Geog. Jour.*, 1942. On the occasion of the Pacific Science Congress at Bangkok in 1957, the Government published a useful summary entitled 'Thailand'. See also R. E. Huke, 'Thailand', *Focus*, **12,** 6, 1962, and R. L. Pendleton, *Thailand*, Amer. Geog. Soc., 1962.

CAMBODIA, LAOS AND VIETNAM

Before the Second World War, Indo-China was part of France's colonial empire, comprising the colony of Cochin-China in the extreme south of the Indo-Chinese Peninsula; the protectorates of Annam and Tongking along the east coast, facing the South China Sea; the protectorate of Cambodia, in the south-west, adjoining southern Thailand and fronting the Gulf of Siam; and the Laos protectorate, an inland territory bordering eastern Thailand. As a result of the war during which the Japanese occupied most of the country these five territories were reconstituted as three independent states associated with France in the French Union. Cambodia and Laos became sovereign states with constitutional monarchies. Cochin-China, Annam and Tongking were combined in the republic of Vietnam and became known respectively as South, Central and North Vietnam; the former Emperor of Annam was recognized as 'Chief of the State'.

There arose in the north, however, a strong Communist organization, the Viet-minh. After a severe struggle, costly both to Vietnamese and French forces, the Communists gained control of Tongking and French troops were withdrawn in 1954. By the armistice of 1954 the Northern (Communist) and Southern Zones of Vietnam became in effect two countries. The boundary is roughly the 17° parallel. The south became a republic in 1955. Cambodia and Laos became independent kingdoms completely divorced from France in 1953-4.

French entry into Cochin-China dates from 1858 and in 1867 that country wrested from the Annamites was annexed by France. Cambodia was added in 1884, Tongking after a longer and more costly

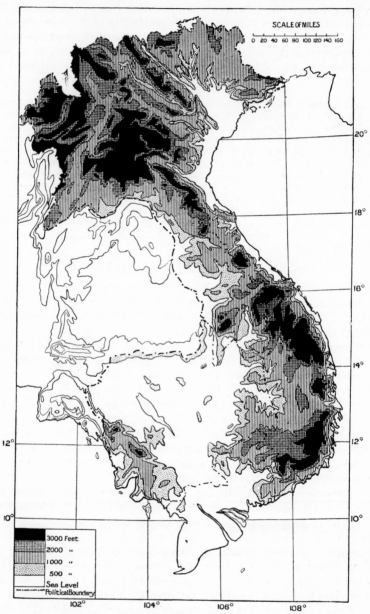

SCALE OF MILES
0 20 40 60 80 100 120 140 160

3000 Feet
2000 "
1000 "
500 "
Sea Level
Political Boundary

FIG. 250.—Physical map of Indo-China (Vietnam, Laos and Cambodia)

conquest in 1884, Laos in 1893. There were later some small adjustments of frontier so that the total area was about 287,000 square miles and the population about 28 million in 1952.

The traditional divisions coincide to a considerable extent with geographical units: Cochin-China and Cambodia include the rice-growing plains of the south; Annam the mountain ridge of the east and its coastal strip; Laos the country behind the Annamese Mountains and cut off by them from the sea; Tongking the Song Kai or Red River Basin in the north.

The whole could formerly also be divided in another way into three economic units which were actually the hinterlands of the three main ports:

(a) The hinterland of Saïgon, comprising Cochin-China, Cambodia, Southern Laos and Annam south of Cape Varella—the great rice-growing countries.

(b) The hinterland of Tourane (now Da Nang), comprising Central Annam between Porte d'Annam and Cape Varella—a narrow strip of coastland backed by high mountains.

(c) The hinterland of Haiphong, comprising Tongking, Northern Annam and Northern Laos.

Physically the whole is divided into great basins by chains of mountains and highlands which form offshoots from the great plateaus of Yunnan and southern China. One branch forms the northern border of the Red River Basin and separates Tongking from China; the other separates the Red River Basin from that of the Mekong. In the north in the 'Haut Laos', many peaks of the latter reach over 6,000 feet and some of the plateaus 4,000 or even 5,000 feet. It is from this centre that the great Annamite Cordillera is given off towards the south-east. This great chain runs parallel to the Annamese coast and separates, in a very effective manner, Annam from Laos. The chain is irregular in height and form; by the spurs which it gives off it forms a series of compartments isolated from one another, or only connected by comparatively high passes. One of the latter is the so-called Annam Gate by which the Annamites of the north were able to invade the territory of their enemies the Cams or Cochin-Chinese of the south. It marks also the division between Northern and Southern Annam. Another pass is the 'Col des Nuages' between Hué and Da Nang (1,500 feet). Communication across the main chain is very difficult: Annam and Laos are almost completely separated, the chief pass being that of Aïlao between Hué and Savannaket on the Mekong. Several peaks of the Annamite Cordillera are over 6,000 feet. To the west the mountainous massif is prolonged into Laos by a series of plateaus, such as that of Cammon in the north and Bolovens (3,000–4,000 feet) in the south. The latter is continued westwards as the chain of Dangkak and eventually turns southwards along the coast of the Gulf of Siam.

Leaving the mountains, Indo-China includes the plains of Tongking in the north and the wide flat basin of Cambodia and the delta plains of the Mekong in the south. A remarkable feature of the Cambodian Plain is the great lake Tonlé Sap. The lake itself is connected with the Mekong by a channel (called also the Tonlé Sap) 40 or 50 miles long. For six months of the year, during the rains, the current is from the Mekong towards the lake; for the other six months from the lake to the Mekong. There is even a short period when the lake is affected by the tidal movements of the sea, 180 miles away. Economically the lake is important because it acts as a regulator of the floods of the Mekong.

Floods are still, however, serious and a gigantic scheme has been formulated for regulating the lower Mekong to the benefit of Laos, Thailand, Cambodia and Vietnam.

In a general way, of course, the climate of Indo-China is dominated by the two great monsoons, the north-east monsoon from November to March which causes the dry season over most of the country—except Annam—and the south-west monsoon from April to October which causes the rainy season. Climatically there are really three distinct provinces. In northern Annam, northern Laos and Tongking the dry season is relatively cold and the rainy season is marked by strong sea breezes and storms. In central Annam it is scarcely correct to say that the seasons are reversed: the conditions suggest rather a comparison with Madras, for the rains are prolonged to January or February, whilst the heat is excessive in May, June, July and August. In Cochin-China, Cambodia and southern Annam the temperatures are higher throughout the year and the hot season is especially trying.

South Vietnam is a republic which includes the delta plains of the Mekong (a region formerly known as Cochin China) and the southern half of the former Annam, another area name now rarely used since the people throughout speak Vietnamese. South Vietnam has received American support as a bulwark against the communism of the north. It has an area of 66,263 square miles and a population estimated in 1962 at 14·2 m. including about 670,000 hill-peoples and 450,000 Chinese and Cambodians. Large areas of the Mekong delta are still occupied by unreclaimed marshes, but 36 per cent. of the whole area is classed as cultivated. Out of the total area cultivated rice occupies nearly 90 per cent.—a proportion which compares with that in the Irrawaddy Delta of Burma. The production of paddy in 1963 was 5·3 m. metric tons from 6·3 m. acres. Ploughing is done mainly by water-buffaloes; other animals include nearly 250,000 pigs, but it is only in the hills of the north that there are a few sheep and goats. Other crops include manioc, maize, sweet potatoes, beans, sugarcane, tobacco, ground nuts, coconuts, betel-nuts, tea, coffee, bananas, etc., and also some cotton. The output of rubber has increased, and in 1963 output in Vietnam amounted to 76,000 metric tons, in 1932 it was only 14,580 tons. River and coast fisheries are actively carried on.

On the eastern fringes of the delta—not on the Mekong itself or one of its distributaries—is the city, port and airport of Saïgon. It is served regularly by ocean liners and commercial vessels. The chief exports are rice, fish and fish-oil, rubber, pepper, cotton, copra and spices.

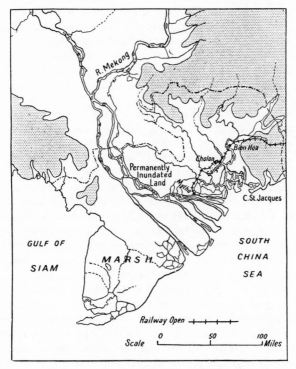

FIG. 251.—Cochin-China (South Vietnam)

Saïgon is, in many ways, a remarkable city. The French transported to the Tropics an essentially French atmosphere in a way which England or Holland never did in their tropical possessions. Saïgon, apart from its populace, became a French provincial town. It had its *pavé* streets, dwelling-houses flush to the roads, its little modiste's shops, its street cafés, where one sat at round marble-topped tables and sipped an apéritif whilst watching the evening promenade, its big flashy stores, and the inevitable Citroën taxis with high-pitched horns. Even the Chinese waiters adopted French mannerisms. With independence it will be interesting to see how far French cultural influence will persist.

Less than a dozen miles away from the old centre of Saïgon is the equally interesting town of Cholon, with over 400,000 Chinese. Cholon is the industrial centre, Saïgon the business and commercial centre and the port. So rapid has been their growth, that Saïgon-Cholon is now a conurbation of over 1,400,000 including about 17,000 Europeans. There are in Cholon and Saïgon a dozen rice-mills—which turn out 3,000 tons of cleaned rice per day—as well as saw-mills, soap and varnish factories.

Cambodia has an area of 67,550 square miles and a population (1962) of 5,749,000. Over 3,500,000 are Cambodians, but there are also 500,000 Chinese, many Vietnamese, Malays and Laotians. Cambodia is a saucer-shaped basin and in this respect compares with the basin of Eastern Siam to the north, but the soil is more fertile and the climate more favourable. Only 4,000,000 acres of the surface are under cultivation, but this is due to shortage of labour, not to infertility. The chief product is again rice, which is exported via the mills of Cholon and the wharves of Saïgon. Rubber-growing for export is extending; the production was estimated in 1963 at 40,000 tons. An important crop, especially near Kampot, is pepper, and about 3,000 metric tons are produced annually. Other crops include maize, tobacco, kapok, coffee and cotton. Cattle-breeding is a flourishing industry, especially around Pnom-Penh. But an even more important local industry is fishing. In the wet season the overflow of the Mekong fills the great lake; in the dry season the lake empties and leaves innumerable pools in which there are enormous numbers of fish suitable for salting and smoking. Much of the fish is exported to China via Saïgon. Valuable forests are said to cover 25,000,000 acres in Cambodia.

The capital and chief town of Cambodia is Pnom-Penh, on the Mekong, below the junction of Tonlé Sap. It has a population of about 400,000 and is accessible by ocean-going vessels; inland the Mekong and its tributaries afford a total of 875 miles of waterways in the high-water season and over 500 miles in the low-water season. Pnom-Penh is also the centre of the road system, there being over 2,000 miles of metalled roads. Roads run from Saïgon via Pnom-Penh to the famous old ruins of Angkor, to Battambang and the Siamese frontier, and to the shores of the Gulf of Siam. On the latter coast is the little port of Kampot, but it is not accessible to ocean-going vessels. A modern port is being developed at Sihanoukville (formerly Kompong Som).

Laos is the least accessible and least developed of the four countries, with an estimated area of 91,400 square miles and 2,500,000 inhabitants. It is a tangle of forested hills and plateaus; there are large areas of valuable teak forests, from which the timber is floated down the Mekong to Saïgon. The soil of the valleys is fertile; minerals, including gold, lead, tin and precious stones, are found. The natural entry to the

country is by the Mekong, but rapids bar continuous navigation at
Khone. Steam launches ply on the upper reaches to Vientiane, the
capital, which has a daily air service from Bangkok.

Annam, the old Annamite kingdom, had an area of about 40,000
square miles and a population (1951) over 6,750,000. It is now divided

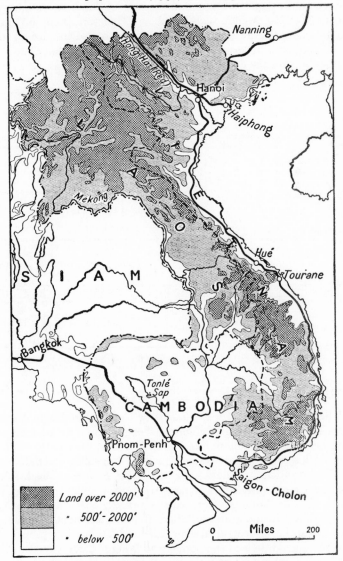

FIG. 252.—Indo-China—political and communications

The heavy lines are through roads. Tourane is now Da Nang and the 17th parallel, dividing North and
South Vietnam, is just north of Hué.

between North Vietnam and South Vietnam. The inhabitants are Annamites in the towns and along the coasts; various tribes of Moïs in the hilly tracts. Reference has already been made to the spurs from the cordillera which divide the coastal strip into a number of separate basins and render communication difficult. Hence the absence of a through railway and the economic linking of Southern Annam with Saïgon, Northern Annam with Haiphong. Hué, former capital, and its port Da Nang (Tourane) and the large town Binh-Dinh are all in the south. Agricultural products resemble those of Cochin-China and Cambodia, with the addition of silk and tea.

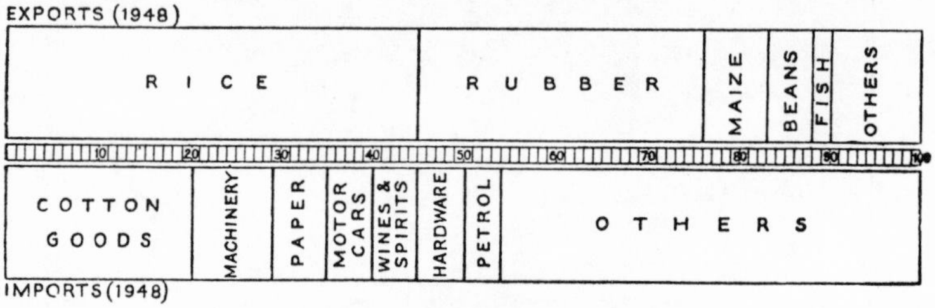

FIG. 253.—The foreign trade of Indo-China

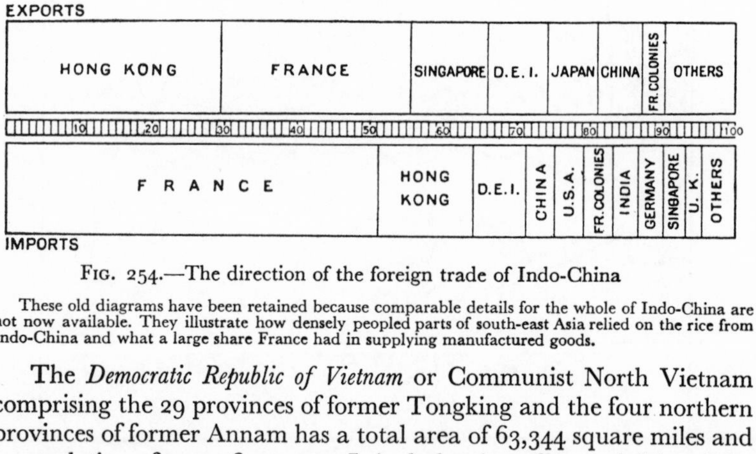

FIG. 254.—The direction of the foreign trade of Indo-China

These old diagrams have been retained because comparable details for the whole of Indo-China are not now available. They illustrate how densely peopled parts of south-east Asia relied on the rice from Indo-China and what a large share France had in supplying manufactured goods.

The *Democratic Republic of Vietnam* or Communist North Vietnam comprising the 29 provinces of former Tongking and the four northern provinces of former Annam has a total area of 63,344 square miles and a population of over 16,000,000. It includes the valley and delta of the Red River and its tributaries, especially the Song bo (Black River). The main river valleys are separated by lofty spurs from the Yun-nanese Plateau. Mining is important, especially coal, zinc, phosphates (12,870 tons), tin and graphite. There are huge limestone quarries, and large quantities of cement are manufactured. The chief crop is rice, normally enough to feed the population. There is, in contrast to Cambodia and Cochin-China, little opportunity for the expansion of rice cultivation, owing to the limited areas of flat land. Other products are maize, sugarcane, arrowroot, tea, coffee and tobacco. There is or was a large production of raw silk, most of which was used locally. The chief town of Tongking is Hanoi, a fine modern city of over 850,000 inhabitants (60,000 Chinese).

Communications and Foreign Trade of Vietnam, Cambodia and Laos. French Indo-China never formed a natural unit and a map of communications illustrates the reason—it being noted that the lines of communication themselves depend on the relief.

Figs. 253–4 illustrate the character of the foreign trade of the former united French Indo-China and the almost overwhelming importance of rice as an export. The present position is that Northern Vietnam trades mainly with China and other Communist countries, but has small barter agreements with Japan, Hong Kong and France; Southern Vietnam had in 1963 an export of rice of 323,000 tons—small compared with former times—69,000 tons of rubber, 4,540 tons of tea, much tobacco and coffee. Trade with Great Britain showed a demand for British manufactured goods; few can yet be supplied by the light industrial factories of Saïgon. The trade of Laos is small—chief export is wood—and the demand for manufactured goods from Thailand, France, Japan and Britain is such that the value of imports is many times that of exports. From Cambodia there is an export of rubber, maize and rice (70,000 tons in 1956). Rice goes mainly to Asian countries. In the troubled years following independence, Laos and Vietnam became a battle-ground between pro-Communist and anti-communist forces, the former supported by China, the latter by the United States.

REFERENCES

Indo-China is a large and interesting tract and the foregoing sketch gives but a very inadequate idea of the country. Amongst readily accessible works of reference from former days is G. Caillard's *L'Indochine* (Paris: Notre Domaine Colonial, 1926). An important general work is *Un Empire Colonial français: L'Indochine*, edited by G. Maspero (Paris: G. van Oest, 1929). See also J. Sion, *Asie des Moussons* (Paris: Colin, Geographie Universelle, 1929), *Indochine*, 2 vols. (Paris: Société d'Editions Géographiques, 1931), and Pierre Gourou, *L'Indochine française* (Hanoi, 1929). Recent changes in political and economic geography are best followed in the *Statesman's Year-Book*, and are summarized in the following:

W. A. Withington, 'Cambodia', *Focus*, **12**, 8, 1962.
L. Unger, 'Laos', *Focus*, **14**, 9, 1964.
F. Hung, 'Vietnam', *Focus*, **16**, 4, 1965.
On the Mekong, see Gilbert White, *Geog. Jour.*, **129**, 1963, 412–36.

CHINA [1]

CHINESE territory extends through thirty-five degrees of latitude, from 18° N. to 53° N., and through no less than sixty degrees of longitude, from 74° E. to 134° E. Since 1949 when the Communists gained control over the whole mainland area and established the 'People's Republic of China', the old distinction between China proper, Manchuria or the North-East and the Outer Territories of Inner Mongolia, Sinkiang or Chinese Turkistan and Tibet has largely disappeared. China of today covers 3,768,100 square miles if Chinese claims on the Indian border are admitted. China, contrasting 1925 and 1965, comprises the following divisions:

		Square miles	
China proper	. . . . .	1,532,800	} 2,647,811 *
Manchuria .	. . . . .	363,700	
Outer Territories			
Mongolia .	. . . . .	1,367,953	—
Sinkiang or Chinese Turkistan	. .	550,579	660,805
Tibet	. . . . .	463,320	349,149
Total	. . .	4,278,352	3,657,765

* Including Taiwan (13,881 sq. miles) and Inner Mongolia.

Until 1907 China proper consisted of eighteen provinces, whilst Manchuria was considered a separate dependency. But by the Imperial Decree of April 20, 1907, the three Manchurian provinces were united as a single viceroyalty, the Viceroyalty of the Three Eastern Provinces. The Chinese hold over Mongolia was slight even in the days of Imperial China, and in the nineteen-thirties Mongolia became closely linked with Soviet Russia. The reconquest of Chinese Turkistan by China in 1877 made this territory more definitely Chinese, but Tibet remained virtually independent till its invasion by the forces of Communist China.

The area of China proper is roughly the same as that of the old Indian Empire (1,550,000 square miles) and latest figures of the population of China give it at least a hundred million more people. A far larger proportion of the surface is mountainous and incapable of utilization than is the case with India, with the result that the population in the fertile plains of China is far denser than in even the thickly populated Ganges Valley.

[1] For comments on this section I am greatly indebted to Dr. T. R. Tregear of the University of Hong Kong who made extensive journeys in China in December 1955. In 1965 he published *A Geography of China* (University of London Press) in which recent developments are described against the geographical background. See also p. 525.

Physiography. Broadly speaking, China proper lies to the east of the great series of plateaus which constitute the heart of the continent of Asia. Excluding Manchuria, the country may be considered as consisting mainly of three river basins—the basins of the Hwang Ho, the Yangtze Kiang and the Si Kiang. These fundamental geographical divisions are useful because they correspond with the popular division of the country into North China, Central China and South China.

The Hwang Ho [1] and the Yangtze Kiang both rise amidst the

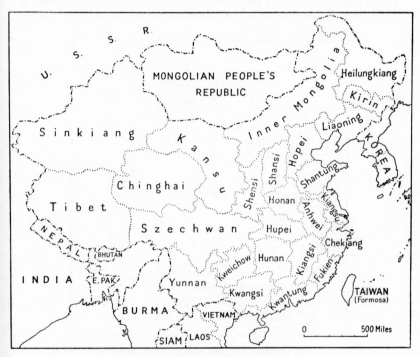

FIG. 255.—The provinces of China

In this map an attempt has been made to give the arrangement and names of provinces in 1965 but there have been so many changes under the Communist régime that it is almost impossible to be exact.

mountains of the high plateau of Tibet, and with their upper courses outside the confines of China proper we are not, for the moment, concerned. The Si Kiang, a shorter river, may be regarded as wholly Chinese, for nearly the whole of its basin lies within the confines of China proper.

In the north-west China includes a very considerable portion of what is, geographically, a part of the Mongolian Plateau, whilst the

[1] An excellent description of the Hwang Ho and its basin is given by G. F. Clapp, 'The Hwang Ho, Yellow River', *Geog. Rev.*, **12**, 1922, 1–18.

Hwang Ho itself makes a long northward detour outside of the confines of China proper into the heart of the plateau.

Separating the Hwang Ho and the Yangtze Kiang basins is the Tsinling Shan, an important spur given off by the central mountainous core of Asia, continued eastwards as the Hwaiyang-shan. Separating the Yangtze Kiang and Si Kiang basins is a broad tract of mountainous country sometimes referred to as the South China plateaus. In the south-west lies the Yunnanese Plateau; in the extreme west the boundary of China includes a large area of the Tibetan mountain system which may be referred to as the Mountain System of the Far West or

FIG. 256.—The partition of China between the principal river basins

the Szechuanese Alps. The old massif of the Shantung Peninsula forms a separate physiographic unit in the east.

Manchuria falls naturally into three subdivisions—the old massif of the east; the central basin; and the western plateaus.

Whilst the broad division of China proper into the three great river basins is clear, the further separation of the country into smaller physiographic units or into natural regions as understood in other countries presents numerous difficulties. There is such a marked contrast between the broad valley floors, often simply wide stretches of alluvium, and the mountainous country which separates the basins that one seems justified in separating the two. Fig. 257 shows a rough subdivision drawn up by the writer some years ago.[1] The scheme agrees very closely with that suggested by the late Professor P. M. Roxby (see below). Dr. Tregear (1965) quoting Hung Fu (1952) uses basically the river basins as shown on Fig. 256.

North China includes:

(1) The Loess Plateau of the north-west, through which the Hwang Ho flows in a deep, narrow valley. Northern Kansu, northern Shensi and most of Shansi are the provinces included.

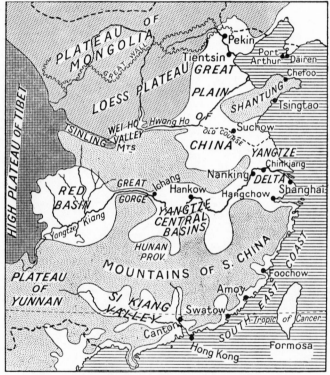

FIG. 257.—The natural regions of China

(2) The edge of the Mongolian Plateau, lying to the north of Peking in the northern part of the province of Hopei.

(3) The Wei Ho Valley—the 'cradle of China'—which lies between the Loess Plateau on the north and the Tsinling massif on the south. This region occupies central Shensi.

(4) The Great Plain of North China, one of the most clearly defined of the physiographical regions.

[1] Reproduced with slight modifications from that first published in L. D. Stamp, *The World: A General Geography for Indian Schools* (Longmans, Green & Co., 1927).

(5) The Shantung Mountains, occupying the eastern two-thirds of Shantung Province. The ancient massif is divided into two halves by a marked valley (the Weihsien-Kiaochow Valley).

Fig. 258.—The natural regions of China according to Cressey

Between North China and Central China lies:

(6) The Tsinling or Central Mountain massif, a broad ridge of mountains separating the Hwang Ho and Yangtze Kiang Valleys and occupying southern Kansu, southern Shensi, south-western Honan and north-western Hupei.

Central China includes:

(7) The mountains of the Far West or the Szechuanese Alps, the fringe of the Tibetan Plateau, occupying the west of Szechwan.

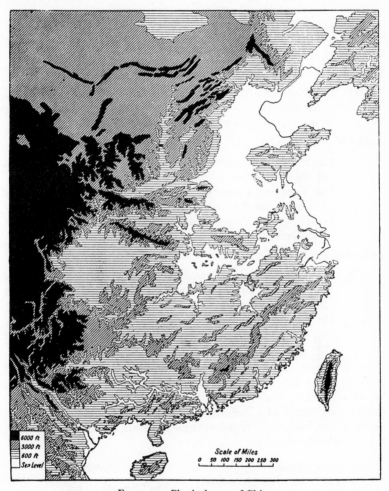

FIG. 259.—Physical map of China

This map shows clearly the extensive northern plain, the Red Basin and the central basins of the Yangtze but demonstrates the comparatively small area of flat lowland—contrast India.

(8) The Red Basin, one of the most famous of the regions of China, occupying the greater part of the province of Szechwan. Near the eastern borders of the province the mountains of the north approach close to the mountains of the south, and

the Yangtze passes between them through the well-known Great Gorge.

(9) The Central Basins of the Yangtze, separated from the Red Basin by the Great Gorge, centre around Hankow and include the most important part of the provinces of Hupei on the north, Hunan and Kiangsi on the south.

(10) The Yangtze Delta Region, lying in An-hwei and Kiangsu, is continuous on the north with the Great Plain of North China.

Between Central China and South China lie:

(11) The Plateaus of South China, a complex region, having as a common feature throughout merely the rugged nature of the country and the geological structure of the ancient massif.

South China includes:

(12) The Plateau of Yunnan occupying the province of Yunnan in the south-west.

(13) The Si Kiang Valley and Delta, occupying the province of Kwangsi and the western half of Kwangtung.

(14) The South-east Coast, occupying eastern Kwangtung, Fukien and Chekiang.

Manchuria includes:

(15) The Eastern Highlands and the Liaotung Peninsula, consisting of ancient rocks and geologically a continuation of the Shantung Peninsula.

(16) The Central Manchurian Lowlands.

(17) The West Manchurian Plateau, representing an extension of the Mongolian Plateau.[1]

In his important work, *China's Geographic Foundations*, first published in 1934, some five years after the first edition of the present book, Dr. G. B. Cressey uses a scheme of regional divisions very closely comparable with those here defined. Cressey's divisions are shown in Fig. 258 and the following tabular statement shows the comparison with the regions described on pp. 525 to 548.

STAMP	CRESSEY
The Loess Plateaus of the North-west ⎫ The Wei Ho Valley ⎬ The Mongolian Plateau edge ⎭	The Loess Highlands The Khingan Mountains

[1] The scheme of natural regions used by Prof. P. M. Roxby is set forth in 'The Distribution of Population in China', *Geog. Rev.*, **15**, 1925, 4–5, and also in an earlier paper, not known to the present writer at the time the above scheme was drawn up, entitled 'Wu-Han: The Heart of China', *Scot. Geog. Mag.*, **32**, June 1916. China is divided into seven regions—N.W. Plateaus, Plain of North China, Highlands of Central China, Red Basin, Region of Yangtze Gorges, Central Basin, South China Plateau.

STAMP	CRESSEY
The Great Plain of North China	The North China Plain
The Shantung Mountains	The Mountains of Shantung
The Tsinling or Central Mountain massif	The Central Mountain Belt
The Szechuanese Alps	The Tibetan Borderland
The Red Basin	The Red Basin
The Central Basins⎫ The Yangtze Delta⎭	The Yangtze Plain
The Plateaus of South China	The South Yangtze Hills
The Plateau of Yunnan	The South-western Tableland
The Si Kiang Basin	The Hills of Liangkwang
The South-east Coast	The South-eastern Coast
The Eastern Highland and Liaotung Peninsula of Manchuria	Mountains of Eastern Manchuria
The Central Manchurian Lowlands	The Manchurian Plain
The West Manchurian Plateau	The Mountains of Jehol

Geology and Minerals.[1] Reference to Fig. 8 shows that forming Shantung and underlying the North China Plain there is an ancient massif, mainly of pre-Cambrian rocks. Folded against this on the west are rocks of various ages. South China consists of a great block of country with a core of Archean rocks. Fundamentally China may be considered as consisting of four main structural units:

(a) The Archean massif of the north-east, the 'Faîte primitif' of De Launay.

(b) The basins of the north-west.

(c) The South China block.

(d) The mountains of the Far West.

The Archean massif of the north-east is best seen in Korea, Liaoning and East Shantung, where pre-Cambrian crystalline rocks occupy most of the surface. On the western flanks infolded sediments of Palaeozoic age occur, and in places include patches of Permo-Carboniferous coal-measures. West Shantung may be considered as a separate sub-region, owing to the greater thickness of Palaeozoic sediments and to the fact that block faulting has warranted Suess's description of the area as a 'shattered horst'. The alluvial plain of North China may be regarded as consisting fundamentally of a down-folded or down-faulted block of the Archean massif.

The Basins of the North-west are important because of the enormous areas of coal-measures which they include. To the north and west of

[1] The work of the Geological Survey of China and of other investigators to that date was summarized by J. S. Lee in his *Geology of China* (London: Murby, 1939). Mention must also be made however of A. W. Grabau's great work, *The Stratigraphy of China* (Geo. Surv. of China I and II, 1926–8), and of Richthofen's famous classic, *The Geology of China* (Berlin, 1882–1912) in which he advanced the sub-aerial origin of loess. Mineral resources were considered by H. F. Bain, *Ores and Industry in the Far East* (Research Publication of the Council on Foreign Relations, New York: new edition, 1933). Later information will be found in N. Dickerman, *Mineral Resources of China* (U.S. Bureau of Mines, 1948). See also T. R. Tregear, *A Geography of China*, 1965.

Peking lie series of anticlinal and synclinal ridges, trending north-east to south-west, that is, parallel to the edge of the sunken portion of the Archean massif. The anticlines have pre-Cambrian cores, but the synclinal basins are filled with Palaeozoic and Mesozoic sediments and the folding apparently took place in the Jurassic. Richthofen and Suess have referred to this succession of folds as the Peking Grid, occupying northern Hopei and northern Shansi. Southwards, in southern Shansi,

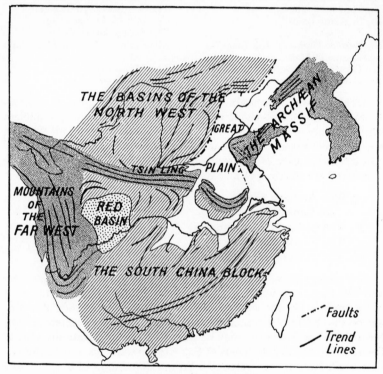

FIG. 260.—The structure of China

the folds broaden out and the sediments in the synclinal basins are often but slightly folded. This is the case with the huge coal basin underlying the Tsin Ho Plateau. Farther west lies the huge basin of northern Shensi, bounded on the south by an anticline to the north of the Wei Ho Valley. Coal-measures of Permo-Carboniferous and possibly also of Jurassic age probably underlie the whole plain, but the thick mantle of loess—often exceeding 1,000 feet—obscures the structure.

The South China Block has its grain running approximately from north-east to south-west or, more correctly, parallel to the coast of south-east China. The coast itself has been supposed by some to be determined by a major line of faulting. Well-marked synclines, important because they are often occupied by coal-measures, follow the dominant trend. It is very probable that the South China Block acted as a stable block during the Tertiary earth movements, but it has been shown that the block is not as old as was formerly supposed. In the New Territories of Hong Kong sediments of Cretaceous age are involved in the folding; the granites of the region are probably of late Cretaceous age. Thus the age of the South China mountains is comparable with that of the Indo-Malayan mountains. There is no doubt, however, that the main grain of the country was determined earlier. In the Mesozoic great lake-basins were formed in Szechwan and Central China. In the

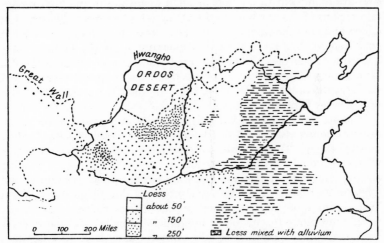

FIG. 261.—Loess of north-west China

Szechwan Basin were laid down not only Rhaetic-Liassic coal-measures but the red Cretaceous sandstones which give the Red Basin its familiar name.

The Mountains of the Far West are believed by many to be of Alpine or Tertiary age, but to enter into this fascinating but dangerous subject is beyond the scope of the present work.

No account of the geology of China, however brief, would be complete without reference to the loess of the north-west. 'Sprinkled over the countryside as though by a giant flour-sifter, a veneer of fine wind-blown silt blankets over a hundred thousand square miles of the north-western provinces.' So writes Dr. Cressey, whose map of the distribution of loess was used as the basis for Fig. 261. The material seems to have been derived from the Gobi, which is now quite free from fine silts, and in a smaller degree from the Ordos Desert.

Minerals. China is by nature a country isolated by barriers of mountains, desert, tempestuous seas and the widest of the oceans. For much of her history she has been out of touch with the rest of the world, self-centred and by design closed to foreigners. Chinese goods which reached the outside world were those of great value for small bulk— rare silks, finely carved jade or exquisite specimens of porcelain. China —so self-centred that she styled herself the Middle or the Central Kingdom—became famed as a land of hidden treasure and vast wealth. The realization that China might be a country poor in many resources came but slowly. Geological exploration over the half-century before 1935 brought many disappointments but intensive work under the new régime is producing more encouraging results. In the noble metals China is particularly poor. Platinum is unknown; placer and reef gold are found but rarely and in small quantities in the high mountain regions of the north and west. Although silver is a noble metal in China and long the chief medium of exchange, the home production is very limited. For more than two thousand years the Chinese have hunted for silver ores and even in the remotest areas—such as the still little known Chinese-Burmese borderland in Yunnan—have worked tiny argentiferous veins. Even the jade—of which it was once the ambition of every Chinese to possess at least one piece—comes from Burma.

Copper has long been worked, especially in Yunnan, from which province comes also the tin which for many years ranked as the leading mineral export. Tungsten and antimony are the two metals in which China is particularly rich. They occur in the eastern part of the Nanling Range, especially in Hunan. The tungsten occurs as wolframite and scheelite and large quantities were produced during the First World War. From 1908 to 1940 China produced over 60 per cent. of the world's antimony (occurring as the mineral stibnite) and the reserves are large. Small quantities of other metals—zinc, lead, molybdenum and bismuth—have been worked and, contrary to earlier pessimistic reports, important oilfields have been developed at Yumen in Kansu, reached by railway from Landow, and at Karamai in Sinkiang. In 1958 rich strikes were reported in Szechwan. Total output 1963 7 m. tons.

Two minerals, however, worthy of very serious study are coal and iron ore. In the famous estimates of world resources of coal published by the International Geological Congress of 1913, China above all countries attracted attention. China's resources were estimated to be 994,987,000,000 tons against 747,508,000,000 tons for the whole of Europe. The figures for other countries of the world were as follows:

United States	3,838,640,000,000 tons
Canada	1,234,270,000,000 ,,
Siberia	173,880,000,000 ,,
Japan	7,970,000,000 ,,
United Kingdom . . .	189,530,000,000 ,,
Germany (post-war boundaries) .	148,220,000,000 ,,
World total	7,397,550,000,000 ,,

This estimate of Drake's for China takes into consideration only seams 1 foot and over in thickness, down to depths of not over 4,000 feet. In 1921 the Geological Survey of China published their first official estimate. Considering only seams of 3 feet and over and only down to 3,000 feet, they arrived at a total of 23,435,000,000 tons—only *one-fortieth* of Drake's figure. But in later years the Survey carried out many detailed studies and published a revised estimate (1945) of 265,000,000,000 tons—of which 80 per cent. is in the loess plateaus of Shensi and Shansi.[1] The following details were given me by Dr. J. S. Lee then of the National University, Peking, who also provided the map, Fig. 262. China's coalfields fall into eleven groups, and the coals range in age from Lower Carboniferous to Tertiary. The Permian and Liassic coals are economically the most important—the coals are thus somewhat younger than in most parts of the world—the Lower Carboniferous and Tertiary coming next. Except in the Fushan field of Manchuria, where good bituminous coal of Tertiary age occurs, the coals of that period are usually better described as lignites.

(1) *The Fields of Shansi and Shensi.* This is undoubtedly the most important group. The structure of the region is simple: there are three blocks arranged longitudinally, the middle block being sunken and itself divided into three basins—the Fenho in the south, the Ningwu in the centre, and the Tatung in the north. In each case coals of more than one age occur below younger sediments. The eastern block is one vast field in which the seams are but gently folded and where conditions may be compared with Pennsylvania—except that the field is as yet scarcely touched by modern methods of mining. The western block has a centre ridge of older rocks, the coal seams dipping away on either side—the field covering 40,000 square miles. In each field numerous seams occur—some inconveniently thick, ranging up to 30 feet. In the old local workings the only coal removed was in large lumps which could be used as an adequate burden for a single coolie. Not only is this first group of coalfields, with an estimated reserve of 200,000,000,000 tons, easily the most important in China economically, but it is politically the most significant, being in the extreme north of China proper and on the borders of Mongolia and accessible from Manchuria.

(2) *The Peking Group.* At the foot of the Taihangshan Range or eastern edge of the Shansi Plateau—that is, along the margin of the North China Plain, from Peking southwards to Honan—there is a long line of small coal basins, those with considerable reserves exceeding forty in number. They are down-faulted blocks of the same character as the plateau above and the coals may extend far under the

[1] Vaguely increased to 1,500,000 million tons in 1959. See D. J. Dwyer, 'The Coal Industry in Mainland China since 1949', *Geog. Jour.*, **129**, 1963, 329–38.

alluvium of the Plain. Owing to the accessibility from the Peking–
Hankow railway and the excellent quantity of the coal (including
much anthracite), working was active some years before the present
régime. The Peking Syndicate, a British concern, opened up in the

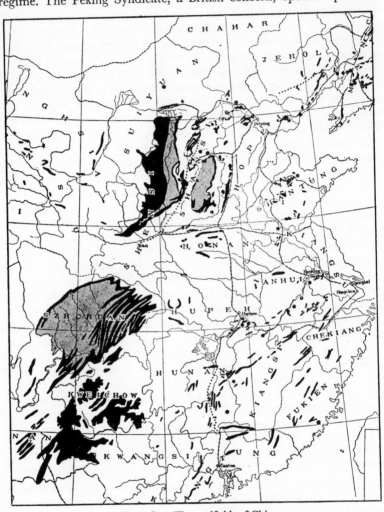

FIG. 262.—The coalfields of China

Exposed coalfields in black, hidden fields stippled.

Siuwu district of northern Honan, the Kailan Mining Administration
(Sino-British) in the Kaiping Basin, where a large plant for recovering
by-products in coking was early established.

　(3) *The Shantung Group*. This group comprises several fields in

Shantung, northern Kiangsu and north-eastern An-hwei, with several modern mines. The coals are bituminous.

(4) *The Northern Group*. This group includes various fields within or near the Manchurian border. The fields are in the mountain zone, the coals poor and often highly folded.

(5) *The Manchurian Group*. These fields are estimated to have a reserve of 5,000,000,000 tons—much of moderate quality only with high ash content and low in fixed carbon.

(6) *The North-western Group*. These fields lie in mountain-locked basins and because of enormous difficulties of transport little attention has been paid to them.

These six groups of fields all lie in Northern China, north of the Tsinling Range, and include all the most valuable areas. South of the Tsinling line conditions are quite different—the strata are usually highly disturbed, the small fields occur in intermontane basins involved in sharp folds or separated into small patches. The coals are usually poor and the seams thin.

(7) *The Red Basin*. A single seam of Jurassic coal is believed to occur almost throughout the basin, but it is usually only 1 foot 6 inches in thickness. More important is the Permian coal of the south of the basin.

(8) *The Central Hunan Group*, with the fields of Hupeh and Kiangsi. There are various small fields with coal of moderate quality.

(9) *The South-eastern Group*. Various small fields occur along the south-eastern coast and in the lower Yangtze Valley, but are not thought to be of much importance.

(10) *The Kwangtung–Kwangsi Group*. These small fields have only thin seams of inferior coal.

(11) *The Yunnan Group*. This area is highly disturbed and the small scattered fields are of doubtful value despite the extensive area.

Summarizing the known coal reserves of China, it would seem that 80 per cent. occur in the Shen-Shan Plateau; 1·8 per cent. only in Manchuria; 4·8 per cent. in the remote north-west; leaving only 13·4 per cent. for the rest of China, of which a total of 8·4 per cent. only is accredited to Southern China.

In the nineteen-thirties the annual output of coal in China was estimated at 30,000,000 tons: a third from native mines, rather less than a third from more modern workings and over a third from two areas only—the Kailan plant and the Japanese-owned Fushun mines of Manchuria. The importance of a field is determined by its accessibility to modern forms of transport. In 1952 production including Manchuria was 66·5 million tons; more than a third from the 'big five'— Kailwan (Kailan), Fushun, Fushin, Huainan and Tatung. This was taken as the base for the First Five-Year Plan. Production climbed rapidly to 110 m. metric tons in 1956 and is believed to have exceeded 400 m. by 1960. There is now a high degree of mechanization.

Iron Ore. The extravagant statements regarding the wealth of China in iron ore were later discounted by detailed work. When this book was first published it was officially stated that 'it is quite clear that China can never be an iron-producing country of any importance'. In contrast it is now stated that known reserves are 19,840,000,000 tons. Cer-

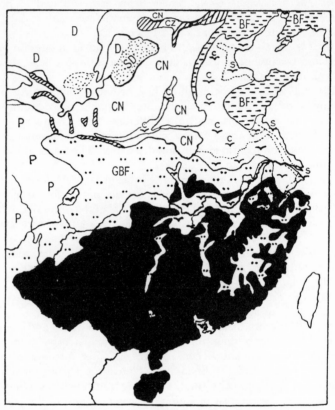

FIG. 263.—Simplified soil map of China

(After James Thorp, 1935.)

P = Podsols; **BF** = Brown Forest Soils; **GBF** = Grey-Brown Forest Soils; **Black** = Red Soils, often with lateritic parent materials; **CZ** = Chernozems; **CN** = Chestnut Soils; **D** = Grey Desert Soils; **SD** = Sand-dunes; ⌄ = Alluvium (**c**, Calcareous; **s**, Saline).

tainly production of ore reached 34·5 m. in 1962, pig iron 19·7 m. and steel 11·8 m. tons. There are haematite-magnetite ores of Archean age of Manchuria, smelted by the famous Anshan Ironworks. Similar ore occurs in north-eastern Hopei within the Great Wall. A large deposit of high-grade ore (50 per cent. metallic iron) in China proper—within the Great Wall—is a haematite occurring in the Hsuanhua and Lungkuan districts in north-western Hopei. The iron industry in China may perhaps be called the oldest in the world, but the small scattered deposits of iron ore used by the early smelters are in general useless as a basis of modern industry. But in the central and lower Yangtze valley are a number of considerable deposits of first-grade ore—developed as a result of contact metamorphism in association with intrusive masses of grano-

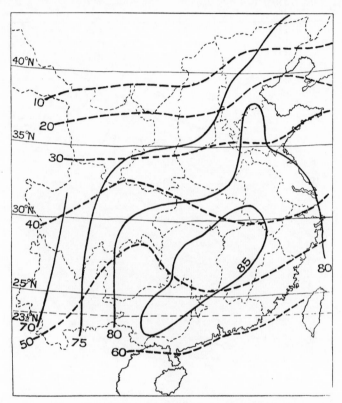

Fig. 264.—The climate of China—January and July isotherms
(*After* Koeppe and Bangs.)

diorite. The most famous of these deposits are the Tayeh deposits near Hankow.

Soils. The first modern study of soils was that by Shaw.[1] He found the major soil regions determined by climate, with leached, non-calcareous soils in the south (associated with rice cultivation) and the generally calcareous soils of the north (associated with wheat and kaoliang). Within the broad climatic zones, the type is determined

[1] C. F. Shaw, 'The Soils of China', *Geological Survey of China*, 1930. To these nine types may be added the loessic soils of the plateau.

by the geological origin of the material, and erosion or deposition is so active that most soils are immature. A few years after Shaw's work James Thorp linked the soils of China with the familiar world grouping as shown in Fig. 263. Shaw distinguished nine soil regions which can be correlated with Thorp's:

1. The *Upland Red Soil Region* of the south with soils of a lateritic

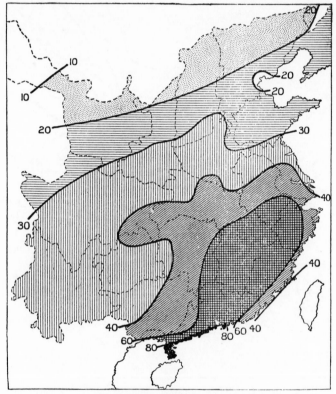

FIG. 265.—The climate of China—annual rainfall in inches
(*After* Koeppe and Bangs.)

character eroding severely when the land is cleared of its natural forest (cf. India). These are the Red Soils of Thorp.

2. The *Claypan Soil Region* has reddish brown soils with a dense clay subsoil and occurs mainly on the northern side of the Yangtze. These are the Grey-Brown Forest Soils of Thorp.

3, 4, 5. The *Soil Regions* of the *Middle Yangtze Flood Plains*, *Yangtze Delta* and *Hwai River Valley* are deep silt loams, clay loams and clays subject to flooding and poorly drained, now calcareous and devoted to rice.

6. The *Brown Soil Region* coincides largely with Shantung and the former Jehol and is naturally a varied area (BF of Fig. 263).

7. The *North China Plain Alluvial Soil Region* has deep, fine-textured soils, calcareous and sometimes saline, poorly drained and liable to flooding but generally productive.

8. The *Old Delta Soil Region* is believed to include more saline soils.

9. The *Sajong Soil Region* of the southern part of the North China

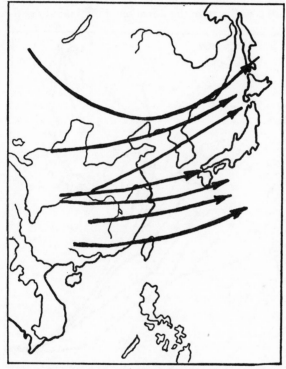

FIG. 266.—Cyclonic storms (1893–1924)

Plain is characterized by an horizon of calcareous concretions or sajong in the subsoil (cf. kankar soils of northern India).

Climate.[1] It is only possible to give the most general account of the climate of China, for detailed records are few and mostly confined to coast stations, whilst observations by travellers in the interior are of a general nature and not infrequently inconsistent.

Winter Conditions. In winter atmospheric conditions in China are dominated by the mass of cold heavy air over the heart of the continent. The barometric gradient over China is steep, so that strong,

[1] See also above the general account of the monsoons: also F. K. Hare, *The Restless Atmosphere* (London: Hutchinson, 1953).

cold winds blow outwards towards the sea. Though warmed somewhat
by their descent from the plateaus, these winds are very cold, especially
over Northern China, where they are at the same time particularly
strong, giving rise to the well-known and hated dust storms. Stormy
weather in the China Sea is a further result. The general direction of
this winter monsoon is from the north-west in Northern China, from
the north in Central China and from the north-east in Southern China,
the direction remaining comparatively constant. The effect of the cold
winter winds is well seen in the direction of the January isotherms. The

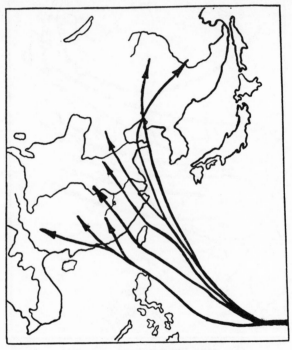

Fig. 267.—Typhoons, 1893–1924

whole of Northern China is below freezing in winter, the January
isotherm of 32° F. reaching its southernmost limit (32° N.) in the
Northern Hemisphere. On the hills, occasional frost is not unknown
even at Hong Kong. On the whole the interior basins are warmer than
the coasts—thus Chengtu in the Red Basin has a January average
temperature of 44° as against 38° at Shanghai on the coast in the same
latitude. In the Red Basin frost and snow are rare, but are usual at
Shanghai. In North China even the largest rivers are generally frozen
over in winter. The winter winds of China, descending from the
deserts of the interior, are, of course, very dry. The skies are almost

cloudless and there is no rain. The winds are strongest in December, January and February, and it is during those months that Peking suffers from the scourge of dust storms. By April the high-pressure system over central Asia is breaking up, and winds over China are light and variable. Occasionally, however, the dry land winds continue over North China right on through the hot months of April and May into June with disastrous results to the crops. In North China the rainlessness of the winter months is well illustrated by Peking, where 91 per cent. of the rain falls in the months May to September, inclusive. The periodicity is of the same character in the Si Kiang Valley of South

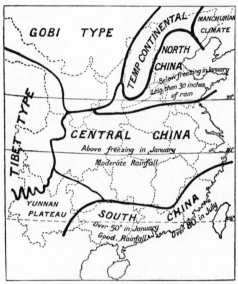

FIG. 268.—The climatic regions of China

China, but in Central China, especially near the coast, there is considerable precipitation in winter. It is believed by some that these winter rains are due to cyclonic disturbances originating in the Red Basin and moving down the Yangtze Valley. The winds which herald the arrival of one of these depressions are easterly and south-easterly, that is, from the sea, and are therefore rain-bearing. The winds in the wake of the depression are very strong, being the north-westerly winds reinforced.

Summer Conditions. After the break-up of the high-pressure system over central Asia in April, depressions form in the interior along what is really a great front or zone of frontogenesis. It lies across South China in May, by June it has moved to the Yangtze Valley and by July is across Manchuria. The summer monsoon or dominance by mT air has set in and continues until September. All over China the prevailing

winds are south and south-east, warm and moist. The summer monsoon winds in China are rarely as strong or as constant as the winter

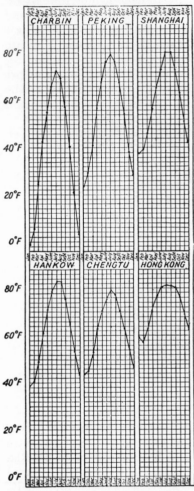

winds—a direct contrast with
India, where the protective
mountain wall cuts off the
strong, cold winter winds which
would otherwise blow from the
heart of Asia. May to September
is the rainy season. Rainfall is
heaviest in the south and east,
the 40-inch isohyet running
along the northern border of the
Yangtze Valley. North China is
drier, Peking having about 25
inches. The moderating influence
of the warm moist monsoon
winds is well seen in the course
of the July isotherms. There
is little difference between the
July temperatures of Peking
(79° F.), Shanghai (80° F.)
and Hong Kong (82° F.). In
Northern and Southern China
the rainfall reaches a maximum
in July and decreases as the
monsoon weakens—a typical
monsoonal régime. In Central
China, however, conditions are
again disturbed by shallow depressions moving down the
Yangtze Valley, and there are
two summer maxima—June and
August. The August maximum
is connected with the typhoons,
which are particularly dangerous
off the coast of Central China

Fig. 269.—Temperature graphs of typical   during that month.[1]
Chinese towns

CLIMATIC REGIONS.[2] The

[1] Indeed, dry spells are associated with *constant* winds.
[2] Climatic changes in other parts of Asia are dealt with elsewhere in this book.
Concerning China in historic times, see Co-Ching Chu, 'Climatic Pulsations during
Historic Times in China', *Geog. Rev.*, **16**, 1926, 274–82. For a summary account of the
climate of China, see C. E. Koeppe and N. H. Bangs, *Monthly Weather Review*, **56**, 1928,
1–7; also Co-Ching Chu, *ibid.*, **44**, 276–81. Published at Shanghai in 1944 and only
rarely seen is the monumental *Climatological Atlas of East Asia* by the Rev. Father
Ernest Gherzi. It includes a remarkable series of maps though some show results
too positive from the scanty data available.

tripartite division of China based on physiographic considerations is corroborated by climatic conditions, and three main climatic provinces may be distinguished.

North China has very cold rainless winters (below 32° in January), with very strong land winds, bringing clouds of dust, and hot, wet summers, nearly as warm as in South China. The rainfall, under 30 inches, is less than in Central and South China.

Central China has cold winters, but mean sea-level temperatures are

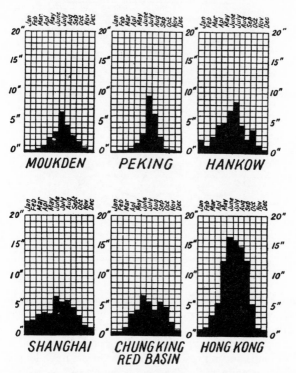

FIG. 270.—Rainfall graphs of typical Chinese towns

above freezing. The principal rainy season is again summer, but local cyclonic disturbances may cause a considerable winter rainfall. The interior in winter is warmer than the coast.

South China has a tropical monsoon climate, comparable in many ways with that of the Ganges Basin, but with rather colder winters. The winters are not, however, sufficiently cold to interrupt vegetative growth, so that more than one crop a year becomes possible.

The *Yunnan Plateau* has a tropical monsoon climate altered by altitude, but with only a small annual range.

The *Tibet Type*—covering the region over 10,000 feet—is described below, under Tibet.

The *Gobi* or *Mongolian Type* is a mid-latitude desert or semi-desert.

Mid-Latitude Continental or *Steppe Type*—grassland or steppe.

Fig. 268 shows the scheme drawn up for the first edition of this book, Fig. 271 the regions distinguished by Co-Ching Chu a few years later.[1] Reference should also be made to Thornthwaite's divisions, given in Chapter III.

FIG. 271.—Climatic regions

Natural Vegetation.[2] In few countries of the world has the natural vegetation been removed as completely as it has over much of China. His devotion to agriculture had not taught the Northern Chinese anything of forestry. The shortage of fuel is second only to the shortage of food, and all readily available forests have long since been destroyed to provide fuel. The people had lived so many centuries without forests that they could not appreciate their benefits. Those who did understand and planted trees found them appropriated for fuel long before they reached any size. The present Government is changing all that and devoting much attention to afforestation. Only in the south-east and Manchuria is there timber in quantity. The barren, eroded

---

[1] *The Climatic Provinces of China.* Memoir No. 1, National Research Institute of Meteorology, Nanking, 1930.

[2] D. Y. Lin, *A World Geography of Forest Resources* (New York, 1956); Norman Shaw, *Chinese Forest Trees and Timber Supply* (London: Unwin, 1914); R. Rosenbluth, 'Forests and Timber Trade of the Chinese Empire', *Forestry Quarterly*, **10**, 1922, 647–72; H. Handel-Mazzetti, *Naturbilder aus Südwest-China* (Vienna and Leipzig, 1927, with numerous coloured and monochrome plates).

hills so characteristic of most of China suggest a rocky desert country rather than one which should, properly, be covered with good forest growth. In Shansi, the patches of woodland which remain by each hill temple afford but a bare suggestion of the normal vegetation, and the same is true of many other parts of China.

The remaining forests of China proper now lie in three main areas:

(a) The Nan Shan or Nanling Mountains, which form an extension of the western plateau of Yunnan and divide the Si Kiang Basin and south-east coast regions from the central basins. The carefully 'cultivated' forests of Fukien and Chekiang in the south-east, with Fukien pine, rosewood and camphor trees and bamboo, offer a remarkable contrast to Central and Northern China.

(b) The Tsinling and Central Mountains, stretching from northern Szechwan through Shensi into Honan and Hupei.

(c) The great western plateau of Szechwan and Yunnan.

The natural vegetation of the lowlands of Southern China should be tropical monsoon forest of hardwoods; such forests do occur in the valleys of southern Yunnan, in the island of Hainan and on the southern slopes of the south-east coastal mountains, and include camphor trees, Cryptomeria and Magnolia. Elsewhere the normal vegetation of the China type of climate is a mixed forest of conifers, deciduous hardwood trees and evergreen hardwoods. The conifers, such as pine, fir, spruce, larch and hemlock, tend to predominate towards the north and at higher elevations in the south. Hardwoods include oaks, chestnut, ash, elm, maple, with birch, beech, poplar and walnut (the last four especially in more northern regions). There are large forests of birch (*Betula utilis*) in north-western Szechwan. Valuable bamboo covers large areas in Central China, and in the same area specially famous trees include the Tallow-tree (*Stillingia sebifera*), from the fruit of which tallow for candles is obtained; the T'ung or wood-oil tree (*Aleurites cordata*) (the oil obtained from the nuts is poisonous when fresh); and the varnish tree (*Rhus vernicifera*), which is tapped to secure the varnish or lacquer of the Far East.

Agricultural Production. Like Indo-Pakistan China is essentially agricultural and, broadly speaking, self-supporting in the matter of foodstuffs. But China includes a far larger proportion of mountainous country not suitable for cultivation, with the result that the valleys and other fertile regions are usually very densely populated. Indeed, the number of people per square mile in the most densely peopled agricultural regions of China is probably far greater than in any other country of the world. In his delightful book *Farmers of Forty Centuries*, King[1] estimated that in many areas 3,000 people and 1,000 domestic

[1] Jonathan Cape, 2nd edition, n.d.

animals find their sustenance on a single square mile of land. In other areas over 4,000 people may be found. These figures cannot, of course, be compared directly with the densely populated regions of Europe where the population is fed on *imported* foodstuffs. Taking China as a whole, there is rather less than 0·4 acre of cultivated land per head of population, whereas one acre is normally regarded as a minimum over the world as a whole.

Messrs. La Fleur and Foscue made an interesting study of agricultural production in China.[1] They pointed out that, if one takes the *whole* of Chinese territory (China proper, Manchuria, Mongolia and Sinkiang, but excluding Tibet), the total area is 2,440 million acres. Half is too arid (1,146 million acres) or too cold (64 million acres); mountains cover a fifth (488 million acres) and infertile soil 36 million acres, leaving 29 per cent. of the whole (706 million acres) suitable for cultivation. Out of the latter they estimated that only about a quarter (176 million acres) was actually cultivated. The authors asked, 'Why should China cultivate only one-fourth of her cultivable land when she is in constant need of food for her teeming millions?' On the other hand, Paul O. Nyhus, of the United States Department of Agriculture, concluded that the Chinese 'have completely taken up the land capable of yielding a good supply'.

Returns published by FAO relating to 1954 (excluding Taiwan) give a somewhat different picture. Out of a total area of 2,412 million acres, 1,503 m. (62·3 per cent.) is classed as 'wasteland and other'. Forests cover 199 m. (8·3 per cent.), arable and tree crops 270 m. (11·2 per cent.), permanent pasture 440 m. (18·2 per cent.). No return is made for unused but potentially productive land.

All these estimates are equally unsatisfactory in one respect. They include together entirely different countries—Mongolia, Turkestan, Tibet, Manchuria and China proper.

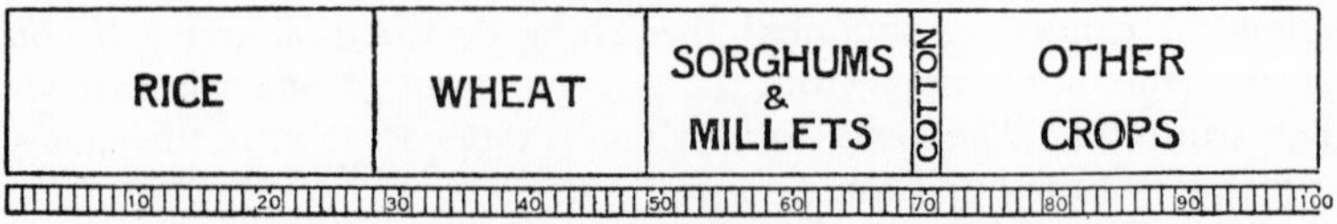

RICE	WHEAT	SORGHUMS & MILLETS	COTTON	OTHER CROPS

FIG. 272.—The areas occupied by the principal crops of China
Because of the higher yield, production of rice is more than double that of wheat.

Taking China proper as the unit, the area including Manchuria is about 1,214 million acres; without Manchuria, 981 million acres. Aridity is not a serious factor except in the north-western loess country but relief certainly is and the mountainous character of the country probably renders half the whole area of China proper not available. Poverty of soil excludes a further percentage. On the whole it is

[1] *Econ. Geog.*, **3,** 1927, 297–308.

probable that about half the possible area of China proper is cultivated. Of land which is purposely and designedly wasted cemeteries are responsible for a large part. The well-known Chinese veneration for ancestors often resulted in the best land being given up for burial

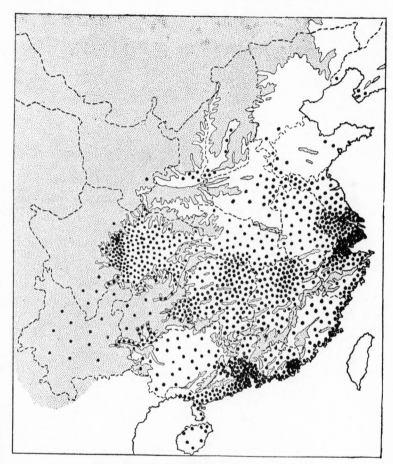

Fig. 273.—The distribution of rice in China

Each dot represents 50,000 acres, out of an estimated total of 70,000,000 acres (1963). All land over 3,000 feet stippled.
(Based on La Fleur, Foscue and Baker.)

purposes. Even in the most densely peopled areas 2 per cent. of the land was used in this way but a great change is now taking place.

Lack of accurate knowledge on the use of land in China inspired Professor J. L. Buck to organize an important survey which resulted in the publication of a report under the title of *Land Utilization in China*.

It is in three volumes—one of text, one of statistics and one of maps (London: Oxford University Press, 1937).

CROPS. There are three great food crops, which together occupy nearly three-quarters of the cultivated lands. Rice occupies rather

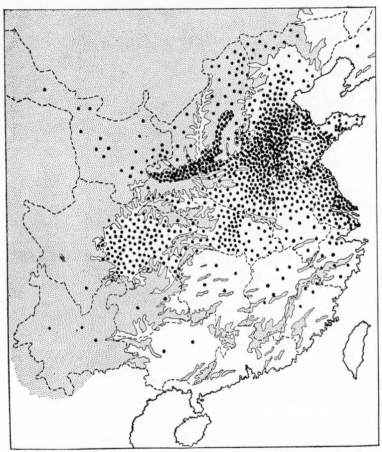

FIG. 274.—The distribution of wheat in China

Each dot represents 50,000 acres, out of an estimated total of 60,000,000 acres (1963). All land over 3,000 feet stippled.
(Based on La Fleur, Foscue and Baker.)

more than a quarter, wheat and millets rather less than a quarter each. The distribution of these three leading crops is shown in Figs. 273–5.

Rice. Rice is the dominant, almost the sole, food crop in Southern China and the south-east coast and occupies there nearly three-quarters of the cultivated land. The yield is about 2,500 lb. per acre. In Central

China—the Yangtze Basin—rice and wheat share the position as lead-ing food grains. In Northern China—north of the 30-inch rainfall line —the proportion of rice is very small. The total annual production for China is recorded as about 80,000,000 metric tons (1955–63).

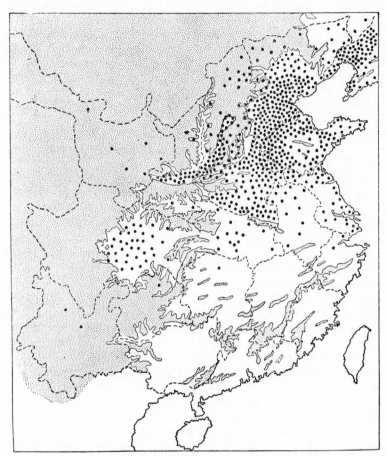

FIG. 275.—The distribution of millet in China

Each dot represents 50,000 acres, out of an estimated total of 60,000,000 acres. All land over 3,000 feet stippled.
(Based on La Fleur, Foscue and Baker.)

Wheat. Very little wheat is grown in Southern China; in Central China it is important; in North China (especially on the Great Plain and in the Wei Ho Valley) a very important crop, and is also grown over considerable areas in Manchuria. Much could be done to improve acre-yields, whilst the drought-resisting varieties of wheat, such as durum wheat, have a great possible future in the development of the semi-arid tracts on the border of the Mongolian Plateau. The annual production of wheat is recorded as about 23,000,000 metric tons (1955–63).

Millets. As in India, the millets become a dominant food grain where the rainfall is less than 40 inches per year. Their concentration in the north-east and in Manchuria is well seen in Fig. 275. The better lands in these drier tracts are occupied by wheat and much land formerly given over to millet is now used for soya-beans. In this map of millets has been included kaoliang, the favourite grain sorghum of the north. It grows to the height of 8 or 10 feet and the brownish coloured grain is of the size of a small pea.

Soya-beans or *Soy-beans.* Although long known in China, it is only of recent years that the proper preparation of the bean, to avoid the rancid taste, has become known. It is rich in oil and extremely nutritious. The acreage devoted to this crop, particularly in Northern China and Manchuria, has increased greatly in recent decades.

Cotton. Most of the cotton of China is grown in the central and northern provinces, and the crop is of considerable importance.

There has been considerable argument concerning the yield per acre of the major crops of China. On incomplete statistics Baker concluded that the yield was 20 per cent. below United States standards and that the adoption of modern methods would go far to alleviate conditions due to food shortage. Later investigations, however, show that the yield per acre is above the world average and considerably above the United States average for practically every crop. The success of the Chinese market gardener in many parts of the world, in areas which have been the despair of others, renders this very probably correct. A bumper harvest was reported for 1958, near famine in 1962–3.

Other Crops. Even after allowing for soy-beans, Fig. 272 shows that a quarter of the land is occupied by 'other crops'. These vary according to location. In the north and centre, barley is significant; in wetter regions, corn. Tea, so indissolubly connected with China, has been of steadily decreasing importance as far as export trade is concerned, but occupies large areas in the Yangtze Basin and the hills of the south-east. Every farm has its patch of vegetables—sweet potatoes are widely grown, but especially in the south-east; potatoes, onions, cabbage and various beans are grown almost everywhere. Most peasants have a melon patch and a few tobacco plants. In the drier, poorer soils peanuts or ground-nuts flourish. In the warm south are many fruit orchards —with oranges (a native of China), and especially mandarins and litchi (lichee), also ginger, bananas and sugarcane. In the silk regions of the Yangtze the necessary mulberry trees are kept trimmed as bushes.

It is a common error to consider all Chinese as rice-eaters. In the north, millions have never tasted rice; to tens of millions it is a luxury only eaten once or twice a year. The Chinese food known in the restaurants of America or Europe is unknown in China, except that it bears some relation to the diet of the Cantonese—who have supplied most of the emigrant Chinese.

AGRICULTURAL REGIONS. It will be obvious from what has already been said that, with Manchuria, four agricultural regions can be distinguished, corresponding to the four climatic provinces:

In South China rice is the staple crop.

In Central China wheat and rice are the two main crops.

In North China millets and wheat are the staple crops, with soyabeans also important.

In Manchuria millets and soya-beans form the leading crops, with some wheat.

ANIMALS. On the whole, the domestic animals of China are widely distributed through these regions, and their distribution is determined by various factors. China has little pasture and no hay—there is no animal husbandry as such. The 9,000,000 horses and mules in China and Manchuria are mainly in the drier north, where they can be used as pack animals, being unsuitable in the wet rice lands of the south. As in India, cattle in China are primarily draught animals. The Chinese eat very little beef and make but little use of milk or other dairy produce. There are about 65,000,000 oxen and water-buffaloes in China, especially in Central China and South China (notably the Si Kiang Basin), where they are essential for ploughing the rice-fields. In many areas there are great possibilities in the establishment of a dairying industry. Of all the non-vegetable foodstuffs of the Chinese, fat pork is easily the most important, and there are probably about 200,000,000 swine distributed through China. Broadly, the density of the pig population varies directly with the density of the human population. Sheep in China are most numerous in the semi-arid north and west, where they are raised primarily for the sake of their coarse, inferior wool. They graze over wide tracts of country under the care of shepherds. Little if any use is made of the meat apart from local consumption. In China nearly every peasant farmer owns at least half a dozen fowls. Again, as in India, the traveller can usually rely upon getting a tough chicken for his dinner and a diminutive egg for his breakfast. There was formerly a large export of eggs and egg products (albumen) from China.

AGRICULTURAL METHODS. The overcrowding in the agricultural lands of China, which has existed for thousands of years, has resulted in highly specialized forms of intensive agriculture. In the United States there are about 3·5 acres of cultivated land per head of population; in China the average is less than 0·4 acre, and over considerable tracts is probably less than 0·2 acre. The two great achievements of the Chinese farmers have been the maintenance of soil fertility and the highly specialized system of intensive cultivation. The secret of the first achievement, accomplished entirely without the aid of chemical fertilizers, is in the use of the wastes of the human body and the wastes of fuel. Some idea of the value placed by the Chinese on human excreta, both liquid and solid—regarded very often merely as waste products in 'civilized' countries—may be gauged by the fact that as long ago as 1908 a Chinese contractor paid £6,500 a year for the privilege of removing the night-soil from the International Concession area of Shanghai. Human manure cannot be applied direct to the soil, but needs careful preparation requiring several weeks. The preparation, often including mixing with river mud or soil, is carried out in a 'compost pit'. In the flat lands, especially of Central and Southern China, the widely practised irrigation has constantly replenished the fields with fertile silt deposited from the flood waters. In the north, the innumerable floods, disastrous though they may be to life and crops, in the long run have proved of incalculable benefit in this way. Apart from the fact that the Chinese have forgotten the natural advantages of a forest cover, in hilly land, the prevention of soil erosion has been brought to a fine art. The hills are not only carefully terraced to prevent the washing away of the soil, but the terraces are so arranged as to arrest the run-off until the suspended matter shall have been deposited. The terracing has required a huge expenditure of human labour, but then there is nearly always a surplus of able-bodied labour even in the most intensely cultivated area. Even more laborious is the actual carrying of soil from one area to another, usually by means of baskets. A barren field may actually be given an artificial layer of soil.

The second achievement may be summed up by saying that every farm is really a large garden. The careful working up of organic matter and soil and then applying it as a dressing makes multiple cropping possible. In India double cropping, where one crop, such as wheat, is grown as a winter crop and another crop in the summer, is common. But in China as many as three crops are sometimes grown simultaneously on one field, all being in different stages of maturity, the first nearing the harvest as another is appearing. The practice of starting rice in 'nurseries' and then transplanting the little rice plants by hand is carried on in China as in India, but has in China a further significance. If a nursery of one acre can supply rice plants for ten acres, then the nine acres can, until the rice is ready for transplanting, be used for another crop. Although the bullock-drawn primitive wooden plough seems absurd to Western eyes,[1] it is essential to Chinese agriculture and could not be replaced by the European or American implement. It only tickles the surface of the soil, but thereby prevents the dreaded soil erosion to which the deep European furrow immediately conduces. It makes a powdery surface layer and thereby conserves moisture as in

---

[1] In the more densely peopled areas hand-digging is the usual method of preparing the land. Chinese farming has been well described as efficient if measured in yield per acre; terribly wasteful if measured in human effort.

the 'dry farming' methods of Australia and America. Further, the ox is invaluable for his manure. The fields on a Chinese smallholding are often divided into parallel ridges and furrows, not only for the purpose of controlling more effectively irrigation water and soil erosion, but to permit the growth of rice in the hollows and such crops as peas, vegetables, ginger, etc., on the ridges. Even the permanent bunds between the larger fields are made useful by the planting of mulberries or pear-trees on them.

Under the present Communist régime *the* great change that has taken place in agriculture is the rapid and apparently successful spread of cooperation now (1966) embracing 85 per cent. of all farms and which is moving on to collectivization.

Fishing. Fish is an article of diet widely used in China. In the days before the present régime the rich man's table would scarcely have been complete without such delicacies as shark's fins and edible sea-weeds, obtained by the intrepid fishermen of the south-east coast. Rivers and lakes throughout the country yield their quota for the masses and nearly every village in south and centre has a fish-pond.

Manufactures and the Industrialization of China. Like other Asiatic countries, China had a wide range of local manufacturers and village craftsmen producing goods often of very high quality and artistic merit. One thinks naturally of silks and porcelain, hand embroidery and jewellery, but the products of village cotton looms or of blacksmiths must not be forgotten. But the industrial revolution in China and the establishment of modern factories dates principally from 1895 with the struggle for 'concessions' between Japan, Russia, Britain, Germany and France or from the opening up of the Treaty ports to foreign trade which was forced upon China from outside. The concentration of modern industries in the coastal cities, notably Shanghai, mainly by foreigners, remained marked until the outbreak of the Sino-Japanese War in 1937.[1] By that time the cotton textile industry was well established and had enjoyed a boom between 1915 and 1920 when European supplies were cut off during the First World War. The industry was concentrated in Shanghai, Tsingtao and Tientsin with roughly half the spindleage and half the looms in Shanghai. Although Chinese ownership had made great strides more than half the cotton cloth produced was from Japanese mills against 8 per cent. from British-owned mills. Other modern industries in 1937 included silk reeling, spinning and weaving (also centred in Shanghai though more widely distributed), woollen textiles, tobacco (dominated by the British-American Tobacco Company), flour-milling (mainly Chinese) and paper manufacture. A start had been made by 1937 with the heavy chemical industry, notably at Shanghai, Canton and in Honan, and a

[1] K. L. Mitchell, 'Industrialization of the Western Pacific' (New York: *Inst. Pacific Relations*, 1942).

plant at Nanking for production of ammonium sulphate. The output of cement was already large.

In Communist China modern factories may appear in remote areas and redistribution is the Government aim. In 1957 the number of factory and office workers was given as 24,000,000. Shabad shows as leading centres Shanghai, Wuhan, Tsingtao, Tientsin, Dairen, Mukden and Harbin. Among newer centres are Lanchow, Chengtu, Chungking, Sian and Chengchow.

The Distribution of Population. The difficulty of estimating the population of China is well known, and a complete Census, as understood in other parts of the world, was first taken in 1953. Curiously enough, one form of the Census is a very old institution in China, the estimates being made on the basis of tax-paying households. It may be generally presumed that all early estimates based on the returns of tax-collectors are well below the real population, since the tax-collector would only have to account for taxes paid by the number of households shown on his returns and would himself grow wealthy on the tithes paid by 'unrecorded' households. A Board of Revenue Census in 1885 gave a population of 377,636,000 for China proper, excluding Manchuria. In 1918–19 the China Continuation Committee compiled a large survey volume entitled *The Christian Occupation of China*. The work included a careful estimate of population, based on official information, and carefully checked by competent missionaries with a knowledge of local conditions. The total was 452,655,836—including 420,926,847 in China proper, 19,998,989 in Manchuria, 7,780,000 in Mongolia, 1,750,000 in Sinkiang and 2,200,000 in Tibet. In 1925 the Chinese Post Office, an efficient modern organization, prepared an independent estimate, which gave a population of 458,779,714 in China proper, together with 24,040,819 in Manchuria and 2,588,305 in Sinkiang.

In 1953 the Chinese People's Republic carried out a Census and published in the Western press a summary. The total was the staggering figure of 602,000,000 [1] including 12,000,000 Chinese resident abroad and 8,000,000 in Formosa. At the first General Election of 1954 there were 323,809,684 registered electors, i.e. men and women 18 years and over, exclusive of 1·64 per cent. deprived of votes for political reasons.

Although the average density in China proper is of the order of 350–370, the mountainous nature of the surface of China and the resulting concentration of the population in the fertile valleys and plains renders this figure of very little significance. Thus the density of population in Kiangsu, mainly agricultural land, is probably about 1,000 per square mile, whilst over considerable areas, as already noted,

[1] Whilst some demographers have questioned the accuracy of the figures, many competent observers accept them. In June 1957 it was officially stated in Peking that the net annual increase was 15,000,000. China excluding Taiwan had reached 760,000,000 by mid-1965. The urban population, 13·3 per cent. in 1953, is increasing rapidly. By 1958 Shanghai had 7 m., Peking 5·5 and 14 other cities exceeded a million.

the density may reach 3,000 or 4,000 per square mile even in purely agricultural country.

Two factors in the main determine the present distribution of population in China. The first is physical. Of necessity the population is concentrated in the non-mountainous areas where intensive agriculture

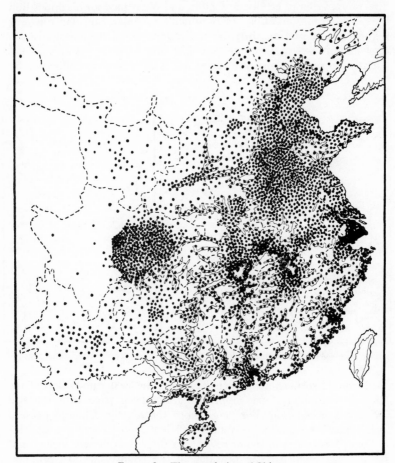

FIG. 276.—The population of China

Each dot represents 100,000 people. The fine line is the 1,500-ft. contour.

is possible. This may be demonstrated in a broad way by superimposing a physical map (on which the 1,500-feet contour is shown) on a population map. The other factor is, or perhaps we should now say was, religious. Ancestor-worship is the universal religion of the country and the first thought of the peasant is: 'Who will tend the graves of my ancestors if I migrate to new lands?' Despite the attractions of cheap, fertile land crying out for cultivation in Manchuria and the fringes of

Mongolia, the Chinese peasant for long elected to starve in his ancestral home, retaining the undivided family and within sight of the graves of his forefathers. It is not that the attractions of the new lands were not known, for every year there was a temporary migration thither of thousands upon thousands of workers. The Chinese peasant lived in direct opposition to economic factors and often paid for his opposition by death from starvation. It is difficult to judge how far the new régime has altered all this: the indications are that Communist indoctrination has in fact penetrated to the remotest corners of the country, already thrown into close touch with modern influences by the necessities of war.

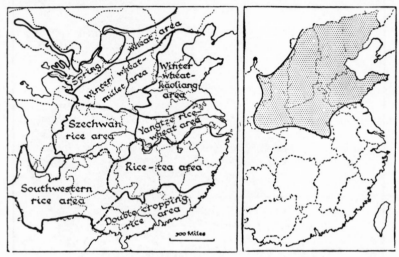

FIG. 277.—The agricultural regions of China   FIG. 278.—The famine region of China

It would seem inevitable that, despite the well-known skill of the Chinese cultivator, food supply does not keep pace with the still increasing population. For generations the average Chinese peasant family has been unable to obtain sufficient food to preserve health.[1] A bountiful harvest does not result in a surplus, it merely means that for at least one year the peasants of the countryside are properly nourished. A failure of the harvest means inevitable famine and starvation—even with modern development of transport. There is no margin. It may be stated here that the normal diet of the Chinese peasant consists of millet and wheat (in the north) or rice (in the south), vegetables, oil and tea, with fish and meat as luxuries rather than necessities. In times of famine, flour made of ground leaves, husk of the ground-nut,

[1] See the interesting account in W. H. Mallory, 'China, Land of Famine', *Amer. Geog. Soc.*, 1926.

bean-husks, sawdust and fuller's earth all have to be used as food, and the boiling water knows no tea leaves

Whilst the Western world is concerned that measures should be taken to control population increase that the people should not starve, the official Communist view (expressed repeatedly at the World Population Congress in Rome held in September 1954) is that it is man's duty to increase production to meet the needs of whatever may be the population increase. China, following this line of thought, actually stated that a desirable net population increase was 12,000,000 a year.[1] There are lands in Mongolia and Manchuria awaiting settlement, and it is probably true to say that under the new régime the Chinese peasant has been released from the age-old ancestor worship which tied him to his native soil. In the past the Chinese who migrated and who are now found in such large numbers in Malaya, Indo-China, Indonesia, Philippines and farther afield in America were Cantonese or people from the south-east coast. Living sometimes on or at least close to the sea they were not tied to the soil in the same way as the people of the north. Even so, many formerly retained close connection with their homeland and often returned in their old age with the wealth accumulated abroad. This is, of course, no longer the case, and foreign-born Chinese are loyal and valuable citizens of their adopted countries.

Reference has already been made to China as a land of famine W. H. Mallory, in his survey of famine conditions in China, mentions the astounding fact that between the years 108 B.C. and A.D. 1911 there are definite records of 1,828 famines or one nearly every year in some one of the provinces. Untold millions have died of starvation through the ages. Even as recently as 1920–1 the great drought in North China claimed half a million victims and rendered 20 million destitute. Mallory divides the causes of famine into economic, natural, political and social. With the economic we have already dealt; of the natural causes it is sufficient to mention droughts due mainly to the irregularity of the rainfall, floods due to the character of the rivers of Northern China, locusts, typhoons and earthquakes. The last-mentioned are un-important, save in the loess districts, where a shock may cause the fall of enormous masses of loess, burying dwellings and destroying fields. Of the social causes of famine, the high birth-rate, which, despite the high death-rate among infants and mothers, results in a large natural increase, the waste of money on ceremonies, the former waste of land for grave mounds, and the family system which prevented co-operation may be specially mentioned.

Although in dealing with physiography, climate and agriculture we have stressed the division into three regions, coinciding with the three great river basins, it is necessary to emphasize the remarkable contrast between the north and the south. The famine map, Fig. 278, suggests

[1] But latterly, as in Japan, the attitude is changing and family planning is advocated.

the line or rather the zone of transition—roughly midway between the Hwang Ho and the Yangtze Kiang. Professor Cressey has so well summarized the contrasts that it is difficult to improve upon his tabular statement (slightly altered):

THE NORTH	THE SOUTH
Limited, uncertain rainfall.	Good or abundant rainfall.
Disastrous floods and droughts.	Water always available.
Climate influenced by Mongolia: cold winters, hot summers, dust storms, a little snow.	Climate influenced by the ocean: cool winters, hot moist summers, typhoons, snow rare.
Four to six months growing season, one or two crops, agriculture precarious if rainfall is deficient.	Seven to twelve months growing season, two or more crops, intensive agriculture, crop failure rare.
Frequent famines.	Relative prosperity, except for overcrowding.
Unleached, calcareous soils; dry terrace cultivation.	Leached, non-calcareous soils; irrigated terraces.
Grassless and treeless; brown and dusty in winter.	Bamboo and abundant vegetation; green at all seasons.
Kaoliang, millet, wheat, beans.	Rice.
Roads and two-wheeled carts, draft animals (donkeys and mules).	Flagstone trails and sedan-chairs, coolie carriers (water-buffaloes in the fields).
Short, sturdy people of uniform race, conservative, speaking mandarin.	Slighter, less sturdy people, mixed with various primitive non-Chinese aboriginals, speaking various dialects, radical and restless.
Seventy-five per cent. rural living in small villages of mud-walled houses with heated brick beds or kangs.	Seventy-five per cent. rural living in huts with woven bamboo walls and thatched roofs.
Cities with wide streets.	Teeming crowded cities with narrow streets.
Foreign intercourse by land, emigration to Manchuria, little use of sea, poor harbours on coast, few fishermen.	Foreign intercourse by sea, emigration overseas, bold sailors and fishermen, good harbours on coast.

Brief Outline of the History of China.[1] The origin of the Chinese people is still a matter of discussion and controversy; but it is widely recognized that the Chinese civilization is one of the oldest in the world.

History, however, may be said to begin with Yao the Great in 2357 B.C., who was the first authentic ruler in China. The subsequent history of China falls roughly into the following divisions: (I) The Feudal Period, 2357 B.C.–221 B.C. (II) The Monarchical Period, 221 B.C.–A.D. 1912. (III) The Republican Period, from 1912 onwards. The early organization was akin to that of feudal chieftainships and the limits of territory never exceeded the bounds of the modern provinces of Shansi, part of Shensi, the southern part of Hopei and a strip only of

[1] See especially T. R. Tregear, *Geography of China*, 1965.

Shantung. But by the second century B.C. the Chinese were masters of lands extending to the Yellow Sea on the east, the Yangtze River on the south and the Kialing River on the west. In 223 B.C. the most powerful state conquered its greatest rival and two years later the Empire of China was united under a single ruler. So we come to the second great stage in Chinese history.

The first Emperor, Ch'in Shin Huang Ti, ordered all records of the past to be destroyed, and had it not been for the disobedience of several hundreds of students no trace might have been left of earlier history. In order to check the incursions of Tartars and other northern tribes, this Emperor united the various existing walls into one Great Wall, which, with branches, attained finally a length of 2,000 miles. Gradually Shantung, Kiangsu, Anhwei, Honan, Hupei and Shensi were added to the Empire.

The Han Dynasty, which ruled from 206 B.C. to A.D. 221, is one of the most famous in Chinese history. The Han era was a time of great prosperity. Literature, art and military studies were among the branches of learning that flourished. During the rule of the Han emperors the Huns became a serious menace and 250 years were spent in wars with the invaders. The Emperor Wu Ti (B.C. 140–86) was an able soldier who succeeded in adding Northern Korea and Kansu to his dominions, while Chinese Turkistan became a tributary province. By the time of Hsian Ti (73–48 B.C.) the whole of central Asia sent tribute to the Emperor, the Huns were driven far westwards and Chinese influence spread even to the Caspian Sea. There followed a period of decline until the dynasty came to an end, only to be followed by other minor dynasties (A.D. 221–589). The Empire was divided into three kingdoms—Shu in the west, Wu in the centre and south, and Wei in the north. In 589 the Empire was again united and peace was restored under the Sui Emperors. From 618 to 907 the Tang Dynasty was in power and contended with enemies in Tibet, Korea and Japan. The Tangs weakened their influence by making the chief governorships of the Empire hereditary. Another age of disintegration followed until the Sung Dynasty brought about reunion in 960. The Northern Sung emperors (960–1127) succeeded in finally subjecting the whole of the South, and the Southern Sungs (1127–1280) were engaged in wars with the Kins. The most deadly of the Empire's foes waited their chance of striking a blow. In 1211 began the great Mongol conquest under Ghenghis Khan, who had helped the Chinese against the Kins, but who then rapidly overran Chihli, Shensi, Shansi and then Honan. His successor, Kublai, invaded the south, conquered Yunnan and annexed Burma. In 1280 the Mongols had wrested the rule of the Empire from the Chinese and were not to be overthrown until 1368. It was the Mongol, Kublai Khan, who received Marco Polo and about whose court we are thus able to gather some interesting information. The year

1356 saw the beginning of the downfall of the Mongols, when the leader of the Chinese rebellion, Chu, captured Nanking. Central China was soon reconquered and in 1368 the Chinese found themselves once again their own rulers.

The Ming Dynasty sat on the imperial throne from 1368 to 1644. The new House in 1421 transferred the capital of the Empire from Ying Tien (Nanking) to Pei P'ing (Peking). During the fifteenth century the Mongols made another bid for power by invading China with some measure of success. The sixteenth century is worthy of note in that it witnessed the real beginnings of relationship between China and European nations. The Portuguese reached Canton and in 1550 or thereabouts were allowed to settle in Macao. The Spaniards, English and Dutch soon followed in the track of the Portuguese merchants in a bid for Chinese trade. Meanwhile the Chinese were yet again occupied with Mongol incursions in the north. Along the coast the Japanese continued their hostile raids and captured many towns. Towards the end of the century the power of the Ming Dynasty began to decline. Foreign elements were creeping in: the Dutch had settled in Formosa, the English had penetrated to Canton and Jesuit missionaries of different nationalities were rapidly gaining ground. With so much to occupy them the Ming emperors ultimately fell victims to Manchu tribes who invaded the Liaotung Peninsula in 1618 from the north-east and set up a capital of their own at Moukden. Subsequently Peking was captured and the Manchus were the rulers of China from 1644 until 1912. The history of these years is partly concerned with further attempts on the part of the English, Dutch and Russians to secure closer relations with China, principally for trade purposes. Embassies from Russia, Holland and Britain met with very little success owing to the many formalities expected of them when approaching the person of the Emperor. In the eighteenth century the Emperor Ch'ien Lung exacted tribute from Burma and warred with the Gurkhas of Nepal in 1790. In 1793 he gave the British permission to trade at Canton. The ill-fated embassy of Lord Amherst in 1816 met with refusal because of the failure of the ambassadors to 'kow tow'. The first war, the 'Opium War', with Great Britain took place in 1840–3 and resulted in the Treaty of Nanking by which Canton, Amoy, Foochow, Ningpo and Shanghai were opened to foreign trade and Hong Kong was ceded to Britain. The disastrous Taiping rebellion (1850–64) began as a religious movement owing to the persecution of Christianity by the Manchus, but it soon became a political rebellion when Hung, the leader, aimed at the overthrow of the Manchus. The rebellion involved twelve provinces and ruined hundreds of cities. In 1856 the second war with Britain was waged and France also took sides against China. In 1860 the Convention of Peking imposed an indemnity on the Chinese and opened Tientsin to foreign trade. Thenceforward it was the West who dictated the terms. In 1875

Ichang, Wuhu and other towns were opened. In 1895 Korea obtained independence, Formosa was ceded to Japan and still more ports admitted foreign ships.

Tsingtao, in Kiaochow Bay, was secured by Germany in 1898, to be captured in 1914 by Japan and in 1922 returned to China. In 1898 also, Great Britain obtained Wei-hai-wei in Shantung and a lease of territory on the mainland opposite the island of Hong Kong. Russia was to hold Port Arthur and Talienwan (or Dairen) on lease. Following the Russo-Japanese War the Liaotung Peninsula and the control of the railway from Port Arthur to Ch'ang-chun were transferred from Russia to Japan. The French in 1898 were granted a ninety-nine years' lease of the Bay of Kwangchow-wan between Hong Kong and the island of Hainan.

The 'Boxer' outbreak in 1900 was a reaction against foreigners, whom it aimed at expelling. It led only to a recognition by the Chinese of the necessity for reform in all commercial administration. The Manchu despotism was nearing its fall. Sun Yat Sen and Yuan Shih-k'ai were leaders of the revolution. They demanded the abdication of the Manchus: the dynasty brought its long reign to an end in February 1912. A republic with Yuan Shih-k'ai as President was established. Yuan died in 1916 and a state of disunion once more set in. Great military war-lords quarrelled over a revision of the constitution and a period of civil war and outlawry ensued. The National Government removed the capital from Peking (renamed Peiping—a former designation) to Nanking in 1928 and began to consolidate its position. Britain restored Wei-hai-wei in 1930 and Belgium their concession at Tientsin in 1931. However, in 1931 the Japanese seized Manchuria and in 1937 invaded China proper. Gradually the Chinese National Government forces were forced to retreat into the interior through a country already torn by civil war—the Red Armies of Communist China were already in full control of many areas. A nationalist capital was established at Chungking in the heart of the Red Basin of Szechwan reached overland from Burma by the famous Burma Road or by airlift. Indeed the necessity of using air routes to a capital unconnected by rail or motor road with the outside world turned the Chinese into an air-minded nation. The defeat of the Japanese in 1945 brought the Second World War to a close and also liberated China from Japanese domination. France returned to China the territory she had leased in 1898 around the Bay of Kwangchowwan, and it was officially renamed Chankiang. But China was already in a state of civil war. The Chinese Communists within a short time gained control of the whole of the mainland: Chiang Kai Shek and the Chinese Nationalists retreated to the stronghold of Formosa. The pattern of Communist control in China follows closely that in Soviet Russia: there are numerous contacts between Chinese and Russians but otherwise the foreigners, once so dominant in the economic life of the country, have been virtually eliminated.[1]

Communications. It is the physiography of China which is mainly responsible for the development of certain special types of land transport in China. The familiar bullock-cart or buffalo-cart of India is of restricted use and distribution in China, being found mainly in the north. In the south either physiography prevents the construction of roads for wheeled traffic—as it does in the Red Basin—or land is too precious for it to be wasted on the construction of a roadway. Or again, why render the problems of 'unemployment' more acute by utilizing an animal where a man could do the work? As a result of these conditions there are three special types of transport still widely used in inner China. One is the wheelbarrow, on which goods can be loaded or passengers carried and full use be made of the narrow pathways. The fare demanded by the owner-driver-steed-and-conductor is but small and the wheelbarrow buses are very popular, especially in the Yangtze Basin. But they are disappearing like the town rickshaw abolished in Shanghai in 1955. Gone too is the palanquin or sedan-chair of the rich. But still characteristic of China is the carrying pole with goods suspended from either end. The carrying pole is much used in towns and in those parts where mountain paths make the wheelbarrow useless. Where watercourses are available junk traffic becomes important. The Yangtze and Si Kiang, and to a less extent the Hwang Ho, are of the greatest importance, and the Chinese do not always get the credit they deserve for seamanship, though it is amazing the voyages which the people of the south-east coast will attempt on the stormy China seas in their little junks. The Yangtze and its tributaries form the great highway of communication in Central China; the Grand Canal and the network of small canals serve the same purpose in the Yangtze Delta and northwards to the Great Plain. Quite a considerable proportion of the population live on their boats. The city of Canton, for example, embraces an extensive floating town of junks, each tenanted by a Chinese family and its picturesque but unfriendly Chow dog.[2]

Turning to the development of modern communications in China, the provision of roads and railways is still one of the greatest needs of the moment. Ocean vessels can reach Hankow; steam launches ply on the Yangtze to Ichang and even into Szechwan, on the Si Kiang and to a more limited extent on other waterways. When this book was first published, in 1929, it was not too much to say that roads fit for motor traffic were absolutely non-existent over enormous areas. But great

[1] The Communists again reverted to the former northern capital so that the city again became known as Peking, which means northern capital. The United States however does not officially recognize Communist China and so in American literature the northern city is still called Peiping.

[2] The rapid extension of railways has proved a severe strain both on available capital and steel, so that Communist China has been paying increased attention to improvement of waterways. See *Geography*, **46**, 1961, 165–7.

progress has been made. In the province of Kwangsi—a remote and sup-
posedly backward area—2,000 miles of motor roads were constructed
in the few years ending 1930. In 1933 it was said that motor-buses plied
for hire in every province of China. By the end of 1957 there were over
100,000 miles usable by motor traffic at least nominally metalled.

By the end of 1935 there were 8,130 miles of railway in China excluding Manchuria, rather more than a third the total in Britain. This may
be compared with about 17,500 miles of railway open for traffic at the

FIG. 279.—The railways, navigable waterways and canals of China

The Trans-Siberian Express now runs direct from Moscow to Peking through Ulan Bator.
For details to March, 1960 see *Geog. Rev.*, **51**, 1961, 534-48.

end of 1957. The railway system did not link Central and Southern
China (Hankow to Canton) until 1936. The chief lines are the Peking–
Hankow and the Peking–Tientsin–Suchow–Shanghai. A branch from
the Hankow line was carried to Changan (Sian) in the Wei Ho Valley
in 1934 and later to Tienshui and Lanchow. In December 1954 a railway was opened from Chengtu to Kwangyuan and continued northwards to Tienshui to meet the Lunghai line linking Lanchow with the
sea. In January 1958 the railhead was already 700 miles beyond Lanchow on its way via Urumchi to link with the Soviet Turk–Sib at

Ayaguz and so with Europe. There is already a line across Mongolia
through Ulan Bator from Peking, which shortens the distance to
Moscow by 600 miles. It is on the Russian gauge. Yunnan is linked
with Hanoi in N. Vietnam by railway, but some idea of the difficulties
of construction may be judged from the statement that in the 289 miles
of this line in Chinese territory there are 152 tunnels and 3,422 bridges.

There are regular aerial services over at least 50,000 miles of route
in China. Peking is linked with 38 major cities but there were, in 1966,
no international services to non-Communist countries.

No account of communications in China, however brief, would be
complete without reference to the 'Treaty ports'. For long Canton was
the only gateway into China open to foreigners; it was not until after
the Treaty of Nanking that Amoy, Foochow, Ningpo and Shanghai, in
addition to Canton, were definitely opened to foreign trade. The opening of other ports followed, so that finally over a hundred were freed to
foreign trade. It should be noted that these included numbers of inland
towns.[1] Two instances alone will be sufficient to show the paramount
importance to China of the Treaty ports and railways. It is emphasized
by Wilfred Smith [2] that all modern iron and coal workings in China
owed their inception and development to modern communications,
so that, conversely, the development of China's resources was impossible
without railways. Professor W. J. Hinton, then of Hong Kong' showed
very clearly that China of the nineteen-thirties fell into three main
economic zones:

(1) The zone of the great Treaty ports and their immediate hinter-
    lands.
(2) The zone along the railways and great rivers.
(3) The great interior—unreached by railways.

It was said very rightly a few years ago that China had four great
needs—stable government, railways, uniform weights, measures and
coinage, and the abolition of the *likin*. The likin was a system of local
taxation or local Customs dues which were levied indiscriminately on
goods in transit by any local authority or even local potentate who
might be in need of funds. The abolition of likin was announced in
January 1931. A standard dollar was introduced in 1933 but suffered
many vicissitudes. The 'People's Bank Jen' introduced in 1955 is
officially rated at 2·46 to one U.S. dollar. The metric system came into
force with Customs in 1934 and has been substituted for native units
all over the country.

Foreign Trade. Two thousand years ago China was exporting
silk to the wondering nations of Europe and over the old 'silk road' of
central Asia passed caravans with porcelain, jade, lacquer and other

[1] E. T. Williams, 'The Open Ports of China', *Geog. Rev.*, **9**, 1920.
[2] *A Geographical Study of Coal and Iron in China*, 1926.

artistic products. As early as A.D. 300 the Arabs had a trading post in Canton—for many centuries the only entry by sea into the country. From those early days right until the latter part of the nineteenth century foreign trade was mainly of exports: every year since 1877, on the other hand, the value of visible imports has exceeded that of exports. Until that date Europe wanted the tea and silk of China, but

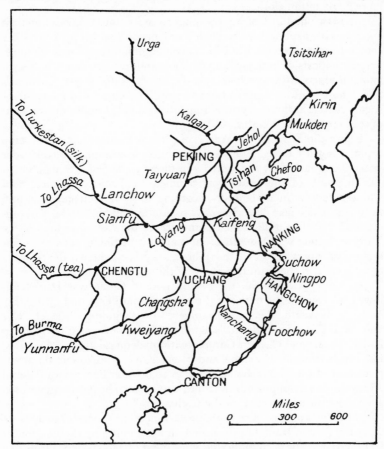

FIG. 280.—Ancient highways

the old Chinese civilization was so self-contained that there were no acceptable imports. China wanted silver, but quantities of the precious metal for shipment to China represented a drain on the resources of Europe and America. Furs were acceptable. Some ships sold ice in South China! Foreign traders encouraged a demand for opium to obviate their difficulties, but international complications followed.

Taking the export trade prior to 1914, tea (54 per cent. in 1871) and silk (42 per cent. in 1899) led during the nineteenth century when beans and bean oil from Manchuria became important. After the First World War raw materials—beans, raw silk, cotton, wool, hides and skins, coal, metals and ores—formed one-half of the total exports; foodstuffs, largely eggs and egg products, nearly one-third; manufactures, one-sixth—a proportion which rose rapidly owing to the increase of cotton cloth.

In 1913 one-third of all the imports were cotton goods (against 0·3 per cent. exports); by 1932 this proportion had dropped to 8 per cent.—less than exports. But China's contempt for foreign manufactures passed; imports of iron, steel, machinery, automobiles (and the petroleum products with which to run them), dyestuffs, paper, chemicals and a host of others bore witness to this. The imports of foodstuffs—sugar, rice, fish, flour—became indicative of the pressure on the land of this agricultural country.

Before the First World War (1914–18) a third of China's foreign trade was with Hong Kong—obviously for transhipment—but later years were marked by the increase in direct trade from Chinese ports.

The bulk of the trade was handled by British, Japanese and Chinese vessels (in that order according to total tonnage). Far and away the chief port was *Shanghai*, handling half the trade. This incredible city of 3¼ million inhabitants served the vast hinterland of the Yangtze Valley with a tenth of all mankind. A line of steel and concrete skyscrapers bordered the Whangpoo River where a dozen miles away were still the primitive farms of the rice cultivators.

Including Manchuria, the second port of China was *Dairen*, followed by *Tientsin*, the outlet of the North China Plain, and *Canton*, the outlet of the south. Tientsin is hampered by a winding silt-laden river and lost much of its trade to Tsingtao (with one of the best harbours in North China) and Chefoo; Canton, with inadequate harbour facilities, lost much trade to Kowloon and Hong Kong. Hankow is the great river port of the Yangtze, accessible to 10,000-ton liners; Swatow and Amoy are the main ports of the south-east coast. The ports enumerated accounted for 90 per cent. of the trade.

Now the whole picture is changed. Since the Japanese invasion of 1937 the foreign trade has dwindled almost to nothing though doubtless there must be a considerable movement of capital goods from the Soviet Union for the industrialization of China. The old foreign concessions have gone: the great International Settlement of Shanghai is essentially Chinese; Shameen Island at Canton, once the preserve of the foreigner, is likewise entirely Chinese. Treaty ports no longer have any meaning and most have decayed: but trade through China's portion of the Iron Curtain is steadily growing.

REFERENCES

Politically, socially and economically China has been so completely changed since the establishment of the Chinese People's Republic in 1949 that most of the earlier literature is now completely out of date, except that the basic physical geography remains unaltered and continues to exert its overriding influence. As noted on p. 480, Dr. T. R. Tregear has considerable experience of modern China and his *Geography of China* (1965) sketches the major changes as well as summarizing the pre-Communist economic geography. Prior to the publication of Tregear's book, Theodore Shabad in 1956 published *China's Changing Map: A Political and Economic Geography of The Chinese People's Republic* based on a critical study of material which reached the news desk of the *New York Times* (London: Methuen, 1956).

It was a few years after the appearance of the first edition of *Asia* (1929) that Professor G. B. Cressey, who had spent some years in university work in China and had travelled some 100,000 miles through the length and breadth of the land, published *China's Geographic Foundations* (New York and London: McGraw-Hill, 1934). It at once became the standard work and established its author's world reputation. As an American Cressey was not able to visit Communist China but spent some time in Taiwan and Hong Kong in 1952 completely rewriting this book which was then published under the title *Land of the 500 Million* (New York: McGraw-Hill, 1955).

Among older books, Little's *Far East* (Oxford: Clarendon Press, 1905) is a classic, and so is Father L. Richards' *Comprehensive Geography of the Chinese Empire* (English translation by M. Kennelly, Shanghai, 1908). Professor J. L. Buck's *Land Utilization in China* (London: Oxford University Press, 1937) is a comprehensive scholarly survey still of great relevance. The trilogy of novels by his talented wife, Pearl Buck (*The Good Earth*, *Sons*, and *A House Divided*) give a fine picture of life amongst the Chinese peasants, especially in the southern part of the Great Plain, before the present regime. R. H. Tawney's *Land and Labour in China* is a masterly summary of the pre-Communist economic position.

The present government of China is publishing in English a range of propagandist literature indicating the various developments in the country—notably the monthly *China Reconstructs*. Numerous works by Chinese scholars emanate from Taiwan (notably the *National Atlas of China* edited by Chang Chi-Yun) which present a different view.

The Loess Plateaus of the North-west.[1] The great German geologist, Baron von Richtofen, was the first to describe in detail for European readers the configuration of North China, and in particular the unique development of the great deposit of loess so characteristic of the region. His theories of the origin of loess, though widely combated in the meantime by those who urged a sub-aqueous origin, are at the present day accepted by the majority of geologists in general as he formulated them. In his great work, *China*, he described how the originally mountainous, rugged outline of the country has been masked by enormous deposits of dust, swept across from the dry steppelands of central Asia by the strong westerly winds which are still such a marked feature of the northern Chinese winter. In the old valleys the loess may even be thousands of feet in thickness; it tails out against the slopes of the old mountains. The lower ranges of the former land

[1] Loess is the hwang-tu or yellow earth of the Chinese.

A.—18

surface are completely covered, the higher ranges still rise above the loess surface. The surface of the plateau is thus divided up into a succession of broad valley-plains separated by rocky ridges. Over northern Shensi and much of Shansi each of these valley-plains constitutes a single *hsien* or county; in the centre lies the 'county-town'—the hsien city or fortress capital of the county. The whole of the province of Shensi was divided traditionally into seventy-three hsiens, Shansi into eighty-six. The sub-aerial origin of the loess is proved by the frequent presence of land shells and bones of animals, by the absence of horizontal

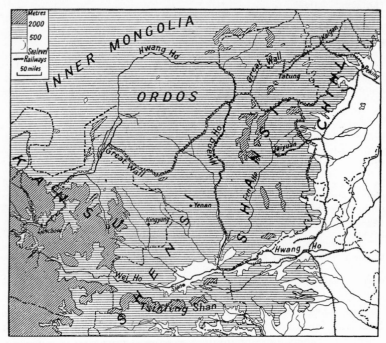

Fig. 281.—The loess plateau of north-west China
The province of Chihli is now known as Hopei.

stratification and the banking up of the deposit against the old mountain ridges. The numerous minute vertical hollows characteristic of the deposit are believed to be due to the roots and stems of successive generations of grasses—as one grass-covered surface was buried and the vegetable matter decayed, another crop sprang up on the new surface. The minute vertical tubes affect the character of the loess in two ways. They result in a sort of vertical jointing, so that, although a very soft deposit, loess stands up in vertical walls. They also assist capillarity and the attraction of moisture, rich in fresh supplies of salts necessary for plant growth, from deep-seated sources to the surface. Hence the extreme fertility of the deposit.

The rivers of the loess plateau, notably the Hwang Ho itself,[1] have naturally cut deep valleys in the soft deposit, valleys with steep, almost vertical, cliffs on either side. Thus the entire course of the Hwang Ho between Shensi and Shansi is inaccessible to wheeled vehicles. In the course of long ages the ceaseless plod of animals and human beings along the cart-tracks has worn the tracks into deep ravines, it may be a hundred feet deep between vertical walls. The erosion has been unequal and, though the surface of the plateau may be level, the roads rise and fall and wind about the country in an amazing way. Along the sunken roads the inhabitants have excavated their dwellings out of the walls. Simple earth caves have now given place to storied houses with wooden doors and windows and often quite elaborate interiors—houses which are warm and dry in winter, cool and dry in summer.[2] To one standing on the surface of the plateau the roads, rivers and dwellings are hidden—the eye sees nothing but a flat or gently rolling surface of cultivated land uninhabited save for an occasional peasant at work in his fields.

It is obvious that such a country of sunken rivers cannot be irrigated—except in certain of the broader valleys—and cultivation depends upon natural rainfall. The natural fertility of the soil makes this a great granary with endless fields of golden wheat, millet, kaoliang, barley and maize, together with cotton, tobacco and groundnuts in normal years, but a region peculiarly liable to famine should the rains fail. Little in his *Far East* stated that a normal crop year had occurred when he wrote only once in every three years, thus accounting for the but moderate density of population in the loess plateau.

The description given above of the loess country applies particularly to northern Shensi. Kansu, to the west, is much drier, with a precarious rainfall, and is but thinly populated.[3] The long north-western extension of the province of Kansu is really only a 'corridor' to the Chinese 'New Dominion', a name commonly applied to Chinese Turkistan. In the province of Shansi the rich loess valleys are smaller, the area of rugged mountains much greater. In fact Shansi consists in the main of a succession of ranges running from south-west to north-east and interspersed by loess-filled valleys. The eastern and southern boundaries of the province coincide with the edge of the plateau, over-looking the Great Plain of North China. It is believed that the reckless deforestation of the once thickly wooded mountains of Shansi has been largely responsible for the decreased productivity of the valleys. The monsoon rainfall runs off rapidly from the mountain slopes and instead

---

[1] F. G. Clapp, 'The Hwang Ho, Yellow River', *Geog. Rev.*, **12**, 1922, 1–18.

[2] Details, with pictures, of these dwellings are given by M. L. Fuller and F. G. Clapp, 'Loess and Rock Dwellings of Shensi, China', *Geog. Rev.*, **14**, 1924, 214–26.

[3] E. Teichman, *Travels of a Consular Officer in North-West China* (Cambridge, 1921), also *Geog. Jour.*, **41**, 1916, and **52**, 1918. The difficulties of transport render impossible the export of bulky produce; hence a considerable production of opium and tobacco.

of fulfilling its proper function of watering the Shansi loess plains, rushes headlong to contribute to the disastrous floods in the Great Plain of North China.

To the north of Shensi lies the Ordos Plateau—an almost desert tract lying in Mongolia, enclosed by the great northward loop of the Hwang Ho.

A huge coalfield underlies a great part of Shansi, of such quality and disposed in such gently folded and easily worked seams that Shansi is often regarded as potentially a second Pennsylvania.

The position of the towns in the loess plateau has already been explained; naturally the larger towns are in the heart of the larger plains. Lanchow may be noted in Kansu; Yen-an (Fushih) in Shensi and Tai-yuan (Yangku), the historic provincial capital, in Shansi. For long the only railways penetrating on to the plateau were to Tai-yuan and the Peking–Paotow line. Northern Hopei, with the historic capital of Shangtu, is really an extension of the region under consideration; here lies also Changkiakow (Kalgan)—frontier town for Mongolia. Lanchow, the capital of Kansu, is built on both banks of the Hwang Ho which was formerly crossed by the 'bridge of boats', over 600 feet in length, and famed throughout China as the most beautiful bridge in the world. It was replaced in 1909 by an American steel bridge. This was the only bridge over the river until the Peking–Hankow railway bridge is reached. The bridge is crossed by the famous old 'silk road' to Chinese Turkistan; the chief industries of the town now are connected with the tobacco and fur brought from the west. The fertile valley round Lanchow is irrigated from the river by so-called 'Persian' water-wheels. The winters in Kansu are sufficiently severe to cause the freezing of the river for six weeks.

The Great Wall [1] forms the northern boundary of China for something like a thousand miles, running across the loess plateau. The inhabitants of Shansi are, to this day, sturdy mountain folk, and that they were greatly feared by the plain-dwellers is evidenced by a branch of the Great Wall which forms part of the eastern boundary of Shansi.

The Wei Ho Valley. This small but important region lies between the loess-covered plateau to the north and the Tsinling Mountains on the south. This east-west strip thus separates the northern portion of Shensi from the southern and centres round Si-an, the provincial capital. The Wei Ho is a tributary of the Hwang Ho which it joins at the great bend of the latter. The Hwang Ho, after a southerly course of about 500 miles through the loess plateau, turns sharply eastwards and forms the boundary between Shansi and Honan before emerging on the Great Plain. Together with the Wei Ho Valley may be considered this easterly course of the Hwang Ho roughly from Paoki to

---

[1] F. G. Clapp, 'Along and Across the Great Wall of China', *Geog. Rev.*, **9**, 1920, 221–49.

Loyang (Honan). A fertile, loess-covered valley, this region is densely populated and intensely cultivated, but its principal call for special consideration is its claim to be the cradle of Chinese civilization. Si-an, in the fertile plain at the foot of the lofty Tsinling range, is famed, under the ancient name of Chang-an, as having been the capital of the Chinese Empire under two dynasties—for 426 years from 206 B.C. to A.D. 220 and again for a short while in the sixth century A.D. Even for the first two thousand years after its emergence from the Wei Valley itself, the old Chinese civilization was confined to the Hwang Ho Basin —including the valleys of such tributary streams as the Fên and Lo.[1]

The Great Plain of North China. Lying between the edge of the loess plateau of Shansi on the west and the Gulf of Chihli or the

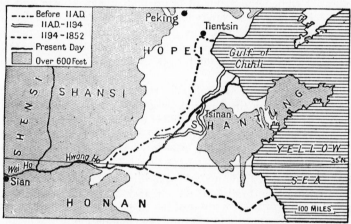

FIG. 282.—The Great Plain of North China and the Shantung Peninsula
The temporary course 1938–47 is far to the south.

Shantung highlands on the east, the Great Plain of North China occupies a large part of the province of Hopei, the western portion of Shantung and the north-east of Honan, whilst southwards it fades into the Yangtze Delta region through the provinces of Anhwei and Kiangsu. Originally occupied by a shallow sea which separated the mountainous Shantung Island from the mainland, the Great Plain is built up of a series of marine gravels and sands covered with a superficial coating of alluvium. The alluvium, which consists largely of redeposited loess, has been laid down by the numerous streams which flow down from the plateau of Shansi and empty themselves into the shallow and decreasing Gulf of Pohai or Chihli. The great Hwang Ho itself, prior to 1852, emptied into the Yellow Sea (Hwang-Hai) south of the Shantung Peninsula. Then it began discharging into the Gulf of Pohai (Pechihli)

[1] C. W. Bishop, 'The Geographical Factor in the Development of Chinese Civilization', *Geog. Rev.*, **12**, 1922, 19–41. Note the importance of the valley as a great east-west route.

till in 1938 it again took a southern course, causing much damage till
turned back in 1947 to the channel of 1853–1937.[1] The behaviour of this
great river may be taken as typical of the rivers of the Great Plain.
In its passage across the plain there is but a slight fall, and the great
burden of fine sediment brought down in the high-water season is
deposited in the bed of the river. In order to confine the water, mud
and straw embankments, sometimes faced with masonry, are built on
either side. Where it is practicable to the peasants who carry out the
work of embankment, the obvious expedient would be to dredge
the river-bed rather than build up artificial sides. Soon the bed of the
river is well above the level of the surrounding plain. Sooner or later
a breach and a serious flood are inevitable and the river which has
temporarily ruined thousands of farms finds a new course and permanently ruins all those lands lying in its new path. Well has the
Hwang Ho been named 'China's Sorrow' and not until the vast
modern river-training works now in hand are complete can the Great
Plain hope to be free from the disastrous floods, at present almost a
yearly occurrence.

But the soil, despite wide marshy tracts in some parts and saline
incrustations through the long dry season in others, is fertile and the
hard cereals—millet and wheat—afford a better diet than the rice of
the south. The cold winters, too, and a strain of Tartar blood have
helped to produce a fine sturdy race. Protected to some extent by the
plateau wall from the extreme force of the biting winter winds, the
plains of Hopei appeared an earthly paradise to the nomadic Mongols
of the plateau. The branch of the Great Wall which now separates
Hopei from Shansi bears witness to the struggle of the plains-dwellers
to keep the Tartar hordes at bay; the very foundation of the northern
capital, Peking, in the north of the Great Plain, was a definite measure
to the same end, and it is only within the last few centuries that the
menace has disappeared. Latterly the tide has turned, and the peaceful
agriculturists of the plain are pushing farther and farther on to the
plateau and adding year by year another and another strip to the
agricultural lands of China. Wanchuan, formerly Kalgan, definitely on
the plateau, is the centre of a thriving agricultural country.

Through the Great Plain from north to south has been cut the
Grand Canal or Grain Canal, the construction of which is associated
with the great emperor Kublai Khan. The network of lakes, canals and
other waterways, into which the canal passes in Kiang-su, is comparable
in character with the Yangtze Delta and the region is more appro-
priately considered with that area.

Foremost among the cities of the Great Plain is the northern
capital, Peking. Founded in A.D. 920, it is quite a modern city compared
with many in China. Successively a capital under the Liao, the Kin

[1] O. J. Todd, 'The Yellow River Reharnessed', *Geog. Rev.*, **39,** 1949, 38–56.

Tartars and the Mongols, it was supplanted in 1341 by Nanking which the conquering Ming made their capital when they had driven the Mongols out of Peking. But renewed Tartar invasions caused the Ming to remove to Peking in 1368, which remained the capital until 1928. The city is in the form of a parallelogram enclosed by high walls of brick. The old Tartar city (the Chinese city is outside) was 5¼ miles from north to south and 4 miles from east to west and in its broad streets and spacious plan resembles a central Asian city rather than one of the typical conglomerations of narrow alleys which make up so many Chinese cities. A forbidden city until 1901, the opening of the sacred Tartar city to foreigners resulted from the Boxer rising and its suppression. The railway invasion of the city dates from the same epoch.[1]

Tientsin, on the Pei Ho, is the port of Peking and a great commercial city of the Northern Plain. The river is here 300 yards wide and lined with wharves for steamers and junks. Cotton-mills have long existed in the city itself. As in Peking, the changes which followed the Boxer troubles were far-reaching. The old walls were pulled down, wide roads constructed and river navigation improved. *Paoting*, although the provincial capital of Hopei, is a relatively unimportant city, and the hundred million people of the plain live mainly in small villages.

The Shantung Peninsula. The province of Shantung, excluding the western strip which forms part of the Great Plain of North China, consists of a mass of ancient mountains rising like an island from the plain on the west and the sea on the east. It was, indeed, actually an island when the sea occupied what is now the Great Plain. Structurally, the Shantung massif of ancient rocks is linked with the Liaotung Peninsula and the mountains of eastern Manchuria and Korea, and the Miao Islands exist to show the former land bridge across the Strait of Pohai (Pechihli). The Shantung highlands are cut into two portions by the Tsingchow-Kiaochow Valley, the eastern portion forming the peninsula, properly speaking. The eastern portion consists of ancient granitic and metamorphic rocks; the western portion of limestones and other sedimentary rocks including some rather poor coals. The precipitous, rocky coastline, not infrequently fog-enwrapped, is interrupted at intervals by magnificent natural harbours. The commanding position of the peninsula and the excellence of these harbours attracted the attention, not only of Japan and Russia, but of the great European powers who had interests, actual or potential, to protect in the Pacific. After her victory over China in 1894–5, Japan occupied part of the peninsula, but withdrew her troops on pressure from Russia, Germany and France. A short while afterwards, in November 1897, however, Germany seized the territory round Kiaochow Bay to indemnify for the murder of two German missionaries. A ninety-nine years' lease was

[1] For recent changes see Sen-Dou Chang, 'Peking: the growing metropolis', *Geog. Rev.*, **55**, 1965, 313–27.

arranged in 1898 and Germany spent huge sums in developing the territory and transforming the fishing village of Tsing-tao into a great port. In particular, the extensive reafforestation of the bare hills, the regulation of watercourses, the constructing of the railway terminating at Tsing-tao and the dredging of the bay are works of permanent importance carried out by the Germans. Early in the First World War (1914) the territory was captured by Japan, but in accordance with the Washington Pact was restored to China in November 1922. It remains a good port and is a manufacturing city with modern textile mills.

The territory of Wei-hai-wei, near the tip of the peninsula, was leased by Great Britain by a convention with the Chinese Government, dated July 1, 1898. The obtaining of this lease was a defensive measure against the Russian lease and occupation of Port Arthur earlier in the same year. The area of the leased territory was 285 square miles and it had 154,416 inhabitants in 1921 (mostly farmers and fishermen). Like much of the remainder of Shantung, the territory consists of rocky hill ranges and picturesque fertile valleys. Much was done in afforestation, the making of roads and the development of trade, before the territory was restored to China in 1930.

The hills of Shantung are barren and useless and illustrate in a very remarkable way the evils of soil erosion resulting from deforestation. In the fertile valleys, the intensive agriculture characteristic of North China is in evidence with populations up to 3,000 and 4,000 per square mile, together with a thousand cows, donkeys and swine. Agriculture depends upon rainfall, or rainfall aided by irrigation from shallow wells. Wheat and millet are among the chief crops. The Shantung silk moths are fed mainly upon oak leaves, though mulberry-trees have been planted and grow well.

The sturdy Shantung people emigrate temporarily in numbers to Manchuria, or as coolies to Shanghai. In Chinese history Shantung is famous as the home of Confucius and of his great disciple Mencius.

The former Treaty port of Yentai (Chefoo) is an important port and trading centre. Amongst inland towns should be noted Yehsien (Laichow), Yitu (Tsingchow) and Weifang (the colliery town). On the border of the Great Plain are Tsinan and Yenchow.

The Szechuanese Alps. This name is a convenient one to use for the belt of mountainous country lying mainly in the province of Szechwan to the north-west, west and south-west of the famous Red Basin. The Min River, which the Chinese themselves regard as the true upper course of the Yangtze and which is of such incalculable value to the Chengtu area of the Red Basin, rises amongst these mountains. The Upper Yangtze itself, as understood by European geographers, after rising in Tibet and racing southwards into Yunnan, turns north-eastwards and follows a tortuous course through this mountain region, forming the boundary between the provinces of

Szechwan and Yunnan and roughly between the mountain zone and the Yunnanese Plateau.

The Chengtu Plateau is bounded on the north and west by the Ching-Cheng Shan, or 'Azure Wall Range', which is indeed a veritable wall. Vertical limestone cliffs rise sheer from the cultivated fields of the plain and through this wall break, in gorges and narrow valleys, the rivers and mountain torrents from which the irrigation waters of the plain are drawn. The Azure Wall, seen from the plain, is two or three thousand feet high, but behind it rise range upon range, culminating in snow-covered peaks of 20,000 feet and over in height in the 'Great Snow Range'—the Himalayas of China. These successive ranges form the steps up on to the north-eastern extension of the Tibetan Plateau which lies beyond.

To the south-west of the Red Basin there lies the tangle of mountains which separate it from the Yunnanese Plateau. Included in this tract is the Liangshan, or Terrace of the Sun, a wild range inhabited by the independent Lolo and round which sweeps the Kinsha (or Upper Yangtze) in a continuous series of rapids.

Needless to say, the Szechuanese Alps as a whole form a thinly populated region, inhabited mainly by independent mountain tribes.[1]

The Red Basin. Occupying the heart of the province of Szechwan, the Red Basin [2] is one of the most remarkable regions in the world. Hemmed in on all sides by a girdle of mountains, the basin was occupied in Cretaceous and Tertiary times by a great lake in which were deposited the red sandstones from which the basin derives its popular name, and which was drained when the outflowing stream cut the famous gorge between Fengkieh and Ichang. The old lake-basin was crossed by a series of limestone ridges, all trending north-north-east and south-south-west. The red sandstones fill in the hollows between these ridges and are banked up against them. When once the main Yangtze Gorge was cut, erosion got to work on the soft sandstones, giving rise to a fantastically rugged landscape, extremely picturesque. Every stream, large and small, has cut its way down and flows in a deep ravine. The Yangtze itself has worn a valley a thousand feet below the level of the sandstones of the basin and cuts through the cross-ridges of limestone in a series of magnificent gorges. The Yangtze flows from west-south-west to east-north-east near the southern border of the basin; flowing in from the north are the tributaries which give rise to the four main valleys in the red sandstone plateau. The name Szechwan actually means 'Four streams'. From west to east there are:

(a) The Min Valley. The Min is regarded by the Chinese as the

---

[1] For a description of some of this country, see H. G. Thompson, 'From Yunnan-fu to Peking along the Tibetan and Mongolian Borders', *Geog. Jour.*, **67**, 1926, 2–27.
[2] A. Hosie, *Szechwan: Its Products, Industries, and Resources* (Shanghai: Kelly and Walsh, 1922).

true upper course of the Yangtze. Though much shorter than the other head-stream (the Kinsha Kiang), it usually has as large a volume of water and is of use as a navigable water-way, which the Kinsha is not. The two unite at Ipin (Sui-fu). The Chengtu Plain, in the upper part of the Min Valley, will be mentioned later.

(b) The Chung Kiang (or Central River) Valley.

(c) The Fu (Fow) Kiang Valley, and

(d) The Kialing Valley. The last two unite a few dozen miles above their junction with the Yangtze at Chungking.

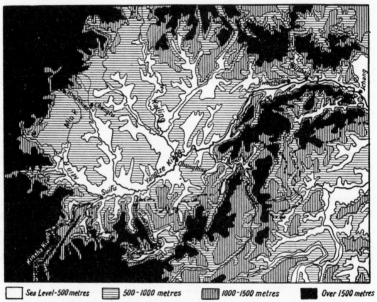

| Sea Level-500 metres | 500-1000 metres | 1000-1500 metres | Over 1500 metres |

FIG. 283.—The Red Basin. Scale: 140 miles to one inch

Kweichow is now Fengkieh.

These four great north and south valleys comprise the richest agricultural land of the Province of the Four Streams.

The whole of the Red Basin, with the exception of the Chengtu Plain, is thus divided up into deep ravines and high ridges. But it is well watered, the rocks almost dripping with moisture, and the hill-sides have been terraced from base to summit. The farmers produce a varied succession of crops: rice, wheat, maize, beans, sugar, hemp and tobacco. Oranges are widely grown, whilst silk is one of the leading products of the region. The well-known 'T'ung yu', or Dryandra oil, comes from this area. In the words of Little: [1] 'The climate of the Red

[1] *The Far East* (Oxford, 1905).

Basin is warm and damp; there is practically no winter, frost and snow being unknown except on the hill-tops, their place being taken by drizzling rains: thus the country is always green and never without crops; no sooner is one crop ready for reaping than another is seen sprouting in the intervening furrows.' But the sun appears so seldom that, according to a local proverb, the dogs bark when the sun shines. The rains in summer are heavy and continuous and landslips are frequent, the terraced hillsides being stripped of their soil, which has then to be carefully replaced by the untiring farmers. Five and six crops a year are rendered possible by the use of cesspool manure from the many populous towns.

Amongst the minerals of this remarkable area, coal has already been mentioned. It crops out frequently on the sides of the ravines, and has long been the principal fuel of the basin. The salt production from the brine wells is an important item in the provincial revenue.

The principal lines of communication in the Red Basin are the rivers. The four main streams and the Yangtze fall about 500 feet in the 200 miles across the basin, but the Chinese boatmen force their craft over apparently hopeless rapids and there is an unending traffic. The land roads traverse the country in all directions, but many are nothing more than narrow tortuous footpaths interrupted by successions of stone staircases, often cut from the solid rock, where they cross the ravines. Modern motor roads now link the main centres, including Chengtu and Chungking, with the outside world, and a railway has been built, as already noted, between these two towns.

The very dense population of Szechwan consists, at the present day, mainly of immigrants from Hupeh, Kiangsi and other eastern provinces who replaced the earlier inhabitants who were virtually exterminated by a Shansi war-lord in the seventeenth century. The pressure on the land from the present immense population is very severe and cultivation is being pushed farther and farther into the surrounding girdle of mountains, especially towards the Tibetan border in which direction Szechwan has been extended.

The Chengtu Plain. Though lying within the limits of the Red Basin, the Chengtu Plain deserves special treatment as a sub-region. It is a tract of about 2,800 square miles of roughly level land in the otherwise mountainous province. Ascending the Min River from its junction with the Kinsha, by a series of rapids one arrives, after a journey of about 200 miles, on to the Chengtu Plateau, which itself has a marked slope from north to south. It is the bed of an old lake and has a subsoil of boulder-filled gravels. Only the ancient and very ingenious irrigation system has prevented the plain from remaining a desert of boulders in the north and a useless swamp in the south.[1] At Kwan-hsien, where

[1] F. O. Jones, 'Tukiangyien: China's Ancient Irrigation System', *Geog. Rev.*, **44,** 1954, 543–59; also Little, *op. cit. sup.*

the Min emerges from its gorge through the Azure Wall Range, Li II, a gentleman of blessed repute, whose very name is unknown, carried out the double scheme of controlling the main stream by caissons and cutting a channel to divert part of the water due east where it intercepts numerous mountain streams and eventually distributes the collected waters over the whole plain. Li II was the son of Li Ping who overthrew the Shu kingdom in 215 B.C., and the success of his irrigation scheme through more than two millennia is largely due to the observance of his maxim 'Dig deep the bars; keep low the dykes'. The Great Plain of North China would have had a much happier history had this maxim been observed there, where the dredging of the river-beds is entirely ignored. One of the great features of the irrigation system is the artificial multiplication of channels and the control of the waters by what appear to be flimsy bamboo fences. Though the principal dykes are elaborate masonry erections dating from the thirteenth century, when molten iron was used to fill the interstices, the use of a bamboo network for temporary works is still of great importance. The density of population made possible by the irrigation works is almost incredible—more than 4,000 to the square mile in places. Unlike many irrigated tracts, the Chengtu Plateau is well-wooded. The watercourses are lined with trees, the numerous fine monasteries are surrounded by groves of forest trees and bamboo thickets, the farms have their orange and other fruit orchards and the agricultural fields appear almost hidden.

The most remarkable feature of the Red Basin, including the Chengtu Plain, remains to be mentioned. That feature is its inaccessibility. Completely shut off from the outside world the Red Basin is self-sufficing, producing all the necessities of life and thus able for centuries to lead a self-contained life. If we exclude the 500 miles of mountain path from Kunming, the chief entrance to and exit from the Red Basin was by the Gorge of the Yangtze—between Fengkieh and Ichang—in the centre of which lies the Great Gorge of Wushan, 22 miles long. Specially constructed boats can pass through the gorge during the greater part of the year; a road has been constructed high up on the flanks. A railway along the same line has long been discussed. But the trade which passes in or out of the Red Basin is still largely in the hands of those intrepid navigators who force their frail craft through the rapids.

The Central Basins. Emerging from the gorges which cut off the Red Basin from the rest of China, a little above the port of Ichang, the Yangtze makes its way across a succession of three level basins before entering the deltaic area near Nanking. These three plains have many features in common and may be considered together as one natural region, that of the Central Basins. It is probable that the waters of the Yangtze originally found their way to the Pacific Ocean through a series of lakes, and the flat alluvial stretches of the Central Basins represent the floors of these infilled lakes. In each of them, there indeed still exists a fragment of the ancient lake and, in times of severe flood, the whole countryside reverts once again to what must have been its prehistoric character.

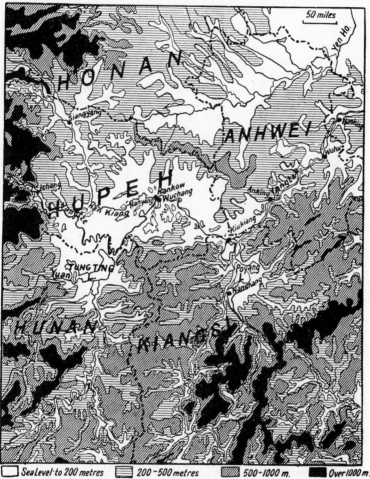

Fig. 284.—Physical map of the Central Basins of the Yangtze

(From the maps published by the Geographical Section of the General Staff.)

(a) The Upper Basin is the largest and is cut into a northern half, lying in Hupeh, and a southern half, lying in Hunan, by the Yangtze itself. The river enters the basin at Ichang and leaves it in the narrow winding channel of 'Split Hill' below

Hankow. The large shallow lake of Tungting, south of the Yangtze, represents the remnants of the original lake, whilst other smaller fragments remain north of the river. Changsha, capital of Hunan, lies south of the lake, on the railway to Canton and is a distributing centre in rice country. In the north the plain is continuous with the lower part of the Han Valley.

(b) The Middle Basin is still more distinctly divided into two parts, a northern and a southern, separated by the Yangtze. In the south is the mountain-girt alluvial plain surrounding the rapidly dwindling Poyang Lake and forming the heart of the province of Kiangsi. North of the river the plain is smaller, and stretches from Wusuch, where the Yangtze emerges from the narrows of Split Hill, to Anking, immediately below which the river flows through the narrows of 'Hen Point'.

(e) The Lower Basin is less distinct and lies mainly to the north of the Yangtze—from below Anking nearly to Nanking. The port of Wuhu may be regarded as its centre, and lies in one of the richest rice-growing regions of China. The Yangtze makes its exit from this basin by the gate known as 'The Pillars'.

In all cases the basins are surrounded by a tangle of mountains and hills, in this part of China largely stripped bare of their original forest cover. The frequent flooding, especially of the Upper Basin, is the obvious result of the inability of the river waters to get away quickly enough through the narrows. At Hankow the normal difference between the summer and winter level is 45 feet.

The climate of the Central Basins is the climate already described as typical of Central China, with colder winters than are experienced in the Red Basin. North of the river, Hupeh grows barley, wheat and cotton, but little rice; cattle are numerous and silk-worm rearing is an important industry. South of the river, the basin of the Tungting Lake in Hunan is a great rice-growing area and large quantities are exported via Hankow to the districts north of the river. Tea and oil-seeds come mainly from the slopes of the surrounding hills. The Poyang Lake basin of Kiangsi is similar in character.

The great highway through the region under consideration is the Yangtze. Ocean-going steamers ascend normally to Hankow; large river craft to Ichang, which after its opening as a Treaty port superseded Shahsi. The lakes are shallow and of little use, but the inflowing river cuts out a navigable channel through them. Thus the Han is navigable to Siangyang; the Yuan across Tungting Lake right through Hunan to the borders of Kweichow; the Kan River right across Poyang Lake into the mountains of the south of Kiangsi Province.

One of the most important centres in China is formed by Wuhan—

the three cities Hankow, Wuchang, Hanyang—with a combined population of between 1½ and 2 million.[1] Hankow and Hanyang are both north of the Yangtze, the former east of the Han, the latter west of the Han. Wuchang faces them and the mouth of the Han and is on the south side of the Yangtze. Hanyang and Wuchang were both walled cities and, normally, administrative centres; Hankow, without walls and free to expand, was the commercial city. Already a focal point on the waterways, the three cities have become a leading railway centre of central China, as well as a leading industrial centre, and are expanding rapidly. Wuhang has had large modern-type cotton-mills since 1901, and the Hanyang iron and steel works using the local Tayeh ores

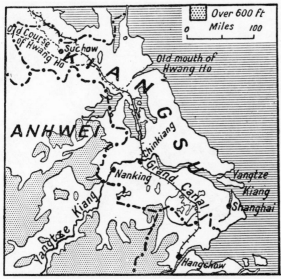

FIG. 285.—The region of the Yangtze Delta

were active until 1920. Destroyed by bombing they have been reconstructed. Wuchang's walls were removed in 1928–9 and since 1951 expansion has been staggering. A rail-road bridge over the Yangtze was opened in 1958 and there are bridges over the Han.

Kiukiang, 140 miles below Hankow, is in the Middle Basin and is another river port and the natural outlet for Kiangsi. *Anking*, or Hweining, the capital of Anhwei, like the other cities of the province, was devastated during the Taiping rebellion (1850–64).

The Yangtze Delta. The natural region of the Yangtze Delta corresponds roughly with the province of Kiangsu. The Yangtze enters the province at 'The Pillars', 20 miles above Nanking, and is tidal to

[1] P. M. Roxby, 'Wu-Han: the Heart of China', *Scott. Geog. Mag.*, 1916. Wuhan is now the name given to the whole. He compared the position with Chicago.

this point, 200 miles from the sea. With the exception of some hills near the river itself along the south bank and a few steep hills rising like islands from the plain, the whole of Kiangsu is a vast alluvial flat. It has been described as the 'Holland of China'—it is traversed by canals and canalized streams in all directions; along the coast the land is actually below high-water level and cultivation is carried on in 'polders'. A tenth of the whole area is still covered with undrained swamps. In the north of the province is the old course of the Hwang Ho and it is there that the Yangtze Delta region fades into the Great Plain of North China. The Grand Canal links the two areas, running

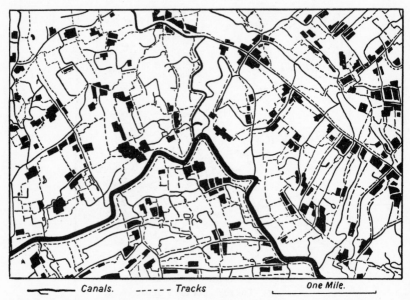

Canals.　－－－－－ Tracks　One Mile.

FIG. 286.—Map of a small portion of the Yangtze Delta region, showing the dense population (each black patch is a village) and the immense numbers of canals. The large canal is the Soochow Canal and the area is west of Shanghai

right across Kiangsu from north to south and crossing the Yangtze at Chinkiang. The banks of the canals are lined with mulberry trees and this is the leading silk-producing region of China. The principal food grain is rice; large quantities of cotton are grown and supply the mills of Shanghai and formerly a surplus for export.

The Yangtze Delta includes within its limits three famous centres: Nanking, the 'Southern Capital'; Chinkiang and Shanghai, the commercial metropolis of China.

Tungshan (Suchow), in the north of Kiangsu Province, belongs more properly to the Great Plain of North China, whilst on the southern limit of the deltaic region, in the province of Chekiang, lies Hangchow.

Nanking is an ancient walled city, the walls 50 feet high, enclosing an area of 35 square miles; it was made the capital of China by the Nationalist Government in 1928, supplanting Peking, but the Communists restored the 'Northern Capital'. A flourishing manufacturing city in the first half of the nineteenth century, it suffered severely during the Taiping rebellion and underwent a protracted siege by the Imperialist forces, capitulating in 1864. During this rebellion, probably half the total population of Kiangsu perished.

Shanghai cannot boast the antiquity of many Chinese cities. Up to the eleventh century it was nothing more than a fishing village and not until the fourteenth century did it become a walled city. Although destroyed by Japanese pirates in the sixteenth century, by the early nineteenth century it had become the leading port of call for sea-going junks. But the prosperity of Shanghai dates from its establishment as a Treaty port in 1843 at the instance of the British Government. The international settlement grew up quite distinct from the old walled city. The safety, cleanliness and well-ordered municipal government of the foreign settlement attracted over a million Chinese, so that the so-called 'foreign' settlement became predominantly Chinese, except in government. Shanghai is not situated on the Yangtze, but on a tidal creek, the Wusung or Hwangpu River, 14 miles from its junction with the main river and 54 miles from the sea. Great blocks of offices, banks and hotels grew up facing the creek along the Bund. Although their European occupants have been replaced by Chinese the Communists have carefully maintained this impressive front door into China.[1]

The South-east Coast. This region corresponds roughly with the provinces of Chekiang, Fukien and the eastern half of Kwangtung. Backed by high mountains, which form an adequate barrier from the centre of China, the outlook of the region is towards the sea. With the exception of the valley bottoms and certain narrow coastal strips, the whole region is mountainous. The productive land, the villages and towns are all concentrated near the coast itself. The region lies between the Yangtze Delta on the north and the Si Kiang Delta on the south-west. At the northern end Hangchow is the liaison city with the Yangtze Delta; at the south-western end Hong Kong is in, but scarcely of, the region.

In contrast with the bare, deforested hills farther north, the mountains and higher hills of this region are forested; the less rugged hills are terraced and covered with tea gardens, orange, lemon and mulberry groves, or with fields of barley, wheat, cotton, or beans. Rice is the chief crop on the flat stretches around the river mouths. The scenery of much of the coast is very fine, especially the Min River. The

[1] Rhoads Murphey, *Shanghai* (Harvard University Press, 1953).

leading ports and towns along the coast are Ningpo in Chekiang; Minhow (Foochow) and Amoy in Fukien, and Swatow in Kwangtung.

The geographical isolation of this region is evidenced in several directions. Like other regions of China, over-population is general; here the obvious outlet is by sea, and so it is the Chinese from this region and the neighbouring Si Kiang Delta who have found their way abroad—to Malaya, the East Indies, India, the Philippines and America. The dialect, especially in Fukien, is entirely distinct from the rest of China, and it was the Fukienese who were the last to be conquered by the Manchus. Even the dress remained slightly different from that affected in other parts of China, especially in the use of a black turban.[1]

An interesting detailed study of north-eastern Chekiang, by Thomas Goodchild,[2] calls attention to a transition region south of the Yangtze Delta and to the position of Ningpo on an alluvial plain in the midst of a district of subdued hills—a level plain from which the hills rise abruptly. The canals form a network over the plains and take the place of roads. The hills are often barren and soil-less.

The Plateau of Yunnan. The province of Yunnan has an area of 162,000 square miles—considerably larger than the British Isles—but has a population of only about 10,000,000–12,000,000. Yunnan is a lofty wind-swept plateau, a continuation of the great plateau of Tibet. Its very name 'South of the Clouds' indicates the contrast with the misty Red Basin to the north-east. In the north-west of the province of Yunnan—which is roughly coextensive with the natural region—is that remarkable area where three of the world's mightiest rivers—the Salween, Mekong and Yangtze—race southwards in huge parallel trenches at the most a few dozen miles apart. These gorges appear to cut the country into north-south ranges and tend to obscure the true plateau character of the country. Farther south the plateau lies at an average elevation of 6,000 to 7,000 feet. Numerous narrow, fertile, but unhealthy valleys interrupt the surface and render communication difficult. The fertility of these valleys attracts farming, but the farmers are compelled to live in villages often many hundreds or even thousands of feet above the fields. Towards the south and east the surface of the plateau drops and the region lies in the drainage of the Red River of Indo-China. This portion of the plateau has been tapped by the railway from Hanoi to Kunming (Yunnan-fu). In the south-west of Yunnan, on the borders of Siam and Burma, the fertile plains are larger and the land richer and rice is an important crop, whereas in the north and east maize is

---

[1] The contrast with other parts of China is emphasized by the development of forestry: almost every Fukien farmer owns a grove of trees—pines and firs—carefully cleared, protected by fire-breaks and tended. Bamboo is also of such importance that it is an old belief that no civilization could exist without it.

[2] 'North-eastern Chekiang, China: Notes on Human Adaptation to Environment', *Bull. Amer. Geog. Soc.*, **43,** 1911.

the chief food grain, rice the diet of the rich. The opium poppy was widely grown in Yunnan. Yunnan is undoubtedly very rich in minerals; it is outstanding in this respect among the provinces of China. Coal of poor quality occurs, and traces of petroleum occur in old lake-basins, but the wealth of the area is in metallic minerals. Gold occurs all over

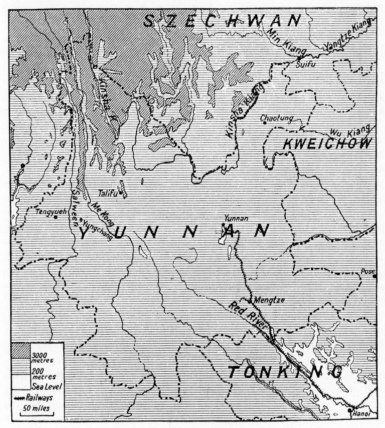

FIG. 287.—The Plateau of Yunnan

Yunnan-fu is now known as Kunming.

Yunnan—it was panned in 430 out of 700 streams tested in 1911–13—but the gold is all alluvial and does not occur in sufficient quantities to justify importation of machinery to so inaccessible a region. For centuries past natives have traded the gold of Yunnan for the jade of Burma. Antimony ores occur in the Chinese Shan States and are worked by modern methods just above Mengtsz on the Tongking–Yunnan Railway. Copper in large quantities is obtained by primitive methods,

Yunnan being the richest copper-producing province of China. Argentiferous galena is worked in various areas, especially near the Burmese border. Spelter—an alloy of copper, lead and zinc—was used extensively in China in making cash currency and was exported in considerable quantity. Tin is mined at Kokin—about 20 miles west of Mengtsz—and has been for many years. Tungsten, arsenic and mercury are among the other minerals of Yunnan, whilst iron ore is mined in almost every part of the province.

It is curious that Yunnan, a province so rich in minerals, and with by no means an unfavourable climate and soils, should remain so undeveloped. Little has compared its situation in elevation and latitude with the Transvaal. A large proportion of the inhabitants are aborigines, allied to the Burmese and Siamese, and known to the Chinese as Miaotse. Difficulty of access and of east-west communication only furnish partial explanations of the backwardness of the province, which never seems to have flourished under Chinese rule. The outlet of the main part of the region, including the large centres of Talifu, Kunming and Mengtsz, is via Tongking (since 1953-4 under Communist control), whilst the south-west, including Teng-yueh (Momein), is more accessible from Burma via Bhamo.[1] It is only the third and fourth of the main approaches which connect Yunnan with the rest of China—the Yangtze route from Kunming to Suifu (Ipin) at the junction of the Min and Yangtze and the Si Kiang route from Kunming via Poseh to the Si Kiang. The remoteness of Yunnan is seen when one remembers it is 2,000 miles from Peking, and that in the old days it took officials appointed from Peking four months to cover the hundred stages necessary to reach their posts.

The Si Kiang Basin. The Si Kiang Basin corresponds roughly with the province of Kwangsi and the western half of Kwangtung. With this region may be included also the coast of western Kwangtung and the island of Hainan. The Tropic of Cancer passes through the heart of the region, and the climate is, on the whole, comparable with that of India and may be classed as tropical monsoon in type. Rice becomes the great staple food crop. The valley of the Si Kiang is much smaller than that of the Yangtze; the area of lowland is limited, but there are many points of resemblance between the two basins. Like the Yangtze, the Si Kiang cuts through the limestone ranges across its path in a series of fine gorges. A northern tributary, the Kwei Kiang, on which stands the town of Kweilin (the capital of Kwangsi), rises on the borders of Hunan and is joined by a short canal with the upper waters of the Siang River, thus affording through water communication with the Yangtze system. A southern tributary, the Tso Kiang, or

---

[1] One motor road from Rangoon through the Shan States reaches the south-west of Yunnan; another farther north is the 'Burma Road' from Bhamo and Lashio to Teng-yueh.

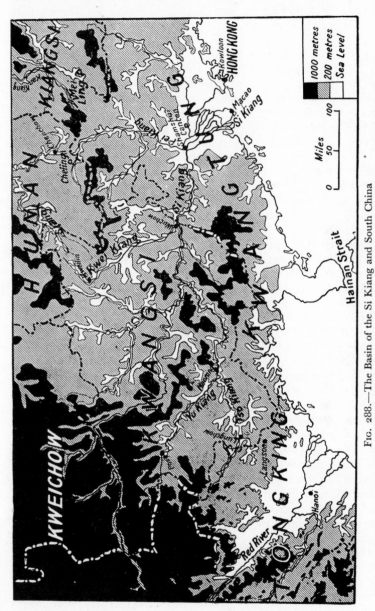

Fig. 288.—The Basin of the Si Kiang and South China

Early in 1958 plans were announced for the building of a giant petroleum city to process large deposits of oil shale in the northern part of Liuchow peninsula in south-western Kwangtung. The aim is to produce a million tons of petroleum a year and a million tons of ammonium sulphate.

Left River, rises in Tongking and affords an easy means of communication to Langson, just on the Viet-nam side of the border, whence there is a railway to Hanoi.

Aborigines (Miao) are numerous in the region; Chinese are largely confined to the fertile river bottoms, where rice is cultivable, and more than half the 'counties' of Kwangsi are normally under 'Miao' headmen. The Communists have recognized this by constituting Kwangsi-Chuang an Autonomous Region. It is interesting to notice that the Chinese long ago recognized the essential geographical unity of the Si Kiang Basin by uniting the Kwangsi and Kwangtung Provinces as one viceroyalty, with headquarters at Canton.

If the Si Kiang Basin is a geographical unity, there is nevertheless a marked contrast in economic development between Kwangsi, the upper part of the basin, and Kwangtung, the lower part. Kwangsi, almost wholly mountainous, as already stated, is still inhabited largely by aborigines. Lungchow is thus of little note. Nanning is more important because it lies on the Pearl River, and thus commands the route up that river to Poseh and Yunnan. Wuchow, the most important town in Kwangsi, occupies a position on the Si Kiang comparable with that of Hankow on the Yangtze. It lies at the junction of the important and navigable Kwei Kiang and Si Kiang and is accessible by steam vessels of considerable size from Canton. Also known as Tsangwu, it is the collecting centre for the cassia, cinnamon and mace, as well as cabinet woods, for which Kwangsi is famous.

The province of Kwangtung by way of contrast, although not one of the largest of the provinces of China, is one of the most densely populated and perhaps the most important. Long before the rise of Shanghai, Canton was the gate to China for the Western world and at least partly open years before other parts of the country. The energetic and active Cantonese are less tied to their native soil, rich as it is, and it is the Cantonese who have penetrated to the new lands of south-east Asia. The energy of the Cantonese sometimes makes itself felt in undesirable channels; piracy by river raiders, whose lairs lie amongst the numerous channels of the Si Kiang Delta, has been a persistent feature. When I first visited China in 1925, it was the Canton River which bore the most warlike appearance, with every little river boat armed—even if only by a rusty rifle sheltered by a battered petrol tin —against the pirates.

The province as a whole is mountainous—with bare deforested hillsides. Granite forms many of the higher ranges such as those which overlook the 'New Territory' of Hong Kong and form the mountainous island of Hainan. In the middle of the mountainous complex is the triangular delta, each of its three sides measuring roughly 100 miles. The delta and the river valleys are well watered—the rainfall being over 60 to 80 inches—and given over to rice cultivation. Subsidiary crops include sugar, tobacco, oil-seeds and silk.

Canton (Kwangchow) is now a clean modern city with wide streets. Lying on the west bank of the Canton River, it is nominally connected with Kowloon (Hong Kong) by rail, but the service has been irregular for many years and Canton is approached by steamer from Hong Kong or direct by ocean-going vessels. When I saw it in 1925 before much destruction by fire and war the heart of the city was a maze of narrow tortuous alleys, lined with shops and paved with large flagstones. No wheeled traffic was possible, but there was a ceaseless stream of foot-passengers and an occasional sedan-chair conveying a rich merchant or a Chinese general—if the latter, probably preceded by a bodyguard with drawn revolvers. Wider streets with large 'stores' surround this old centre, and just to the north, separated from the city by a stream only a few feet wide, is the island of Shameen, formerly the residential and business quarter of Europeans, now with its European-type bunga-lows occupied by families of Red officials. Until the opening of the coast ports Canton was the port of entry for the whole of China: the road to the interior lies up the North River (Pei Kiang) to the Meiling (Plum-tree Pass), a low notch only a thousand feet high, which separates the headwaters of the Pei Kiang from those of the Kan of Kiangsi. Farther west is the Lesser Meiling or Cheling Pass, leading to Hengyang in Hunan. The long-promised Canton–Hankow Railway completed in 1936 follows approximately this line; but human beings are still the beasts of burden, bearing merchandise suspended from the inevitable pientan, or carrying pole.

Canton overshadows the other urban centres, which include Sam-shui, a port at the junction of the West and North Rivers, with a large junk trade; Chaoking (Koyiu), on the West River, once the residence of the viceroy; and Namhoi (Fat-shan).

To the east of the mouth of the Canton River lies Hong Kong, to the west the Portuguese territory of *Macao*. The Portuguese obtained permission to settle in Macao under the Ming Dynasty in 1557 and Portuguese sovereignty was finally recognized in 1887. Macao (or Macau) is a rocky peninsula, which is now almost entirely occupied by the town, linked to the mainland of Communist China by a narrow sandy isthmus. To the west is a shallow arm of the sea teeming with fishing vessels (fishing provides a livelihood for a quarter of the popula-tion) and with wharves from which steamers ply several times daily to Hong Kong and from which launches serve the two small islands, also part of the 'province', which has a total area of six square miles. Macao was not occupied by the Japanese in 1941–5 and its population was swollen to 600,000 by refugees (it was 187,772 at the Census of 1950 but only 169,299 in 1960). Though Europeans number less than 10,000 (7,974 Portuguese in 1960) there has been considerable inter-marriage. With the old fort of Gura dating from 1626, its numerous churches, fine modern cathedral, historic town hall and fine library, Macao is a remarkable cultural outpost where the leisurely pace of life contrasts strangely with the bustle of Hong Kong. It has never been an important trading port and land reclaimed from the sea on the east remains unused. There are local handicrafts, especially the making of fire-crackers, matches and incense-sticks, and much fish is dried and exported. Its quiet charm—and its gambling saloons—attract a number of visitors, especially from Hong Kong.

The Plateaus of South China. The Si Kiang Valley and the south-east coast of China are cut off from the Yangtze Basins by a series of rugged, largely deforested mountains which broaden in some parts to form plateaus. Practically the whole of the province of Kwei-chow is occupied by such a plateau: it is continuous with, but distinct from, the Yunnan Plateau to the west and is also distinct from the basins to the north and south. Kweichow, like Yunnan, has numerous high plains surrounded by amphitheatres of mountains, and each has been made the seat of the capital of one of the thirty-three counties into which the province was divided—wherein a comparison with Shansi may be noted. Rice, maize and tobacco are the principal crops, together with opium. Nut-galls are collected from the oak forests and exported; the province is famous for its silk and is rich in minerals, though only silver and iron have been extensively worked. But Kweichow remains one of the least known and least accessible parts of China. The proportion of 'Miao', or aborigines, is large, but there is a steady immigration from overcrowded Szechwan.

Note on Chinese Place Names. Very great difficulty exists in the use of Chinese place names. In the first place there are several systems for the transliteration of Chinese characters into English letters which may result in such differences as Tsinghai or Chinghai, Chenchow or Hengchow, -peh or -pei. Then the names are often descriptive, especially of the status of a town or other settlement, which may change from time to time. Older maps (e.g. *Times* Atlas of 1919) add -fu (roughly city), -chow (head of a district), or -hsien (county town) to the actual place name but in many cases these syllables form part of the name itself (compare Newtown in English). Some names have been changed (e.g. Peking, Peiping as noted above on p. 520) because the description no longer applies: others for political reasons. Other names vary according to the Chinese language or dialect used. Many places have conventional names which differ in spelling and pronunciation in English, French, German and other European languages. Often these conventional names were derived through Cantonese and not through the local language. Canton itself is a conventional name for a city otherwise known as Punyu or Kwang-chow-fu. Finally pronunciation is far from phonetic: thus kiang should be pronounced jee-ong and pai is bai.

MANCHURIA OR THE 'NORTH-EAST'

Historical Introduction. The land to the north-east of China proper has long been known to Europeans as Manchuria—the land of the Manchus. The Manchus were nomadic tribesmen, allied to the Tungus, and were numbered amongst the raiders who periodically harassed the settled peoples of northern China. It was as a protection against such raids that Chao Hsing, about 244 B.C., commenced the building of that barrier, completed during the Ming Dynasty, universally famous as the Great Wall and which extends for 2,000 miles from eastern Turkistan to northern Hopei, reaching the sea at Shanhaikwan. In time the Manchus of the plains acquired the arts of cultivation and developed a marked cultural life of their own, though they retained their virility, their superb horsemanship and their military organization. The invasion of China by the Manchus in the seventeenth century took place at a time when the Chinese were weakened by internal struggles and the once powerful Ming Dynasty (1368 to 1644) had suffered from the successive Mongol incursions (see p. 518). The virile Manchus provided just the stimulus that China needed at the time. 'Flushed with victory and with long-desired power over her southern neighbour, Manchuria determined to mark the whole empire with her personality. The arts were encouraged and special schools for research were established. The Manchus were fully alive to the necessity for continuing Chinese customs and a form of government which, by long usage, had become not merely palatable but sacrosanct to the Chinese.' From the advent of the Manchu Dynasty in 1644 the Manchu tribesmen formed a sort of hereditary militia and penetrated to all parts of China. By intermarriage the erstwhile conquerors were thus absorbed physically and culturally by the Chinese, with the result that the Manchus in China no longer exist. For long Manchuria was the recruiting ground for the garrisons with which the Dynasty held China and Chinese immigration was strictly forbidden. In 1776 this prohibition was relaxed as far as the southern part of Manchuria was concerned. The dense agricultural population of northern China began to filter into the Manchurian plain—a land never very densely peopled and whose population had been greatly depleted by the continual drain of men to China. The Chinese immigrant farmers were mainly men who intermarried with the Manchu women. Thus in Manchuria also, the Chinese absorbed the Manchus, and if today there are any Manchus left it is in the extreme north where soldier colonies were long ago planted on the Amur River frontier. By the end of the nineteenth century the population of Manchuria was estimated at 14,000,000—

more than 90 per cent. Chinese—but it was not until the Imperial Edict of 1907 that Manchuria was formally recognized as part of China. Thus the viceroyalty of the 'Three Eastern Provinces' (as Manchuria then became known) under a Chinese Governor-General was only established four years before the fall of the Manchu Dynasty and the establishment of the Republic.

In the meantime several foreign powers had become interested in Manchuria. The Russian penetration of Siberia—originally attracted by the fur trade—had proceeded as far as Tobolsk by the fourteenth century and in the succeeding centuries was pushed steadily eastwards. In 1852 a Russian military expedition explored the Amur, and by 1857 Cossacks and peasants were established all along the river. This fact was recognized by China in 1857 (in 1860 by a treaty). For Czarist Russia, Manchuria was to be the eastern outpost of her empire and the eastern terminus of the Trans-Siberian Railway (begun in 1891) which was to bind that empire together. But Japan, with an over-flowing population and with only limited resources, had a more vital interest than Russia in Manchuria. As the southern key to Manchuria interest centred on the Liaotung Peninsula. Japan demanded the peninsula as the prize of her victory in the Sino-Japanese War of 1894-5, but Russia, backed by France and Germany, forced her to abandon this claim to the peninsula, which, commanding the seaward approach to Peking, has been described as a 'veritable pistol pointed at the head of China'. But three years later (1898) Russia secured a lease of Kwantung at the tip of the peninsula with the naval station of Port Arthur and what became the great port of Dairen. After her victory in the Russo-Japanese War of 1904-5, Japan secured this lease as well as the right to construct railways in southern Manchuria—to be vested in the South Manchuria Railway Company. Even before the war of 1904-5 Russia had built the Chinese Eastern Railway across northern Manchuria—a short cut to Vladivostok—and was pushing railway construction towards Port Arthur, especially important because Vladivostok is ice-bound in winter. Although neither the South Manchuria Railway nor the Chinese Eastern Railway were nominally Government concerns, the Japanese Government appointed the officials of the South Manchuria Railway from amongst the shareholders (who were either Japanese or Chinese citizens). Investment in the Chinese Eastern Railway was restricted to Russians and Chinese, so that in effect southern Manchuria became a Japanese 'sphere of influence' and northern Manchuria a Russian sphere. The famous 'Twenty-one Demands' presented to China by Japan in 1915 confirmed 'the predominant position of Japan in South Manchuria and eastern (Inner) Mongolia'.

During the Chinese Civil War, which broke out about 1922, Japan continued to exercise a controlling influence, and the presence of

Japanese troops in the railway zone was the chief factor in the main-tenance of peace in the country. As the Chinese National Government at Nanking grew in stability, it sought to re-establish Chinese authority over Manchuria, but on September 18, 1931, a Japanese army occu-pied Mukden. Military operations followed, and in February 1932 the 'Three Eastern Provinces' (Fengtien, Kirin and Heilungkiang), together with Jehol, were, with the assistance of Japan, proclaimed a nominally independent state under the title of 'Manchukuo', with a capital at Hsinking (Chang-chun). The League of Nations sent a com-mission of inquiry under the chairmanship of Lord Lytton in 1932, and the Lytton Report favoured the claims of China. Japan 'recog-nized' the State of Manchukuo six months after its formation. In January 1933 Japan decided to make Henry Pu (the Chief Executive and scion of the old Imperial Manchu house) hereditary Emperor. He was crowned on March 1, 1934. During 1933 and 1934 the boundaries of Manchukuo were extended westwards so as to include 'outer' Mongolia and southwards to the Great Wall. Early in 1935 Japan completed the purchase of the Chinese Eastern Railway from Russia, thus eliminating the old Russian sphere of influence in the north. On the defeat of Japan by the Allies in 1945 Manchuria was nominally restored to China, but the state of civil war existing in China and the occupation of Manchuria by Russian forces hindered the effective reunion till the Communist victory.

Position and Area.—Since it is the policy of the Chinese People's Government to merge Manchuria into China and to ignore old boundaries, it can only be said in general terms that Manchuria as formerly understood lies between Lat. 38° 43′ and 53° 50′ North and Long. 115° 20′ and 135° 20′ East, being bounded naturally on the north by the Amur River; on the east by the Maritime Province of Siberia and by Korea; on the west by Inner Mongolia. There has been much regrouping of Manchuria's provinces and the inclusion or other-wise of parts of the neighbouring provinces of China proper. As con-stituted in 1956 Manchuria had three provinces: Heilungkiang in the north, Kirin in the centre and Liaoning in the south. Manchuria corre-sponds in latitude to the region around the mouth of the St. Lawrence and the north-eastern United States—from Washington to Labrador or the south part of Hudson Bay. Like the North American region, Man-churia has a marked 'East Coast' climate, but rendered more extreme by the greater land mass of Asia, the influence of Mongolia and the physical isolation from the Pacific Ocean.

Physical Features. Physically, Manchuria consists of three parts. There is a great central plain, narrow in the south, where it is drained by the lower course of the Liao Ho and by the Hun Ho; broad in the north, where it stretches from the Khingan scarps on the west to the forested mountains of eastern Manchuria on the east. This broad northern region is drained by the tributaries of the Sungari, which itself flows into the Amur. The mountains of eastern Mongolia are prolonged southwards into the Liaotung Peninsula. The greater part of

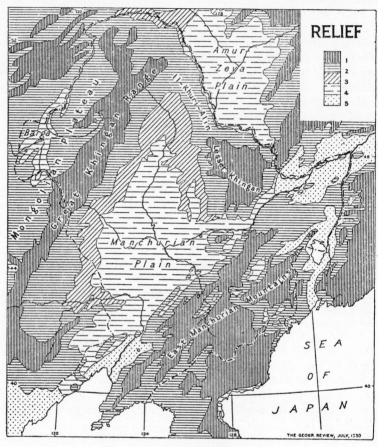

FIG. 289.—The relief of Manchuria

1 = Mountains. 2 = Uplands and higher foothills. 3 = Lower foothills.
4 = Plains.   5 = Lowlands.
(*After* E. E. Ahnert.)

(*Reproduced from the 'Geographical Review', published by the American Geographical Society of New York.*)

northern Manchuria is a complex of wooded hills and mountains, including the Lesser Khingan.

It is possible to distinguish, within the present boundaries of the country, seven natural regions—primarily physical regions, but in which physiography is reflected in all phases of human activity. These regions are:

(1) The forested eastern mountains, south of the Sungari Valley. The forests consist mainly of oak, ash, walnut, poplar, spruce, fir, pine and larch, and are largely untouched except near the railways.

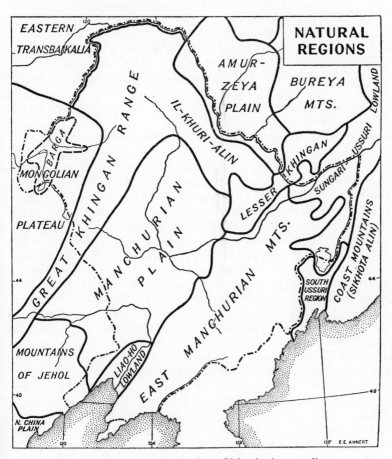

FIG. 290.—The geographical regions of Manchuria, according to E. E. Ahnert

(2) The Liaotung Peninsula, which is physically a continuation of the last region towards the south-west and which is structurally allied to the Shantung Peninsula. Here are the great coal and iron ore resources of the country—the Fushun coalfield worked 22 miles south-east of Mukden with the thickest seam of bituminous coal in the world (over 400 feet) and an output for a time nearly equal to that of the whole of China proper.

(3) The fertile central plains, naturally grass-covered, comprising the Liao Plain in the south and the Sungari Plain in the north. These plains are different in character from the North China Plain which is largely alluvial, whilst the Manchurian Plain is a plain resulting from long-continued denudation and so has a more irregular surface.

(4) The Khingan mountains—the forested mountains of the north and west. In the forests the principal trees are fir, larch, aspen, elm, oak, birch and pine, with spruce to the south.

(5) The mountains of Jehol, stretching south-westwards to the Great Wall.

(6) The Mongolian steppelands occupy that part of the country beyond the Khingan mountains.

(7) The narrow Amur Valley occupies the extreme north.

Minerals. Before the introduction of foreign capital for development work, alluvial gold was the only mineral extensively mined. The alluvial gold appears to have come from widely disseminated gold-bearing gneisses. For centuries the alluvials of small streams have been panned, but much metal still remains in deposits actually already worked over. The most extensive deposits lie in the tributaries of the Yalu and the Upper Sungari and amongst the valleys of Heilungkiang. Manchuria has large coalfields, and although coal was worked by Koreans and Chinese probably as early as the fourteenth century, modern coal-mining was inaugurated by the Russians and flourished after the Japanese took over the principal collieries with the South Manchuria Railway. These are the Fushun open-cast mines. The field occupies the valley of the Yingpan, and in an area 10 miles by 2 is estimated to have reserves of 1,200,000,000 tons of bituminous coal. The seams include some of the thickest in the world. In 1907–8, immediately after the taking over of the mines by the South Manchuria Railway Company, the production was under 200,000 tons; it increased almost steadily (except for 1914–15 and 1915–16) to 3,700,000 tons in 1919–20 and 5,540,000 tons in 1924–5, and still higher figures have been reached, being about 8,000,000 tons in 1934. There has been a steady increase in the amount of coal consumed in Manchuria, in addition to a steady export trade. Another field developed by the Railway is Yentai. Other mines formerly independently owned are Hsintai and Penhsihu. The total output of coal from Manchuria first exceeded 10,000,000 tons in 1930 (Fuhsun and Yentai mines). It is now about 25,000,000 tons from 40 mines (notably Fuhsun and Fushun).

Next to coal, iron is the most important mineral product of Manchuria. There are said to be numerous haematite-bearing veins in the metamorphic rocks of the country, some of which have been worked by native methods on a small scale. But interest centres on the mines of

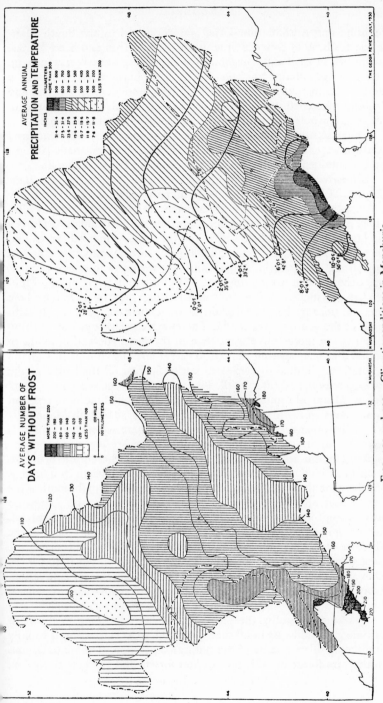

FIGS. 291 and 292.—Climatic conditions in Manchuria

Penhsihu and Anshan. The latter was developed by the South Man-churia Railway in connection with the Anshan Iron and Steel Works, established in 1918 and reorganized as the Showa Steel Works in 1933. The total production of iron ore in Manchuria realized nearly a million tons in 1931 and 1932, and pig-iron production at Anshan and Penhsihu exceeded 430,000 tons in 1933. Total pig-iron produced in China as a whole was 4·9 million tons in 1956; 19·7 m. in 1962.

Amongst other minerals may be mentioned salt, manufactured from sea-water along the coasts, and oil distilled from oil-shale. Natural soda is obtained from the low plains of eastern Inner Mongolia.

Climate. In the south, on the shores of the Yellow Sea, the tem-perature of Dairen ranges from a January average of 23° F. to a July or August average of 76° F. Farther north the winters are much colder, whilst in summer the temperatures are not quite so high. At Harbin the January average is below zero, the July 75°. As in northern China, the winds of winter, and especially of spring, are not only very cold but very strong. Manchuria is still within the region of monsoon rainfall, hence the summer is the rainy season. But the total fall is small—Muk-den has 26·5 inches, Harbin 19·7, and Tsitsihar only 10·2. On the whole the conditions in the central plain of Manchuria compare closely with those in the prairies of Canada. The climate is rigorous but healthy, conducive to more active work than in the more enervating plains of China, and one especially suited to cereal farming. But as in Canada agriculture is limited by two great sets of factors: (a) the length of the growing season, and (b) rainfall. Two maps have been reproduced from Nobuo Murakoshi and G. T. Trewartha's study.[1] One hundred and twenty days' growing season is ample for wheat, so that all Manchuria except the north-west lies within the area where wheat cultivation is possible, but aridity limits the area in the west (see Fig. 291).

Vegetation and Soils. The typical black chernozem does not occur in Manchuria, the organic matter being insufficient in quantity. But the content of valuable mineral salts is high; the main fault of the soils is that after rain they are so fine grained as to be somewhat heavy except in the more arid west where sandy soils are widespread. In this area, too, considerable tracts—probably 10 per cent. of the whole plain—are rendered unproductive by alkalinity. Indeed, the extraction of soda from these soils in the north is an old industry. In other areas poor drainage renders large tracts unsuitable for cultivation. Away from the plains the soils are brown or yellow and in general thinner and poorer—as for example in the Liaotung Peninsula.

Speaking generally, the plains of Manchuria belong to the mid-latitude grasslands. As in all such grassland areas cultivation is rapidly eliminating all remnants of the natural vegetation. The mountainous borders are forested, with the thickest forests and the best timber on

[1] *Geog. Rev.*, **20**, 1930, 480–93.

the eastern mountains. The most valuable timber is the Manchurian pine (*Pinus mandshurica*); often reaching 200 feet in height and 5 feet in diameter. Larches rank second in importance to the pines.

Agricultural Development. The most complete agricultural development of Manchuria has taken place in a belt from 100 to 150

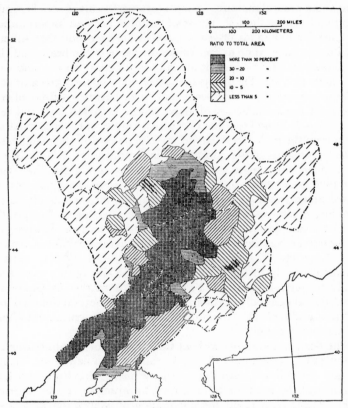

Fig. 293.—The proportion of cultivated land in Manchuria

(*After* Murakoshi and Trewartha.)

miles wide stretching from the Gulf of Liaotung north-eastwards, as shown in Fig. 293.

In 1934 it was calculated that 35 per cent. of the southern province of Fengtien (now Liaoning) could be classed as arable, and of this no less than 73 per cent. was actually under crops. In Heilungkiang 22 per cent. was classed as arable, of which only 32 per cent. was already farmed. The north of Manchuria is still the 'land of promise' and it is clear why immigration of recent years has been so largely to the north.

A.—19

In order of acreage the chief crops are soya beans, kaoliang, millet, maize, wheat and rice.

Soya or Soy Beans. Undoubtedly the outstanding crop of Manchuria is the soya bean; indeed, the rapid rise of this crop to importance in the world's commerce is one of the most remarkable agricultural developments of the last half-century. The plant itself is a valuable fodder plant and a natural manure—being a legume, the plant enriches rather than impoverishes the soil. The soya bean has been an important food in China for thousands of years, but it is only recently that America and Europe have come to appreciate the value of the beans and their oil. Actually the first shipment abroad of the beans—to England—was only made in 1908. The beans themselves may be used green as vegetables or canned; the dried beans may be cooked in a variety of ways or used for the manufacture of soups, sauces, breakfast food and vegetable milk—it being possible to prepare a variety of cheeses, milks and casein from the milk. The bean oil can also be used in the manufacture of food products—butter substitutes, lard substitutes, salad oils, etc., but its main importance is in industry. It was during the First World War that huge quantities of soya-bean oil were imported into the United States to supply essential raw material for the manufacture of glycerine, explosives, soaps, paints, varnishes, celluloid and printing inks. The bean meal is valuable, not only as stock feed and fertilizer, but also for human consumption, being prepared as breakfast foods, diabetic foods, flour, etc. The expansion of the soya-bean industry must be accredited largely to the South Manchuria Railway; the export was mainly through Dairen, the beans finding a market in China and Japan, the oil especially in America and Europe. Several hundred mills of all sizes and types exist in southern Manchuria for crushing the beans and extracting the oil.

The bean cannot grow without the existence of certain bacteria in the soil and so cannot immediately be cultivated in new areas. But soils are now 'inoculated' with the necessary bacterial culture and huge quantities of the bean are being grown, for example, in the American Middle West. As a result the elimination of Manchuria as a world source has had but a limited effect.

Kaoliang (Sorghum-millet) is the staple food of the people and of the animals engaged in farm work and transport, and, prior to the extension of bean cultivation, was the leading crop and occupied half the cropped land. It requires a growing season of at least 150 frost-free days and so becomes of small importance northwards. A strong, colourless spirit is prepared from the grain; the stalks find a use as a roofing material, in the manufacture of matting and as fuel.

Millet. Italian and common millet rank next to kaoliang as human food, whilst the straw is universally used as fodder. It is to the people of northern Manchuria what kaoliang is in the south.

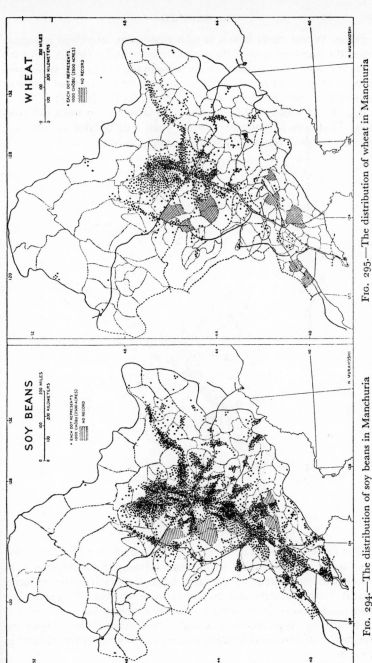

FIG. 294.—The distribution of soy beans in Manchuria

FIG. 295.—The distribution of wheat in Manchuria

These maps relate to the period of Japanese expansion and show how cultivation followed the railways.

Wheat. Wheat ranks fourth or fifth among the crops and is a great crop of the northern part of the plains, whereas *maize* (which vies with it in importance) is of greatest importance in the south. The wide open plains of Manchuria are suitable for large-scale mechanized methods of agriculture, which were in fact introduced by the Japanese.

Rice. The Chinese of Manchuria are neither rice-growers nor rice-eaters. That which is grown is more than half upland or hill rice; production was developed by Korean immigrants.

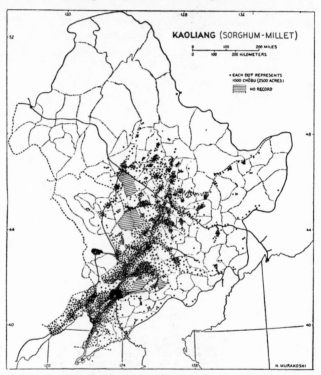

Fig. 296.—The distribution of kaoliang in Manchuria

Other Crops. Work has not been restricted merely to opening up new areas; much has been done to improve existing crops—especially to increase the oil content of the soya bean—to teach better cultural methods to the farmers and to introduce new crops. In particular, arboricultural work is notable; a country formerly barren of trees is now dotted by large orchards of apples and other fruits all over the south, whilst willows and Chinese poplars have been widely planted in the north.

Barley has been cultivated mainly since the Russo-Japanese War, when it was required as food for the horses of the Japanese Army.

Buckwheat, hemp, tobacco, cotton, sugar beet and fruit are other important crops.

It is difficult to assess the importance of opium. In November 1932 a State opium monopoly was created with the avowed intention of gradually eliminating its use. The areas in which the poppy may be cultivated were fixed and lie almost entirely in Liaoning and north-eastern Kirin.

The cultivation of cotton has been encouraged, but the quality is said to be indifferent.

Sericulture. Much attention has been directed both to the rearing of 'wild' silk-worms (for tussore silk) and to the introduction of sericulture as a side-line in general farming. Production of silk is largely restricted to the Kwantung area around Lu-ta (formerly Dairen).

Pastoral Farming and Stock Rearing. As in most of the world's grass-lands, stock raising preceded agriculture in Manchuria and was the principal occupation of the Manchus, though they do not seem to have used milk. Pigs, cattle, horses, sheep, donkeys and mules are all numerous, being kept by the Chinese as farm animals. The horses are almost entirely of Mongolian breeds, small but sturdy.

The Population of Manchuria. Figures from official sources relating to October 1952 gave a population of about 43,000,000 for Manchuria including 6,000,000 in Jehol, since divided between Man-churia, Inner Mongolia and Hopei. In 1934 the total was given from Japanese sources as nearly 31,000,000 including 590,760 Japanese and 98,431 'other nationals' (mainly Russians). The population of Kwantung and the railway zone was, in addition, 1,408,755, of which 309,029 were Japanese and 2,185 'other nationals'. It would seem that the figures for Chinese (described as Manchus) included the 680,000 immigrant Koreans.

About 80 per cent. of the inhabitants of Manchuria can be described as 'rural'; the chief cities are Hsinking (formerly Chang-chun), the capital, Pinkiang (Harbin), Shenyang (Mukden) (1,550,000), Kirin, Tsitsihar, Yingkow and Antung. Lu-ta, formed of the union of Dairen (Russian Dalny) and Port Arthur, boasts over a million inhabitants. One of the most remarkable cities of Manchuria is Harbin—at the beginning of the present century it scarcely existed and its spectacular rise was mainly due to Russian enterprise. Side by side with a thor-oughly modern Western city, at one time boasting the largest white population of any city in Asia (over 100,000 Russians), has grown an old-style Chinese town. But Dairen could claim to be as remarkable in its way as Harbin. It was as much Japanese as Harbin was Russian and in its expanding wealth of fine modern buildings far surpassed the northern city.

The Sino-Soviet Treaty of 1950 recognized Manchuria as an integral part of the Chinese People's Republic but the Chinese in 1952 'requested' the U.S.S.R. to retain control of Port Arthur for defence purposes. Transfer was finally effected in May 1955.

Communications. The railway has played, and is playing, a remarkable part in the development of Manchuria. The three chief systems were the Chinese Eastern in the north, the South Manchuria in the south-east, and the Peiping–Liaoning (Peking–Mukden) in the

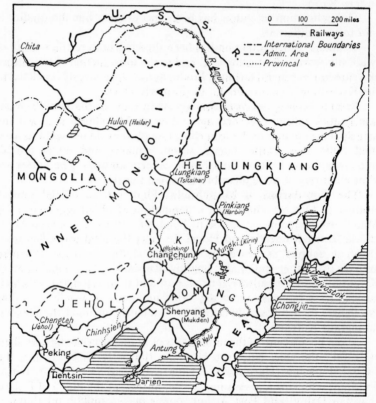

FIG. 297.—The communications of Manchuria

For Darien read Dairen. Jehol has been partitioned between Manchuria, Mongolia and Hopei.

south-west—representing Russian, Japanese and Chinese influence respectively. With the purchase of the Chinese Eastern in 1935, the South Manchuria was left with practically the whole of Manchuria as its sphere—as long ago as 1917 the whole of the Korean system was put under its management.

The part which the South Manchuria Railway played in the development of Manchuria may be likened to that played by the Canadian Pacific in the opening up of Canada. Like the Canadian Pacific, the South Manchuria Railway was far more than merely a railway company. Taking the position in 1931 when the Japanese entered into territorial possession of Manchuria, only 27 per cent. of its capital expenditure had been on railways; 11 per cent. being for mines (Fuhsun coal mines and iron mines), 3 per cent. for steel works (Anshan), 8 per cent. for harbours, its other activities including land, buildings, local institutions, hospitals, schools, hotels, steamships, electricity, gas and other industries and workshops, research bureaus for agriculture, minerals, public health and civic planning. The total capital of the company was 440,000,000 yen (£44,000,000 roughly), half of which was held by the Japanese Government, the other half by Japanese and Chinese investors—but mainly Japanese. After the inauguration of Manchukuo, railway construction was pushed on with great rapidity.

A great scheme for the construction of 37,000 miles of roads in ten years was put into operation in March 1932. When the Chinese regained Manchuria in 1945 they found a country already well developed along modern lines. It was a ripe Japanese plum which fell into Chinese—and Russian—mouths. The main purpose of the roadways was to encourage bus services. Horse carts now have pneumatic tyres.

Already the normal means of travel for many purposes was by air, and now as in China proper there is a network of internal routes.

Extensive use is made of navigable waterways—regular cargo services are operated on the Sungari, Amur, Liao, Non and Yalu, though climate limits navigation to seven months of the year or less.

Luta has the only ice-free port of Manchuria. After long use as a naval base, Port Arthur was opened to commerce, but was never greatly used. *Dairen* was the great port for the whole country. Before the present régime its traffic ranked second only to Shanghai on the eastern coast of Continental Asia. The port is located near the south-west point of the peninsula, the mouth of the naturally protected harbour opening to the south-east. *Antung*, the third port of Manchuria, lies on the Yalu River—which is blocked by ice for four months or more—25 miles from its mouth. It is limited to small vessels.

Industries and Trade. The ushering in of a new industrial era in Manchuria was mainly the result of Japanese initiative. Bean-oil milling, flour milling and the preparation of tobacco took the leading place. Other industries include cotton textiles. Anshan has been created by the iron and steel industry, Fushun by the collieries, Shakaka-kon by railway workshops. The distilling of kaoliang liquor and the brewing of beer are other important industries, and a wide variety of minor industries has been established. During the period of close association with Japan from 1931 onwards half of all the exports went to Japan, though China and Germany were large purchasers of soya beans. By that time the United States, until 1929 a very large purchaser of soya beans, was growing her own. Beans, bean cake and bean oil represented more than half the exports, followed by coal and coke. The imports then included particularly such consumption goods as cotton textiles and a wide range of capital equipment such as machinery required by a rapidly developing country. The importance then attached by Japan to Manchuria is too obvious to need stressing and there is no doubt that both China and Soviet Asia today benefit greatly from the surplus of foodstuffs and raw materials available from Manchuria.

Since 1951, under the First Five Year Plan, strenuous efforts have been made to develop heavy industries and by-products in the North East, as Manchuria is now called. Anshan has eight modern automatic blast-furnaces with an output of 3,500,000 tons and the adjacent steel rolling mills are vast by any standards. They were built by the U.S.S.R. and are now being copied by the Chinese. Seamless steel tubing is an important product. Fenghsiang (Mukden) has new machine-tool works specializing in the production of lathes.

It must be emphasized that Manchuria is now integrated with the rest of the Chinese People's Republic and has no separate political existence. Much of the preceding matter is now mainly of historical interest. For the past the following references may be found useful.

REFERENCES

G. B. Cressey's *China's Geographic Foundations* (McGraw-Hill, 1934) includes excellent chapters on Manchuria. There are numerous publications on Manchuria issued from Japanese sources which naturally stress the Japanese viewpoint. Amongst these the *Japan-Manchukuo Year Book* is an invaluable source of material which may be supplemented from older sources such as the Report on *Progress in Manchuria, 1907-28* (South Manchuria Railway Company, 1929). The *Manchurian Year Book* was replaced by the *Far East Year Book* in 1941. Much use has been made in the foregoing account of an important series of crop maps by N. Murakoshi and G. T. Trewartha in the *Geog. Rev.*, **20**, 1930, 480-93. See also *The Pioneer Fringe* (various authors), American Geographical Society; Owen Lattimore: *The Mongols of Manchuria* (London, 1935) and *Manchuria, Cradle of Conflict* (New York, 1932). More recent material will be found in R. T. Moyer, 'The Agricultural Potentialities of Manchuria', *Foreign Agriculture*, **8**, 1944, 171-91, and A. Rodgers, 'The Manchurian Iron and Steel Industry', *Geog. Rev.*, **38**, 1948, 41-54.

TAIWAN (FORMOSA)

THE island of Taiwan lies off the south-east coast of China from which it is separated by the Taiwan Kaikyo or Formosa Strait averaging about a hundred miles in width. The Tropic of Cancer almost bisects the island. Because it tapers towards the south rather less than half of its 13,840 square miles lie actually within the Tropics but the ameliorating influences of winds and ocean currents justify its being considered a tropical island. It is about 240 miles in extreme length from north to south. Included administratively with the island are the

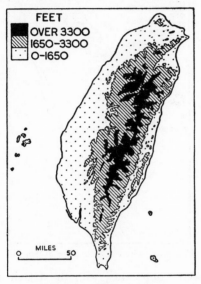

FEET
■ OVER 3300
▨ 1650-3300
· 0-1650

MILES
0   50

Fig. 298.—Taiwan—relief

Pescadores (former Japanese Hokoto, 49 square miles) lying in the strait, and various small islands, notably Quemoy, off the coast.

The main island is traversed from north to south by a great range of mountains with the main crest nearer the east coast than the west. Very broadly the island may be regarded as a tilted fault block. Mount Niitaka or Mount Morrison (which gives its name to the whole range) rises to 12,939 feet; other peaks reach almost that level. Slopes to the east descend precipitously but between the central part of the range and the Pacific is the narrow but important Taito lowland parallel to the coast and separated from it by a long ridge. From the crest of the Niitaka range the descent to the western plains is more gentle and so the western half of the island is by comparison flat, fertile, well settled and cultivated.

The aboriginal inhabitants, now restricted to the forest mountainous core or its margins, belong to some eight or nine different tribes all ethnologically allied to the Malays. Chinese settlement began along the west coast about 1621 and Chinese control over the island became effective from 1683 onwards. For the next two centuries Chinese settlemen took place steadily all over the western lowlands. The name Formosa, long applied by westerners to the island, is a Portuguese word meaning beautiful and dates from the seventeenth century when

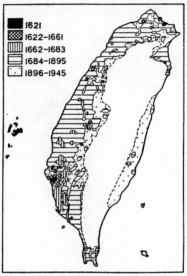

Fig. 299.—Chinese settlement at Taiwan

the Portuguese were contestants, with the Dutch and Spanish, for possession. Taiwan is the ancient name and the present official name. In 1895 the island was claimed as a prize of war by the victorious Japanese after the Sino-Japanese war, 1894–5. For the next fifty years it was developed as a tropical dependency of Japan, sending much-needed rice, sugar and other food to the homeland. Though the Japanese opened up parts of the east coast, the population remained predominantly Chinese—the quarter of a million Japanese settlers representing less than ten per cent. of the number of Chinese. After the Second World War the island was restored in 1945 to China. When the Chinese Communists overthrew the Kuomintang or Chinese Nationalists under Chiang Kai-Shek on the mainland, Taiwan became the last stronghold of Nationalist China and so, from 1949 onwards,

really became a separate country—the 'China' officially recognized by
the United States and member of the United Nations. All Japanese
have been expelled and there has been a large influx of pro-Nationalist
refugees from the mainland. Under the Japanese the aborigines lived
for the most part within an electrically charged barbed wire fence
enclosing about half the island. They remain unabsorbed and largely
uncivilized, though small groups may be found settled on the south-
western plains. The settled parts of Taiwan are essentially Chinese.

It is probably true to say that Taiwan is better known scientifically
than any part of China. Many *intelligentsia* came with the influx of

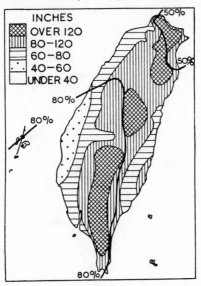

INCHES
OVER 120
80–120
60–80
40–60
UNDER 40

FIG. 300.—Taiwan—Rainfall

Nationalists and members of the National Taiwan University have
made intensive studies of the island, its resources and population.[1]

Though Taiwan is less than half the size of Scotland or the State of
Maine its rugged and varied relief results in marked climatic contrasts
between one part and another. The southern part of the island comes
under the influence of the south-west monsoon and the rainy season is
in the summer. But the winds are usually slight and variable in direction though thunderstorms are frequent and destructive typhoons occur.
Wide deviations from both the annual and monthly averages are consequently general. The south is sheltered from the strong north-east

[1] A magnificent *Atlas of Land Utilization in Taiwan* was prepared by Cheng-Siang
Chen at the Institute of Agricultural Geography (of the University) at Taipei and
in 1963 appeared Vol. I of his sumptuous and monumental *Taiwan, an economic and
social geography*. See also his brief summary, 'The changing economy of Taiwan',
Pacific Viewpoint, **6**, 465, 179–90.

monsoon which blows during the winter and brings a heavy rainfall to the north with a long period of depressing cloudy weather. The northerly gales may do harm to field crops and along the north-west coast lines upon lines of wind breaks are planted.

Ground frost may occur in some winters on low ground in the north and limits the cultivation there of sugarcane, but only once since records were started in 1895 has ice been known to form. Generally, the range of temperature is small: the January average of coastal stations ranging from 60° to 65 F., the July from 80° to 85° F.

Since 80 per cent. of the total value of all production from the island is in agricultural products and more than half the islanders are

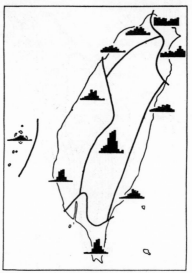

Fig. 301.—The climatic regions of Taiwan
(*After* C. S. Chen.)

directly engaged in farming, special interest attaches to the agro-climatic regions into which the country has been divided by C. S. Chen. He distinguishes the seven regions shown in Fig. 301.

(1) The North-East Corner. The prevailing north-easterly winds bring rather more rain in the winter half of the year than the summer, though every month is wet. Fine days may be fewer than 20 a year and sunshine is rare: river flooding is a constant menace. Double-cropped rice-fields represent the bulk of the cultivated low ground, tea gardens are important on the hill slopes.

(2) The North Region. This might better be called the north-west region. It is hilly, exposed to cold winds of continental origin

and so has the lowest winter lowland temperatures of the island with a February average below 59° F. It is the main area of tea and citrus fruit production.

(3) The West Plain. This is the most important agricultural region, producing more than two-thirds of both the rice and sugar of the island. By comparison with other parts rainfall is light because of protection from the north-east monsoon and heavy falls occur only in summer, beginning at the end of April and showing maxima in June and August—the latter due in part to typhoons. Rainfall variability is marked and irrigation is very important for successful agriculture. The winter is dry and warm and everywhere sunshine exceeds 2,200 hours per annum. Double cropping of rice in the northern half gives place southwards to single cropping.

(4) The South Region. This has a real tropical climate—the average of the coldest month exceeding 68° F. and between 80 and 90 per cent. of the 60 to 100 inches of rain falls in summer. Because of the long dry winter with high evaporation resulting from frequent gales rubber cultivation has been proved impossible despite the suitability of the temperature but bananas and pineapples do well and there are areas of tobacco and sisal cultivation as well as taro.

(5) The East Coast. In this narrow belt two-thirds of the heavy rainfall (60 to 80 inches) comes in summer. Floods are frequent and double-cropped rice is the main form of cultivation.

(6) The Central Mountain Region. Here elevation and exposure are the main factors in determining the character of local climates. Rainfall usually exceeds 150 inches and frosts are frequent. Most remains forested and the region is unsettled except by groups of aborigines.

(7) The Pescadores or Penghu Islands. These flat, windswept islands have summer rainfall less than elsewhere and growth of trees and crops is severely restricted by the cold north-east monsoon of winter.

The natural vegetation of Taiwan is forest. Over the densely settled lowland areas the tropical forest has been almost completely removed. On the lands marginal to cultivation are considerable areas of scrub with some bamboo thickets. Over the central mountain region a forest of broad-leaved trees predominates, giving place at higher levels to a mixed forest and finally, above 6,000–8,000 feet, to coniferous forest. Much of the scrub is the result of reckless felling and much of the good forest land remains the domain of the head-hunting aborigines but scientific forestry for both hardwoods and conifers was developed by the Japanese east of Kagi and Taichu, light railways being run into the forests from the cities.

Special interest attaches to the camphor trees of Taiwan. The Japanese instituted a Government monopoly in 1899 to prevent the rapid felling of the trees and the manufacture of camphor and camphor oil was licensed to the Formosa Manufacturing Company. A great expansion of the industry took place with the development of the celluloid industry until synthetic substitutes were found which caused a collapse of the demand.

The agriculture of Taiwan remained essentially Chinese in character and never took on the features familiar in Japan. On every farm are pigs and ducks; water-buffalo are almost exclusively used; the farm implements, methods of farming and the two-wheeled cart are all typically Chinese. Agriculturally Taiwan was important to Japan in two ways. First, despite the large population, rice could be grown in excess of requirements and the surplus was available for export. Secondly, tropical crops which can scarcely be grown in Japan proper could be grown in Taiwan. The Japanese worked strenuously to put the sugar industry on a firm basis and the industry grew from small beginnings to give a yield of over a million tons of sugar before the liberation.

The total area of cropland, at rather over 2 million acres, is just under one-quarter of the surface. By far the most important crop of the island is rice. Lowland paddy fields occupy a million acres and upland cultivation a similar area, but owing to double cropping the equivalent of 1,300,000 acres are under lowland rice. The sweet potato is important as a staple article of diet and occupies about a third of a million acres; it can be used as a source of industrial alcohol. On the drier western plains bananas, pineapples, ground-nuts, tobacco, soya beans, wheat, cassava and corn are all important, sometimes strongly localized. An interesting crop in the west also is jute. Except for parts of Brazil this is almost the only considerable area of jute cultivation outside Bengal. The citrus orchards—different types of orange and pomelo (grapefruit)—are mainly in the north and so are the tea gardens. The 'Oolong' tea of Taiwan is famous for its delicacy of flavour and was formerly much appreciated in Britain and the United States.

The natural richness of the surrounding seas in fish has given rise to an important fishing industry which was naturally stimulated by the Japanese.

The island is rich in minerals including coal, gold, silver, copper, aluminium, sulphur and phosphorus. The mining was in the hands of the Japanese: in particular they developed coal mines near Keelung and maintained an output of between 1 and 2 million tons. A little oil has long been obtained from one area in the north but intensive drilling revealed no other fields though several gas fields were discovered.

Cement is manufactured and some exported; salt is obtained by evaporation along the west coast.

At the time when the Pilgrim Fathers were busy clearing the forests of New England and disputing possession with the North American Indians the first waves of Chinese settlers were similarly engaged in western Taiwan. The aborigines were inveterate head-hunters and

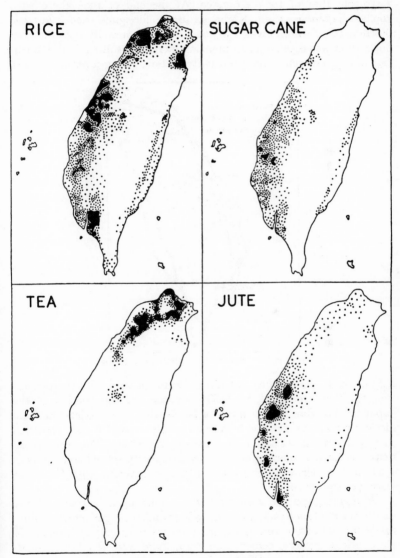

Figs. 302–5.—Crops of Taiwan

have preserved much of their life and tribal customs to the present day, but were probably never numerous. Immigration from Fukien and Kwangtung was encouraged after the Manchu conquest of China in 1683 and by the middle of the next century there were probably a million Chinese on the island. When the Japanese took possession in 1895 this had increased to 2 million. A census in 1905 gave a total of 3,156,700; that of 1925 4,147,500. At the end of 1936 there were 299,280 Japanese, 1,985 Koreans, 46,373 foreigners and 5,261,404 'Formosans' of whom about 150,000 were aborigines. By 1943 the total population was 6,585,841, an amazing increase resulting from a birthrate of 4·44 per cent. and a mortality of 2·01, giving a net increase of

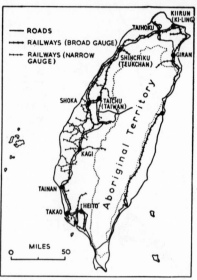

FIG. 306.—Taiwan—communities and towns

2·43 per cent. per annum. A Chinese census of 1949 after the restoration to China recorded 7,026,883—despite the repatriation of the Japanese, but due to the influx of Nationalist mainlanders the total already exceeded 9,240,000 by mid-1956. The census of 1962 recorded 11,375,085 and a net annual increase of 3·3 per cent. Thus the overall density is 820 per square mile; the average over the settled areas exceeds 1,000 and in terms of cropland (2,164,000 acres in 1956) is about 3,400 per square mile.

Although Japanese rule resulted in some urbanization and the development of such manufactures as flour milling, sugar refining, pineapple canning, iron working, aluminium smelting and the making of glass, bricks, pottery, cement and soap, there were few large towns. Now, the capital Taipei (Taihoku) in the north, with 450,000 in 1950, had 964,000 in 1962. Other towns, now all over 150,000, include

Kao-hsiung (Takao), Tainan, Ki-lung (Kurun)—the port of Taipei—
and Taichung.

The Japanese created a network of roads and railways over the
western plains but the first—a road—to cross the mountains dates from
1957. The main east coast settlements are linked by motor road with
Taipei in the north but not by rail. The main lines are on the Japanese
gauge of 3 feet 6 inches with feeders of smaller gauge. A great development of hydro-electric power has taken place and there is a main trans-
mission line from north to south of 154,000 volts. This, like the improved
communications, has encouraged town development. Industrial expansion has been focused on home needs such as textiles for clothing and
fertilizers to raise production on the little farms which, under recent
reforms, are almost entirely owned by the occupiers.

It will be seen that Taiwan though tiny by comparison with mainland China of 60 times the population and a hundred times the area
is a 'viable' unit able to feed itself and provide a surplus of commodities
for export, though no longer one of the granaries of Japan.

Note.—Place names in Taiwan present considerable difficulty since there is usually
the Chinese name which has been transliterated in several ways, the Japanese name,
and frequently conventional European names which vary from one language to
another.

A Note on Chinese overseas. The Chinese Census of 1953 included an estimate of
11,743,000 for Chinese settled overseas. Since the sixteenth century there has been a
steady stream of emigrants, especially to the countries of south-east Asia, known
collectively to the Chinese as Nanyang (South Seas). Ninety per cent. of the migrants
are from the two maritime provinces of Kwangtung and Fukien and the island of
Hainan. The five main dialect groups tend to remain distinct and in order of numbers
are:

      Hokkien (from Amoy and south Fukien)
      Teochew (from Swatow and district)
      Cantonese (from Canton and the delta)
      Hakka (from northern Kwangtung)
      Hailam (from Hainan)

Chinese who left their native land were formerly regarded rather as deserters and
many became closely identified with their adopted countries—by citizenship, intermarriage and in other ways. The great reformer, Dr. Sun Yat Sen, having himself
been brought up overseas, initiated the present trend which is to keep close contact
with all Chinese overseas, to ensure that they learn and use the national language
Knoyü and to encourage students to come to China for higher education.

Apart from the two million Chinese in Hong Kong, *The Times* of May 5, 1956,
gave the following details of Chinese overseas:

North Vietnam .	100,000	
South Vietnam .	800,000	
Siam	3,000,000	Much intermarriage and fusion with Siamese and adoption of Siamese language
Cambodia . . .	180,000	
Laos	15,000	
Philippines . .	200,000	
British Borneo . .	250,000	
Indonesia . . .	2,200,000	
Singapore . . .	920,000	
Malayan Federation	2,300,000	Distinction between Malayan-born and recent immigrants
Burma	350,000	Much intermarriage

In addition there are considerable Chinese communities in India, Pakistan, Mauritius,
the Caribbean, South America and the United States.

HONG KONG [1]

ALTHOUGH Britain had been trading with South China for more than two centuries from that great centre of trade, the city of Canton, official Chinese policy remained one of indifference, even hostility, to foreign trade. In 1839 this attitude culminated in an attempt to drive all foreigners away from the China coast. The British refused to be intimidated and the success of British naval action resulted in the occupation by them in January 1841 of the rocky mountainous island of Hong Kong. Its cession in perpetuity to the British Crown was formally recognized by the Treaty of Nanking in 1842. At that time the island of 32 square miles was uninhabited save by a few hundred fishermen—and some pirates—and British official opinion had no faith in its future. The leader of the British forces, Captain Charles Elliot, R.N., and a number of merchants on the spot, however, were men of vision. They realized the immense significance of a perfectly protected harbour unrivalled along the China coast, which lay between the island and the mainland, offering anchorage to ships drawing up to 36 feet and large enough in its 17 square miles to accommodate all the merchant navies of the world.

The city of Victoria, now the heart of a large urban area and usually called loosely Hong Kong or simply the central district, was founded on the north shore facing the mainland and separated from it by the central part of the anchorage, there only about a mile wide. Elliot was made the first governor and the colony prospered from the start. It became the chief port of call for all ships trading with South China and commercial firms from Canton and Macao quickly sought the security of British rule. In 1860 3¼ square miles of the mainland in Kowloon—the peninsula facing Victoria—and Stonecutters' Island were ceded permanently to Britain whilst in 1898 the area known as the New Territories, including a considerable mainland tract, the large island of Lantau and several smaller islands, was leased to Britain for 99 years. This brought the total area of the colony up to its present extent of 396 square miles—almost exactly a quarter of a million acres or the size of a small English county such as Huntingdon.

On Christmas Day, 1941, shortly after celebrating its centenary, Hong Kong fell to the Japanese and was occupied by them until liberated by the British Pacific Fleet on August 30, 1945.

In the first hundred years of its existence as a colony the growth of Hong Kong was truly remarkable: in the few years since liberation it

[1] This section was written in Hong Kong whilst I was enjoying the delightful hospitality and expert help of Professor and Mrs. S. G. Davis.

has been phenomenal. From 4,350 on the island in 1841—plus two
or three thousand boat-dwellers and temporary labourers—the population increased to 1,615,629 in 1941 though the latter total it is true was
artificially swollen by refugees from the Japanese invasion of China.
Yet there were never more than 20,000 Europeans and a few thousand
Indians: all the rest, over 98 per cent., are Chinese, mainly Cantonese
and Hakkas. From the first Hong Kong was developed on the basis of
law and order, free trade and equal opportunities for all. Dr. Sun Yat
Sen, founder of the Chinese Republic, who was educated in Hong
Kong, said to students there in 1923 that he marvelled 'how it was that
foreigners, that Englishmen, could do such things with the barren rock

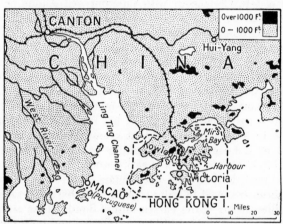

Fig. 307.—Hong Kong, showing the mountainous nature of the island and the
situation of the magnificent harbour between the island and mainland

of Hong Kong within 70 or 80 years while China, in 4,000 years, had
no place like Hong Kong'.

The three years and eight months of Japanese occupation saw much
destruction, a stifling of trade and industry, the population reduced
by over a million to about 650,000, neglect of education, much pillag-
ing and deforestation of the island for fuel. It is noteworthy that the
Japanese invasion had been preceded by an infiltration so that Japanese
numbered 3,500 in 1941. Yet recovery was so rapid after the war that
by 1951 the population had topped 2 million. By 1955 another half
million had been added by natural increase (75,000 a year) and the
constant stream of refugees (at least 25,000 a year) from Red China.
The Census population of March 1961 was 3,133,131; by January 1966
it was nearing four million. By good government this vast influx has
been housed and to a great extent absorbed into a useful economy of
which the most obvious sign is the great growth of small industries of
all sorts.

In its physical geography Hong Kong, with the New Territories,
does not differ from neighbouring parts of south and south-east China.

Developments since liberation in 1945 epitomize what might be done over vast areas of the mainland. Hong Kong is a great pilot experiment under a paternally-guided democracy to be compared and contrasted with Red China.

Geologically the whole colony is a complex of acid volcanics and intrusive masses of granite, porphyry, granodiorite and syenite. Associated metamorphosed sediments and later sedimentary rocks do not occupy more than 5 per cent. of the area and the few recorded fossils suggest that the oldest rocks are Permian. The structure is complicated: probably three great earth-movements have helped to shape the present picture. These are the Jurasside of late Jurassic times and the Laramide of late Cretaceous with superimposed Alpine or Tertiary folding believed by some to have been mainly responsible for the common, even dominant, south-west to north-east trend lines. The granites are of different ages but the Laramide Hong Kong granite is both interesting and important. There are exposures which afford excellent building stone but in many areas the microscope reveals a kaolinization of the felspars which causes the stone to break down easily on exposure—with resultant pock-marking and staining of many new granite-faced buildings. *In situ* it has resulted in the 'rotting' of the granite to a great depth so that granite outcrops can often be picked out by the occurrence of granitic 'badlands'. These consist of boulders of granite in a matrix of easily eroded sand derived from the quartz and clay derived from the felspars. Where the natural forest cover has been removed hillsides remain quite bare and seamed with erosion gullies. Many of the barren hills of South China are probably of this nature. Yet if the boulders are collected and built into terrace walls, the remaining quartz-clay mixture can quickly be converted by the addition of organic matter into a first-class market-garden soil to be cultivated by a modified system of hydroponics. This has only recently been realized in the course of the work of settling new immigrants but opens up vast possibilities.

Mineralization is associated with shatter-belts, intrusive quartz veins and dykes. Deposits of lead ore, magnetic iron ore, wolfram and tin ore have been worked irregularly for a long time and the deposits have assumed a new significance since the cutting off of Chinese supplies. There are many and varied deposits of clay important in the local brick, tile and ceramic industries. Some excellent white clays are exported to Japan. Late acid volcanics cap many of the hills.

Such a complex geology has given rise to a highly accidented relief. On Hong Kong island itself the Peak rises to 1,823 feet, Lantau Peak is 3,065 feet and Tai Mo Shan on the mainland reaches 3,130 feet. Hill-slopes are often precipitous and boulder-strewn and frequently plunge straight into deep water. A few alluvial fans and plains, most extensive in the north-western part of the New Territories, afford paddy lands but most of the vegetable cultivation is on terraced slopes. The city of Victoria expanded as best it could up the steep slopes of the Peak, now dotted to the top with modern residences or blocks of flats which seem in imminent danger of slipping off their tiny artificial ledges and are reached by well-designed but winding and hair-raising roads. At lower levels many of the crowded bazaar-streets are in fact flights of stone stairs. Seawards the city has had to rely for its expansion on piecemeal reclamation so that most of the commercial and industrial area is situated on a belt of made-ground some nine miles long and averaging between 200 and 400 yards wide. Few sights surpass in ever-changing beauty that of Hong Kong harbour. By night the characters of the Chinese language lend themselves to neon lighting and the coloured blaze of the water-front passes naturally into twinkling lights which dot the hill-slopes or outline the ships at anchor. By day both sea and land present a spectacle of constant animation backed by most varied cloud effects on the hills.

Excellent wharves, mainly on the Kowloon side, have been built out into the harbour with material derived from levelling the foot-hills, but in such a mountainous area the provision of an adequate air-port has proved extremely difficult. Kaitak airport on the north shore of Kowloon Bay, surrounded by mountains, with limited runways and frequent restrictions by fog or mist, was extended in 1958 by removing a considerable hill and using the material to build out seawards a run-way capable of taking all types of aircraft—with 679,000 international passengers in 1963–4. The increased use of air transport for both passengers and goods has been one of the factors in shifting the focus of activity from the island to the mainland.

The virtual closing of Canton and Shanghai to foreign trade has focussed both shipping and trade on Hong Kong, but until there is freedom of trade with Communist China the port is unlikely to reach its old levels. In 1963–4 nearly 12,000 ocean-going vessels of 38·5 million net tons were entered and cleared, but these figures are still under those of the old peak year of 1921. In addition the port is used by thousands of river craft and junks. In addition to its protected anchor-age the harbour has specially enclosed typhoon shelters for junks. The harbour enjoys mixed double tides which give long periods of slack water: at those times when the two sets of tides coincide the maximum tidal range is still only about 8 feet.

It is broadly true to say that Hong Kong, situated rather less than a hundred miles within the Tropics, enjoys a tropical monsoon climate. The old statement that frost is unknown on low ground was shattered by the low temperatures of January 1955 when several degrees of frost were recorded at Fanling and other parts of the New Territories as well as over much of Victoria Peak. There are those who claim to remember a powdering of snow over the Peak but some of the oldest inhabitants deny this, though hail is admitted. Climatic records for exceptionally long periods are available for Hong Kong and are correspondingly valuable in the interpretation of conditions all along the South China coast. The figures are for the Royal Observatory situated at Kowloon and established in 1884.

ROYAL OBSERVATORY: HONG KONG, 1884–1939, 1947–50

	Jan.	Feb.	Mar.	April	May	June	July	Aug.	Sept.	Oct.	Nov.	Dec.	Year
Temperature, °F.													
Mean	60	59	63	70	77	81	82	82	81	76	69	63	72
Max.	65	64	68	75	82	86	87	87	85	81	75	68	77
Min.	56	56	60	67	74	78	78	78	77	72	65	59	68
Wind direction, ° from North	76	79	84	90	100	147	139	137	82	74	64	67	
Rainfall, in.													
Normal	1·3	1·8	2·9	5·6	12·1	15·7	14·4	14·4	9·7	4·9	1·7	1·0	85·7
Max.	8·4	7·9	11·5	17·2	48·8	34·4	30·1	34·3	30·6	24·0	8·8	4·9	119·7
Min.	0	0	0·2	1·2	1·2	2·3	4·4	4·0	0·6	0	0	0	45·8
Humidity, %	75	79	83	85	84	83	83	84	79	72	67	70	79
Cloudiness, %	64	75	82	80	76	78	69	67	60	52	54	56	68
Sunshine, hours	145	98	95	114	156	161	210	201	198	217	186	171	1952

The dominant winds are easterly throughout the year.

The importance of these records is that they stress the considerable variability, even unreliability, of the weather from day to day and year to year over much of South China. The cold air mass of winter over the Asian mainland has an irregular and fluctuating margin which is a zone of frontogenesis. Whilst the two winter months of December and January are normally cold or cool and dry, the four months February to May inclusive are characterized by fog, mist, low cloud and drizzle—often unpleasant—but with fine warm spells or cold dry spells. The rainy season from June to September is hot and humid, oppressive, and marked by thunderstorms and occasional typhoons (Chinese: *tai*, big; *fung*, wind). In the pleasant months of October and November temperatures and rainfall are lower.

Heavy rainfalls combined with high temperature are responsible for the leaching of the dominant soils which are commonly yellow or red in colour. They belong to the group which some now prefer to call latosols to avoid the confusion which has grown up around the word laterite. Only on the low paddy lands are there grey or dark grey clay soils. But the cultivated soils are, as everywhere in China, in large measure the result of prodigious human effort and especially the use of carefully prepared human manure. The characteristic country smell of cow-dung which dominates so many agricultural countries is replaced by a somewhat different but equally all-pervading odour.

The main primary product of the colony is fish. After liberation a decision was taken in October 1945 to set up the Fish Marketing Organization to control the transportation and marketing of all marine fish and so to assist the previously uneducated fishermen who, numbering some 50,000 by 1955, had long been the prey of middlemen. By early 1955 more than a thousand of the total of 6,000 fishing junks had been mechanized and steam trawlers to the number of thirty or more were working the continental shelf as far away as Taiwan to the north and the Philippines in the south. A remarkable variety of dried fish is a feature of Hong Kong's fish markets but with modern developments the proportion of dried fish marketed through the Organization dropped from 86 per cent. in 1946–7 to 20 per cent. in 1953–4. The total production of fish climbed steadily in the post-war years to reach 70,000,000 lb. or over 30,000 tons in 1952–3 and 1953–4. In addition fish culture in ponds is growing. A recognized aim is to provide the inhabitants of the colony with at least 2 ounces of fish per head per day.

Vegetables rival fish in importance as a primary product. As with fish the small producer has been greatly aided by a Marketing Organization and remarkable progress has been made. By the end of 1964 90 per cent. of the vegetables consumed in the colony were locally produced, compared with 20 per cent. of a much smaller total in pre-war years. The uncertainty of supplies from Red China, the settlement of refugees on the land, improved methods of production and marketing combined to raise the local production from 21,355 tons in 1947–8 to 52,308 tons in 1953–4. White cabbage, flowering cabbage, turnips, tomatoes, sweet potatoes, water spinach and watercress are among the chief locally grown vegetables, but there are many others such as beans, cucumbers, onions, bringals and chives. In addition there is a wide range of fruits and nearly 100,000 fruit trees have been counted in the small area of the colony—various types of orange, lime, lemon, papaya, guava, lychee, banana, peach and a dozen others. One of the great changes in the food habits of the Chinese in recent years has been the increased consumption of fruit. The cultivation of pineapples has not it may be noted proved successful and once important tea has disappeared but water chestnuts are grown and canned for the American market. There are numerous specialized vegetable farms—many less than an acre but supporting a family—but the mixed paddy-vegetable farms averaging $2\frac{1}{2}$ to 3 acres are a common feature. The general rule is to plant the first paddy crop early in March and harvest it in July. A second paddy crop follows, sown in July or August and harvested in November. This in turn is succeeded by vegetables in the winter. Much work has been done to improve paddy yields, now nearly a ton per acre per harvest. Both in Hong Kong and in the neighbouring Chinese province of Kwangtung it is commonly reckoned that one-third of an acre of such paddy-vegetable land will support one person. This is equivalent to a rural population density of 2,000 per square mile. The New Territories can show some remarkable examples of prosperous peasant farmers who have risen from penniless refugees with the aid of small loans from such an organization as the Kadoorie Agricultural Aid Association. They have built themselves substantial houses of local stone, terraced and irrigated steep hillsides by the process of abstracting the stones from previously worthless land, and in particular have taken to the successful breeding of pigs, chickens and ducks. An enterprise of a different character but now of wide scope is that known as The Dairy Farm Limited. Milk (little used however by the Chinese) is produced in quantity and quality from stall-fed cattle for which guinea grass is specially grown.

The barren hillsides of China, long since denuded of timber by peasants in search of fuel, are notorious. By contrast the steep slopes on Hong Kong island, protected from such depredations at least until the Japanese occupation, offer a delightful contrast and the water-gathering grounds are carefully protected thus from soil erosion. The New Territories had not been so fortunate but the post-war policy of the Government has been to afforest all land not otherwise required—especially water-gathering grounds, eroded areas and lands liable to erosion. Quick-growing eucalypts (*E. robusta*) suitable for firewood at the lower levels, the pretty feathery Casuarina on higher slopes and the local *Pinus massoniana* at higher levels are the three chief trees being planted. It is an offence to cut firewood and, although it is difficult thus to break the habits of centuries, already there is a marked change in the landscape. In particular the catchment area of the big Tai Lam Chung dam, a large project designed to help the ever-present water supply problem (for many years there have been restrictions on use of water), is to be completely forested. The existing contrast between the forested island slopes and the scrub-covered mainland and the correlation between badly eroded lands and the granite outcrops are among the features well shown in the fine land-utilization map prepared by Dr. T. R. Tregear.

Turning to Hong Kong's industries, shipbuilding and especially ship-repairing (aided by a 750-foot-long dry dock) form the largest single industry and the naval dockyard has been a feature of the colony from its earliest days. The first stimulus to the now wide range of other industries was afforded by World War I. By 1941 there were 1,200 factories and the earlier European-controlled cement works (using raw material from Indo-China), rope works and sugar refinery had become over-shadowed by the Chinese-controlled factories covering spinning, weaving and knitting of silk and cotton, engineering, small metal works, furniture making, brewing, tin-refining, printing, plastics and the making of batteries, fireworks, cigarettes and cosmetics. Ginger preserving is a Hong Kong monopoly, joss-sticks mark a survival of the old sandalwood industry, but the old camphor stills are illicit because all camphor trees are the property of the Government.

The congested quarters of the city of Victoria can probably lay claim to be the most densely populated urban area in the world with as many as 2,000 persons per acre in places. At all hours of the day or night passage, often possible for pedestrians only, through the narrow

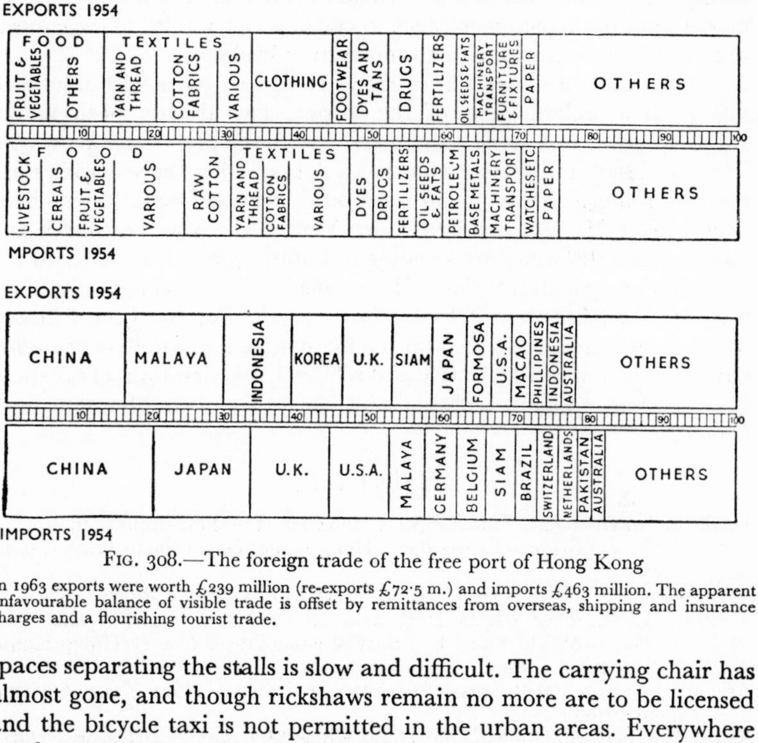

EXPORTS 1954

IMPORTS 1954

EXPORTS 1954

IMPORTS 1954

Fig. 308.—The foreign trade of the free port of Hong Kong

In 1963 exports were worth £239 million (re-exports £72·5 m.) and imports £463 million. The apparent unfavourable balance of visible trade is offset by remittances from overseas, shipping and insurance charges and a flourishing tourist trade.

spaces separating the stalls is slow and difficult. The carrying chair has almost gone, and though rickshaws remain no more are to be licensed and the bicycle taxi is not permitted in the urban areas. Everywhere goods are transported by the inevitable carrying pole with loads of all sizes, shapes and weights. A ten-mile-long tramway still runs along the main road parallel to the water-front, but elsewhere both on the island and mainland an excellent service of buses uses the magnificent network of roads. Fishing villages such as Aberdeen and Stanley have a bus every few minutes to the centre. The ferries across the harbour are among the most frequent and frequented in the world and an underwater tunnel has long been planned. Europeans early sought the cool breezes of the Peak, and the Peak Railway (now cable and electric) to 1,306 feet has operated since 1888. Now the island is saturated with cars and Kowloon is scarcely less congested. The future may see the development of the yet little-used Lantau Island.

From Kowloon a standard-gauge railway runs to Canton, 114 miles away, and Kowloon could serve as the rail port for the whole Chinese system northwards to Hankow and beyond. At present there is no through running, even to Canton. A closely guarded barbed-wire fence with a strip of restricted territory separates the colony from Communist China.

Hong Kong remains a free port with no customs duties except those on liquors, tobacco, oils and proprietary medicines. The former reliance on entrepôt trade has given place to one in which a third of the exports are local manufactures with cotton textiles leading.

At present the expansion of Hong Kong continues with unabated vigour. The enlargement of the airport has already been noted. Either a tunnel or a bridge is planned to join the island with Kowloon. The erection of multi-storey blocks of flats—and schools—never stops and the refugee shanty towns disappear. New industrial towns have been built at Kwun Tong and Tsuen Wan in the New Territories and land is being reclaimed by levelling hills and tipping the spoil into the sea. On the agricultural side a determined effort is being made to re-suscitate tea cultivation. Chinese love of gambling has been focussed on horse-racing where a levy on the many millions of dollars changing hands on the tote is an effective and relatively painless form of taxation. A permanent problem is shortage of water, now being brought from China.

REFERENCES

Davis, S. G., *Hong Kong in its Geographical Setting* (London: Collins, 1949).

Davis, S. G., *The Geology of Hong Kong* (Hong Kong: Government Printer, n.d.) (1952).

Ingrams, Harold, *Hong Kong* (London: H.M.S.O., Corona Library, 1952).

Tregear, T. R., *Land Use in Hong Kong and the New Territories with Map 1 : 80,000*. World Land Use Survey Monograph No. 1 (Hong Kong: University; London, Macmillan, 1958).

Annual Departmental Reports of various departments (Hong Kong: Government Printer).

Royal Observatory, Hong Kong: Hong Kong Meteorological Records 1884–1939 and 1947–50, also various papers (Hong Kong: Government Printer).

Hong Kong Annual Report (Hong Kong: Government Printer).

Ginsburg, N. S., 'Hongkong', *Focus, Amer. Geog. Soc.*, Nov. 1953 (with detailed map of the harbour).

Tregear, T. R., and Berry, L., *The Development of Hong Kong in Maps* (Hong Kong, 1959).

Hughes, R. H., 'Hong Kong—Far Eastern Meeting Point', *Geog. Jour.*, **129**, 1963, 450–65.

THE DEAD HEART OF ASIA

PART I. TIBET

THE mysterious land of Tibet has long appealed to all classes of mankind. Its inaccessibility and the exclusiveness of its inhabitants have proved in a high degree attractive to explorers; the rivers which take their rise within its mountain fastnesses have become the sacred rivers of Hinduism; it is also the site of many of the most sacred shrines of Buddhism.

Tibet consists essentially of a huge stretch of upland plains, lying at a height of more than 12,000 feet above sea-level, surrounded by walls of mountains rising to even greater heights and situated between 27° N. and 37° N. and 78° E. and 103° E. The boundaries are, in many cases, ill defined as, for example, in Bhutan, where the junction between the pine forests and bamboo forests marks the limit between the Tibetans' grazing land and the Bhutanese territory. Geographically and ethnographically north-eastern Kashmir—the province of Ladakh —is part of Tibet. Sikkim was originally under Tibetan rule, and so was the Indian district of Darjeeling. The whole area is between 700,000 and 800,000 square miles, with a population estimated at 4,000,000 or 5,000,000, the majority of whom live in the districts between Lhasa and the Chinese border. The western half of Tibet supports a density of population of only about 1, for even the plains and valleys, lying at over 15,000 feet above sea-level, are too elevated for crops to ripen. The slope of the country is in general towards the east, and parts of the eastern and south-eastern districts descend in places to below 5,000 feet, making possible the cultivation of barley, wheat and peas (the staple crops of central Tibet), as well as maize and occasionally even rice.

Tibet may be divided into four great physical regions:

(1) The Northern Plains (Chang Tang) form a tangled mass of plains and valleys, with an elevation averaging more than 10,000 feet and rising several thousand feet higher in its mountain peaks and ridges. The region is bounded on the north by the Kunlun and the steppes of Tsaidam and stretches as far south as the valley of the Tsangpo. The Chang Tang is studded with lakes of varying size, sometimes in groups, fed by waters from the surrounding mountains and valleys, but with no outlets. The streams provide fresh water; the lakes are salt. Many of these lakes have an area of more than 100 square miles; Tengri Nor is more than 1,000. The plains are treeless because of the elevation; the vegetation consists of scanty grass, but sufficient

583

to support numbers of wild yaks, asses, sheep, goats and other animals, as well as the herds of yaks and sheep tended by nomads. A few radishes and potatoes can be grown, but no grain, so that food for the herdsmen has to be brought from more favoured parts. As a result this vast stretch of country, 1,500 miles from east to west and 400 or 500 broad, is almost uninhabited and forms one of the main barriers of central Asia.

(2) Southern Tibet consists of the valleys of the Upper Indus and Sutlej in the west and the great valley of the Tsangpo—the Brahmaputra of India—in the south and east. The three rivers all rise in the same region, near the sacred lake of Manasarowar. For 400 miles of its course on the plateau (from Lhatse to below Tsetang) the Tsangpo, though flowing at an elevation of 12,000 feet above sea-level, is navigable. The Tibetan craft is a coracle, made from the hides of yaks and other cattle stretched over a framework, generally of willow. The loads possible are amazing—a whole Tibetan family with the family donkey. This country is Tibet proper—known to the people as Pö (in contrast to the Chang Tang on the north)—and here are found the chief towns —Lhasa, Shigatse and Gyangtse; it includes the seat of the Dalai Lama and his government.

(3) Eastern Tibet comprises the mountains and valleys lying between the Chang Tang and the old China proper. On the eastern slopes of the Chang Tang rise the great rivers of south-eastern Asia—the Salween, Mekong and Yangtze; a little to the north the Hwang Ho. The three first mentioned flow through eastern Tibet and leave by the three famous parallel gorges only a couple of dozen miles from one another. Eastern Tibet for long was partly under the sway of Lhasa, partly under the influence of China and is divided into a number of states very different from one another. Eastern Tibet is a land of considerable natural resources—grazing is abundant, there are extensive forests, agriculture is possible on a large scale, and there is known to be considerable mineral wealth.

(4) The great Tsaidam Basin with the Tsaidam swamp and the Koko Nor Basin to the north-east may be regarded as a fourth region of Tibet.

For long Tibet was loosely part of Greater China. In the post-war period the Chinese Communists invaded the country and established their suzerainty. Eastern Tibet had comprised the two provinces of Sikang and Chinghai: in 1954-5 the Sikang was absorbed into Szechwan. Tibet as now politically defined as an 'autonomous region' of the Chinese People's Republic (Fig. 255) covers only 350,000 square miles.

The climate of Tibet is exceptionally severe, the natural severity due to elevation being accentuated by the violent biting winds which blow during the greater part of the year, especially about midday and in the early afternoon. In the wide, open spaces of Tibet there is nothing to break their force, and travellers in autumn and winter prefer to brave the keen frosts of early morning than the winds of later

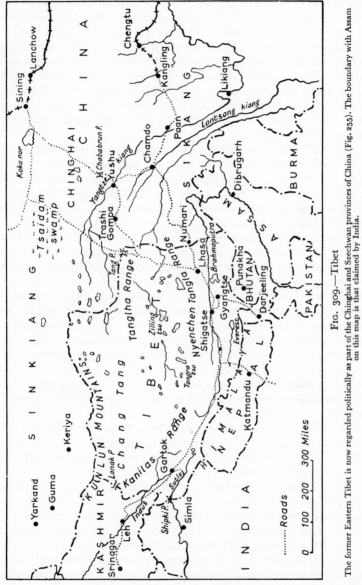

FIG. 309.—Tibet

The former Eastern Tibet is now regarded politically as part of the Chinghai and Szechwan provinces of China (Fig. 255). The boundary with Assam on this map is that claimed by India.

in the day. In the lower lands, such as the Chumbi Valley, below 12,000 feet, the climate is dry, bracing, agreeable and healthy and the air extraordinarily clear. Amongst the effects associated with the rarity of the atmosphere at great elevations are the differences between sun and shade temperatures. Rocks in the sun are often too hot to touch, whilst it may be freezing in the shade. The great height of the snow-line—20,000 feet in central Tibet, compared with 17,000 feet on the Himalayas in Sikkim—is due to the greater dryness of the atmosphere. Sikkim and Darjeeling have an annual precipitation of 80 to 250 inches, but Gyangtse, though only between fifty and a hundred miles to the north, has an average annual fall of about 8 inches, whilst a fall of 12 inches during an exceptional year was sufficient to cause extensive flood damage. To the north the fall increases; Lhasa has 14 inches, sixty miles farther north it is probably 18 or 20 inches, but decreases on the northern plains.

The Tibetans are keen traders, and the country is well supplied with trade routes; the more important trading posts are shown in Fig. 309. There is the Srinagar-Leh-Shigatse-Lhasa 'road' which is joined at Leh by the 'Hindustan-Tibet' road via Simla.[1] But the most important route from India is from Kalimpong (Darjeeling district) across the Dzelep La via the Chumbi Valley to Phari and thence by two routes to Lhasa. Another route is from Assam via Tsetang to Lhasa. From Lhasa a great route strikes north past Nagchuka and the Chang Tang, eventually reaching Urga. From Lhasa a well-used route goes to Chamdo, whence there are two routes to Tachienlu: the southern via Batang and Litang, the northern via Kanze and Dango. Tachienlu is on the ethnographic frontier between Tibet and China and the chief entrepôt of trade. Here the wool of Tibetan sheep is exchanged for the tea of China, which the Tibetans prefer to Indian tea. Twice a year also caravans assemble together for mutual protection near Koko Nor, and merchants and pilgrims together make the adventurous crossing to Lhasa, arriving in August or January. In the northern plateau camels and yaks are used for riding and transport, but it is not permitted to bring camels to Lhasa. Yaks are unsurpassed on seemingly impossible tracks over rocks and boulders, but the small sturdy Tibetan mule is better on slippery grass. Shaggy ponies and donkeys are also used for riding, whilst the poorer Tibetans attach their possessions to the back of a solitary sheep which they drive before them.

The preceding paragraph on trade routes is to a considerable degree past history. Under the Communist régime two main routes have been converted to motor roads and lorries now reach Lhasa direct from the Lanchow railhead in the north and from Chengtu in the east. An air service from Peking to Lhasa was inaugurated in May 1956.

The Buddhism of Tibet entered the country from India mainly between the seventh and ninth centuries, but was reformed from within. Tsong Kapa, born in 1358, was the reformer, but it was two centuries

[1] For the old trade on these routes, see H. L. Shuttleworth, *Geog. Rev.*, **13**, 1923, 552–8.

later that Sönam Gyatso received from the Mongol chieftain, Altan Khan, the title of Dalai Lama Vajradhara, 'The All-embracing Lama; the Holder of the Thunderbolt'. So arose the rule of the Priest-Kings of Tibet and the Buddhist monkhood so essentially characteristic of the country till disrupted by the Communist take-over of 1950. The Dalai Lama fled to India in 1959.

REFERENCES

After his flight from Tibet the Dalai Lama wrote his own account in *My Land and My People* which was edited by D. Howarth and published in London, 1962. A recent work is H. E. Richardson's *Tibet and its History* (London: Oxford University Press, 1962). Earlier travel books on Tibet are numerous, but two of the most useful summaries of the country's geography are Sir Charles Bell's *Tibet, Past and Present* (Oxford: Clarendon Press, 1924), and F. Grenard's *Tibet: The Country and its Inhabitants* (English translation, London: Hutchinson, 1904). Amongst noteworthy geographers and explorers may be noted Eric Teichman, F. Kingdon Ward, J. W. and C. J. Gregory, the Duke of Abruzzi and Sven Hedin.

The Pamirs

Although the broad lands of Tibet are often referred to as 'the roof of the world', more correctly that name is applicable to the still loftier dissected plateau of the Pamirs. The origin of the word Pamir is doubtful, and the most varied interpretations have been given not only of the origin of the word but of the character of the Pamir region. Correctly, a pamir is a mountain valley of glacial origin, differing in the main from other mountain valleys by its superior altitude—its floor lying from 12,000 to 14,000 feet above sea-level—and 'in the greater degree to which its trough has been filled up by glacial detritus and alluvium and has thereby approximated in appearance to a plain'. Each pamir is thus characterized by a border of snow-crowned peaks, 'sometimes seamed with ice-fields, and terminating in steep shingle slopes or boulder-strewn undulations lower down; in the bottom of the valley a river or stream or mountain torrent, noisily spreading itself over a stone bed or meandering in a peaty track, and sometimes feeding a lake or succession of lakes; and on either bank of the stream or lake a more or less level expanse of spongy soil, usually covered with coarse, yellow grass, and frequently broken up by swampy patches exactly like the ground on a Scottish moor. With the grassy stretches, which are green and flower-bestrewn in the summer only, and during the rest of the year—when not covered with snow—are sere and yellow, are interspersed expanses of sand and clay and stones, very often overlaid with a powdery incrustation of salts which glitter in the sun like hoar-frost. The main and differentiating features, therefore, of a Pamir are the abundance of pasturage, affording excellent food for every variety of animal and the almost total absence either of timber or of cultivation.' Thus, from one point of view, the Pamirs are rich and fertile, but from the absence of cultivation, habitations and fuel, and from the scourge of icy blasts of the winter months, they are often described as savage, inhospitable and desolate. Lord Curzon, from whose account [1] these particulars are taken, states that there are eight true pamirs lying in an area about 150 miles from north to south and the same distance from east to west, the peaks of the tract lying at elevations of over 20,000 feet. Almost the sole inhabitants are nomadic Kirghiz. Politically the region lies between Russian and Chinese Turkistan and Kashmir, mainly actually in Soviet territory.

PART II. THE TARIM BASIN AND ASSOCIATED BASINS

The detailed exploration of the central part of the dead heart of Asia is associated, in particular, with the name of Sir Aurel Stein. Sir Aurel has published the results of his journeys in a series of volumes, [2] but in the first 'Asia Lecture' of the Royal Geographical Society he gave a brief résumé of the geography of the region, which is of the utmost value to the student. The following descriptive account is based mainly on that summary account, which has a most instructive map of the whole region, and to which reference should be made. [3]

The central belt of the dead heart of Asia consists of a series of elevated and drainageless basins stretched out in an east and west line. Their northern limit is well defined by the big rampart of the Tien Shan—the 'Celestial Mountains'; on the south they are separated from the high plateau of Tibet by the still loftier Kunlun with its eastern continuation the Nan Shan. On the west the basins abut on the mighty mountain mass of the Pamirs; the eastern border of the region may be placed where the Nan Shan forms the watershed towards the drainage area of the Pacific Ocean.

The series of basins consists of the huge Tarim Basin in the west, at the eastern end of which is the salt-encrusted sea-bed of the old Lop Sea (Lop Nor is the present-day marshy remnant), and the two small basins of the Sulo Ho and the Etsin Gol in the east. The whole area may be called Chinese Turkistan (as contrasted with Soviet Turkistan on the far western side of the Pamirs)—the outer Scythia (*extra Imaon*) of Ptolemy and the Outer Tartary of a century ago.

We will examine, in the first place, the mountains which border this series of depressions. In the west, joining the Tien Shan on the

---

[1] 'The Pamirs and the Source of the Oxus', *Geog. Jour.*, **8**, 1896. Many accounts of later explorations will be found in the volumes of the *Geographical Journal*. See also W. R. Rickmers, 'The Pamir Glaciers', *Geog. Jour.*, **131**, 1965, 217–20.

[2] *Ancient Khotan*, 1907; *Serindia*, 1921; *Ruins of Desert Cathay*, 1912; *Innermost Asia*, 1928.

[3] 'Innermost Asia: its Geography as a Factor in History', *Geog. Jour.*, **65**, May–June 1925. For a later interpretation see Chang Chih-Yi, 'Land Utilization and Settlement Possibilities in Sinkiang', *Geog. Rev.*, **39**, 1949, 57–75.

north with the Kunlun on the south, is that great mass of mountains and bleak uplands—the Pamirs, known to the Ancients by the name of *Imaos*. Precipitation on the Pamirs is but slight and glaciation very limited; the high plateau-like valleys drain on the west into the Oxus and its tributaries, on the east into the Tarim Basin. Great importance attaches to the lines of communication through the Pamirs, which served in ancient times as arteries of trade and cultural relations between the Oxus region and the Tarim Basin, and thus eventually between Greece and Rome on the one hand and China on the other.

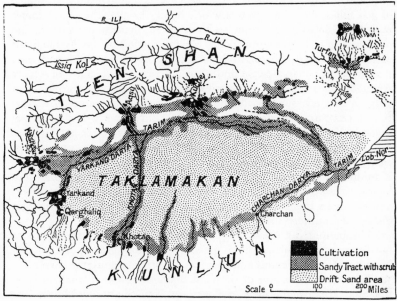

FIG. 310.—The Tarim Basin
(*After* Sir Aurel Stein.)

Despite the general east-to-west trend of the Pamir valleys, apparently only two routes were of real importance:

(a) The southern route is up the main Oxus Valley, through Sarigol to Kashgar and Yarkand. This is the route followed by Marco Polo in his famous journey in 1273 and before him by the great Buddhist pilgrim Hsüan-tsang returning to China from India in 644.

(b) The northern route is from the the ancient centre of Bactra (modern Balkh) up the Surkh Ab or Qizil Su, crossing the saddle to the headwaters of the river of Kashgar and so down to the oasis of Kashgar. This route was far more important as a trade route and is the one which was followed by the

ancient caravans bringing silk from China in the days of
Greece and Rome. It is this route which accounts for the
remarkable part played by the Tarim Basin 'for close on a
thousand years as the main channel for the interchange of
cultural influences between China, India and the Near East'.

On the southern flank of the basins lies the great mountain rampart
of the Kunlun. In the west the chain starts as a series of buttresses to
the glacier-clad Karakoram; farther east it rises to form a practically
impenetrable barrier with a crest-line of about 20,000 feet for a distance
of 300 miles. The few streams which break through the outer ranges
into the basin to the north do so by deep-cut, inaccessible gorges. The
outer slopes of the Kunlun in the Khotan section of the Tarim Basin
are extraordinarily barren and forbidding. 'Here by the side of wide
loess-covered peneplains we find areas where a perfect maze of steeply
serrated ridges and deep-cut gorges has been produced by erosion. Yet
only on rare occasions do these barren slopes, unprotected by vegetation, receive any heavy rain or snow fall. But when it does come the
great aridity of the climate helps to make its erosive force all the more
effective.' Eastwards for some 400 miles the Kunlun takes on a north-
easterly trend as far as Lop Nor, where the outermost range of the
Kunlun is the Astin (Altyn) Tagh. Whatever may be the morpho-
logical relation between the systems, the Kunlun here becomes lower,
easterly in its trend and begins to merge imperceptibly into the Nan
Shan, the 'southern mountains' of the Chinese.

Throughout the whole length of the Kunlun chain, the foot of its
northern slopes is formed by a 'glacis of piedmont gravel, attaining in
parts a width of 40 miles and more and everywhere utterly barren'.

The western portion of the Nan Shan overlooks a small basin—
the Sulo Ho trough. Here the western Nan Shan reproduces very
closely the features of the Kunlun—with their arid northern slopes and
marked erosion. But there is a more marked division with successive
parallel ranges growing higher towards the south and, although reaching heights of 20,000 feet in the south, giving easier access to the open
uplands beyond than in the Kunlun.

East of the Sulo Ho trough the central portion of the Nan Shan
shows evidence of a moister climate. The moisture which penetrates
from the Pacific affords excellent summer grazing in the high valleys
and still farther to the south-east there are forests in the valleys drained
by the Kanchow River. Immediately to the east is the watershed
between the inland drainage and the Pacific Ocean drainage of the
Hwang Ho Basin.

The water from the central Nan Shan drains into the Etsin Gol.
The Etsin Gol Basin is the easternmost of the basins of inland drainage
in this central belt.

Turning now to the northern rim of the basins, to the north of the Etsin Gol and Sulo Ho Basins, are low, uniform desert hills—very insignificant when compared with the snowy heights of the Nan Shan to the south.

Northwards and westwards of these ridges lies a huge desert area— the barren ranges and plateaus of the Pei Shan (the 'Northern Mountains' of the Chinese). This is a vast, stony, waterless tract, still little known in detail, devoid of life and swept by violent icy winds from the north-east in winter and even late in spring.

To the east of the Hami oasis there starts the great mountain chain of the Tien Shan, which extends unbroken westwards far beyond the Tarim Basin and throughout forms its northern rampart. This is the dividing line between the central and northern tracts of central Asia. To the north the wide, open plateaus are moister and capable of supporting nomadic races who, in times past, have found it worth while to cross the Tien Shan and raid the oasis settlements of the Tarim Basin. The Tien Shan is not, as may be gathered from this statement, as impenetrable as the Kunlun. The leading passes include the Barköl Daban, and the low saddles of Tashihto and Tapancheng at either end of the Bogdo Ula massif. Farther west, too, are routes leading down to the cultivated tracts of Kucha, Aqsu and the open valley of the Taushquan Darya, as well as via the Terek and Turug Art passes to Kashgar.

Having completed the circuit of the encircling walls, we now turn to the basins themselves. By far the most important is the great Tarim Basin itself; the small, narrow Sulo Ho and Etsin Gol Basins are mere appendages like an eastern tail.

The *Tarim Basin* is a pear-shaped area about 900 miles from east to west and a width from north to south of as much as 330 miles. Despite the huge area, the arrangement of the basin is comparatively simple.

(1) By far the largest area is occupied by the huge central desert of bare sand-dunes, popularly known as the Taklamakan. This is perhaps the most formidable of all the dune-covered wastes of the globe—a 'true' desert as opposed to what has been called 'tame' desert.[1] The drifting soil of the Taklamakan is referred to as sand for want of a better name. It consists really of fine, disintegrated particles of rock and is of the character of alluvial loess. It is very fertile in itself, and wherever irrigated is capable of producing excellent crops. Hence there is no danger of sand-dunes approaching close to the irrigated fields of the margin of the basin, for the moisture binds the fertile soil and thereby stops the further advance of the dunes. In addition to individual dunes whose form and position is determined by the prevalent wind direction (mainly from the north-east), there are big hill-like ridges

[1] A tame desert may in years of good rainfall become partly covered with grass or herbs and so support life. Compare the plain of Dera Ismail Khan in India.

rising to a height of 300 feet or more known as 'Davans'. In general they seem to lie parallel to the old watercourses.

(2) On the west, north and east the central waste is bounded by the belts of vegetation along the Tiznaf, Yarkand and Tarim Rivers. On the south a line of oases, mostly small, stretches along the foot of the gravel glacis of the Kunlun, continued eastwards by patches of sandy jungle intermittently watered by small streams. Thus there is a narrow belt of vegetation right round the basin—in places with areas of sand-dunes beyond it. Where the cultivated ground or the jungle belt begins to fade into the lifeless Taklamakan there is first a zone with desert vegetation—tamarisks, wild poplars or reeds—and in this zone a peculiar feature is the 'tamarisk cone'—hillocks of drift sand

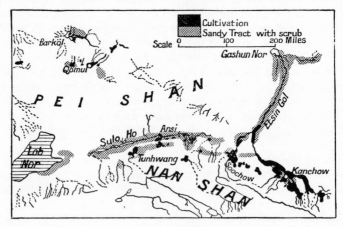

Fig. 311.—The Sulo Ho and Etsin Gol Basins—the eastern 'tail' of the great Tarim Basin

(*After* Sir Aurel Stein.)

around a tuft of tamarisk which may, after centuries of growth, reach a height of 50 feet or more. 'Further out in the Taklamakan there emerge from the dunes only shrivelled and bleached trunks of trees, dead for ages, or sand cones with tamarisk growth from which life has departed.'

(3) At the foot of the encircling mountains is a belt built of gravel swept down from the mountains, especially on the south along the Kunlun. From each gorge a huge fan of gravel spreads out, though the streams are rarely permanent. Much of the water is lost by evaporation or absorption on its way across the huge glacis of gravel; a stretch which is unsuitable for irrigation. All cultivated areas along the southern margin of the desert are thus 'terminal oases'—they occupy the farthermost ground to which water from the rivers of the Kunlun

can be brought for irrigation. 'Not one of the numerous rivers descending from the snowy Kunlun succeeds in making its way through the Taklamakan, except the Khotan River, and that, too, only during a few summer months. All the rest are lost in this "sea of sand" at a greater or lesser distance from the line occupied by the oases or the areas of desert vegetation which they adjoin.'

Special interest attaches naturally to the oases of the Tarim Basin— the only habitable parts of the basin—although on a map they appear as mere specks in the great expanse of the whole basin. There are two clearly marked belts of oases:

(a) The western and northern marginal arc, containing the important oases of Yarkand, Kashgar, Kalpin, Aqsu and Kucha. Owing to the position of these main oases and the convenient stages at which the smaller ones are strung out between them, the route passing along this belt has from the earliest historical times to the present day been the chief line of communication and trade within the Tarim Basin.

(b) The southern marginal arc, stretching along the foot of the Kunlun, has only one oasis of note, that of Khotan. The main reason for this has been mentioned above—the unsuitability of the gravel fans for irrigation—but there is also the added difficulty of maintaining canal heads where the shifting river-courses pass over their fans of gravel.

Owing to the uniform aridity of the climate and the comparatively small variation in altitude—all the important oases mentioned above lie between 3,300 and 4,500 feet above sea-level—all the oases are strikingly similar. 'Whatever their position or size, the traveller sees everywhere the same fields of wheat, maize, or cotton, slightly terraced for irrigation; the same winding lanes lined with white poplars and willows; the same little arbours or orchards inviting with their shade and their plentiful produce of European fruits.' It must be emphasized that the whole Tarim Basin is extremely arid. Kashgar is favoured, when compared with districts east and south, by its relatively large precipitation of about 2 inches per annum. Hence there are in the Tarim Basin no open grazing grounds, but only the carefully irrigated oases and the narrow strips of riverine jungle which can support life, either human or animal. A peculiar feature of the atmospheric conditions is the constant dust haze which hangs over the basin and rarely allows the traveller to catch a glimpse of the great enclosing ranges. When the air is still this fine dust settles and adds naturally to the fertile soils of the oases. When the wind is strong—the strong winds are the north-easterlies—this dust is carried on to the slopes of the Kunlun where true aerial loess several hundreds of feet in thickness occurs up to elevations of 12,000 to 13,000 feet. Much of this loess is in turn washed down into the streams and so back to the basin from which it was removed by wind erosion.

At the eastern end of the Tarim Basin is the depression of Lop [1] —the most desolate of all the natural divisions of the basin. It comprises the stretch of marshes (Lop Nor) into which the waters of the Tarim pass and finally disappear and the great salt-encrusted bed of the dried-up Lop Sea beyond, together with the wastes of gravel, drift sand and wind-eroded clay which surround it. A handful of Lopliks fish and hunt in the Tarim marshes, and a few hundred people live in the little oases along the Kunlun, otherwise the whole vast area is uninhabited.

The *Sulo Ho Basin* has a length of about 220 miles from east to west, but is a narrow trough bounded by the slopes of absolutely bare gravel descending from the western Nan Shan on the south and the utterly barren Pei Shan on the north. The Sulo Ho is fed by the glaciers and snows of the central Nan Shan and descends into the basin at its eastern end. Its sole affluent, the Tang Ho, provides water for irrigating the main oasis of the basin, the oasis of Tunhwang or Sachow. The importance of the Sulo Ho Basin is that, flanked by high mountains on the south and desert wastes on the north, it forms a natural and easily defended corridor leading from north-western China into central Asia. This importance is emphasized by the existence of remains of the ancient Chinese *Limes* or border wall along the trough.

The tiny basin of the Hwahaitze or Yingpan oasis lies between the eastern end of the Sulo Ho Basin and the Etsin Gol Basin.

The *Etsin Gol Basin* stretches east and west from the Pacific watershed to Suchow, whilst the Etsin Gol itself flows away to the north-north-east far towards Mongolia before losing itself in the Gashun Nor. We are now within the influence of moisture-laden breezes from the Pacific: a continuous line of villages lies along the northern foot of the eastern Nan Shan. Cultivation is carried on with the help of rainfall and snowfall only (especially east of Kanchow), as well as by irrigation from the mountain streams. The course of the Etsin Gol to the north is important, because it furnished a convenient line of approach for raiders from the Mongolian steppes.

We cannot leave the Tarim Basin without referring to the fascinating problem of the supposed desiccation of central Asia. Sir Aurel Stein, reviewing the evidence afforded by archaeological discoveries, says that two conclusions are inevitable. 'One is that climatic conditions quite as arid as the present ones prevailed within the big trough of the Tarim Basin as far back as ancient remains and available records can take us. The other conclusion is that the amount of water carried by its rivers has greatly diminished during the same historical period.'

[1] For details, see Ellsworth Huntington, 'Lop-Nor, a Chinese Lake', *Bull. Amer. Geog. Soc.*, **39**, No. 2, 1907.

One explanation of these apparently contradictory conclusions has been suggested independently by Sir Sidney Burrard and Dr. Ficker. It is that the diminished volume of the rivers is due to the shrinkage of the glaciers of the high ranges which are their main feeders. This shrinkage is explained by supposing the glaciers themselves are great relics of ice which were left behind by the great Ice Age and have since been undergoing slow but continuous reduction through milder climatic conditions. This is borne out by the enormous thickness of débris which overlies the Kunlun glaciers. It will be noted that this explanation is really equivalent to saying that of course there has been a gradual climatic change since the Ice Age—a progressive desiccation —but that alterations in the amount of atmospheric moisture reaching the Tarim Basin cannot be detected within historic times.

REFERENCES

Amongst many books dealing with Chinese Turkistan there are numbers of interesting travel books from which geographical information may be extracted:

M. Cable and F. French, *Through Jade Gate and Central Asia*, 1927.
C. P. Skrine, *Chinese Central Asia*, 1926.
Ella and Percy Sykes, *Through Deserts and Oases of Central Asia*, 1920.
Peter Fleming, *News from Tartary*, 1936.
Sir Eric Teichman, *Journey to Turkistan*, 1937.
Ellsworth Huntington's well-known work, *The Pulse of Asia* (1908), deals with the travels of a trained geographer through the area, and contains that author's now famous theories of cyclic climatic changes.
See also below pp. 600–1.

PART III. MONGOLIA

The vast, indefinite tract of country called Mongolia may be said to comprise broadly the north-eastern half of the central mass of Asia's plateaus; bounded by Siberia on the north, Manchuria on the north-east, China on the south-east and Chinese Turkistan on the south-west. The Khingan Mountains form its natural boundary on the east, the Altai and Khangai Mountains penetrate into its heart from the west. The area is roughly 1,875,000 square miles, the total population probably under a million—consisting of nomadic Mongols and Kalmucks, who range the deserts with camels, horses and sheep.

From the broadest possible point of view Mongolia consists of the great central desert of Gobi or Shamo, continuous with that of Chinese Turkistan to the south-west, but fringed on the north-west, north-east and east by a more fertile belt. The results of the expeditions of the American Museum of Natural History, under the leadership of R. C. Andrews, added much to the general knowledge of the whole area. Two geologists of the expedition, Messrs. Berkey and Morris, have given a general account of the topography and geology.[1]

[1] *Geology of Mongolia: Natural History of Central Asia*, Vol. II, 1927.

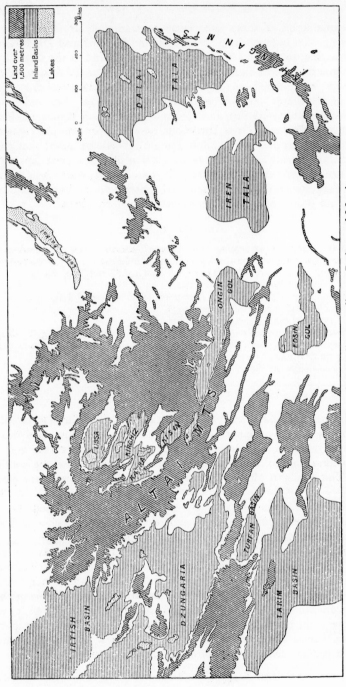

Fig. 312.—The Basins of Mongolia, according to Berkey and Morris

The great basin of the Gobi contains many minor basins, which Berkey and Morris have called 'talas'. They distinguish the Dalai Nor tala, the Iren tala, the Etsin Gol tala, the Kirghiz Nor tala and the Ubsa Nor tala. Each tala has its own local interior drainage and is bounded by inconspicuous warp divides or by mountain ranges. Within each tala are still smaller basins which contain late Mesozoic or Tertiary sediments. These Berkey and Morris have termed 'gobis'. It would seem that underlying Mongolia is an immense pre-Palaeozoic floor, probably a granite batholith, perhaps of unrivalled dimensions. Central Mongolia was a continental mass standing above sea-level during the Lower and Middle Palaeozoic, submerged during the Carboniferous and Permian, since when it has formed a land mass and a long succession of continental deposits has been laid down on the

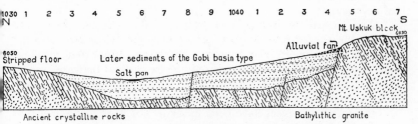

FIG. 313.—Cross-section of a typical Mongolian basin. The basin north of Uskuk Mountain

surface of the plateau and in the basins, and these beds have yielded a wonderful series of fossils, notably of land animals. The erosion of the shallow basins which is going on at the present day and has probably been in progress for ages, is wind erosion. It is from these arid wastes of the dead heart of Asia that the winter winds bring their load of dust, which, in course of time, has built up the great loess deposits of northern China. The cliffs on the edges of the eroded basins are often grotesque in the extreme and afford beautiful examples of the erosive action of wind, frost and rain.[1] The north of the desert, the grassland fringe, is comparatively level. Belts of sand-dunes occur locally in the desert, one of the most remarkable areas being a strip 100 miles long but only 2 or 3 miles wide near the northern foot of the Eastern Altai. Sand-dunes are also found on the southern or western shores of almost every desert lake.

The fringe of Mongolia is rolling pasture land, varying in the quality of the pasture; the heart is desert. In the south-west 'tamarisk and sand' summarizes the character of the desert. An interesting

[1] Berkey and Morris attribute the peneplanation of surfaces so characteristic of Mongolia to stream action during flood, but recognize the transporting power of wind.

account of a journey through the southern part of Mongolia is given by Owen Lattimore in his *Desert Road to Turkestan* (London: Methuen, 1928). In the great central desert, the floor is composed of rock rather than of sand—a circumstance which permits the extensive use of motor transport—and the desert vegetation consists of short wiry grass, camel sage, and low thorny bushes. Great stretches of the surface are almost flat, and a shower of rain will produce almost miraculous changes— the dry, yellow, gravelly surface becomes tinged with a delicate green as far as the eye can reach. The slopes of the mountains, such as the Eastern Altai, are either bare or covered with short grass, so too are the enormous alluvial fans of débris washed out by the occasional torrential rains which fall on the higher peaks of the mountains. The only places where trees are found in the Gobi are in the few river bottoms. They are all old trees—especially elms—and there is no sign of new growth.

The climate of Mongolia is severe in the extreme. During the winter the temperature drops to 40° or even 50° below zero, and the summer is very short. The American Expedition found that, for climatic reasons, scientific work could only be carried out between April 1 and October 1. A blanket of snow covers the peaks of the higher ranges, such as the Altai, except for a few weeks in August.

Repeated references have been made in this book to the fact that the heart of Asia has been a continental mass since remote times. Dr. Chaney, of the American Expedition, considered the Khingan Mountains acted as a climatic barrier in the Cretaceous and Tertiary times, just as they do today, permitting the growth of sequoia forest 'whose moisture requirements were about 40 inches a year' on the windward side, whilst arid and semi-arid conditions on the northern side limited tree growth to scattered conifers and poplars.

For long the hypothesis that central Asia was the ancestral home of man rested upon theoretical evidence only. Remarkable confirmation is afforded by the discovery in the heart of Mongolia of no less than five cultural horizons—'Eolithic', Upper Palaeolithic (with stone implements of Mousterian and Aurignacian types), Mesolithic, Neolithic and later. Special interest attaches to the Mesolithic-Neolithic cultures, the remains of the one found superimposed upon the other in an old sand-dune belt in the heart of the Gobi Desert. From the location of the remains the people have been called the Mongolian 'Dune-Dwellers'. The relatively moister conditions indicated by these discoveries have been confirmed by the discovery of scratched rock surfaces in the grasslands of north central Mongolia, showing representations of game animals no longer living in the region. On the whole the results of the American Expedition's work confirm the sequence of climatic changes worked out by Ellsworth Huntington in the more southerly parts of central Asia.

At the present day a distinction must be drawn between Outer Mongolia, which, after the revolution of 1924, became independent with a Soviet form of government (in north-west Mongolia the Soviet republic of Tannu-Tuva was absorbed by U.S.S.R. in 1945), and Inner Mongolia, an autonomous region within China. The Mongolian People's Republic (the old Outer Mongolia) was formally recognized as independent by both China and U.S.S.R. in 1946. The Mongols of Outer Mongolia are typical nomadic steppe-dwellers; in Inner Mongolia the vanguard of the Chinese agriculturists is penetrating year

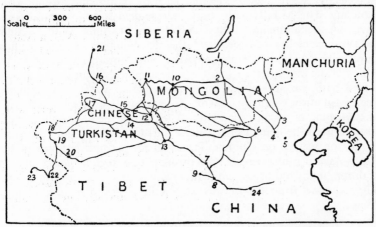

Fig. 314.—The principal routes of Mongolia and Chinese Turkistan

1. Kiakhta.	9. Sining.	17. Kuldja.
2. Ulan Bator (Urga).	10. Uliassutai.	18. Kashgar.
3. Dolon Nor.	11. Kobdo.	19. Yarkand.
4. Kalgan.	12. Barköl.	20. Khotan.
5. Peking.	13. Ansi.	21. Semipalatinsk.
6. Kweihwa.	14. Turfan.	22. Leh.
7. Liangchow.	15. Urumtsi.	23. Srinagar.
8. Lanchow.	16. Chuguchak.	24. Sian.

These routes may be traced out on a good physical map. Ku Ch'eng-tze, mentioned in the text, is situated at the junction of routes between **12** and **15**; the route to Tashkent goes westwards from **17**.

by year farther and farther, pushing the nomadic Mongols before them. The railway penetrates from Peking right across Inner and Outer Mongolia to link with the Russian system (opened January 1, 1956).

The capital and only city of the Mongolian People's Republic is Ulan Bator, formerly Urga, with a quarter of the country's 1,045,000 inhabitants (1964). Ulan Bator is 170 miles south of the Siberian frontier at Kiakhta, and there is an important trade with Kiakhta and Kalgan (now Changkiakow). A motor service between Kalgan and Urga was inaugurated as long ago as 1917 and regular running was carried on in summer months. Wools, hides and skins, furs, horns, etc., are the chief items of export. It is interesting to note that in the early part of the nineteenth century, before the opening of northern Chinese ports to foreign trade, considerable quantities of British goods found their way from Nijni-Novgorod, across Siberia, and into China by this route. Now that a through railway service has been established trade has been freed from many of its former difficulties.

In a brief but informative article entitled 'Economic Advance in Mongolia' (*The World To-Day*, **16**, No. 6, June 1960, 257–70) C. R. Bawden gives a map of the Mongolian People's Republic showing main highways now radiating from Ulan Bator to the capitals of each of the *aimaks* or provinces. The traditional stockbreeding—an early attempt at collectivization failed—is giving place to an agricultural-industrial economy. The M.P.R. is the only independent state in central Asia, developing as a satellite of the U.S.S.R., not of China. With a system of 'rural economy co-operatives' the development of crop-farming (especially wheat) is being combined with improvement of stock. Many of the industries, such as three biochemical factories, are closely linked with the agricultural programme. Ulan Bator, with 250,000 people out of the country's total of 1,045,000, is showing the world-wide phenomenon of urbanization with at least some of its people moving straight from the nomad's felt tent or yurt to a flat in a lofty block.

In the section on Chinese Turkistan an account is given of the Trans-Asiatic routes which pass through that region. There are, in addition, many old trans-continental caravan routes across Mongolia.[1] They all start from the railway at Kweihwa and diverge at Pailing Miao.

(1) The Uliassutai-Kobdo Road runs to the north of the Altai.
(2) The Great and Small Mongolian Roads which join at Khara-niuto run to the south of the Altai and have Ku Ch'eng-tze as their objective.
(3) The Winding Road or the 'Desert Road' runs farther south, also to Ku Ch'eng-tze.

The first of these roads leads on across the mountains north of the Altai to Barnaul; the second and third run together to Urumchi and afterwards fork, the northern branch going via the famous Dzungarian Gate to Sergiopol (whence the railway at Semipalatinsk is easily reached), the southern branch through Semireychensk to Tashkent.

It would be surprising if such a vast area as the heart of Asia did not prove to have resources, especially of minerals, as yet unknown. A reference to Fig. 255 shows that the province of Sinkiang as at present defined under Communist China includes not only the Tarim Basin described on pp. 588–94 but also a huge area of mountains and plains to the north—between the Tien Shan and the Altai on the Soviet border. The focus of this country is Urumchi through which now passes the railway from Lanchow which serves the Yümen oilfields in

[1] See Owen Lattimore, *The Desert Road to Turkestan* (Methuen, 1928).

Kansu. Already a small oilfield has been opened up at Tushantze near Wusu: the Chinese are confident that other promising structures will prove productive both in this area and in the Tsaidam basin (p. 584).

It is unfortunately impossible in the limited space here available even to attempt an adequate account of the great heart of Asia. Until recently so little known, the stories of exploration by travellers, some still living, afford fascinating reading. Among the classics comes Sir Francis Younghusband's account of his early journeys in the eighties and nineties of last century, *The Heart of a Continent* (London: Murray, 1896).[1] For an account of the rugged Mongolian-Russian borderlands there is Douglas Carruthers' *Unknown Mongolia* (2 vols., London: Hutchinson, 1913). See also the summary of work carried out in 1917–20 by Finnish geographers and published as the first part of *Acta Geographica* (Geographical Society of Finland)—summarized in *Geog. Jour.*, **71**, 1928, 502–3. Langdon Warner's *The Long Old Road in China* (New York: Doubleday, Page, 1926) deals with the old North-west Road. A very important work is W. Karamisheff's *Mongolia and Western China* (Tientsin: La Librairie française). In this are given full details of trade, trade centres and trade routes, as well as analyses of the economic possibilities of Mongolia. For a full scientific treatment of central Mongolia there are the voluminous reports of the Expeditions of the American Museum of Natural History. Berkey and Morris's *Geology of Mongolia* has been mentioned; their preliminary summary 'Basin Structures in Mongolia' (*Bull. Amer. Mus. Nat. Hist.*, **51**, 1924, 103–27) will be found of especial value to geographers. A general summary is given by R. C. Andrews in *The New Conquest of Central Asia*, 1932. For some details of trade routes, see M. Cable, 'The Bazaars of Tangut and the Trade Routes of Dzungaria', *Geog. Jour.*, **83**, 1934, 17–32. Owen Lattimore, now Professor in the University of Leeds, has continued his studies in Mongolia for more than forty years and has brought our information up to date in a succession of papers, many including a broader area (notably his inaugural address at Leeds, 1964). See *Geog. Jour.*, **91**, 1938, 1–20 (history), *ibid.*, **132**, 1966. For Urumchi see H. G. Wiens, *Ann. Ass. Amer. Geog.*, **53**, 1963, 441–64.

[1] Reissued in part with additional material, 1937.

KOREA (CHOSEN) [1]

THE important peninsula of Korea is nearly as large as the main island of Japan proper and has an area of 85,228 square miles. In the south it is separated from Japan by a strait only 120 miles wide, with the historic island of Tsushima forming a stepping-stone between the two. On the east coast the Gulf of Jinsen and on the west the river Tadong divide the peninsula into Northern and Southern Korea. The northern boundary is formed by the Tumen and Yalu Rivers and White Mountain.

The mountainous backbone of Korea lies nearer the east coast than the west; the rivers flowing into the Yellow Sea are longer than those of Japan and some are navigable for considerable distances, especially at flood-tide. The tides on the west coast are very high—even as much as 33 feet. The south-western part of the peninsula is the best land and is generally well cultivated.

Climate. Broadly speaking the climate of Korea is comparable with that of northern China. Practically the whole country has at least one month with a mean temperature below freezing. Seoul has two and the Manchurian border has five. The east coast faces the northerly winds, which blow across the sea from the neighbourhood of Vladivostok, and receives considerable snow in winter. But the normal rainy season is summer. Korea shares with Japan and the Yangtze Valley the early rainfall maximum in June (Bai-u or Plum rains of Japan) and in the south of Korea there is a distinct short season of rains in April. The April rains are important since they furnish water to irrigate the rice-fields, and make this part of Korea ideal paddy land. Thornthwaite's classification of Korean climates is shown in Fig. 331 on page 627.

Jones and Whittlesey recognize three climatic regions: (*a*) north-east with heavy winter snowfall; (*b*) south, from Jinsen and Seoul southwards, with nine months' growing season and winter sub-zero temperatures rare; (*c*) north-west continental and resembling the neighbouring parts of Manchuria. The cold winter climate has led to the development of a simple but effective form of central heating. The flue from the kitchen of a village hut is led under the mud floors of the living-rooms to the far end of the building.

[1] J. W. Baylor, 'The Geography of Chosen', *Econ. Geog.*, **7**, 1931, 238–51.
R. B. Hall, 'Agricultural Regions', *Econ. Geog.*, **11**, 1935, 44–52.
J. W. Coulter and B. Bong Hee Kim, 'Land Utilization Maps of Korea', *Geog. Rev.*, **24**, 1934, 418–22.
C. A. Fisher, 'The Role of Korea in the Far East', *Geog. Jour.*, **120**, 1954, 282–98.
Shannon McCune and George M. McCune, *Korea Today* (New York, 1950).
Alice Taylor, 'Korea', *Focus*, **12**, 4, 1961.

Natural Vegetation. The natural vegetation of Korea is forest: in the south resembling that of southern Japan with pines mixed with oaks, walnuts, etc.; in the north resembling that of northern Japan with conifers such as *Chamaecyparis*, *Larix*, *Abies*, *Pinus*, as well as birch. Forests would normally cover 70 per cent. of the surface but as a result of reckless felling and neglect the mountains of central and much of southern Korea are bare. There has been a considerable amount of

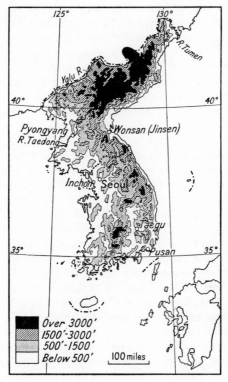

FIG. 315.—Physical map of Korea

re-afforestation. Nevertheless the country as a whole is a maze of green checkerboard valleys set amongst gaunt eroded hills.

Before dealing with agriculture and other industries, it will be desirable to outline the history of Korea in order that the present position may be intelligible.

Historical. The history of Korea has been very largely the natural result of the geographical situation of the country, with China on the west, Japan on the east, and Russia on the north. Herself the possessor of advantages, especially of good natural harbours, coveted by her neighbours, the history of Korea has been the chequered history of a typical buffer state.

When the Chinese statesman, Ki-tze, invaded Korea in the twelfth century before Christ, it is said that he found the country occupied by cave-dwellers in a state of savagery, and little is known of the early history of the Koreans themselves. But for more than two thousand years Korea wavered between a state of independence and a state of suzerainty under China or Japan. The country was repeatedly invaded from the north, by China under both the Chinese and Manchu Dynasties, and by nomadic tribes. In 1592 Japan attacked Korea with an army of 300,000 men as part of a general campaign against China. These various invasions and raids, coupled with the prevalence of piracy in Korean waters, led Korea for several centuries to adopt a policy of absolute national seclusion, so that Korea became known throughout the world as the Hermit Kingdom. Whether Korea was a vassal state of China was never quite decided. When it suited the Koreans to claim the protection of China they did so; when China sought to make its suzerainty effective the Koreans claimed that the annual tribute was paid on sentimental grounds in perpetuation of an ancient custom. But at the same time China disclaimed any responsibility for the acts of Koreans which gave rise to the French and American punitive expeditions of 1866 and 1871. This state of affairs was particularly irritating to Japan, and when, in 1875, a Korean shore-battery fired on a Japanese warship without provocation, Japan took the opportunity of defining and establishing Japanese-Korean relations. The Treaty of Kwangha, 1876, provided for mutual trade, the mutual opening of ports and the recognition by Japan of Korean independence. But China continued to interfere in Korea's domestic affairs and in 1894 Korea asked China's help in subduing a serious rebellion. Chinese troops were sent and Japan sent a bodyguard to protect her minister at Seoul. Japan's suggestion that the Chinese and Japanese troops should work together was rejected and the Sino-Japanese War of 1894–5 became inevitable. Japan was completely victorious and the Treaty of Shimonoseki recognized the absolute independence of Korea, but the intervention of France, Germany and Russia compelled Japan to withdraw her troops from the Chinese peninsula of Liaotung. But what these European powers prevented Japan from doing they immediately proceeded to do themselves and established colonial outposts on Chinese soil. Theoretically an independent Korea protected Japan from the aggression of Russia. But Russia proceeded to develop the powerful naval base of Vladivostok, occupied Port Arthur and the Liaotung Peninsula, dominated Manchuria and formulated obvious designs on Korea. In the meantime Japan quietly improved her land and sea forces. In 1903 and 1904 Russia showed her unwillingness to effect an amicable settlement with

Japan and to guarantee Korean independence. The Russo-Japanese War therefore followed and resulted in the complete victory of Japan. According to the declaration made in 1905 the 'relations of propinquity have made it necessary for Japan to take and exercise, for reasons

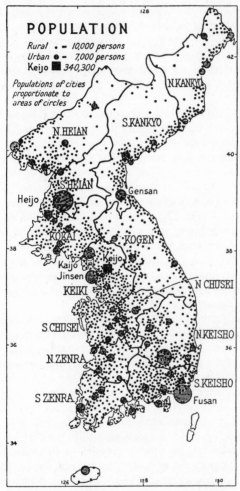

Fig. 316.—Map showing the population of Korea

(By J. W. Coulter and B. B. H. Kim)

closely connected with her own safety and repose, a paramount interest and influence in the political and military affairs of Korea'. The protectorate thus established was unsatisfactory. The assassination of a United States citizen and of the Japanese Prince Ito induced certain classes of Koreans to petition for annexation, which was finally carried into effect on August 29, 1910. From 1910 to 1919 Japan ruled Korea with a fair but harsh and inflexible military rule. The Independence Movement of 1919 was stamped out with a cruel but effective vigour, but it marked the dawn of a new era for Korea. Under the humane and sympathetic governorship of Viscount Ito, Korea made marked economic and social progress. Mr. Alleyne Ireland, passing an American's judgment on the matter in 1925, was able to say, 'Korea is today infinitely better governed than it ever was under its own native rulers, better governed than most self-governing countries, and better governed than most British, American, French, Dutch and Portuguese dependencies.' [1]

From one point of view Korea, as any map suggests, is a pistol pointed at the very heart of Japan, its ice-free numerous safe harbours a prize long coveted by the Russians. From the Japanese point of view Korea's importance was twofold. In 1910 despite a population of some 13 million the density was much lower than in Japan and it was estimated that only 10 per cent. of the cultivable land was under the plough, whilst in the north were unworked deposits of iron ore and anthracite. Korea offered not so much an area of settlement to a rapidly expanding Japan as a source of vital food and raw materials. Secondly Korea was the ideal bridgehead for Japanese plans of continental expansion. Japan built as early as 1906 the railway from Pusan, opposite Shimonoseki, through Seoul to the border of Manchuria: the Yalu River was bridged in 1911 and through running with Manchurian railways became possible.

The system served Japan well in the invasion of Manchuria in 1931. Later Korea and Manchuria were developed, one may say exploited, to supply the ever-growing needs of the Japanese homeland. Not till the outbreak of the Second World War was there extensive industrial development—large hydro-electric installations on the Yalu River and various heavy chemical industries supplying fertilizers and explosives.

With the defeat of Japan in 1945 the Yalta decision to establish Korea as an independent state was temporarily shelved when the country was arbitrarily divided along the 38th parallel so that Russian troops could take the Japanese surrender in the north, American in the south, and supply the necessary occupation forces. This temporary arrangement steadily assumed a more and more permanent character. The Republic of Korea in the south, with its capital at Seoul, was proclaimed in August 1948; the Korean People's Democratic Republic (on a Soviet model) or North Korea with its capital at Pyongyang a month later.

On June 25, 1950, the North Koreans attacked the South, which appealed to the United Nations against the aggression. The burden

[1] *The New Korea* (New York: E. P. Dutton & Co., 1926).

of the ideological war between United Nations forces and Communist armies from China supported by the U.S.S.R., fell mainly on the United States. The truce of 1953 left a division into North and South Korea not far from the former line and subsequent developments have heightened the contrast between what are at present two very distinct countries.

Population. The Censuses of 1963 gave a total population of 38,170,000. This was an increase of 18,650,000 over the Census total of 1925 so that the population is growing at the rate of 500,000 per annum. Until the war of 1904–5 Japanese settlers numbered only 40,000–50,000; by 1935 they had increased to 583,000 though they were mainly in the towns. Seoul, known to the Japanese as Keijo, with a population then of 404,000, had over 100,000 Japanese. At the conclusion of the North-South struggle in 1953 the mass movements of civilian population which had taken place away from the main areas of conflict gave place to movements dictated partly by choice of régime, with a balance of movement to the south. The estimated result on population is shown in the annexed table. Seoul had been reduced to ruins and only about 50,000 people remained, but refugees swarmed back with the staggering result that the population at the Census of December 1963 was recorded as 3,370,030.

	Total	North Korea	%	South Korea	%
Area, square miles	85,266	46,814	55	38,452	45
Population, 1949	29·57 mn.	9·17 mn.	31	20·40 mn.	69
„ 1963	38·17	11·04	29	27·13 „	71
„ density, 1963	447	236		705	
Rice production	3·8 mn. tons ⎫		36	2·0	64
Other grains	4·0 „ „ ⎬ 6·6		37		63
Soya beans	0·4 „ „ ⎭		69		31
Fish catch	1,950,000 tons	1,500,000	77	450,000	23
Tungsten	12,000	5,000	42	7,000	58
Anthracite and coal	22·9 mn. tons	14·0		8·9 mn.	32
Iron ore	4·4 „ „	3·9	89	0·5 mn.	11
Output:					
Chemical industries			88		12
Metal industries			85		15
Textiles industries			14		86
H.E. installed power capacity	2,500,000		96		4
Thermal capacity	313,000 „		30		70

This table refers in the main to 1963; the figures for output of industry are from earlier estimates. The North has the minerals and water power, the South has the food, but is much more densely peopled.

Occupations. Between 80 and 85 per cent. of the inhabitants of Korea are engaged in farming—especially of rice, which is the staple food. Fishing is an important subsidiary occupation; the west and south coasts have numerous and excellent harbours though suffering from an exceptional tidal range—exceeding 30 feet in places. These marked tidal movements combined with the conditions resulting in the meeting of cold and warm currents off the coasts are responsible for the wealth and variety of the catch. The value of fishery products increased greatly through the introduction of modern gear and methods—including deep-sea fishing—by the Japanese, though the Japanese themselves took little part in either fishing or agriculture.

Agriculture. Arable land covers about 11 million acres.

The chief crops are rice, barley, millet, wheat, soya beans and red beans. There are also such special crops as cotton, tobacco, hemp and ginseng. The cultivation of fruit has also produced excellent results. Radishes are popular for making 'kinchi', an important item of the Korean menu. Most Koreans subsist on a diet of rice if they can afford it, barley or millet if they cannot. Dried fish, pork and occasionally chicken, together with bean sprouts and curd, add variety, but kinchi adds zest to every meal. It is essentially a relish, very hot, with pepper and garlic, and strong smelling.

The rice crop steadily increased under Japanese influence to an average of about 100,000,000 bushels in the nineteen-thirties. Out of this 40 per cent. went to Japan (where it formed some 8 per cent. of consumption) and the *per capita* amount left to the Koreans diminished rather than increased. It is not difficult to see why the distribution of the former Japanese estates among Korean peasants after 1945 was a popular move. As the table above shows, output of other grains— mainly millet, barley and wheat—in total exceeds that of rice. There is also a large production of American upland cotton and of native cotton; of apples and of pears. Double-crop farming is limited to South Korea.

The importance to Japan proper of the surplus agricultural products was of course immense, and agricultural development of the country was mainly due to Japanese enterprise. It was a group of Japanese who first experimented with cotton in 1905; until 1920 or 1930 fruits produced in excess and of fine quality, because of the drier climate, compared with Japan, were exported to China and Japan. Sericulture was also stimulated and production of cocoons rose from 715,645 kilograms in 1909–13 to 23,000,000 in 1937.

Livestock is raised as a by-product of agriculture—over $1\frac{1}{2}$ million cattle and $1\frac{1}{4}$ million pigs. The cattle are well known for their size and quality, especially those reared in Hamkyong, North Korea, and there was a large export to Japan.

An interesting product of Korea is ginseng, a medical root highly

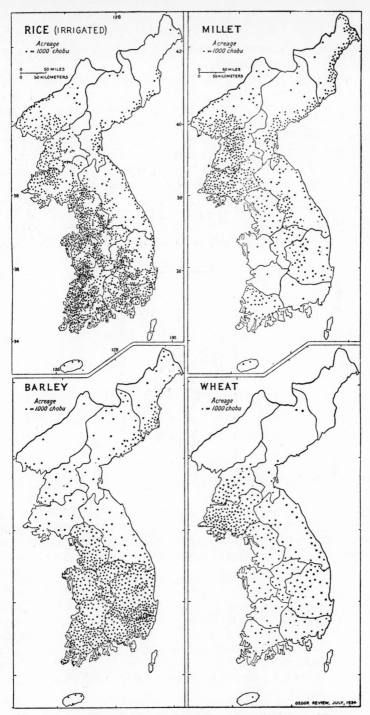

FIGS. 317–20.—Maps showing the distribution of the chief crops of Korea

(By J. W. Coulter and B. B. H. Kim.)

One chobu or chungbo = 2·45 acres or practically one hectare.

valued by the Chinese. The cultivation is a Government monopoly. Tobacco is another monopoly.

Minerals. Northern Korea is rich in minerals and those worked include anthracite, iron ore, tungsten ore and gold. The bulk of the gold is from two mines, the Unsan mine and Suian mine—both were controlled by American interests. Whanghai is the centre of iron ore mining. The Pyongyang Colliery is famous as working the richest anthracite mine in the Far East. The output of coal exceeded a million tons for the first time in 1932 and continued to expand. It reached nearly 7,000,000 tons during the Second World War.

Natural Regions of Korea. The crop distribution maps here reproduced from Coulter and Kim's paper suggest wide variations in agricultural production with a millet-wheat-bean region in the north-west, and a rice-barley region in the south. A division of the country

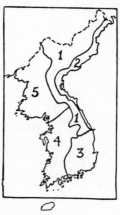

FIG. 321.—The natural regions of Korea, altered from Baylor

into five regions has been proposed by Baylor; these are shown with modifications in Fig. 321. It will be noted that South Korea coincides closely with Regions 3 and 4 together with the southern section of the mountains. North Korea embraces Region 5 and most of 1 and 2.

(1) *The Central and Northern Mountain Region.* This is a sparsely in-habited, wild and inaccessible region of mountainous country with peaks rising to over 8,000 feet and the lofty Kaima plateau passing southwards into the Taihoku Range. The few superstitious hill peoples, living in two- or three-roomed clay huts with thatched roofs, attempt a little cultivation in the valleys. The region has largely been despoiled of the forests it should possess and presents barren foothills where larch should flourish.

(2) *The Eastern Coastal Strip*. This narrow, isolated region is inhabited along the coast by villagers whose main interest is
in fishing from tiny boats by primitive methods. The tides on
this coast are small, but harbours suitable for large craft are
absent. There is a narrow belt of arable country behind the
coastal tract where rice and millet are the staples.

(3) *The South-eastern Silk Area*. This comprises the Naktong Basin
and its surrounding foothills and is one of the areas where
sericulture has made great strides. Having Pusan (formerly
Fusan) as its outlet and enjoying excellent communications,
further development may be prophesied for this region.

(4) *The South-western Agricultural Basins*. The western agricultural
basins of Korea are by far the most important parts of
the country. The central Han Basin, radiating in three
directions from the mouth of the river near Inchon, has long
been the economic and political heart of the peninsula. This
river separates roughly the south-western from the north-
western basins. The south-western region is, like the south-
east, a two-crop region. October is not only the month of the
rice harvest but is marked by great activity in the ploughing
of the rice lands and the sowing of large quantities of barley,
and some wheat to be reaped in June or July when the monsoon rains break and prepare the land for transplanting the
little rice plants. Sericulture and the growing of mulberry
trees are carried on throughout the western basins.

(5) *The North-western Agricultural Basins and the Mining Regions*.
North of Seoul the severity of the winters makes autumn or
fall sowing either impossible or unwise; thus the land is
single cropped. There is little barley but much wheat, millet
and soya beans, with a relatively smaller quantity of rice.
The mining areas occur as enclaves in this region.

Commerce. The bulk of the commerce was with Japan. The
former large trade with 'China' was actually with Manchuria.

Pusan (Fusan), 1,391,000 in 1963, is the oldest and largest port of
Korea; it has been modernized and has excellent railway facilities. It is
a western-type city—like Seoul—in contrast with most of the towns and
villages of the country. Inchon (Jinsen) is the second port. Though there
is an increasing mileage of roads, much of the country is still inaccessible and transport in the interior is by porters, pack-horses or oxen.

Enough has been said to indicate that Korea, despite its very considerable population, was producing a large excess of foodstuffs and
raw materials which were being exported to Japan. It follows that an
independent Korea has the land resources to develop a much higher
standard of living for its people, as well as mineral and power reserves.

JAPAN [1]

THE island kingdom of Japan has sometimes been called the 'Britain of the East'. Both Britain and Japan are groups of islands lying in middle latitudes and a short distance off continental masses, but there the comparison may almost be said to end. Britain lies to the north-west, Japan to the north-east of the great continental mass of Eurasia; consequently whilst Britain has a 'west coast' climate, benefiting to the full from the warming influence of the North Atlantic drift and the westerly wind belt, Japan has an 'east coast' climate, suffering from cold winter winds and heavy summer monsoon rains and only benefiting partly from the warming influence of the Kuro Siwo or Kuro-shio—the Gulf Stream of the Pacific.

Japanese mythology claims that the empire, with its focus around the Inland Sea, was founded in 660 B.C. by Jimmu Tennō, the first Emperor of the present dynasty. Bearing the title of Dai Nippon Teikoku Tennō (Imperial Son of Heaven of Great Japan), the old emphasis on the divine character of the Emperor led to his remaining in complete seclusion, the control of the country being in the hands of the family of Shoguns who ruled it on a feudal system. In 1867 the Emperor assumed temporal power; in 1871 the feudal system was abolished and there followed a rapid westernization and urbanization of the country. The capital was moved to Tokyo in 1868—then in the midst of a relatively little-developed part of the country—and there followed a phenomenal increase of population over the country as a whole, but especially northwards from Tokyo and the Kwanto Plain. The Japanese proved themselves adept in copying Western methods in industry and developed a wide range of factory goods at prices with which Western nations with higher standards of living were unable to compete. Soon pressure on the restricted land area of Japan became intense. War with China (1894–5) brought Japan control over Formosa, war with Russia in 1904–5 brought control over Korea and initiated Japanese activities in Manchuria, culminating in the invasion of the country in 1931 and the setting up of the puppet state of Manchukuo in 1932–3. In the meantime Japan, in accordance with the existing Anglo-Japanese alliance, participated in the First World War

[1] I am greatly indebted to the Japanese National Committee for Geography and especially its chairman, Professor Fumio Tada, for making possible a brief visit to Japan in the spring of 1955—exactly thirty years after my first geographical studies there. Professor Fumio Tada and Professor Torao Yoshikawa have also made valuable comments on this revision. In August and September 1957 I carried out extensive journeys on the occasion of the Japanese Regional Conference of the International Geographical Union. The present chapter has been reviewed also by Professor R. Ishida of Hitotsubashi University, Tokyo, on behalf of the International Society for Educational Information to whom I am greatly indebted.

but doubtless considered her spoils of war meagre—a mandate over certain former German island possessions in the Pacific.

The Japanese do not take kindly to emigration and the Japanese Empire was organized on the basis of an inner ring, broadly speaking Old Japan, densely populated and highly industrialized, and an outer 'ring'—Hokkaido, Karafuto, Korea, Manchuria and Formosa—organized to supply foodstuffs and raw materials. Not content with Manchuria, Japan took advantage of a disorganized China to invade that country in 1937, gaining control of most except the Far West.

Striking a severe blow at the United States fleet by the unheralded

JAPANESE EMPIRE: CENSUS OF OCTOBER 1, 1935

	Area, including adjacent small islands, sq. miles	%	Population
Japan Proper	147,201	56·56	69,254,148
Mainland (Honshu or Hondo)	87,805	33·74	—
Shikoku	7,246	2·78	—
Kyushu	16,174	6·21	—
Hokkaido (Yezo)	30,115	11·57	—
Chishima isles (Kuriles)	3,970	1·53	—
Other islands	1,891	0·73	—
Chosen (Korea)	85,228	32·75	22,899,038
Taiwan (Formosa)	13,840	5·32	5,212,426
Hōkotō (Pescadores)	49	0·02	—
Karafuto (Japanese Sakhalin)	13,934	5·35	331,943
Japanese Empire	260,252	100·00	97,697,555
Kwangtung (leased)	1,438	—	1,656,726
South Sea mandated islands	830	—	102,537
Manchuria (Manchukuo)	503,427	—	31,000,000

JAPAN: CENSUS OF OCTOBER 1, 1955

Japan	142,748	—	89,275,529

attack at Pearl Harbour in 1941, Japan rapidly overran much of south-east Asia in 1942–4—Hong Kong, the Philippines, French Indo-China, Malaya, British territory in Borneo, the Dutch East Indies, Burma and the Andaman-Nicobar islands—and established a 'Greater East Asian Prosperity Sphere'.

With the collapse of Japan in 1945 and the unconditional surrender which followed the dropping of the first atomic bomb on Hiroshima, not only did Japan lose her temporary gains of the war years, but also

the Empire as it had existed in the nineteen-thirties. The present
position of the lost parts of the Empire—Formosa, Korea, Karafuto,
the Kuriles, Manchuria and the South Sea islands—is separately con-

FIG. 322.—The Japanese Empire, political, in 1935

Japan proper dotted; possessions lined. In addition Japan had a lease over the Liaotung Peninsula
and controlled Manchuria. The Empire also included the Kurile Islands, off the map to the north-east,
and the tiny Ogasawara (Bonin) Islands, not marked in long. 141° and lat. 25–28°.

sidered. American forces entered into temporary occupation of Japan
itself but were withdrawn and Japanese independent sovereignty
restored in 1952 over Japan proper, comprising the three islands of
Old Japan, Hokkaido or the Northland, and the Ryukyu islands.

The contrast in area and population of the Japanese Empire of 1935 and present-day Japan is shown in the tables on p. 613. By 1940 the Empire is estimated to have had a population of 105,226,000. Japan proper had about 72,270,000 on V-J Day, 1945. During 1946 the Americans repatriated all Japanese from the Philippines, Western

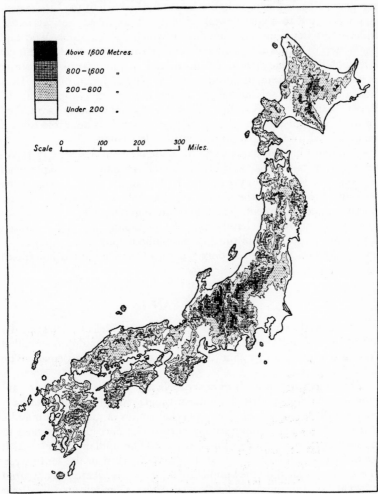

FIG. 323.—A physical map of Japan proper

Pacific and Korea (nearly a million) and by 1948 Japan proper had 78,627,000 people.

Japan proper extends from about 30° N. to 45° N., but running through the island of Taiwan (Formosa) is the Tropic of Cancer, whilst Japanese territory in Sakhalin extended to 50° N. The Japanese Empire thus covered a wide latitude, but the whole was nearer the

Equator than are the British Isles. In all there were nearly 1,700 small islands in the Empire.

Broadly speaking, the Japanese Empire comprised two economic zones. There was an inner, densely populated—one might say over-populated—central zone, unable to produce sufficient food to be self-supporting and to a considerable extent industrialized, and an outer, under-populated zone, the function of which was to supply food and raw materials to the inner zone. The inner zone is practically identical with Old Japan; Hokkaido, the 'northland' of Japan, is still a frontier or pioneer land although administered as part of Japan proper. Thus Hokkaido may be said to belong to the outer zone, which included Korea, Taiwan and Karafuto. There will be, obviously, a marked contrast between the two zones; for that reason it is desirable to deal separately with Old Japan and then with Hokkaido.

An interesting comparison can be made between present-day Japan and Great Britain. Japan and Britain both have about an acre per head of population. In Japan 15 per cent. of this is arable, 4 per cent. grass, 67 per cent. woodland; in the United Kingdom the corresponding figures are 18, 19 and 6 per cent. (excluding rough grazing which amounts to 17 per cent.). Overall density was 622 in Japan, 537 in the United Kingdom; 30 per cent. of the Japanese labour force was employed in agriculture and fisheries but only 5 per cent. in the United Kingdom. See also p. 630.

OLD JAPAN

Of the lands which remain to Japan after her defeat in 1945 at the end of the Second World War only Hokkaido (Hokaidō), once called Yezo, is part of the 'outer zone' of comparatively recent settlement. The rest is Old Japan.

Physiography and Structure. Nearly all parts of Japan are mountainous and at first sight the arrangement of the mountains is irregular. Broadly, however, two parallel chains of mountains may be distinguished, each forming a long curve. The one curve lies close to the west coast, the other to the east coast. The midland valley which lies between the two chains is most clearly marked in the south-west, where it is occupied by the famous Inland Sea. Elsewhere it is obscured by great volcanic piles, and volcanoes show a tendency to lie along the island arcs and folded chains. The midland valley is completely obliterated by the great knot of mountains in the heart of Honshu, forming the 'Japanese Alps', of which more than a dozen peaks rise to over 8,000 feet. Some of these central peaks are active or extinct volcanoes. To the south rises the most familiar and perhaps the most famous of all mountains, the sacred mountain of the Japanese, Fujisan, wrongly translated and known to foreigners as Fujiyama. In Hokkaido there is a central knot of mountains, due to the meeting at right angles of the Japanese fold ranges and the fold range which forms the Kurile festoon. Similarly in Kyushu, the Ryukyu fold chain crosses the Japanese folds—all with their attendant volcanic piles.

An excellent physiographic diagram of Japan was prepared by Guy-Harold Smith and published with explanatory notes by G. T.

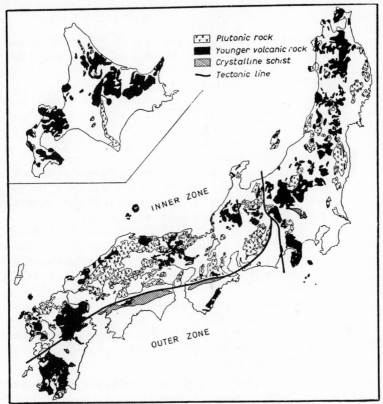

Plutonic rock
Younger volcanic rock
Crystalline schist
Tectonic line

INNER ZONE

OUTER ZONE

FIG. 324.—Outline geological map of Japan
Map supplied by Fumio Tada and Torao Yoshikawa.

Trewartha.[1] He pointed out the essential youthfulness of Japanese relief and noted that the small plains are not structural but are patches of riverine or wave-worked sediments developed in mountain basins or coastal indentations. Often these delta plains terminate abruptly against the surrounding foothills; only in some cases is there a piedmont belt of coarse-textured alluvial fans. Numerous terraces bear evidence of

---

[1] *Geog. Rev.*, **24,** 1934, 400–3. An authoritative work is now available in G. T. Trewartha, *Japan, a Physical, Cultural and Regional Geography* (University of Wisconsin Press, 1948, new edition, 1965).

recent uplift; they consist of unconsolidated material undergoing rapid erosion and so exhibit narrow, canyon-like valleys with flat to gently sloping inter-stream uplands.

Trewartha distinguishes four geomorphological 'zones' in Japan, which can be followed in Fig. 324.

The 'Outer' and 'Inner' Zones are parallel zones of contrasted geological structure; fault scarps and tectonic depressions mark their contact.

(a) The south-western Outer Zone (Pacific Folded Mountains) consists of well-developed longitudinal ridges and valleys often bounded by parallel fault lines and consisting of old, highly folded strata forming rugged mountains.

(b) The south-western Inner Zone consists of dissected block plateaus, mostly rugged hill country, and is marked by widespread granitic rocks. Eastwards it terminates in a tremendous fault scarp shown on Fig. 324.

(c) The Outer Zone (Pacific) of Northern Japan is separated from the Inner Zone by the line of tectonic depressions extending from the Ishikari-Yufutsu lowland in Hokkaido to the bay-head plain of Kwanto. The complicated structure resembles that of the south-western Inner Zone.

(d) The Inner Zone of Northern Japan consists of two parallel ranges of highland, separated by a series of detritus-floored fault basins. The central range forms the backbone and watershed of Northern Japan and consists largely of Tertiary sediments.

(e) The 'Fossa Magna' east of the scarp on Fig. 324 has been interpreted as a great rift valley—a line of weakness naturally developed at right angles to the folded chains. The valley has been largely filled by the huge volcanic piles of which Fuji-san is the best known.

It is already clear that Japan can boast no large plains. Indeed, land inclined at angles of less than 10 degrees (equal to a slope of 1 in 7) does not exceed a quarter of the whole. The only extensive plain is that known as the Kwanto Plain, around Tokyo, which supports 22 million people. The smaller Nobi Plain contains Nagoya and 6 million people; the Kinki Plains, Kyoto, Kobe and Osaka and 8 million people. The fertile land of Japan is to be found in these and other small plains and in the valleys of the larger rivers. But only a fifth of this mountainous country may be classed as cultivable or, at the most optimistic estimate, only a little over a quarter. The rivers of Japan are short and swift, of little or no value for navigation, but of considerable significance as a source of power and for irrigating the rice-fields.

From the irregular nature of the coast-line Japan is well supplied with harbours. Indeed, the Inland Sea may be described as one gigantic harbour penetrating to the heart of the most fertile part of the country; few rivers drain into it to cause silting; it has but a very small tide (2 feet) in the eastern part (though a large one with strong tidal currents in the west) and is protected from winds and storms from all directions.

The intense nature of the Alpine folding and the extraordinary

DISTRIBUTION OF ROCK-TYPES IN JAPAN

	Per cent. of surface
Sedimentary Rocks	67·84
Crystalline	3·78
Palaeozoic	10·24
Mesozoic	7·95
Cainozoic and Quaternary	45·87
Igneous Rocks	32·16
Older	11·24
Tertiary and Recent	20·92

development of vulcanicity have resulted in a very complex geological map of Japan. Igneous rocks occupy nearly a third of the surface, as shown in the preceding table.

It will be noticed to what a large extent Alpine material enters into the Alpine folds, and that a relatively small area of the Archean core is exposed.[1]

No account of Japan would be complete without a reference to the seismic disturbances which are the curse of the country. Japan has been described as a land of volcanoes and earthquakes. It is well known that the portion of the Pacific Ocean which borders the southern and eastern shores of Japan is there extraordinarily deep; and that the high mountains of Japan are in close juxtaposition with one of the great ocean deeps. The principal Japanese earthquakes are associated with the resulting line of weakness; the seismic foci are associated with the convex or outer side of the Japanese arc and only rarely with the inner or concave side. Some smaller shocks are also associated with volcanic eruptions, but it is a mistaken idea to suppose that the major quakes are caused in this way. On the contrary, volcanoes act as safety-valves, and places in their immediate vicinity are rarely visited by destructive shocks. Though ten years may elapse between serious quakes, in Tokyo a sensible shock occurs on an average every three days. The prevalence of earthquakes has affected Japanese architecture from earliest times, the familiar bell tower (Kanetsukido), five-storied pagoda and temple gate (sammon) being built in such a way as to withstand the most

[1] For a brief account of the geology of Japan reference may be made to an official summary by the Imperial Geological Survey, *The Geology and Mineral Resources of the Japanese Empire* (Tokyo, 1926), which was written to accompany the revised edition of the 'Geological Map of the Japanese Empire', scale 1/2,000,000.

severe shocks. Indeed, the principle of the five-storied pagoda is that
of the duplex pendulum seismograph. The epicentres of Japanese earthquakes are frequently situated under the sea and deaths from tidal
waves may exceed those from the earthquake itself. Amongst the more
severe disasters may be noted that of A.D. 1498, when Tokaido was

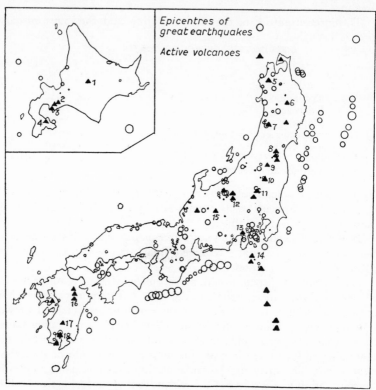

FIG. 325.—The active volcanoes and seismic foci of Japan

Volcanoes:

1 Tokachi	6 Iwate	11 Shirane Nikko)	16 Aso
2 Tarumae	7 Chokai	12 Asama	17 Kirishima
3 Usu	8 Zao	13 Hakone	18 Sakurajima
4 Komagatake	9 Bandai	14 Oshima Island	
5 Iwaki	10 Nasu	15 Yakedake	

Notice that Fuji, in common with an immense number of other dormant or extinct volcanoes, is not
shown.

visited by a severe earthquake and 20,000 perished; that of 1792 (Hizen
and Higo), when 15,000 were killed or drowned; that of 1847 (Shinano),
when 12,000 died; that of 1855 (Tokyo), 6,700 deaths; that of 1891
(Mino-Owari), 7,300 deaths; that of 1896, when tidal waves drowned
over 27,000 in the Sanriku district. But in point of magnitude of
damage inflicted on life and property the great earthquake of September 1, 1923, which had its epicentre in the northern part of Sagami

Bay, is without a rival in the world history. The earthquake and the disastrous fire which followed razed Yokohama to the ground and destroyed half Tokyo, resulting in the destruction of 558,000 houses and causing the death of 91,344 people. It is perhaps only natural that Japan should have taken a foremost place in seismological investigations, but it was after the 1923 disaster that serious attention was given to the construction of earthquake-resisting buildings. Light wooden buildings of the old type may be ideal in the country, but the danger of fire renders them totally unsuited for use in towns. There seems little doubt that the most suitable buildings are steel-framed buildings with rigid reinforced concrete walls.

Associated with vulcanicity in Japan are numerous mineral springs —at least 1,200 are known—mostly hot springs, many of which are radioactive. Numbers of popular health resorts are centred round the more famous of the hot springs.

On the whole Japan is not rich in minerals. Associated with the Tertiary sedimentary rocks are small coalfields and oilfields and small seams of anthracite are found in Mesozoic rocks. Of the metallic minerals copper is economically the most important and, after it, gold, silver and iron. The metallic minerals are associated, in the main, either with the Tertiary volcanics or with the Archean and Palaeozoic rocks.

Coal. Of the Tertiary coalfields those in Kyushu and Hokkaido are the most extensive and valuable. In Honshu there is a small field of inferior coal extending over Iwaki and Hitachi, but the fields of northern Kyushu (in Hizen, Chikuzen and Buzen) are believed to have about two-thirds of the reserves in Japan and the fields of Ishikari in Hokkaido one-sixth of the reserves. A peak production of 57·5 million long tons was reached in 1943: it is now between 50 and 55 million tons. The coalfields are not well situated relative to the industrial centres; transport facilities are indifferent; workers not very efficient and wages high. These factors encourage the development of hydro-electric power. Coking coal is imported. Hakodate is the port of shipment for Hokkaido coal; Nagasaki, Wakamatsu and Kanda are the bunkering ports for Kyushu coal.

Petroleum. Japan's oil comes from two main areas—the Akita and Niigata oilfields, bordering the Japan Sea in north-west Honshu. Petroleum has been known to exist for a very long time, but it was not until about 1900 that the industry began to assume its modern activity. The peak of production was reached about 1912, and later years were marked by a steady decline in output (103 million gallons or about 400,000 tons in 1918 to about half that in the thirties, but 300,000 in 1954). Production is only about one per cent. of requirements, hence a large import from the Middle East, Indonesia and elsewhere, especially of crude oil for refining in Japan.

Copper. Copper is mined in several areas and Japan formerly figured as the world's seventh largest producer. The ores are widespread, being found especially on the inner arc on the Japan Sea side, but also on both sides of the outer arc. As in most countries of the world, the production has varied considerably; from high levels of over 100,000 tons it fell to a quarter or less, but in 1956 amounted to 77,000 tons. In the inter-war years the smaller producers dropped out and in the thirties 75 per cent. of the output was from five mines: Ashio (Tochigi district), Besshi (Ehime district), Kosaka (Akita district), Hitachi (Ibaraki district) and Saganoseki (Ōita district).

Copper was the only metal which Japan produced in excess of

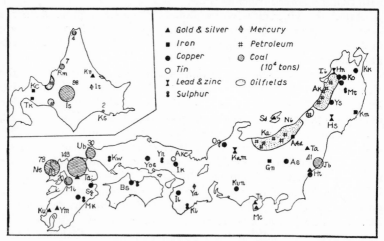

FIG. 326.—The chief mines of Japan

Ak: Akita Oilfield, Aka: Akatani, Ake: Akenobe, As: Ashio, Bs: Besshi, Ck: Chikuho Coalfield, Gn: Gunma, Hn: Hanaoka, Hs: Hosokura, Ht: Hitachi, Ii: Iimori, Ik: Ikuno, Is: Ishikari Coalfield, It: Itomuka, Jb: Joban Coalfield, Ka: Kashiwazaki, Kam: Kamioka, Kc: Kucchian, Ki: Kishu, Kk: Kamikita, Km: Kamaishi, Kn: Konomai, Ko: Kosaka, Ku: Kushikino, Kun: Kune, Ks: Kushiro Coalfield, Kw: Kawayama, Mc: Mochikoshi, Mi: Miike Coalfield, Mk: Makimine, Mt: Matsuo, Ni: Niigata Oilfield, Ns: Nishikyushu Coalfield, Og: Ogoya, Rm: Rumoi Coalfield, Sd: Sado, Sg: Saganoseki, Ta: Takatama, Tai: Taio, Th: Tohi, Ti: Taira, Tk: Tokushunbetsu, Ub: Ube Coalfield, Ya: Yamato, Ym: Yamagano, Yn: Yanahara, Ys: Yoshino, Yos: Yoshioka.

home requirements, but the home demand increased and now production is only about a third of domestic requirements.

Gold and Silver. Gold and silver not infrequently occur together, or in veins of similar origin in sedimentary or volcanic rocks of Tertiary age. The production was never large enough to satisfy home demand. In 1954 it was equivalent to 237,000 fine ounces of gold and 6,040,000 fine ounces of silver.

Iron. Japan is poor in iron ores but built up a large iron and steel industry by buying scrap all over the world and importing ores from abroad. Japan when in control of Manchuria had there a large source of supply. A war-time peak using Empire resources was reached in

1944 of 4·4 million tons of iron ore and Japan's open-hearth steel capacity during the war was 9·4 million tons. Output of iron ore in 1956 was 1·9 million tons; pig-iron 6·2 million tons; steel 10·9 million tons. The last figure has been climbing rapidly. Yet in 1926 only one iron ore mine was listed in Japan; in 1963 there were six.

Other minerals of varying importance in Japan include salt, iron pyrites, sulphur, manganese, chromite, barytes, gypsum, lead, zinc, mercury, tungsten and molybdenum.

Climate. In general the climate, or more correctly the climates,

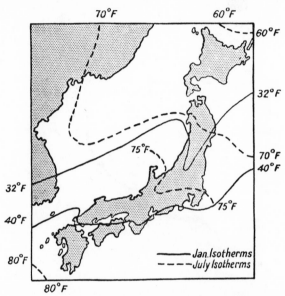

FIG. 327.—The climate of Japan—January and July isotherms

More accurate data, expressed in Centigrade, are now available in Okada's *Climate of Japan.*

of Japan are comparable with those of China but modified locally by Japan's insular position. As in China, there are very strong north-west winds in winter, and feebler south-east winds in summer.

Winter Conditions. The Japanese archipelago is warmer in winter than corresponding latitudes on the mainland and the country is divided roughly into two halves, a northern and a southern, by the January isotherm of 32° F. Although the west coast is exposed to the full force of the cold winds from the Asiatic mainland in winter, it is warmer than the east coast. The explanation of this surprising fact is found in the ocean currents bathing the Japanese shores. An important branch of the warm Kuro-shio hugs the west coast, but the east coast is washed by the cold Okhotsk current from the north. Actually, it is the north-west winds that are warmed in crossing the warm waters which are in the main responsible for the warming effect on the west coast. There is naturally a great difference between the winter temperature in the north of the Japanese chain and the south. January temperatures in Sakhalin and the interior of Hokkaido are below 15° F., whilst Southern Japan has mild winters with an average January temperature of over 45°. Over most of Japan the winter is dry, though

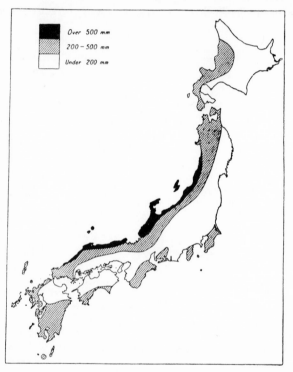

FIG. 328.—The winter rainfall of Japan (for the three months December, January and February)

Note.—25·4 mm. = 1 inch.

not so dry as in northern China. In crossing the Japanese Sea the north-west winds, however, pick up a considerable amount of moisture and give a heavy precipitation, mainly in the form of snow, as they rise to cross the Japanese mountains. The east coast is comparatively rainless. In the north of Japan the air is, however, damp in winter and the raw cold contrasts with the dry cold of North China. Some localities on the west coast of Japan have over 30 inches of rainfall in the three winter months—considerably greater than the precipitation in the summer months. Since the 30 inches of rain fall actually as 30 feet of snow, the winters can be described as very snowy.

Summer Conditions. In July the temperatures decrease steadily from just below 80° F. in the south to 60° F. in the north of Hokkaido and in Sakhalin. The south-east monsoon commences to blow about May and reaches its height in August, dying away in September and October.

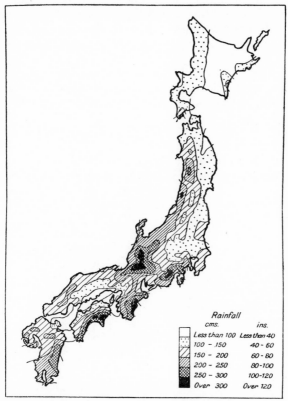

Fig. 329.—The annual rainfall of Japan
(Based on T. Okada, *The Climate of Japan*, Tokyo, 1931.)

A curious feature of the climate of Japan, not fully explained, is that the maximum rainfall does not coincide with the height of the monsoon. There are, instead, two rainfall maxima, one in June and one in September. In Japan proper (except Hokkaido) the first rainy season begins towards the middle of June and lasts till mid-July. Rain is more or less continuous, skies are overcast, the air is so damp that everything tends to become mouldy and the weather is distinctly depressing. These early 'plum-rains' (Bai-u, so called because they come when the plums are getting ripe) are important in cultivation, for preparing the fields for the transplanting of the young plants. In most parts of Japan August is the hottest month, a feature definitely associated with the lessened rainfall (compare October in Rangoon, Calcutta and other Indian towns). The Bai-u are now regarded as resulting from the stagnation of a front formed between the Okhotsk air mass (mP) to the north (wet and cold) and the warm moist Ogasawara air mass (mT) to the south. The second rainfall maximum coming in September is due to a some-what similar front between the Siberian air mass which has now estab-lished itself over the continent (cP) and the Ogasawara mass (mT). It is also helped by the typhoons which travel along this frontal zone.

On the whole the rainfall of Japan is greatest along the south coast, where it may exceed 80 inches, and decreases northwards to less than 30 in northern Hokkaido, but the west coast has a very wet strip due to the winter rains. Throughout the length of Japan the interior valleys (including that portion which constitutes the Inland Sea) are drier than either of the coasts.

Climatic Regions. In the first edition of this book it was remarked that the complicated relief of Japan resulted in rapid and marked local

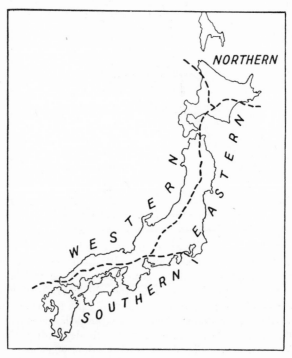

Fig. 330.—The main climatic regions of Japan

variations in climate but that four broad climatic regions could be distinguished as in Fig. 330.[1]

    (*a*) *Southern Japan* or the sub-tropical region embraces the islands of Kyushu and Shikoku as well as of Honshu or Mainland as far north as 35° N.—that is, roughly, to the south of the main divide. This region includes all the country round the

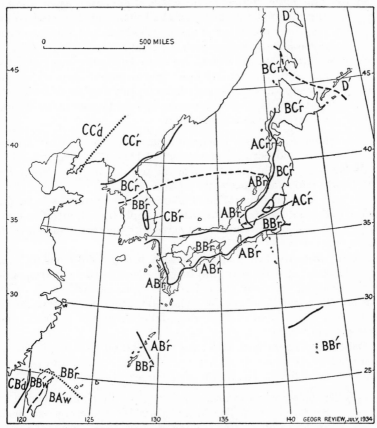

Fig. 331.—The climatic regions of Japan according to Thornthwaite's scheme
For explanation of lettering, see Fig. 20.

    Inland Sea and the south coast. The winters are mild (January average about 40° or 45° F.) and dry, the summers hot (July average 75°–80° F.). Although the winters are colder, it is perhaps better to include the Tokyo Plain in Southern Japan, since the winters are not so cold as to prevent winter sowing of crops.

  [1] Japanese geographers now prefer a division into the four climatic provinces of Hokkaido, Tohoku (or northern Honshu), Pacific with Inland Sea, and Japan Sea.

(b) *Eastern Japan*, embracing Honshu east of the main divide, north of 35° N., and including a small part of southern Hokkaido. The winters are dry but cold, owing to the influence of the cold Okhotsk current. Over the northern half of the area the January temperature is below freezing point (25°–32° F.), over the southern half about 32°–38° F.

(c) *Western Japan*, embracing the whole of the west coast of Honshu and the southern portion of Hokkaido, and characterized by the winter precipitation and by cloudiness and fog. The north is considerably colder than the south.

(d) *Northern Japan*, or strictly northern Hokkaido, together with Sakhalin, has bitterly cold raw winters (below 25° F. in January) and rather cool summers (July average, 66°–68° F.). The same type of climate may be said to exist in the Alpine region in the heart of Honshu.

According to Köppen's scheme (see Fig. 19) Hokkaido, the extreme north and northern mountains of Honshu belong to his Dfc (sub-arctic, constantly moist), whilst the rest of Japan belongs to his Cfa (warm temperate, constantly moist).

Shortly after the publication of Thornthwaite's general scheme (as shown in Fig. 20) an attempt was made to apply it, with modifications, to Japan, but Thornthwaite did not agree with the results and drew up the detailed scheme shown in Fig. 331.

Apart from the fact that the division between AB′r and BC′r is placed somewhat to the west, this scheme shows a general correspondence with Fig. 330—Western Japan comprising AB′r and AC′r, Eastern BC′r, and Southern BB′r and AB′r. Hokkaido appears to be generously treated, and one feels doubtful of the justice of placing the Western and Southern coasts together.

Natural Vegetation. The natural vegetation of Japan is forest; as a result of the mountainous nature of the surface two-thirds actually remains under forest. The forests of Japan are of three types:

(a) The sub-tropical forests, which occupy the climatic region of Southern Japan. They include broad-leaved evergreens, such as the camphor tree (*Cinnamomum camphora*), evergreen oaks (*Quercus abuta*) and *Pasania cupidata*, as well as deciduous oaks (*Q. serrata* and *Q. glandulifera*) and several species of pines.

(b) The temperate forests, which occupy the climatic regions of Eastern and Western Japan, and which are mixed coniferous and deciduous forests. Conifers include *Cryptomeria japonica*, *Chamaecyparis obtusa*, *C. pisifera*, *Tsuga sieboldii*, *Abies firma* and several species of pine; the deciduous trees include oaks, chestnuts, maples, *Zelkowa serrata*, *Fagus sylvatica* and *Magnolia*. These forests are economically the most important in

Japan and are now found especially on the mountain slopes overlooking the Sea of Japan on the one hand and the Pacific on the other.

(c) The cold temperate forests which cover a large part of Hokkaido and occur also above 4,000 or 5,000 feet on the mountains of Honshu. They are coniferous forests and the trees include *Abies veitchii, A. sachalinensis, Picea jezoensis, Larix kurilensis* and also the 'creeping-pines' (*Pinus pumila*) of the high mountains of Honshu.

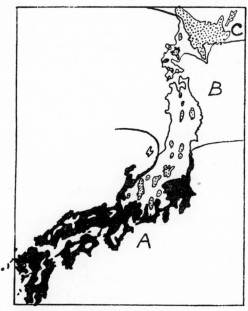

FIG. 332.—Map showing the forest and soil belts of Japan

A. The Zone of Sub-Tropical Forests with red and yellow soils.
B. The Zone of Temperate Forests with brown forest soils.
C. The Zone of Boreal Forests with podsolized, partly podsolized, and bog soils.

(*After* O. N. Mikhailovska.)

Investigations have shown a close correlation between these vegetation belts and soil types.

(a) Yellow and red soils occur in the sub-tropical forests.

(b) Brown and slightly podsolized soils occur in the temperate forests

(c) Podsols occur in the cold temperate or boreal forests.

In Japan proper there are roughly 63,000,000 acres of forest—more than two-thirds of the total land area of 91,000,000 acres. Half are privately owned, a third by the State, the rest by communities of different sorts. A quarter of the forest land is artificial (i.e. planted).

Much attention has been paid in recent years to scientific forestry, and Japan's forests form one of her great natural assets. In recent years the forests yielded 1,400,000,000 cubic feet of timber, also faggots, bamboo, and various by-products (especially charcoal). Of the timber trees there are three of special importance. Sugi (*Cryptomeria japonica*) represents over a quarter of the total quantity of timber and over 40 per cent. of the value; pine more than a fifth of the quantity and of the value; Hinoki (*Chamaecyparis obtusa*) only 4 per cent. of the quantity, but over 9 per cent. of the value.

Despite the area and importance of her forests, Japan figures on the balance as a timber importer.

Agriculture in Japan. From time immemorial rice cultivation has been the prime occupation in Japan, and the country was essentially an agricultural one. Within the last half-century changes of the most far-reaching character have taken place. It is unnecessary to stress the westernization and industrialization of Japan—these are too familiar to require emphasis. The point to be stressed is the rapid growth of the population which from 1720 to 1840 had remained practically constant at 30,000,000, but which, by 1950, had risen to 83,200,000. From a self-supporting country Japan has become one dependent upon imported foodstuffs and raw materials and one in which the population problem is extremely acute. The position may be judged by comparison with England and Wales. There are in Japan (World Agricultural Census, 1950) 12·6 million acres of cultivated land (or 15·5 including pasture) to support 83,200,000 people; in England and Wales 24 million acres of arable land and permanent pasture to support 44,000,000 people. For each person in Japan there is only 0·2 acre of farmland; in England and Wales 0·55 acre. Yet in England and Wales only about 55 per cent. of the foodstuffs required are produced at home. Even allowing for a lower standard of living the utter dependence of Japan on food supplies from outside the country is at once apparent. The Japanese farming families number 5,875,000 (1962), so that the average size of a farm is only a little over 2½ acres. Out of this 2·05 acres are devoted to cropland but owing to double cropping 3·1 acres are harvested. Even in Hokkaido the average area per family is only 7½ acres.

Great changes in cultivation have taken place since the end of the Second World War. Although hand labour is still important by 1964 30 per cent. of Japan's farmers owned their own powered cultivators (hand tractors) and many more hired them as required or used communally owned ones. It is now rare to see horses or oxen used in cultivation. Much that has been said as to Chinese agriculture applies also to Japan; human excreta, farmyard manure, fish guano, wood ash and rice bran are, or were, the chief types of manure. Phosphate manures are manufactured from phosphatic rocks imported from Christmas

Island (Indian Ocean) and the islands of Oceania. Although from 1880 to 1950 there was only a 12 per cent. increase in the area of arable land, yield of rice was nearly doubled. The manufacture of chemical fertilizers is now one of the country's major industries.

In 1872, when the feudal system of government was peacefully replaced by the Imperial régime, a great change was effected in the land system. Before that date the feudal lords and their vassals owned the land and let it to the farmers. In the peaceful revolution of 1872 the land passed into the possession of the tenants. About three-fifths of the arable land is now cultivated by peasant proprietors. Later years saw the rise of a *nouveaux riches* class of landowners, perhaps less considerate to their tenants than the old feudal lords. It should be noted that the owner of 75 acres would be classed as a great landowner. In 1945 General MacArthur, head of the American occupying forces, ordered all large estates to be divided up for sale to the peasants. Over 5,000,000 acres were redistributed from 2,440,000 landlords to 4,260,000 tenant farmers, but nearly 2,000,000 farmers still had less than $1\frac{1}{4}$ acres. In order to economize valuable land villages are often built on steep hillsides and terracing is practised wherever possible. Nevertheless, great waste results from excessive fragmentation of holdings (compare India) and progress is slow in consolidating over 90,000,000 separate strips.

Rice is, *par excellence*, the staple farm product of Japan. Cultivation is almost entirely in irrigated paddy-fields, the production in ordinary dry fields being insignificant. As a second crop wheat, barley, rape, beans and peas are grown. The principal crops in upland farms are wheat, barley, rye, buckwheat, sweet potatoes, as well as vegetables, fruits, etc. Amongst the crops of comparatively recent introduction are oats, flax, onions, cabbage, asparagus, as well as, surprising as it may seem from the association of Japan with cherry blossom, apples, cherries and small fruit. Tobacco growing is a Government monopoly. Cotton has almost gone out of cultivation and so has indigo. The clearcut distinction between paddy-fields and fields for other crops is recognized in the official classification of arable land into 'rice-fields' and 'fields for other cereals',[1] in addition to which there are 'pastures' and 'plains' (Genya). The 'genya' are regions with an inferior soil situated at high levels, naturally covered with a growth of bushes but used for raising weeds for manure, growing fodder (one-third of whole) or for pasture. Rice occupies 59 per cent. of the cultivated area, but because much land is double cropped—the barley and wheat being grown in the paddy-fields—this is reduced to almost 40 per cent. of crop area. Though the yield is the highest in Asia at about $1\frac{1}{2}$ tons per acre, it is below that of European countries.

For irrigation of paddy-fields, rivers supply water for over 64 per

[1] The first is the 'ta', or wet cultivation, the second the 'hata', or dry cultivation.

cent., reservoirs for 21 per cent. and old-fashioned primitive methods of irrigation supply water for most of the remainder. The raising of winter crops—naked barley, wheat, rape and various millets—is by no means universal on the paddy lands. In recent years not only has the acreage under rice steadily increased but so has the yield. In round figures the annual yield of rice is 250,000,000 bushels, which is about 40,000,000 bushels less than the domestic consumption, including that required for the manufacture of saké.

The chief secondary grains are wheat, barley and rye, occupying together about 28 per cent. of the crop area, or two-thirds that of rice. Wheat is now decreasing; 1·5 m. tons in 1953, 0·7 m. in 1963. The soy or soya bean is used, not only for human consumption, but also to make soy—essential in Japanese cooking—soup and *tofu*—a bean curd with the consistency of cream cheese and a popular and important article of diet.[1]

The sweet potato, important because of its high calorific value, is a leading crop of the uplands. It is naturally sub-tropical and does not flower in Japan itself. In consequence Okinawa was the former centre of breeding. By way of contrast a third of all the ordinary potatoes are grown in Hokkaido.

Tea occupies a decreasing acreage—now under 27,000 hectares, or 67,000 acres—but there are over 10,000 small manufactories and efficiency has increased the output. Most of the tea produced is green tea, especially the variety known as Sencha. The tea gardens are in South Japan.

Special interest attaches to the sericulture of Japan. The position occupied by sericulture in Japanese agriculture bears a strong similarity to that taken by poultry-farming in mixed farms of Europe and America. It is carried on by farmers as an adjunct to crop-raising, the farmer's wife and children supplying much of the skilled labour necessary. The female of *Bombyx mori* is a sluggish moth which lays about 500 eggs and then dies. The minute eggs are covered with a gelatinous material and are usually washed before being incubated. For incubation the eggs are kept for eleven months at an even temperature of 64° F. The worms are about one-twelfth inch long when hatched, and are born with ravenous appetites. They feed for four days before becoming torpid, bursting their skins and starting afresh. During their brief life of seven weeks the skin is shed four times. Although the worms themselves can be, and are, kept under glass, a genial spring is still of very great importance in providing a continuous supply of fresh mulberry leaves. Each pound of eggs will require about 10 tons of leaves, so that every spring the silkworms of Japan consume 4,000,000 tons of fresh young mulberry leaves, thirty or forty trees being needed to yield

[1] For details of the distribution of the various crops see G. T. Trewartha, *Japan*, with an excellent series of crop-distribution maps.

1 ton of leaves. Hence mulberry trees once occupied 1,750,000 acres. If the worms themselves are kept out in the open a minimum average temperature of at least 60° from April onwards is required. When fully grown each caterpillar should be placed by hand on clean straw or twigs in a suitable position. It is unnecessary to emphasize further the skill and patience required at every stage in the production of raw silk. Not only must labour be abundant and cheap, but inherited delicacy of manipulation is virtually a necessity. The fact that silkworm rearing is essentially dependent upon skilled manual labour has been a vital factor in the prosperity of this industry in Japan, as it has baffled the inventive ingenuity of Western nations to devise labour-saving substitutes for skilled human manipulation. The discovery that the hatching season may be freely regulated by keeping the eggs in cool places has made it possible to undertake summer and autumn rearing and to double the output of cocoons. At present, since sericulture has seldom succeeded when conducted on a large scale, it seems specially designed to assist the otherwise hard-driven small farmer. Lack of uniformity as to the quality of the filaments is the chief drawback of the present domestic system of sericulture. The production of cocoons in Japan (including Korea) in 1921–5 averaged 260,000 metric tons out of a world's total (excluding China) of 350,000 metric tons. Amazing progress was then made so that production in the thirties rose to over 400,000 tons. The importance of the summer crop is shown by the following table:

	Spring eggs, %	Spring cocoons, %	Autumn eggs, %	Autumn cocoons, %
1909–13	52·5	60	47·5	40
1925	43	48	57	52
1927	40·5	50·8	59·5	49·2
1936	44·7	50·0	55·3	50·0

Whilst the yield of silk from spring cocoons is greater than from autumn cocoons, more than half Japan's silk is now obtained from the later crop, safe from the vagaries of spring. There has also been a remarkable increase of yield of silk per unit weight of eggs incubated. Roughly 1 lb. of raw silk is obtained from 10 to 11 lb. of cocoons. It is scarcely necessary to add that there is now very little hand reeling of silk.

To restore the industry after the war, the Ministry of Agriculture was ordered by the American Occupying Forces to plant 50,000,000 mulberry trees. By 1963 production of pure silk yarn was back to 9,725,300 lb. and of pure silk fabrics 141,655,000 square metres.

Owing to the lack of pasturage Japan is not a great stockbreeding country. Among horses native-breds have largely given place to cross-breds, stallions being imported from Australia and England. Similarly the native horned cattle are being replaced by cross-breds. Devon, Ayrshire and Shorthorn cattle were imported and, more recently, Holstein and Simmenthal. The increased demand for dairy produce has given rise to the breeding of dairy cows, and of the 1964 total of 3,446,000 cattle, one-third were dairy cattle. Sheep, goats and pigs are all, however, being bred in increasing numbers. In 1916 there were only 3,000 sheep—almost entirely on Government farms. In 1953 there were 700,000 but only 274,000 in 1964. In the same period pigs have increased from 327,000 to over 3·4 million (1964).

CROPS OF JAPAN—1960

	Area 1,000 acres	Percentage to total farmland
Rice	8,272	51·9
Wheat	1,505	9·5
Barley	2,095	13·2
Beans	800	5·0
Sweet potato . . .	825	5·2
White potato . . .	510	3·2
Vegetables	1,136	6·0
Fruits	532	3·3
Mulberry	410	2·6
Tea	121	0·8
Total farmland . . .	15,935	100·0
Total arable and orchard .	13,200	

Fisheries. The continental shelf around Japan is one of the great fishing-grounds of the world and fish forms an important supplement to the diet of rice and vegetables.[1] The Buddhist aversion to a meat diet has tended to confirm the importance of the fisheries. Upwards of 400,000 boats, mostly small open craft, are engaged on the Japanese fishing-grounds, but steam trawlers are gradually coming into use. Nearly 600,000 people are engaged in the fishing industry, including 200,000 women and children. The annual catch of 4–5,000,000 tons is a sixth of the world's total. The chief food fishes include herring, sardine and anchovy, mackerel, bonito, tunny, yellow tail, sea bream, cuttle-fish, flatfish, squid and octopus, lobsters, prawns, etc. In addition to the food fish, secondary products are worth large sums annually; fish guano, dried bonito, dried cuttle-fish and squid being some of the chief items. Sea-cucumber or bêche-de-mer is found round the coasts of Honshu and in Hokkaido and was formerly exported to China, together with sharks' fins. Seaweeds are collected and dried

---

[1] For a good map see Ada Espenshade, *Geog. Rev.*, **39**, 1949, 77. The Japanese also have distant whaling and 12 per cent. of the fish catch—including salmon and crab for canning—is from distant waters.

and sold as a relish for soup, fish or rice. Seaweed is also turned into a kind of jelly as well as being used in the manufacture of isinglass. Japan developed a unique industry in the breeding of pearl oysters and of 'culture pearls'. Grains of mother-of-pearl are introduced between the shells of three-year-old oysters, causing the oyster to secrete a pearl round the irritating body. In four years a pearl of considerable size is formed and is indistinguishable from a pearl naturally formed. These 'culture pearls' are grown on rafts in the Bay of Ago, where Mr. Mikimoto had the monopoly before the Second World War temporarily ruined the business, now again on the upgrade.

Industry. The industrial revolution in Japan—the replacement of household industry by the factory system and of handwork by machines —made the most marked strides after the war with China in 1894–5. The change was most conspicuous in the spinning industries.

The Russo-Japanese War (1904–5) brought into prominence the chemical industries, whilst during the First World War all Japanese industries were stimulated into great activity and reached a state of amazing prosperity, Japanese goods obtaining a firm hold on all Eastern markets. In the first instance a slavish imitator of Western ideas, Japan has long since shown her own creative genius in the field of industry and can no longer be regarded as an imitator. The appalling disaster of 1923 seriously dislocated Japan's industry and trade: Yokohama silk mercers migrated temporarily to Kobe and Osaka. There was a decline in the years which followed, but from about 1925 to the present, despite the depressions and war, there has been a steady increase in the number of factories and output (only a few are now run by manual power).

Hydroelectric Power. In a mountainous country such as Japan, with a good rainfall and numerous swift streams and at the same time a country deficient in coal, it is not surprising that extensive use should have been made of water-power resources. The development dates from 1891 and the war with China in 1894–5 acted as a spur. The electrical undertakings in operation at the end of 1924 numbered 4,472, developing 2,230,000 kilowatts, of which 1,470,000 kw. represented water-power. By 1933 this had increased to 67,400 developing 5,000,000 kw., of which 3,110,000 kw. represented water-power. By 1951 the figures were 10,523,000 kw., of which 6,559,000 were hydroelectric, and consumption in 1952 was 51,647 million kwh., of which 40,327 million were hydroelectric. There are, theoretically, large reserves of power awaiting development. Of rivers draining to the Japan Sea the following are the most important: Shinano, Agano (each capable of developing over half a million horse-power), Jintsu, Kurobe, Sho, Mogami, Hime, Kuzuryu, Joganji and Tetori. Of those draining into the Pacific Ocean, the Kiso, Tenryu (both over 500,000 h.p.), Fuji, Tone, Oh-i, Kitakami, Abukuma, Yoshino and Kumano are the chief. It will be noted that these rivers are all conveniently situated for the chief power-using centres—the eastern zone with Tokyo and Yokohama and the western zone with Nagoya, Kyoto, Osaka and Kobe.

Can Japan Develop Industrially? Under this title Dr. J. E. Orchard presented some years ago [1] an impartial survey of Japan's industrial position, and shortly afterwards elaborated the subject in an invaluable book.[2] He pointed out that Japan was attempting to solve her population problem as Britain did a century or more ago—by becoming the 'England of Asia', making every effort for the encouragement of industrialization and distributing her manufactured goods to all the markets of the world in exchange for foodstuffs and raw materials.

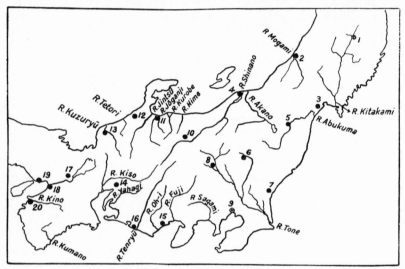

Fig. 333.—Principal hydroelectric schemes in Middle Japan

Enormous progress has been made in industry: Japan increased her foreign trade during the great depression, whereas that of every other great power declined. But Japan faced difficulties such as England never had. Resources in iron and steel—the bases of modern industry—are poor, resources in most raw materials except silk are limited, and Japan entered into a world already highly industrialized and every year becoming more so. It is interesting to compare the assessment made by E. A. Ackerman in 1953.[3] He contends that it will be necessary for 'the Japanese to become more efficient in production than any nation in history has been'.

Though supplies of coal are reasonable and of hydroelectric power

[1] *Geog. Rev.*, **19,** 1929, 177–200.
[2] *Japan's Economic Position* (New York, 1930). See also Freda Utley, *Japan's Feet of Clay* (London, 1936).
[3] *Japan's Natural Resources* (University of Chicago Press, 1953).

good, the lack of industrial raw materials remains acute. Over half of the country's needs in wood and fibres, half the iron, all the aluminium and many other vital items must be imported. They must be paid for, like the food required, in exports of manufactures.

The Manufacturing Regions of Japan. Japan's manufacturing belt extends, as shown in Fig. 334, from Nagasaki and northern Kyushu and the western entrance to Setouchi (the Inland Sea), along both shores of that sea and to the Tokyo Plain in the east.

There are four main foci within this belt:

(1) The Tokyo Industrial Region, roughly coincident with the Kwanto or Tokyo Plain and centring around Tokyo and

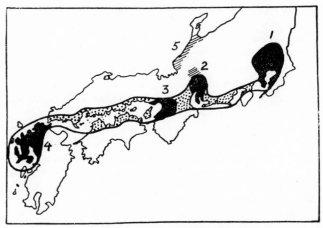

FIG. 334.—The manufacturing belt of Japan

The four main foci are shown in solid black; the numbers correspond with the regions listed in the text. The area marked 5 is that important for silk-weaving.

Yokohama. A great variety of manufactures are carried on here, and this is pre-eminently the region of small industries and small factories.

(2) The Ise Bay or Nagoya Industrial Region, with its main centre at Nagoya, is concerned especially with the reeling of raw silk, cotton and porcelain.

(3) The Kobe-Osaka Region, at the eastern end of the Inland Sea, produces a third of all the manufactured goods of Japan, Osaka being the great cotton centre, and having many other industries, notably the manufacture of small metal goods and machinery.

(4) The Northern Kyushu Region, situated on or near the coal-fields of Kyushu and conveniently placed for the import of iron ore or pig-iron from overseas, is associated with the heavy industries; the textile industry is unimportant.

The Textile Industries. The early history of the Japanese cotton industry was one of continuous expansion. From 1912 to 1934 not a single
year passed without an increase in the number of spinning mills and
spindles—from 147 mills with 2½ million spindles in 1912 to 267 mills
with over 9 million spindles in 1933. In addition there were the Japanese
mills in China (especially Shanghai)—over 2 million spindles—and in
Manchuria. The development in Japan is all the more remarkable as
Japan has had to depend upon foreign supplies of raw material and
machinery. The raw cotton comes from India, the United States, China
and Egypt, the first two supplying 80 to 90 per cent. of the total. Of
later years there was a marked tendency to the spinning of finer counts
with a consequent rise in imports from the United States and a lower
or stationary demand for the coarse Indian cotton. Cotton-weaving is
a somewhat later development but is now as important as the spinning.
The textiles—both cotton and silk—intended for domestic consumption are made in widths often of only one foot and the specialization
for export is a noteworthy feature of Japanese industry. In this, too,
there is a marked flexibility. Until about 1924 China took half of
Japan's export. In the next eight years the value of the goods purchased
by China fell to one-fifth of the 1924 total, whilst production within
China trebled. Japan sought new markets and found them in India,
the East Indies, South Africa and the Near East. But India was already
making her own coarse cloths, and so Japan specialized in the finer
materials, thus clashing directly with Lancashire's exports. During the
great depression of the thirties the Japanese industry went ahead
unchecked: the output of cotton cloth leapt from 1,500,000,000 square
yards in 1932 to nearly 1,800,000,000 in 1934. Severely hit during the
war, the industry was reduced to about a fifth of its strength in 1945 but
had recovered by 1954 to turn out 2,810,000,000 square yards of cloth,
of which a third was exported.

The lack of raw materials, machinery and skilled labour retarded
the development of a woollen industry, although it was started as long
ago as 1876 by a Government factory. Again, the First World War
provided the necessary stimulus—not only because of the demand for
woollen cloths for uniforms but because of the disappearance of the light
fabrics previously made in France and Germany especially for Far
Eastern markets. The export of these light fabrics from Japan first
appears in returns for the year 1905; imports appear for the last time
in 1917.

Japanese production of rayon or artificial silk started in 1919 and
the output increased by at least 30 per cent. yearly for many years.
The really phenomenal rise was from 90 million lb. in 1933 to over 140
million in 1934, so that Japan became second only to the United States
in this industry. By 1936 Japan led the world. Yet the industry had to
fight the opposition of the silk manufacturers and the prejudice of the

purchasing public. Both have been overcome and the industry is located in famous silk centres such as Kanazawa and Fukui on the Japan Sea Littoral, at Kyoto and in the northern part of the Kwanto industrial region. Even here Japan has another industry dependent mainly on imported raw materials—wood-pulp from Canada—against a small quantity of home wood-pulp from the north. But Japan has introduced soft shiny rayon for the first time to such poverty-bound but inherent lovers of the luxurious as the Ethiopians, the natives of the Congo and the 'savages' of Borneo. The industry was reduced to 30 per cent. during the war but by 1953 was producing over 1,000,000 square yards of rayon or rayon mixture cloths. Though far below the United States, Japan is now the world's second producer.

The silk industry occupies a position different from that of cotton. It is not an industry imported from the West but one indigenous to the country. The rearing of silkworms is a branch of agriculture, the reeling of silk is a simple mechanical process requiring skill and patience but little power and no complicated machinery. The product, raw silk, is in reality a raw material—the one raw material exported in large quantity from Japan. As much as 80 per cent. of the silk produced used in some years to be exported—especially to the United States. In the silk-weaving industry a distinction must be made between the heavy and often costly fabrics—satins, silk crêpes and brocades—for the domestic market, which are produced generally by women on hand-machines, and the cheaper, lighter fabrics made almost exclusively for export. The thin 'Jap silk' and 'Fuji' so well known abroad were rarely used in the country itself. Although silk spinning is separate, weaving may be carried on as a subsidiary business by the cotton-mills, but silk-weaving business is also a semi-domestic one and carried on largely *outside* the main industrial belt. Thus the Fukui and Ishikawa prefectures, along the north coast, produce a third of the output.

It was estimated that 22 per cent. of all industrial capital in 1954 was invested in the textile industries. Iron, steel and machinery ranked second with 18 per cent. Textiles have since decreased relatively.

The Paper Industry. Japan from very early times has produced a variety of hand-made papers, but the modern factory industry dates from 1872, and is now one of the major ones of the country. The output exceeds a million tons of paper and cardboard. The pulp is produced in Hokkaido, but is supplemented by an import from Canada and the United States.

The Chemical and Associated Industries. The chemical industry has been described as the 'most polygamous of all industries' in that its products are required by nearly all other industries. Thus the products are very varied: the availability of cheap hydroelectric power favours the electro-chemical production of fertilizers, calcium carbide, caustic soda, bleaching powder, electrolytic copper, etc. The extensive production of glass and glassware, dyestuffs, matches, paper, celluloid, soaps, etc., is to be regarded in part as an offshoot of the chemical industries.

The Iron and Steel and Engineering Industries. The difficulty of the iron and steel industry and its size have been noted. There are numerous iron-using industries—including new electrical machinery, ship-building, locomotive works and locomotives. The manufacture of toys has changed from a domestic to a factory industry: bicycles once imported in large numbers are now exported in huge numbers to China, the South Sea Islands and many Asiatic countries.

Other Industries. An old and important industry is the manufacture of porcelain and pottery. Japanese lacquer is also well known in most parts of the world. Cement, brewing (of both beer and saké), flour milling, sugar refining, preparation of oils, fats and waxes, rubber goods, leather goods, mats, brushes and bamboo are all significant. Hokkaido has developed an interesting production of peppermint.

The Population of Japan. 'Japan labours with a perplexing problem. Her population is increasing at a rate so rapid that it threatens soon to pass beyond the productive capacity of the nation's soil and resources. Pressure of the population on subsistence is the basis of the present economic unrest within the country. Search for relief is the keynote of Japan's domestic and foreign politics.' So wrote Professor Orchard as long ago as 1928.[1] The rapid increase dates from the sixties and seventies of last century, but it was in the nineteen-twenties that the position became serious. In 1925 the net increase for Japan proper was 875,000; in 1926 over 900,000; in 1927 over a million. In the next four years the annual increase averaged nearly 900,000; in 1932 it again exceeded a million; in each year, 1932–40, well over a million. The net increase has been 1·2 per cent. per annum, and at that rate the population doubles in 40 years. No longer is the rapid increase regarded with pride as evidence of a vigorous nation; such sentiments are overruled by the fear for the food supply. For many years the *per capita* consumption of the staple food, rice, has been about 5½ bushels, whilst the yield of Japanese paddy-fields is about 38 bushels per acre. The 7,000,000 acres under rice could thus support about 50,000,000 people, but the new acreage being brought under rice annually is only sufficient to support about a quarter of the actual increase. Up to the present internal reorganization has supplied much of the increasing need of foodstuffs and, despite a definite increase in the standard of living, only 10 per cent. of the food consumed within the country is imported. But this cannot continue.

The increasing urbanization of Japan has lowered rather than increased the death-rate. Turning to solutions of Japan's population

[1] J. E. Orchard, 'The Pressure of Population in Japan', *Geog. Rev.*, **18,** 1928, 374–401.

problem, the physical configuration of Japan proper prevents extensive agricultural expansion; even in Hokkaido the amount of available land is but small and the very rigorous winters are not only hated by the Japanese but demand a radical alteration in the mode of living. It has been officially stated that Hokkaido cannot support more than another 2,000,000. The climate of Korea was more to the liking of the Japanese, but Korea was already rather densely populated (238 per square mile in 1931) and the Japanese farmer could not compete with the Korean farmer, with a far lower standard of living. The Japanese in Korea were mainly merchants and town-dwellers. Land in Formosa suitable for occupation and cultivation was strictly limited. Thus these parts of the pre-1945 Empire had strict limitations.

For many years Manchuria was regarded by the Japanese as 'the land of promise', and Japan obtained a footing in the region after the war with Russia (1904–5) by taking over the lease of the Liaotung Peninsula (1,500 square miles) and the control of the South Manchuria Railway. The Japanese Government announced its intention of settling 1,000,000 colonists in the territory under her control within ten years, but twenty years later there were less than 100,000 Japanese in the peninsula (nearly all living in the cities of Dairen and Port Arthur), about the same number in the railway zone and about 35,000 in other parts of Manchuria—less than half being farmers. Despite the ties of the family system which prevented rapid Chinese settlement in Manchuria, it is the Chinese who made the greater strides in settlement. Apart from the difficulties of competing with the Chinese farmer, with a lower standard of living, the Japanese farmer did not take kindly to the rigorous Manchurian winters.

Despite the population pressure at home, Japanese emigration to foreign lands has always been small compared with that from many European countries. An official record is kept of Japanese emigrants or 'Japanese resident abroad'—the total number was less than a million in 1936. The main field of Japanese emigration was then to the Brazilian plateau. To this area the migrants averaged 10,000 per year, more than half the total emigrating. Many Japanese lived in the Hawaiian Islands and on the Pacific coast of the United States and in 1950 they still numbered 185,000 and 142,000 in those two areas.

The post-war years have been marked by a phenomenal drop in the birth-rate—from 34 per 1,000 in 1950 to only 19 per 1,000 in 1955. Though the death-rate has also dropped phenomenally—to 7·8 in 1955—the population by mid-1967 was regarded as likely to exceed 100,000,000.

Settlements. Throughout its history Japan has been essentially an agricultural country. Even with the modern dependence on industrialization 30 per cent. of the people are still farmers, and the commonest unit of settlement is the agricultural town with between 2,000 and

10,000 people. Nearly half the people live in villages or such towns. R. B. Hall in his study of rural settlement forms in Japan [1] finds that in the rice lands there is an even distribution of small compact villages except where areas are liable to violent floods when there are isolated settlements on safe or dry spots (dry-point settlements). In areas of dry-crop cultivation the farms are disseminated. The Japanese home is the plot of land: the house is almost subsidiary to it; the walls are for winter use and are partly movable in the summer, so that the living-rooms become part of the garden. This renders the house, to Western ideas, ill adapted for the cold of winter. The house is essentially a light wood-bamboo structure, unaffected by earthquakes but liable to fire very easily. It is basically of three rooms, but a house is the home of a united family and increases in size accordingly.

Japanese towns have been divided by Trewartha into (a) the indigenous towns, and (b) the six metropoles. The indigenous towns present a flat appearance with small, closely spaced individual family houses, the only large buildings being the temples and, where present, the castle. Many of these 'indigenous' towns are daimyo towns—that is, they date from the days of feudal Japan when the local lord or daimyo ruled from his castle which was surrounded by the quarters of the samurai or soldiers, and became the nucleus of a large civilian settlement. Other cities are religious centres or shrine cities; others are 'post' cities on main highways. There are also the old 'free' ports—free in the sense that they were controlled by the resident merchants.

Japan owes not a few of its cities to the ancient custom that each new Emperor should build a new capital on the death of his predecessor. Japan has thus actually had 60 capitals, mostly between Lake Biwa and the Inland Sea. By far the most important, however, is Kyoto, where the Court was established in A.D. 794 and remained till the revolution of 1868. It is today the western capital.

There are now (1965) 7 cities in Japan with over a million; 3 between 500,000 and a million; 41 with between 200,000 and 500,000. The great cities are Tokyo (8,527,000), Osaka (3,119,000), Nagoya (1,907,000), Kobe (1,196,000), Kyoto (1,376,000), and Yokohama (1,619,000). These figures show the populations in 1965, when, in contrast to 1950, the effects of war-time bombing had been overcome. Next in order of size are Kita-Kyushu (1,072,000) and Fukuoka (718,000) which, though growing very rapidly, has still much of the character of the group of 'indigenous' cities. The six great metropoles are strikingly Western in character, being modelled on American rather than European prototypes.

Tokyo between 1950 and 1955 surpassed London and New York as the largest city in the world.[2] A large section was destroyed by the earthquake of 1923, but the modern steel and concrete skyscrapers withstood the shocks. Tokyo is the business centre of the country as well as a manu-

---

[1] *Geog. Rev.*, **21**, 1931, 93–123.   [2] Population over 10 m. (Greater Tokyo).

facturing town. It is now continuous with the iron and steel centre, oil refining and modern port of Kawasaki which links it with Yokohama.

Yokohama was completely razed to the ground by the 1923 earthquake and the business of the port was transferred temporarily to Kobe, but the population by 1935 was nearly 50 per cent. greater than in 1920.

Osaka was primarily the port of Kyoto and its region but has supplanted the old inland centre in size and importance. It is preeminently the cotton town and hence is called the 'Manchester of Japan'. From another point of view, owing to the many waterways, it has been called the Venice of Japan.

Kobe is the deep-water port adjoining Osaka.

Nagoya and *Kyoto* both combine the ancient and modern, Kyoto in particular being famed for its many temples.

Communications. The first railway in Japan was built in 1872 between Tokyo and Yokohama, a distance of 18 miles. In 1933 the railway mileage was 13,500, or more than half that of the British Isles. The mileage in 1963 was about 17,500. A Railway Nationalization Programme was adopted in 1905–6, and three-quarters of the railways are State-owned. The gauge is 3 feet 6 inches but trains are fast and very efficiently run. The Tokyo suburban lines are electrified and the steep Usui Pass section is also electrically operated. Now most local lines and 17 per cent. of the State railways are electrified.

Japan has been slower than might have been expected in the adoption of motor transport—largely due to the mountainous nature of the country and to the difficulty of building and maintaining roads. In addition, land is very precious for food production. In 1953 only 850 out of 15,000 miles of national roads and 600 out of 70,000 miles of prefectural roads were fully paved. The other roads are often, indeed usually, too narrow for vehicles to pass without one stopping and drawing off. In 1932 there were about 100,000 motors in the country—two-thirds cars and one-third trucks. Most of the cars were taxis. Twenty years later, in 1953, the number was still under a million but it was exceeded the following year and in 1964 there were 1,285,000 cars and 1,960,000 trucks. Great use is made of 100,000 country buses.

Aerial transport has been developed mainly since the Second World War.

Japan has three great ports—Yokohama, Kobe and Osaka. These three handle 75 to 80 per cent. of the export trade and about 60 per cent. of the import trade. Kobe leads (about 33 per cent. of the total foreign trade), followed by Yokohama (20 per cent.) and Osaka. Nagoya, Tokyo and Moji each have about 3 or 4 per cent. of the foreign trade, so that the minor ports such as Kawasaki, Shimizu, Yokkaichi, Wakamatsu and Moji have in each case less than 1 per cent. of the foreign trade, though there may be a large coastal trade.

Japan's merchant marine exceeds 9,000,000 tons (1963) and Japan now leads the world in shipbuilding.

Foreign Trade. Reference has already been made to Japan's attempt to solve her population problem by becoming the outstanding manufacturing country of the East and by selling her manufactures in the world's markets to pay for her imports of foodstuffs and raw materials. Thus the expansion of her foreign trade has been an essential feature of Japanese policy for many years. The Japanese yen was put on a gold basis at Y1·00 = 24·5 pence in 1897, so that the trade expansion before the First World War is accurately shown in pounds sterling or in gold dollars:

	Value in million sterling		Value in million gold dollars	
	Imports	Exports	Imports	Exports
1891–5	11·51	12·61	55	60
1901–5	35·92	30·23	175	150
1906–10	46·40	43·70	230	215
1911–13	64·63	55·51	320	275
1925–9 [1]	213·48	187·55	1,050	925

[1] 1 yen = 1s. 10d., or 10·8 yen = £1.

The expansion after the First World War is shown in the diagram below, Fig. 335–6. Measured in yen Japanese foreign trade, unlike that of any other country, expanded continuously throughout the world depression (1931–4). The expansion of the export trade during the First World War was clearly due to the inability of European nations—

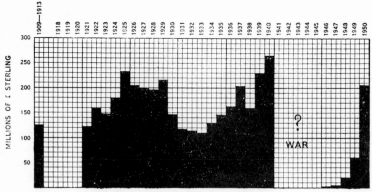

Fig. 335–6.—The fluctuations in the value of the exports of Japan
The value of the imports moved in sympathy.

including Great Britain—to feed the countries of the Orient (notably India) with textiles and other manufactures. Japan stepped into the breach. After that war some of the new markets were retained, others

1946
1947
1948
1949
1950
1951
1952
1953
1954
1955
1956
1957
1958
1959
1960
MILLIONS OF U.S. DOLLARS
4500
4000
3500
3000
2500
2000
1500
1000
500
0
EXPORTS
IMPORTS

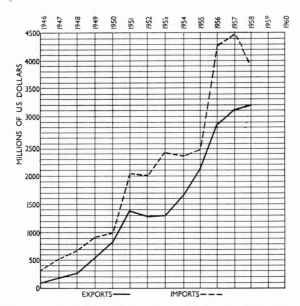

FIG. 337.—The revival of Japanese trade after World War II

Imports 1959, 3,600 m.; 1960, 4,491 m.; 1961, 5,810 m.; 1962, 4,546 m.; 1963, 6,736 m. Exports 1959, 3,456 m.; 1960, 4,054 m.; 1961, 4,236 m.; 1962, 4,787 m.; 1963, 5,447 m.

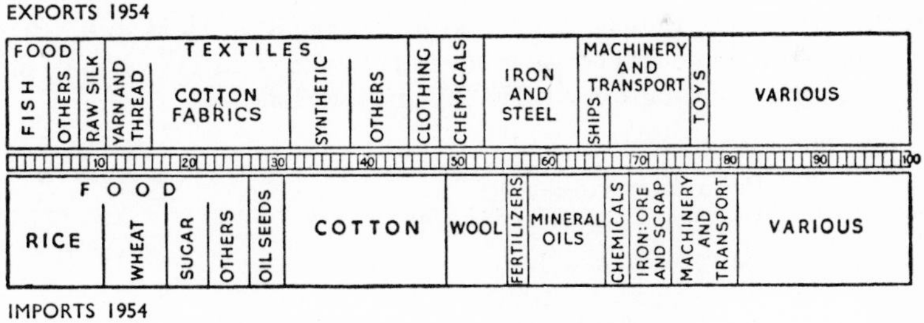

EXPORTS 1954
FOOD
FISH
OTHERS
RAW SILK
TEXTILES
YARN AND THREAD
COTTON FABRICS
SYNTHETIC
OTHERS
CLOTHING
CHEMICALS
IRON AND STEEL
MACHINERY AND TRANSPORT
SHIPS
TOYS
VARIOUS
10
20
30
40
50
60
70
80
90
100
FOOD
RICE
WHEAT
SUGAR
OTHERS
OIL SEEDS
COTTON
WOOL
FERTILIZERS
MINERAL OILS
CHEMICALS
IRON: ORE AND SCRAP
MACHINERY AND TRANSPORT
VARIOUS
IMPORTS 1954

FIG. 338—9.—The foreign trade of Japan

lost. Japan has sought continuously for new lands to which to send her manufactures, with the result that Japanese trade became almost world-wide. Before the First World War raw silk represented a third of all the exports, other silk another 10 per cent. A third of all the exports went to the United States, a quarter to China and 10 per cent. to France.

Fig. 338–9 show the position in 1954 since when there has been a marked decrease in the imports of corn and the exports of cotton goods. In 1963 the direction of foreign trade was as follows:

Imports. U.S.A. 30·8%, Australia 7·6%, Canada 4·7%, Malaysia 4·3%, Kuwait 3·7%, W. Germany 3·3%, Saudi Arabia 2·7%, India 2·4%, U.K. 2·2%, Iran 2·0%, Mexico 2·0%, U.S.S.R. 2·4%.

Exports. U.S.A. 27·6%, Hong Kong 4·5%, Thailand 3·3%, Malaysia 3·1%, S. Korea 2·9%, Australia 2·9%, India 2·9%, U.K. 2·9%, Philippines 2·8%, Ryukyus 2·5%, Liberia 2·4%, Canada 2·3%, W. Germany 2·1%, Taiwan 2·0%, U.S.S.R. 2·9%.

THE NATURAL REGIONS OF JAPAN

'Complexity and fineness of pattern are the keynote of the geology and geomorphology of Nippon.' So wrote G. T. Trewartha in his *Reconnaissance Geography of Japan.*[1] In view of the youthfulness of the Japanese relief and the exceptionally mountainous nature of the country, the human population is of necessity restricted to the small areas of lowland or plain and any regional division of the country based on human occupancy features must not only reflect the 'complexity and fineness of pattern' of the geomorphology, but any division so based must bear an unusually close correlation with that based on physical features. It is therefore difficult to suggest a division of Japan into natural regions without getting an inordinately large number. Fortunately an excellent detailed treatment of the regional subdivisions of Japan is now available in English and the account which follows is summarized essentially from Trewartha's work and may be looked upon as an introduction to his fuller account. It has not seemed necessary to deal as fully with the regions of Hokkaido, where a simpler division has been adopted, and in some areas Trewartha's subdivisions have been grouped. His scheme is as follows:

A. Hokkaido.
    1. Peninsular Hokkaido.
    2. Ishikari-Yufutsu Lowland.
    3. Eastern Hokkaido.
B. Ou (or Northern Honshu).
    1. Eastern Highlands.
    2. Eastern Lowlands.
    3. Central Mountain Range.
    4. Western Intermontane Basins.
    5. Western Mountains and Hills.
    6. Western Plains.

[1] University of Wisconsin Studies in the Social Sciences and History, 1934; later replaced by the same author's *Japan, a Physical, Cultural and Regional Geography* (University of Wisconsin Press, 1948, new edition, 1965).

C. Chubu (or Central Honshu).
1. Central Mountain Knot.
2. Lowlands of the Japan Sea Littoral.
3. Lowlands of the Pacific Coast (including the Kwanto or Tokyo Plain and the Nagoya Plain).
D. Inner Zone of South-west Japan.
1. Kinki or Eastern Setouchi.
2. Central Setouchi (Inland Sea).
3. Sanin Littoral.
4. Northern Kyushu.
E. Outer Zone of South-west Japan (Pacific Folded Mountains).
1. Southern Kyushu.
2. Southern Shikoku.
3. Kii Peninsula.

In most cases these subdivisions are actually groups of small units, thus the 'Western Intermontane Basins' of Ou comprise nine separate basins.

OU, TOHOKU OR NORTHERN HONSHU [1]

This division comprises the portion of Honshu lying north of approximately 37° and is thus the northern part of 'Old Japan'. Structurally and topographically it consists of the three north-south ranges separated by longitudinal depressions described on p. 618, and the limit of the region has been chosen on a topographical basis— where the ranges give place to the great Kwanto Plain. Climatically, most of the region has a January average below 32° and the frost-free season is 160 to 200 days. The southern limit also approximates roughly to the limit of the temperate forests (with deciduous trees predominating) and the brown soil region. There are contrasts between this northern region of Old Japan and Hokkaido in that farms are smaller, settlements are in the form of small villages rather than isolated farms. But when compared with regions farther south there are also marked differences—there are few large towns, only Niigata and Sendai having more than 350,000, whilst there are no first-class ports and manufacturing is poorly developed. Agriculturally there is little tea or sweet-potato cultivation; mulberry cultivation becomes unimportant about Lat. 39° or 40°.

1. **The Eastern Highlands** form part of the Outer Zone of

[1] Although the main administrative unit is the préfecture of which there are 46 the Japanese recognize nine administrative regions which are to a large extent natural regions. For example Tohoku is one.

Northern Japan mentioned on p. 618, and consist of two mountain masses, the Kitakami and the Abukuma, separated by the Sendai Lowland. The small population is found in the small valleys and on the tiny delta fans. In the old rocks of the northern hill mass is one of the two significant iron-ore deposits of Japan; adjacent to one of the intrusive masses of the southern hill mass is the copper deposit of

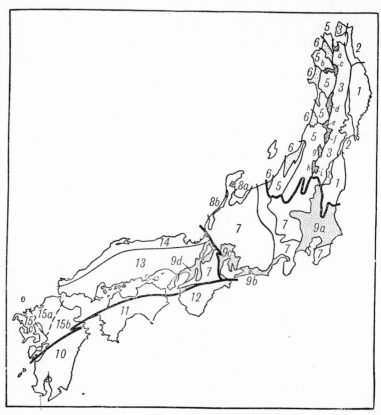

FIG. 340.—The natural regions of Japan

(*After* G. T. Trewartha.)

(Numbers correspond with textual descriptions.)

Hitachi. Along the coastal strip in the south is the Joban coalfield, the third in order of importance of the fields of Japan.

2. **The Eastern Lowlands** include three separate tracts : (*a*) the Mutsu Plain in the north; (*b*) the Kitakami or Sendai Lowland which separates the two hill masses just described and extends northwards to border the Kitakami hill mass; and (*c*) the Abukuma Lowland, a

river valley which borders the Abukuma Highland on the west. The northern area suggests certain comparisons with south-eastern Hokkaido—especially in the extensive horse breeding carried on in the moor-like areas. In the Kitakami Lowland the mulberry tree first appears, the low, wet, alluvial lands are occupied by wide stretches of paddy, but the winter cold prevents double cropping of the paddy lands with fall-sown crops. Where the plain reaches the coast is the famed resort of the pine-clad islands of Matsushima Bay, but the metropolis of the region, Sendai, is inland. Sendai is the seat of an important University and the largest city in northern Honshu, but is not a manufacturing town. The southern, Abukuma Lowland is warmer in winter, the mulberry is more abundant and winter cropping of paddy-fields is practised.

3. **The Central Mountain Range** is the climatic divide of the northern part of Japan and the range is accentuated by a line of seven fine volcanic piles, one at least reaching a height of over 6,000 feet. There are forest and mineral resources, but more important is the heavy precipitation which affords a source of irrigation water and of power to the basins lying to the east and to the west.

4. **The Western Intermontane Basins** are nine in number and form an irregular string west of the central divide. Each basin has a flood-plain floor and a small surrounding piedmont belt of alluvial fans. They have dark, gloomy winter weather with abundant snow which interrupts traffic and prevents the cultivation of winter wheat or barley. The houses have various devices against the heavy snow—wide eaves and covered side-walks. The basins from north to south are Aomori (with Aomori, the ferry port for Hokkaido through Hakodate), Hanawa, Odate, Yokote (the largest), Shinjo, Yamagata, Yonezawa, Wakamatsu, and Inawashiro. (These are numbered *a* to *i* on Fig. 340.)

5. **The Western Mountains and Hills** consist of an elongated mass with a crystalline core, the whole separated into a number of blocks by four transverse river-valleys. In the Dewa Hills are mineral deposits; among the foothills to the west, bordering the Japan Sea, are the small Akita oilfield and, farther south, the Niigata oilfield on the borders of the Echigo Plains.

6. **The Western Plains** suffer also from dark, stormy winter weather with much snow. The strong winter winds and the heavy seas have prevented the formation of a continuous coastal lowland; there is instead a succession of small infilled depressions. Natural harbours are naturally few; Niigata is the only considerable port-town. Rice is the chief crop; the winter weather prevents the cultivation of the winter cereals. Even the houses have to be protected against winter storms and large boulders are used to weigh down the roofs. From north to south the plains are: Tsugaru (Iwaki) (6*a*), Noshiro-Omono (6*b*), Shonai (Mogami) (6*c*), Echigo or Niigata (6*d*) and Takata (6*e*).

CHUBU, OR CENTRAL HONSHU

Chubu includes the broadest part of Honshu and is occupied mainly by a confused mass of mountains, mainly of volcanic origin. Through the centre of the knot, and running from coast to coast in a direction north-north-west to south-south-east, is the great rift valley referred to above as the Fossa Magna. It is partly filled with young volcanic rocks, including Fujiyama, and sediments. On the Pacific side of Chubu are three large bays of faulted origin; two of them now largely infilled and forming the very important Nobi and Kwanto Plains.

There is, of course, a marked difference between the Pacific and Japan Sea sides, but the whole region has abundant rain, long hot summers, a frost-free season of 180 to 260 days, a January average of well above freezing (and with minimum temperatures only a few degrees below). On the lowlands the sub-tropical woodlands of broad-leaved evergreen trees reach their poleward limit. Tea cultivation and mulberry trees reach their maximum, for more than half the acreage of mulberries is within this region, which is thus the focus of Japanese sericulture. Kwanto is the largest as well as the most densely populated of Japan's plains.

7. **The Central Mountain Knot** includes (*a*) the Fossa Magna and its associated volcanic piles, including Fuji; (*b*) the mountain masses to the east; and (*c*) to the west of the depression. Where the depression meets the Japan Sea is the natural 'back door' to the heart of the country, but formidable mountains guard the approach to Tokyo and the developed Pacific coast. Much of this country is famed for its hot mineral springs and there are many spas and resorts. The mountain streams supply water for electric-power installations, but the population is naturally concentrated in the frequent tiny basins. In many of these sericulture overshadows in importance the other activities of the farmers. The Suwa Basin [1] is thus the largest single silk filature centre in Japan. Each basin boasts a town of considerable size—often approaching or exceeding 100,000. The chief basins with their towns include Matsumoto (Matsumoto), Suwa (Okaya), Kofu (Kofu), Nagano (Nagano City, a famous Buddhist shrine), and Ueda.

Amongst the volcanic highlands east of the depression lies the celebrated town of Nikko, with its wonderful Buddhist temples, and Karuizawa, a hill station well known to foreign visitors. The Ashio mountains are noteworthy for one of the largest copper mines of the country.

Amongst the mountains of the west of the depression are numerous mining settlements.

8. **The Lowlands of the Japan Sea Littoral** lie on either side

[1] This basin has been made the subject of a detailed study by Trewartha—see *Geog. Rev.*, **20**, 1930, 224–44.

of the Noto Peninsula. To the east of the peninsula is the Toyama Alluvial Piedmont which differs from the other lowlands along the Japan Sea coast in that it is not a wet low area but a region of steep alluvial fans and lacks the wide belt of parallel beach ridges and dunes usually found. It is further a region of dispersed settlement—a feature indicative of comparatively recent utilization of the coarse rather poor soils. Despite the soil rice is the dominant crop. The different character of the coast is due to the protection afforded by the large rocky Noto Peninsula, and the local port, Fushiki, seeks its shelter also. Toyama and Takaoka are the two commercial centres, the former a textile town also.

To the west of the peninsula are narrow alluvial plains, protected from the strong winter winds by wind breaks of conifers planted along the beach ridges. Kanazawa, a silk-weaving town, is the metropolis of the plain and of the whole west coast of Honshu as well. Its industry is shared with Fukui and many smaller centres.

9. **The Lowlands of the Pacific Coast** include some of the most important parts of Japan.

9a. The *Kwanto* or *Tokyo Plain* has an area of rather over 2,500 square miles and supports over 22,000,000 people. A great depression in the solid rocks has become largely filled in with fresh-water or marine gravels, sands and clay, overlain by several feet of volcanic ash laid down in shallow water or subaerially. Slight elevation has resulted in steep bluffs along the river valleys and parts of the coast and two major terraces can be distinguished. The infertility of the recent ashes was partly responsible for the late settlement of the plain, which remained a wilderness whilst Kyoto was at the height of its glory. The development followed the establishment of the residence of the ruling Tokugawa Shoguns at Yedo (Tokyo) in the latter part of the sixteenth century. Even today, despite the enormous population, rural density is less than what it is on the older plains.

In some of the lower levels drainage is imperfect and villages are strung out along drainage dykes. Elsewhere, too, villages are of the 'Strassendorf' type because of the advantage of easy access to fields. In the easily irrigated lowlands rice is naturally the chief crop, but the paddy-fields lie fallow or with a leguminous fodder crop in the cool season. At slightly higher levels mulberry trees and dry crops take the place of rice. Large areas of slightly elevated ground have no rice at all, but are devoted to vegetables, beans, peas, sweet potatoes, millet, autumn-sown wheat and barley. Tea gardens occupy a small acreage and there are large tracts of specialized tobacco culture and many of the higher terraces are in woodland or moor.

At least a hundred cities and towns on the Kwanto Plain have over 30,000 inhabitants, but they are overshadowed by the great conurbation of Tokyo–Kawasaki–Yokohama. The industrial development since the Second World War of the whole area has been phenomenal but perhaps especially so at the new deep-water port of Kawasaki, now with 768,000 people. Tokyo is not only a convenient centre for the whole of Japan, but as ports Tokyo and Yokohama include within their hinterland the whole of Northern Japan—due largely to the absence or poverty of harbours in northern Honshu.

9b. *The Sun-en Littoral* is the coastal strip from the Izu Peninsula to Ilse Bay and consists of a succession of densely populated delta fans devoted to rice cultivation alternating with beach or dune settlements supplying market garden produce to the readily accessible metropolitan centres. Very mild winters and heavy rainfall favour the growth of citrus fruits, and this is the home of Japan's famous Mandarin oranges, whilst three-quarters of Japan's tea-crop (including the green tea) is grown on the neighbouring hillsides. The region lies on the main routes—the Tokkaido Railway and Highway—between the plains of Kwanto and Kinki and forms part of the great manufacturing belt, enjoying the advantages of easy access, cheap hydroelectric power and abundant clean water. Shizuoka City has tea-packing and cotton industries. Hamamatsu is also a cotton textile town.

9c. *The Nobi or Nagoya Plain* (Ise Bay lowland) resembles the Kwanto Plain in its origin; again, the low new alluvium is in paddyfields, the smoother lower terraces in rice and dry crops—including tea, oranges and mulberry—while the higher terraces suffer badly from erosion and support but few people. Nagoya is the metropolis of this plain as Tokyo is of Kwanto, and is now Japan's fourth port. Yokkaichi exports the porcelain largely produced in the plain, and imports raw cotton for Nagoya's mills; since World War II it has become a great centre of the chemical industry.

THE INNER ZONE OF SOUTH-WEST JAPAN

This region comprises the lands on either side of Setouchi or the Inland Sea together with the whole of the western end of Honshu, including the Japan Sea coast. Northern Kyushu has the larger part of Japan's reserves of coal, but otherwise minerals are unimportant. Climatically the region has a January average of about 40° F., a July average about 75° to 78° F., with a frost-free season of 200 to 240 days. There is naturally a contrast between the Japan Sea coast, with its winter clouds and snow—lying on the ground to the depth of an inch or two—and the Inland Sea coast, with bright clear winters and no snow.

The basin of the Inland Sea is the heart of Old Japan. Here are the old capitals with their temples, shrines and palaces: here population density and pressure on the limited amount of cultivable land reaches its maximum. Terracing of the hillsides has reached a maximum; most fields are double cropped with rice in summer and wheat or barley in winter. Here, too, is half of Japan's industrial belt and such great modern centres as Kobe and Osaka.

9*d*. **Kinki** [1] **or Eastern Setouchi** includes a number of semi-isolated alluvium-filled basins and associated hill lands. The basins, which are graben or fault basins, are five in number—Biwa (Omi), Yamato (Nara), Kyoto (Yamashiro), Osaka (Settsu) and Kino Kawa.

(*a*) *The Biwa* (*or Omi*) *Basin* is the largest and contains Lake Biwa, Japan's largest lake. The basin extends almost to the Japan Sea on the north and thus almost breaks through the northern mountain barrier. It has thus been from ancient times an important route-way; the railways of today tunnel through the hill barriers at the northern and southern ends and place the Japan Sea coast within the hinterland of Osaka and Kobe. The basin is typical of those of Kinki as a whole. There are three 'zones': an alluvial zone with rivers controlled between dykes; an intermediate zone of low terraces with a good soil; an outer zone of higher terraces often with a gravelly soil and exhibiting 'bad-land' features. The lake is attractive scenically and many tourists visit Mt. Hieh with its Buddhist temples and wonderful panoramic views.

(*b*) *The Yamato or Nara Basin* [2] is a very thickly populated tract, marked by its innumerable small rectangular villages not infrequently enclosed by moats. This results from a rectilinear partition of the land which took place before the seventh century. The low-lying paddy lands lie fallow in winter, but three-quarters of the better drained terrace land are double cropped—some treble cropped. The metropolis of the basin, Nara City, although boasting only about 150,000 people, is famed as the first permanent capital of Japan, and its temples are visited by 3,000,000 tourists a year.

(*c*) *The Kyoto or Yamashiro Basin* resembles in general features the others; bamboo grows extensively along the river courses, pears flourish along the eastern margins and the region is famed for the excellence of its teas. The land utilization shows the remarkable rectangular pattern resulting from its partition. Kyoto, the city of this basin, is one of Japan's six great cities and for eleven centuries (until 1869) was the site of the Imperial residence. It is an old city of great charm, full of delightful temples and temple gardens, and has not been ruined by modern industrialization. Instead, it remains the city of craftsmen catering to the wealthy and the artistic.

(*d*) *The Osaka or Settsu Plain* differs from the last three in that it is a coastal plain—the bayhead delta of the broad, dyked Yodo River. The plain is densely populated and intensively cultivated, but is chiefly remarkable in that it has become the leading industrial region of Japan.

---

[1] The Japanese tend to apply the derivation Kinki to the whole area from Japan Sea to Pacific.

[2] See R. B. Hall, 'The Yamato Basin', *Annals Assoc. American Geographers*, **22**, 1932, 243–91.

The Osaka-Kobe industrial region, including Sakai and Kishiwada as secondary foci, has a quarter of Japan's factory workers and produces a third of the nation's manufactured goods. Many industries are represented, with cotton textiles of outstanding importance. Osaka, the 'Manchester' of Japan, is the centre of the cotton trade, with 3 million people, and if one includes domestic traffic, is the leading port of Japan, though surpassed by Kobe and Yokohama in foreign trade. Kobe, 16 miles down the bay, has deep water, is a modern city on a narrow coastal strip and is a port and commercial rather than industrial centre. It handles much of the raw cotton which comes in and much of the raw silk which goes out of the country.

(e) *The Kino Kawa Graben*, a narrow rift valley, is famed for its orange groves. At the seaward end is Wakayama, an outlier of the Osaka industrial region.

13. **Central Setouchi** (the Central Inland Sea region) is a name conveniently applied to the lands on either side of Japan's Mediterranean. It is an area of subsidence which had been a maturely dissected lowland and is now a tract of calm, blue water dotted with innumerable islands. The neighbouring hills are bare and show up in contrast with the small cultivated plains and the closely spaced settlements with their carefully terraced slopes behind. The innumerable towns which lie between the great metropolitan agglomeration of Kobe-Osaka at one end of the sea and the Moji-Shimonoseki area are mostly small and carry on a great variety of industries—shipbuilding, iron and steel, spinning, rubber, chemical, metal and brewing (of beer and saké) are some. Along the coasts are numerous salt pans and an aquatic plant is cultivated for the manufacture of 'reed' mats. The quietness of the waters, the ten-foot tide and cheap local coal from Ube favour the salt-boiling industry. Hiroshima is the metropolis of the region and a city with a colourful past. Kure is a military and naval station, with steel mills and the largest dry dock in the country. Okayama is a local manufacturing centre, whilst Takamatsu, Tokushima and Matsuyama are the leading centres on the Shikoku side of the Inland Sea.

14. **The Sanin Littoral of Northern Chuguko** is well described by its Japanese name, Sanin, meaning 'shady side'. It refers to the darker, gloomier and stormier weather of the Japan Sea Littoral when compared with the Setouchi. In most other respects it presents a contrast—smoother coastline, fewer people, fewer cities, limited development of manufacturing. It lacks extensive plains, so that general subsistence agriculture is the rule, with moderate numbers of cattle. The coastal villages are agricultural-fishing settlements but three towns have more than 100,000 people. Of these Matsue is the chief. The hill country is still largely forested, so that charcoal burning is there a significant industry.

15. **Northern Kyushu** is geologically and morphologically a very

complex region, with the result that its human geography is both complex and varied. The region ought naturally to be divided into a large number of small units—there are barren granite hills, dissected ash and lava plateaus and volcanic cones, and small but important basins. Climatically the region is partly exposed to the north-west monsoon: it shares in some of the stormy cloudy weather of the northern coasts and has less sunshine than the Inland Sea regions.

15a. *The Tsukushi Hill Lands and Associated Plains* include the most important coalfield in Japan, the Chikuho Basin. Railways connect the numerous mines and take the coal northwards to the ports of Wakamatsu and Moji and to the important industrial belt, including Yawata, Tobata, and Kokura, which lies along the coast between them. The five towns are now united as Kita-Kyushu. This is the focus of Japan's 'heavy' industries—including iron and the other metals. Its favourable situation relative to coal and for the import of heavy and bulky raw materials (including iron ore and pig-iron) is the significant factor with iron and steel concentrated at Yawata. Moji guards the entrance to the Inland Sea—the entrance being little over a mile wide and under which there is a rail tunnel. The Miike coalfield occurs in another part of the region; here the chief town is Omuta.

15b. *The Northern Volcanic Region*, with its wild undeveloped lava plateaus and very varied scenery, offers great contrasts with the coalfields. Frequently the scenery is very beautiful and hot springs have given rise to resort centres, whilst the great pile of Mt. Aso is almost a rival to Fuji.

15c. *Insular and Peninsular North-western Kyushu* includes the Hizen Peninsula and the Amakusa Islands and is again a very complex region. The northern part of Hizen includes the coalfields of Sasebo and Karatsu. Sasebo City is a fortified naval station with dockyards and an arsenal, whilst the coal from the second basin leaves by the small port of Karatsu. The towns of Imari and Arita produce much of Japan's fine porcelain from local kaolin. The southern part of Hizen consists of three sprawling peninsulas and the old port city of Nagasaki occupies the head of one of the deep indentations. As a coaling station, it has suffered from the growing use of oil, and in foreign trade has dropped from third to a much lower place amongst Japan's ports. But it is the nearest port to China and was the first of Japan's ports open to foreign trade. Except for one great shipbuilding establishment, it is not a manufacturing town but a picturesque overgrown village, straggling over steep hillsides and with evidences of its early foreign intercourse.

OUTER ZONE OF SOUTH-WEST JAPAN

This region lies south of the great fault line which separates the Inner and Outer Zones of South-west Japan. It consists mainly of ancient crystalline schists and old sedimentary rocks and is a region of rugged mountains and hill country. There are well-developed longitudinal ridges and valleys with a general trend from N.E. to S.W.; but the valleys are narrow and steep-sided and the areas of lowland very restricted. Climatically this is the most nearly tropical region of Old Japan—the humid summer months have temperatures averaging nearly 80° F., eight months (250 days) are frost-free, while light frosts only occur on 30 or 40 days, even in the winter. There is a heavy summer rainfall and hurricanes are frequent in the late summer. The natural vegetation is sub-tropical forest with dense undergrowth: palm and camphor trees are represented in the indigenous flora. But the rugged nature of the region has prevented extensive settlement; there are no important ports and manufacturing is undeveloped. The two channels which connect the Inland Sea with the Pacific Ocean divide the region into three parts.

10. **Southern Kyushu** differs from the other parts of the region in the prevalence of ash and lava plateaus. Forests clothe large areas and forest industries are important; the region includes some mining country, notably the copper-gold mines of Saganoseki. On the ash beds are tracts of grass supporting numbers of horses. Owing to soil and relief rice is relatively less important than beans, sweet potatoes, winter grains and tobacco, whilst this is the only part of Japan where sugarcane is extensively grown. Certain more fertile coastal strips were until recently difficult of access. The construction of a railway to Miyazaki resulted in an immigration, whilst other sections have long had a close association with the Ryukyu Islands.

11. **Southern Shikoku** consists of ridges and valleys of folded sedimentary rocks. The amount of cultivable land is very limited and a very interesting 'cottage industry', with which the farmers supplement their income, is the manufacture of Japanese paper from the fibres of two local shrubs. The mines of the region include Besshi, the copper from which is smelted on a small island in the Inland Sea in order to prevent damage by the fumes to growing crops.

12. **Kii Peninsula** is a rugged, isolated region, almost uninhabited except round the margins.

THE RYUKYU (LOO CHOO OR NANSEI) ISLANDS [1]

The islands of the Ryukyu arc are the summits of a submerged mountain chain. In many cases the islands are surrounded by coral reefs. Although administered as part of Japan proper, these islands have had a different cultural history, with long centuries of contact with China, a virtually complete autonomy under their own kings until recent times and an agriculture influenced by the almost tropical conditions—comparable with those in Taiwan. Thus today the sweet potato is the chief sustenance crop, occupying 40 per cent. of all the

[1] S. McCune, 'The Ryukyu Islands', Focus, **15,** 7, 1965.

arable land. Under Japanese influence and the needs of Japan sugar-cane came to be the chief money crop and exceed rice in importance—rice only occupying 12 per cent. of the cultivated ground. As in Taiwan, various tropical fruits such as pineapples, bananas and papaya (paw-paw) are grown. They are exported to Japan. The limited area under rice and the poor yield due to inadequate use of fertilizer has led to a food problem and a consequent emigration to Old Japan. The largest of the group is Okinawa and it was the capture of this island by United States forces on June 22, 1945, which marked the beginning of the end of the Second World War. It remains an important American Pacific base and the islands though nominally Japanese territory are under American administration. Those north of 29° N. were returned to Japan in 1953.

HOKKAIDO [1]

Hokkaido, the northland of Japan, differs strikingly from the rest of Japan proper. Prior to the era of modern Japan, ushered in by the reign of Emperor Meiji (1868–1912), there were few Japanese on the island, and these were almost entirely confined to fishing villages along the southern coasts. 'Most of the island was the unprotected domain of Ainu tribes who supplemented hunting and fishing with some primitive agriculture.' The early attempts at settlements and agricultural development were not encouraging, despite the help of experts from America and Europe. The railway eventually proved to be the essential pioneer, and today the population is not only concentrated along the railways but exhibits all stages from the pioneer fringe along the newer lines to the settled communities in older areas.

Topographically, in the small area of lowland available, Hokkaido resembles Japan proper. The south-western or Oshima Peninsula is structurally a continuation of the central ranges of northern Honshu. Northwards the most extensive lowland is the Ishikari Plain, from which a narrow plain extends towards the northern tip of the island between the two north-south ranges which form its backbone. The structure lines of the Kurile arc, associated with much vulcanicity, cross these from east to west and from the central knob there is a radial drainage. The streams have built up considerable plains bordering the coasts and there is also an important development of marine terraces.

Climatically, the rough divisions drawn up for the first edition of this book seem satisfactory in that they parallel the agricultural regions later established by Davis (though E. Fukui and A. Watanabe both find different regions).

[1] W. D. Jones, 'Hokkaido, the Northland of Japan', *Geog. Rev.*, **11**, 1921, 16–30. D. H. Davis, 'Present Status of Settlement in Hokkaido', *Geog. Rev.*, **24**, 1934, 386–99. R. B. Hall, 'Agricultural Regions of Asia, the Japanese Empire', *Econ. Geog.*, **11**, 1935, 40–3. A. Watanabe, 'Hokkaido', *Regional Geography of Japan*, **1** (I.G.U., 1957).

(a) Northern Hokkaido has not only bitterly cold or raw winters with a January average below 25° F., but has four months or more with mean temperatures below freezing.

(b) Western Hokkaido resembles western Honshu in its winter snowfall, winter cloud and fog, clear and warm summers.

(c) South-eastern Hokkaido, with its moister and consequently cooler summers (often foggy just when sun would be valuable for ripening crops), is inimical to arable farming.

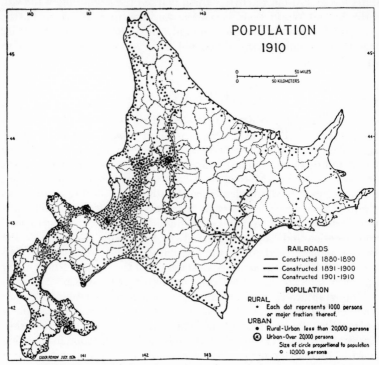

POPULATION
1910

RAILROADS
—— Constructed 1880-1890
—— Constructed 1891-1900
——— Constructed 1901-1910

POPULATION
RURAL
• Each dot represents 1000 persons or major fraction thereof.
URBAN
• Rural-Urban less than 20,000 persons
⊙ Urban-Over 20,000 persons
Size of circle proportional to population
○ 10,000 persons

FIG. 341.—Settlement in Hokkaido, following the pioneer railways
Prior to the construction of railways, settlement was mainly coastal.

Davis's agricultural regions are similarly:

(a) The northern or 'Mixed Farming Region', where rice occupies 25 per cent. or less of the cropped area and where oats occupy about the same area, followed by beans, potatoes, peas, rye, buckwheat and some wheat.

(b) The western or 'Rice and Oats Region', where rice is the leading crop—occupying up to 60 per cent. of the cropped land—with oats a close second.

(c) The southern or 'Stock-raising Region', where (owing to the climatic conditions of the summer) there is little crop production and where the rearing of horses is a leading occupation. Hokkaido has a quarter of a million horses, and horses are not only the chief draught animals and beasts of burden but were reared for the Japanese Army. There has, however, been a great development of dairying, specially from Holstein cattle.

Hokkaido is still a frontier land. The land is still cheap, so that the farms, with an average size of twelve acres, are four times the area

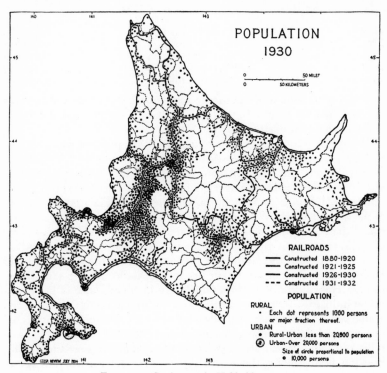

FIG. 342.—Settlement in Hokkaido, 1930

common in Old Japan. The northward extension of rice cultivation has been made possible by the perfecting of varieties that will mature in as short a frost-free season as 90 days. But much of the land—even the 18 per cent. available for crop production—is topographically unsuited to rice and there is serious danger of crop failure in unfavourable years. The scattered patches of cultivation and isolated farms in Hokkaido with a gridiron pattern of roads contrast with the continuous culture of Old Japan, its villages and irregular road patterns.

D. H. Davis, in the paper already quoted, has demonstrated the really remarkable way in which settlement in Hokkaido has followed the building of railways. Two of his maps—for 1910 and 1930—are here reproduced. Lumbering is the first occupation—timber is still an important product; then the cut-over areas are prepared for agriculture; in the older settled areas such as the Ishikari Plain near Sapporo the forest has entirely disappeared. The aboriginal inhabitants, the Ainu, who lived along the coasts and engaged in fishing, have decreased in numbers from an estimated 50,000 in 1600 and 20,000 in 1800, to about 15,000 now. By way of contrast the total population has shot up in a remarkable way:

1869	58,000	1920	2,359,183
1880	191,172	1930	2,812,342
1890	321,118	1939	3,273,342
1900	786,211	1950	4,295,567
1910	1,609,546	1960	5,139,206

Actually these figures are not large remembering the extreme pressure on land in Old Japan. In truth the Japanese do not take kindly to living in this cold northland.

It will be noticed that after 1930—when the position was as shown in Fig. 342—immigration, settlement and development slowed down. It was in 1931 that the Japanese went into Manchuria and the vast possibilities there led to the neglect of Hokkaido. There was even migration from Hokkaido to Manchuria. But the position in 1945, at the end of the Second World War, was entirely different and once more the full use of the resources of Hokkaido became a vital part of national planning. In ten years a million migrants moved in to swell the natural increase. Half of all the land to be reclaimed under the National Land Development Project for Japan lies in Hokkaido. At the same time, though Hokkaido differs from Old Japan in the absence of light consumer industries, including textiles, and traditional crafts there has been a marked urbanization with development of hydroelectricity, coal mining, and the processing of the primary products of the forests (saw mills, pulp and paper), fisheries (canning), and farms (beet-sugar mills, brewing, flour-milling, cheese and butter making). Sapporo, the capital, has shot up from 313,850 in 1950 to 523,839 in 1960, Hakodate from 228,994 to 243,012 in the same ten years. Sapporo is a modern solid-built city—so different from many in the warmer southern islands—the heart of the agricultural region of the Ishikari Plain. Hakodate has a good deep-water harbour and is a ferry port, but does not handle as much trade as Otaru. Muroran is the port for Yūbari coal, and has iron and steel mills; Kushiro is the lumber port of the south-east. Asahigawa is an inland railway centre. The smaller towns act as foci for agricultural expansion.

SOUTHERN SAKHALIN

The southern half—south of 50° N.—of the island of Sakhalin was ceded to Japan under the Treaty of Portsmouth in 1905. Known to the Japanese as Karafuto, it passed back into Soviet possession in 1945. It covered an area of 13,254 square miles (almost half the island) and in the south is separated from Hokkaido by a strait 24 miles wide. The island consists of subdued mountain ranges with a north and south alignment. The main western range extends to the southernmost tip of the island, whereas the eastern ranges are interrupted by a wide bay.

The climate of Karafuto is against extensive settlement. In all parts there are at least five months with an average temperature below freezing, whilst in the north the mean *annual* temperature is below freezing. The sea-level temperature, below zero in January, may frequently rise to 90° F. in July. Northern Sakhalin, which includes the Manchili Plain as its only important area of low relief, is virtually a tundra inhabited by nomadic Gilyak tribes with herds of reindeer. Southern Sakhalin has land capable of cultivation—with potatoes, oats, rye, buckwheat, hay and vegetables. But only 0·7 per cent. of the island is arable—2 per cent only of the south—and less than a quarter of the population is engaged in farming. Grazing is relatively important.

The inhabitants include a small and dwindling number of aborigines—less than 2,000—and rather under 300,000 Japanese immigrants had settled in the southern part.

Fishing is the oldest industry and by far the most important: the fishing is for herring, cod, trout, salmon, whilst crab are also valuable. Seaweed is collected for manufacture into fertilizer—the fate also of many of the herrings—whilst the crab is tinned for export to Europe and America. Fisheries are still largely in Japanese hands.

Forests cover half the area, mixed stands of larch, *Abies* and *Picea* being the usual rule.

There are three fields of Tertiary coal and the output now exceeds half a million tons a year, and a little oil in the north—the half of the island which has remained Russian since Sakhalin was occupied in 1854.

THE KURILES

The island arc of the Kuriles extends from Hokkaido to the tip of the Kamchatka Peninsula and consists of thirty-one volcanic islands. The two southernmost islands have coniferous forests and, as in Hokkaido, fishing villages are scattered along the coasts. The remaining islands are practically uninhabited, support but a tundra vegetation and are fog-bound during much of the summer. Known to the Japanese as the Chishima or Thousand Islands District, they were surrendered in 1945 to the U.S.S.R. by Japan which had held them since 1875.

THE FORMER JAPANESE SOUTH SEA ISLANDS

After World War I Japan was given the mandate over the former German possessions of the Marianne, Marshall and Caroline groups which had early been occupied by a Japanese naval force. There are nearly 1,500 islands, islets and reefs scattered over a wide area of the Pacific Ocean—between 0° and 22° N. and 130° and 175° E. The total area is less than a thousand square miles and the population had reached nearly 70,000 by 1930 and over 80,000 by 1933 owing to the influx of Japanese (over 30,000 in 1933). Nearly half the Japanese were in Saipan Island, where they engaged in sugarcane cultivation or sugar manufacture. From the Augaur Islands is an important production of phosphate. Copra is also an article of export.

The Japanese developed naval and air bases amongst the islands which they used during the Second World War. The United States had held Guam, the largest of the Marshall Islands, since 1898, and on the defeat of the Japanese the Americans became Trustees of the whole group under the United Nations.

REFERENCES

A full-scale description of Japan is contained in G. T. Trewartha, *Japan, a Physical, Cultural and Regional Geography* (University of Wisconsin Press, 1945). This may be supplemented from *Japanese Natural Resources: A Comprehensive Survey* (prepared in the General Headquarters of the United States Army, 1948, and printed in Tokyo, 1949) and from E. A. Ackerman, *Japan's Natural Resources* (Chicago, 1953). On the occasion of the Regional Conference in Japan of the International Geographical Union held in 1957 a series of Guidebooks were prepared including a summary entitled *Geography of Japan*. This is the first geography of the country in English prepared by Japanese geographers themselves and serves to correct views expressed by outside observers. As a main purpose of the conference was to bring to the attention of the western world the work of Japanese geographers, the bibliography published in the I.G.U. News Letter, 1958, is important. See also H. Kublin, 'Japan', *Focus*, **14**, 6, 1964, and the *Proceedings* of the 1957 Conference.

An important Economic Atlas of Japan was published in 1954 and the Department of Geography, University of Chicago, published a guide and translation of the map legends into English. The International Society for Educational Information publishes at intervals a bulletin entitled 'Understanding Japan' with much useful information. See also *Bibliography of Standard Reference Books for Japanese Studies with descriptive notes*, Vol. II, 'Geography and Travel', edited by R. Isida, 1962.

ASIATIC RUSSIA [1]

PRIOR to the Revolution of 1917 the Russian Empire included practically the whole of Asia lying to the north and west of the great central mountainous triangle, together with considerable tracts of the latter itself. The name Siberia (Sibir), which was originally the Russian name given to the settlement of Isker on the Irtysh, came gradually to be applied to the whole vast stretch of Asiatic Russia. The south-western tracts have long been known as Russian Turkistan—the Inner Tartary of older geographers—and were frequently excluded from the area covered by the loose term Siberia, as were also some of the moun-tainous tracts bordering Mongolia.[2] Since the Russian Revolution of 1917 a more restricted meaning has been applied to the term Siberia. In this chapter it is proposed to consider all the territory which, before the First World War, formed the Asiatic portion of the Russian Empire. We shall consider it in two portions:

(a) Siberia, from the Arctic to the Mongolian-Manchurian frontier.
(b) Russian Turkistan or Russian Central Asia.

SIBERIA

Siberia lies between the inhospitable waters of the Arctic Sea on the north and the almost equally inhospitable mountains and deserts of central Asia on the south. Its outlets are thus through European Russia on the west and across the formidable coastal ranges to the Bering and Okhotsk Seas on the east. Siberia's chief drawback is its inaccessibility; its other drawback is its vast size. Five thousand miles from east to west, and in the west as much as 2,300 miles from north to south, it has an area of about 5,200,000 square miles. Even allowing for the doubtful value of enormous tracts, there is enough left to justify the statement that Siberia has the largest area in mid-latitudes still awaiting development. There are two main problems awaiting solution: one is the problem of low-cost transport to consuming centres; the other is the augmentation of the population. Given these, Siberia has immense capabilities for the production of all types of mid-latitude agricultural products, an enormous area of softwood forest at present

[1] Although in this book we consider only the 'Asiatic' parts of the Union of Soviet Socialist Republics (U.S.S.R.) lying east of the Urals, these low mountains and hills do not coincide with any existing political boundary. Europe is essentially a peninsula of Asia and the use of the line of the Urals to separate two continents is a geographical convention little related to either physical or political facts.
[2] Siberia is interpreted in this sense in the Admiralty *Handbook of Siberia and Arctic Russia*, 1918.

untouched, and mineral resources still being unexplored. The inter-war population (Census of 1933) was about 20,000,000; the farming lands for their adequate development required another 20,000,000;

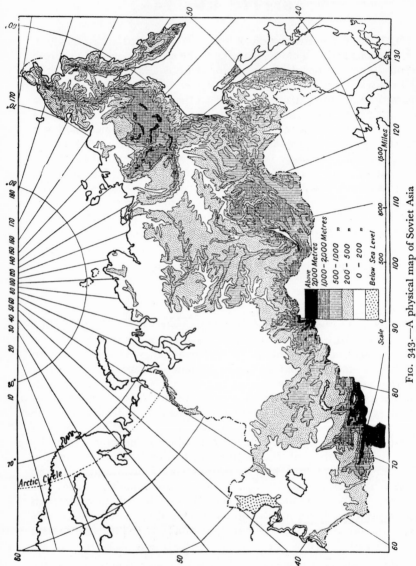

FIG. 343.—A physical map of Soviet Asia

The central and western portions are taken from *The Times Atlas*, but the eastern portion was specially drawn by Miss E. Sandercock, B.A.,

double this number was the estimated need for the development of trade, transport and manufactures. The amazing urban development, hastened by the Second World War, is mentioned below. Siberia before the incidence of the First Five Year Plan (1928–32) might have been compared with Canada of a few decades ago, but without the features of accessibility and ready markets which have favoured the very rapid progress of the Canadian prairies and Far West.

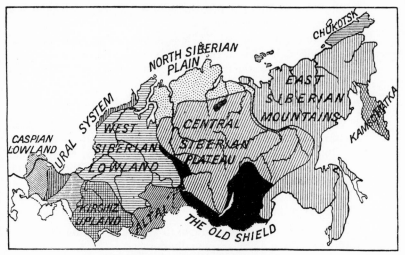

FIG. 344.—The physical divisions of Siberia
(*After* Schultz.)

Orography.[1] Siberia may be divided primarily into Western, Central and Eastern Siberia.

Western Siberia, from the Urals on the west to the Yenisei River on the east, comprises:

(1) A huge plain on the north, roughly the basin of the Ob and its tributaries (West Siberian Lowlands).

(2) The Kirghiz Uplands or foldlands, lying to the south of the plain, and passing westwards into the Turgai Plateau.

(3) The Altai and Western Sayan mountain region, on the Chinese borders.

[1] Since the first edition of this book was published there has appeared the excellent volume in the *Geographie Universelle* (Vol. V), *États de la Baltique, Russie*, by P. C. d'Almeida (1932). See also article 'Russia', *Encyclopædia Britannica*, 14th Edition. A valuable source of information concerning later development is N. Mikhaylov's *Soviet Geography* (Methuen, 1935). Simple modern accounts are given by G. D. B. Gray, *Soviet Lands* (1947), and by J. S. Gregory and D. W. Shave, *The U.S.S.R., a Geographical Survey* (1944). For a recent appraisal see G. B. Cressey, *How Strong is Russia?* (1954). *The Oxford Regional Economic Atlas: The U.S.S.R. and Eastern Europe* (1956) is a veritable mine of recent information and quite indispensable. In 1957 the Central Statistical Board of the U.S.S.R. published a very useful volume of statistics in English under the title *National Economy of the U.S.S.R.* A standard work now available in an English translation is S. P. Suslov, *Physical Geography of Asiatic Russia* (New York: W. H. Freeman, 1961). *Information U.S.S.R.*, edited by Robert Maxwell, Pergamon Press, 1962, is a huge reference work translated from the great Soviet Encyclopædia.

Central Siberia, from the Yenisei River on the west to the Lena River on the east, comprises:

(4) The North Siberian Plain, along the borders of the Arctic Ocean.

(5) The Middle Siberian Plateau—the Angaraland of the geologists.

(6) The Old Shield of Asia, a mountainous region of old rocks around Lake Baikal, including both the border ranges and also portions of the central Asia plateaus (Vitim Plateau and Yablonoi Mountains).

Eastern Siberia lies east of the Lena River and comprises:

(7) The mountain lands of Eastern Siberia, which include several great festoons of mountains, about which little is known— Stanovoi Mountains, Verkhoyansk Mountains, Kolyma and Anadyr Mountains, as well as the mountains of the Maritime Provinces.[1]

(8) The peninsula of Kamchatka.

(9) The peninsula of Chukotsk.

Figs. 343 and 344 have been drawn to show side by side the actual topography and these physiographic divisions.

Structure. It must be admitted that the physiographic regions just enumerated are based partly on topography, but primarily on the structure which is reflected in the topography. If we examine the now classic tectonic map of Siberia given by Obrutschev,[2] we find he distinguishes the following geomorphological regions:

Western Siberia:

(1) West Siberian Lowland.[3]

(2) The Kirghiz Steppelands.

(3) The Altai-Takbagatai.

Central Siberia:

(4–5) Angaraland.

(6) The Old Shield of Asia.

Eastern Siberia:

(7) Verkhoyansk-Kolyma Region.

[1] Much of the intensive exploration of this region has been carried out in recent decades. As late as 1926, S. V. Obrutschev discovered a hitherto unknown range rising to heights of 10,000 feet, which forms an inner arc parallel to the outer arc composed of the Verkhoyansk-Kolymsk-Anadyrsk range. See Obrutschev, *Geog. Jour.*, **86**, 1935, 422–40. Reference should be made to the maps in the Great Soviet World Atlas. In recent years hundreds of geologists, organized by the Russian Academy of Sciences, have carried out detailed mapping.

[2] W. A. Obrutschev, 'Geologie von Sibirien' (Berlin: Borntraeger, 1926).

[3] See a note on the structure of this plain in *Geog. Rev.*, **17**, 1927, 494–5.

(8) Peripheral Tracts to the east of the Old Shield, including Kamchatka, Sakhalin and the ranges of the Maritime Provinces.

In view of the very great importance of Obrutschev's work on the tectonics of Siberia an attempt has been made to reproduce the main features of his tectonic map.

Climate. The climate of the whole of Siberia is essentially continental. So much prominence has been given to the Siberian winter that some common misconceptions must be dealt with. The winter is very long and very cold, but the air is dry [1] and bracing, and the skies cloudless. Precipitation in the winter is but slight, so that the snowfall is measured by inches rather than feet.

In winter the 'cold pole' of the earth is located in Eastern Siberia. The mean temperature of Verkhoyansk in January is — 59° F.; in February 1892 — 90° F. was recorded, this being then the lowest reading ever taken on the surface of the earth. It may be that these extremely low temperatures belong only to valleys in which the cold air collects, and neighbouring hills may be much warmer. From this cold pole there is a steady increase in temperature in all directions. The high-pressure centre which is largely the result of the extreme cold lies farther to the south, and a wedge of high pressure extends through western Asia and eastern Europe roughly along latitude 50° N. This wedge of high pressure is a well-known wind divide. To the south of it (in Turkistan) the winds are north, north-east and east, very cold and dry. To the north of it the winds are west and south-west, and the ameliorating influences of the North Atlantic thus penetrate to the north-west of Siberia. It is these winds which bring the winter cyclones, responsible for the small snowfall of northern Siberia.

In summer the whole of Siberia is comparatively warm and the isotherms run roughly east and west except where they curve suddenly southwards on nearing the Pacific Ocean. Siberia in summer comes under the influence of the low-pressure system of central Asia, but the pressure gradient is gentle, and the winds, which are westerly, are light.

Over the whole of Siberia the precipitation is light. Over most of the country it is between 10 and 20 inches; dropping to less than 10 inches along the northern coasts and in the arid south-west; rising to 20 inches and over on the Altai Mountains and in the Maritime Provinces of the east. More than half the precipitation is in the summer months—June, July and August being the wettest months. This is important because the moisture is available for crops.

There are two factors in operation in Siberia which have an

[1] Strictly speaking, the relative humidity is as high as it is in the humid winters of England, but the temperature is so low that the absolute humidity is very low. When the air comes in contact with the human body it is greatly heated, and its relative humidity drops, so that as far as man is concerned, it is physiologically dry.

important influence on climate. One is the influence of such bodies of water as Lake Baikal, which cause a marked amelioration of winter cold and a lowering of summer temperature. The other is the character of Siberian rivers, which, owing to the gentle northern slope, flow but

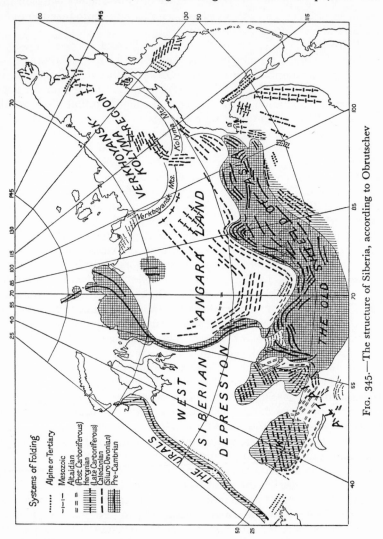

FIG. 345.—The structure of Siberia, according to Obrutschev

sluggishly, and in spring overflow their banks owing to the ice which at that season still blocks their mouths and lower courses. This gives the country a far more humid aspect than one would expect judging by rainfall alone.

The warm summers permit agricultural operations to be carried far to the north in Siberia. The only country where climatic conditions are in many ways comparable with those in Siberia is Canada. As is well known, one of the great problems in Canadian agriculture is the necessity for extending agriculture northwards. The critical line, which limits farming in the Prairie Provinces, is that of 110 days of growing season, i.e. 110 days with a temperature of 50° or over. Experiments in Canada are directed largely towards producing a wheat which will mature with a growing season of 100 days or even less. The Russians are fully alive to the problem and under the First and Second Five Year Plans numerous agricultural research stations were established

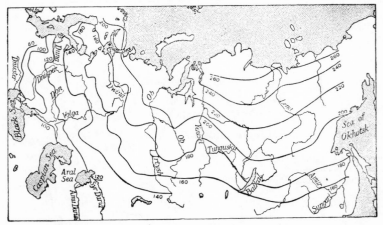

FIG. 346.—Lines showing the mean number of days the rivers are ice-bound each year in the U.S.S.R.

in the far north. At present sufficient data do not exist to enable the line of 100 days above 50° F. to be drawn. The trend of the isotherms for the one hottest month does not really affect the problem. In July temperatures of 90° F. and over have been recorded even in the tundra.

The freezing of Siberian rivers is a most important factor in the life of the people. In the whole of Siberia the rivers are frozen for at least five months; in the extreme north they only flow for about three months. Most of the rivers are frozen solid. The north coast of Siberia is ice-bound for most of the year: the permanent Arctic ice nearly reaches Taimyr Peninsula (Cape Chelyuskin).[1] Nikolaievsk, at the mouth of the Amur, is blocked for 220 days of the year, Vladivostok from the

[1] The seaway along the Arctic Coast is usually open for a short time each year. Two vessels in each direction made the passage in 1935 and since then the Russians have used the route with considerable regularity. On development in the Arctic, see H. P. Smolka, *Geog. Jour.*, **89**, 1937, 327, and *40,000 against the Arctic* (London, 1937).

middle of December to the beginning of April. Lake Baikal is frozen for 4½ months from December

Climatic Regions of Siberia. Several schemes for climatic regions of Siberia are in common use. The broad one given earlier in this book divides Siberia into—Tundra, Cold Temperate, Mid-Latitude Continental, and Mid-Latitude Desert, and has the advantage of coinciding with the main vegetation regions (Tundra, Coniferous Forest, Steppe, Desert). Under this scheme the Cold Temperate Climate may be divided into the climate of eastern Siberia with great extremes (Feuchtswinterkaltes Klima of the Germans), and that of western Siberia and the Pacific Coastal Strip (Wintertrochenkaltes Klima).

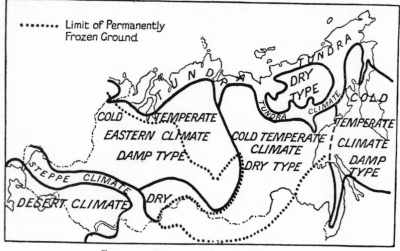

FIG. 347.—The climatic divisions of Siberia

(*After* Schultz.)

For a more accurate delineation of permanently frozen subsoil, or permafrost, see d'Almeida, *op. cit.*, Fig. 45, or Stamp, *Our Undeveloped World*, 1952.

Kendrew distinguishes the same four primary types, but divides the Coniferous Forest or Cold Temperate Belt into three. His classification is as follows:

1. The Tundra Climate is characterized not so much by its cold winters—those of central Siberia are far colder—as by its cool summers. The ground is frozen hard most of the year and only the surface thaws for a few months in summer, and is then waterlogged. The precipitation is small, but the air is damp and raw.

2. The Cold Temperate or Coniferous Forest Climate has a cold winter, but a warm summer. It includes:

  (*a*) West Siberia with very cold winters (January between − 15° F. and 10° F.). Rainfall 8–16 inches—less in the north than the south. The summers are cooler in the north (less than 65° F.) than in the south. (2Ca and 2Cb of Fig. 348.)

(*b*) Central Siberia with the coldest winters known anywhere and an extreme range of temperature. The air is dry and clear in winter, the sky less cloudy than in West Siberia. The rainfall is also less and again decreases from south to north. (2Da and 2Db.)

(*c*) East Coastal Siberia with a damp, cloudy, cool summer and much fog and drizzle. The winters are not as cold as in the interior. Strong north-west winds make the climate more trying than in the interior. (2Ea and 2Eb.)

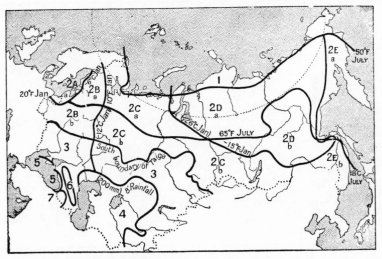

FIG. 348.—The major climatic regions of Asiatic Russia, according to Kendrew

3. The Steppe Climate (Mid-Latitude Continental) has a rainfall of 8-16 inches, falling mainly in spring and early summer in heavy thunderstorms, so that the run-off is excessive, and much of the water is lost to vegetation. Evaporation, also, is very serious west of 90° E. The prevailing winds are north-east, dry and strong throughout the year, and reaching gale force (the Buran) in winter. The snow of winter is swept away by the wind, and the bare ground exposed to the severe winter frosts. Spring is warm, summer hot. The winds, winter frost, and the character of the rainfall combine to make the climate unfavourable to trees and favourable to grass.

4. The Mid-Latitude Desert Climate in the south (in Turkistan) has a rainfall of less than 8 inches. The summers are extremely hot, but the winters are cold for the latitude, with mean temperatures well below freezing. The air is very dry and the skies cloudless.

The Soils of Siberia. Russian scientists have been pioneers in the scientific study of soils, but it was not until the nineteen-twenties that some of the far-reaching results of their studies could be appreciated by scientists familiar only with the languages of western Europe.[1] It is largely owing to the influence of Russian studies that we are getting away from what may be called the geological bogy. In the majority of cases climate takes a much more important part in the making of a soil than does the geology of the underlying rocks. In tropical climates with alternating wet and dry seasons—let us say, for example, the tropical monsoon climate of the wetter parts of Burma—it is impossible to distinguish a laterite derived from an underlying alluvium and one

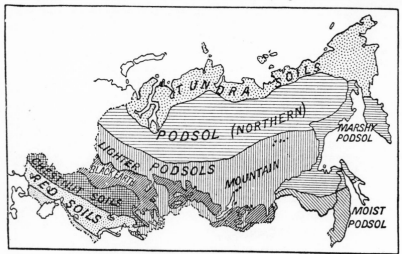

Fig. 349.—The soils of Siberia (*after* Schultz)

For a more accurate and detailed soil-map, see *Oxford Regional Economic Atlas: U.S.S.R.*, 1956, 221–5. In western Siberia it is now usual to recognize a belt of brown earths between the podsols and black earths.

formed from a gneiss or a slate. It is the climate which determines the soil. In those regions, such as the Mediterranean regions, where the hot and wet seasons do not coincide, the formation of soil is a much slower process and geology plays a more conspicuous part in the character of the soils.

The soils of Siberia are determined more by climate than by the geological formations, and hence the belts of soil run across the country from west to east, following the climatic belts.

(*a*) The Tundra soils are definitely the result of Arctic conditions. Rainfall is low but humidity great, owing to the low temperature, and the great feature is the accumulations of water in

[1] K. D. Glinka's classic work, *The Great Soil Groups of the World and their Development*, was translated into English and published only in 1928 (London: Thos. Murby & Co.).

the surface layers overlying the permanently frozen subsoil or permafrost.

(b) The Podsol soils occur in the forest belt; they are ash-coloured and low in fertility, and are generally sandy in character. There is a well-marked soil profile or differentiation in horizons and there is a thin black surface layer with much vegetable matter (A_0), a leached ash-coloured layer (A_1) below which is the B horizon of secondary deposition. In the Podsol or Podsolized soil belt are vast strips of bog-soils.

(c) The Black Earth Belt extends into Siberia from European Russia, and is a narrow but a very important zone, and includes the richest agricultural land in Siberia. The soil is a deep loess, rich in humus, hence the dark colour. The Black Earths (Chernozems or Chernozyoms) are not necessarily formed on loess, however. The essentials for their formation are high evaporation with consequent desiccation of the soil in summer and long freezing of the subsoil in winter. During winter the water accumulates and provides for the luxuriant spring vegetation. Later the subsoil also thaws so that there is not impeded drainage as in the tundras. The abundant humus is derived from the well-developed roots of the steppe grasses whose decay is retarded by the drought of late summer. Downward movement of water and consequent leaching is approximately balanced by upward so that there are no distinct soil horizons in the profile.

(d) The Chestnut-coloured Soil Belt lies to the south of the Black Soil Belt, and is much less fertile. This is the soil of the true steppelands.

(e) The Red Soil Belt differs characteristically from the last in its colour. Saline or slightly saline soils pass into highly saline ones with salt pans, whilst much of the soil itself is sandy. This belt is better described as the Alkaline Soil Belt because the soils are different from the typical Red Soils of the Tropics.

(f) The Grey Soil Belt occupies a more southerly zone in the region of the Turanian depression and is characteristic of still greater aridity (desert soils).

The Vegetation Belts of Siberia.[1] The vegetation of Siberia remains very largely in its original state, for man has effected but few changes except in the southern taïga and steppeland belts. Broadly, there are but three vegetation belts—the tundra, the taïga and the steppe, the latter fading into desert in Turkistan.

The Tundra occupies a belt from 30 to 200 miles wide along the shores of the Arctic Ocean. The term is used loosely to cover the treeless

[1] See A. Schultz, *Siberien*, and *A World Geography of Forest Resources* (Amer. Geog. Soc.).

Arctic plains north of the forest limit. The perpetually frozen lower layers of the soil prevent the filtration of surface waters to deeper levels, and when not frozen the surface layers are waterlogged. In low-lying areas moss often forms a cover five feet thick; lichens, including the famous Reindeer 'moss', replace moss in drier areas. Moss and lichens are the chief plants in the east; in the west grasses, sedges, perennial herbs, including numerous bulbs, are found. Except in sheltered nooks, the only trees are dwarf birches (*Betula nana*) and willows growing to a height of a few inches and generally creeping on the ground. Bushes of heath, azalea and arbutus are also found. The tundra is frozen and snow-covered for eight or nine months of the year; during the few

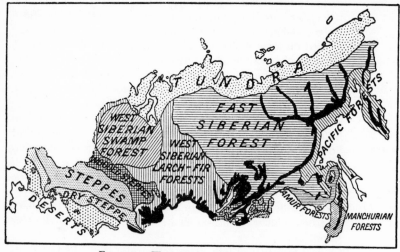

FIG. 350.—The natural vegetation of Siberia

For a more detailed map see *Oxford Regional Economic Atlas: U.S.S.R.*, 1956, 26–7.

weeks of spring and summer it is alive with birds, and swarms of mosquitoes make life unbearable for man should he attempt to penetrate the almost impassable swamp. The waters of the rivers and the Arctic Ocean abound in fish—salmon, cod and sturgeon—and the sparse population derives its livelihood very largely from fishing. Reindeer may also be raised: wild animals include a few Arctic species (such as the lemming, Arctic fox and polar bear) in winter, and a host of carnivores which move north after the wading birds in summer.

The Taïga or Coniferous Forests cover by far the largest area of Siberia. Nearly all the forests are full of fur-bearing animals—bear, lynx, fox, wolf, sable, squirrel and ermine—and the scanty population is mainly engaged in hunting and fishing. Placer-mining (for gold) is important, especially in the Lena Basin. The commercial exploitation of the forests is retarded by difficulty of access.

Five types of taïga may be distinguished:

(1) The West Siberian Swamp Forest occupies the middle and lower basin of the Ob. The forest is marshy and has impenetrable undergrowth. The Siberian fir predominates; larch is rare, but there is an admixture of deciduous trees (birch and aspen). Thickets of willow, alder and poplar fringe the streams, and berry-bearing bushes (whortle-berry, bilberry) are common. The south part of this area includes the well-known Vasyugan swamps.

(2) The West Siberian Larch-Fir Forest occupies the greater part of the Yenisei Basin, and the basin of the Upper Ob, stretching on to the Altai Mountains. The chief trees are the Siberian fir, the stone pine (*Pinus cembra*), the spruce (*Picea obovata*), the silver fir, and the Siberian larch. Undergrowth is frequently absent, and the forests are com paratively dry. The forests on the Altai are more open and the trees are taller. Obviously these forests are of greater commercial value than the swamp forests.

(3) The East Siberian Forests extend from the Yenisei Basin to the Stanovoi Mountains. Growth is poorer than in the western forests, owing to the long and very severe winter and the dry cold winds. Marshy areas are rare, owing to the hillier nature of the country, and undergrowth is infrequent. Siberian fir and Eastern larch (*Larix daurica*) are the chief trees; *Pinus cembra* and Scots pine also occur. The spruce extends as far east as the Lena.

(4) The Amur Forests are characterized by an admixture of num-erous deciduous trees—oak, elm, lime, maple, walnut, ash, aspen, willow, etc.—all of Eastern species typical of China and Japan. The coniferous trees include those of the East Siberian forests as well as yew, ayan pitch pine (*Picea ayanensis*) and the white cedar or Manchu pine (*Pinus mandshurica*); but *Pinus cembra* is absent.

(5) The Pacific Forests occupy the Pacific slopes from Sakhalin in the south to (and including) Kamchatka in the north. The Eastern larch, *Larix daurica*, is the prevailing species, but Siberian fir and Siberian cedar are also common. In Kamchatka the trees are widely spaced and some natural meadows occur.

The Wooded Steppes lie between the true forests and the true steppes. Southwards from the forest belt firs gradually disappear, and their place is taken by birches, aspens and willows. But the trees occur mainly in clumps, or along river-banks, separated by broad expanses of rolling grasslands. It is this belt which has the fertile black earth, and which forms the most valuable agricultural region in Siberia.

The Steppes lie to the south of the wooded steppes, in the region of the Kirghiz uplands. Feather grass (*Stipa*) is the characteristic plant; flowering herbs are numerous; trees are rare, except in a few damper spots, but dwarf thorny bushes—broom, hawthorn and tamarisk—are common. Southwards the steppes pass into the semi-desert of Turkistan.

In eastern Siberia steppes reappear in the Transbaikal Region (south of Lake Baikal).

Population. In December 1926 a complete Census of Russia was taken for the first time. Another was taken in January 1939 and official estimates for the constituent republics of the Union and of all principal towns have been published relating to April 1956. The population of the area here described as Siberia was about 15,000,000 in 1926; it is difficult to state exactly because the 'Ural Territory' strides the Urals and lies partly in Europe, partly in Asia. In the thirty years 1926–56 the average rate of population increase in the U.S.S.R. is 1·0 per cent. per annum but with the great development in Siberia one may hazard a guess that the total now exceeds 40,000,000 out of the total of 229,000,000 in 1965. Huge areas however remain uninhabited or very sparsely settled; only where accessible by rail or road does the density exceed 2·5 per square mile. The population comprises three groups:

(1) The descendants of the prehistoric inhabitants, known as the Palaeo-Siberians and including the tribes of the Chukchis, Koryaks,[1] Kamchadals (all in the extreme north-east), Gilyaks (of the Pacific Coast), Yukaghirs and Yenisei Ostyaks. They are allied to the Ainus of Japan, Aleutians, and Eskimos of North America (number about a million).

(2) The races who settled in Siberia during the great movements of population which took place from about the third to the thirteenth centuries, and who came mainly from central Asia. The races are known as the Neo-Siberians and include the Voguls, Ugrian Ostyaks, Samoyedes and allied tribes, the Siberian Tartars, the Kirghiz of the Steppes, the Yakuts of the Lena Valley, the Buryats of Lake Baikal, the various Tungus tribes of the Yenisei Valley and the north-east (number in all probably about a million).

(3) The Russian immigrants, the inflow of whom started in the sixteenth century, but scarcely gathered force until the opening years of the present century.

The Aborigines. Space prevents us from considering the aboriginal tribes, interesting as they are; but a good account of them is readily available in the Admiralty *Handbook of Siberia and Arctic Russia*. The Chukchis, Koryaks, Kamchadals and Samoyedes are hunters, fishers and reindeer breeders; the Tungus tribes are occupied chiefly in hunting. The Buryats raise livestock and engage in a little agriculture; the Yakuts breed livestock, and of course the Tartars and the Kirghiz of the steppes are stock-rearers.

The Russian Colonists. The bulk of the colonists are found in the agricultural belt of western Siberia, where before the Revolution density was estimated to range as high as 20 or 25, and in the areas industrialized during and since the Second World War. The Russian

[1] The plural form is more correctly Koriaki, Kamchadaly, Tungusy, Buriaty, etc.

colonization of Siberia dates from the sixteenth century, the first settlers arriving in 1593 after the conquests of Yermak in the reign of Ivan the Terrible. The first colonists were traders who were attracted by the fur trade, and Cossacks who formed a sort of military guard for the traders. The use of Siberia as a place of exile for criminals, political or religious, dates from about 1648. Between 1823 and 1898 700,000 exiles with 216,000 voluntary followers passed into Siberia. A distinction should be made between criminal exiles (187,000 of the above total plus 107,000 companions) who were condemned to hard labour, and who were confined mainly in the Far East, and political exiles who formed enlightened, energetic and valuable settlers. Religious exiles—especially dissenters or raskolniki—were especially predominant in Transbaikal, and became so numerous that it is said that before the Revolution dissenters constituted 10 per cent. of the entire population of Russia.

The colonization of Siberia by free settlers progressed very slowly until about 1896. The abolition of serfdom in 1861 enabled the Russian peasant to leave his native soil; the nominal abolition of criminal exile to Siberia in 1900, the building of the Trans-Siberian Railway in 1902 and the directing of attention to Siberia by the Russo-Japanese War in 1904–5, and the active Government support of the colonists, were all factors encouraging settlement. The following figures show the progress of colonization by free settlers:

1870–1890	500,000
1896–1905	1,078,000
1906	141,294
1907	427,339
1908	664,777
1909	619,320
1910	316,163
1911	189,791
1912	201,027
1913	234,877

In the latter part of this period the percentage of returning colonists had fallen to about 4 per cent. a year. The immigrants were nearly all Russian peasant farmers who settled in the Black Soil Zone, along the railways, and in certain of the river valleys. According to the Census of 1926, about 85 per cent. of the population was rural, living in villages of log-huts arranged on both sides of a single street. Urban communities developed later, and only in the ten years before the Revolution did the towns of Siberia commence to carry out modern schemes of water supply, sewerage and lighting. In 1926 only three towns—Omsk (161,600), Novo-Sibirsk (120,700) and Vladivostok (107,980)—had a population over 100,000; six others had a population between 50,000 and 100,000. These were Irkutsk, Tomsk, Chita, Krasnoyarsk, Blagovyeshchensk and Barnaul. All these, it will be noted, are on, or closely linked with, the Trans-Siberian Railway. Tobolsk, advantageously situated at the junction of the Tobol with the Irtish, with its 18,500 inhabitants, was the only town of any size away from the railway. Places like Verkhoyansk in the far north were merely villages of wooden huts. The Census of 1939 showed some remarkable increases—Omsk to 281,000; Novo-Sibirsk to 278,000; Vladivostok to 206,000; Irkutsk to 243,000; Tomsk to 141,000; Krasnoyarsk to 190,000 and Barnaul to 148,000. During the Second World War growth was even more phenomenal, as the figures given below indicate, and many completely new towns have been built, such as Karaganda (founded 1928).

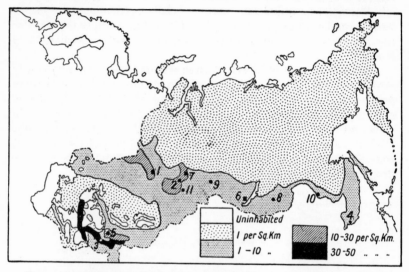

Towns with populations in 1926 and 1956: **1.** Omsk (161,600—505,000); **2.** Novosibirsk (120,700—731,000); **3.** Samarkand (105,200—170,000); **4.** Vladivostock (108,000—265,000); **5.** Tashkent (323,600—778,000); **6.** Irkutsk (99,000—314,000); **7.** Tomsk (92,400—224,000); **8.** Chita (61,500—162,000); **9.** Krasnoyarsk (72,400—328,000); **10.** Blagovyeshchensk (61,200—100,000); **11.** Barnaul (74,300—255,000). The above map does not include the old Ural Territory on the eastern flanks of which are the large towns of Chelyabinsk (612,000 in 1956), Sverdlovsk (707,000), Nizhry-Tagil (297,000) and Magnitogorsk (284,000). Towns under 50,000 in 1926 and not shown on the above map include the following all over 200,000: Karagamda (350,000), Stalinsk (347,000), Alma-Ata (330,000), Khabarovsk (280,000), Prokopyevsk (260,000) and Kemerovo (240,000). There are a dozen others now over 100,000

FIG. 351.—Asiatic Russia—density of population and chief towns, Census of 1926. and estimate of 1956

The Far East is dominated by the port of Vladivostok and the city of Khabarovsk where the Trans-Siberian Railway crosses the Amur. Both have now over a quarter of a million people. The latter acts as a collecting centre for the restricted but still significant agriculture of the Amur Valley.

Agriculture. Fig. 352 shows the marked concentration of agriculture in the Black Earth Region, and its absence alike in the cold and forested north, and in the arid south-west. Relief, as well as soil and climate, is an important factor in limiting agriculture to the Forest-Steppe belt of western Siberia; here are vast plains of low altitude, whereas in eastern Siberia there are few plains, and only narrow valleys. In general the conditions are closely comparable with those in the prairies of North America—in Minnesota and the Dakotas, or the southern parts of the Prairie Provinces of Canada. The Census taken in 1917 just prior to the Revolution showed that there were nearly 2,000,000 farmsteads, 81 per cent. belonging to peasants, 15 per cent. to natives and 4 per cent. to Cossacks. The acreage under crops was 27,400,000. In addition about 18,000,000 acres previously tilled and used for hay remained uncultivated, and 9,000,000 acres was fallow land in accordance with the general system of rotation. At that time grains occupied 94 per cent. of the sown area (spring wheat 48, oats 28, rye 14, barley 4), potatoes 2 per cent., flax and hemp 1 per cent. each, miscellaneous crops 2 per cent.[1] In common with other parts of the U.S.S.R. the years 1917–22 saw a heavy drop in farm production in Siberia though perhaps less than where the big private, royal and church estates were expropriated and there was no adequate organization to carry on. Siberia was then a land of small peasant proprietors—it was transport and marketing which broke down. Under the New Economic Policy of 1922–8 the rights of the peasants to grow what and how they pleased were recognized, but this temporary measure gave place in 1928 to the collective farm and the State farm. Within two years a quarter of the peasant householders and a third of the crop area were incorporated in collective holdings, including State. The process was practically complete—99·9 per cent. of the crop area—by the outbreak of war in 1940. According to the 'Spring Sowing Plan' 30,000,000 acres were to be sown in the area called Siberia in this book; of that total 5,500,000 acres were in State farms. The post-War period has been marked by the rapidly increasing mechanization of farm equipment. According to official statements in 1956 'engines made up 94 per cent. of all capacities used in agriculture'. Amongst major reclamation schemes is a diversion of the Ob and the farm settlement of the steppes north-west of the Caspian.

The crops vary according to the varieties of soil. Wheat grows best on the sandy black soil; barley and spring rye on the brownish rather infertile soil of central Tomsk; oats are most abundant along the great Siberian road. The yields in Siberia are considerably lower than on similar land in Canada or the United States, and wide fluctuations from year to year are due to cold blasts from the north, or hot winds from the arid lands to the south.

[1] Map showing the distribution of crops in western Siberia and details of acreage up to 1938–9 will be found in L. Volin, *A Survey of Soviet Russian Agriculture*, U.S. Dept. of Agriculture monograph 5, 1951, and maps based on 1950 figures will be found in the *Oxford Regional Economic Atlas*.

It is still common to sow the land for two or three years, then to leave it fallow for a year; then to sow again for one or two years. This process is repeated until the land shows signs that it needs a rest. Intensive agriculture is practised on irrigated lands but these are mainly in Soviet Central Asia.

Dr. Baievsky, writing in 1927, estimated that in Siberia there were an additional 200,000,000 acres suitable for crop raising; sufficient to accommodate 4,000,000 families, or 20,000,000 people. Thus the acreage under wheat might reach 150,000,000 acres (compare Canada, 26,000,000 acres in 1952; United States 71,000,000 acres in 1952) and

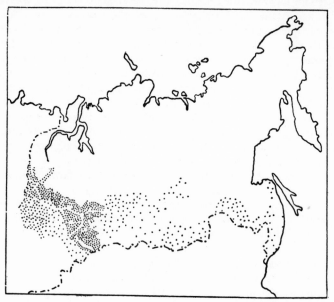

FIG. 352.—The distribution of agricultural land in Siberia
Each dot represents 27,000 acres.

the acreage under oats 75,000,000 acres (compare Canada, 11,060,000 acres in 1952).

A very interesting and important calculation was made some years later by the late Dr. C. F. Marbut, then head of the United States Soil Survey, as to the possibilities of expansion of the wheat area in Russia.[1] Basing his calculations on the area covered by chernozem and chestnut soils, he came to the conclusion that the possible wheat area on the steppelands of European and Asiatic Russia was 854,500,000 acres compared with only 234,500,000 acres in the United States. Thus Russia alone *could* produce, at a very moderate yield of half a ton or

[1] 'Russia and the United States in the World's Wheat Market', *Geog. Rev.*, **21**, 1931, 1–21.

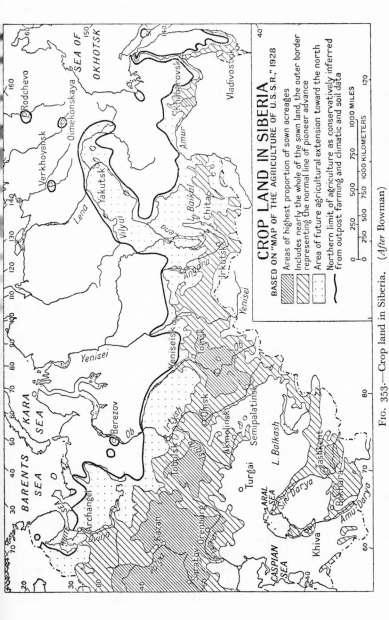

CROP LAND IN SIBERIA. (*After Bowman*)

This map may be compared with the detailed maps of agricultural distributions published in the *Oxford Regional Economic Atlas* of the U.S.S.R. and which are based primarily on 1950 figures. Experience over the last twenty-five years has in general confirmed the northern limit of agriculture shown on the above map with one major restriction—the area around Yakutsk would seem to be an 'island' rather than an extension of the main belt. 'New wheatlands' planned in 1954 are indeed restricted to the area south of a line joining Tyumen, Omsk and Tomsk.

Fig. 353.—Crop land in Siberia.

18 bushels per acre, nearly four times the present total world production of wheat. Several authors,[1] however, regarded Marbut's calculations as unduly optimistic and held that he paid insufficient attention to unfavourable climatic conditions and the presence of harmful alkali in some of the soils. But even with the present great population increase in the U.S.S.R. there is no fear of starvation.

Among the minor crops of Siberia may be noted buckwheat, millet, peas, beans, sugar-beet, sunflowers, linseed and other oil seeds, and tobacco.

Livestock is especially important in the Khirghiz steppelands, the southern portion of Siberia proper and Transbaikal. As long ago as 1917, before the Revolution, a census showed the following:

Cattle	.	.	.	.	.	11,400,000
Sheep	.	.	.	.	.	14,700,000
Pigs .	.	.	.	.	.	3,400,000
Goats	.	.	.	.	.	1,000,000
Horses	.	.	.	.	.	7,800,000

The rapid rise to importance of co-operative dairying was in large measure due to the fact that the produce is relatively more valuable, and could stand higher transport charges. The success of the industry was due in large measure to the quality of the milk, only 20 lb. of milk being required to produce 1 lb. of butter compared with 28 lb. for the same period in Denmark. The excellent pastures are responsible for this. The industry is concentrated west of Krasnoyarsk; in summer many refrigerator trains weekly run from Novo-Sibirsk.

Forests.[2] Apart from the forested slopes of the Urals, Raphael Zon considers that the forests of Siberia fall into a western area (west of Lake Baikal) and an eastern. Western Siberia has 75,000,000 acres of productive forests with a total stand of merchantable timber of 3,500,000,000 cubic metres and a possible annual cut of 16,000,000 cubic metres or about 10,000,000 tons. The timber is larch and fir and the high-class Siberian 'cedar' (*Pinus cembra*) of which there are 17,000,000 acres. Eastern Siberia is believed to have over 700,000,000 acres of merchantable timber totalling 19,000,000,000 cubic metres with a potential annual cut of 37,000,000. Because of their relative accessibility and variety of species, including many hardwoods, the forests of the Far East, accessible from the Pacific, are more important than the vast but inaccessible forest lands of the interior.

The exploitation of Siberia's forests was seriously undertaken as part of the First Five Year Plan (1928-32). According to Mikhaylov, production during that period was increased by 70 per cent. in the Urals, 110 per cent. in eastern Siberia and 210 per cent. in western

[1] See V. P. Timoshenko, *Geog. Rev.*, **23**, 1933, 479-81.
[2] See Raphael Zon, *The U.S.S.R.* in *A World Geography of Forest Resources*, Amer. Geog. Soc., 1956.

Siberia. In 1928–9 out of a total production in the U.S.S.R. of 55,000,000 cubic metres (approximately 1,942,000,000 cubic feet), 7·6 per cent. came from Siberia, and 3·1 per cent. from the Far Eastern Region, with the addition of 10 per cent. from the Urals. According to the Second Five Year Plan, the total out-turn for 1937 was to be 6,000,000,000 cubic feet and it was planned that the Urals should produce 14·8, West Siberia 6·2, East Siberia 6·5 and the Far Eastern Region 7·1 per cent. of this. This would give about 1,500,000,000 cubic feet for the area under consideration—one-seventh of that given above as theoretically possible. Wood-working industries are developing in Siberia itself, especially at Krasnoyarsk. Much timber, despite the short open season, is floated down the Yenisei to the Arctic port of Igarka. There some of it is worked, but the bulk taken by the 'caravan' of timber-carrying ships accompanied by ice-breakers and aeroplanes through the Kara Sea to Europe.

With the forest wealth of Siberia may be associated the fur trade. In some areas of the taïga and tundra, trapping is the chief means of livelihood of the people and, as in all parts of the world, the numbers of animals are rapidly diminishing. Sables are now rare; squirrels, most important of all, are rapidly becoming scarcer. Other important fur-bearing animals include fox, hare, ermine, marten and bear. The value of the fur trade is difficult to assess, as most of the furs pass through European Russia or through the countries of Asia. It was claimed in 1935 that Soviet Russia supplied 30 per cent. of all furs entering international trade.

Fisheries. Siberian rivers and lakes abound in fish, but the most important fisheries are those along the Pacific Coast, especially round Kamchatka. The annual catch between 1909 and 1922 was between 110,000 and 130,000 tons, with a marked tendency to increase. Ninety per cent. of the catch was salmon, and the salmon fisheries and canneries were in Japanese hands. Although Japan has lost Sakhalin and the Kuriles to the U.S.S.R. this is still true.

Minerals. The mineral wealth of Siberia is second only to its agricultural resources. The distribution of minerals reflects closely the structural geology, and there are three main mineral-bearing regions:

(1) The Altai Mountains—Kirghiz Upland Region of western Siberia, with copper, gold, zinc, silver, etc.

(2) The Old Shield of Asia—a very important region—including the regions round Lake Baikal, with coal, iron, gold, etc.

(3) The Eastern Mountain Region, especially in the upper basin of the Amur, which because of its accessibility is the most important region.

Coal [1] resources have been estimated at a minimum of 400,000 million metric tons, equal to a quarter of the total resources of Asia, or a half of those of Europe. The chief basins are:

- (*a*) Kuznetzk (Kuzbas) Basin.
- (*b*) Irkutsk Basin.
- (*c*) Minusinsk Basin.
- (*d*) Kirghiz Steppe Basins (Karaganda Basin in Kazak Republic).
- (*e*) Sakhalin Island.

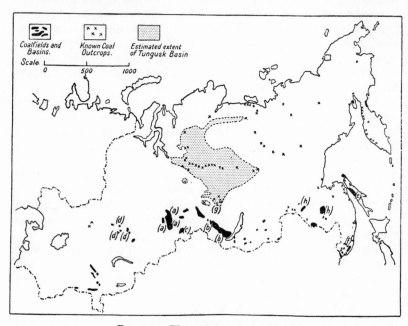

FIG. 354.—The coal resources of Siberia

The letters correspond to the fields listed in the text.

- (*f*) Maritime Provinces.
- (*g*) Tungusk Basin.
- (*h*) Bureinsk (Bureya) Basin.

In 1950 the chief producing fields were the Kuznetzk or Kuzbas Basin (43,000,000 tons); Karaganda (17,000,000 tons); the Irkutsk Basin, stretching for 300 miles along the Trans-Siberian Railway; and

[1] P. P. Goudkoff, 'Economic Geography of the Coal Resources of Asiatic Russia', *Geog. Rev.*, **13**, 1923, 283–93. N. Mikhaylov, in his *Soviet Geography* (Methuen, 1935), adds to these the Yakutia area near the Lena River (shown by scattered crosses in Fig. 354) and estimates the total reserves in Asiatic Russia at nearly 1,080,000,000,000 tons, allowing 400 billion tons in the Kuznetzk Basin and 400 billion in the Tungusk.

the easily accessible basins of Sakhalin and the Maritime Provinces near Vladivostok.

Petroleum occurs in the northern half of Sakhalin, and its exploitation was a matter for negotiation between the Japanese (then controlling southern Sakhalin) and Russians. Kamchatka may also have important fields, but the remainder of Siberia is not particularly promising. The Caucasus belt, however, extends eastwards into Turkistan, and there are many large oilfields the whole length of the Urals.

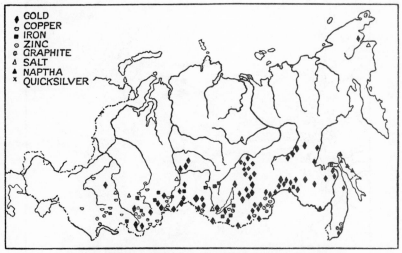

FIG. 355.—The mineral deposits of Siberia (excluding coal)
For modern detailed maps see *Oxford Regional Economic Atlas, U.S.S.R.*, 1956.

Gold is very widely distributed in Siberia; the principal gold-mining districts for long were in the Olekma-Vitim region of the Lena Basin. The deposits worked are all placer deposits. The Lena goldfields were for long exploited by a company mainly with British capital. In 1935, after long negotiations, terms were agreed for the compensation of this company. Total production averaged 1·5 million ounces in 1910–14; in 1940 it had reached 4 million. Then came remarkable discoveries in the Upper Lena and Kolyma and there is good reason for believing output in 1957 was between 17 and 19 million ounces—over half the world's total.

Copper is especially important in the Kirghiz Steppes, in the Altai Region, and in the southern part of the Yenisei Province.

Zinc, Lead and Silver are most important in the Altai Region, in Transbaikalia, and the south-eastern coasts of the Maritime Territory.

Iron Ores are widely distributed, and are now being worked Specially important deposits include those of Telbes in the Kuznetzk coal basin, Minusinsk in Yenisei, Olga district in the Maritime Territory and in the Irkutsk Province.

A.—23

Other minerals include tin, manganese, rare metals, such as platinum, iridium and osmium, and numerous non-metallic minerals. The U.S.S.R. is probably more nearly self-sufficient in minerals than any other country in the world.

Industrial Development. The Russian immigrants into Siberia

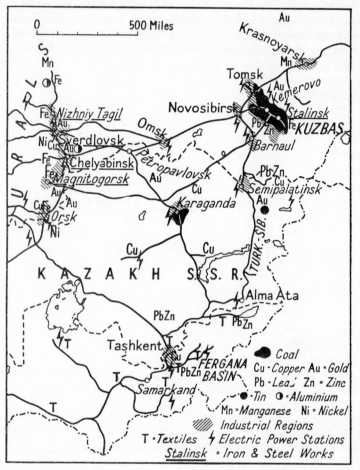

Fig. 356.—The coalfields and new industrial regions of western Soviet Asia

took with them their *Koustar* (peasant) industries and they found in their new homes an even greater need for these occupations in the long severe winter. Woodwork, the dressing of sheep-skins and furs, the spinning and weaving of wool, metal-working and rope-making are all widespread. More localized are the boot industry of the Irkutsk district, the making of metal containers for milk and of skin coats in the Barnaul district, the pottery industry of Yeniseisk and the specialized metal and woodwork of Kuznetzk and Tomsk. But in recent years factory industries have been increasing with the growth of urbanization. Not only is there the need for preparing local commodities for distant markets—hence the numerous creameries and butter factories—but distances are so vast in Russia that local factories for local needs are concerned with brewing, distilling, weaving, glass-making, brick and cement making. The localization of boat-building at Minusinsk, on the upper Yenisei, and carriage-building at Omsk and Tomsk is also to be expected.

Not only did the First (1928-32) and Second (1933-7) Five Year Plans aim at the industrialization of Russia but they aimed also at a better distribution of industries. Hence the amazingly rapid growth of the new industrial areas shown in Fig. 356. This proved of very great importance in the Second World War when German armies swept over and devastated European Russia as far east as Moscow and Stalingrad. The chief areas are:

(a) The Southern Urals, with two main centres around Magnitogorsk and Orsk, devoted to iron, steel and heavy industries.
(b) The Central Urals, with the great centres of Chelyabinsk, Sverdlovsk and Nizhniy Tagil.
(c) The Novo-Sibirsk area.
(d) The Kuzbas coalfield with Stalinsk, Kemerovo (iron and steel).
(e) The Krasnoyarsk region making machinery.
(f) The Barnaul area, textiles and clothing.

To these may be added the textile industries developing in Turkistan, in the home of cotton. The great use made of electric power, both hydroelectric and carboelectric, is noteworthy.

Communications. It will have been gathered already that no factor plays, indeed no factor will play in the future, such an important part as communications. In a country which is 5,000 miles from end to end low-cost transportation is a prime problem. To the north are the Arctic wastes, to the south are the sparsely inhabited regions of central Asia which offer no outlet to Siberia's products. With the exception of the important Amur, the rivers of Siberia flow from south to north: consequently the railways and the highways must provide the outlets to east and west.

Siberia's trade with the outside world practically started only with the construction of the first railway—the great Trans-Siberian. This is the longest single railway line in the world; from Leningrad to Vladivostok is over 5,400 miles, and the cost to the Russian Government was over £200,000,000. It was built in six sections simultaneously. The main line runs via Omsk, Novo-Sibirsk, Krasnoyarsk, Irkutsk, Tschita (Chita) and Khabarovsk to Vladivostok. At first the trains were ferried across Lake Baikal, or crossed the ice in winter, but later the line was built round the southern shore of the lake. From Chita to Vladivostok the North Manchuria Railway, formerly the Chinese Eastern Railway, affords a shorter route, but through Manchuria via Harbin. The most

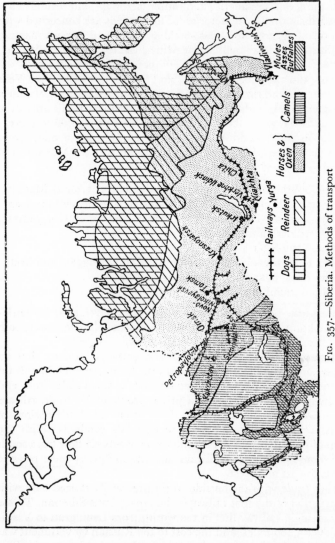

Fig. 357.—Siberia. Methods of transport

(*After* Schultz.)

Note.—Novo-Nikolayevsk is now Novo-Sibirsk.

For a recent account see George Kish, 'Railroad Passenger Transport in the Soviet Union', *Geog. Rev.*, **53**, 1963, 363–76.

important branches are Targa-Tomsk, Petropavlosk-Kokchetav and Verkhne-Udinsk-Kiakhta. From Altan Bulak which faces Kiakhta across the border there is a railway to Ulan Bator (Urga), the capital of Mongolia and now through to Peking on the Russian broad gauge.

Other important lines include the Altai Railway from Novo-Sibirsk to
Semipalatinsk through fertile agricultural land; the Kuznetzk coalfield
line from Yurga, and others. The line from Semipalatinsk was linked
with the Turkistan railways in 1930—the Turk-Sib Railway thus
formed making possible an interchange of foodstuffs from Siberia with
semi-tropical products.

Siberia has only a few thousand miles of paved roads, but owing
to the flatness of the country and the low rainfall the unimproved
'wagon roads' are open for wheeled traffic, including now motor-cars,
for most of the year. There are 90,000 miles of such roads. One of the

FIG. 358.—Physical map of Russian Turkistan
A = Plain of Ferghana.

most famous of Siberian roads is the Great Siberian Military Road or
Trakt from Moscow to Vladivostok—the track followed by so many
thousands of hapless exiles.

About 6,000 miles of Siberia's rivers are said to be navigable in the
open-water season. The east-west tributaries are often more important
than the main north-south streams. Before the war a commission in-
vestigated and favourably reported on a scheme to link the waterways
and allow uninterrupted navigation from the Pacific to the Urals, and
thence by linking the Ob with the Volga to Europe. The North Coast
Sea route is possible and, indeed, is quite commonly used, but is only

open for one or at the most two months of the year. Consequently the chief ports are Vladivostok and Nikolayevsk on the Amur, but in recent years Igarka has developed, as a result of great expenditure, into a large river port on the Yenisei, north of the Arctic Circle, accessible to ocean vessels. Enormous use is made of aerial transport—the aeroplanes landing on skis in winter—but details are not published. Nakhodka as a commercial port rivals Vladivostok.

SOVIET CENTRAL ASIA

Soviet Central Asia lies between the Caspian Sea on the west, the great Pamir–Tien Shan mountain divide on the east, Siberia on the north and Persia and Afghanistan on the south. The whole area has

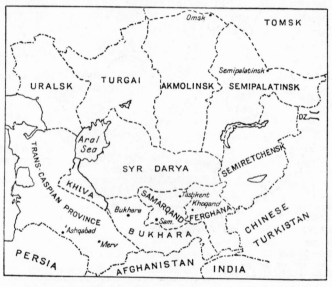

Fig. 359.—The old political divisions of Russian Central Asia

conventionally been called Russian Turkistan, a name which indicates one salient feature—that it is inhabited mainly by Turkish races. The Russian expansion into Turkistan in the eighteenth and nineteenth centuries has already been mentioned (see Fig. 73)—but the greater part did not come under Russian dominion until about ninety years ago. In 1866 Tashkent was occupied, and in 1868 Samarqand. In 1873, the Emir of Bukhara recognized the suzerainty of Russia. Until 1917 Russian Central Asia was divided politically into:

(a) The Transcaspian Province of Russia proper—the desert country east of the Caspian Sea.

(b) The Khanate of Khiva, south of the Aral Sea, along the left bank of the Amu Darya or Oxus.

(c) The Emirate of Bukhara or Bokhara—roughly the upper basin of the Amu Darya.

(d) The Governor-Generalship of Turkistan, which included the fertile lands of Samarqand and Ferghana.

(e) The Provinces of Semiretchensk and Semipalatinsk, the latter bordering Siberia but whose southern part drains to Lake Balkash.

(f) The Provinces of Akmolinsk, Yurgai and Uralsk—the drier Kirghiz Steppes south of the more fertile Black Earth steppes of Siberia.

The divisions (a), (b), (c) and (d) together were broadly equivalent to the old land of Turan and constitute the area commonly known to geographers as the Turanian Basin.

Professor d'Almeida, whose excellent description should be consulted,[1] considers the area geographically under four headings—(a) The Kirghiz Steppes; (b) the Mountainous Border; (c) the Cultivated Lands; (d) the Aralo-Caspian Deserts and Turkmen. Perhaps a simpler geographical division is into—

(A) The Kirghiz Steppes.

(B) Russian Turkistan proper—the Turanian Basin and its borders.

(A) The Kirghiz Steppes

South of the Black Earth Belt is a wide tract of much drier and less fertile steppeland. This tract connects the southern end of the Urals on the one hand with the branches of the Altai and Tien Shan on the other, and occasional outcrops of granite, basic igneous rocks and older sedimentary strata indicate a structural connection. In many other ways this is a zone of transition, a passage-way. It connects the steppes of southern European Russia with the steppes of Mongolia (through the Dzungarian Gate). With a rolling topography, few water-courses and an absence of trees it was a naturally cleared route-way along which journeyed the hordes of Mongols under Jenghiz Khan in the Middle Ages. Over the whole area January average temperatures range from about zero Fahrenheit in the north to 14° or 16° F. in the south; July averages from 72° F. in the north to 81° F. in the south. The nomadic steppe dwellers are the Kazaks or Kirghiz, and the essential unity of the region and of its people was recognized by the creation in 1920 of the Kazak Soviet Socialist Republic within the U.S.S.R. As subsequently enlarged this Republic has an area of 1,048,000 square miles and a population of 11,600,000 (1964), of whom 60 per cent. are described as 'rural'. Within the Kazak Republic, two Autonomous

[1] *Geographie Universelle*, Tome V, 1932, pp. 267–319.

Regions were established, in the interests of distinct groups of Kirghiz tribesmen—that of Kara-Kalpakia extending south-east of the Sea of Aral, and Kirghizia covering most of the old Semiretchensk Province. Kara-Kalpakia later became an autonomous region in the Uzbek S.S.R. (63,920 square miles; 586,000 population in 1964); Kirghizia in 1927 (77,000 square miles; 2,500,000 in 1964). The capital of Kazakhstan is Alma Ata.

FIG. 360.—The present political divisions of Russian Central Asia. These divisions are on a racial basis

Kara-Kalpak is an autonomous republic within the Uzbek S.S.R.; Badakshan within the Tajik S.S.R. For later boundary adjustments see *Oxford Regional Economic Atlas: U.S.S.R.*

(B) Russian Turkistan proper

Russian Turkistan, excluding the northern portion now lying within the Kazak Republic, 'is a country of almost desert plains for three-quarters of its area, and a country of mountains, in part very lofty, for the remainder. These mountains, with their snows and their glaciers, are a source of life for the valleys and plains, for they furnish water for artificial irrigation, and allow the creation of flourishing oases in the midst of the desert. The translation from desert to oasis is generally abrupt, once seen it is never forgotten.' Irrigation has been practised since remote antiquity; in a country in which rain is very scarce in the hot season, it is practically indispensable. Crops can be cultivated without irrigation in the mountain valleys, but not on the plains, where pulses, fruit, rice and fodder all depend on artificial water supply.

Russian Turkistan includes the following geomorphological units:

(1) The Plateau of Ust Urt, about 500 or 600 feet above sea-level formed of horizontal Tertiary rocks, lies between the Caspian and Aral Seas, from which it is separated by sharp escarpments. In spring, after the melting of winter snows and the spring rains, there is a sparse covering of vegetation which rapidly disappears.

(2) The Desert of Kara-Kum (black sand) lies to the south and south-east of the Ust-Urt Plateau, and stretches almost to the Persian

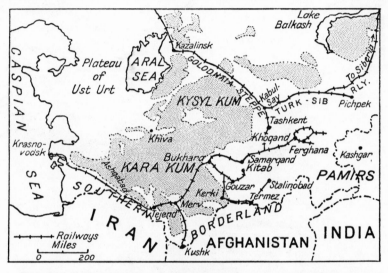

FIG. 361.—Russian Turkistan, showing the extent of desert areas (dotted) and the railways

(*After* Woeikof; the *Atlas of Russian Agriculture* gives a very much more optimistic map of this area)

and Afghan frontiers and from the Caspian on the west to the Amu Darya on the east. It is an irregular plain covered with shifting sands which form into horseshoe-shaped dunes 15–40 feet high and tend to become gradually fixed by the growth of vegetation, forming a very poor type of steppe, unless destroyed by grazing animals. There are also clayey depressions (takyrs) with salt efflorescences and almost without vegetation.

(3) The southern borderland stretches along the frontiers of Persia and Afghanistan. Where the surface commences to rise from the Kara-Kum desert to the mountains of Kopet-Dagh, there are fertile loess soils; a little herbaceous vegetation appears and where streams descend from the mountains oases have been established. But the quantity of

water is small; along 300 miles of the Transcaspian Railway there are only twenty-seven springs of any size, and all water is absorbed in the irrigation of fields and gardens. In the neighbourhood of Tejend and the river Murgab (around Merv) the grassy steppes are more extensive, and larger areas are irrigated.

(4) The Desert of Kysyl Kum ('red sand') stretches between the Amu Darya and the Sir Darya, south-east of the Sea of Aral. It is more varied than the Kara-Kum; there are small ranges of mountains and stretches of grassy steppe. Special attention has been directed of recent

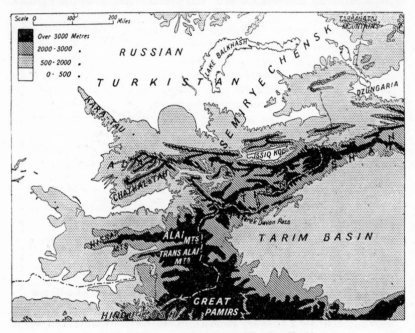

FIG. 362.—The mountain border of Russian Turkistan

years to the 'Golodnaia Steppe' along the Sir Darya and the Tashkent Railway. It is a stretch of level land with a clayey or loamy soil, in spring covered with vegetation, which can easily be irrigated from the Sir Darya, and is regarded as having an important future.

(5) The Plain of Ferghana is a small oval-shaped plain, with its long axis from east to west, almost completely surrounded by mountains. The snows of the mountains furnish abundant water, and this is one of the most flourishing regions of Turkistan, and the centre of cotton cultivation. It is watered by the Kara Darya flowing from the east, and the Naryn from the north-east, the two streams uniting to form the Sir Darya. The route across the Terek Davan Pass is the chief

route from Russian to Chinese Turkistan, from Samarqand and the plain of Ferghana to Kashgar.

(6) The Mountain Border occupies most of the remainder of Soviet Turkistan. The Tien Shan and its westward continuations lie between Turkistan proper and Semiretchensk. Amongst the mountains of the Pamir-Alaï Group is the well-known valley of the Alaï, famous for its fine pastures. In the south-west of Turkistan special mention should be made of the Balkhan Mountains as being the Transcaspian continuation of the much loftier Caucasus.

To sum up, deserts or very dry steppes and mountains occupy most of Turkistan; the fertile areas wherein most of the population is found cover less than 15 per cent. of the surface; the extension of cultivated land is a question of utilizing to the full the river water of the country, notably that of the two great rivers—the Amu Darya (or Oxus of the Ancients) and the Sir Darya. The most fertile soil is the loess, comparable in origin with the loess of China, which occupies especially the strips at the foot of the mountain ranges.

Soviet Turkistan has long been famed for a supposed richness in minerals. Placer gold occurs and some copper deposits; salt is abundant as a precipitation from the salt lakes; indifferent coal occurs, and there are indications of oil near the eastern shores of the Caspian and in Ferghana, but in the latter locality the disturbed condition of the rocks is against the presence of large oil-pools.

The climate of Turkistan has already been mentioned in outline. The January temperature is usually below freezing; the July usually over 80° F. Skies are most clouded—but only about half—in January, and clearest in August. Northerly, north-easterly and north-westerly winds predominate, except among the mountain valleys where local winds mask the general circulation. The winds in the Ferghana 'gate' are particularly interesting. In winter calm days are fine, but cold; on breezy days the wind is an easterly wind of Föhn type, and is accompanied by a marked rise in temperature. In summer on the plains, strong but dry west winds are dominant which scorch up any vegetation left from spring. On the plains the rainfall ranges from about 3 or 4 inches to about 6 inches, increasing in the east among the hills to 14 inches at Samarqand and Tashkent and more at greater heights. Nearly all localities show a marked spring maximum.

Five belts of natural vegetation may be distinguished: the desert belt, the steppe belt, the loess foothill belt, the mountain sparse-forest belt, and the Alpine zone. The vegetation of Turkistan has been well studied; attention has been drawn to the fact that nine-tenths of the trees grow on sandy soil where their roots can penetrate easily to great depths to touch deep-seated supplies of water. It has been indicated that this circumstance should be taken advantage of, and the cultivation of vines and deep-rooted fruit-trees extended.

Amongst crops cultivated wheat occupies a leading position, followed in acreage by cotton, then by barley, rice, millets, and maize. Special interest and importance attaches to the cotton cultivation of Ferghana, where, as in the southern United States, Cotton is King. At the time of the Russian conquest only short-fibred native cotton was grown; later attempts were made without success to grow Sea-Island, but the introduction of American Upland proved more successful. As early as 1911 more than 1,000,000 acres of Turkistan were under cotton—a very important source of supply for Russian mills. Special interest attaches, also, to the vine, and fruit-tree orchards of favoured Turkistan.

After the 1917 Revolution several parts of Russian Turkistan assumed independence temporarily, but, as Soviet influence spread, became Soviet Socialist Republics. These were reorganized and their boundaries rearranged on a national basis, and there came into existence three new republics—Uzbekistan, Turkmenistan and Tajikistan— each a member of the U.S.S.R.

Uzbekistan (Uzbek Soviet Socialist Republic) was formed in 1924 from parts of Khiva and Bukhara and the provinces of Samarqand and Bukhara. The Uzbeks, who form the majority of the population, are Sunni Muslims and were long the ruling race over much of central Asia till the arrival of the Russians. The area of the republic is only 173,546 square miles, but it has a population of over 9,700,000 (1964), of whom more than a third are urban dwellers. Towns include the capital, Tashkent, Bukhara,[1] Khiva, Kokand and Samarqand. These are essentially irrigation settlements.[2]

Tashkent (1,073,000 in 1964) is the largest city in Asiatic Russia and ranks fifth in size amongst all the cities of the U.S.S.R. Samarqand (Samarkand), with 226,000 people, is also a large city: it combines ancient and modern in the presence of the native town on the east and the Russian town on the west with the fortress in the centre. Khoqand (Kokand) (117,000) is typical of all these irrigation-oasis settlements; its position may be compared with the cities of the Tarim Basin. The oasis of Khiva has over half a million people.

Turkmenistan (Turkoman Soviet Socialist Republic) was formed in 1924 from the old Trans-Caspian Province and neighbouring parts of Khiva and Bukhara. The people are Turkoman tribes who speak allied dialects of the Turkoman language and are Sunni Mahommedans. They number 1,500,000 (1964) and the country has an area of 189,370 square miles. The capital is Ashkhabad ('Ashqabad), another large town being Merv.

Tajikistan [3] (Tajik Soviet Socialist Republic) was formed in 1929

---

[1] The ancient importance of Bukhara has been noted in Part I; on its later importance see F. M. Bailey, 'A Visit to Bokhara in 1919', *Geog. Jour.*, **57**, 1921, 75–95.
[2] For a recent appraisal of irrigation prospects see N. C. Field, 'The Amu Darya, a Study in Resource Geography', *Geog. Rev.*, **44**, 1954, 528–42.
[3] Now usually spelt Tadzhikistan.

of those portions of Bukhara and Turkistan inhabited mainly by Tajiks, who speak a language allied to Iranian. They are Aryans and numbered 2,341,000 in 1964. The area of the country is 55,700 square miles. The capital is Dushanbe (formerly Stalinabad) and the state is remarkable for the development of motor roads. Stalinabad is now not only linked by rail with Termez but has regular air services. During the Czarist régime literacy was only 0·5 per cent. It has now risen to 60 per cent. The eastern part of this republic is Badakshan, lying amongst the Pamirs. The Russians have recently carried out intensive searches for minerals, with important results.

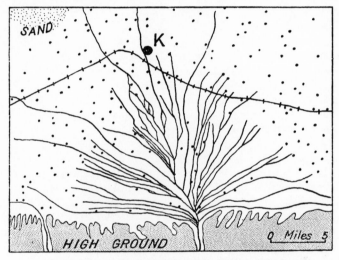

FIG. 363.—Irrigation canals of the Khoqand Oasis

(*After* d'Almeida.)
Dots = settlements.

Foreign Relationships of Turkistan. The natural outlet of Turkistan is to European Russia. There is direct rail communication from Leningrad and Moscow to Tashkent and so to Samarqand. There is also communication by the Caspian Sea and the Transcaspian Railway. On the south-south-east, east and north-east, Turkistan is shut in by mountains. The trade with Persia and Afghanistan is limited, that with Chinese Turkistan and Siberia still more so; hence the trade of Russian Turkistan would naturally be with Russia apart from political ties.

The whole area now has a special significance for Soviet Russia. The Soviet Union has an area of 8·65 million square miles and over 230 million inhabitants. Yet it is only in this south-eastern corner that tropical crops can be cultivated, and an economically independent

Russia falls to the ground without an assured supply of products of tropical or sub-tropical origin. Hence the very definite policy of improving communications with Turkistan, educating the people and encouraging them to draw their foodstuffs from Siberia and to use their own land for the growing of cotton for export to Moscow's mills. As typical of efforts made in this direction, it is said that rubber has been successfully grown under specially adapted conditions in Turkistan. The Turkistan-Siberian (Turk-Sib) Railway was planned to play, and is playing, a large part in the free interchange of produce. There is a little river traffic on the Sir Darya, and on the lower Amu Darya as well as on the Aral Sea.

INDEX

The numbers in black type refer to passages that contain an important mention of the subject of reference.